PRINCIPLES OF MANAGEMENT: AN ANALYSIS OF MANAGERIAL FUNCTIONS

Fifth Edition

HAROLD KOONTZ
Graduate School of Management
University of California, Los Angeles
CYRIL O'DONNELL
Graduate School of Management
University of California, Los Angeles

McGraw-Hill Book Company
New York   St. Louis   San Francisco   Düsseldorf   Johannesburg
Kuala Lumpur   London   Mexico   Montreal   New Delhi   Panama
Rio de Janeiro   Singapore   Sydney   Toronto

This book was set in Melior by Black Dot, Inc., and printed and bound by Kingsport Press. The designer was Richard Paul Kluga; the drawings were done by Hank Iken. The editors were Richard F. Dojny, Hiag Akmakjian, and Sally Mobley. John F. Harte supervised production.

contents

v

PART FOUR   STAFFING

PART FIVE   DIRECTING

PART SIX   CONTROLLING

preface

It is the purpose of this book to present the basics of an operational theory of management. While the authors would not pretend to put in one book all knowledge that may be useful to a practicing manager, they hope to furnish a framework of basic knowledge organized and presented in a useful way. As a first classification of this knowledge, they have chosen to deal with it under the functions of planning, organizing, staffing, directing, and controlling. Each function, in turn, is dealt with by further classifications of knowledge pertaining in a basic way to it. Experience has proved that any new knowledge, whether from the behavioral or quantitative sciences or from the innovations of practice, can be placed within this framework. It is hoped in this way to make a start toward management as a science—organized knowledge—and to make this science useful to those who must apply it, as practitioners, to reality.

It should be emphasized that even though the authors find the organization of knowledge in first-order classifications by function most useful, this does not overlook a systems approach. The functions of managers represent an interlocking system. Each functional area represents within it a number of systems and subsystems. With the eclectic inclusion of pertinent knowledge and techniques from other areas of scientific inquiry, the authors likewise recognize the need for interconnecting elements between such information and the task of the manager. Moreover, it should be emphasized that this book does not look at the enterprise and the manager's role within it as a closed social system. Even though the emphasis is on the manager's role in creating and maintaining an internal environment for performance, it would be foolish indeed for him or the authors not to consider his task as interacting with the entire external environment—economic, technological, social, political, or ethical.

It has been suggested that there be some distillation and organization of knowledge through the device of formulating major principles found in managing. In undertaking this task, the authors have drawn freely upon the discoveries, formulations, and researches of many managers and scholars who have studied various aspects of the subject. While attempting to formulate additional principles from their long managerial experience, observation, and research, the authors readily acknowledge a heavy debt to the many who have made contributions to this important field of human endeavor.

As they have done in previous editions, the authors would like again to make certain aspects of their position clear at the outset. While they recognize that managers seldom, if ever, spend all their time and talents in managing, it is their conviction that the functions of a manager, as manager, are essentially the same whether he is a first-line supervisor or the top executive of an enterprise. The reader will find, therefore, no basic distinction made among managers, executives, administrators, or supervisors. To be sure, the environment of each may differ, the scope of authority held may vary, the types of problems dealt with may be considerably different, and a person in a managerial role may also act as a salesman, engineer, or financier. But the fact remains that, as managers, all who obtain results by establishing an environment for effective and efficient performance of individuals operating in groups undertake the same basic functions.

Moreover, the principles related to the task of managing apply to any kind of enterprise in any kind of culture. The purposes of different enterprises may vary, but all which are organized do rely on effective group operation for efficient attainment of whatever goals they may have. It is true that many of the case examples and techniques used in this book are drawn from business enterprises. In doing so, however, the authors have no intention of overlooking the fact that the same fundamental truths are applicable elsewhere.

Principles are used here in the sense of fundamental truths applicable to a given set of circumstances which have value in predicting results. They are thus descriptive and predictive and not prescriptive as so many erroneously have believed. An attempt has been made to cast most of these fundamental truths in the form of propositions with independent and dependent variables. In a few cases, principles are very little more than concepts. In other instances, concepts and basic truths are introduced without elevating them to the status of major principles. In any event, however, an attempt has been made to recognize the indisputable fact that clear concepts are the initial requirement of science and understanding. The structure of major principles emphasized, to the extent that they reflect fundamentals in a given area, may be referred to as "theory"—a body of related principles dealing systematically with a subject. Even though principles and theory are referred to throughout the book, the reader must not gain the impression that they are impractical. If accurately formulated and properly used, principles and theory should be eminently practical. The real test of their validity is in the crucible of practice.

There are those who object to using the term "principles" for fundamental truths not supported by elaborate and complete verification of their validity. Such persons would prefer to see these principles characterized as hypotheses. Perhaps, strictly speaking, many are. However, even far more statistically verified principles in the so-called exact sciences are virtually always regarded as subjects for further verification. Moreover, the authors are completely aware that the formulation of many principles made here represents essentially a preliminary attempt to codify a number of basic truths and, by placing them in a framework believed to be logical, an attempt to move toward a theory of management. Being preliminary, these summaries are not intended as a final scheme of a theory of management. But they are believed to be a convenient and useful way of packaging some of the major truths that experience and research have found to have a high degree of credibility and predictability.

In this fifth edition, as in those preceding it, the authors have attempted to respond to two major influences. One is the continuing help from a comprehensive survey of teachers and scholars who have honored them by using the past editions of this book at various levels of academic and practical management education in a wide variety of universities and operating enterprises. Another is the burgeoning volume of research, new ideas, and advanced techniques, particularly those being applied to management from the behavioral and physical sciences. The authors have consequently been led to sharpen concepts, rearrange certain material, and add much new material while still placing it within the framework of the managerial functions.

In this particular edition, there has been some rearrangement of subjects. In order to give emphasis to the fact that managers operate in an open social system, a chapter on the environment of managing is included in the first part. Also, because it has been found that readers can better appreciate the distinction between management science, enterprise sciences, cultural factors in managing, and managerial practice by looking at the basics of comparative management, a largely new chapter on this subject is placed in the first part.

In the area of planning, considerable new material has been incorporated. This includes, in part, the theory and practice of managing by objectives and newer decision theory and applications. It also broadens the subject of premising to cover the entire enterprise environment, introduces much that is new on strategies, and makes other important changes brought about by increasing sophistication in this field. Likewise, in the parts on organizing, staffing, and directing, many more of the applicable findings of the behavioral sciences have been incorporated. In managerial appraisal, an entire new chapter reflects the growing use of appraising against verifiable objectives and introduces a new approach to supplement this aspect of performance by appraising managers as managers. Similar new approaches and techniques have been introduced in the chapters on controlling.

By rewriting so much of this edition and recasting the material on management, the authors wish to keep faith with those teachers, students, and practitioners whose appreciated acceptance of this book has been so great in previous editions. Yet, through careful and often painful choosing and pruning, an attempt has been made to make this edition as concise as possible. In answer to a strong demand by many users, the authors have developed a fairly large number of case incidents which teachers and especially students may find helpful. By placing them in the back of the book along with selected references, rather than within its main body, it is hoped that these will not distract those who wish to use the book as a statement of basic management theory rather than as a teaching tool.

As might be expected in a book of this kind which now enters its fifth edition, the authors are indebted to so many persons that a complete acknowledgment would be encyclopedic. Some managers and scholars are acknowledged through footnotes and other references to their contributions. Many managers with whom the authors have served in business, government, education, and other enterprises have contributed by word and precept. Thousands of managers in all levels and kinds of enterprise have honored the authors over the years by allowing them to test their ideas in executive training classes and lectures. To the executives of the various companies with which they have been privileged to work as directors or consultants, the authors are grateful for the opportunity to continue the clinical practice of management.

In previous editions, special appreciation has been expressed to a number of individuals who have contributed materially to the writing of the book. While they are not again named here, their contributions, by shaping many parts of earlier editions, have also been important to this one. In particular, however, the authors would like to express appreciation for the thoughtful, helpful, and sometimes brutal criticisms offered in comprehensive reviews made by Professor Richard Babcock of the University of Illinois, Professors Lloyd E. Bowman and Alex S. Pomnichowski of Ferris State College, Dean B. K. Marks of Sam Houston State University, Professor Jack L. Mendelson of Arizona State University, Professor Roger R. Stanton of California State College at Long Beach, and Professor Thomas L. Watkins of Wayne State University. The authors are also grateful for the assistance of Dr. F. Cesar Toscano of the International Business Machines Corporation for his review and suggestions on quantitative approaches to management. Help in certain aspects of the book was given by Professor A. L. Springfield of the University of Tulsa, Mr. W. Sidney Taylor of the Department of Defense, and Mrs. Diane Steubing of the University of Cincinnati. The authors also wish to acknowledge and thank Mrs. Ilana Seginer who cheerfully and intelligently assumed the wearisome task of preparing the manuscript of this edition for publication.

Harold Koontz
Cyril O'Donnell

PRINCIPLES OF MANAGEMENT:
AN ANALYSIS OF MANAGERIAL FUNCTIONS

part one
THE BASIS OF MANAGEMENT

This book undertakes the study of management by utilizing analysis of the basic managerial functions as a framework for organizing knowledge and techniques in the field. Managing is defined here as the creation and maintenance of an internal environment in an enterprise where individuals, working together in groups, can perform efficiently and effectively toward the attainment of group goals. Managing could, then, be called "performance environment design." Essentially, managing is the art of doing, and management is the body of organized knowledge which underlies the art.

Each of the managerial functions (planning, organizing, staffing, directing, and controlling) is analyzed and described in a systematic way. As this is done, both the distilled experience of practicing managers and the findings of scholars are presented. This is approached in such a way that the reader may grasp the relationships between each of the functions, obtain a clear view of the major principles underlying them, and be given the means of organizing existing knowledge in the field.

Part 1 is an introduction to the basis of management through a study of the nature and operation of management principles (Chapter 1), a description of the various schools and approaches of management theory (Chapter 2), the functions of the manager (Chapter 3), an analytical inquiry into the total environment in which a manager must work (Chapter 4), and an introduction to comparative management in which approaches are presented for separating external environmental forces and nonmanagerial enterprise functions from purely managerial knowledge (Chapter 5). Each succeeding part of the book takes up one of the five managerial functions: planning, organizing, staffing, directing, controlling. If the reader keeps in mind the fact that all managerial knowledge can be organized under these five categories, he will provide himself with a useful tool which will help him in his understanding of a complex subject.

The first chapter of this part discusses the role of management princi-ples. These are defined as fundamental truths of general validity which have value in predicting the results of managerial action. These principles aid in furnishing the groundwork for a science of management. A management principle distills and organizes knowledge that has been built up through experience and analysis. While the authors agree that a science of manage-ment is only now developing and is still very inexact, they nonetheless be-lieve that understanding and applying such principles can materially improve the quality of management practice. Although management, like all social sciences, has far to go to become an exact science, it is hoped that research and reflection will continue to improve it. If the reader understands at the outset that this book is not a description of an exact science but rather an endeavor to codify, as accurately as possible, an extant body of knowledge, his task will be lighter. Even the physical sciences which we now regard as mature and "exact" went through a long period of inexact experimentation and probing for principles. These principles eventually led to the discovery of scientific laws. Managing, like engineering and the practice of medicine, will never be wholly scientific. Rather, it will remain largely an art in which the practitioner uses whatever scientific knowledge is available but must supplement it with a great deal of personal judgment. To many, this very re-liance on personal ability makes managing a very rewarding career.

Chapter 2 of this part describes the various schools or approaches to management theory. There is a danger that the reader will become puzzled about the orientation of the authors. There is a mathematical school, a social system school, a behavioristic approach, and others. What then is the school of the authors? This book adheres to the "operational" school. It looks at managing as a series of actions which are taken to achieve a predetermined goal. In other words, managing is an intelligent, purposeful activity—a proc-ess, not a series of unrelated actions which occur as a result of accident or sociological or psychological pressures. This approach has the advantage of being realistic and therefore "operational" in that it deals with the whole subject of management in the language and from the point of view of the practicing manager. Yet the authors are aware that others approach the study of management differently. In fact, these differing approaches have resulted in different meanings for a number of words used very frequently in manage-ment literature. Chapter 2 seeks to give the reader a picture of the various approaches to management. If he grasps the differing orientations of these approaches, the manner in which they use the language of management will become clear.

Chapter 3 very briefly defines and describes the five basic functions of the manager—planning, organizing, staffing, directing, and controlling—and serves primarily as an orientation to the remaining five parts of the book. The authors believe that these five functions are the same for every manager in all kinds of enterprise and at all levels. The president of a large American corporation is a manager. His Holiness the Pope also manages. Both men must plan the results to be obtained and lay out the means, organize accordingly, staff their organizations by choosing and developing adequate subordinates, direct them in the accomplishment of work, and control (check on performance and correct deviations from planned action). Thus, the process itself is a system, a complex of interrelated and interacting elements and activities. Although the functions of managers are the same, the specific content of the work is not. For instance, a general plans but he usually does so in a state of comparative calm (peace) for a sudden, normally short period of activity to begin in the future (war). The business manager is most often forced to plan continuously amid a continuous flux of daily work. The other functions vary too, according to the specific nature of the job. This superficial difference has helped to obscure the universality of the five management functions and has delayed the development of sound management principles.

Underlying the managerial task is the concept of organizational authority and responsibility also dealt with in Chapter 3. The authors see authority as the right to exercise discretion in making operational decisions. As the right to exercise discretion, it is a means to be creative, to design, and to maintain an environment conducive to individual performance. Responsibility is the obligation to use this discretion for the purposes desired by those who bestow it. Authority does not necessarily imply arbitrary or dictatorial use of it, but it does imply that final responsibility for accomplishment rests with the manager.

In Chapter 4, the authors wish to make it clear that managers do not operate in a "closed" system, responding only to the forces inside their organization or their department. Rather, as should be readily apparent, they operate in a total environment that goes beyond their enterprise and encompasses economic, technological, social, political, and ethical elements of the society in which they operate. While the concern of this book is primarily with the enterprise internal environment, it would be foolish indeed if a manager were not at all times responsive to external environmental forces.

In the final chapter of this part, the authors intend to make even more clear the necessity for separating managerial from nonmanagerial factors in both studying and practicing management. The focus of this chapter is the problem of analyzing the universality and transferability of management. Clearly, if management is becoming a science as the authors believe it is, basic management fundamentals should have applicability to all managerial situations in varying cultures and subcultures. By identifying what is managerial, the small but increasing volume of research is proving that basic management theory is universal and transferable.

1
managing and management science

Perhaps there is no more important area of human activity than managing, for it is the task of the manager to establish and maintain an internal environment in which people working together in groups can perform effectively and efficiently toward the attainment of group goals. In other words, it is the manager who is charged with the responsibility of undertaking those actions calculated to make it possible for individuals to make their best contributions toward group objectives. While the emphasis is on the internal environment of the enterprise or a department of it, clearly no manager can perform this task well unless he has an understanding of and is responsive to the many elements of the ethical, social, economic, political, and technical environment which affect his area of operations.

How the manager does his task and what basic science underlies it are the focus of this book. As many managers in all types of enterprises and many scholars in the field have found, this analysis is facilitated by breaking down the total managerial task into its primary functions and organizing the principles, techniques, and knowledge of managing around these functions.

In undertaking this task, the authors have utilized the functions of the manager—planning, organizing, staffing, directing, and controlling—as a logical framework within which to classify the basic practice and knowledge of management. It is recognized that there are other classifications of managerial functions which differ slightly, and with most of these the authors have no quarrel. It does seem, however, that the classification used here has the advantages of being comprehensive, of being divisible into enough parts to permit logical analysis, and of being operational in the sense that it portrays functions as managers themselves see them. Moreover, these sharply distinguish the task of the manager from the nonmanagerial activities of the specialist or technician.

4

WHY GROUP ACTIVITY?

Our modern civilization has increasingly become one of cooperative endeavor. Whether in business, government, the church, philanthropic institutions, or other forms of enterprise, the effectiveness with which people work together toward the attainment of enterprise goals is largely determined by the ability of those who hold managerial positions. It is of little avail to have scientific knowledge, engineering skills, technical abilities, or vast material resources unless the quality of managing organized groups permits effective coordination of resources.

Group activity exists because man has found it necessary to cooperate with others. Due to his own physical, biological, and psychic limitations, he must unite with others in order to attain most of his personal goals. Also, any individual wishes to maximize personal goal satisfaction with the least expenditure of time, money, unpleasantness, or other unsought consequences. This desire to accomplish goals through cooperation, and to do so efficiently, applies whether group action involves business, military, religious, charitable, social, or other objectives.

WHY MANAGEMENT?

Not all groups believe that they need managing. As a matter of fact, certain critics of modern management feel that people would work together better and with more personal satisfaction if there were no managers. They prefer to refer to the ideal group operation as a "team" effort. They apparently do not realize that in the most rudimentary form of team play, individuals playing the game have clear group goals as well as personal ones, are assigned to positions, follow play patterns, allow someone to call the plays, and follow certain rules and guidelines. Indeed, it is a characteristic of every effective group effort designed to attain group goals at the least cost of time, money, material, or discomfort, that it adopts the basic process and principles of management.

Managing is essential in all organized cooperation, as well as at all levels of organization in an enterprise. It is the function not only of the corporation president and the army general, but also of the shop foreman and the company commander. In working with many enterprises and organizations, the authors have heard repeatedly that the "trouble" with the enterprise is "the management," meaning persons at a higher level in the organization. There have been instances where even vice-presidents of a company have made this observation. While weaknesses and difficulties may appear at any level of management, effective and perceptive management demands that all those responsible for the work of others, at all levels and in any type of enterprise, regard themselves as managers. It is in this sense that this term is used in this book.

Thus, the reader will find no basic distinction between managers and executives, or administrators, or supervisors. To be sure, a given environment may differ considerably between various levels in an organization or various types of enterprise, the scope of authority held may vary, the types of problems dealt with may be considerably different, and a person in a managerial role may also be a salesman, engineer, or financier; but the fact remains that, *as managers,* all who obtain results by establishing an environment for effective group endeavor undertake the same functions.

Even so, there is seldom anyone in a managerial role who spends all his time and talents in managing, and the organization roles which individuals fill almost invariably involve nonmanagerial duties. One has only to look at the duties and performance of perhaps the most complex managerial role in our society—that of the President of the United States—to realize that much of his work is nonmanagerial. Even in a business corporation, a company president finds himself doing a considerable amount of nonmanagerial work. And, as one goes down the organization ladder, the number of nonmanagerial duties tends to increase. Nevertheless, this fact of life should not detract in any way from the key significance of managing.

THE GOAL OF ALL MANAGERS

It is sometimes said by nonbusiness executives that the top business manager has it easy. They say that he has profit as his goal. As will be elaborated in later discussions, profit is only a measure of the surplus of business income results over costs. In a very real sense the goal of every manager must be surplus. His task must be so to establish the environment for group effort that individuals will contribute to group objectives with the least costs—whether money, time, effort, discomfort, or materials. By the very definition of his task, this becomes his goal. But if he is ever to know whether the efforts of those for whom he is responsible are effective and efficient—attaining goals with least costs—he obviously must know what group goals are. Not only must these be known, preferably to all those for whom he is responsible as well as to himself, but they should be known in a verifiable way. Otherwise, he cannot ever measure his and his group's effectiveness or efficiency.

Thus, the goal of managers, as managers, is fundamentally the same in business and nonbusiness enterprises. It is also the same at every level. The corporation president, the city administrator, the hospital department head, the government first-line supervisor, the Boy Scout leader, the bishop, the baseball manager, the university president or dean, all, as managers, have the same goals. The purposes of their enterprise or their department of it may vary, and these purposes may be more difficult to define in one situation than in another, but their basic managerial goal does not vary.

IS MANAGING A SCIENCE OR AN ART?

This question is often raised. Actually, the practice of managing, like all other arts—whether medicine, music composition, engineering, baseball, or accountancy—makes use of underlying organized knowledge—science—and applies it in the light of realities to gain a desired, practical result. In doing so, practice must design a solution which will work, that is, get the results desired.

Art, then, is the "know-how" to accomplish a desired concrete result. It is what Chester I. Barnard has called "behavioral knowledge."[1] Those who diagnose "by the book" or design wholly by formula or attempt to manage by memorization of principles are almost certain to overlook practical realities. As such it can be seen that, with the possible exception of formulating science itself, art is the most creative of all human pursuits. When it is appreciated how important effective and efficient group cooperation is in any society, it is not difficult to argue that managing is the most important of all arts.

The most productive art is always based on an understanding of the science underlying it. Thus, science and art are not mutually exclusive but are complementary. As science improves, so should art, as has happened in the physical and biological sciences. The physician without a knowledge of science becomes a witch doctor; with science, an artful surgeon. The executive attempting to manage without a theory, and knowledge structured by it, must trust to luck, intuition, or what he did in the past; with organized knowledge he has a far better opportunity to design a workable and sound solution to a managerial problem. However, mere knowledge of principles or theory will not assure successful practice because one must know how to use them. Since there is no science in which everything is known and all relationships proved, science cannot be a comprehensive tool of the artist. This is true in diagnosing illness, designing bridges, or managing a company.

One of the common errors in utilizing theory and science is overlooking the necessity of compromising, or blending, in order to achieve a total desired result. An airplane designer must make a compromise between weight and strength on the one hand and cost on the other. A manager may wisely assign an employee more than one superior—breaking the principle of unity of command—if he is certain that *total* results attained will be better that way. But in disregarding principles and the other elements of science, one must calculate the cost and weigh it against the total result. The ability to compromise with the least of undesired consequences is the essence of art.

Another problem often results from the attempt to solve a practical situation by applying a principle not designed to cover it. One would not apply a theory of metal stresses to an engineering problem where stresses were unimportant and the cost of material was. Nor would one be likely to apply a principle of management to a problem of medical diagnosis. One of the difficulties of many management scholars and practitioners is that they try to force a principle into a situation which it was not designed to explain.

[1] As Barnard says in The Functions of the Executive (Cambridge, Mass.: Harvard University Press, 1938), pp. 290–291: "It is the function of the arts to accomplish concrete ends, effect results, produce situations, that would not come about without the deliberate efforts to secure them. These arts must be mastered and applied by those who deal in the concrete and for the future. The function of the sciences, on the other hand, is to explain the phenomena, the events, the situations, of the past. Their aim is not to produce specific events, effects, or situations, but explanations which we call knowledge. It has not been the aim of science to be a system of technology, and it could not be such a system. There is required in order to manipulate the concrete a vast amount of knowledge of a temporary, local, specific character, of no general value or interest, that it is not the function of a science to have or to present and only to explain to the extent that it is generally significant."

SCIENCE AND MANAGEMENT

Although the organization of human beings for the attainment of common objectives is ages old, a science of management is just now developing. Since World War II there has been an increasing awareness that the quality of managing is important to modern life, resulting in extensive analysis and study of the management process, its environment, and its technique.

The importance of management is nowhere more dramatized than in the case of many underdeveloped or developing countries. Review of this problem in recent years by economic development specialists has shown that provision of capital or technology does not bring development. The limiting factor in almost every case has been the quality and vigor of managers.

The culture of present-day society is characterized by revolutionary improvements in the physical and biological sciences, while the social sciences have lagged far behind. Yet, unless man can learn to harness human resources and coordinate the activities of people, inefficiency and waste in applying technical discoveries will continue. One has only to look at the incredible waste of human and material resources, in the light of unfulfilled social objectives, to realize that the social sciences are far from doing their job of guiding social policy and action.

Certain of the social sciences have progressed further than others. With all its deficiencies, economics, for example, has progressed far in explaining what courses of action will yield optimum output at the least expenditure of labor and capital. But economic principles *assume* that economic objectives can be attained through the coordination of human activity and that the enterprise, as well as groups of enterprises, will be well managed. Other social sciences, such as sociology and anthropology, have gone far in explaining man's cultural environment. Even though the foundations of these sciences suffer from incompleteness and inexactness, the theories have helped man to understand his society.

The study and analysis of management have lagged behind other sciences until recent years. Yet, as in other fields, the development of an underlying science must precede an improved practice.

Science and the Scientific Method

Science explains phenomena. It is based on a belief in the rationality of nature, on the idea that relationships can be found between two or more sets of events. The essential feature of science is that knowledge has been systematized through the application of scientific method. Thus, we speak of a science of astronomy or chemistry to indicate accumulated knowledge formulated with reference to the discovery of general truths in these areas. Science is systematized in the sense that relationships between variables and limits have been ascertained and underlying principles discovered.

Scientific method involves determination of facts through observation of events or things and verifying the accuracy of these facts through continued observations. After classification and analysis of the facts, the scientist looks for and finds some causal relationships which he believes to be true. Such generalizations, called hypotheses, are then tested for their accuracy. When hypotheses are found to be true and to reflect or explain reality and therefore to have value in predicting what will happen in similar circumstances, they are called principles.

Application of scientific method to the development of principles does not totally eliminate doubt. Every generalization, however proved, may be subject to further research and analysis. Even so long-standing a generalization as Newton's law of gravitation might be modified with new knowledge and phenomena. But without new facts, induction from them of significant relationships, testing of hypotheses, and development of principles, man would never understand his universe.

Principles and Causal Relationships

As has been properly pointed out by a student of management theory, if principles are to explain management behavior, they should be formulated to predict results.[2] In connection with many of the principles in this book, it is not explicitly stated that a certain course of action will bring "good" results. This is implied. Since principles are designed to predict results in given circumstances, the reader must be aware of what the authors regard as "good." The standard used in this book—one with which managers would certainly agree— is the efficient and effective attainment of enterprise or departmental objectives, whether economic, political, educational, social, or religious.

This includes the objective of maintaining the organized enterprise as an effective joint effort over time, that is, of providing for the survival of the group until basic goals are reached. For most enterprises, these goals are so continuing, of so long a duration, that this means indefinite survival. Thus, a business enterprise—set up for a specific short-term purpose, such as building a bridge—has a continuing goal of making profits and justifying the confidence of investors, just as an educational or religious enterprise pursues continuing goals of educating or furthering spiritual life.

Even though the principles as stated in this book may not always be established as complete causal propositions, the reader should interpret them as such. They can always be read in the sense that if this or that is done, the result will be more efficient and effective attainment of objectives.

Management As an Inexact Science

It is often pointed out that the social sciences are "inexact" sciences, as compared to the "exact" physical sciences. It is also sometimes indicated that management is perhaps the most inexact of the social sciences. It is true that the social sciences, and management in particular, deal with complex phenomena about which too little is known. It is true, likewise, that the structure and

---

[2]John F. Halff, "Applying Scientific Method to the Study of Management," *Journal of the Academy of Management,* vol. 3, no. 3, pp. 193–196 (December, 1960). The authors are indebted to Mr. Halff for his insistence on clarifying this point.

behavior of the atom are far less complex than the structure and behavior of groups of people.

But we should not forget that even in the most exact of the "exact" sciences—physics—there are areas where scientific knowledge must be replaced with speculation and hypothesis. As much as is known of bridge mechanics, there are still cases where bridges fail through such causes as vibrations set up from wind currents. And as we move from the longer-known areas of physics into the biological sciences, we find that areas of exactness tend to diminish.

Since virtually all areas of knowledge have tremendous expanses of the unknown, people working in the social sciences should not be defeatist. A scientific approach to management cannot wait until an exact science of management can be developed. Had the physical and biological sciences thus waited, man might have still been living in caves.

Certainly, the observations of perceptive managers must substitute for the desirable laboratory-proved facts of the management scientist, at least until such facts can be determined. Statistical proof of principles of management is desirable, but there is no use waiting for such proof before giving credence to principles derived from experience. After all, no one has been able to give statistical proof of the validity of the Golden Rule, but people of many religions have accepted this fundamental precept as a guide to behavior for centuries, and there are few who would doubt that its observance improves human conduct.

In looking at general management from an intellectual and scientific point of view, the earliest contributions came from such experienced business managers as Fayol, Mooney, Alvin Brown, Sheldon, Barnard, and Urwick. Many of the propositions offered in this book are based on the distilled experience of these and other practitioners. Admittedly, much of the research has been done without questionnaires, controlled interviews, laboratory experiments, or mathematics, but it can hardly be regarded as "armchair" or lacking in experienced observation. To be sure, management is an inexact science. But the questions one must ask are these: Does the use of such theory as is available or postulated help us understand management and aid in improving management practice now? Are we better off using such theory now—for guidelines in research and practice—or waiting until that perhaps distant future when the science can be "proved"? Does such theory help in substituting rationality for confusion? Does it increase objectivity in understanding and practicing of management?

PRINCIPLES AND THEORY

Principles are thus fundamental truths, or what are believed to be truths at a given time, explaining relationships between two or more sets of variables. In its purest form, a principle embodies an independent and a dependent variable. Thus, in physics, as Galileo discovered, if gravity is the only force acting on a falling body, it will fall at a uniformly accelerated speed (at 32.16 feet per second at the latitude of New York City). Or take the much less physical example of Parkinson's law that work tends to expand to fill the time available; thus work depends on time available.

March and Simon point out that propositions explaining relationships may be of various forms.[3] One type comprises propositions that state the dependence of one variable on one or more other independent variables. Another kind is propositions embodying a qualitative, descriptive generalization about a subject. They use an example of this as: "One of the important activities that goes on in an organization is the development of programs for new activities that need to be routinized for day-to-day performance."[4] As can be seen, this is little more than the concept type of proposition. A third type of proposition mentioned by these authors is one where a particular phenomenon performs a particular function, such as: "Rigidity of behavior increases the defensibility of individual action."[5] Although all three types of the March and Simon propositions might be used to indicate principles, the most meaningful type of principle is one which involves causal relationships with dependent and independent variables.

Theory is a systematic grouping of interrelated principles. Its task is to tie together, to give a framework to significant knowledge. Scattered data, such as the miscellaneous numbers or diagrams typically found on a blackboard after a group of engineers has been discussing a problem, are not information unless the observer has a knowledge of the theory which explains their relationships. With this knowledge he can tie them together and probably comprehend what they mean. Theory is, as Homans has said, "in its lowest form a classification, a set of pigeon holes, a filing cabinet in which fact can accumulate. Nothing is more lost than a loose fact."[6]

The importance of theory to the development of organized knowledge has been dramatically indicated by the various essays of Talcott Parsons. In one, he says:[7]

It is scarcely too much to say that the most important index of the state of maturity of a science is the state of its systematic theory. This includes the character of the general conceptual scheme in use in the field, the kinds and degrees of logical integration of the different elements which make it up, and the ways in which it is actually used in empirical research.

Any system of principles or theory requires clarity of concepts—mental images of a thing formed by generalization from particulars. Obviously, a clear definition of a word is an elemental type of concept. Concepts are the building blocks of theory and principles. Unless concepts are clear, meaningful to those who use them, and used consistently, what may be said by one person who attempts to explain knowledge will not transfer to another

---

[3] J. G. March and H. A. Simon, *Organizations* (New York: John Wiley & Sons, Inc., 1958), pp. 7–9.

[4] *Ibid.*, p. 8.

[5] *Ibid.*

[6] G. C. Homans, *The Human Group* (New York: Harcourt, Brace & World, Inc., 1950), p. 5.

[7] *Essays in Sociological Theory, Pure and Applied* (New York: The Free Press of Glencoe, 1949), p. 17.

in the same way. Indeed, this is one of the major difficulties with management as a science. As will be noted in the next chapter, the same word or term does not imply the same phenomena to various persons. One need only reflect on the term "organization" to see how true this is.

Principles are often referred to as being "descriptive," "prescriptive," or "normative." As might be drawn from these terms, a principle is descriptive if it merely describes a relationship between variables. It is referred to as being "prescriptive," or "normative," if it is stated in such a way as to indicate what a person *should* do. Obviously, the principle of falling bodies, referred to above, is purely descriptive. It has no implication as to whether a person *ought* to jump off a high building, but is only an indication that, so far as gravity is concerned, if he does, he will fall at a certain speed. On the other hand, when principles are applied against some scale of values, they may be referred to as prescribing action or as being "prescriptive," or "normative." If the reader agrees with the thesis of the authors that it is the goal of all managers so to operate as to gain organization purpose effectively and efficiently, he has a value against which to apply management principles. It is consequently easy to make management principles "normative" as well as "descriptive." Indeed, with the standard of effectiveness and efficiency in mind, we have difficulty in not doing this.

MANAGING AND SYSTEMS THEORY

As is so customary in a developing field, new terms and approaches often come into vogue leaving practitioner and student alike feeling that a whole new body of knowledge has been discovered. This has certainly been the case with the popularity of systems management in recent years. The emphasis on systems has brought into the field of management concepts, theory, and techniques which have been so basic and fruitful in the physical sciences. It has introduced a rigor of analysis that is valuable to managing.

What Systems Are

However, systems are neither new nor startling in their fundamentals. A system has been defined in the *Oxford English Dictionary* as simply "a set or assemblage of things connected, or interdependent, so as to form a complex unity; a whole composed of parts in orderly arrangement according to some scheme or plan." To see anything as a system, then, is to see it as an interrelated set of interacting components. Managing, like almost every aspect of life itself, is systematic, and managers long accustomed to seeing their operations and problems as a network of interrelated parts may be surprised to hear of the "new" systems management.

A business, government, or other type of enterprise, or a department within it, is a system, and managing itself represents a system. Also, management plans are systems involving interacting components of people, authority, information flow, markets and customers, materials and facilities.

Barnard saw the executive as a component of a system of formal organization, and the latter as a part of an entire cooperative system involving bio-logical, physical, social, and psychological elements. Social psychologists likewise see managing as a subsystem of a social system—an interconnected, interacting set of social forces and elements "anchored in the attitudes, per-ceptions, beliefs, motivations, habits and expectations of human beings."[8] But Barnard's inclusion of biological and physical, as well as social and psy-chological, elements in the system a manager operates is perhaps a more accurate portrayal of a total managerial system. To be sure, most of the inter-actions of a manager have to do with social and psychological forces or ele-ments. It is difficult, however, not to see him interacting with other elements, particularly such physical ones as money, materials, and facilities.

Open and Closed Social Systems

A social system is regarded as open when there are constant relationships or transactions between it and its environment, where there are inputs from the environment and outputs to the environment. Closed systems are the reverse. Although it may be possible to conceive of a physical system such as an auto-mobile as being fairly "closed," it is inconceivable that one could think of a social system as being so. Whether one talks of a business enterprise or a university as a social system, it is not possible to think of it not having signifi-cant interaction with its environment.

In the light of these self-evident truths, it is surprising to any manager or theorist to find that management theory is sometimes criticized for regarding an enterprise or a department as a closed system. For example, two prominent scholars have said.[9]

Traditional organizational theories have tended to view the human organization as a closed system. This tendency has led to disregard of differing organizational environ-ments and the nature of organizational dependency on the environment. It has led also to an overconcentration on principles of internal organizational functioning, with consequent failure to develop and understand the processes of feedback which are essential to survival.

Surely no person interested in management as a practitioner, theorist, or student could ever overlook the open-system nature of managing. Neither objectives nor plans can possibly be set in the vacuum of a closed company system. Markets, government regulations, competitors, technology, and too many other elements of an enterprise environment affect these ever to overlook them. Likewise, no manager with any experience with people could disregard the fact that they are products of and are influenced by their entire cultural environment.

It is true that, in order to carve out an area of knowledge and make it manageable, operational management theory emphasizes the functions of

---

[8] D. Katz and R. L. Kahn, *The Social Psychology of Organizations* (New York: John Wiley & Sons, Inc., 1966), p. 33.

[9] *Ibid.,* p. 29.

managers in an enterprise or department. But never can this theory disregard the impact of the external environment.

The Value of the Systems Approach to Management

Saying that systems are not new is not to say that modern systems thinking and new special systems approaches have not been valuable to both theory and practice. The advantage of approaching any area of inquiry or any problem as a system is to see the critical variables and constraints and their interaction with each other. It forces scholars and practitioners in the field to be constantly aware that one single element, phenomenon, or problem should not be treated without regard for its interacting consequences with other elements.

This is nowhere better exemplified than in the case of the functions of managers, to be discussed in Chapter 3. While we can define and organize knowledge around the functions of planning, organizing, staffing, directing, and controlling, a moment's reflection will show how interlocked they are. A manager, for example, plans his organization structure, develops staffing programs, and bases his controls on plans. And this is true in various ways with all functions.

Almost all of life is a system. Our bodies certainly are. Our homes and universities are, as are our government agencies and our businesses. These, in turn, are interconnected with various other systems, and each has within it a number of subsystems. No one can or should disregard the network nature of the components in any company, department, problem, technique, or program. Certainly, the theory and practice of management presented in this book do not.

THE NEED FOR THEORY AND PRINCIPLES OF MANAGEMENT

Obviously, principles of management can have a tremendous impact upon the practice of management, simplifying and improving it. Since in all fields of human cooperation, efficiency of group effort lags far behind that of machines, application of principles of management will further human progress.

The need for a clear concept of management and for a framework of related principles has been recognized for many years by such practical scholars of management as Henri Fayol, Chester Barnard, and Alvin Brown.[10]

To Increase Efficiency

When management principles can be developed, proved, and used, managerial

---

[10]In *General and Industrial Management* (New York: Pitman Publishing Corporation, 1949), pp. 14–15, Fayol bemoaned the lack of management teaching in vocational schools, but ascribed it to a lack of theory, since, as he said, "without theory no teaching is possible." Likewise, Barnard (*op. cit.*, p. 289) deplored the lack of literature and instruction for executives and, above all, the lack of "an accepted conceptual scheme with which to exchange their thought." Alvin Brown, in *Organization of Industry* (Englewood Cliffs, N.J.: Prentice-Hall, Inc., 1947), p. vi, held that the understanding and development of the art of management must be a study "grounded in principle."

efficiency will inevitably improve. Then the conscientious manager can become more effective by using established guidelines to help solve his problems, without engaging in original laborious research or the risky practice of trial and error.[11]

It is not always appreciated that what can be learned from experience and transferred to new situations are only the fundamentals involved. The kind of experience on which many managers rely too heavily is only a hodgepodge of problems and solutions existing in the past and never exactly duplicated. Two management situations are seldom alike in all respects, and a manager cannot assume that exact techniques applicable in one situation will necessarily work in another. However, if a manager can *distill* experience, seek out and recognize the *fundamental* causal relationships in different circumstances, he can apply this knowledge to the solution of new problems. In other words, solutions become simplified if dealt with in terms of principles. The value in understanding management as a conceptual scheme of principles is that it lets one see and understand what would otherwise remain unseen. Theory can solve future problems arising in an everchanging environment.

The value of knowing principles might be shown by several examples. We know from principles that having individuals report to more than one boss involves certain costs and disadvantages, even though doing so may justify the costs and by knowing principles we may be able to minimize these costs. Principles tell us that no manager can develop controls without basing them on plans, that a manager must have organization authority necessary to accomplish the results expected of him, and that no manager can develop a meaningful plan without a clear idea of the goal to be accomplished and the future environment premised for its operation. While principles are, as they should be, distilled knowledge, awareness of them can help managers avoid making mistakes. It is obviously wasteful for every manager to have to learn these truths from his own experience.

To Crystallize the Nature of Management

Lack of understanding of the principles of management makes it difficult to analyze the management job and to train managers. Principles act as a check list of the elements of management. Without principles, the training of managers depends upon haphazard trial and error. To some extent, this will be the case until an adequate science of management has been developed. Meanwhile in business, government, and other enterprise a considerable body of management principles does already exist and serves increasingly to crystallize the nature of management and to simplify manager training.

To Improve Research

As pointed out above, all hypotheses can be used to further research. And if research is undertaken to build further theory or otherwise to expand the

---

[11] As Urwick has aptly said: "And we should not forget that in the field of management our errors are other people's trials."

horizons of knowledge, establishment of a structural framework of knowledge would appear to be useful for productive research.

In view of the rush of interest in management in the past two decades and the tremendous amount of study by students and managers, better channeling of research is bound to be productive. Since management deals in part with people, and groups of people are unpredictable and complex, effective research is difficult. Management also deals with the planning of action, the devising of controls, and the grouping of activities, in all of which progress in research is slow and costly. The need for tested knowledge of organized enterprise is great, and anything which makes management research more pointed will help improve management practice.

To Attain Social Goals

In a broad sense, managing coordinates the efforts of people so that individual objectives become translated into social attainments. Development of management principles, by increasing efficiency in the use of human as well as material resources, would unquestionably have a revolutionary impact on the cultural level of society. To illustrate this point, nations with a high material standard of living tend to have a high level of intelligence and skill in their management of business. Although ample raw materials and favorable political climate have been important in accounting for the economic productivity of the United States, equally significant, particularly in the twentieth century, has been the relatively high quality of management.

Reasons for Delay in Development

Considering the pressing need for principles of management, it seems surprising that the development of a theory of management has been confined to the past few decades and that businessmen and others generally have been awakening to the need only since World War II.

In pointing to some of the reasons for this delay, one cannot overlook those centuries in which business was held in low esteem. Although business institutions of insurance, credit, and marketing were developed in the Middle Ages and although these and still others were well formed by the time of the industrial revolution, business itself was regarded as a degrading occupation. Aristotle's characterization of buying and selling as "unnatural" money-making,[12] Adam Smith's disparaging remarks concerning businessmen,[13] and Napoleon's castigation of England as a "nation of shopkeepers" are evidences

---

[12]In *Politics and Ethics*, Aristotle wrote: "Of the two sorts of money-making, one is a part of household management, the other is retail trade; the former necessary and honorable, the latter a kind of exchange which is justly censured, for it is unnatural, and a mode by which men gain from one another."

[13]In *Wealth of Nations* (New York: Modern Library, Inc., 1917), p. 250, Adam Smith said of certain businessmen that they are "an order of men, whose interest is never the same with that of the public, who have generally an interest to deceive and even to oppress the public, and who accordingly have, upon many occasions, both deceived and oppressed it."

of this fact. Even in the past century, business was often regarded by the educated as a somewhat inglorious occupation. Indeed, one can say that only in the past half century has the businessman begun to hold a place of respect.

Another reason for the delay has been the preoccupation of economists with political economy and the nonmanagerial aspects of business. In their analysis of business enterprise and the development of philosophical precepts concerning business, the early economists generally followed the lead of Adam Smith, whose concern was for measures to increase the wealth of a nation; of Ricardo, whose emphasis was upon the distribution of wealth to the factors of production; and of Alfred Marshall and others, who refined some of the marginal analyses in competitive and monopolistic marketing. The modern treatment of the economics of the individual firm is largely a development of the past three decades. Even the work of Chamberlin and Robinson, which has so changed the course of economic theory since 1933, assumes the existence of an effective business management. These preoccupations kept economists from examining the theoretical implications of the significant job of business management until recent years.

One might expect that political science would have been the father of a theory of management, since the administration of policies is one of the major tasks of government and government itself is the oldest and most comprehensive form of social organization. Yet, despite its obvious importance, early political theorists were slow to turn their attention to the problem of administration. They, like the early economists, were too preoccupied with policy making on a national and international level; therefore, they largely overlooked the executive process, at least until recent years. Some of the early contributions to the theory of management, nevertheless, have come from scholars in the field of public administration, and important contributions have continued to come from this source at an accelerated pace.

To some extent the delay has also been due to the tendency to compartmentize the disciplines within the broad field of social science, as in the failure to apply the research of sociologists to the area of management. The theories of sociology concerning formal and informal organizations have only recently been applied to the functions of the manager. Likewise, research of psychologists in the fields of individual motivation, reactions to authority, and the meaning and measurement of leadership has extended to the area of management only in the past few years.

In addition to these reasons, there has been a widespread belief among managers in business, government, and other organizations that management is not susceptible to principles—that management is an art, not a science.

Moreover, businessmen themselves have in the past discouraged the development of a theory of management. Too often their emphasis has been on technology, price, and the balance sheet—an orientation hardly conducive to the understanding of, and inquiry into, the job of the manager.

It is interesting to note that the opening wedge to the study of management as a science was driven by the so-called scientific management school of Frederick W. Taylor.

Recent Impetus

Impetus to the development of a theory of management has come in the past four decades as the result of the recognition that one missing link in the attainment of an effective enterprise system is human relations. The Great Depression following 1929 brought forth such symptoms of human unrest as the New Deal and national unionism and emphasized to alert businessmen that among the deficiencies of American industrial development, perhaps the greatest was the concentration on the mere manipulation of resources. It is probably not too much to say that the upheaval of the 1930s and the attack by government and other social groups upon the institution of free private enterprise were instrumental in forcing business managers to examine the nature of their job.

World War II and the subsequent defense programs were of even greater importance in the development of a theory of business management. The emphasis upon production with the least cost in materials and manpower focused attention on the job of the manager—at every level in an organization —as the strategic factor in accomplishing the objective. The importance of the manager has increased in the postwar years. For one thing, the siphoning off of some of the best young men into military programs during the war left a shortage of promotable manpower after the war. For another thing, the technical advances which accompanied the war exaggerated the lag between managerial knowledge and technical knowledge.

The decade of feverish productive activity set off by military preparation accelerated the movement toward larger and more complex business enterprises. The challenge to effective management increases as business size increases. As business methods and products become more complex and relationships with other businesses, consumers, workers, and the government become more intricate, the need for skilled management, even in the small firm, expands materially.

In more recent years, tremendous impetus to the development of management theory and to the search for scientific underpinnings to improve practice has come from the world-wide rivalry for markets, power, and progress. This might be called the "era of supercompetition." Increasingly severe competition has resulted from such factors as (1) dissemination of technical knowledge, which has allowed an increasing number of firms and nations to compete for world markets; (2) the freeing of trade; (3) the change from sellers' to buyers' markets; (4) the increase of capital investment and capacity and the rise in the level of break-even points; and (5) the rapid rate of technological change, which can make a product obsolete or lower its costs virtually overnight.

In addition to the growth of competition from these factors, both within the United States and on an expanding world front, businessmen have been faced with cost-price squeezes. The pressure for wage and fringe increases has raised costs to a point where businesses which fail to use modern techniques of management are at the mercy of those which do. With the tendency of wages to rise faster than labor productivity, the firm which would continue to enjoy profit dares not be content to be mediocre, but must aggressively attempt to be more efficient than its competitors.

This intense rivalry applies not only to business firms. In government, universities, churches, and other enterprises, one sees forces at work which indicate that group effectiveness may be a key to continued survival. In government, the demand for public services tends to outstrip the tax resources available to support them, and the same atmosphere of pressure exists in other nonbusiness enterprises.

These forces, always important but now of such magnitude as to affect survival, have placed heavy emphasis on management effectiveness. It may be that technical know-how will become less important to the maintenance of high living standards in the United States and elsewhere than the continued improvement of management. The present effort to develop management principles reflects this possibility.

EARLY CONTRIBUTIONS TO MANAGEMENT PRINCIPLES

Management naturally has been of some concern to organized society throughout civilized history. Most of the earlier contributions came, of course, from practitioners, not theorists. Since early in the century, particularly through the work of Taylor and Fayol, there have been scattered but significant contributions to management theory. But the epoch of upsurge in management inquiry and research, in which academicians have participated with practitioners, is largely a development of recent years.

Management in Antiquity

Interpretations of early Egyptian papyri, extending as far back as 1300 B.C., indicate the recognition of the importance of organization and administration in the bureaucratic states of antiquity.[14] Similar records exist for ancient China. Confucius's parables include practical suggestions for proper public administration, and admonitions to choose honest, unselfish, and capable public officers.[15]

Although the records of early Greece do not give much insight into the principles of management, the very existence of the Athenian commonwealth, with its councils, popular courts, administrative officials, and board of generals, indicates an appreciation of the managerial function. Socrates's definition of management as a skill separate from technical knowledge and ex-

---

[14] See A. Lepawsky, *Administration* (New York: Alfred A. Knopf, Inc., 1949), pp. 78–81, and numerous original and secondary sources there quoted.

[15] L. S. Hsu, *The Political Philosophy of Confucianism* (New York: E. P. Dutton & Co., Inc., 1932), p. 124. For excerpts from this study as well as other sources of early Chinese works on administration, see Lepawsky, *op. cit.*, pp. 82–84.

perience is remarkably close to our current understanding of the function.[16]

The records of management in ancient Rome are incomplete, although it is well known that the complexity of the administrative job evoked considerable development of managerial techniques. The existence of the Roman magistrates, with their functional areas of authority and degrees of importance, indicates a scalar relationship characteristic of organization. Indeed, it is thought that the real genius of the Romans and the secret of success of the Roman Empire lay in their ability to organize. Through the use of the scalar principle and the delegation of authority, the city of Rome was expanded to an empire with an efficiency of organization that had never before been observed.[17]

The Roman Catholic Church

If one is to judge by age, the most effective formal organization in the history of Western civilization has been the Roman Catholic Church. Its long organizational life has been due not only to the appeal of its objectives but also to the effectiveness of its organization and management techniques. The development of the hierarchy of authority with its scalar territorial organization, the specialization of activities along functional lines, and the early use of the staff device are striking examples of these techniques. It is remarkable that, for centuries, their successful employment by the Church had virtually no influence on other organizations. In his study of this, Mooney expresses the belief that "nothing but the general neglect of the study of organization" can explain why the staff principle, so important to the organization of the Catholic Church, did not take root in other organizations until fairly recently.

Military Organizations

As might be expected, some of the more important principles and practices of modern business management may be traced to military organizations. Except for the Church, no other form of organization in the history of Western civilization has been forced, by the problems of managing large groups, to

---

[16] In his discourse with Nicomachides (*Plato and Xenophon: Socratic Discourses*, book III, chap. 4, New York: E. P. Dutton & Co., Inc., 1910), Socrates is reported to have made the following observations on management: "I say that over whatever a man may preside, he will, if he knows what he needs, and is able to provide it, be a good president, whether he have the direction of a chorus, a family, a city, or an army. . . . Is it not also the duty . . . to appoint fitting persons to fulfill the various duties . . . ? To punish the bad, and to honour the good. . . . Do not, therefore, Nicomachides, despise men skillful in managing a household; for the conduct of private affairs differs from that of public concerns only in magnitude; in other respects they are similar, but what is most to be observed is, that neither of them are managed without men; and that private matters are not managed by one species of men, and public matters by another; for those who conduct public business make use of men not at all differing in nature from those whom the managers of private affairs employ; and those who know how to employ them, conduct either private or public affairs judiciously, while those who do not know, will err in the management of both."

[17] For an excellent analysis of the Roman genius for organization, see J. D. Mooney, *The Principles of Organization*, rev. ed. (New York: Harper & Row, Publishers, Incorporated, 1947), pp. 62–72.

develop organization principles. Yet despite the need, military organizations failed to put much theory to use before the past two centuries.

Although military organizations remained fairly simple until recent times, being limited largely to refinements of authority relationships, they have, over the centuries, gradually improved their techniques of direction. Early armies, even those composed of mercenaries, were often characterized by adequate morale and the complementary relationship of individual and group objectives. History is replete with examples of military leaders who communicated their plans and objectives to their followers, thereby developing what Mooney calls a "unity of doctrine" in the organization. Even as autocratic a commander as Napoleon supplemented his power to command with a careful explanation of the purpose of his orders.

More recently, however, military organizations have applied other management principles. Among the most important of these has been the staff principle. Although the term "general staff" is found in the French army of 1790 and certain staff functions have characterized military organizations for many centuries, the modern concept of general staff can be traced to the Prussian armies of the nineteenth century. This group, organized under a chief of staff, furnished specialized advice and information and supplied auxiliary services which have come to be essential features of military as well as all other types of enterprises.

The Cameralists

The cameralists were a group of German and Austrian public administrators and intellectuals who generally held, from the sixteenth to the eighteenth century, the same tenets as the British mercantilist and the French physiocratic schools of political economy. They all believed that to enhance the position of a state, it was necessary to maximize material wealth. But the cameralist school alone emphasized systematic administration as a source of strength and was one of the earliest groups to do so.[18]

The cameralists believed as well in the universality of management techniques, noting that the same qualities which increased an individual's wealth were called for in the proper administration of the state and its departments. In developing management principles, they emphasized specialization of function, care in selection and training of subordinates for administrative positions, establishment of the office of comptroller in the government, expedition of legal processes, and simplification of administrative procedures.

Taylor's Principles of Management

Although Frederick W. Taylor is properly called the founder of modern scientific management, the roots of his principles are found in earlier writings. As in other fields of knowledge, the principles of scientific management were

---

[18]For one of the most scholarly analyses of cameralism, see A. Small, *The Cameralists* (Chicago: The University of Chicago Press, 1909).

discovered as the occasion for their use arose. The rise of large industry and the factory system and the introduction of expensive machinery occasioned new interest in problems of management.

Taylor's famous work *The Principles of Scientific Management* was published in 1911. Despite his apparent intent to provide principles applicable to management, his main concern was with achieving efficiency of human beings and machines through time and motion study, which has been referred to as the "cornerstone of scientific management."[19]

Perhaps Taylor's principal contribution to management theory is his insistence upon the application of scientific method. Thus, Taylor held that *The Principles of Scientific Management* had been written:[20]

First: To point out, through a series of simple illustrations, the great loss which the whole country is suffering through inefficiency in almost all of our daily acts.

Second: To try to convince the reader that the remedy for this inefficiency lies in systematic management, rather than in searching for some unusual or extraordinary man.

Third: To prove that the best management is a true science, resting upon clearly defined laws, rules, and principles, as a foundation. And further to show that the fundamental principles of scientific management are applicable to all kinds of human activities, from our simplest individual acts to the work of our great corporations, which call for the most elaborate co-operation. And, briefly, through a series of illustrations, to convince the reader that whenever these principles are correctly applied, results must follow which are truly astounding.

In developing his theory, Taylor pointed out that a new philosophy of management was involved, a philosophy under which management would take more responsibility for planning and supervision and for reducing the knowledge of labor and machine techniques to rules, laws, and formulas, thereby "immensely" helping employees to work at lower cost to the employer and with higher returns to themselves.

Taylor saw several new functions for managers: (1) replacing rule-of-thumb methods with scientific determination of each element of a man's job; (2) scientific selection and training of workmen; (3) cooperation of management and labor to accomplish work in accordance with scientific method; and (4) a more equal division of responsibility between managers and workers, with managers planning and organizing the work.

Taylor's contributions, however, were not an unmixed blessing. Through his stress on efficiency at the shop level and economies gained through time and motion study, he caused attention to be drawn so completely to the shop that for a time the study of management became in effect the study of shop management, while the more general aspects were overlooked, particularly in the United States and Great Britain. As discussed below, had the work of

---

[19] R. F. Hoxie, "Scientific Management and Labor Welfare," *Journal of Political Economy*, vol. 24, p. 838 (November, 1916).

[20] Frederick W. Taylor, *The Principles of Scientific Management* (New York: Harper & Brothers, 1911), p. 7.

Henri Fayol not been overshadowed by enthusiasm for Taylorism, the history of management theory might well have been different and the principles of general management advanced much earlier.

Fayol's Theory

Perhaps the real father of modern management theory is the French industrialist, Henri Fayol. Although there is little evidence that management scholars, either in England or in the United States, paid much heed to, or knew about, Fayol's work until the 1920s or even later, his acute observations on the principles of general management first appeared in 1916 in French, under the title of *Administration Industrielle et Génefale.* This monograph, reprinted in French several times, was not translated into English until 1929; even then it was printed by the International Institute of Management at Geneva, and only a few copies were made available for sale outside Great Britain. No English translation was published in the United States until 1949, although the work of Fayol was brought to the attention of American management scholars in 1923 by Sarah Greer's translation of one of Fayol's papers, later incorporated in a collection of papers by Gulick and Urwick.[21] In this same collection, the more general aspects of Fayol's works were referred to in a paper by the British management consultant and scholar, Lyndall Urwick.[22]

Thus, even though Fayol's monograph did not appear in the United States in a form for general reading until 1949,[23] and despite the fact that few in this country knew of Fayol's work until 1937—more than two decades after its original publication and more than a decade after the author's death —a study of Fayol's monograph, with its practical and clear approach to the job of the manager and its perception of the universality of management principles, discloses an extraordinary insight into the basic problems of modern business management. Indeed, even though the thinking of certain students of management was clearly affected by Fayol long before his work was brought to the attention of the general public, one regrets that few serious students of business management had the advantage of Fayol's analysis. Most of those who have contributed to the principles of business management— such as Sheldon, Dennison, Mooney, and Barnard—show no evidence of having been familiar with the work of Fayol.

Fayol wrote as the practical man of business reflecting on his long managerial career and setting down the principles he had observed. In doing so, he made no attempt to develop a logical theory or a self-contained philosophy of management. His observations, however, fit amazingly well into the currently developing mold of management theory.

---

[21] L. Gulick and L. Urwick (eds.), *Papers on the Science of Administration* (New York: Institute of Public Administration, 1937). Fayol's paper was translated by Miss Greer as "The Administrative Theory of the State."

[22] "The Function of Administration," in *ibid.*

[23] H. Fayol, *General and Industrial Administration* (London: Sir Isaac Pitman & Sons, Ltd., 1949). Most of the biographical material used here has been drawn from Urwick's interesting introduction in this edition.

Fayol found that all activities of industrial undertaking could be divided into six groups: (1) technical (production); (2) commercial (buying, selling, and exchange); (3) financial (search for, and optimum use of, capital); (4) security (protection of property and persons); (5) accounting (including statistics); and (6) managerial (planning, organization, command, coordination, and control).[24] Pointing out that these activities exist in businesses of every size, Fayol observed that the first five were well known and consequently devoted most of his book to an analysis of the sixth.

Because there will be many occasions to refer to Fayol in succeeding pages, it will be helpful at this point to outline briefly the contents of his remarkable monograph. The book may be divided into observations on managerial qualities and training, general principles of management, and elements of management. Fayol distinguished between principles and elements by reserving the former term for rules or guides and the latter for functions.

Managerial qualities and training   Fayol considered the qualities required by managers to be physical ("health, vigor, address"); mental ("ability to understand and learn, judgment, mental vigor, and adaptability"); moral ("energy, firmness, willingness to accept responsibility, initiative, loyalty, tact, dignity"); educational ("general acquaintance with matters not belonging exclusively to the function performed"); technical ("peculiar to the function"); and experience ("arising from the work proper").[25]

With insight, confirmed in more recent studies, Fayol observed that, while the most important ability for a worker is technical, the relative importance of managerial ability increases as one goes up the scalar chain, becoming the most important skill for top-level executives. On the basis of this conclusion, Fayol recognized a widespread need for principles of management and for management teaching, and decried the lack of the latter in the technical schools of his time. He held that managerial ability should be acquired as technical ability is, first in school and later in the workshop. In the absence of a well-developed and accepted theory of management, he set himself early in the twentieth century to fill this need in a manner which, if followed more assiduously by succeeding scholars of management, would probably have gone far toward closing a gap which still exists today.

General principles of management   Noting that principles of management are flexible, not absolute, and must be usable regardless of changing and special conditions, Fayol listed fourteen based on his experience. They may be summarized as follows:

1.   Division of work. This is the specialization which economists consider necessary to efficiency in the use of labor. Fayol applies the principle to all kinds of work, managerial as well as technical.
2.   Authority and responsibility. Here Fayol finds authority and responsi-

[24] *Ibid.,* p. 3.
[25] *Ibid.,* p. 7.

bility to be related, with the latter the corollary of the former and arising from the former. He sees authority as a combination of official—deriving from the manager's position—and personal—"compounded of intelligence, experience, moral worth, past services, etc."

3. Discipline. Seeing discipline as "respect for agreements which are directed at achieving obedience, application, energy, and the outward marks of respect," Fayol declares that discipline requires good superiors at all levels.

4. Unity of command. This means that employees should receive orders from one superior only.

5. Unity of direction. According to this, each group of activities having the same objective must have one head and one plan. As distinguished from No. 4, it relates to the organization of the "body corporate," rather than to personnel.

6. Subordination of individual to general interest. This is self-explanatory; when the two are found to differ, management must reconcile them.

7. Remuneration. Remuneration and methods of payment should be fair and afford the maximum possible satisfaction to employees and employer.

8. Centralization. Without using the term "centralization of authority," Fayol refers to the extent to which authority is concentrated or dispersed. Individual circumstances will determine the degree that will "give the best over-all yield."

9. Scalar chain. Fayol thinks of this as a "chain of superiors" from the highest to the lowest ranks, which, while not to be departed from needlessly, should be short-circuited when its scrupulous following would be detrimental.

10. Order. Breaking this into "material" and "social" order, Fayol follows the simple adage of "a place for everything (everyone), and everything (everyone) in its (his) place." This is essentially a principle of organization in the arrangement of things and people.

11. Equity. Loyalty and devotion should be elicited from personnel by a combination of kindliness and justice in managers dealing with subordinates.

12. Stability of tenure. Finding unnecessary turnover to be both the cause and the effect of bad management, Fayol points out its dangers and costs.

13. Initiative. Initiative is conceived of as the thinking out and execution of a plan. Since it is one of the "keenest satisfactions for an intelligent man to experience," Fayol exhorts managers to "sacrifice personal vanity" in order to permit subordinates to exercise it.

14. Esprit de corps. This is the principle that "in union there is strength," as well as an extension of the principle of unity of command, emphasizing the need for teamwork and the importance of communication in obtaining it.

In concluding his discussion of these principles, Fayol observed that he had made no attempt to be exhaustive but had tried only to describe those he had had the most occasion to use, because some kind of codification of principles appeared to be indispensable in every undertaking.

Elements of management Fayol regarded the elements of management as its functions—planning, organizing, commanding, coordinating, and controlling.[26] A large part of his treatise is given to an examination of these functions, and his observations are, on the whole, still valid, after more than five decades of study and experience of others in the field. Throughout Fayol's treatise, there exists an understanding of the universality of principles. Again and again, he points out that these apply not only to business but also to political, religious, philanthropic, military, or other undertakings. Since all enterprise requires management, the formulation of a theory of management is necessary to its effective teaching.

THE EMERGENCE OF MODERN THOUGHT

Since the time of Fayol and Taylor, a universally applicable theory of management has been developing at an increasing rate. Although long neglected in favor of research into the more technical and functional aspects of behavior, the realization of the peculiar role of the manager and the desire to improve his effectiveness through selection and training and, gradually, through self-appraisal, have resulted in increasing research. Impossible as it is to recount here all the significant contributions to a theory of management, some of the most important ones can be noted.

Contributions of Public Administrators

Coincident with the scientific-management movement and encouraged by it, a number of scholars attempted to bring about increased efficiency in government by improved personnel practices and better management. One of the leading apostles of this movement was Woodrow Wilson, who, as early as 1885 and on many occasions later, sounded the call for efficient government.[27] In a quest for economy and efficiency, those interested in public administration have naturally stressed organization, personnel practices, budgetary controls, and planning; to these fields many public administrators and political scientists have made major contributions. Among these are such scholars as Luther Gulick, with his observations on government organization and his research in the application of scientific methodology to public administration,[28] as well as such other noteworthy pioneers in the field as White,[29]

---

[26] *Ibid.*, chap. 5.

[27] See, for example, Wilson's *Congressional Government* (Boston: Houghton Mifflin Company, 1885) and "The Study of Administration," *Political Science Quarterly*, vol. 2, pp. 197–222 (June, 1887). Note also, with regard to developments in Great Britain, D. B. Eaton, *Civil Service in Great Britain* (New York: Harper & Brothers, 1880).

[28] See "Notes on the Theory of Organization" and "Science, Values, and Public Administration," in L. Gulick and L. Urwick (eds.), *Papers on the Science of Administration* (New York: Institute of Public Administration, 1937).

[29] L. D. White, *Introduction to the Study of Public Administration* (New York: The Macmillan Company, 1939).

Gaus,[30] Friedrich,[31] Stene.[32] Dimock,[33] Simon,[34] and Merriam,[35] who have approached the field not only as practical public administrators but as university scholars.

Contributions of Business Managers

The most significant contributions to the field of management theory have been made by businessmen, including Taylor and Fayol. One of these early writers was Russell Robb, who in 1910, at the Graduate School of Business Administration at Harvard, gave a special group of three lectures on organization.[36] Drawing from his business experience, Robb saw organization as a tool for the efficient utilization of manpower and materials, a tool which had to be suited to the circumstances of each enterprise. Robb was one of the first to warn of overorganization.[37] Emphasizing the importance of definite authority, harmony, and "team play," Robb warned that too much functional specialization would result in problems of coordination.

Of the comprehensive works on management, perhaps one of the most significant is *The Philosophy of Management*,[38] written in 1923 by the scholarly British industrial consultant, Oliver Sheldon. Like Fayol, Sheldon sought to formulate a theory of "management as a whole," through defining its purpose, tracing its line of growth, and spelling out the principles governing its practice. Sheldon thought of management in broad terms, as including the determination of policy and coordination of functions (administration), the execution of policy and employment of organization (management proper), and the combination of the work of individuals or groups "with the faculties

[30] J. M. Gaus, "The Responsibility of Public Administration," in J. M. Gaus, L. D. White, and M. E. Dimock (eds.), *The Frontiers of Public Administration* (Chicago: The University of Chicago Press, 1936), pp. 26–44; also (with L. O. Wolcott), *Public Administration and the U.S. Dept. of Agriculture* (Chicago: Public Administration Service, 1941).

[31] C. J. Friedrich, *Constitutional Government and Politics* (New York: Harper & Brothers, 1937); also *Responsibile Bureaucracy* (Cambridge, Mass.: Harvard University Press, 1932); and "Public Policy and the Nature of Administrative Responsibility," in *Public Policy* (Cambridge, Mass.: Harvard University Press, 1940).

[32] E. O. Stene, "An Approach to a Science of Administration," *American Political Science Review*, vol. 34, pp. 1124–1137 (December, 1940).

[33] M. E. Dimock, "The Criteria and Objectives of Public Administration," in Gaus, White, and Dimock, *op. cit.*, pp. 116–133.

[34] H. A. Simon, *Administrative Behavior* (New York: The Macmillan Company, 1950); also, *Determining Work Loads for Professional Staff in a Public Welfare Agency* (Berkeley, Calif.: University of California Bureau of Public Administration, 1941); and *Public Administration* (New York: Alfred A. Knopf, Inc., 1950).

[35] C. E. Merriam, *Political Power, Its Composition and Incidence* (New York: McGraw-Hill Book Company, 1934); also, *The New Democracy and the New Despotism* (New York: McGraw-Hill Book Company, 1939).

[36] *Lectures on Organization* (privately printed, 1910); incorporated in Catheryn Seckler-Hudson (ed.), *Processes of Organization and Management* (Washington, D.C.: Public Affairs Press, 1948), pp. 99–124, 269–281.

[37] Ibid., p. 45. In speaking of organization to control costs, Robb sagely remarks: "While it pays to know costs, it also pays to find out how much it costs to know costs."

[38] O. Sheldon, *The Philosophy of Management* (London: Sir Isaac Pitman & Sons, Ltd., 1923).

necessary for its execution" (organization).[39] Although Sheldon stressed such matters as the social responsibilities of managers and examined functional fields of management, such as personnel ("labour management") and production management, many of his principles are similar to those of Fayol. One receives the impression from Sheldon's work, however, that he did not have Fayol's breadth of understanding and that, except for organization, he did not see the functions of managers as having universal application. For example, his discussion of planning revolves primarily around factory planning.[40]

Another important contribution by a businessman to the development of management theory is that of Henry Dennison, a Massachusetts industrialist whose advanced management techniques in the Dennison Manufacturing Company permitted him to explore the principles of management. In a book published in 1931,[41] Dennison set out to study the scientific aspects of management, particularly organization, and ascertain whether the methods of the engineer might not be applicable. In doing so, Dennison developed concepts of motivation, leadership, and teamwork and analyzed the structural factors of organization in their effects on personalities. Although Dennison did not develop a theory of management, his emphasis upon human engineering and the role of leadership made his contribution significant.

Perhaps the most illuminating attempt by businessmen to develop a logical framework for the theory of organization is in the work of Mooney and Reiley.[42] Drawing upon lessons from history, particularly that of the church and military organizations, these authors undertook to combine the elements of organization into a logical pattern of principle, process, and effect. Starting with the principle of coordination, they moved into the concepts of scalar organization and functionalism, arriving at a total of nine principles. While the work of Mooney and Reiley has been criticized as being too doctrinaire,[43] it represents a logical approach for relating fundamental principles of organization to one another.

One of the most influential and comprehensive treatises in this field is Chester I. Barnard's *The Functions of the Executive*, published in 1938.[44] During his long career as a business executive, Barnard was impressed with the need for some universal fundamentals to explain the executive's job and help him to improve his ability as a manager. Drawing heavily upon the research of sociologists and, to some extent, of psychologists, Barnard produced an extraordinarily provocative work. His treatise is, as he points out in the introduction, really two short treatises, one dealing with the theory of organi-

---

[39] *Ibid.*, p. 32. It is interesting that Sheldon drew these concepts of the function of management from an American, J. N. Shultze, in a paper read before the Taylor Society in 1919.

[40] *Ibid.*, p. 218. Note that Sheldon defines planning as "the business of directing and controlling the processes of production to a given end."

[41] H. S. Dennison, *Organization Engineering* (New York: McGraw-Hill Book Company, 1931).

[42] First published as J. D. Mooney and A. C. Reiley, *Onward Industry* (New York: Harper & Brothers, 1931), this work later appeared with slight modifications as *The Principles of Organization* (New York: Harper & Brothers, 1939). A later edition, in 1947, appeared with only the name of Mooney as author.

[43] Lepawsky, *op. cit.*, p. 253.

[44] (Cambridge, Mass.: Harvard University Press, 1938.)

zation, the other with the functions of executives. His theory of organization, heavily sociological in approach, moves from the principles of group cooperation to those of formal organization. His principles of executive functions lean on this theory and consequently place great stress on leadership and the importance of communication. His examination of decision making, with particular attention to the search for strategic factors, is also penetrating. Barnard's work is so comprehensive that it cannot well be summarized. However, his contribution is as much a matter of provocation as it is of content, for he opens many vistas for the further pursuit of management principles.

Another contribution by a practicing business executive is Alvin Brown's *Organization of Industry*, published in 1947.[45] This treatise is essentially an analysis of the delegation of authority, with an attempt to construct a theory of organization and a division of the managerial functions into the "phases of administration" of planning, doing, and seeing. Although Brown often refers to "responsibility" when he means authority or authority plus an assigned activity, his work is outstanding as a thorough analysis of authority delegation and an attempt to codify a number of principles of management.

Among other contributions by business and professional management people, one should not overlook the crisp reasoning and syntheses of Lyndall Urwick,[46] the papers of Mary Parker Follett,[47] and the pioneering work of Ordway Tead[48] and Paul Holden,[49] to mention only a few. Nor should one overlook the tremendous force which has been exerted by the Society for the Advancement of Management and the American Management Association. The latter organization, particularly, has its roots in the top managerial group in this country, its members being drawn mostly from among the alert business managers who seek a scientific foundation for their jobs. The Society for the Advancement of Management, another important group, is an outgrowth of the Taylor Society, and much of its early emphasis was upon the production management aspects of general management.

The fact that so many of the major contributions to management theory have come from persons to whom the practice of management has been a real and challenging task speaks well for the importance of the field and the realism with which it is being approached.

Contributions of the Behavioralists

Spurred on by the Hawthorne experiments of 1927–1932 and the awakened interest in human relations in the 1930s and 1940s, there has been a tremen-

---

[45] (Englewood Cliffs, N.J.: Prentice-Hall, Inc., 1947.)

[46] See especially *The Elements of Administration* (New York: Harper & Row, Publishers, Incorporated, 1943) and *Management of Tomorrow* (New York: Harper & Row, Publishers, Incorporated, 1933).

[47] H. C. Metcalf and L. Urwick (eds.), *Dynamic Administration: The Collected Papers of Mary Parker Follett* (New York: Harper & Row, Publishers, Incorporated, 1941).

[48] *The Art of Leadership* (New York: McGraw-Hill Book Company, 1935).

[49] With L. S. Fish and H. L. Smith, *Top-management Organization and Control* (New York: McGraw-Hill Book Company, 1951).

dous influx of behavioral scientists into the study of management in recent years. The Hawthorne experiments, undertaken by Mayo and Roethlisberger of the Harvard Business School, disclosed that attitudes toward people— people being regarded as people—may be more important to efficiency and productivity than are such material factors as rest periods, illumination, and even money.[50] This disclosure, as well as the more basic work done by psychologists and sociologists in prior years, resulted in a considerable volume of academic writing by the behavioral scientists.

Much of the focus of the behavioral scientists was stimulated by the belief that every management theorist had assumed that people were "inert" instruments and the human organism a "simple machine." One finds this accusation at the base of many of the behavioral studies on management. Perhaps it is true that practicing followers of the early management writers did overemphasize the mechanistic aspects of so-called classical theory. But careful review of these "classicists" will show that the leaders did not do so. Even in the writings of Frederick Taylor, the importance of the human element was recognized.[51] And Fayol,[52] Henry Gantt,[53] Mary Parker Follett,[54] and Urwick,[55] to mention only a few classicists, took positions many years ago which support points emphasized by behavioralists in recent years with understandably greater sophistication and insight. And one of the leading "classicists," Lillian M. Gilbreth, wrote one of the earliest treatises on industrial psychology.[56]

Although one cannot say prior to the 1940s sociologists, anthropologists, psychologists, and social psychologists were particularly interested in the problems of management, by now their contributions to management theory have been considerable. While those in all areas of behavioral science who have made significant contributions to management are too numerous to detail,[57] a few can be named.

[50] For a complete account of the studies, see F. J. Roethlisberger and W. J. Dickson, *Management and the Worker: An Account of a Research Program Conducted by the Western Electric Company, Hawthorne Works, Chicago* (Cambridge, Mass.: Harvard University Press, 1939).

[51] See, for example, *Principles of Scientific Management* (New York: Harper & Brothers, 1911), p. 29.

[52] For example, *General and Industrial Management* (New York: Pitman Publishing Corporation, 1949), p. 40.

[53] See A. W. Rathe (ed.), *Gantt on Management* (New York: American Management Association, 1961), pp. 60–66, 211–236.

[54] *Freedom and Coordination* (London: Management Publications Trust, Ltd., 1949), pp. 47–76. These two papers on "The Essentials of Leadership" and "Coordination" were actually given in 1933. It is interesting that in Miss Follett's paper on coordination, she emphasized that, "The fair test of business administration, of industrial organization, is whether you have a business with all its parts so coordinated, so moving together in their closely knit and adjusting activities, so linking, interlocking, inter-relating, that they make a working unit, not a congeries of separate pieces." (At p. 61.)

[55] *The Elements of Administration* (New York: Harper & Row, Publishers, Incorporated, 1944), pp. 32–33, 49–51, 89–94.

[56] *The Psychology of Management* (New York: The Macmillan Company, 1914).

[57] For an inventory of scientific findings in the behavioral sciences, but with particular reference to contributions of psychologists, see B. Berelson and G. A. Steiner, *Human Behavior* (New York: Harcourt, Brace & World, Inc., 1964).

Sociologists have contributed much to understanding the anatomy of organizations through their work on groups, cultural patterns, group cohesiveness, and cooperation. Among the sociologists who might be mentioned are Weber,[58] Bakke,[59] Selznick,[60] Homans,[61] Dubin,[62] Dalton,[63] and Katz and Kahn.[64]

Psychologists have likewise contributed to management understanding through their illumination of the aspects of rational behavior and influence, the sources of motivation, and the nature of leadership. Among the many in the area of individual and social psychology who have contributed materially to management are McGregor,[65] Likert,[66] Argyris,[67] Leavitt,[68] Blake,[69] Sayles,[70] Tannenbaum and his associates,[71] Bennis,[72] Fiedler,[73] Stogdill,[74] and Hertzberg.[75]

These scholars and others have shown how the human being brings to his task aspects of behavior which the effective manager should profitably understand. After all, it is individuals and groups with which a manager is concerned and, while organizational roles are designed to accomplish group purposes, these roles must be filled by people. Likewise, as will be pointed out later, the most effective manager is a leader, and understanding how leadership emerges is a key to understanding management itself.

Contributions of the Systems Scientists

As noted above, better realization of the managerial process and environment as a series of systems has led to increased sophistication of management. While

[58] *The Theory of Social and Economic Organization* (Fair Lawn, N.J.: Oxford University Press, 1947).

[59] See, for example, *Bonds of Organization* (New York: Harper & Row, Publishers, Incorporated, 1950).

[60] See, for example, "Foundations of the Theory of Organization," *American Sociological Review*, vol. 13, pp. 25–35 (February, 1948).

[61] *The Human Group* (New York: Harcourt, Brace & World, Inc., 1950).

[62] For example, *The World of Work: Industrial Society and Human Relations* (Englewood Cliffs, N.J.: Prentice-Hall, Inc., 1958).

[63] *Men Who Manage* (New York: John Wiley & Sons, Inc., 1959).

[64] *The Social Psychology of Organizations* (New York: John Wiley & Sons, Inc., 1966).

[65] *The Human Side of Enterprise* (New York: McGraw-Hill Book Company, 1960).

[66] *New Patterns of Management* (New York: McGraw-Hill Book Company, 1961).

[67] For example, *Integrating the Individual and the Organization* (New York: John Wiley & Sons, Inc., 1964).

[68] *Managerial Psychology* (Chicago: The University of Chicago Press, 1958 and 1964).

[69] R. B. Blake and J. S. Mouton, *The Managerial Grid* (Houston, Texas: Gulf Publishing Company, 1964).

[70] *Managerial Behavior* (New York: McGraw-Hill Book Company, 1964).

[71] See, for example, R. Tannenbaum, I. R. Weschler, and F. Massarik, *Leadership and Organization: A Behavioral Science Approach* (New York: McGraw-Hill Book Company, 1961).

[72] *Changing Organizations* (New York: McGraw-Hill Book Company, 1966).

[73] *A Theory of Leadership Effectiveness* (New York: McGraw-Hill Book Company, 1967).

[74] *Individual Behavior and Group Achievement* (London: Oxford University Press, 1959).

[75] See, for example, with B. Mausner and B. B. Snyderman, *The Motivation to Work*, 2d ed. (New York: John Wiley & Sons, Inc., 1959) and *Work and the Nature of Man* (Cleveland: The World Publishing Company, 1966).

it is difficult to select specific contributors in this field because so many contributions have been made by physical, biological, and social scientists of a wide array of interests, a few major threads may be identified.

Perhaps the major contribution of the systems approach to managing came with the introduction of operations research[76] into the areas of planning and control. Through its use, management planning and control have been given the more rigorous treatment required by clear-cut goals, measures of effectiveness and mathematical models, and the attempt to develop quantified answers. Other types of problem simulation have developed with the modeling and manipulative techniques of mathematics, with speed and memory capacities of computers playing a major part. In addition, seeing plans as networks of interacting events has sharpened managerial perceptiveness in planning and control.[77]

One of the major contributors to the expansion of systems theory to all science was von Bertanfly[78] in 1951 and, with special reference to management, Boulding in 1956.[79] Many others have made significant contributions to various aspects of systems theory as it may apply to management. Among them one might mention the work of Katz and Kahn in social systems,[80] and of Forrester in industrial systems;[81] and the operations research contributions of Stafford Beer,[82] Churchman and his associates,[83] Hertz,[84] McCloskey,[85] and Morse.[86] Nor should one ever underestimate the influence of Wiener on developing and emphasizing feedback theory which had such an influence on systems theory.[87] Likewise the contribution of Johnson, Kast, and Rosenzweig in forcefully relating systems theory to management through their early textbook should not be overlooked.[88]

FOR DISCUSSION

1. How would you expect a theory of management to differ from a theory of mechanics? To what extent would a profession of management have elements similar to the professions of medicine, law, or engineering?

[76] See chap. 9.

[77] For a discussion of network planning and control, see chap. 30.

[78] "General Systems Theory: A New Approach to Unity of Science," *Human Biology*, vol. 23, pp. 303–361 (December, 1961).

[79] "General Systems Theory: The Skeleton of Science," *Management Science*, vol. 3, no. 4, pp. 197–208 (April, 1956).

[80] *The Social Psychology of Organizations* (New York: John Wiley & Sons, Inc., 1966).

[81] *Industrial Dynamics* (New York: The M.I.T. Press and John Wiley & Sons, Inc., 1961).

[82] For example, *Decision and Control* (New York: John Wiley & Sons, Inc., 1966).

[83] For example, with R. L. Ackoff and E. L. Arnoff, *Introduction to Operations Research* (New York: John Wiley & Sons, Inc., 1957).

[84] See, for example, with A. H. Rubenstein, *Research Operations in Industry* (New York: King's Crown Press, 1953).

[85] See, for example, with F. N. Trefethen, *Operations Research for Management* (Baltimore: The Johns Hopkins Press, 1954).

[86] See, for example, with G. E. Kimball, *Methods of Operations Research* (New York: The M.I.T. Press and John Wiley & Sons, Inc., 1951).

[87] *Cybernetics* (Cambridge, Mass.: The M.I.T. Press, 1948).

[88] *The Theory and Management of Systems* (New York: McGraw-Hill Book Company, 1963).

2. Must a principle be valid in all circumstances to which it is designed to apply in order to be a true principle?
3. Look up the terms "theory" and "principle" in an acceptable dictionary and determine how they are used.
4. It is sometimes said that a manager must believe in theory since he has nowhere else to turn. Do you agree?
5. Theory and principles are sometimes referred to as descriptive or normative. How would you classify management theory or principles?

2
patterns of management analysis

Because of the extraordinary interest in management in recent years, there have developed a number of approaches to its study. Their variety and the large number of persons, particularly from universities, who espouse them have resulted in much confusion as to what management is, what management theory and science are, and how management should be studied. One of the authors has called the present situation "the management theory jungle."[1]

THE APPROACHES TO MANAGEMENT

Some may believe that it is no more important that there be one approach to management than that there be a single approach to psychology or trout fishing. But no one can doubt that it is important for students and managers to be able to classify and recognize the various patterns of management analysis. Management is a difficult enough field without those in it being forced to face confusion and apparent contradiction.

The approach adopted in this book might best be referred to as "operational" since it attempts to analyze management in terms of what managers actually do.[2] This book considers management to be a process of designing and maintaining the internal environment for organized effort to accomplish group goals. In this context, the authors believe that they analyze management in a way most useful to the manager, reflecting the way he sees his job. The

[1] See Harold Koontz, "The Management Theory Jungle," *Journal of the Academy of Management,* vol. 4, no. 3, pp. 174–188 (December, 1961). See also Harold Koontz, "Making Sense of Management Theory," *Harvard Business Review,* vol. 40, no. 4, pp. 24ff. (July–August, 1962). Much of the material in these chapters has been drawn from these articles.

[2] For a discussion of the operational approach to concepts and analysis, see P. W. Bridgman, *The Logic of Modern Physics* (New York: The Macmillan Company, 1938), pp. 2–32.

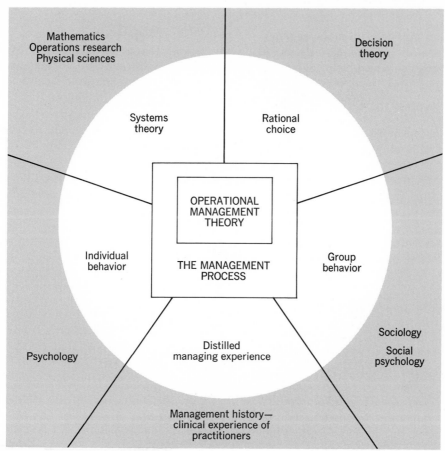

Figure 2.1 *Management theory as a system drawing on other areas of organized knowledge. . . . The "operational" school of management represents an organized body of knowledge and theory, but it also draws techniques and theoretical knowledge from other disciplines. This diagram shows the major areas which make contributions. The area of management theory not only includes the central discipline, but also is eclectic in that it draws on other disciplines. The area of the diagram shown in white is the area of management theory.*

authors nevertheless recognize that other analyses of management are useful and important and that contributions made by proponents of other approaches have been significant.

The various approaches to management are here grouped into the following categories: (1) the operational (management process) approach, (2) the empirical or case approach, (3) the human behavior approach, (4) the social system approach, (5) the decision theory approach, (6) the communications center approach, and (7) the mathematical approach. In the following summary, the authors do not attempt to deal with all the nuances of the different patterns of analysis or do more than sketch the theory of each.

The Operational Approach

This approach attempts to relate the body of management knowledge to the nature of the managerial task. Although various first-order classifications of knowledge could be used, it has been found most helpful to utilize managerial functions. It has, therefore, often been called the "management process" school. Utilizing these functions as the major conceptual framework, the second order of classification is to analyze all these functions essentially by asking basic questions about each. These include (1) What is the nature and purpose of the function? (2) What are the structural properties of each? (3) How is each undertaken? (4) What are the underlying principles and theory in each area? (5) What are the techniques most useful in each area? (6) What are the difficulties involved? (7) How is an environment for performance created in each?

The authors have found that even the newest ideas of management can be placed in this framework.

The operational approach regards management as a universally applicable body of knowledge with principles and theory applicable to all types and levels of enterprise. At the same time, the approach recognizes that the actual environment and problems faced by managers may vary between enterprises and levels and that application of science by a perceptive practitioner must take these into account. Theory, then, is looked upon as a way of organizing knowledge and experience so that practice can be improved through research, empirical testing of principles, and the teaching of fundamentals.[3]

Often referred to, especially by its critics, as "traditional" or "universalist," this school was fathered by Henri Fayol, although many of his offspring did not know of their parent, since Fayol's work was eclipsed by the bright light of his contemporary, Frederick Taylor, and clouded by the lack of a widely available English translation until 1949. Other than Fayol, most of the early contributors to this school dealt only with the organizing function of management, largely because of their greater experience with this function and the simple fact that planning, controlling, and staffing were given little attention by managers before 1940.

In summary this approach bases its analysis of management on the fundamental beliefs that:

1. Managing is an operational process best dissected intellectually by analyzing managerial functions.
2. Long experience with managing in a variety of enterprise situations can be grounds for distillation of basic truths or principles having a clarifying and predictive value in the understanding and improvement of practice.

---

[3]It is interesting that one of the scholars strongly oriented to the human relations and behavioral approaches to management has recently noted that "theory can be viewed as a way of organizing experience" and that "once initial sense is made out of experienced environment, the way is cleared for an even more adequate organization of this experience," See Robert Dubin in "Psyche, Sensitivity, and Social Structure," critical comment in Robert Tannenbaum, I. R. Weschler, and Fred Massarik, *Leadership and Organization: A Behavioral Science Approach* (New York: McGraw-Hill Book Company, 1961), p. 401.

3. These principles can become focal points for useful research both to ascertain their validity and to improve their applicability.

4. Such principles can furnish elements, at least until disproved and certainly until sharpened, of a useful theory of management.

5. Managing is an art that, like medicine or engineering, should rely on thorough grounding in principles.

6. Management principles, like those of logical and physical sciences, are nonetheless true even if a practitioner in a given situation chooses to ignore them and the costs involved in so doing, or attempts to accomplish some other benefit that offsets the costs incurred.

7. While the total culture and the physical and biological universe variously affect the manager's environment, as they do every field of science and art, management theory need not encompass all knowledge in order for it to serve as a scientific foundation of management practice.

To make the area of management theory intellectually manageable, subscribers to this school do not include in their theory entire areas of sociology, economics, biology, psychology, physics, chemistry, or other sciences, not because these have no bearing on management, but because all progress in science has entailed partitioning of knowledge. Yet it would be foolish not to realize that an activity dealing with people's production and marketing of anything from bread and money to religion and education cannot be completely independent of their physical, biological, and cultural universe.

The Empirical Approach

The empirical approach analyzes management by a study of experience, sometimes with intent to draw generalizations, but usually merely as a means of transferring knowledge to the student. Typical of this school are those who teach management of "policy" by the study and analysis of cases and by Ernest Dale's "comparative approach."[4] To some extent, this school also uses an operational approach.

This approach is based upon the premise that through study of the successes and mistakes made by managers in individual cases, and of attempts to solve specific problems, students and practitioners will somehow come to understand and learn to apply effective techniques in comparable situations. No one can deny the importance of analyzing past experience or the "how-it-was-done" of management. But management, unlike law, is not a science based on precedent, and future situations exactly resembling those of the past are unlikely to occur. Indeed, there is a positive danger in relying too much on past experience and on undistilled history of managerial problem solving, for the simple reason that a technique found "right" in the past may be far from an exact fit for a somewhat similar situation of the future.

The empiricists are likely to say that in analyzing cases or history they draw from them certain generalizations to be applied as useful guides for

[4] *The Great Organizers* (New York: McGraw-Hill Book Company, 1960), pp. 11–28.

future thought or action. As a matter of fact, Ernest Dale, after claiming to find "so little practical value" in the principles enunciated by the operationalists, drew such generalizations or criteria from his valuable study of a number of great managers.[5]

By the emphasis of the empirical approach on the study of experience, it appears that the research and thought so engendered may hasten a verification of principles. It is also possible that the empiricists may establish a more useful framework of principles than that of the operational approach. But, to the extent that the empirical approach draws generalizations of what is fundamental from research into past cases and finds it necessary to do this to avoid exchanging meaningless and structureless experience, the empirical approach tends to be the same as the operational approach.

The Human Behavior Approach

This analysis is based on the thesis that since managing involves getting things done with and through people, its study should be centered on interpersonal relations. Variously called the "human relations," "leadership," or "behavioral sciences" approach, this school brings to bear "existing and newly-developed theories, methods, and techniques of the relevant social sciences upon the study of inter- and intrapersonal phenomena, ranging fully from the personality dynamics of individuals at one extreme to the relations of cultures at the other."[6] In other words, this approach concentrates on the human aspect of management and the principle that, when people work together to accomplish group objectives, "people should understand people."

The scholars in this area are heavily oriented to individual and social psychology. Their focus is the individual and his motivations as a sociopsychological being. Their emphasis varies from those who see psychology as a necessary part of the manager's job—a tool to help understand and get the best from people by responding to their needs and motivation—to those who use the psychological behavior of individuals and groups as the core of management.

In this school are those who emphasize human relations as an art that the manager should understand and practice. There are those who focus attention on the manager as a leader and sometimes equate managership with leadership, thus, in effect, treating all "led" activities as "managed" situations. There are those who see the study of group dynamics and interpersonal relationships as simply a study of sociopsychological relationships and seem, therefore, merely to be attaching this term "management" to the field of social psychology.

That managing involves human behavior can hardly be denied. That the study of human interactions, whether in the context of management or otherwise, is important and useful cannot be disputed. And it would be a serious

---

[5] *Ibid.*, pp. 11, 26–28, 62–68.
[6] Tannenbaum, Weschler, and Massarik, *op. cit.*, p. 9.

mistake to regard good leadership as unimportant in good managership. But to assert that the field of human behavior is equivalent to the field of management is quite another thing.

The Social System Approach

This approach is closely related to the human behavior approach and is often confused or intertwined with it. It includes those who look upon management as a social system, that is, a system of cultural interrelationships. Sometimes, as in the case of J. G. March and H. A. Simon,[7] system is limited to formal organizations, the term "organization" being equivalent to enterprise, rather than used in the structured role sense employed most often in management. In other cases, formal organization is not distinguished, and any kind of system of human relationships is encompassed. Strongly sociological in flavor, this pattern of analysis does essentially what any study of sociology does: It describes the cultural relationships of various social groups and attempts to integrate them into a system.

Perhaps the spiritual father of this school of theorists is Chester I. Barnard.[8] In seeking fundamental explanations of the management process, this thoughtful executive developed a theory of cooperation grounded in the need of the individual to offset, through cooperation, the biological, physical, and social limitations affecting him and his environment. Barnard's idea of formal organization, quite unlike that usually held by management practitioners, is defined as any cooperative system in which people are able to communicate with each other and are willing to contribute action toward a conscious common purpose.

The Barnard concept of cooperation pervades the work of many contributors to the social system school of management. For example, Herbert Simon[9] at one time defined human organizations as "systems of interdependent activity, encompassing at least several primary groups, and usually characterized, at the level of consciousness of participants, by a high degree of rational direction of behavior toward ends that are objects of common knowledge." Simon and others have subsequently seemed to expand this concept to include any cooperative and purposeful group interrelationship or behavior.

This approach has made many noteworthy contributions to management. The recognition of organized enterprise as a social organism, subject to all the pressures and conflicts of the cultural environment, has been helpful to both theorist and practicing manager. Among other helpful aspects are the awareness of the institutional foundations of organization authority, the influence of informal organization,[10] and such social factors as those Wight

[7] *Organizations* (New York: John Wiley & Sons, Inc., 1958).

[8] *The Functions of the Executive* (Cambridge, Mass.: Harvard University Press, 1938).

[9] "Comments on the Theory of Organizations," *American Political Science Review*, vol. 46, no. 4, p. 1130 (December, 1952).

[10] For a discussion of the nature of informal organization, see pp. 408.

Bakke has called the "bonds of organization."[11] Likewise, many of Barnard's insights, such as that into the economy of incentives and his theory of opportunism, have brought the power of sociological understanding into the realm of management practice.

Basic sociology—analysis of social behavior and study of group behavior in social systems—does have great value in the field of management. But one may ask whether this is management. Is the field of management coterminous with the field of sociology? Or is sociology an important underpinning, like language or psychology?

The Decision Theory Approach

This approach concentrates on rational decision—the selection, from among possible alternatives, of a course of action. Decision theorists may deal with the decision itself, with the persons or organized group making the decision, or with an analysis of the decision process. Some limit themselves essentially to the economic rationale of the decision; others regard anything that happens in an enterprise as a subject for analysis; and still others expand decision theory to cover the psychological and sociological aspects and environment of decisions and decision makers.

The decision theory school is apparently an outgrowth of the theory of consumer's choice with which economists have long been concerned. It has arisen out of such economic considerations as utility maximization, indifference curves, marginal utility, and economic behavior under risks and uncertainties. It is, therefore, no surprise that most of the members of this school are economic theorists. It is likewise no surprise to find the content of this theory oriented to model construction and mathematics.

The decision theory school has expanded its horizon considerably beyond the process of evaluating alternatives. That has become for many only a springboard for examination of the entire sphere of enterprise activity, including the nature of organization structure, the psychological and social reactions of individuals and groups, development of basic information for decisions, and analysis of values—particularly, value considerations with respect to goals. As one would expect, when the decision theorists start with study of the small, but central, area of decision *making*, they are led by this keyhole look at management to consider the entire field of enterprise operation and its environment. The result is that decision theory is no longer a neat and narrow concentration on decision but becomes a broad view of the enterprise as a social system.

There are those who believe that, since management is characterized by decision making, the future development of management theory will use

[11] *Bonds of Organization* (New York: Harper & Row, Publishers, Incorporated, 1950). These "bonds" or devices of organization are identified by Bakke as (1) the functional specifications system (a system of teamwork arising from job specifications and arrangements for association); (2) the status system (a vertical hierarchy of authority); (3) the communications system; (4) the reward and penalty system; and (5) the organization charter (ideas and means which give character and individuality to the organization).

the decision as its central focus and that the rest of management theory will be hung on this structural center. This may occur, and certainly the study of the decision, the decision process, and the decision maker can be much extended. Nevertheless, one wonders whether this focus could not also be used to build around it the entire area of human knowledge. For, as most decision theorists recognize, the problem of choice is individual as well as organizational, and most of pure decision theory could be applied to the existence and thinking of a Robinson Crusoe as well as the United States Steel Corporation.

The Communications Center Approach

Another approach, closely related to the decision theory approach, is one of looking at the manager as a communications center and building the knowledge of managing around this concept. While this approach is not widely utilized and is not yet well defined, the manager's role is sometimes seen as that of receiving information, storing and processing it, and disseminating it. It has occasionally been likened to a telephone switchboard. As an approach, its real significance is to apply computer technology to managing. By casting the manager in the role of a communications center, the application of the computer to both programmed and unprogrammed decision making falls neatly into place.

This approach does have some attractions. It emphasizes the role of communication in managing as well as the central importance of decision making. It is likewise a means by which computer science can be geared to management thought and action. But as an approach to the science and theory of management it seems to suffer from some of the same deficiencies as the decision theory approach. If defined narrowly, it is not realistically usable as a means of classifying all pertinent management knowledge; if interpreted broadly enough to encompass all managing, it does not seem to be very helpful in giving a base for an operational management science.

The Mathematical Approach

Although mathematical methods can be used by any school of management theory, we refer here to those theorists who see management as a system of mathematical models and processes. Perhaps the most widely known of these are the operations researchers or operations analysts, who sometimes call themselves "management scientists." The belief of this group is that if management or organizing or planning or decision making is a logical process, it can be expressed in mathematical symbols and relationships. The focus of this school is the model, for through this device the problem is expressed in its basic relationships and in terms of selected goals. It is, thus, closely related to the decision theory approach since, particularly in the area of managing, the primary use of mathematics has been to develop various kinds of decision models. However, because of the almost complete absorption with mathematics (and sometimes the extreme belief that "if you cannot express it mathematically, it is not worth expressing") in management, it is separated here.

There can be no doubt of the great usefulness of the mathematical approach to any field of inquiry. It forces upon the researcher the definition of a problem or problem area; it conveniently allows the insertion of symbols for unknown data; and its logical methodology, developed over years of scientific application and abstraction, furnishes a powerful tool for solving or simplifying complex phenomena.

But it is hard to see mathematics as a truly separate approach to management theory, any more than it is a separate school in physics, chemistry, engineering, or medicine. It is dealt with here as such only because there has developed around mathematical analysts a kind of cult which has, at times, appeared to presume that this encompasses the whole area of management.

In pointing out that mathematics is a tool, rather than a school, there is no intention of underestimating the impact of mathematics on the science and practice of management. By bringing to the important and complex field of management the techniques of the physical sciences, mathematicians have already made an immense contribution to orderly thinking. They have forced on people in management the means and desirability of seeing many problems more clearly; they have pressed on both students and managers the need for establishing goals and ways of measuring effectiveness; they have been extremely helpful in promoting the concept of management as a logical system of relationships; and they have caused people in management to review and occasionally reorganize information sources and systems so that mathematics can be given sensible quantitative meaning. But even with this contribution and the greater sharpness and sophistication of planning which are resulting, it is difficult to see that mathematics is management science any more than it is astronomy.

FACTORS CONTRIBUTING TO DIFFERENCES

Like the widely differing and often contentious denominations of the Christian religion, the various patterns of management analysis all have essentially the same goals and deal with essentially the same world. Two of the main differences in approach are semantics and varying definitions of management.

Semantics

As is so often true when intelligent men differ in their interpretations of problems, some of the trouble lies in key words. In the field of management, there are even differences in the application of the word *management*. Most people would agree that it means getting things done through and with people. In this book, the reference is to establishing an effective environment for people operating in formal organizational groups; in other studies, the reference is expanded to apply to people in any kind of group. And there are even treatises purporting to deal with management which cover all kinds of interpersonal relations.

Perhaps a major point of confusion lies in the word *organization*. Most members of the operational approach apply it to the intentional structure of roles. In this case, organization represents the formal framework for the role environment in which people perform within an enterprise. Certainly, in the experience and observation of the authors, most managers believe they are organizing when they establish such a framework. Yet, many organization theorists conceive of organization as the sum total of human relationships, thus making it equivalent to social system. And some use "organization" to mean enterprise.

Other semantic differences might be mentioned. By some theorists, decision making is regarded, as it is in this book, as the act of choosing a course of action from among alternatives; others include in decision making the total managerial task and its environment. Leadership is differentiated from managership in this book; others often make them synonymous. Communications may mean anything from written or oral reports to a vast network of formal and informal relationships.

Differing Definitions of Management

While it is generally agreed that managing involves getting things done through and with people, does it deal with all human relationships? Is a street peddler a manager? Is a leader of a disorganized mob a manager? Is a parent a manager? Does the field of management equal the fields of sociology and social psychology combined?

Certainly if a field of knowledge is not to become bogged down in a quagmire of misunderstandings, the first need is for definition of the field, not in sharp, detailed, and inflexible terms, but rather along lines which will give it fairly specific content. The authors have suggested that the field of management be defined in the light of the able and discerning manager's frame of reference, because theoretical science unrelated to the practical art it is designed to serve is unlikely to be productive.

In defining the field of management, care must be taken to distinguish between tools and content. Thus, mathematics, operations research, accounting, economic theory, sociometry, and psychometrics, to mention a few, are *tools* of management but are not, in themselves, a part of its *content*. This is not to say that these fields are unimportant to the study and practice of management, as important contributions have been made from them. Nor does it mean that they may not further push back the frontiers of knowledge of management. But they should not be confused with the basic content of the management field.

In defining the field, too, it seems imperative to draw some limits for purposes of analysis and research. If one is to call the entire cultural, biological, and physical universe the field of management, he can make no more progress than could have been made if chemistry or geology had undertaken to cover such a broad field rather than to carve out a specific area for inquiry. In general, one might say that the field of management should deal with an area of knowledge and inquiry that is manageable. No great advances in scientific knowledge were made as long as man contemplated the whole universe. In other words, knowledge of the field of management must be recognized as a part of and interacting with a larger universe of knowledge but need not encompass that universe.

MANAGEMENT AS A SYSTEM

It is sometimes forgotten that management, even as defined here, is a system just as a space satellite is a system, or an automobile, a thermostat, an assembly line, or a company. To analyze management and its various parts as systems enables the student to apply the essentials of systems theory, so profitably applied in engineering, to the appreciation and practice of management.

Systems may be open loop or closed loop. The open-loop system is characterized by a one-way cause-and-effect relationship, while the closed-loop system is characterized by a feedback of information to correct errors which might go unnoticed in the open loop. Closed loop can be illustrated by the system of controls on a diesel locomotive. Because there is danger of burning out generators or motors by applying too high an amperage of electricity, most locomotives are equipped with an automatic cutout which will keep the amperage at tolerable levels despite what the engineer does. Again, when a company has a set of quality-control specifications for a product and the inspector is instructed simply to reject products which do not meet the specifications, a straight cause-and-effect relationship or open-loop system exists. But if, as *should* be the case, the observance of variances from standard is accompanied by some information feedback which assures that action is taken to correct the cause of production below standard, then it is a closed-loop system.

Systems have certain characteristics. In the first place, every system is part of a still larger system, or it encompasses many subsystems. A company is a system, but it is a part of an industrial system, a social system, a system of government, and, ultimately, of the systematized universe. Likewise, within the company, the marketing department is a system and within it the sales department, and so on. In the second place, every system—whether physical, biological, or social—has a specific purpose to which all its parts are designed to contribute. Without such a common purpose, the interrelationships would be meaningless. The third essential characteristic of a system is that it is complex, in the sense that a change in one variable will effect change in others.

Norbert Weiner, who has made considerable contribution to systems theory, has given us certain systems principles which are as applicable to management as to any mechanical or biological system.[12] He notes that all systems tend to lose energy at an increased rate, particularly as systems become more complex. This energy loss is due primarily to the frictional effects

---

[12] *The Human Use of Human Beings: Cybernetics and Society,* 2d ed. (Garden City, N.Y.: Doubleday & Company, Inc., 1956).

of communication (or energy transfer) between the various components of a system. As a result, the designed structure of a machine or organization is an index of the performance which may be expected from it. In a machine this performance might depend upon the design of gears, the kinds of lubricants, the strength of metals, the tolerances of moving parts, and similar factors. In an organization structure, performance might depend upon the clarity of goals and authority delegations, the way activities are grouped, and other variables that affect the means by which inputs are translated into desired outputs.

The systems approach to management, then, simply recognizes that a management system—a formal, systematically organized complex of relationships between people—has, as a system, characteristics similar to physical and biological systems. It recognizes that there are total systems and subsystems; that a system is characterized by an arrangement of variables and constants; that there are interactions and communications problems; that there are inputs and outputs; that a closed loop is the best assurance of getting desired results; and that, above all, the effective manager must, in a very real sense, be a scientific and creative designer of workable systems.

FOR DISCUSSION

1. Taking any four articles or books on management you like, determine how the authors are defining "management," "organization," "leadership," and "decision making." Why is semantics a problem in management theory?
2. Are there really various "schools" of management, are these simply ways of approaching the subject, or do they merely represent an intellectual division of labor?
3. Taking each approach to, or "school" of, management, discuss how the major concerns and findings of each can be integrated into the area outlined by the operational school.
4. By reference to a company or department with which you are familiar, sketch some of the major system and subsystem relationships and determine whether they involve open loops or closed loops.

3
the functions and authority of the manager

The overall job of a manager is to create within the enterprise an environment which will facilitate the accomplishment of its objective. He will, of course, be also vitally affected by the external environment in which the firm must operate, but he will have little, if any, power to influence government policy or economic, social, and ethical conditions. Within the enterprise or his department, however, the manager is responsible for the environment in which his subordinates work. In cooperative enterprises—whether these be government, universities, churches, hospitals, or business firms—the able manager creates conditions conducive to effective work. In doing this, the manager plans the operations of his subordinates, selects and trains them, organizes their role relationships, directs their work, and evaluates the results.

CLASSIFICATION OF FUNCTIONS

In classifying the functions of managers, one must distinguish clearly those of functional operation, such as selling, manufacturing, accounting, engineering, and purchasing. These differ from one enterprise to another but the basic tasks of the manager, as a manager, are common to all.

Although the development of a theory and science of management suffers from disagreement among scholars and managers as to the classification of managerial functions, a general pattern of practice and terminology has emerged. Adopted here and used by managers in many fields, this pattern avoids artificial terminology, so that students and managers need not learn new definitions—rather, they may use common terms with greater precision. It is also hoped that managers, using common terms with ordinary meanings, will be encouraged to adopt an increasingly scientific approach to their important task.

The authors believe that the most useful method of classifying managerial functions, at least for purposes of classifying knowledge, is to group them around the activities of planning, organizing, staffing, directing, and controlling. In practice it is not always possible to slice all managerial activities neatly into these categories, since the functions tend to coalesce; however, this classification is a helpful and realistic tool for analysis and understanding.

Some authorities suggest representation as a distinct management function. They have in mind the manager who represents his firm in trade association and government relationships with a view to modifying the external environment or committing the firm to a contractual obligation, or the manager who represents his division or department in committee meetings which may affect the internal environment. There is also the larger problem of the "corporate image," which is influenced by the behavior of all employees, whether managerial or not. The authors have excluded representation as a separate function, partly because it appears to be a complex made up largely of communication and of the exercise of authority (included in direction and organization, respectively) and partly because nonmanagers exert influence on the corporate image.

Occasionally, scholars concern themselves about the order in which the managerial functions should be undertaken. Theoretically, planning comes first, and organizing, staffing, directing, and controlling follow. But according to this logic, an enterprise carries out only one master plan, each part of which, once completed, never has to be revised or modified. This conception is unrealistic. In practice, managers oversee many plans in various stages of execution; they are at least likely to be engaged in solving a control problem or a motivation problem at any moment in time. They move easily from one function to another and devote their attention to the most pressing issues. Managing is, after all, a systematic network and not a sequentially undertaken set of duties.

Moreover, the question of what managers actually do is really secondary to what makes an acceptable and clear first breakdown of management knowledge. As pointed out in the opening chapter, our major concern is to organize knowledge with respect to managing, as an indispensable approach to developing a science of management. In utilizing the functions of managers as this first step, it is believed that a logical start can be made in setting up some "pigeonholes" for classifying knowledge, recognizing, of course, that in management as in all areas of knowledge the classification is not airtight and that there are interlocking and even overlapping elements. This first classification is further dissected by looking at the essential elements in each function, as is done in the succeeding parts of this book.

Planning

Planning involves selecting objectives—and the strategies, policies, programs, and procedures for achieving them—either for the entire enterprise or for any organized part thereof. Planning is, of course, decision making, since it involves selecting among alternatives. There are, for example, policies relating to authority, prices, and competition; programs of production, management succession, and internal audit; and procedures requiring a specific method of handling paper, products, and people.

Considerable confusion has arisen about who should plan and when. Ever since the work of F. W. Taylor, executives have toyed with separating planning from performance, a practice that may be unworkable when two managers command the same subordinates. If, however, the planning is undertaken as an advisory service to the manager in charge of performance, this kind of separation is often highly productive. The responsibility for planning cannot be completely separated from managerial performance because all managers plan, whether they are at the top, middle, or bottom of the organization structure.

Organizing

Organizing involves the establishment of an intentional structure of roles through determination and enumeration of the activities required to achieve the goals of an enterprise and each part of it, the grouping of these activities, the assignment of such groups of activities to a manager, the delegation of authority to carry them out, and provision for coordination of authority and informational relationships horizontally and vertically in the organization structure. Sometimes all these factors are included in the term "organization structure"; sometimes they are referred to as "managerial authority relationships." In any case, it is the totality of such activities and authority relationships that constitute the organizing function.

There are several implications of this concept of organizing. In the first place, the one-man business cannot possibly be organized. Since the owner or operator himself performs the business functions, he delegates no authority. Let him, however, split off the buying activities, assign them to a subordinate, and provide coordination of activity between the buyer and himself, and the enterprise will have become organized.

A second implication is that every manager, when he decides to organize an enterprise or a department, is involved basically in the same task. Whether he is president, sales manager, controller, or office manager, he will reflect the goals toward which he is striving by identifying and grouping activities essential for their accomplishment, assigning some of them to subordinates, delegating the requisite authority to accomplish results, and providing for their coordination.

The organization structure is, of course, not an end in itself but a tool for accomplishing enterprise objectives. Efficient organization will contribute to the success of the enterprise, and for this reason the application of principles is very important. But striving for a "pretty" structure, without regard for its precise use, is futile. The organization structure must fit the task—not vice versa—and must reflect any compromises and limitations imposed on the manager by people, since organizational roles must be manned.

Staffing

Staffing involves manning, and keeping manned, the positions provided for by the organization structure. It thus necessitates defining manpower requirements for the job to be done, and includes inventorying, appraising, and selecting candidates for positions; compensating; and training or otherwise developing both candidates and incumbents to accomplish their tasks effectively. Since this book is devoted to managers, the staffing function will primarily be dealt with as it concerns managers rather than nonmanagers, but the needs and principles involved apply in most instances to both groups. In doing so, there is no intent whatsoever to imply that the first-line supervisor is not a manager.

Directing

Directing involves guiding and leading subordinates. Although this concept is very simple, the methods of directing may be of extraordinary complexity. The superior manager inculcates in his subordinates a keen appreciation of enterprise traditions, history, objectives, and policies. Subordinates learn the organization structure and the interdepartmental relationships of activities and personalities, their duties and authority. Once subordinates are oriented, the superior has a continuing responsibility for clarifying their assignments, guiding them toward improved performance, and motivating them to work with zeal and confidence.

The methods a superior will employ are, of course, various. The successful direction of subordinates results in knowledgeable, well-trained people who work efficiently toward enterprise objectives.

Controlling

Controlling is the measuring and correcting of *activities* of subordinates to assure that events conform to plans. Thus it measures performance against goals and plans, shows where negative deviations exist, and, by putting in motion actions to correct deviations, helps assure accomplishment of plans. Although planning must precede control, plans are not self-achieving. Carrying them out means prescribing the activities of employees at designated times. The plan guides the manager in the timely use of resources to accomplish specific goals. Then activities are monitored to determine whether they conform to planned action.

In the past, control activities generally related to the measurement of objective achievement. Such control devices as the budget for controllable expense, inspection records, and the record of man-hours lost are generally familiar. Each has the characteristic of objective counting; each shows whether plans are working out. If abnormal deviations persist, correction is indicated. But what is corrected? Activities through persons. Nothing can be done about reducing scrap, buying according to specifications, or sales returns until the personal responsibility for deviations has been determined. Compelling events to conform to plans means locating the persons who are responsible for negative deviations from planned action and then taking the necessary steps to improve performance. Thus, things are controlled by controlling what people do.

COORDINATION, THE ESSENCE OF MANAGERSHIP

Many authorities consider coordination as a separate function of the manager. It seems more accurate, however, to regard it as the essence of managership, for the achievement of harmony of individual effort toward the accomplishment of group goals is the purpose of management. Each of the managerial functions is an exercise in coordination.

Need for Coordination

The necessity for synchronizing individual action arises out of differences in opinion as to how group goals can be reached or how individual and group objectives can be harmonized. Even in the case of a church or a fraternal organization, individuals often interpret similar interests in different ways, and their efforts toward mutual goals do not automatically mesh with the efforts of others. It thus becomes the central task of the manager to reconcile differences in approach, timing, effort, or interest and to harmonize cooperative and individual goals.

The best coordination occurs when individuals see how their jobs contribute to the dominant goals of the enterprise. This implies knowledge and understanding of enterprise objectives, not just on the part of a few at the top but by everyone throughout the enterprise. If, for example, managers are not sure whether the basic goal of their firm is profit, quality, advanced techniques, or customer service, they cannot coordinate their efforts to achieve the true objective. Each would be guided by his own ideas of what is in the interest of the firm or, without any such conviction, might work for self-aggrandizement. To avoid such splintering efforts, the dominant goal of the enterprise should be clearly defined and communicated to everyone concerned. And, naturally, goals of subordinate departments should be designed to contribute maximally to enterprise goals.

Principles of Coordination

Perhaps the most original and constructive thought on the concept of coordination has been that of Mary Parker Follett,[1] who has sifted principles from techniques and clarified the conditions for creating synchronized effort.

The principle of direct contact states that coordination must be achieved through interpersonal, vertical, and horizontal relationships of people in an enterprise. People exchange ideas, ideals, prejudices, and purposes through direct personal communication much more efficiently than by any other method, and, with the understanding gained in this way, they find means to achieve both common and personal goals. This recognized identity of ultimate interests then tends to bring agreement on methods and actions. For instance, rivalry and consequent criticism, which all too frequently mar the relationships of employees in sales and manufacturing departments, are evi-

---

[1] H. C. Metcalf and L. Urwick (eds.), *Dynamic Administration: The Collected Papers of Mary Parker Follett* (New York: Harper & Row, Publishers, Incorporated, 1941), pp. 297ff.

dences of poor coordination. Salespersons are understandably interested in offering products that will suit the customer. On the other hand, production personnel think in terms of permissible tolerances, straight-line manufacturing, and the minimum in variety and design. Unless the personnel of these departments exchange ideas and reach an understanding, there can be little coordination between them. No *order* to coordinate can achieve coordination.

A second principle stresses the importance of achieving coordination in the early stages of planning and policy making. It is clear that *after* departmental plans are put into operation it becomes more difficult to unify and time them properly. There is the treasurer, for example, who suddenly tightens up credit without first clearing with the sales department; or the engineer who specifies tighter tolerances without consulting the production department or waiting until the proper equipment, men, and training can be provided. The cry, "Why doesn't someone tell me about this?" thus becomes a common refrain.

The third principle states that all factors in a situation are reciprocally related. When A works with B, for instance, each influences the other, and both are influenced by all persons in the total situation. The people in the marketing research department are influenced by others in the sales department or by the attitude of those in production or finance. A department that has not entrenched itself is highly sensitive to the criticism of other units, and its planning and practices are likely to be trimmed accordingly.

These principles indicate, finally, that the method of achieving coordination is largely horizontal rather than vertical. People cooperate as a result of understanding one another's tasks, and the line officer's dictum, "Coordinate!" is both unrealistic and unenforceable.

The need for continuous interchange of information can hardly be overemphasized. Enterprise never stays put. It is continually being modified by alterations in the external environment and by internal actions and decisions. The achievement of coordination itself modifies the strength of contending forces, often creating new ones and not infrequently deflating the old. Issues crumble before the adjustments of interested personnel; compromises are reached by interchange of information or modification of details. When these adjustments are made, problems disappear. New strengths and weaknesses may be uncovered and, in time, may build up again to the stature of a problem—a critical relationship of numerous complex forces. Good coordination will attack the problems as they arise; excellent coordination will anticipate them and prevent their occurrence.

Techniques of Coordination

The oldest as well as the most important device for achieving coordination is the supervisor. His chief duty to his own superior is to see that his subordinates are achieving a high quality of coordinated effort among themselves and in their relationships with other groups. This does not mean that supervisors directly coordinate the work of their subordinates. It does mean that they employ directional devices, teach principles of coordination, illustrate their application, and apply tests to determine the quality of synchronized effort.

Because the span of management limits the number of subordinates that a supervisor can properly direct[2] and because enterprises may be of a size which requires the services of many supervisors, organization is a very important device for achieving coordination. Careful attention to its principles will produce a structure in which the authority and functions of the several divisions will be clearly defined and whose framework will facilitate the interaction essential to correlation of activity.

Although personal contact is perhaps the most effective means of achieving such coordination, many supplementary devices are also utilized. These include all types of written communications, such as procedures, letters, and bulletins, as well as modern electronic or mechanical devices for the transmission of ideas. Since skill in the use of such timesavers varies, employees need instruction in expressing ideas in the absence of personal contact. They must learn what information it is essential to pass on to others without loss of time.

Group meetings are effective for achieving coordination. They represent a deliberate effort on the part of the superior to bring into personal contact the people especially concerned with a subject. Their purpose is not to "tell" the members something—since coordination cannot be imposed from the top—but to encourage members to integrate their own efforts.

Finally, there is the not unusual device of using liaison men to facilitate coordination. Indeed, there were few firms during World War II that did not have their expediters, and expediting continues as an important activity in many firms. However, this device on any but a temporary basis is often evidence of poor planning or a poor organization structure.

Managerial Functions and Coordination

What the manager does to accomplish synchronized effort of subordinates is to carry out managerial functions, that is, to plan, organize, staff, direct, and control. It is the manager's responsibility, then, to achieve coordination. He achieves it in two ways. First, he ensures that the environment facilitates coordination by creating an appropriate organization structure, selecting skillful subordinates and training and supervising them effectively, providing and explaining the integrated plans and programs that subordinates will carry out, and establishing means to determine whether plans are being carried out properly and programs are on schedule. Second, he makes certain that his subordinates understand the principles of coordination and the importance of acting upon them.

THE NATURE OF MANAGING

At least three groups have an interest in understanding the nature of managing. Those who occupy managerial positions obviously need a clear under-

---

[2] For discussion of this point, see chap. 13.

standing of their duties: a blurred concept frequently results in time lost in nonmanagerial activities, to the neglect of executive duties. A second group is that of employed persons who do not manage—laborers, clerks, and others. Because their goals derive from the firm, they want to feel confident that their managers know how to manage, and their favorable evaluation is an important source of support for any superior. If, on the other hand, workers commonly believe that managers "do nothing," it reflects a failure to understand that executives get things done primarily by working through others. The third interested group includes students, teachers, and scholars in this field.

Writers describing the nature of managing and the separate activities of managers and nonmanagers have adopted the technique of observation and comparison—that of eliminating activities common to both and classifying the remainder. Similar results can be obtained by deductive reasoning.

Managers may sometimes engage in activities that are not managerial. For example, a manager may type his own letters, try his hand at writing advertising copy, sell a house account, write a book, act as staff expert to his superior, or handle bank relationships at one time or another. But these activities are not managerial. Differentiating between managers and nonmanagers involves recognition of their characteristic functions. Although executives may, at their discretion or whim, engage in nonmanagerial activities, those who are not managers do not undertake executive functions.

Universality of Managerial Functions

As was pointed out in the opening chapter, managers perform the same functions regardless of their place in the organization structure or the type of enterprise in which they are engaged. Acting in their managerial capacity, presidents, department heads, foremen, supervisors, college deans, bishops, and heads of governmental agencies all do the same thing. As managers, they are all engaged in part in getting things done with and through people. As a manager, each must, at one time or another, carry out all the duties characteristic of managers. This is the principle of the universality of managerial functions.

The implications of this principle are several. In the first place, it means that anything significant that is said about the functions of one manager applies to all managers. As a consequence, it is now possible to develop a theory of management applicable to all executives in all occupations.[3] This is a significant forward step, for if the principle failed to hold, writers could report only fragmentarily on managerial activities.

In the second place, the principle implies that managerial knowledge and experience are transferable from department to department and from enterprise to enterprise: merchandising executives may be shifted to manufactur-

---

[3] Compare Urwick's remark in H. R. Light, *The Nature of Management* (London: Sir Isaac Pitman & Sons, Ltd., 1950), p. 10: "Knowledge of a particular branch of business was, and still is in many instances, the sole criterion of competence. It has only recently been recognized that there is a general ability to manage which can be made the subject of a recognized 'discipline' based upon objective research."

ing; the military commander to peaceful pursuits; foreman from flour milling to warehousing; and production managers to sales. To the extent that their tasks are managerial rather than technical, and with the proper motivation and orientation to the environment of managing, executives may employ their skill as well in one occupation as in another.

Functions versus Techniques

It is useful to distinguish between functions and techniques, because of the tendency to classify techniques along with functions in describing what managers do. Functions are the characteristic duties of the manager, while techniques refer to the way these functions are carried out. Thus a manager may be engaged in the function of directing but he may use the technique of command or persuasion. His function of controlling a subordinate's activities may be exercised through the technique of a budget; or he may organize his department with the help of the technique of written job descriptions or charts showing lines of authority.

Functions versus Nonmanagerial Skills

The failure to distinguish executive functions from nonmanagerial technical skills is another source of confusion. Technical skills, acquired through study and practice, are attributes of such experts as the chemist, the statistician, the physicist, the accountant, and the engineer. These people are, of course, vitally important to the success of their enterprises, a fact recognized in the often-heard statement that the day of the unspecialized worker is over. The technician applies his skill to any problem assigned to him in his field. A lawyer is employed to draw up sales contracts; a physicist, to undertake research in natural science; an accountant, to keep records; an engineer, to design an electronic instrument. Their skills are by no means managerial in nature. Rather, the manager employs these men, because they can do the technical work which contributes to the achievement of the enterprise objective.

The manager himself will not be using these kinds of technical skills as he plans, organizes, staffs, directs, and controls. This does not mean that he is without them. Everyone will recall that the typical individual is introduced to organized productive life by being hired as an engineer, technician, technical writer, salesman, machinist, accountant, or other specialist. In this work he applies and augments his technical skills and often goes into other work that requires other technical abilities. When he becomes a supervisor and eventually progresses upward through the managerial levels, he still has technical skill though in many cases it tends to erode quickly. He is unlikely to use these old skills in any way except as he is better fitted to ask technical questions and understand technical relationships. Since no one lives long enough to acquire many skills, the manager cannot have all the skills of those he is directing. But if he can rely upon and successfully use the technical abilities of others, he need not possess any nonmanagerial skill.

Can the possession of technical operating skills be a handicap to managers? Evidence points in both directions. Most businessmen can list accountants, lawyers, engineers, or other technical experts who are corporation presidents, but always the sample is too small to indicate reliably whether they make better or worse presidents than men with a broad production or sales background. In American business history there has been a tendency for corporations seeking presidents to name production men when their problems were those of production, sales managers when their problems were marketing, and engineers when their problems concerned research and development. This practice has generally escaped criticism, either because it was not known what the managers were supposed to do or because those selected either were already qualified as managers or they developed into good managers after their appointment.

The primary problem of the technically skilled manager involves time spent in acquiring and practicing his specialty. Continued application of a skill for ten or twenty years may narrow one's outlook. The specialist may either neglect to keep up in his own field or lose sight of the relation of his activities to those of the department or enterprise. What is more, in his capacity as an expert he is given no opportunity to practice *managing*. As managers, such men are poor risks, becoming too often, in F. C. Hooper's characterization, "one-eyed specialists in life-long grooves and niches."[4]

There are, however, two things a manager must know about technical skills. In the first place, he must know which skills should be employed in his particular enterprise and be familiar enough with their potentiality to ask discerning questions of his technical advisers. For instance, the president of a firm that manufactures a hair restorer may well read about the research on this subject being carried on at Johns Hopkins University. His technical advisers may not know about this or, as is frequently the case, may not be able to see its commercial application. This independent source of information, however, will enable the president to counsel with his advisers and broaden their viewpoint.

In the second place, a manager must understand both the role of each skill employed and the interrelationships between skills. The physicists, the chemist, the engineer, and the lawyer may delve into the same problem from different points of view. The manager then must know what to assign to and expect of each and whether all phases of the issue are being studied. He must also determine the relationship of the work of each technician to that of the others and to all other phases of the enterprise process. He decides such questions as the number of specialists in each activity, the ratio of their progress to budget, and their individual and group effect upon the product, its quality, price, and market.

In addition, most managers, particularly at lower levels in the typical organization, have technical as well as managerial functions. The director of purchasing is likely to be also the president's chief adviser on procurement policy. The head of the market research department will probably serve as the company's principal technical expert in this area. But in all such cases, it is important that the distinction be drawn between that portion of the job

---

[4]F. C. Hooper, *Management Survey* (London: Sir Isaac Pitman & Sons, Ltd., 1948), p. 150.

which is managerial and that which is technical. Only the latter part depends upon competence as a technical expert.

THE FUNCTION OF ASSEMBLING MATERIAL RESOURCES

It must be recognized that when a manager designs and maintains an environment for the performance of individuals working together in groups, he must be sure that he furnishes material as well as human resources. It is likewise true that planning, for example, requires assembling and organizing both human and material instrumentalities to assure that goals are achieved. Therefore, as the authors are fully aware, it would not be logically improper to add to the functions utilized here, the function of assembly of material resources. The system with which a manager deals includes material as well as human elements. Obviously, the manager without an office and desk, the salesman without a telephone or automobile, or the supervisor without a factory would be quite powerless.

This extensive area has, however, been excluded as a special function of managers in this book for several reasons. In the first place, the execution of other managerial functions is the *means* by which material resources are obtained and utilized, and a manager ordinarily obtains them through employing the nonmanagerial services of people. A manager does not manage capital and land; he uses them. But he does deal widely in his managerial role with people.

In the second place, by including much more than a reference to assembly of material resources, the area of knowledge it is intended to organize would be so large that it could hardly be encompassed in one brand of science. There are other fields of science that deal extensively with assembly of material instrumentalities as there are other sciences that attempt to explain such enterprise functions as marketing, manufacturing, accounting, and engineering.

All these are important to the manager who would take responsibility for any enterprise or any department of it. They interface and interlock with his managerial role. Some may be so interwoven as hardly to be separable. In presenting the material in this book, the writers are ever mindful that providing, either directly or indirectly, for material resources is an important aspect of managing. This function will be noted whenever appropriate in discussing planning, organizing, staffing, directing, and controlling. But in order to keep the subject presented here within "manageable" limits, this aspect of managing will not be dealt with as a separate major function.

AUTHORITY AND THE MANAGERIAL ROLE

Authority is the key to the management job. It is the right inherent in a position to utilize discretion in such a way that enterprise or department objectives are set and achieved. It is in this sense that authority is, to use a standard dictionary definition, a "right" and sometimes the "power to influence" behavior or action. Organization authority inheres in positions and not in people.

The power connotations of authority frequently do not exist in the same person. Power implies force, and there are few managers who really have the personal ability to enforce a decision. If matters reach a point where force is necessary, resort is usually had to the courts, the police, or other sources of coercive ability. Actually the authority vested in a managerial position is the right to use discretion, the right to create and maintain an environment for the performance of individuals working together in groups. The true implication of this ability to create is then not autocratic. It is, perhaps, no accident that "authority" derives from the same Latin root word that "author" does.

As will be seen later in the discussion of organization, authority is the basis for responsibility and is the binding force in organization. The process of organizing encompasses grouping of activities for purposes of management and specification of authority relationships between superiors and subordinates and horizontally between managers. Consequently, there are authority and responsibility relationships in all undertakings where the superior-subordinate link exists.

Despite the importance of authority, managers tend to avoid using the word, perhaps because of its connotation of power. Thus, subordinates are spoken of as having responsibility delegated to them, even though it is authority, rather than responsibility, that is delegated. The essence of responsibility is obligation—the obligation to one's superior to perform assigned duties. Similarly, one hears of managers being assigned responsibilities, when what is meant is that they are assigned duties or activities. This misused terminology may be corrected by noting that managers have authority *delegated* to them, responsibility *exacted* from them, and duties *assigned* to them, all as pertain to their position.

SOURCE OF AUTHORITY

Some disagreement has developed in the field of management as to the source of authority, experts being mainly divided between those who subscribe to the formal authority theory and those who subscribe to the acceptance theory.

The Formal Authority Theory

Until recent years, it rarely occurred to writers on management that there could be any argument about the source of a manager's authority. One had only to trace authority delegations upward from any managerial position. Thus, the supervisor of cash control obtained his authority from the assistant treasurer, who obtained his from the treasurer, who in turn got his from the president of the company, whose authority was delegated by the board of directors, who obtained theirs from the stockholders, who held theirs by virtue of the institution of private property as modified by incorporation and other laws. Thus, in a business firm, the ultimate source of authority lies principally in the institution of private property—a complex of rights, laws, mores, and folkways vesting in a person power over material resources. Naturally, this authority arises also from other social institutions. The manager, as well as the stockholder, finds himself limited by laws, by political and ethical considerations, and by such economic institutions as competition, banking, and labor unions. Governmental controls—whether in the form of direct regulations or such indirect controls as fiscal policies—constitute an institutional framework that gives added meaning and substance to the authority of corporate executives. Social institutions—whether political, economic, religious, or educational—define the bounds and content of private property and, in so doing, define the authority of the person who has the property rights. Moreover, in political or religious organizations, the authority of managers (whether governors or bishops) originates from such social institutions as representative government, the federal system of government, or the various elements of church doctrine and organization.

The origin of authority, then—whether in economic enterprises or in other enterprises where private property is nonexistent—may be traced to the elements of basic group behavior. As these elements change, the social institution of authority must change. One has only to look at the recently changing nature of private property to see how a social institution responds to the desires, objectives, and practices of the group.

The concept of authority as being a right transmitted from basic social institutions to individual managers has been called formal authority.[5] For example, in the case of private business, this authority is hierarchical, originating from the top of the institution of private property and being delegated through owners to their representatives, the managers, and through them to their subordinates.

Most formal authority theorists emphasize the legal aspects of private property as the source of authority, though good sociological analysis would broaden the source to include all related social institutions.[6]

Under our democratic form of government the right upon which managerial authority is based appears to have its primary source in the Constitution of the United States. Since the Constitution is the creature of the people, subject to amendment and modification by the will of the people, it follows that the total society, through government, is the source from which delegated authority flows to ownership and thence to managers. Indeed, the entire social institution of private property is molded not only by the Constitution, but by many federal and state legislative and administrative regulations, and by the mores of the entire American society.

The Acceptance Theory

The notion that the real source of managerial authority is acceptance by subordinates of the power the manager holds over them can be traced directly

---

[5] C. I. Barnard, *The Functions of the Executive* (Cambridge, Mass.: Harvard University Press, 1938), pp. 162ff.

[6] Note that "institutions," as here used in the sociological sense, means a complex of laws, codes, mores, and folkways by which a social group attains and enforces group purpose.

from the syndicalists through Laski to the American business executive Chester I. Barnard and is perhaps best expressed by Barnard's definition of authority:[7]

. . . the character of a communication (order) in a formal organization by virtue of which it is accepted by a contributor to or "member" of the organization as governing the action he contributes; that is, as governing or determining what he does or is not to do far as the organization is concerned. According to this definition, authority involves two aspects: first, the subjective, the personal, the accepting of a communication as authoritative . . . ; and, second, the objective aspect—the character in the communication by virtue of which it is accepted.

Barnard argues that ". . . the necessity of the assent of the individual to establish authority *for him* is inescapable."[8] Barnard's position is that a subordinate will "accept" the authority of a command if he understands it, if he believes it consistent with organization purpose and compatible with his own interests, and if he is mentally and physically able to comply with it. A subordinate must, then, determine if these conditions exist before obeying. But even Barnard thinks this improbable, for he carefully explains that, in enduring organizations, orders usually conform to the above conditions; within an "indifference zone" in each individual, orders are acceptable without question, and group pressure is on the side of accepting orders. Thus, instead of the subordinate making a complex decision to obey or disobey, as required by the bald statement of the acceptance theory, Barnard makes it easy for him by saying that most orders are automatically acceptable, the subordinate doesn't care really, and group pressure will make him comply anyway. Moreover, Barnard dilutes his own theory somewhat by admitting that a "fiction"—which is nonetheless real—of superior authority exists and is necessary; he also admits that "authority in the aggregate arises from *all* contributors to a cooperative system."[9]

It is difficult to adopt the acceptance theorists' hedonistic formula for the source of managerial authority.[10] The very fact that some of the most important advantages of accepting and disadvantages of not accepting authority arise from the manager's power to grant or withhold rewards or to dismiss the subordinate makes the theory unreal. The soldier's obedience to commands —because the alternative is the guardhouse or the firing squad—is hardly genuine acceptance, nor is acceptance more genuine where a civilian's alternative is to quit his job or be fired.

Moreover, the implications of the theory are serious for the continuation of order in organization. If acceptance were the source of authority, the manager would, strictly speaking, be in the position of not knowing from one command to another whether he would be obeyed, for until he was obeyed, he would have no authority to command. Furthermore, if subordinates confer managerial power, they must also confer power to levy sanctions.

[7] Barnard, *op. cit.*, p. 163.
[8] *Ibid.*, p. 167.
[9] *Ibid.*, pp. 170 and 168n.
[10] For an extended analysis of this problem, see Cyril O'Donnell, "The Source of Managerial Authority," *Political Science Quarterly*, vol. 47, pp. 583–588 (December, 1952).

The basic error of the acceptance theorists consists not only in conceiving authority without sanctions but also in overlooking the powerful effect of social institutions, which confer powers that supersede individual desires. The authority of ownership involved in the institution of private property, for example, carries with it the right to contract for services or to grant or withhold remuneration, except, of course, as the right has been circumscribed by such other institutional developments as labor unions and labor legislation.

Order in organized behavior cannot be achieved without authority, since this force unifies the social group. The alternative, as Malinowski has pointed out,[11] is chaos: "Submission to laws as well as the power to enforce laws and rules are indispensable to human behavior." In a free society, the person who contracts to work for another agrees, *at that time,* to obey the proper orders of superiors while in their employ. Also, in a free society, the employee may resign if he no longer wishes to obey. But, during the period of employment, he has no power to confer authority on his superior. In unfree societies, the subordinate has no choice but to obey if he wishes to escape jail or other punishment.

It appears, then, that the acceptance theorists are not discussing authority at all, but leadership—the ability to persuade others to work well to accomplish a group goal.

But the uses of authority are much more comprehensive than merely to secure the compliance of subordinates. Managers use authority to contract with labor unions concerning working conditions and practices, with financial firms for raising capital, and with vendors for the acquisition of land and capital. The acceptance theory fails entirely to explain the source of authority to accomplish these ends.

The Competence Theory

In addition to the formal and acceptance theories of the source of authority, although perhaps more closely related to the latter, is the belief that authority is generated by personal qualities or technical competence.[12] Under this heading is the individual who has made, in effect, subordinates of others through sheer force of personality and the engineer or economist who exerts influence by furnishing answers or sound advice. These may have no actual organizational authority, yet their advice may be so eagerly sought and so unerringly followed that it appears to carry the weight of an order.

But, above all, one cannot discount the importance of formal authority with its institutional foundations. Buttressed by the qualities of leadership

---

[11] Bronislaw Malinowski, *Freedom and Civilization* (New York: Roy Publishers, 1944), p. 27. Ranyard West, in speaking of primitive organizations, has observed that "the prime requisite and firm creator of any community life is a law of order maintained by force." See his *Conscience and Society* (London: Methuen & Co., Ltd., 1942).

[12] L. F. Urwick, *The Elements of Administration* (New York: Harper & Row, Publishers, Incorporated, 1944). In a discussion on p. 47, Urwick speaks of "formal" authority as being "conferred by organization," of "technical" authority as being "implicit in special knowledge or skill," and of "personal" authority as being "conferred by seniority or popularity."

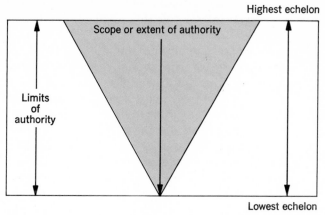

Figure 3.1 *Limits of authority of various echelons of an organization structure.*

implicit in the acceptance theory, formal authority is basic to the managerial job. Once possessed, it may be delegated or withheld, used or misused, and effective in capable hands or ineffective in inept hands.

LIMITS OF AUTHORITY

The generality of the right to command decreases as it proceeds from the highest to the lowest echelon of an organization structure, as illustrated in Figure 3.1. One may visualize this characteristic of authority as an inverted pyramid, with the front-line manager at its bottom point. His right to command is severely restricted in every direction. But as one follows the chain of command to the top of the organization structure, the area of authority of the executives at each level gradually expands.

However, the institutional foundation of authority implies that this power is never absolute but that it, like private property, changes with shifts in group behavior. Within an enterprise, the exerciser of authority must remember that his right is limited by the mores of his subordinates. A minority racial group, for example, or a small-town group will each react to authority in its own individual way, while the managerial subordinates and the nonmanagerial employees of a highly organized company may react differently from a group of stockholding subordinates. These are examples of social limitations on the exercise of authority.

There are also biological limitations placed on authority by the fact that human beings do not have the capacity to do certain things; one can hardly, for instance, order a person to walk up the side of a building. Other limitations are physical—climate, geography, physical laws, and chemical elements; an order to make gold from copper would be futile. In addition, there are technological constraints; a factory would not be ordered on the moon—at least not until technology had made this possible. There are also economic limitations on managerial authority: competitor prices and service levels determined by the market, and ownership by a rival of an advantageous resource or location, for example.

There are other diverse and complex limitations upon executive authority. The right to change enterprise objectives and methods is frequently hedged about in partnership agreements and in articles of incorporation. The statutes reserve to stockholders certain broad rights; bylaws frequently delimit authority, as when the right to employ an auditor is reserved to the board of directors; and policies, procedures, and programs further guide action. Obviously, every manager, whether of high or low degree, must respect such restrictions, which affect all managers alike; no one is ever free to ignore a procedure, violate a policy, or modify a program. Changes can be made, of course, but not at the whim of any individual.

Each manager, in addition, is subject to specific limitations ordinarily found in his delegation of authority. As will be noted in a later discussion,[13] these are usually specific limits on his ability to commit the enterprise in dollar expenditures, or limitations may be imposed by certain approval rights of others, or they may be circumscribed by various approved policies or procedures.

RESPONSIBILITY

Responsibility is one of the most misunderstood terms in the literature of management. It is common to hear and read about "delegating responsibilities," "holding a person responsible," "discharging responsibility," and "carrying out a responsibility." Responsibility is variously used to mean duty, activity, obligation, or authority.

Viewed internally with respect to the enterprise, responsibility may be defined as the obligation of a subordinate to perform assigned and implied duties. The essence of responsibility is, then, *obligation*. Responsibility has no meaning except as applied to a person; a building, a machine, or an animal cannot be held responsible.

Responsibility arises from the superior-subordinate relationship, from the fact that someone (in this case, a manager) has the authority to require specified services from another person. This authority in business normally results from a contractual arrangement by which the subordinate agrees to perform such services—perhaps using delegated authority—in return for monetary and other rewards. Thus, authority flows from the superior to the subordinate manager when duties are assigned; and responsibility is the obligation simultaneously exacted from the subordinate for the accomplishment of those duties.

Responsibility may be a continuing obligation, or it may be discharged by a single action and not arise again. The relationship between a president

[13] See chap. 18.

and his sales manager is typical of a continuing obligation; on the other hand, the president may hire, for an organization study, a consulting management engineer whose obligation will cease when the assignment is completed.

A problem in responsibility sometimes arises when informal leadership appears. For example, a sales manager may have as subordinates an advertising manager, a sales promotion manager, and three district sales managers. For many reasons—among them, perhaps, the powerful position of the production manager—some of the sales manager's subordinates may look to the production manager for guidance. This informal relationship may have the effect of reducing the influence but not the authority of the sales manager over his subordinates. Unless this shift is made with the approval of the president or the sales manager—thus constituting a change in the organization structure itself—the basic responsibility relationships would not be changed. The president would still hold the sales manager responsible for the department's performance, and the subordinates would still be responsible to the sales manager.

Responsibility and Delegation

Responsibility cannot be delegated. While a manager may delegate to a subordinate authority to accomplish a service and the subordinate, in turn, may delegate a portion of the authority received, neither delegates any of his responsibility. Responsibility, being an obligation to perform, is owed to one's superior, and no subordinate reduces his responsibility by delegating to another the authority to perform a duty.

No manager, then, can shift responsibility to his subordinates. The president employed by the board of directors cannot avoid total responsibility for the conduct of the enterprise. If employees are derelict in their duties, enrage customers, or carry on warfare with a trade union, the president must answer to the board for these things and all other actions of any employee. He cannot claim to have "delegated the responsibility" to a manager, who may, indeed, have caused the trouble.

This inability to delegate responsibility is illustrated by an incident at a company developing a careful financial plan, where a simple arithmetic error made by a clerk affected the projection of cash needs so much that, when discovered, it caused considerable embarrassment. The error was disclosed at the meeting between the board finance committee and bankers arranging the loan. The finance vice-president who had presented the forecast could hardly waive responsibility by explaining that a clerk in a unit of the planning section of the assistant treasurer's office in the treasurer's department had made the error. The finance vice-president was responsible to the board for the mistake, the treasurer was responsible to the vice-president, the assistant treasurer to the treasurer, the planning section chief to the assistant treasurer, the forecast unit head to the planning chief, and the clerk to the forecast unit head. Although authority had been delegated and duties assigned at each level, no one was relieved of his responsibility.

Accountability

A few writers in the field of management use the term "accountability" to indicate liability for the proper discharge of duties by the subordinate. The concept of accountability is also widely used in military organizations to indicate the duty of an officer to keep accurate records and to safeguard public property and funds. Although this concept may be useful in military organizations, it clearly has strong overtones of a control technique. Even so, accountability is really an aspect of responsibility, and since the latter term has much wider currency in management practice, it will be employed here exclusively.

AUTHORITY AND LEADERSHIP

In pointing out the central role of authority in making organization and managership possible and in recognizing authority as a socially given right to command or act, it must be emphasized that the existence of authority does not imply authoritarian use of it. A manager may literally order his subordinates, or he may ask, suggest, or persuade them; he may also use such techniques of directing as counseling, teaching, suggesting, or allowing a decision to arise naturally from a discussion. But regardless of how the authority is applied, the manager must have it, and its dispersal in the organization must be coordinated. Managers, to be effective, cannot and should not shy away from the fact of their having authority. Those who find authority distasteful and pose as operating "democratically" seldom deceive subordinates, who readily understand that their chief has, and must have, as an occupant of his position, certain rights of decision that can affect their jobs.

Subordinates respond to direction in all organized activities. They respond because, on balance, they stand to gain net advantages in meeting their physical, social, and psychic needs. Disregard of authority tends to exclude them from the enterprise. In a democratic society, they may be free to join another cooperative group, but here also they would be required to deal with superiors. Even with numbers large enough to revolt successfully, a new cooperative arrangement would develop, requiring response to superiors who would ultimately obtain authority from the members of the society.

Moreover, it is sometimes overlooked that the most essential use of managerial authority is to give the manager the means by which he can create and maintain an environment for performance. By having the authority either to specify or to work out meaningful goals with subordinates, to give them the power in turn to accomplish these goals and the means and assistance to do so, to give them training and understanding of their role in the enterprise and of their relationships to others, and to reward them through promotion, pay increases, and improved status, the manager is truly using authority in a creative way.

Authority is not a social invention to give people power for prestige or authoritarian conduct, but an instrument to place in an organizational role the means of doing something creative. It behooves the intelligent manager never to forget this simple fact.

However, the purpose of authority is to make sure that plans will be co-ordinated and tasks assigned to persons able to do them. Good employees respond best to leaders who plan soundly; organize clearly; select, train, and direct subordinates well; and bring plans to fruition. Undue emphasis on human relations often befogs the fact that the best human relations grow out of successful group accomplishment. This is not to regard interpersonal relations and the human element as other than extremely important aspects of the managerial job. But managerial leadership requires much more than smooth interpersonal relationships. In other words, able managing usually gives rise to a situation in which subordinates find that their best interests lie in following superiors they can respect.

Most of the aspects and techniques of leadership are encompassed in the managerial function of directing, which will be discussed in later chapters.

FOR DISCUSSION

1. Do you see any advantage in attempts to classify the functions of managers? Is there any advantage in the use of the same classifications by scholars and managers?
2. Propose a scheme of classification which appeals to you and explain your preference.
3. Why should the functions of integrating, motivating, and coordinating not be included in the functions of managers?
4. Can you see how the five functions of managers are really an integrated social system?
5. When you are accepted for a position, what authority are you agreeing to obey? Can you later take back your agreement to abide by this authority?
6. What use do you think the word "accountability" serves?
7. Where would you say the authority of a manager originates?
8. How can managerial authority be used creatively?

4

the manager and his environment

Enterprises, like men, do not live unto themselves alone. No manager operates in a closed social system. This may not have always been so. In the dim past, even the family, man's first and continuing institution, may have existed in the short and happenstance fashion of our ancient forebears. But at the dawn of history, this institution was well established, as was the tribe. Increasing population and the agricultural revolution were new forces with which men had to deal. These could not be managed by the individual alone, and he gradually created institutions, such as the town, government, army, education, and religion, to help him. The proliferation of institutions has proceeded down to our own day, where they often exist in bewildering confusion.

However institutions and enterprises are created, they securely enfold the individual beyond any possibility of escape. As Gotshalk sees it:[1]

Every human being is born into a social order. This order begins with the family, or at least with the parent-child relation, but it is actually as extensive as the human race. This complex order with its many interior orders provides the setting and chief condition of the individual's existence. . . . Romantics have dreamed of escaping it. Not only is there no place one can go, on earth or elsewhere, independent of society, but for a good segment of the individual's life . . . he is incompetent to go.

Our own experience confirms this view. The one great and overriding social institution is the state. It was created as the most desirable means of maintaining peace and justice for citizens and residents alike. Subservient to the state are uncounted groups and enterprises of varying scope and purpose. They include educational, subgovernmental, religious, and business institutions; health and recreation organizations; trade unions; professional societies; farm unions; war veterans' associations; political parties; charter parties; and bridge clubs. No individual is a member of every group, but each is a member of many. His membership often shifts with age and time, but his whole life

---

[1] D. W. Gotshalk, *Patterns of Good and Evil* (Urbana, Ill.: University of Illinois Press, 1963), p. 128.

is spent as an active or passive member of several groups simultaneously. From this fact of our lives there emerges a number of major problems.

Membership in several groups is bound to create a conflict in loyalties for the individual. As a member of a union, he may support the leadership in striving for higher wages, but his family may suffer from a strike; he may have to weigh the advantages of a higher living standard against pressures to make religious or charitable contributions; he may want a "welfare state" but dislike paying the taxes to support it. These and many other sets of circumstances pose difficult psychological problems. Some individuals respond by being consumed with frustration; most seem able to cope with diverse purposes, seeking refuge in compromise and in their lack of discernment.

The tyranny of the majority is a major trial. In the United States, our tradition is to strive vigorously for what one thinks is right but to submit to the majority if one loses. In small matters, this is a convenient formula; but in large matters, especially those wherein principles are at stake, the very life of the institutional group may be risked by an undiscerning majority. Resigning from a group may not solve the problem—nonmembership may be even worse—and at the very highest level, one cannot resign his citizenship without becoming an expatriate. For those who find themselves in a hopeless minority in vital matters, only a life of difficulty awaits.

Man being man, there is always a sense of lost freedom of action among members of institutional groups. It is not merely because man is romantic or nostalgic about the past days of freedom. He wants to make his own decisions, act as he feels he ought, be free of social pressures—follow his own rational and emotional drives. He wants to self-actualize in his own way. Of course, one must be realistic even while sympathizing with man's struggle for individuality. There are few places on this earth where real freedom can be found. Society has been organized to the point that one can no longer satisfy his basic needs by his own means. This means that man will be forever responding to social pressures to live in the "right" way, to work at certain hours—in short, to conform. Men can learn to do a certain amount of this; they will have to learn to do more. As they do so, the bright light of freedom will continue to fade away.

The foregoing problems stress the issues which men face as organization members. This view of interpersonal relationships is often contested by those who see no difference between the interrelationships of organizations and of their members.[2] This position is difficult to accept, however, since no organization can act unless the men who occupy its power center act. It has no personality, no conscience of its own. Although it is convenient to personify the state, the corporation, the church, or the university, it is readily understood that these organizations are lifeless without the actions of the men who make decisions in their name. Thus, the actions of groups are, in reality, the actions of the men who manage them, and these actions emanate from their principles and convictions.

[2] Cf. B. W. Dempsey, "The Roots of Business Responsibility," in E. C. Bursk (ed.), *Business and Religion* (New York: Harper & Row, Publishers, Incorporated, 1959), p. 111.

EXTERNAL ENVIRONMENTAL FORCES

The managers who are responsible for the success of any organized effort are also concerned about the external forces which impinge upon them. They have never been free of these influences. Even in the most primitive circumstances a family, unconcerned about distant neighbors, was nonetheless concerned about the changing conditions of its physical environment. Weather, the availability of food and water, and personal safety occupied a large place in its conscious concern. In our own day we are still not free from the impact of these same external realities on decision making; but they have been aggravated and complicated beyond measure by man himself.

Managers cannot control the "external environment." They must identify, evaluate, and react to those forces external to the enterprise which may affect its welfare. But what is the identification process? There is a strong temptation to take into consideration those forces that others have compiled, or simply consider those forces of which they themselves are conscious. In either approach they would have a feeling that maybe they were missing something important. There is clearly a need for classification.

Some have suggested that external forces be grouped into political, economic, social, and technological sections. Others want to add international forces, religions, and education. There are others who wonder why history, culture, and ethics are not included. The point of view of the classifier dictates these suggestions. The bishop, the teacher, and the bureaucrat see the problem differently; so also do the specialists within each of these fields. The authors of this book approach the problem from the viewpoint of the manager of an organized enterprise. Through the area of every one of these, whether he is the head of a business, a church, a government agency, a university, or a hospital, there runs the common thread of utilizing resources to effect a social purpose. Consequently, the tentative classification of the external environment is composed of the forces that affect the market for the product or service and those that influence the availability of the productive resources required; the quality, supply, and cost of ancillary services; and the influence of the social systems. The secondary and tertiary breakouts from this classification entail environmental forces of bewildering complexity. Furthermore, these categories are by no means distinct: some forces, such as technology and the nature of society, deeply influence every one of them.

Since all enterprises have a product or a service to distribute, they are all concerned about the market for their product. Demographic factors have a predominant influence on the location of a facility. The buying power or tax-paying ability of the community to be served is never overlooked. The competition of others for this market is evaluated. For instance, the location of a church in a community that is already being fully served by competing religious organizations could be a good move if its proselyting ability were matched with apathetic communicants in the community.

Sometimes the literacy of the product market population is critical to success. It certainly influences how the product is promoted, how potential customers are instructed in the use of the service or product, and how the product will be received. And sometimes literacy is not enough. There are religious taboos that may be respected. It used to be an important business consideration that Catholics could not eat meat on Fridays and Jews could not eat pork at any time.

Public support for the goods and services offered by every organized enterprise is very much a matter of external forces. World-wide instant propaganda can be generated by the communication devices that bind the world so tightly. In a matter of moments the opinion of millions of people can be changed by someone, often irresponsibly, telling them that the French have wrecked NATO, that the Japanese are destroying American textile businesses, that a product of the General Motors Corporation is unsafe, that the credit of a firm is shaky. Public support is the very lifeblood of every institution, and the risk of its erosion is a nightmare to enterprise managers.

Illustrations of the effect of external forces on the factor market abound. Physical resources tend to become more and more scarce as population increases. Competition for their use can be intense. Their nature can be changed, to some extent, by technological improvements. The source of needed resources is sometimes world-wide, and their availability often depends upon transportation facilities, international politics, conservation and antipollution movements.

It is very difficult to grasp the full impact of technological change on the factor market. As Henry B. Schacht, president of Cummins Engine Company, observes:[3]

It staggers our imagination to realize that 95% of all the scientists and engineers who have ever existed from the beginning of history are alive and hard at work today. The sheer bulk of their annual work is overwhelming and guarantees that the place of innovation, invention, and the onset of change will speed up, not slow down.

The new materials and equipment that appear upon the heels of expanding technical knowledge create obsolescence and an enormous demand for capital. If an enterprise is to keep alive, it must compete in new products, new approaches in materials and design, and new techniques for producing the end product.

The operators of all enterprises, whether organized or not, compete with each other for land, capital, and labor in ways that change from day to day. Competition for the air above us, for the minerals and space of land and sea, for money and credit, and for human skills is deeply affected by the expansion of knowledge. The factor market tends to expand around the world. Manufacturers and financial houses borrow Eurodollars; businessmen and governments explore for resources in every land and every ocean; merchants buy in world-wide markets; the International Monetary Fund affects the exchange rates of the world's currencies; and international agreements affect the flow of goods and investments.

For most of the enterprises in the United States, ancillary services are provided by third parties and are therefore external to the firm. Government,

[3]"The Impact of Changes in the Seventies," *Business Horizons*, vol. 13, no. 4, p. 30 (August, 1970).

for example, supplies mail service, a monetary system, credit and insurance of some types; utilities are expected to provide power, water, telephone service, and sometimes transportation; private enterprises provide for markets, banks, entertainment, and sometimes religious and educational services. All these services are required, in one way or another, in the operation of a given organization. It is quite clear that no enterprise could exist unless these services were made available either by the enterprise itself or by others. And in either case, the importance of keeping up with technological change is obviously a vital matter. Any enterprise could be ruined by slow and problematical mail and transportation service, the inadequate supply of power and water, and the facilities to house, feed, and entertain people. They affect the product and factor markets and predetermine the availability of labor and financial services.

The social system within which every enterprise must operate is immensely complex. There are government systems that establish the legal apparatus, give aid and comfort to some enterprises and limit or prohibit others, decree the tax structure and assessment levels, reflect the political arrangements that the people want or are forced to accept, decree the type of economic organization that will prevail, and supposedly see to the safety of persons and property. The political factor is a dominant social arrangement within which enterprises must operate. It reflects the attitudes of a people toward government, religion, education, business, freedom, ethics, foreign relations, and power. Sometimes these attitudes are a compromise of differing viewpoints; sometimes they are imposed by a few strong men. However derived, they establish the climate and the rules for those who operate enterprises of all types.

There is a rather widespread belief that enterprise managers can cope with the external forces if they only know what they are and, even better, forecast them. To a considerable extent this is true. In fact this is why there is as much success in the operation of organized effort as can be observed. We do have successful businesses, universities, religions, hospitals, and many other types of enterprises. Perhaps if a people intend that there will be success, then that success will be realized. However, this view is probably too sanguine. There are many areas in which the people's viewpoint is changing, and there are several areas in which the demands upon institutions are unjust on the one hand and reflect the need for principle on the other. For instance, the demand for socially responsible action proceeds from assumptions that are often unacceptable; and the demand for ethical action assumes that there are generally acceptable principles in this area of social concern. In the face of these types of external forces, the enterprise manager is often at a loss to know how to respond. Let us look at a case in point.

Business Enterprise: A Case in Point

When a business enterprise is the subject of discussion, it is probable that most people conjure up visions of a manufacturing firm, a department store, a railroad, or a brokerage house. These and similar enterprises are rather clearly defined, but their listing does not convey the extent and variety of

business. It is necessary to turn to the economist for a comprehensive definition. He conceives a business to be any activity that is concerned with the
production (or purchase) for sale of scarce goods and services. Such an enterprise may be conducted by one person or thousands, and may be owned and
operated in many different ways.

The purpose of economic activity is always the same: it is to employ
human and natural resources, and the capital that is accumulated through
savings, in the production of goods and services which the ultimate consumers
want. So far as we know, the wants of consumers are infinitely expansible,
even while particular wants for any individual may well become satiated.
Because resources are not free but are scarce, a decision has to be made concerning how they are to be employed, that is, what will actually be produced.
What we know as high living standards result from the skillful use of relatively
opulent capital and skilled human as well as natural resources to produce
large volumes and wide varieties of goods and services relative to the number
of consumers. Thus, the purpose of business is to satisfy the economic wants
of people, and, since resources are scarce, their efficient use is a socially responsive requirement.

Economic Organization

There are a variety of ways in which economic activity may be organized.
The typical classifications include free enterprise, socialism, communism,
and the welfare state. If enterprise is really free, it permits individuals to establish and operate a business as they see opportunities to profit from the exchange of goods or services. Of course, totally free enterprise has never existed.
Even Adam Smith reserved to government such functions as protection of the
people from foreign and domestic aggression, the administration of justice,
and the production of services or goods that private business was unable to
accomplish.

A fundamental assumption of a free enterprise system is the existence
of effective and responsible competition. Thus, the "invisible hand" of competition will lead sellers to produce those things desired by buyers—as expressed by their purchasing choices—at the lowest possible prices. If any seller
either makes too much profit or produces goods inefficiently, it is postulated
that competitive forces will bring other sellers into the market. The result is
that competition plus desire for goods at lowest prices and desire for profits
will give rise to a total system where those products and services most desired
will be made available at the lowest possible prices.

The British socialists advocated an economic organization wherein the
state would own and operate the basic means of production, by which they
meant enterprises concerned with transportation, power, steel, and textiles.
These were typically large enterprises whose power the socialists feared. Free
enterprise would be permitted elsewhere in the economy, however. Communist theory, on the other hand, requires that the state own and operate all types
of enterprises. Thus, communists would go further down the road to state
ownership and simply prohibit almost all kinds of private economic activity.

But this does not mean that business does not exist in a purely socialistic country. It means, rather, that the state owns and operates business enterprises. Thus, economic goods and services are produced, as they always must be, but this is accomplished through a system of public ownership and distribution.

None of the foregoing types of economic organization really describes accurately the relationships that currently exist in the United States. Beginning with almost totally free enterprise, restrictions upon the freedom of businessmen to make decisions have been gradually introduced. These limitations relate to central banking, regulation of monopolies, control of price-fixing, and prevention of certain advertising and fraudulent practices. On the positive side, legislation now requires such things as bargaining with trade unions under certain conditions, collecting taxes without recompense, and fair employment practices. In addition, the state provides a wide variety of services, such as social security and medicare. Fortunately, the state has not seen fit to own and operate many businesses. The special genius of Americans is to modify free enterprise through regulation rather than through public ownership and operation. This suits the American temperament, is more in line with our economic traditions, and can be made workable provided that the following principles are adhered to:[4]

1. *Primacy of Free Enterprise: Government interference in free enterprise is permissible only after a clear public advantage has been demonstrated.*
2. *Democratic Action: Every instrument designed to limit, channel, or coerce private economic activity must be instituted by the democratic process.*
3. *Clarity and Unity of Purpose: The purpose of government interference in private economic activity should be clearly stated, be integrated, and be periodically reviewed.*
4. *Provision for Authority: Administrative authority should be adequate for the purpose and be indirectly applied.*

The Business of Business

There is no doubt whatever that the function of business is to make economic goods and services available for consumption. Neither is there any question about the magnitude and complexity of this work. It is one of the historical trio of major functions of society, the others being government and religion. But it is not enough to produce economic goods; the first duty of business is to produce them efficiently. As Donald K. David remarked:[5]

I feel strongly that operating a successful business is the first responsibility of a business leader. The simple fact is that in our society the businessman is primarily responsible for organizing the production and distribution of the nation's goods and services. He can meet that responsibility only through the competent management of business enterprise and through the creation and development of healthy business

---

[4] Cyril O'Donnell, "Coordination des Plans des Enterprises et des Objectifs Economiques de la Nation," *Economie Appliqée*, Tome XVIX, I, II, pp. 209–233 (1965).

[5] Quoted by Dempsey, *op, cit.*, p. 110.

concerns. To me it is unrealistic to presume that the business leader can discharge any other responsibility if he fails in this, his foremost job.

Since businessmen obtain control of scarce resources by the purchase or lease of land and capital and hire human services, they have a moral responsibility for using them efficiently in the production and distribution of consumer goods. Only in this way can every person in society obtain access to its resources, and this is their right.

Quite irrespective of the type of economic organization, the moral responsibility remains with those who own and operate or regulate business enterprise. It is the business of society to prescribe which type of economic organization best discharges the responsibility for use of resources. Efficiency in resource employment is undoubtedly best achieved through free enterprise.[6] It is the business of the state to make sure through legislation and regulation that the private economy does not fail in its function to efficiently utilize resources to maximize the satisfaction of consumer wants for economic goods and services. The state is not equipped to accomplish this result by means of a monolithic bureaucracy.

CRITICISMS OF THE PRIVATE PROFIT MOTIVE

The accomplishments of the relatively free enterprise system, with appropriate regulation in the United States, are tremendously impressive. The volume and quality of goods and services which it has produced were inconceivable in even the recent past and there is little question that these will continue to be expanded into the future. And yet, in this plethora of wealth that surrounds us, there are many individuals who take serious exception to our accomplishments, who are dissatisfied with the economic organization which produced these results, and who would have us so modify the system, through changing the ground rules, as to make it more like the social systems found in Eastern Europe. These critics are willing to give up an efficient system they know for a system that has not worked efficiently and with which they have had no experience.

The Critical Positions

Central to the criticisms directed toward the economic organization of this society is the attack upon the private profit motive. It matters little whether these people are regurgitating the views of Marx, Lenin, or Sydney Webb; whether, as Levin thinks,[7] they are ignorant of economics and are victims of self-pity; or whether they desire power and have an immense envy of success. The profit motive is attacked because, allegedly, it is responsible for material-

---

[6] M. Friedman, "The Market v. the Bureaucrat," *National Review*, vol. 22, no. 19, pp. 507–510, 525–528 (May 19, 1970).

[7] R. I. Levin, "Profits and Responsibility," *Mississippi Valley Journal of Business and Economics*, vol. 1, no. 1, p. 92 (Fall, 1965).

ism and because, as Galbraith asserts,[8] it provides the motivation for producing goods that consumers should not want to want.

Materialism

If the charge of materialism proceeds from those who are envious, it does not merit a reply. But if it is made by those who are seriously concerned about the direction of man's efforts, it is important to inquire into the bases for their position and into what they think men "ought" to do. These critics of materialism rest their case upon personal conviction; they have no authority of position or of uncontestable source. They have suggested, at one time or another, that men should be devoted to the spiritual life, to humanitarianism, to aestheticism, to stoicism. To these people, these ends seem superior to an asserted devotion to materialism. Their views are based upon various assumptions about man's nature and his purposes. They are selective in stressing certain facets of man's nature, such as his wish for immortality, his tolerance and compassion, his striving for beauty, and his pride in emotional repression, each of which is considered admirable.

Poor Choice of Goods

Galbraith's view that people cannot be trusted to determine what they want because they do not want what they should proceeds from a monolithic egotism. The point at issue here is: Who is to judge? In our society, we do have certain laws that restrict or prohibit the production and consumption of goods that are dangerous to personal well-being. This is a proper test to apply. Beyond this, it is important to remember that man is a wanting animal and that none of us is endowed with either the right or the prescience to restrict these desires in others.

Dislike of the Economic System

Perhaps the positions taken by the critics of profit making are not real. It may well be that they really want to destroy the profit objective of business. If this is true, the question merely becomes one of economic organization. Students already know what the alternatives are. The free enterprise, regulated in fairness to all, utilizes scarce resources most effectively. This is what an economic system is supposed to do. Those who receive business profits are the men and women who successfully risk their capital by investing in small business or in the stock of large businesses; all others concerned with these enterprises are employees who receive their income from wages and salaries. No one has ever calculated the return on total investment in any country, but it must be very small, considering the large number of failures that must also be included. It is the individual opportunity which attracts investment. If the question is to be decided on the basis of efficiency of the function and not on political or

[8]J. K. Galbraith, *The Affluent Society* (Boston: Houghton, Mifflin Co., 1958), chap. 22.

imperialistic grounds, there is no question of the superiority of the responsibly competitive free enterprise system.

Fear of Power

There are other critics who are impressed with the great power of large-scale corporations and assert that if they are to retain this power, they should be held responsible for supporting other commendable institutions, such as the community, government, and education. Looking internally at any large business enterprise, one is bound to be impressed with the scope of these powers.[9] But the large firm finds itself considerably restricted in their use. First, there is the competitive structure of industry. In this environment any one firm must be aware of the competition of thousands of other firms for land, capital, and personnel. As it acquires resources, it must compete with many others who are in the market for them. As it sells its products, it must compete for the buyers' dollars. In this situation, no firm can be arbitrary.

Second, there are important legal safeguards. There are laws against collusion, monopolies, and various forms of unfair competition. The right of eminent domain gives governmental bodies access to the land they need. And there is always the threat that antisocial activity will result in further limiting their freedom of action.

Third, there is the force of voluntary restraint. For instance, the pension and investment funds do have power to vote the shares they own in corporations. In this way, they, being few but potent, could easily control numerous businesses. To date they have not chosen to exercise this right, perhaps because they fear potential regulation by government, or perhaps they realize that they may be expert in fund management but not in the management of other enterprises.

Social Irresponsibility

There are other critics of business who stoutly maintain that these enterprises do not discharge their social responsibilities. All of the critics are extremely vague and the terms used are rarely defined. It seems that business is supposed to be a better citizen by taking better care of employees, consumers, and the community; by solving social problems; by contributing more to religious institutions, charity, and education; and by helping government carry the social load.

RATIONAL VIEW OF SOCIAL RESPONSIBILITY

A clear understanding of the terminology selected to describe a concept is very difficult to attain. The phrase "social responsibility" is widely used in

[9]See A. A. Berle, Jr., *Power without Property* (New York: Harcourt, Brace & World, Inc., 1959), p. 79. See also K. Davis, "Can Business Afford to Ignore Social Responsibilities?" *California Management Review*, vol. 2, no. 3, pp. 70–76 (Spring, 1960).

the literature of sociology, anthropology, economics, politics, and business management. One writer defines the concept as the ". . . obligation [of managers] to pursue those policies, to make those decisions, or to follow those lines of action which are desirable in terms of the objectives and values of our society."[10] Despite the seeming clarity of this definition, it still contains vague phrases and assumes everyone knows those to whom an obligation is owed and the meaning of social values. Presumably, managers are obliged to make decisions that are within the framework of the nation's social values, about which there is no consensus, and whatever they do, they must support all values whether they approve of them or not. Clearly, there is much to be desired that is not present in this "definition."

Since an obligation can only be owed by one person to another, social responsibility is an interpersonal relationship that exists when people are continuously or discontinuously dependent upon one another in both an organized and an unorganized way. As a working definition, social responsibility, as used in this book, is the personal obligation of everyone, as he acts in his own interests, to assure that the rights and legitimate interests of all others are not impinged. It is perhaps, unfortunate that this concept is stated negatively, but it is convenient to conceive of social responsibility in this way.

Thus, the socially responsible person will obey the laws of the land because the rights of others are at stake. He is free to support the institutions and individuals of his choice, or he may take a neutral stand, neither supporting nor interfering with the well-being of institutions and individuals. But he may not by word or deed attempt to destroy institutions or impinge upon the rights and interests of individuals except through legal processes.

The implications of this view of social responsibility are several. First, the neutral and negative aspects of personal behavior are as important as the positive. For instance, an individual nonmember is not obliged to support a trade union. He may be quite neutral, but he may not set forth to destroy it except through the legislative or judicial process. Similarly, a person is not obliged to support a church, a charity, a university, or a community, so long as there is no legal requirement for membership or for the payment of taxes in their behalf.

The same view is held on interpersonal relationships. Except for unlawful discrimination on the basis of race, sex, or religion, one person may well give preference to another in terms of a job (other than those covered in a union contract), a promotion, or an advance in status, because none of these acts, and similar marks of interest, restricts the rights of others.

A second implication is that the social obligation is owed by individuals and not by organizations. A club, a church, a university, or a corporation does not discharge a responsibility; it can act only by means of the persons who invoke its name. Social responsibility is a personal attribute; there is no action without personal action. To be sure, this viewpoint is frequently obscured by our habit of personifying enterprises and by the legal fiction that clothes a

---

[10] H. R. Bowen, *Social Responsibilities of the Businessman* (New York: Harper & Row, Publishers, Incorporated, 1953), p. 6.

corporation with personality. But this is no reason why students should not make the appropriate distinction. When a state university uses its funds to engage in politics, a church expels a member, a club blackballs a candidate for membership, a business corporation violates antitrust legislation, or a charity supports the indigent, some individual or a group of individuals made each decision. No individual can escape his social responsibility by the artifice of the fictional person; neither can the totality of social responsibility be increased by adding thereto the obligation of the fictional person. As will be seen later, this concept is absolutely essential if we are to make sense of ethical responsibilities.

A third implication is that every person in society has a social responsibility to discharge. The same rules apply to professors, churchmen, lawyers, and doctors as apply to the men who act for and in the name of corporations, governments, and other organized enterprises. Businessmen have long been criticized for their lack of social responsibility, and only in recent years has censure been aimed at professors who do not distinguish between academic freedom and propaganda, judges who use legal processes to reflect personal biases, ministers who substitute social action for preaching the Word of God, and union members who resort to autocratic pressures.

The Business of Business Is Business

The people of societies create many institutions to accomplish their purposes. Governmental institutions have many purposes, among them protection from foreign intrusion, the administration of justice, the amelioration of gross inequities, and aid for the unfortunate, all designed to protect and encourage the people of the society in their pursuit of happiness. Religious institutions are designed to care for the spiritual needs of their memberships. Educational institutions are a society's great teaching and research arm. Labor and farm unions look to material benefits for their memberships.

Economic enterprises are designed to produce goods and services to satisfy the material wants of man. Their managers' first responsibility is efficiency in the use of resources to produce economic wealth. Their second responsibility is to accomplish this purpose in such a way that no restriction is placed upon the legitimate rights and interests of any person. Their third responsibility is to observe, by word and deed, the ethical standards of society.

Some who want businessmen to accept a wider social responsibility than is suggested here insist that business enterprises discharge their "obligations" to employees for better-than-competitive wage and fringe benefits, those to consumers through uneconomical prices and quality of merchandise, those to educational endeavors through gifts, those to the community by donating services and maintaining uneconomic operations, those to the unemployed by placing them in jobs they cannot perform, those to government through free tax collections and donations of the services of gifted managers, and those to unions by sacrificing the right to manage.

These critics want businessmen to do more than operate efficiently; they want business to engage in activities which many other institutions are organized to achieve. For businessmen to do this would certainly blur responsibility for results. The way to make certain that each enterprise achieves the results it was designed to secure is to have it properly managed. If the results are unsatisfactory, perhaps subsidies are appropriate, or perhaps the enterprise should be abandoned.

There is another reason for keeping businessmen within their own function. They are not experts in everything. The choices they would make and the support they would choose to provide might fail to meet the expectations of those who manage other enterprises. The late Senator Robert Taft said several years ago that businessmen are not wanted in politics because they do not understand the political processes. It is equally certain that businessmen are not always wanted at decision-making levels in other enterprises for similar reasons. The critics want the financial support of businessmen but not their influence at decision levels.

The appropriate way out of this dilemma is to distinguish between the business firm and the businessman. It is clearly the function of the firm to produce wealth efficiently because, as Levin[11] says, the maximization of profits and social benefits are interdependent. Furthermore, the managers of the modern firm are typically employees of the firm and not its owners. Thus, managers must act in a trustee relationship for those who risk their capital in the business venture.[12] Morally, they are not free to use corporate resources for any purpose which, in their prudent judgment, does not redound to the welfare of the owners. In practice, corporate managers go far beyond this standard. With the blessing of the Supreme Court, they can make donations out of profits to educational institutions;[13] they are under extreme pressure from federal agencies to employ unemployables; they make large grants to charities.

Where a business manager engages in or supports nonbusiness enterprises at company expense, there is ever a danger, of course, that he may be using the property of owners in ways to which they would not consent. On the other hand, support of such nonbusiness enterprises as education and research may have a direct relationship to the future of a business by making more available better trained human resources or advanced knowledge which will be beneficial to the business. Also, if the support of such nonbusiness enterprises as charities is regarded as wise responsiveness of the business enterprise to its social environment, such responsiveness may well be in the owners' long-range self-interest. No enterprise exists in isolation from its external environment whether social, economic, technological, political, or ethical.

Feasibility of the rational view   It is all very well to build a theoretical structure that compartmentalizes nicely the activities of man in his social environment. The view that the business firm should confine itself to the

[11] Levin, *op. cit.*, p. 88.

[12] See A. W. Lorig, "Corporate Responsibilities," *Business Horizons*, vol. 10, no. 1, pp. 51–54 (Spring, 1967).

[13] Probably first advocated and implemented by Frank W. Abrams. See A. H. Cole, *Business Enterprise in Its Social Setting* (Cambridge, Mass.: Harvard University Press, 1959), p. 241.

production of wealth, that individuals and not institutions have obligations of an interpersonal nature, and that the businessman acts in his personal capacity when he supports other institutions may be criticized as simplistic. The question is, Can a system of relationships which embodies these views be made to work?

In the present-day world they clearly are not working this way. Institutions overlap in purpose and activity, they support and harm each other, depending upon what is conceived to be their interests; the business enterprises that produce wealth and thereby have the resources are sometimes unreasonably taxed and pressured to support other causes, and the concept of trusteeship is fading. In some cases this situation was produced because there has been no clear set of principles to guide action; in others, the principles were simply smothered and ignored.

Despite these circumstances which, in the short run, seem to overwhelm us, pessimism is not in order. Efforts are being directed toward the development of a science wherein principles will provide standards for governing the conduct of interpersonal affairs. Even more important is the realization that perhaps man does not take too kindly to rational governance. He will need persuading that rationality, in separating out his social responsibilities, can lead to their integration with his emotional life.[14]

ETHICS AND THE MANAGER

It was pointed out above that the practice of ethics is one of the social responsibilities of managers. This is a problem of universal concern. Unethical conduct is highly publicized wherever it is found, but most of the "sharp" practices remain hidden within the organizational structures.[15] Also, it is a problem very difficult to get hold of because there is not yet a science of ethics resting, as one should, upon principles having general acceptance.

The Causes of Confusion

There are several factors that have led us into the present state of uncertainty about ethical standards. In the first place, the successive waves of immigration have brought to the United States masses of people with widely varying practices of ethical behavior. Their cultures have not yet been wholly integrated into a national culture and, until this occurs, there is very little reason to anticipate any *national* ethical standards. In the second place, there is no recognized source of ethical standards. In nations that have a state religion, there does exist a central source of authority to teach ethical practices. In the United States, with its myriad cultures and religions, no one can look to

[14] Perhaps this statement needs clarification. It is believed that much of man's actions are explainable in rational and emotional terms. The direction of our civilization is to stress the former. Thus, a manager will operate rationally and will include in his calculus an attempt to manage as rationally as possible his own and others' emotions.

[15] See, for instance, "Wall Street's Own Watch Dogs," *Business Week*, pp. 90–96 (July 29, 1967).

church, government, educational institution, or private association as the center of ethical teaching. And, in the third place, there is little effort on the part of teachers of ethics to develop a science.

Definition

In the consideration of this subject, the student is first beset with terminological problems. Such words as "ethics" and "morals" seem to be used interchangeably, but neither is consistently employed. Indeed, in our own day, "ethics" seems to be a term chiefly referring to high standards of professional conduct. This narrow application is unfortunate, for it leaves us without a similar word with which to characterize high standards of conduct in other affairs. For the purposes of this analysis, it is perhaps best to define ethics as the collective term for principles of personal conduct. Being principles, they should be universally applicable and they should also provide the standards with which the conduct of all persons, including businessmen, may be compared. Being principles, they can also be taught and, in this way, help to establish general standards of personal conduct throughout the land.

Morals are often quite a different matter. While ethics are grounded on moral standards, "morals" can refer to any generally accepted customs of conduct and right living in a society. There are many societies and there are many changes in these societies. Furthermore, within a society numerous local customs emerge. Therefore, what is moral in one society may be immoral in another; and what is moral in one sector or province may be immoral in another area within the same society. For our purposes, then, there can be no prescriptive *science* of morals; there are merely customs having a high degree of social acceptance. There is every reason to suspect that the moral practices of a given society are probably more closely adhered to than are any universal principles of ethics. Furthermore, what is considered moral in certain groups or societies may well be contrary to some more universally held ethical principle. For instance, in some countries it is a moral practice to bribe an official to secure a favor, but surely an ethical principle is fractured in the process.

Need for a science of ethics   The need for a set of generally accepted and practiced standards of personal conduct is evident in all parts of the world. The need is plainly evident in the conduct of heads of state, politicians, judges, professors, churchmen, lawyers, accountants, and just plain workers.

This situation is especially distressing because one really does not know what ethical standards will guide the conduct of the man he votes for, of his lawyer, of the judge who tries his case, of the teacher of his children, of the minister of his church, of the labor union leader, of the businessman he deals with, or even of his neighbor and his neighbor's wife. In the United States, the assumption is chiefly made that others will abide by the same principles as one's self. To a considerable extent, this is all to the good because it assumes a certain degree of commonality of ethical standards. But care must be taken. For instance, the *now* is a point in history. What has been the trend of ethical experience? Since the seventeenth century it has probably declined, but in the last fifty years it may have improved. Again, the uncertainty concerning another's ethical standards establishes a situation in which we learn of them through trial and error.

In the world as it stands today, relationships are world-wide in scope. We make treaties with unknown heads of state and commercial agreements with distant and often foreign strangers; we send our children to distant colleges to be instructed by unknown professors. In these and many similar situations, trial-and-error methodology is, perhaps, often disastrous.

If ethical standards could be incorporated in statutes, there would be much less reason to feel the vacuum created by the lack of a science. But even here it is simply not possible to establish such needed standards by law. By their very nature, laws tend to deal with specific acts, and these must be in the billions. No legislature could hope to deal with them all. Perhaps only a theocratic state would undertake the codification of a set of ethical principles.

The lack of a science of ethics is a cause of suffering by every person in a society except those at the no-ethics end of the scale. The pressing populations of our times, the small world constricted by communications networks and fast travel time, the pressing interpersonal relationships, all are forces that demand the development of ethical principles. Fortunately, these same forces will provide the pressure on individuals to practice right conduct once this is taught. A world packed with people will force the standardization of ethical practices—but this state of affairs will be a long time coming.

Variant sources of ethical teaching   The search for the sources of ethical teaching in the United States leads us back to the major religious contributions.[16] It is not that this is necessarily true, because it is conceivable that lay scholars could develop a science of ethics. This they have not done. Even lay writers on this subject return to the prominent religions for guidance, for they, like most everyone else in this country, have been touched by an admonishing finger in their youth.

Protestant contributions to the teaching of ethics have had an outstanding influence upon the American people. The religion of most early colonists was a strong force in molding their behavior. With the passage of time, these original immigrants achieved and maintained positions of wealth and power in all walks of life. From pre-Revolutionary times to the present, the impact of the Protestant Ethic has been of great importance. Men were taught to perform good works, to practice the virtues of austerity, frugality, and industry, and to act as stewards in the management and disposition of wealth. Even in recent times these virtues have been practiced by businessmen who may not even know their origins. In the opinion of Kenneth E. Boulding, "Looking at a perspective of three or four hundred years, the Protestant economic gospel has been a fantastic success."[17]

---

[16] For an excellent summary see J. W. Clark, *Religion and the Moral Standards of American Businessmen* (Cincinnati: South-Western Publishing Company, 1966), part I, pp. 1–75.

[17] "Our Lost Economic Gospel," *Christian Century*, vol. 67, no. 33, p. 972 (Aug. 16, 1950).

Clark[18] believes that the contribution of the Jewish faith has been more than proportional to the population of those who profess it. In attempting to identify a set of values that can be attributed to these people, an important problem presents itself: there is no single set of universally accepted values. The Jewish community is divided on the scope of Judaism—whether it should be viewed as a whole way of life, or whether it should be viewed as wholly religious. Illustrative, but assuredly not comprehensively, the religious teaching of the Jews seems to include an appreciation for the love of life and the importance of social consciousness. These values have been modified in the American environment to the point where there is positive acceptance of wealth as a value in itself, even though, to be sure, the literature of the Old Testament emphasizes the importance of charity and stewardship.

According to Clark,[19] much of Catholic social theory is derived from a basic concept of man that regards him as possessing both individual and social aspects. The dignity of the individual is given its just due, but the point is made that it may not be achievable outside the social organization established by man. These values are expressed in Catholic social doctrine in rather specific ways. The concept of justice guides human beings on the interpersonal level and on the social level. The first is concerned with giving to another what is his due; the second involves the individual's duties to society and vice versa. For instance, private property is strongly supported because it is not only natural to the individual but it also contributes effectively to his development and to his dignity. At the same time, it must be used in ways that advance the social good. Thus, the element of stewardship, common also to the Protestant Ethic and to Jewish doctrine, is strongly stressed. Similarly, the concept of fair price guides the interrelationships of individuals in such a way as to make certain the mutual advantage from exchange and its potential contribution to society as a whole.

Ethical standards and the law   The absence of a set of ethical principles has not impeded the effort of government to regulate interpersonal standards of conduct. Most people have some concept of what is ethical, at least in particular cases, and on many of these there is considerable agreement. Our legislative representatives assess this consensus and act to establish statute and administrative laws in critical areas of interpersonal conduct where the safety and personal welfare of the people can be vitally affected by unethical practices. Government cannot, by any means, cover all cases in point because, by its very nature, a law is aimed at specific unethical acts and not at the establishment of a principle. This accounts for the long list of criminal and civil laws aimed at practices that seriously affect the rights of individuals to life and liberty.

The effect of the just administration of such laws is important for the development of a future science of ethics. The mere fact that a people is required to obey this legislation develops in them a strong agreement about the

[18] *Op. cit.,* p. 28.
[19] *Op. cit.,* p. 58.

relevant ethical standards. Mistakes, of course, are bound to develop, but the remedy is to change the law through the processes provided. In this way agreement is achieved about a large body of ethical practices, and from these a start can be made to deduce the principles upon which they rest.

Business and professional codes   Another phenomenon that has some potential in the area of furthering ethical practices is the rather widespread tendency of business groups, professional people, and even politicians to adopt or to consider the adoption of codes of conduct.[20] Examples abound in the codes adhered to by the medical, legal, and accounting professions and the many business codes usually developed by trade associations, and in various proposals for codes to govern the conduct of professors, politicians, and legislators.

Purpose   The usual reasons for the development of these codes are two. In the first place, it is considered that the publication of a code of ethics will improve the confidence of the customer, client, patient, or voter in the quality of service he may expect. A reason of this type must assume that past practices of the group membership have undermined the trust of the very people whose custom is essential for the support of the group. This is why education, which is presumed to be the best safeguard against quackery, is stressed. So also are truth-in-advertising, something more than *caveat emptor*, conflicts of interest, and similar matters covered in the codes.

A second reason for the development of this practice concerns the interrelationships of the members themselves. Business simply cannot be carried on in its present complexity without trust in the ethical standards of vendors and suppliers, of financial houses, and of government agencies. It is believed that their business risks will be somewhat minimized if the competitors within the group, and between groups, can rely upon at least some expectation of a given standard practice.

McGuire[21] believes that there are two additional reasons for codes. They can be used as a crutch for the weak, who, if approached to undertake some unethical act, can point to the code to underwrite their refusal. And then there is the practical result that codes simplify the detection of unethical behavior in competitors and employees.

Voluntary nature of codes   Since there is no legal requirement that anyone subscribe to an ethical code, reliance must be placed on the voluntary action of the group membership. People are notoriously slow to volunteer, not usually because they are indeed unethical, but because they feel codes to be a restriction upon their freedom and subscribing to them would imply a

---

[20] For a good summary of these codes, see B. Y. Landis (ed.), "Ethical Standards and Professional Conduct," *The Annals of the Academy of Political and Social Science,* vol. 297, pp. 1–124 (January, 1955).

[21] J. W. McGuire, *Business and Society* (New York: McGraw-Hill Book Company, 1963), p. 285.

reflection upon their practices. In the face of these problems, means are sought to "require" voluntary adherence. Penalties are sought in the legislatures against the nonconformist; preferences are granted for those who do sign the code by way of according the legal right to make audits, in the administration of legislation affecting the group, and in protecting the fundamental right to practice a profession. Members are protected through limitation upon the persons admitted to the profession and, as with the case of the medical profession, through bringing pressure on hospitals, for example, to admit only members to their staff positions. And if the group feels strongly enough about it, it may terminate the membership of defectors, as was done in 1970 when the New York Stock Exchange expelled certain members who, it was believed, did not live up to the exchange's conduct rules.

Provisions of ethical codes   McGuire is of the opinion that the provisions of codes of ethics are either dogmatic or meaningless.[22] He feels that dogmatic provisions do not permit adjustment to change in a dynamic and complex world. To avoid this dilemma, many groups resort to a meaningless statement of generalities that could be interpreted in ways to suit the convenience of the individual.

Even more important is the question: Are ethical codes really codes of ethics? In general, they are not. They are concerned with local custom in respect to particular circumstances. For example, in summary form, the chief provisions of the code for professional accountants include:[23]

A. Professional conduct.
   1. An appropriate firm name, style, and description.
   2. Practice as a corporation is forbidden.
   3. Occupations incompatible with public accounting are prohibited.
   4. If engaged in another business, the same rules of conduct apply.
   5. Advertising and solicitation of business are prohibited.
   6. Members of the American Institute of Accountants must observe the rules of State societies, where they exist, on competitive bidding.
   7. Offers of employment to employees of other accountants are forbidden.
B. Confidence of clients.
   1. Confidential relationship must not be violated.
   2. Splitting fees with, or paying commission to, the laity is forbidden.
   3. Excepting partners and employees, members may not permit others to use their names on financial documents.
   4. Members may not sign the work of others, excepting their own associates or other accredited accountants.
C. Confidence of third parties.
   1. Members must conform to generally accepted accounting and auditing standards in certifying statements.
   2. Contingent fees relating to audits are prohibited.
   3. Members must not vouch for the accuracy of earnings forecasts.
   4. Members may not express an opinion on financial statements of an enter-

---

[22] Ibid., p. 286.
[23] Landis, op. cit., p. 2.

prise financed by public issues of securities if they, or their immediate rela-
tives, have a substantial financial interest. With private financing, their
interests must be exposed.

Much of what is called "professional accountancy" conduct should more properly be called "competitive" conduct. Certain requirements and proscriptions relate to intermember competition, and they have the effect of reducing the area of competition between accounting firms. The same may be said of fee-splitting and contingent audit fees. The remainder of the items deal chiefly with potential fraud and, therefore, are concerned with an ethical principle. But there are few truly *ethical* principles involved.

Enforcement of ethical codes   The reader will infer from the foregoing discussion that the difficulties of enforcing ethical codes are monumental. Some kind of board, elected by the membership, would have the problem of trying to determine what is really the standard and assessing the occurrence of an actual offense against it. Words, terms, and lack of principles would work against them. Loyalty to members, even when accused, may be found to have a higher value than enforcement of the code. Sanctions against a member may well result in the disintegration of the group. For all of these reasons, the ethical codes are often pointed to with pride but are ignored in practice.

Conclusion   Most so-called ethical codes are, at best, a stopgap and, at worst, deceptions. As a stopgap, they are employed as a means of trying to provide some assurance of ethical conduct on the part of a membership. In this sense they may be making a contribution if only in pointing up the critical need for the development and teaching of a science of ethics. As a deception, they easily give the appearance of restricting the behavior of members to some recognized standard, but in fact they are incapable of so doing. In this sense they are notoriously misleading, especially to the customer, patient, consumer, and voter.

This state of affairs does not mean that managers are helpless. Even though they recognize that virtue does not always triumph, that kindness may not be its own reward, and that ethical practices are not necessarily profitable, the manager who is really convinced that he must and will operate ethically can do many things. For instance, he can establish clear policies and enforce them; he can exert strong pressures on his subordinates and his superior; he can take a position of leadership among his peers in persuading them to follow ethical standards; and, above all, he can think through to his own position and resolve to cultivate the character needed to adhere to his principles. Indeed, in the real world, there are many businessmen who are doing just this. As McGuire states:[24]

Like other men, businessmen sometimes succumb to [these] temptations. This should not surprise us. What should surprise us is that so many businessmen withstand the

[24] *Op. cit.,* p. 280.

temptations and that they have an ethical code of values which would do justice to men in any occupation.

TOWARD THE GOOD SOCIETY

This is not good enough. It is urgent that scholars set out now to develop a science of ethics, for this can offer the standard for the teaching and practice of the desired quality of interpersonal conduct. Scholars do not have to start from zero. They may proceed inductively by synthesizing such evidences of ethical standards as are found in the Golden Rule, the Ten Commandments, legal standards, and codes of associations. Others, if they prefer, may proceed deductively and develop a system of ethical principles based upon their conceptions of accepted morals. Through research, teaching, and interchange of ideas, it is not too much to hope that there will some day emerge a science of ethics.

FOR DISCUSSION

1. Some people fear the power of large corporations. How do such organizations exercise power? Are people safe in a world of big business? Of big government?
2. Can an enterprise act responsibly, as distinguished from the behavior of its managers?
3. In what sense are social responsibilities a product of interpersonal relationships?
4. Do you think there is really a good way to distinguish ethics and morals?
5. What problems do congressmen face in developing and applying a code of ethics to themselves?

5

comparative management

As the area of management has increasingly commanded world-wide interest and recognition, the question whether it is a science with universal application has concerned scholars and practitioners alike. A real science should explain phenomena regardless of national or cultural environments. Thus, the science of mechanics knows no boundaries, providing it applies to the reality being considered. Principles of the building sciences are no different if applied to a small house or a large building and whether these structures are built in the tropics or the arctic.

Unless basic management science can be useful for practitioners in varying circumstances, it is certainly suspect. For the task of an *operational* science is so to organize pertinent knowledge as to make it applicable, and thereby useful, to those who would achieve intended, real results.

The authors have taken the position that management fundamentals—theory and principles—have universal application in every kind of enterprise and at every level of an enterprise. Yet they have constantly acknowledged that the specific problems with which a manager deals, the individuals and groups with which he interacts, and the elements of the external environment will differ. One would expect, therefore, that given techniques and approaches, even though based upon the same fundamentals, would vary because of these differences, just as engineering design would vary if a mechanical engineer were planning a bridge rather than a precise pressure-measuring instrument.

It is true that most studies of management fundamentals have been made without regard to specific external cultural environments. It is likewise true that most have been made against the backdrop of culturally well-developed and predominantly private enterprise societies. However, in approaching the study of comparative management, two basic questions may be posed: (1) Do management fundamentals, in contrast to specific techniques and approaches, vary with external cultural—social, economic, political, technological, or ethical—differences? (2) To what extent should we expect managerial practice —the art of managing—to differ with variations in the external environment?

These questions have not yet been answered conclusively, but recent studies have cast some interesting light on them.

MANAGEMENT AS A CRITICAL ELEMENT IN ECONOMIC GROWTH

In the increasing concern with what makes for economic growth, it is natural for social scientists to look for its underlying causes. Why is it that one country has a higher per capita national income than another? Why is it that only eighteen countries of the world were found in 1966 to have a gross national product per capita of more than $1,000 per year, while thirty-three had GNP per capita of $201–$1,000 per year, and sixty-six had GNP per capita of less than $200 per year?[1]

Because of the disparity of national incomes and the problems caused in much of the world by incomes which do not allow for adequate subsistence, let alone the raising of cultural standards, attention of world leaders and development economists has naturally turned to the need for increasing productivity and production. Indeed, one author has described this widespread movement as "one of the great world crusades of our time."[2] Until recent years, the necessities for development were thought to be the transfer of technology, education, and capital. But as important as these are, it has come to be recognized that advanced managerial know-how[3] is probably the most critical of all elements responsible for growth. As one Chilean executive has put it:[4]

Perhaps it is time to alter our concept of underdevelopment and think in terms of management. This would focus our attention on helping mismanaged areas to improve their organizations and knowledge. No amount of capital investment will succeed in furthering human progress if such wealth producing resources are mishandled or undermined through lack of fundamental concepts. This lack of knowledge exists and the modern tools of finance, marketing, etc. are not common knowledge in underdeveloping areas and their absence prevents the rapid and successful expansion of areas. Capital alone will not replace this information, but likewise the lack of such capital will make it impossible to bring about the looked for development.

This opinion is buttressed by other findings. Rostow recognized the importance of entrepreneurial skills in management and economic growth when he pointed out that "a small professional elite (of entrepreneurs and executives) can go a long way toward initiating economic growth."[5] Sayles expresses the

---

[1] R. N. Farmer and B. M. Richman, *International Business: An Operational Theory* (Homewood, Ill.: Richard D. Irwin, Inc., 1966), p. 39.

[2] M. D. Bryce, *Industrial Development* (New York: McGraw-Hill Book Company, 1960), p. 3.

[3] "Know-how" is used differently by various authors. Here it is used to connote the ability to apply knowledge effectively in practice; it therefore includes both knowledge of underlying science and the artful ability to apply it to reality.

[4] J. Ross, "The Profit Motive and Its Potential for New Economies," *Proceedings, International Management Congress, CIOS XIII* [New York: Council for International Progress in Management (USA), Inc., 1963].

[5] W. W. Rostow, *The Stages of Economic Growth* (Cambridge, Mass.: Harvard University Press, 1962), p. 52.

same viewpoint even more strongly when he concludes that "in the world race for economic growth and for the allegiance and stability of lesser-developed sections of the globe, United States management 'knowhow' is a crucial factor."[6]

These conclusions are not difficult for a person knowledgeable in management to understand. The goal of managing is making it possible for people to operate in groups in such a way as to gain the most, in terms of objectives sought by an enterprise or a part of it, with the human and material resources available. Clearly, ineffectual managership leads to inefficient use of these resources. And whether the goal of an enterprise is economic, political, or other, it is not difficult to see that waste of resources will occur with poor managing.

Although one must grant that technical knowledge is necessary for economic growth, this is fairly transferable between countries and no nation long holds a monopoly on it. Even so sophisticated a technology as the atomic bomb, whose secrecy was actively protected by the United States, became known in Russia, France, China, and elsewhere in less than two decades. Most advances in technology are neither as complex nor as well-guarded, so that their transfer is not likely to be difficult, particularly when one realizes that in any country few people need to have this knowledge to make it available for use.

On the other hand, a cultural factor such as the level of education, particularly knowledge of skills, has an important impact on economic progress. Also, such cultural variables as desire for more of the products and services that a country can provide can be significant. Similarly constraining on economic progress are a large number of political factors, such as fiscal policy, labor regulations, business restrictions, and foreign policy. But even with these and other constraints, which may limit managerial effectiveness, qualified managers can do much to bring economic progress to a society by identifying them and by designing a managerial approach or technique to take them into account.

Two prominent scholars of comparative management have said in this connection:[7]

We view management as the single most critical social activity in connection with economic progress. Physical, financial, and manpower resources are by themselves but passive agents; they must be effectively combined and coordinated through sound, active management if a country is to experience a substantial level of economic growth and development. A country can have sizeable natural and manpower resources including plentiful skilled labor and substantial capital but still be relatively poor because very few competent managers are available to put these resources efficiently together in the production and distribution of useful goods and services.

The United States leads the world in per capita gross national product and is generally credited as being the world leader in the development of

---

[6]L. R. Sayles, *Managerial Behavior* (New York: McGraw-Hill Book Company, 1964), p. 17.
[7]R. N. Farmer and B. M. Richman, *Comparative Management and Economic Progress* (Homewood, Ill.: Richard D. Irwin, Inc., 1965), p. 1.

management know-how. It is, therefore, not surprising that American management is regarded widely as the standard of the world and that most scholars regard the problem of comparative management as one of transferring American management knowledge and practice to less developed countries.

This may be a justifiable point of view. But the authors of this book do not base any of their position on management universality on such a premise. After all, the earliest and most perceptive managerial insights were those of a Frenchman, Henri Fayol. Many early and present management pioneers were British, and many other management scholars have come from a host of other countries and cultures. It is rather the authors' position that effective management knowledge and art are not uniquely American. In their writing on management and in their experience in leading seminars for managers and scholars throughout the world, it has never been the position of the authors that their task was to export American management, but rather to identify and discuss management fundamentals.

IS MANAGEMENT CULTURE-BOUND?

A few scholars of management have concluded that management is culture-bound. In other words, the facts that management practices differ and people and their environment vary are believed by some to be persuasive evidence that management theory and principles—the framework of management knowledge—are applicable only in developed societies similar to that existing in the United States. Also, there are some who believe that the structure and content of management science are not transferable, and that the application of these to specific enterprise situations in the same national culture is not necessarily possible.

The Differing Views

The findings of Gonzalez and McMillan are among those that are often quoted to show that management is culture-bound. These scholars, on the basis of a two-year study in Brazil, concluded that "American management experience abroad provides evidence that our uniquely American philosophy of management is not universally applicable but is a rather special case."[8] Note that these authors refer to "philosophy" and not to "science" or "theory" or "principles," and have emphasized that "that aspect of management which lacks universality has to do with interpersonal relationships, including those between management and workers, management and suppliers, management and the customer, the community, competition and government."[9]

On the basis of similar research, Oberg appears to agree with Gonzalez and McMillan and expresses doubt that the "game" of management in Brazil, being so different from that played in the United States, would permit appli-

[8]R. F. Gonzalez and C. McMillan, Jr., "The Universality of American Management Philosophy," *Journal of the Academy of Management*, vol. 4, no. 1, pp. 33–41 (April, 1961), at p. 41.
[9]*Ibid.*, p. 39.

cation of management principles, useful in the United States, to Brazil.[10] It is Oberg's belief that the applicability of management principles may be limited to a particular culture or situation and that it may be fruitless to search for a common set of "principles," "absolutes," or "determinate solutions." It is even argued that since management principles appear not to be adaptable between cultures, they may not even be applicable between subcultures such as those of a rural businessman versus the manager of a large corporation within the United States.[11]

On the other hand, even those who question the transfer of managerial knowledge have admitted that it has often been successfully applied. For example, Gonzalez and McMillan, in their article indicating belief that the American philosophy of management is culture-bound, stated that:[12]

The science of management has reached its highest state of development in the U.S., and it is for this knowledge, this know-how, that American management is most highly respected abroad. Transferred abroad, this know-how is first viewed with skepticism. Foreign national employees and partners are slow to respond and understand the American scientific approach to management problems. However, once fully indoctrinated, they accept and support this way of doing things. The superiority of this more objective, systematic, orderly and controlled approach to problems is seen and appreciated. For the host country, for American international relations, and for the American parent firm itself the export of American managerial know-how as well as technological know-how has yielded great dividends.

Also, Harbison and Myers, in their study of management in a number of countries of the world, have concluded that there is a "logic of industrialization." They moreover indicated that "organization building has its logic, too, which rests upon the development of management. And this brings us to the fundamental premise of our study: there is a general logic of management development which has applicability both to advanced and industrializing countries in the modern world."[13] While offered as a premise, their study of management in twelve foreign countries supports it.

Interesting and consistent findings were made in another study in which the behavior of some 3,600 managers in fourteen countries was probed. This study, undertaken by Haire, Ghiselli, and Porter, found a high degree of similarity in managerial behavior patterns and that many of the variations disclosed were due to identifiable cultural differences.[14] It is interesting, also, that Richman, in reporting on the developing interest in management in the Soviet Union in 1965, found that the evolving Soviet approach to management utilized the functions of managers—planning, organizing, coordination, control, direction, leadership, motivation, and staffing—which were essentially the

[10] W. Oberg, "Cross-cultural Perspectives on Management Principles," *Academy of Management Journal*, vol. 6, no. 2, pp. 129–143 (June, 1963), at p. 120.

[11] *Ibid.*, pp. 142–143.

[12] Gonzalez and McMillan, *op. cit.*, p. 39.

[13] F. Harbison and C. A. Myers, *Management in the Industrial World* (New York; McGraw-Hill Book Company, 1959), p. 117.

[14] M. Haire, E. E. Ghiselli, and L. W. Porter, *Managerial Thinking: An International Study* (New York: John Wiley and Sons, 1966).

same as long-held American concepts.[15] As will be pointed out below, other studies, particularly those carried on by the Comparative Management Program of the University of California, Los Angeles, also support this view.

The Problem of Semantics in Assessing Transfer of Management

In looking over the altogether too scant evidence on the transferability of management knowledge between countries and cultures, one is struck by the fact that differences of opinion seem to arise largely from semantics. The concepts of "management philosophy," "management know-how," "management theory," "management principles," and "management knowledge" are often left undefined. The authors of this book have attempted to give the concepts of management theory, principles, and science careful definition. In essence, science is organized knowledge, theory is a structure of fundamental concepts and principles around which knowledge in a field is organized, and principles are regarded as fundamental truths which can be used to describe and predict the results of certain variables in a given situation.

On the other hand, it is the authors' belief that management "philosophy" has such a variable meaning as almost to defy definition. Strictly speaking, philosophy is the love, study, or pursuit of knowledge and is sometimes used, but certainly not always, as equivalent to science. On the other hand, in looking at the studies of comparative management, one finds "management philosophy" sometimes used to indicate attitudes of managers toward such groups as consumers, stockholders, suppliers, unions, and government.[16]

As can be seen, if a concept of management science includes underlying basic knowledge of management and, in addition, the application of this knowledge in given situations and cultures, differences in interpretation of what a researcher finds in comparative societies would naturally exist. Likewise, if a concept of management philosophy includes not only basic management theory and principles, but also beliefs as to such societal matters as ownership of property and attitudes toward individuals, one would expect that the resultant concept would vary between cultures as attitudes on fundamental social matters differ. In this context, it is easy to understand how Gonzalez and McMillan could come to the conclusion that American business philosophy is culture-bound, while they admit that the export of American managerial know-how has yielded great dividends.

The essential point is simply this: Cultural differences exist between various countries and societies, sometimes to a marked degree. There are even subcultural variations of an important nature in the same country or society. It is therefore important in any study of the transferability of knowledge to separate the fundamentals of management from their application to given situations. For example, one might well expect, as these authors do, that

[15] B. M. Richman, "The Soviet Educational and Research Revolution: Implications for Management Development," *California Management Review*, vol. 9, no. 4, p. 12 (Summer, 1967).

[16] A. R. Negandhi and B. D. Estafen, "A Research Model to Determine the Applicability of American Management Know-how in Differing Cultures and/or Environments," *Academy of Management Journal*, vol. 8, no. 4, pp. 309–318 (December, 1965), at p. 312.

basic management theory and principles would have universal applicability, and yet equally expect that management approaches and techniques would vary in different cultures. In other words, the only approach toward comparative management believed to be valid is to distinguish carefully between management fundamentals, or the science of management, and management practice.

When the distinction is made between management fundamentals, as expressed in basic concepts, theory, and principles, and management practice—the application of management fundamentals to a given situation—progress can be made in determining the extent of management universality and the transferability of managerial fundamentals. With variations in cultures, one would not expect that *application* of management fundamentals to these varied cultures would always be the same.

The importance of this distinction cannot be overlooked, particularly if basic knowledge of management in one culture is to be transferred to another. However, this does not mean that a management technique or approach successful in one society may not work with few, if any, changes in another. It simply means that the manager who would succeed in a different culture should ascertain the extent of change in technique or application required to meet any existing differences. The same is true in any field of science. One would not necessarily expect an automobile designed for use in deserts or jungles to be the same as one planned for high-speed superhighways, even though the physical science which underpins both remains the same.

INTRODUCING THE EXTERNAL ENVIRONMENT: THE FARMER-RICHMAN MODEL

In order to fill the gaps which exist in the discussions of management theory, including that in this book, a few scholars have attempted to establish models for the analysis of comparative management, taking into account the influence of external environments. In doing so, they have recognized that external cultural environments do affect the *practice* of management, whether an environment is a subculture such as that of a public utility versus that of a soap and detergent company within the United States, or whether one is considering environments in different countries.

Several promising approaches have been made to the subject. One of these is the model developed by Professors Farmer and Richman. Another is that developed by Professors Negandhi and Estafen. While similar in many particulars, both models attempt to identify and weigh the effect of cultural factors on the functional elements of the management process. As such, they furnish tools for assessing the operation of management theory and principles in varying environments.

In the model offered by Professors Farmer and Richman, their approach is, first, to identify the critical elements in the management process, and attempt to evaluate their operation in individual firms in different cultures. Second, they have attempted to identify the various environmental factors which are believed to have a significant impact on the management process and management effectiveness, classifying these constraints as (1) educational variables, (2) sociological-cultural variables, (3) political and legal variables, and (4) economic variables.

The Concept of Managerial Effectiveness

Hypothesizing that management of productive enterprises is directly related to the external environment in which a manager operates and that managers may, at times, affect this environment, Farmer and Richman believe that management practice and its effectiveness will depend to a major extent upon external environmental characteristics.

Assuming that one of the major goals of any society is productivity (even though this appears sometimes to be unrealistic), managerial effectiveness is defined as simply how well and efficiently the managers of an enterprise in a given environment accomplish enterprise objectives. If we can assume that the objective is productivity, then efficiency is given by $E = O/I$, where E is efficiency, O is output, and I is input. While this concept is clear, Farmer and Richman realize that, in measuring the efficiency of management, an analyst will encounter extremely difficult problems in measuring inputs and outputs. These include (1) the problem of uncertainty, since management decisions and customs ever deal with the future; (2) the problem of clearly defining goals, since, if not so defined, outputs cannot be accurately measured and a knowledge of efficiency becomes impossible; (3) the problem of subsystem optimization, since the conceptual ability and measuring techniques are seldom available to evaluate adequately the enterprise as a total system over time; and (4) the problem of resource mobility, since inputs, such as labor and capital, cannot be easily shifted from less profitable opportunities to more profitable ones.

Although difficulties of measuring and other deficiencies exist, there are a number of means by which efficiency of a country or a firm's operation can be assessed. From the standpoint of a country, they include (1) the level of real per capita gross national product; (2) the rate of growth of real per capita gross national product; (3) the rate of utilization of inputs (how well are labor, capital, and land utilized?); (4) the usability of outputs (are they needed, and how usable are they?); (5) the level of competition (how much rivalry is there to force entrepreneurs to be efficient?); and (6) the adequacy and accuracy of planning (are outputs available for unwanted and unneeded items in some sections of the economy while shortages exist in others?).

The efficiency of an individual firm may be ascertained by looking at a number of factors. One of these is profitability as measured either by the return-on-net-worth or assets employed. Another is how well the firm competes in export markets. A third is the output per employee, such as tons of steel. A fourth measure is the extent to which a firm utilizes its plant capacity. A fifth factor, where applicable, is the level of cost and prices and their relationship to those of another firm. A final type of measurement involves the matter of long-run innovation and whether policy and actions are optimizing short-range performance at the expense of long-range, or vice versa.

It does seem that these measures of management effectiveness, both in a nation and within a firm, are appropriate. Fairly accurate data exist for some. Data subject to various degrees of inaccuracy exist for others. And, for still others, credible data may not currently be available. Also, there is the danger that different statistical and accounting treatments between countries and firms may be such as to make comparisons difficult or invalid.

Managerial Elements

In order to separate the elements of the management process from the external constraints of the environment, Farmer and Richman use the framework of management and most of the fundamentals outlined in this book. Thus they pick the critical elements of the management process as follows:

Critical Elements of the Management Process

Planning and innovation

1.1   *Basic organizational objectives pursued and the form of their operational expression.*

1.2   *Types of plans utilized.*

1.3   *Time horizon of plans and planning.*

1.4   *Degree and extent to which enterprise operations are spelled out in plans (i.e., preprogrammed).*

1.5   *Flexibility of plans.*

1.6   *Methodologies, techniques, and tools used in planning and decision making.*

1.7   *Extent and effectiveness of employee participation in planning.*

1.8   *Managerial behavior in the planning process.*

1.9   *Degree and extent of information distortion in planning.*

1.10 *Degree and extent to which scientific method is effectively applied by enterprise personnel—both managers and non-managers—in dealing with causation and futurity problems.*

1.11 *Nature, extent, and rate of innovation and risk taking in enterprise operations over a given period of time.*

1.12 *Ease or difficulty of introducing changes and innovation in enterprise operations.*

Control

2.1   *Types of strategic performance and control standards used in different areas; e.g., production, marketing, finance, personnel.*

2.2   *Types of control techniques used.*

2.3   *Nature and structure of information feedback systems used for control purposes.*

2.4   *Timing and procedures for corrective action.*

2.5   *Degree of looseness or tightness of control over personnel.*

2.6   *Extent and nature of unintended effects resulting from the over-all control system employed.*

2.7   *Effectiveness of the control system in compelling events to conform to plans.*

Organization

3.1   *Size of representative enterprise and its major subunits.*

3.2   *Degree of centralization or decentralization of authority.*

3.3   Degree of work specialization (division of labor).

3.4   Spans of control.

3.5   Basic departmentation and grouping of activities. Extent and uses of service departments.

3.6   Extent and uses of staff generalists and specialists.

3.7   Extent and uses of functional authority.

3.8   Extent and degree of organizational confusion and friction regarding authority and responsibility relationships.

3.9   Extent and uses of committee and group decision making.

3.10 Nature, extent, and uses of the informal organization.

3.11 Degree and extent to which the organization structure (i.e., the formal organization) is mechanical or flexible with regard to causing and/or adapting to changing conditions.

Staffing

4.1   Methods used in recruiting personnel.

4.2   Criteria used in selecting and promoting personnel.

4.3   Techniques and criteria used in appraising personnel.

4.4   Nature and uses of job descriptions.

4.5   Levels of compensation.

4.6   Nature, extent, and time absorbed in enterprise training programs and activities.

4.7   Extent of informal individual development.

4.8   Policies and procedures regarding the layoff and dismissal of personnel.

4.9   Ease or difficulty in dismissing personnel no longer required or desired.

4.10 Ease or difficulty of obtaining and maintaining personnel of all types with desired skills and abilities.

Direction, leadership, and motivation

5.1   Degree and extent of authoritarian vs. participative management. (This relates to autocratic vs. consultative direction.)

5.2   Techniques and methods used for motivating managerial personnel.

5.3   Techniques and methods used for motivating nonmanagerial personnel.

5.4   Supervisory techniques used.

5.5   Communication structure and techniques.

5.6   Degree and extent to which communication is ineffective among personnel of all types.

5.7   Ease or difficulty of motivating personnel to perform efficiently, and to improve their performance and abilities over time (irrespective of the types of incentives that may be utilized for this purpose).

5.8   Degree and extent of identification that exists between the interests and objectives of individuals, work groups, departments, and the enterprise as a whole.

5.9   Degree and extent of trust and cooperation or conflict and distrust among personnel of all types.

5.10 Degree and extent of frustration, absenteeism, and turnover among personnel.

5.11 Degree and extent of wasteful time and effort, resulting from restrictive work practices, unproductive bargaining, conflicts, etc.

In addition, these authors expand their listing of critical elements of the management process to include major policy areas of management planning in order to obtain a view of the policies followed by various companies. These policies are classified as those related to marketing, production and procurement, research and development, finance, and external relations. Each of these in turn is broken down into a number of elements. In the area of marketing policy, for example, channels of distribution and types and locations of customers are listed. In the area of production and procurement, policy with respect to making or buying items is one of those listed, and in the area of finance, policy with respect to distribution of earnings is an example.[17]

External Environmental Constraints

Farmer and Richman divide external and environmental constraints into four classes: educational, sociological-cultural, legal-political, and economic.

Educational constraints Among the major educational constraints noted are literacy level, the availability of specialized vocational and technical training and secondary education, higher education, management development programs, the prevailing attitude toward education, and the extent to which education matches requirements for skills and abilities. Mere reference to these educational factors indicates how they may support or limit effective management. Moreover, where education is inadequate, not only will economic enterprises themselves tend to suffer thereby, but political and legal systems are likely to be poor. Even in advanced societies, where education appears to be more closely matched with requirements, there is always the phenomenon of a shortage of educational brain power, since it is a characteristic of all societies that the more that is available, the more is needed.

Sociological-cultural constraints In the sociological-cultural area, Farmer and Richman identify a large number of factors. These include (1) the general attitude of the society toward managers (for example, is a career in the profession of medicine or law, or in government, regarded as of higher status than in business management?); (2) the dominant views of authority and subordinates (for example, are subordinates expected to follow the all-knowing, paternalistic decisions of the top manager, or is participation of subordinates accepted and encouraged?); (3) the extent to which cooperation between various groups is a way of life (for example, are class structures rigid or are the means for advancement open to a person who is capable regardless of his class affiliation?); (4) the extent of union-management cooperation; (5) the view of achievement and work (for example, does the society value economic achievement through hard work as a desirable personal trait, or is achievement in the arts or preparation for life-after-death regarded as paramount?); (6) the extent of inflexible class structure and individual mobility (for example, are individuals moved to positions on the basis of their abilities, or are they restricted by caste systems or other forms of discrimination not related to ability?); (7) the dominant view of wealth and material gain, such as attitudes toward saving and the desire for material wealth versus religious satisfaction, the "good life," or other nonmaterial stimuli; (8) the view of sci-

---

[17]For a full listing of these policy areas, the reader is referred to R. N. Farmer and B. M. Richman, *op. cit.,* pp. 348–349.

entific method (for example, is the society interested in preserving traditional cultures and patterns or in following a given ideology regardless of the logic involved or the empirical evidence and new discoveries available, or does the society understand the basic relationships between such economic factors as demand, price, wages, training, absenteeism and turnover, etc.?); (9) the view of risk taking (for example, are nations, enterprises, and individuals willing to take reasonable risks?); and (10) the view of change (for example, do the people in a society maintain their basic faith in traditions—old ways of doing things—or do they embrace change which promises to improve productivity?).

Legal-political constraints   The major legal-political constraints in an external environment have been identified by Farmer and Richman as falling into six categories: (1) relevant rules of the game; (2) defense policy and national security; (3) foreign policy; (4) political stability; (5) political organization; and (6) flexibility of law and legal changes.

There are, as one might expect, a number of legal rules in any business game. One is the general business law which provides a framework within which the firm must work. Important factors in this framework are codes of fair and effective competition, the law of contracts, and laws pertaining to trademarks, copyrights, and patents. Likewise, general laws governing society, such as those affecting health, welfare, and safety, have their effect, as automobile and pharmaceutical manufacturers, among others, in the United States are well aware.

Another legal area constraining the manager is that dealing with prices and competition. The United States has been the leader in the work of framing and enforcing laws to require a responsible level of competition, and these have had both a constraining and a constructive effect on a manager's environment. But elsewhere in the world these laws differ, ranging from those coming somewhat close to American legislation in enforcing competition to laws which permit and encourage monopoly or monopolistic practices.

Still another area which has a far-reaching effect on management is labor law. In most countries these laws are extremely complex. They usually apply to hours and conditions of work, use of women and minors, tenure and job security, employer responsibility for health and welfare, use of nationals, and unemployment compensation. But differences in requirements may be considerable. In the United States, for example, a company manager is normally permitted to discharge or lay off an employee with little or no difficulty or cost. But in many other countries he may find it virtually impossible to do so, especially if the employee has fairly long tenure. Furthermore, in one country the cost of social benefits may be virtually nonexistent while in another it may amount to nearly half of the payroll costs.

Tax law variations are also significant. Tax regulations and the impact of taxes are different in various jurisdictions. Some may even materially affect whether a business operates as a proprietorship, partnership, or corporation. Possibilities of evasion differ considerably. It is customary for businesses in many countries to evade taxes to a great extent. This is epitomized by the statement of a foreign business owner to one of the authors that he kept three sets of books: one for the tax collector, one for the person who might wish to buy his business, and one for himself. Also, the extent of tax benefits or penalties to encourage or discourage a business obviously has a significant effect on management policy.

Another political factor affecting management is the country's policy toward defense and national security. Where huge sums are spent toward this end, as in the United States, the effect is obvious. Defense policy often has considerable impact on the allocation of manpower and resources. Draft of manpower and allocation and rationing of materials are cases in point.

Foreign policy also has its influence on the management of enterprises. Tariffs and quotas, economic aid, protection of local businesses by restricting foreign ownership, monetary exchange controls, and control of imports or exports are conspicuous and widespread examples. Managers always have to contend with these influences, and companies domiciled in one country and doing business in another, either through export or through license, joint venture, or wholly owned subsidiary, have special problems in dealing with them.

Still another environmental factor is the extent of political stability which a country enjoys. Where political systems and leadership are highly unstable, the manager faces an area of uncertainty which cannot help but materially affect his planning. Even moderate political uncertainties can have consequences. The changing policy in Great Britain with respect to nationalizing the steel industry, as Labor and Conservative elements come into and lose power, cannot help but have a detrimental effect on planning in this industry —planning which in many respects unavoidably involves commitments of a long-range and inflexible nature.

Likewise, the type of political organization has an important influence on managers. If a country is operated under a federal system, as are the United States and Australia, the environment is different from one operated under a highly centralized political organization, such as France. The more government levels and functions with power to affect a manager's operation, the more complicated his task may be in meeting legal requirements. But it is also likely that he will receive more local understanding of his problems in a federal system than under a highly centralized government.

Farmer and Richman further identify as an important factor in the political environment the flexibility of law—the ease with which legal changes are brought about in a society. Law is notably conservative, largely because it is designed to correct past abuses and conditions. But as conditions change, if the law itself is not flexible or cannot be changed readily, the manager may have a critical problem on his hands.

Economic constraints   Farmer and Richman likewise identify a number of economic constraints which differ between countries and affect the practice of managing. Among these are the basic economic system, whether predominantly private or public in ownership, whether competitive, whether exchange is based on sound money, and the extent to which the government controls economic activities.

There are economic differences in whether the central banking system and national monetary policy work to help or to thwart managers. Does the banking system provide needed money and credit expansion as businesses grow? Does it control monetary supply to avoid unsettling inflation? Does it operate to stabilize the economy, or does it contribute to excess booms? Does it support or hinder export business? These questions are closely tied in with fiscal policy in the extent to which the public sector of an economy creates price stability, tax fluctuations, booms, and recessions. Obviously, this element of a manager's environment greatly influences his managerial policies.

Economic stability is a significant economic variable. A degree of price stability is highly desirable, since a manager is required to make many fairly long-range commitments and is almost forced to rely very largely upon financial data for much of his planning and control. Utilization of production factors is an environmental matter of importance; cycles in employment of capital and land can understandably have a disturbing effect on enterprises that must use, and plan to utilize for some time, these resources. While no manager would expect perfect stability in either prices or the economy and would normally prefer a growing economy, and while he is usually able to live with moderate price changes, uncertainty in these economic elements cannot help but hinder planning effectiveness and compel shortening the time span of decision commitment.

Since capital is the lifeblood of any business enterprise, organization of capital markets is an important environmental factor. The manager operating in an environment where capital is reasonably available has, of course, a tremendous advantage over one who operates in an environment where capital is scarce and expensive. Even in completely government-planned and controlled economies, this problem exists. Capital needs may be furnished as a government service, but with all the problems of restriction and bureaucratic friction which exist.

In addition to the above economic controls, Farmer and Richman identify three all-pervasive economic constraints. One they refer to as factor endowment—the extent to which a country has available natural resources, adequate and useful labor, and capital which can be employed for efficient production. Another is the size of markets. Obviously, to take advantage of many of the economies of large-scale production, the size of a market open to a firm is important. Closely related are the extent to which competition exists and whether there are legal or other limitations on a manager reaching a market.

A third major pervasive economic constraint which they stress is the extent to which social-overhead capital is available, that is, the supply and quality of public utility-type services. These refer to a host of services necessary to support production, distribution, and consumption. They include transportation, communication, energy production and transmission, warehousing, and sewer and water facilities.

The Farmer-Richman Model

From their identification of the various elements of the management process and of a manager's external environment which affect the way he manages, Farmer and Richman have constructed a model. While probably subject to

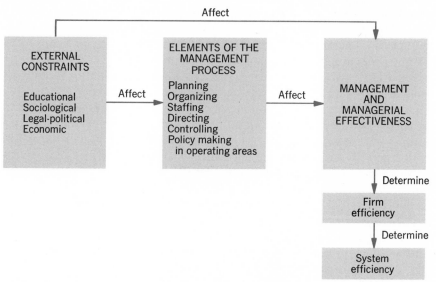

Figure 5.1 *Farmer-Richman model for analyzing comparative management.* SOURCE: *Adapted from R. N. Farmer and B. M. Richman,* Comparative Management and Economic Progress *(Homewood, Ill.: Richard D. Irwin, Inc., 1965), p. 35.*

revision in the future, this model nonetheless distinguishes the management process from the environment of managing. In doing so, it appears to be a useful tool for evaluating management as management and for understanding what may make effective management practice differ as between varying cultures.

The model may be depicted as in Figure 5.1.

The Farmer-Richman Model and Principles of Management

Farmer and Richman express the belief that external conditions of the type outlined above will affect both managerial effectiveness and the elements of the management process. Managerial effectiveness will, in turn, determine a firm's efficiency and consequently the efficiency of a given country or society (a "system").

They put it in this way. If a country has a negative attitude toward education, it presents a manager with staffing difficulties if a level of unavailable education is important to his operations. If a population has a negative attitude toward scientific method, staffing with people having abilities to analyze and act rationally will be difficult. Or if a law against pollution of streams exists in a country, this will, in turn, affect production policies and activities. A lack of an established communications system will also have an effect on the efficiency of many firms. While they may furnish their own system, this is likely to be less efficient.

Other factors may only affect the operation of the management process. The planning time horizon may be limited by political instability or rapid inflation. A paternalistic attitude toward people may influence organizational patterns by restricting delegation. Or an accounting system based on tax evasion may so contort financial data as to make managerial control information misleading. Likewise, management development and promotion may be thwarted by a caste system or racial or religious discrimination. As can be seen, these and many other cultural variables may materially influence management functions and the way a manager undertakes them.

But there is no evidence in the Farmer-Richman model or in their study of comparative management that the *fundamentals* of managing are changed by these environmental constraints. For example, the limitation of the planning horizon caused by rapid inflation does not invalidate the principle of commitment.[18] It only means, as many Brazilian businessmen have found, that the period and means of obtaining recovery of costs plus return-on-investment are shortened. Nor does a level of education affect the principle of job definition,[19] although its application in terms of a given structure of roles and provisions for incentives will vary. Also, even though a caste system or an attitude of racial or religious discrimination may not permit operation of the principle of open competition and promotion,[20] this does not mean that the principle is untrue. It means, rather, that managerial efficiency is hampered by these external constraints, since a manager is not able to apply the principles completely.

INTRODUCING THE EXTERNAL ENVIRONMENT: THE NEGANDHI-ESTAFEN MODEL

Another model for separating the influence of the external environment from the analysis of management fundamentals has been formulated by Professors A. R. Negandhi and B. D. Estafen. First offered in 1965,[21] the Negandhi-Estafen model differs somewhat from the Farmer-Richman model although it still includes as a major independent variable external cultural factors affecting managerial action. However, Negandhi and Estafen believe that the Farmer-Richman model does not go far enough in indicating major influences on managerial practice and that another independent variable, that of management philosophy, should be given weight.

Introduction of Management Philosophy

Negandhi and Estafen believe that it is a mistake to regard management philosophy as only a product of the cultural environment. In their paper, the

[18] See discussion of this principle in chap. 6.

[19] See discussion of this principle, under the alternate title of "functional" definition, in chap. 18.

[20] See discussion of this principle in chap. 22.

[21] Negandhi and Estafen, *op. cit.* Also see further refinements and research results in A. R. Negandhi, "A Model for Analyzing Organizations in Cross-Cultural Settings: A Conceptual Scheme and Some Research Findings," *Comparative Administration and Research Conference* (Kent, Ohio: Kent State University, 1969), pp. 55–87. Estafen has recently developed another comparative model in which he sees environmental forces as limitations, rather than determinants, and emphasizes systems transfer characteristics (the firm environment interface). See "Systems Transfer Characteristics: An Experimental Model for Comparative Management Research," *International Management Review*, vol. 10, no. 2–3, pp. 21–34 (1970).

opinion was expressed that certain elements of management philosophy can be and have been successfully imported from one culture to another. In this paper, management philosophy was defined as "the expressed and implied attitude or relationships of a firm with some of its external and internal agents" such as consumers, stockholders, suppliers, distributors, employee unions, community, and local, state, and federal governments. To support that position, Negandhi and Estafen have given as an example the finding of two researchers with respect to two textile mills in India.[22] One mill had a philosophy of "quick profit," which is hardly a culturally limited attitude, while the other had a similarly culturally widespread philosophy in being "product conscious" and embracing "long-range profit." These two philosophies had a considerable and different impact on employee morale, productivity, organization structure, delegation of authority, span of management, and communication patterns.

Thus, it is Negandhi and Estafen's position that certain areas of management philosophy should be introduced as a variable which may or may not be influenced by cultural differences. These are the expressed and implied attitudes toward such agents as: (1) the consumer (does the company regard consumer loyalty as important?); (2) the company's involvement in community welfare activities and educational institutions; (3) the company's relationship with local, state, and national governments; (4) the company's attitude toward and relationship with unions and union leaders; (5) the company's relationship with employees; and (6) the company's relationship with suppliers and distributors.

The Negandhi-Estafen Model

Consequently, the Negandhi-Estafen model may be essentially depicted as in Figure 5.2 on page 104.

The Two Models

It is interesting that so little difference exists between the Farmer-Richman model and the Negandhi-Estafen model. Both recognize, and do so properly, the fact that the external cultural environment does have an effect on the operation of the management process. Such a way of managing will then affect management effectiveness. As has been pointed out, the only difference in the Negandhi-Estafen position is that managerial attitudes ("philosophy") are believed to be important enough to identify separately as independent variables. Farmer and Richman, on the other hand, place policy making in operating areas as elements of the management process, and thereby they imply that the benefits or attitudes which lead managers to follow one policy rather than another are affected by the same external constraints as affect the functions of managers.

There is much to be said for both types of models. There can be little doubt that policies are influenced by external cultural factors. On the other

[22] K. Chowdhry and A. K. Pal, "Production Planning and Organization Morale," in A. H. Rubenstein and C. J. Haberstroh (eds.), *Some Theories of Organization* (Homewood, Ill.: The Dorsey Press, Inc., and Richard D. Irwin, Inc., 1960), pp. 185–196.

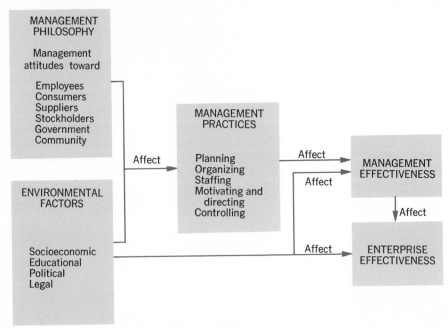

Figure 5.2 *Negandhi-Estafen model for analyzing comparative management.* SOURCE: *Adapted from A. R. Negandhi and B. D. Estafen, "A Research Model to Determine the Applicability of American Management Know-how in Differing Cultures and/or Environments," Academy of Management Journal, vol. 8, no. 4, pp. 309–318 (December, 1965), and from A. R. Negandhi, op. cit.*

hand, many of these policies do not appear to be culture-bound. One finds, for example, both the "quick profit" and the "long-range profit" attitude in many cultures. Likewise, the same attitudes toward such things as product quality, community relations, and fair dealing tend to exist in various cultures. Where these similar attitudes exist, they are simply reflections of like characteristics found in different cultures. Thus, as everyone dealing in international business knows, similar attitudes toward accepting business bribes (as we understand this term by standards applied in the United States) as a way of life exist in otherwise widely varied cultures.

What concerns the authors of this book regarding the Farmer-Richman model is that the inclusion in the management process of policies with respect to operational matters (marketing, production and procurement, research and development, finance, and public and external relations) tends to detract from the more meaningful focus on the management process itself. To be sure, policy making as a function is a part of management planning. But the type of policy pursued in given instances will probably be strongly influenced by factors external to managing itself. Consequently, for purposes of determining the transferability of fundamentals of the management process between nations or cultures, it would be preferable to separate as a variable the types of policies pursued. But the process of policy making itself and the fundamentals underlying it are proper elements of planning and should be included in the management process.

SEPARATING ENVIRONMENTAL FACTORS FROM MANAGEMENT FUNDAMENTALS: A PROPOSED MODEL

From the point of view of studying comparative management to determine the universality and transferability of the basics of management and thus to make a start in separating science from practice in this field, neither of the above models seems to be suitable. Both make major contributions in recognizing the importance of environmental factors and in attempting to show how they affect the practice of management, but neither is as useful as it might be in dealing with the problem of transferability. Likewise, many other studies that have contributed much to an understanding of comparative management suffer from similar disabilities.

There are several difficulties with the generally used models. The problem of separating the art and science of management has been noted. Also, the effectiveness of an enterprise's operation not only depends upon management but on other factors. Management knowledge does not by any means encompass all the knowledge that is utilized in an enterprise. The specialized knowledge, or science, in such basic areas of enterprise operation as marketing, engineering, production, and finance, is essential to enterprise operation. Many are the enterprises that have been successful despite poor management, because of brilliant marketing, strong engineering, well organized and operated production, or astute financing. Even though it is the authors' firm judgment, based on an analysis of the histories of many companies, that effectiveness of management will ultimately make the difference between continued success and decline, at least in a competitive economy, it is still true that enterprises have for a time succeeded entirely through nonmanagerial factors. It is also probably true that, if an enterprise has excellent capabilities in nonmanagerial areas, effective managing would greatly enhance and would surely assure this success.

In total, then, enterprise activities fall into two broad categories, managerial and nonmanagerial. Either or both can be the causal factors for at least some degree of enterprise effectiveness. Also, nonmanagerial activities will be affected by relevant underlying science or knowledge, just as managerial activities will be affected by underlying management science. Both types of activities will be affected by the availability of human and material resources and by the constraints and influences of the external environment, whether these are educational, political-legal, economic, technological, or sociological-ethical.

If the factors affecting enterprise effectiveness and the role of underlying management science are to be brought to light more clearly than has been done, it would appear that we need a model of the kind shown in Figure 5.3.

As is clear, this revised model is far more complex than those used by previous researchers in the field of comparative management. It is also be-

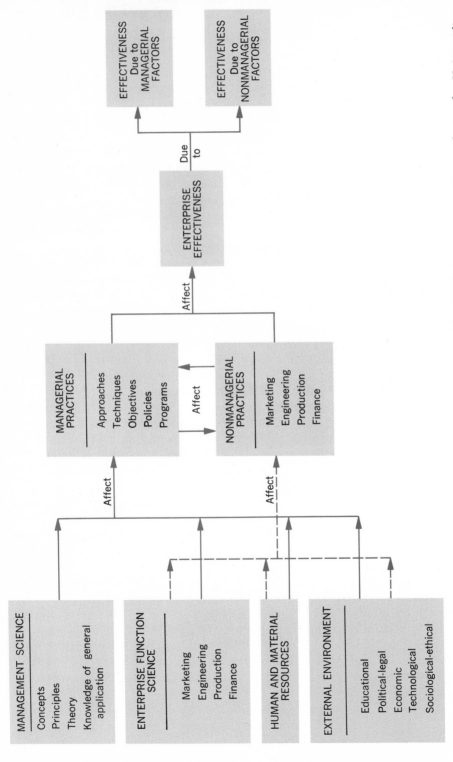

Figure 5.3 *Koontz model for analyzing comparative management.* SOURCE: *From H. Koontz, "A Model for Analyzing the Universality and Transferability of Management." Academy of Management Journal, vol. 12, no. 4, pp. 415–429 (December, 1969).*

lieved to be far more accurate and realistic. If the purpose is to study comparative *management*, something like this must be done in order to understand and see the elements of universality in management.

The real problem is not only to separate the influence of environmental factors but also the importance of managerial, rather than nonmanagerial, factors in determining enterprise effectiveness. This is obviously difficult. If an enterprise were in a laboratory where all input variables except managerial could be controlled, it would then be possible to ascribe effectiveness to the quality of managing. But this is impossible. However, if comparative management researchers would try to identify enterprise function factors as well as they have external environment variables, a closer, even though crude, recognition of *managerial* effectiveness could be made.

This may not be as difficult as it appears. If we could take enterprises (whether business, government, or other) operating in essentially the same external environment and trace their primary causes of effectiveness to managerial and nonmanagerial factors, we might be surprised at what would be disclosed. The authors have had the occasion to analyze several companies in the United States that had had a profitable growth only to find in some instances the quality of managing was rather poor and the success—often erroneously ascribed to astute managing—was really due to genius in marketing or in engineering, or in clever financial manipulation.

It will be noted that managerial attitudes are not included in the model as an independent variable. While they are recognized as very important and must be taken into account, it is believed that they are resultants of cultural factors and environment. Many sociological consultants, for example, on being asked to help change attitudes in an enterprise, have found that they cannot do so without making certain environmental changes.

EVIDENCES OF UNIVERSALITY

Despite the difficulties in separating the variables involved in enterprise effectiveness or ineffectiveness, there has been persuasive evidence that the fundamentals of managing are universal. While much of this represents conclusions and opinions, it has arisen from studies and analyses of well-qualified scholars. While the studies are too numerous to be summarized here, some references may be noted. The conclusion of Harbison and Myers that "organization building has its logic" has been noted.[23] The work of Farmer and Richman[24] covering a number of different cultures is particularly noteworthy and indicates the universality of basic management theory and principles. Likewise, the work of Negandhi points in the same direction.[25] The same kind of inferences can clearly be drawn from the work of Fayerweather on Mexico,[26]

---

[23] Harbison and Myers, *op. cit.*, p. 117.

[24] *Comparative Management and Economic Progress*, *loc. cit.* See also many other publications by the same authors, either jointly or individually presented.

[25] See, for example, his paper on "A Model for Organizations in Cross-Cultural Settings: A Conceptual Scheme and Some Research Findings," *loc. cit.*

[26] J. Fayerweather, *The Executive Overseas* (Syracuse: Syracuse University Press, 1959).

the various publications of the National Planning Association,[27] the work of Abegglen on Japan,[28] the studies of Prasad,[29] and many others.

Also, a number of studies on comparative management have been made in recent years by doctoral students. Most of these have found a high degree of universality in the application of management concepts and principles. For example, a series of studies undertaken at the University of California, Los Angeles, indicate quite persuasively that well-managed American-owned companies, operating in less developed countries, have generally shown superiority in management and economic effectiveness.[30]

The universal nature of management fundamentals is also apparent in the specialized books on administration for business, government, and other types of enterprises. While semantic differences may exist, one finds that, at the fundamental level, authors are talking about the same phenomena.

Persons like the authors who have led management seminars for various types of enterprises find that the identical concepts, theory, and principles, and often the same techniques (such as variable budgeting or management by objectives) apply with equal force in widely different enterprise environments. Also, it is interesting that most of the basic propositions inventoried from the behavioral sciences have universal application where relevant to managerial situations.[31]

THE SIGNIFICANCE OF UNIVERSALITY FOR MANAGEMENT RESEARCH, TEACHING, AND PRACTICE

It is hoped that increasing effort will be made to separate the underlying science of management from the art of managing. By so doing, we should then become increasingly able to recognize fundamentals of universal application and transferability. And, in doing so, many of the clouds that have obscured

[27] See, for example, F. Brandenberg, *The Development of Latin American Private Enterprise* (1964); T. Geiger, *The General Electric Company in Brazil* (1961); T. Geiger and W. Armstrong, *The Development of African Private Enterprise* (1961); and S. Kannappan and E. Burgess, *Aluminum Ltd. in India* (1967).

[28] *The Japanese Factory* (New York: The Free Press of Glencoe, 1958).

[29] See, for example, "New Managerialism in Czechoslovakia and the Soviet Union," *Academy of Management Journal*, vol. 9, no. 4, pp. 328–336. (December, 1966).

[30] These include such unpublished dissertations as B. D. Estafen, "An Empirical Experiment in Comparative Management: A Study of the Transferability of American Management Policies and Practices into Firms Operating in Chile" (1967); A. J. Papageorge, "Transferability of Management: A Case Study of the United States and Greece" (1967); F. C. Flores, Jr., "Applicability of American Management Know-How to Developing Countries: Case Studies of U.S. Firms Operating Both in the United States and the Philippines in Comparison with Domestic Firms in the Philippines" (1967); John Jaeger, "A Comparative Management Study: Organization Patterns and Processes of Hotels in Four Countries" (1965); Y. K. Shetty, "A Comparative Study of Manpower Management Practices in American and Indian Industrial Enterprises" (1967).

[31] See, for example, the inventory of propositions in J. L. Pierce, *Organizational Effectiveness: An Inventory of Propositions* (Homewood, Ill.: Richard D. Irwin, Inc., 1968) and B. Berelson and G. A. Steiner, *Human Behavior: An Inventory of Scientific Findings* (New York: Harcourt, Brace & World, Inc., 1964).

the analysis, teaching, and practice of management may be lifted and the jungle of management theory made into orderly rows of trees at last.

Managing as a science and practice is complex enough. But when it is put in the operating framework of enterprise functions and surrounded by a myriad of environmental influences, its complexity becomes virtually incomprehensible. With growing recognition of the importance of competent managing for effectively and efficiently reaching group and social goals, those whose role is to research, teach, or practice in the field have an obligation at least to clarify the field.

Much research has been done. Teaching of basic management has greatly expanded in the past fifteen years. Management practice has become far more sophisticated and effective. But only the surface of this important field has been touched. Meanwhile, a great waste of human and material resources continues through inept research, ineffective teaching, and too much seat-of-the-pants managing. It is believed that much can be accomplished through the simple, but largely unaccomplished, approach of clearly and purposively separating underlying science from its artful application to reality.

FOR DISCUSSION

1. Why is management quality a crucial factor in economic growth? Can a country thrive economically with poor or average management?
2. From your knowledge of any foreign country, outline the major elements of its culture that would in your judgment influence the kind of management you would expect in a typical firm.
3. Take any selected management technique or approach (such as budgeting, a training program, participative management, an executive committee operation, or engineering project management) and divide it into management fundamentals and those aspects which might be affected by cultural variables.
4. Compare and contrast the Farmer-Richman and Negandhi-Estafen comparative management models. Which do you prefer? What are the advantages and disadvantages of each?
5. Taking some enterprise—whether business or other—with which you are familiar, apply the model proposed in this chapter to see whether you can ascertain whether its success or failure is due to managerial or nonmanagerial factors.
6. Do you agree with the position taken in this chapter that attitudes, or values, are not independent variables? Why? Why not?
7. In accepting or rejecting the concept of universality of management, do you agree that separation of fundamental management knowledge from application to practice is a useful and logical approach to comparative management?

part two
PLANNING

The reader is now familiar with the development of basic management theory and has been introduced to the five managerial functions: planning, organizing, staffing, directing, and controlling. The six chapters on planning which follow form Part 2 of the book.

Planning is the most basic of all management functions since it involves selection from among alternative courses of action. Not only is planning a basic function for all managers at all levels in the enterprise, but the four other functions of the manager must reflect it. Thus a manager organizes, staffs, directs, and controls to assure the attainment of goals according to plans.

Planning involves selection of enterprise and departmental objectives as well as determination of the means of reaching them. It is thus a rational approach to preselected objectives. Since this approach does not take place in a vacuum, good planning must consider the nature of the future environment in which planning decisions and actions are intended to operate.

In the first chapter of this part, the reasons for planning and the general kinds of plans are explained. The logical process of planning is discussed and attention is given to such practical matters as the length of time for which a manager should plan.

This is followed by a chapter on objectives—the determination of which decides the basic nature of total planned action and, through a hierarchy of derivative goals, determines a host of supporting plans which are developed by the component units of the organization.

Plans are made to operate in the future. Therefore, a key part of planning is the establishment of clear planning premises. To assure coordination among all managers who make plans in a given organization, these premises should be used by all concerned. Premises spell out the "stage" of the expected future events which it is believed will exist when plans operate. They are the expected environment of plans. Chapter 7 gives the reader a clear view of "premising" in management, including methods of making these important planning determinants clear to enterprise planners.

The next chapter of this part analyzes the decision-making process, which is an essential part of planning. Of course, every manager must make decisions throughout his working life. But decisions are at the core of planning since they represent that part of the process where a selection of a course of future action is made. Therefore, decision making is treated in the planning section of this book rather than elsewhere. As will be seen, one of the major developments in decision making is the increasing use of the research methodology of the physical sciences and a greater reliance on mathematics.

Policy and strategy formulation is the subject of Chapter 8. Policies, written or unwritten, may be thought of quite simply as guides to thinking in decision making. They act as guidelines so that all managers in an organization make consistent decisions that contribute to the achievement of goals in an orderly way. Strategies are broad overall concepts of an enterprise operation. Together they constitute a general program of action, including the deployment of resources to attain ultimate objectives, and thus include the selection of major goals and overall policies that indicate what the enterprise is trying to achieve or to become. Since both policies and strategies are designed to guide thinking and action they are dealt with in the same chapter.

The last chapter of this part deals with some of the major considerations involved in putting plans into action, such as coordination of plans, communication for planning, and the importance of getting participation in making plans. The problems of limitations in plans and the difficulties encountered in making plans operate effectively are analyzed, and suggestions are offered as to the major elements necessary for an effective planning environment.

6
the nature and purpose of planning

The most basic of management functions is planning, the selection from among alternatives of future courses of action for the enterprise as a whole and each department within it. Every manager plans, and his other functions depend upon his planning. Plans involve selecting enterprise objectives and departmental goals and determining ways of reaching them. Plans thus provide a rational approach to preselected objectives.

As Billy E. Goetz[1] has said, planning is "fundamentally choosing" and "a planning problem arises only when an alternative course of action is discovered." In this range, it is essentially decision making, although, as will be seen, it is also more. Indeed, actual and final choosing between alternatives may be the easiest part of planning. Planning presupposes the existence of alternatives, and there are few business decisions for which some kind of alternatives does not exist—even when it comes to meeting legal or other requirements imposed by forces beyond the manager's control.

Planning is deciding in advance what to do, how to do it, when to do it, and who is to do it. Planning bridges the gap from where we are to where we want to go. It makes it possible for things to occur which would not otherwise happen. Although the exact future can seldom be predicted and factors beyond control may interfere with the best-laid plans, without planning events are left to chance. Planning is an intellectual process, the conscious determination of courses of action, the basing of decisions on purpose, facts, and considered estimates.

A strong aspect of the managerial revolution of the past two decades has been a tremendous interest in planning by all forms of enterprise—business, government, education, and others. Note that this strong interest is primarily a phenomenon of the past quarter century, although in areas such as factory operations production planning has been stressed for a half century.

---

[1] Billy E. Goetz, *Management Planning and Control* (New York: McGraw-Hill Book Company, 1949), p. 2.

Production managers found early that, without planning, their mistakes showed up within days as production lines came to a halt through a misfit part or the absence of a needed component. Also, well-managed companies have long planned to meet cash needs before their checks bounced. But, generally speaking, planning as a widely recognized and actively pursued managerial function is a fairly recent development.

Now, nearly everyone plans. Enterprises of all kinds plan further into the future, plan more aspects of their operations, plan less by intuition or hunch, and lean more heavily on forecasts and studies. In fact, a few years ago, an economic consulting firm advising a large company board stated that the development of business planning has been as revolutionary a movement as the technological revolution or the revolution in expansion of income.

We are in an economic, technological, social, and political era in which planning, like the other functions of managers, has become requisite for enterprise survival. Change and economic growth bring opportunities, but they also bring risk, particularly in an era of world-wide rivalry for markets, resources, and influence. It is exactly the task of planning to minimize risk while taking advantage of opportunities.

With all the interest in planning and all the sense of urgency brought about by modern supercompetition, there is danger that planning could become merely a costly fad, not very useful, and even disillusioning. To plan well, to make plans that will succeed, planning—again, like the other managerial functions—must take place in a context of fundamental principles.

THE NATURE OF PLANNING

The essential nature of planning can be understood through four major aspects of planning: contribution to objectives, primacy of planning, pervasiveness of planning, and efficiency of plans.

Contribution to Objectives

The purpose of every plan and all derivative plans is to facilitate the accomplishment of enterprise objectives. This principle derives from the nature of organized enterprise, which exists for the accomplishment of group purpose through deliberate cooperation. This principle was emphasized by Goetz when he said:[2]

Plans alone cannot make an enterprise successful. Action is required; the enterprise must operate. Plans can, however, focus action on purposes. They can forecast which actions will tend toward the ultimate objective . . . , which tend away, which will likely offset one another, and which are merely irrelevant. Managerial planning seeks to achieve a consistent, co-ordinated structure of operations focused on desired ends. Without plans, action must become merely random activity, producing nothing but chaos.

[2] Ibid., p. 63.

Primacy of Planning

Since managerial operations in organizing, staffing, directing, and controlling are designed to support the accomplishment of enterprise objectives, planning logically precedes the execution of all other managerial functions. Although all the functions intermesh in practice, planning is unique in that it establishes the objectives necessary for all group effort. Besides, plans must be made to accomplish these objectives before the manager knows what kind of organization relationships and personal qualifications are needed, along which course subordinates are to be directed, and what kind of control is to be applied. And, of course, each of the other managerial functions must be planned if they are to be effective.

Planning and control are inseparable—the Siamese twins of management. Unplanned action cannot be controlled, for control involves keeping activities on course by correcting deviations from plans. Any attempt to control without plans would be meaningless, since there is no way anyone can tell whether he is going where he wants to go—the task of control—unless first he knows where he wants to go—the task of planning. Plans thus furnish the standards of control.

Pervasiveness of Planning

Planning is a function of every manager, although the character and breadth of planning will vary with his authority and the nature of policies and plans outlined by his superior. It is virtually impossible so to circumscribe his area of choice that he can exercise no discretion, and unless he has some planning responsibility, it is doubtful that he is truly a manager.

Recognition of the pervasiveness of planning goes far in clarifying the attempt on the part of some students of management to distinguish between policy making (the setting of guides for thinking in decision making) and administration, or between the "manager" and the "administrator" or "supervisor." One manager, because of his authority delegation or position in the organization, may do more planning or more important planning than another, or the planning of one may be more basic and applicable to a larger portion of the enterprise than that of another. However, all managers—from presidents to foremen—plan. The foreman of a road gang or a factory crew plans in a limited area under fairly strict rules and procedures. Interestingly, in studies of work satisfactions, a principal factor found to account for the success of supervisors at the lowest organization level has been their ability to plan.[3]

Efficiency of Plans

The efficiency of a plan is measured by the amount it contributes to objectives as offset by the costs and other unsought consequences required to formulate

---

[3] D. Katz et al., *Productivity, Supervision and Morale among Railroad Workers* (Ann Arbor, Mich.: Survey Research Center, Institute for Social Research, University of Michigan, 1951).

and operate it.[4] A plan can contribute to the attainment of objectives, but at too high or unnecessarily high costs. This concept of efficiency implies the normal ratio of input to output, but goes beyond the usual understanding of inputs and outputs in terms of dollars, man-hours, or units of production to include such values as individual and group satisfactions.

Many managers have followed plans, such as in the acquisition of certain aircraft by airlines, where costs were greater than the revenues obtainable. Companies have inefficiently attempted to attain objectives in the face of the unsought consequence of market unacceptability, as happened when a motorcar manufacturer tried to capture a postwar market by emphasizing engineering without competitive advances in style. Plans may also become inefficient in the attainment of objectives by jeopardizing group satisfactions. The new president of a company that was losing money attempted quickly to reorganize and cut expenses by wholesale and unplanned layoffs of key personnel. The result in fear, resentment, and loss of morale led to so much lower productivity as to defeat his laudable objective of eliminating losses and making profits. And many attempts to install management appraisal and development programs have failed because of group resentment of the methods used, regardless of whether these methods, if accepted, would have developed better managers.

TYPES OF PLANS

Identifying the types of plans in the typical enterprise illustrates the breadth of planning. They may be classified as objectives, policies, strategies, procedures, rules, programs, and budgets.

Objectives

Objectives, or goals, are the ends toward which activity is aimed. They represent not only the end point of planning, but the end toward which organizing, staffing, directing, and controlling are aimed. While enterprise objectives constitute the basic plan of the firm, a department may also have objectives. Its goals naturally contribute to the attainment of enterprise objectives, but the two sets of goals may be entirely different. Thus, if the objective of a business is to make a profit in electronics, the goal of the manufacturing department might be to produce the required number of television sets of a given design and quality at a given cost. These objectives are consistent, but they differ in that the manufacturing department alone cannot assure a profit.

The nature of objectives and their relationship to planning are discussed in the following chapter. It is enough to emphasize here that objectives, or goals, are plans, that they involve the same planning process as any other type of planning, even though they are also end points of planning. A profit

---

[4]The authors are indebted to Chester I. Barnard for having so clearly pointed out the applicability of concepts of effectiveness and efficiency to systems of human cooperation. See *The Functions of the Executive* (Cambridge, Mass.: Harvard University Press, 1938), pp. 19–20.

goal, for example, cannot be guessed at or wished but needs to be determined in the light of purpose and circumstances. Likewise, a plan to accomplish a certain profit goal will have within it, or as derivatives of it, project or departmental goals.

Policies

Policies, also, are plans in that they are general statements or understandings which guide or channel thinking and action in decision making of subordinates. One can hardly refer to all policies as "statements," since they are often merely implied from the actions of managers. The president of a company, for example, may strictly follow—perhaps for convenience rather than as policy— the practice of promoting from within; the practice may then be interpreted as policy and rigorously followed by his subordinates. In fact, one of the problems of the manager is to make sure that subordinates do not interpret as policy minor decisions which he makes without intending them to serve as precedents.

Policies delimit an area within which a decision is to be made and assure that the decision will be consistent with and contributive to objectives. Policies tend to predecide issues, avoid repeated analysis, and give a unified structure to other types of plans, thus permitting managers to delegate authority while maintaining control. For example, a certain railroad has the policy of acquiring industrial land to replace all acreage sold along its right of way. This permits the manager of the land department to develop his acquisition plans without continual reference to top management, which is nevertheless furnished with a standard of control.

Policies ordinarily have at least as many levels as organization, ranging from major company policies through major departmental policies to minor or derivative policies applicable to the smallest segment of the organization. They may also be related to functions—such as sales and finance—or merely to a project—such as that of designing a new product with materials to meet a specified competition.

The varieties of policies are legion. Examples are company policies to promote from within, to conform strictly to a high standard of business ethics, to compete on a price basis, to insist on fixed rather than cost-plus pricing, or to shun publicity; and department policies to hire only university-trained engineers or to encourage employee suggestions for improved cooperation.

Being guides to thinking in decision making, it follows that policies must allow for some discretion. Otherwise, they would be rules. Too often policies are established as a kind of Ten Commandments which leave no room for discretion. Although the discretion area, in some instances, is quite broad, it can be exceedingly narrow. For example, a policy to buy from the lowest of three qualified bidders leaves for discretion only the question of which bidders are qualified; a requirement to buy from a certain company, regardless of price or service, is a rule.

Because policies are so often misunderstood, the authors have selected examples from a company's policy manual. It will be noted in each case that there is an area for a person in a decision-making capacity to use discretion. The following are interesting examples.

1. *Gifts from suppliers. Except for token gifts of purely nominal or advertising value, no employee shall accept any gift or gratuity from any supplier at any time.*
2. *Entertainment. No officer or employee shall accept favors or entertainment from an outside organization or agency which are substantial enough to cause undue influence in his selection of goods or services for the company.*
3. *Outside employment. It is improper for any employee to work for any company customers, or for any competitors, or for any vendors or suppliers of goods or services to the company; outside employment is further prohibited if it: (a) results in a division of loyalty to the company or a conflict of interests, or (b) interferes with or adversely affects the employee's work or opportunity for advancement in the company.*
4. *Pricing. Each territorial division manager may establish such prices for the products under his control as he deems in the division's interest so long as (a) these prices result in gross profit margins for any line of products which are consistent with his approved profit plan; (b) price reductions will not result in detrimental effects on prices of similar products of another company division in another state or country; and (c) prices meet the legal requirements of the state or country in which the prices are effective.*

The area of discretion in most of these policies is fairly general. However, in the pricing policy shown, the discretion area is fairly specifically defined. Likewise, in the outside employment policy, that portion dealing with employment with any vendors or suppliers leaves no discretion and is, consequently, a rule.

Policy should be regarded as a means of encouraging discretion and initiative, but within limits. The amount of freedom possible will naturally depend upon the policy, which in turn reflects position and authority in the organization. The president of a company with a policy of aggressive price competition has a broad area of discretion and initiative in which to interpret and apply this policy. The district sales manager abides by the same basic policy, but the interpretations made by the president, the vice-president for sales, and the regional sales manager become derivative policies which narrow his scope to where, for example, he may be permitted only to approve a special sale price to meet competition not exceeding a 10 percent reduction.

Making policies consistent and integrated enough to facilitate the realization of enterprise objectives is difficult for many reasons. First, policies are too seldom written and their exact interpretations too little known. Second, the very delegation of authority that policies are intended to implement leads, through its decentralizing influence, to widespread participation in policy making and interpretation, with almost certain variations among individuals. Third, it is not always easy to control policy, because *actual* policy may be difficult to ascertain and *intended* policy not always clear.

Strategies

For years strategies were used by the military to mean a grand plan made in the light of what it was believed an adversary might or might not do. While

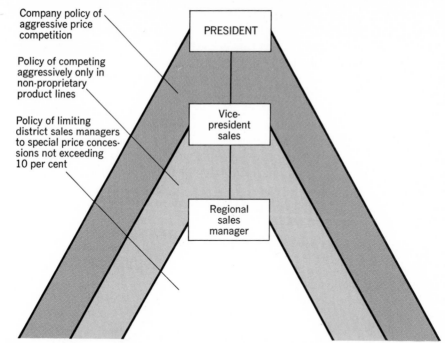

Company policy of aggressive price competition

Policy of competing aggressively only in non-proprietary product lines

Policy of limiting district sales managers to special price concessions not exceeding 10 per cent

PRESIDENT

Vice-president sales

Regional sales manager

Figure 6.1   *How definition of policies may be successively limiting.*

this type of plan still usually has a competitive implication, it has been increasingly used as a term to reflect broad overall concepts of an enterprise operation. Strategies therefore most often denote a general program of action and deployment of emphasis and resources to attain comprehensive objectives. Anthony defines them as resulting from ". . . the process of deciding on objectives of the organization, on changes in these objectives, on the resources used to attain these objectives, and on the policies that are to govern the acquisition, use, and disposition of these resources."[5] And Chandler defines a strategy as "the determination of the basic long-term goals and objectives of an enterprise, and the adoption of courses of action and the allocation of resources necessary to carry out these goals."[6]

Thus, a company may have an objective of profitable growth at a certain percentage per year. Supportive of this might be a determination that the company will be of a certain kind, such as a transportation company rather than a railroad company, or a container company rather than a paper box manufacturer. A strategy might include such major policies as to market directly rather than through distribution, or to concentrate on proprietary products, or to have a full line such as General Motors decided to have years ago for its automobile business.

The purpose of strategies, then, is to determine and communicate, through a system of major objectives and policies, a picture of what kind of enterprise

[5] R. N. Anthony, *Planning and Control Systems: A Framework for Analysis* (Boston: Division of Research, Harvard Business School, 1965), p. 24.

[6] A. D. Chandler, Jr., *Strategy and Structure* (Cambridge, Mass.: The M.I.T. Press, 1962), p. 13.

is envisioned. Strategies show direction and general deployment of emphasis and resources. They do not attempt to outline exactly *how* the enterprise is to accomplish its objectives, since this is the task of countless major and minor supporting programs. But they are a useful framework for guiding enterprise thinking and action. This usefulness in practice and importance in guiding planning do, however, justify their separation as a type of plan for purposes of analysis.

As a matter of fact, most strategies, particularly in business, do fit the traditional military concept by including competitive considerations. A foreign automobile manufacturer, for example, selected the strategy of offering on the highly competitive American market a low-priced and small car, easy to drive in congested areas and easy to park in order to meet a demand by consumers who were not being served in these respects by native manufacturers. In this strategy were all the elements of the traditional military concept: (1) competitors, (2) a market not large enough to satisfy all competitive manufacturers, and (3) a gap that offered an adversary an opportunity. But even this kind of strategy is not really an independently separate type of plan because it is actually a combination of objectives (to secure a given market share), a major policy (produce and market a small low-priced car), and various programs (for example, exporting and marketing).

Procedures

Procedures are plans in that they establish a customary method of handling future activities. They are truly guides to action rather than to thinking, and they detail the exact manner in which a certain activity must be accomplished. Their essence is chronological sequence of required actions.

Their pervasiveness in the organization is readily apparent. The board of directors follows many procedures quite different from those of the foremen; the expense account of the vice-president may go through quite different approval procedures from that of the salesman; the procedures for carrying out vacation and sick-leave provisions may vary considerably at various levels of organization. But the important fact is that procedures exist throughout an organization, even though, as one might expect, they become more exacting and numerous in the lower levels, largely because of the necessity for more careful control, the economic advantages of spelling out actions in detail, the reduced need for discretion, and the fact that routine jobs lend themselves to obtaining greater efficiency through prescription of the one best way.

As in other types of plans, procedures have a hierarchy of importance. Thus, in a typical corporation, one may find a manual of "Corporation Standard Practice," outlining procedures for the corporation as a whole, a manual of "Division Standard Practice," and special sets of procedures for a department, a branch, a section, or a unit.

Procedures often cut across department lines. For example, in a manufacturing company, the procedure for handling orders will almost certainly encompass the sales department (for the original order), the finance department (for acknowledgment of receipt of funds and for customer credit determination), the accounting department (for recording the transaction), the production department (for order to produce or authority to release from stock), and the traffic department (for determination of the shipping means and route).

The relationship between procedures and policies may best be indicated by a few examples. Company policy may grant employees vacations; procedures established to implement this policy will schedule vacations to avoid disruption of work, set methods and rates of vacation pay, maintain records to assure each employee a vacation, and provide means of applying for the vacation. A company may have a policy of shipping orders quickly; particularly in a large company, careful procedures will be necessary to assure that orders are handled in a specific way. Company policy may require clearance by the public relations department of public utterances of its employees; to implement this policy, procedures must be established to obtain clearance with a minimum of inconvenience and delay.

Rules

Rules are plans in that they are a course of required actions which, like other plans, are chosen from among alternatives. They are usually the simplest type of plan.

Rules are frequently confused with policies or procedures, although they are entirely distinct. A rule requires that a specific and definite action be taken or not taken with respect to a situation. It is thus related to a procedure, in that it guides action, but it specifies no time sequence. A rule may or may not be part of a procedure. For example, "no smoking" is a rule quite unrelated to any procedure; but a procedure governing the handling of orders may incorporate the rule that all orders must be confirmed the day they are received. This rule allows no deviation from a stated course of action and in no way interferes with the procedure for handling orders. It is comparable to a rule that all fractions over half an ounce are to be counted a full ounce or that receiving inspection must count or weigh all materials against the purchase order. The essence of a rule is that it reflects a managerial decision that certain action be taken—or not be taken.

Rules should also be distinguished from policies. The purpose of policies is to guide thinking in decision making by marking off areas of discretion. Although rules also serve as guides, they allow no discretion in their application.

Programs

Programs are a complex of goals, policies, procedures, rules, task assignments, steps to be taken, resources to be employed, and other elements necessary to carry out a given course of action; they are ordinarily supported by necessary capital and operating budgets. Programs may be as major as that of an airline to acquire a 400-million-dollar fleet of jets, or the five-year program embarked upon by the Ford Motor Company several years ago to improve the status and quality of its thousands of foremen. Or they may be as minor as a program formulated by a single foreman in a parts manufacturing department of a farm machinery company to improve the morale of his workers.

A primary program may call for many derivative programs. For example, an airline program to invest in new jets, costing many millions of dollars for the aircraft and the necessary spare parts, requires many derivative programs if the investment is to be properly used. A program for providing the maintenance and operating bases with spare components and parts must be developed in detail. Special maintenance facilities must be prepared and maintenance personnel trained. Pilots and flight engineers must also be trained, and, if the new jets mean a net addition to flying hours, flight personnel recruited. Flight schedules must be revised and groundstation personnel trained to handle the new airplanes and their schedules as service is expanded to new cities in the airline's system. Advertising programs must give adequate publicity to the new service. Plans to finance the aircraft and provide for insurance coverage must be developed.

These and other programs must be devised and effected before any new aircraft are received and placed in service. Furthermore, all these programs necessitate coordination and timing, since the failure of any part of this network of derivative plans means delay for the major program with consequent unnecessary costs and loss of revenues. Some of the programs, particularly those involving hiring and training of personnel, can be accomplished *too soon* as well as too late, since needless expense results from employees being available and trained before their services are required.

Thus one seldom finds that a program of any importance in business planning stands by itself. It is usually a part of a complex structure of programs, depending upon some and affecting others. This interdependence of plans makes planning very difficult. The results of poor or inadequate planning are seldom isolated, for planning is only as strong as its weakest link. Even a seemingly unimportant procedure or rule, if badly conceived, may wreck an important program. Coordinated planning requires extraordinarily exacting managerial skill.

Budgets

A budget as a plan is a statement of expected results expressed in numerical terms. It may be referred to as a "numberized" program. As a matter of fact, the financial operating budget is often called a "profit plan." It may be expressed either in financial terms or in terms of man-hours, units of product, machine-hours, or any other numerically measurable term. It may deal with operations, as does the expense budget; it may reflect capital outlays, as does the capital expenditures budget; or it may show flow of cash, as does the cash budget.

Since budgets are also control devices, the principal discussion of them is reserved for the chapters on control. However, *making* a budget is clearly planning. It is the fundamental planning instrument in many companies. A budget forces a company to make in advance—whether for a week or five years —a numerical compilation of expected cash flow, expenses and revenues, capital outlays, or man- or machine-hour utilization. The budget is necessary for control, but it cannot serve as a sensible standard of control unless it reflects plans.

Although a budget usually implements a program, it may actually be a program. One of the authors recalls a company in difficult financial straits installing an elaborate budgetary control program, designed not only to control expenditures but to instill cost consciousness in managing. A budget may also encompass the entire enterprise program, with all other programs reflected in it.

THE IMPORTANCE OF PLANNING

Four concrete reasons for the paramount importance of the planning function are: to offset uncertainty and change, to focus attention on objectives, to gain economical operation, and to facilitate control.

To Offset Uncertainty and Change

Future uncertainty and change make planning a necessity. Just as the navigator cannot set a course once and forget about it, so the business manager cannot establish his goal and let the matter rest. The future is seldom very certain, and the further in the future the results of a decision must be considered, the less the certainty. An executive may feel quite certain that within the next month orders, costs, productive capacity, output, cash availability, and other factors of the business environment will be at a given level. A fire, an unforeseen strike, or an order cancellation by a major customer could change all this, but in the short run this is unlikely. However, as this manager plans further in advance, his certainty about the internal and external business environment diminishes, and the rightness of any decision becomes less sure.

Even when the future is highly certain, some planning is usually necessary. In the first place, there is the necessity of selecting the best way to accomplish an objective. With conditions of certainty, this becomes primarily a mathematical problem of calculating on the basis of the known facts, which course will yield the desired result at the least cost. In the second place, after the course has been decided, it is necessary to lay out plans so that each part of the business will contribute toward the job to be done.

Even when trends indicating change are easily discernible, difficult planning problems arise. The manufacture of television sets is a case in point. The change away from black-and-white to color television did not take place overnight. The manufacturer had to determine what percentage of his production should be assigned to color sets and what to black-and-white and how to retain efficient production of both lines. There came a time when the declining business of black-and-white consoles became uneconomical, an obvious cutoff point. However, the manufacturer could have chosen an entirely different course. Having satisfied himself of the certainty of the change, he might have deliberately sacrificed black-and-white business in order to concentrate on the design and development of color sets, with the hope of becoming the leader among color set manufacturers.

When trends are not easily discernible, good planning can be even more difficult. Many businessmen missed the significance of inflationary prices, increasing interest rates, and reduction in certain defense and aerospace spending in the late 1960s, with the result that they were not ready for certain market shifts and business losses that occurred. Even the long concern with air pollution did not reach urgent proportions until the end of the 1960s.

To Focus Attention on Objectives

Because all planning is directed toward achieving enterprise objectives, the very act of planning focuses attention on these objectives. Well-considered over-all plans unify interdepartmental activities. Managers, being typically immersed in immediate problems, are forced through planning to consider the future and even consider the periodic need to revise and extend plans in the interest of achieving their objectives.

To Gain Economical Operation

Planning minimizes costs because of the emphasis on efficient operation and consistency. It substitutes joint directed effort for uncoordinated piecemeal activity, even flow of work for uneven flow, and deliberate decisions for snap judgments.

The economy of planning is plainly seen at the production level. No one who has watched the assembly of automobiles in one of the larger factories can fail to be impressed with the way that the parts and subassemblies come together. From one overhead conveyor system comes a body and from others various appurtenances. Exactly the right engine, transmission, and accessories fall into place at the exact appointed time. This implies extensive detailed planning without which the manufacture of automobiles would be chaotic and impossibly costly. Although every manager sees the imperative economy of planning at the production level, planning of equal or sometimes greater importance in other areas is occasionally left to chance and too great individual discretion.

To Facilitate Control

A manager cannot check on his subordinates' accomplishments without having planned goals against which to measure. As a top executive told one of the authors, "After I leave my office at five o'clock in the evening, I will not care what happened today, for I cannot do anything about it; I will only care about what will happen tomorrow or the next day or next year, because I can do something about it." Perhaps this is an extreme position, but it emphasizes the point that effective control is that which looks to the future.

STEPS IN PLANNING

Although the steps in planning are presented here in connection with major programs such as the acquisition of a plant or a fleet of jets or the development of a product, essentially the same steps must be followed in any thorough planning. As minor plans are usually simpler, certain of the steps are more easily accomplished, but the following six practical steps are of general application. Obviously, the discriminating manager would not use 100 dollars worth of time to make a decision worth 50 cents, but what is shocking is to see 50 cents worth of time used to make a planning decision involving millions of dollars.

Being Aware of Opportunity

Although preceding actual planning and therefore not strictly a part of the planning process, awareness of an opportunity[7] is the real starting point for planning. It includes a preliminary look at possible future opportunities and the ability to see them clearly and completely, a knowledge of where we stand and our strengths and weaknesses, an understanding of why we wish to solve uncertainties, and a vision of what we expect to gain. Setting realistic objectives depends on this awareness. Planning requires realistic diagnosis of the opportunity situation.

Establishing Objectives

The first step in planning itself is to establish planning objectives for the entire enterprise and then for each subordinate unit. Objectives specifying the results expected indicate the end points of what is to be done, where the primary emphasis is to be placed, and what is to be accomplished by the network of policies, strategies, procedures, rules, budgets, and programs.

Enterprise objectives should control the nature of all major plans, which, by reflecting these objectives, define the objectives of the major departments. Major department objectives, in turn, control the objectives of subordinate departments, and so on down the line. The objectives of lesser departments will be better framed, however, if subdivision managers understand the overall enterprise objectives and the implied derivative goals.

Premising

A second logical step in planning is to establish, obtain agreement to utilize, and disseminate critical planning premises. These are forecast data of a factual nature, applicable basic policies, and existing company plans. Premises, then, are planning assumptions—in other words, the expected environment of plans in operation. This step leads to one of the major principles of planning: *the more individuals charged with planning understand and agree to utilize consistent planning premises, the more coordinated enterprise planning will be.*

---

[7]The word "problem" might be used instead of "opportunity." But, in the view of the authors, a state of disorder or confusion and a need for a solution to gain a given goal can more constructively be regarded as an opportunity. In fact, the authors know of a very successful and astute company president who does not permit his colleagues to speak of problems, but only of opportunities.

Forecasting is important to premising: What kind of markets will there be? What quantity of sales? What prices? What products? What technical developments? What costs? What wage rates? What tax rates and policies? What new plants? What policies with respect to dividends? How will expansion be financed? What political or social environment? Planning premises include far more than basic forecasts of population, prices, costs, production, markets, and similar matters.

Some premises forecast policies not yet made. For example, if a company has no pension plan and no policy with respect to one, planning premises sometimes must forecast whether such a policy will be set and, if so, what it will contain. Other premises naturally grow out of existing policies or other plans. For example, if a company has a policy of paying out 5 percent of its profits, before taxes, for contributions and if there is no reason to believe that this policy will be changed, the policy becomes a planning premise. Or, if a company has made large investments in special-purpose fixed plant and machinery, this becomes an important planning premise.

A difficulty of establishing complete premises and keeping them up to date is that every major plan, and many minor ones, become premises for the future. The plan to establish a factory in Kansas City, for example, becomes a premise for plans in which plant location is important. Or a Pacific Northwest railroad, for instance, would make little sense in premising future plans on Florida markets without reasonable expectation of expanding to the southeast. And when an airline equips its long-haul routes with one type of aircraft for which it builds maintenance and overhaul facilities, this becomes a critical premise for other plans.

As one moves down the organization hierarchy, the composition of planning premises changes somewhat. The basic process will be the same, but old and new major plans will materially affect the future against which managers of lesser units must plan. Superior plans affecting a subordinate manager's area of authority become premises for his planning.

Because the future environment of plans is so complex, it would not be profitable or realistic to make assumptions about every detail of the future environment of a plan. Therefore, premises are, as a practical matter, limited to those which are critical, or strategic, to a plan, that is, those which most influence its operation.

It would be surprising if all members of a company's management at all levels agreed independently about the company future. One manager might expect world peace to last ten years, another, world war for the same period. One manager might expect prices to go up 10 percent in five years; another, 50 percent; and another might expect prices to drop.

Lack of planning coordination, through use by managers of different sets of premises, can be extremely costly to a company. The use of consistent premises should, therefore, be agreed upon. A single standard for the future is necessary for good planning, even though this standard includes several sets of premises, with the instruction that different sets of plans be developed on each. Some companies, for example, customarily develop plans in prospect of both peace and war, so that, regardless of what occurs, the company will be ready. Obviously, however, a plan actually put into operation for any future period can use only one set of premises if coordination of its elements is to be achieved.

Since agreement to utilize a given set of premises is important to co-ordinated planning, it becomes a major responsibility of managers, starting with those at the top, to make sure that subordinate managers understand the premises upon which they are expected to plan. It is not unusual for chief executives in well-managed companies to force top managers with differing views, through group deliberation, to arrive at a set of major premises that all can accept. But whether they are acceptable to all or not, no chief executive can afford to chance a situation where his lieutenants are planning their portions of the company's future on substantially different premises.

The importance of premising is illustrated by the case where a company president, believing that planning should start from the bottom, issued instructions that all departments should develop their own budgets and submit them to him. When he received them, he was surprised and dismayed to find that the budgets did not fit, and he had a complex of inconsistent plans on his hands. Had he been aware of the importance of premises, he would never have asked for budgets without first giving his department heads their guidelines.

Determining Alternative Courses

The third step in planning is to search for and examine alternative courses of action, especially those not immediately apparent. There is seldom a plan for which reasonable alternatives do not exist, and quite often an alternative that is not obvious proves to be the best.

The more common problem is not finding alternatives, but reducing the number of alternatives so that the most promising may be analyzed. Even with mathematical techniques and the computer, there is a limit to the number of alternatives that may be examined. It is therefore usually necessary for the planner to reduce by preliminary examination the number of alternatives to those promising the most fruitful possibilities or by mathematically eliminating, through the process of approximation, the least promising ones.

Evaluating Alternative Courses

Having sought out alternative courses and examined their strong and weak points, the fourth step is to evaluate them by weighing the various factors in the light of premises and goals. One course may appear to be the most profitable but requires a large cash outlay and a slow payback; another may be less profitable but involves less risk; still another may better suit the company's long-range objectives.

If the only objective were to maximize profits immediately, if the future were not uncertain, if cash position and capital availability were not worrisome, and if most factors could be reduced to definite data, this evaluation should be relatively easy. But typical planning is replete with uncertainties, problems of capital shortages, and intangible factors, so evaluation is usually very difficult, even with relatively simple problems. A company may wish to enter a new product line primarily for purposes of prestige; the forecast of expected results may show a clear financial loss; but the question is still open as to whether the loss is worth the gain in prestige.

Because the number of alternative courses in most situations is legion and the numerous variables and limitations are involved, evaluation can be also exceedingly complex. Because of these complexities, the newer method-ologies and applications of operations research and analysis, discussed in Chapter 9, are helpful. Indeed, it is at this step in the planning process that operations research and mathematical and computing techniques have their primary application to the field of management.

Selecting a Course

The fifth planning step, selecting the course of action, is the point at which the plan is adopted—the real point of decision making. Occasionally an anal-ysis and evaluation of alternative courses will disclose that two or more are advisable, and the manager may decide to follow several courses rather than one best course.

Formulating Derivative Plans

At the point where a decision is made, planning is seldom complete, and a last step is indicated. There are almost invariably derivative plans required to support the basic plan. In the case where an airline decided to acquire a fleet of new planes, this decision was the signal for the development of a host of derivative plans dealing with the hiring and training of various types of per-sonnel, the acquisition and positioning of spare parts, the development of maintenance facilities, scheduling and advertising, financing and insurance.

THE PLANNING PROCESS: RATIONAL APPROACH

As seen in the planning steps outlined above, planning is simply a rational approach to the future. The process can be illustrated as shown in Figure 6.2. In this diagram, progress (toward more sales, more profits, less costs, and so forth) is on the vertical axis and time on the horizontal axis. X indicates where we are (at t_o) and Y where we want to be—a goal for the future (at t_n). Since we ordinarily have to study where we are in advance of t_o, particularly with the lag of accounting and statistical data, we may actually have to start our study of the future at X_1 (at t_{-n}). The line XY indicates the decision path which will take us from X to Y.

If the future were completely certain, the line XY would be relatively easy to draw. However, in actuality, a myriad of factors in the environment in which a plan is to operate may push events away from or toward the desired goal. These are the planning premises. Again, because we cannot forecast or consider everything, we try to develop our path from X to Y in the light of the most critical premises.

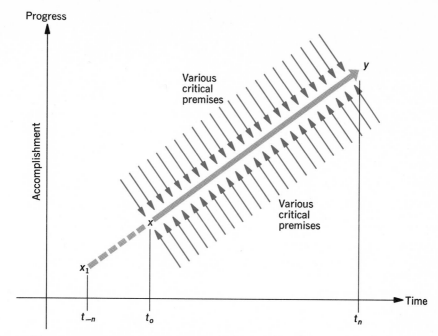

Figure 6.2   *Progress, time, and critical planning premises.*

The essential logic of planning applies regardless of the time interval between t_o and t_n, whether five minutes or twenty years. However, the clarity of premises, the attainability of goals, and the lessening of other planning complexities are almost certain to be inversely related to the time span.

Decision making may be the easiest part of planning, although it involves techniques of evaluation and approach and considerable skill in applying these. The real difficulties arise primarily from sharpening and giving meaning (preferably verifiable) to objectives, spelling out and giving meaning to critical premises, seeing the nature and relationships of the strengths and weaknesses of alternatives, and communicating goals and premises to those throughout the enterprise who must plan.

THE PLANNING PERIOD: LONG-RANGE PLANNING

Shall plans be for a short period or a long one? How shall short-range plans be coordinated with long-range plans? These questions suggest a multiple horizon of planning—that, in some cases, planning a week in advance may be ample and that, in others, the desirable period may be a number of years. Even within the same firm at the same time, various planning periods may exist for various matters.

The National Industrial Conference Board, reporting on a survey of business planning some years ago,[8] disclosed, as might be expected, that businesses

[8] "Industry Plans for the Future," *Conference Board Business Record*, vol. 9, pp. 324–328 (August, 1952).

varied considerably in their planning periods. In some instances, long-range plans were confined to two years, while in others they spanned decades. But three to five years appeared to be most common for long-range planning, and few companies planned less than a year in advance. Later surveys showed more companies engaging in long-range planning, with the planning period being extended. A survey made by McGraw-Hill in 1956 disclosed that the number of large firms laying plans three to five years in advance had doubled in the prior few years and that even small and medium companies were increasingly undertaking long-range planning.[9] Approximately one-third of the companies interviewed had established their formal long-range planning programs in the previous two or three years. However, an increasing number of companies were laying their plans on forecasts of a future ten to twenty years ahead.

Long-range planning has continued to increase until today it is almost a badge of alert management to have some kind of long-range planning department. Yet, as late as 1962, a study by the American Management Association reported that five years seemed to be the norm of long-range planning,[10] although planning periods ranging to twenty-five years and more did exist. In analyzing case studies, the AMA report concluded that companies seem to base their period on a future that can reasonably be anticipated. Another study published by the National Planning Commission in 1966 showed that 16 percent of the 420 companies surveyed had no corporate plan, 53 percent planned on the basis of five years, 6 percent on less than five years, and 17 percent for ten years or more.[11]

The Commitment Principle

There should be some logic in selecting the right time range for company planning. In general, since planning and the forecasting that underlies it are costly, a company should probably not plan for a longer period than is economically justifiable; yet it is risky to plan for a shorter period. The answer as to the right planning period seems to lie in the "commitment principle," *that logical planning encompasses a period of time in the future necessary to foresee, through a series of actions, the fulfillment of commitments involved in a decision.*

Perhaps the most striking application of this principle is the setting of a planning period long enough to anticipate the recovery of costs sunk in a course of action.[12] But since other things than costs can be committed for various lengths of time and because a commitment to spend often precedes an expenditure and may be as unchangeable as sunk costs, it seems inadequate to refer to recovery of costs alone. Thus a company may commit itself, for

---

[9] "In Business, Everyone's Looking Ahead," *Business Week*, p. 113 (Jan. 5, 1957).

[10] Stewart Thompson, *How Companies Plan*, Research Study No. 54 (New York: American Management Association, 1962), pp. 23–31.

[11] "The Use of Economic Projections in Long-Range Business Planning: Results of a Questionnaire Survey," National/Regional Economic Projection Services, Report No. 66-J-5 (Washington: December, 1966), p. 29.

[12] As a matter of fact, in the first edition of this book this was referred to as the recovery-of-cost principle. See Harold Koontz and Cyril O'Donnell, *Principles of Management* (New York: McGraw-Hill Book Company, 1955), p. 442.

varying lengths of time, to a personnel policy, such as promotion from within or retirement at age sixty-five, or to other policies or programs involving commitments of direction and not immediately tangible in terms of dollars.

One can readily grasp the logic of planning far enough in the future to foresee, as well as possible, the recovery of capital sunk in a building or a machine. Since capital is the lifeblood of an enterprise and is normally limited in relation to the firm's needs, its expenditure must be accompanied by a reasonable possibility of recovering it, plus a return on investment, through operations. For example, when Lever Brothers sank 25 million dollars into a new factory on the West Coast, they, in effect, decided that the detergent business would permit the recovery of this investment over a period of time. If this period was twenty years, then logically the plans should have been based upon a projection of business for such a time. Of course, as will be discussed presently, they might have introduced some flexibility and reduced their risk (as they did) by spending extra funds to make the plant useful for other purposes.

What the commitment principle implies is that long-range planning is not really planning for future decisions but rather planning the future impact of *today's* decisions. In other words, a decision is a commitment, normally of funds, direction of action, or reputation. And decisions lie at the core of planning. While studies and analyses precede decisions, any type of plan implies that some decision has been made. Under these circumstances, then, the astute manager will recognize the validity of gearing all planning into present decisions. To do otherwise is to overlook both the basic nature of planning and that of decision making.

Application of the Commitment Principle

There is no uniform or arbitrary length of time for which a company should plan or for which a given program or any of its parts should be planned. An airplane company embarking on a new commercial jet aircraft project should probably plan this program some twelve years ahead, with five or six years for conception, engineering, and development and as many more years for production and sales in order to recoup total costs and make a reasonable profit. An instrument manufacturer might need to plan revenues and expenses some six months ahead, since this may represent the cycle of raw-material acquisition, production, inventorying, sales, and collection of accounts. But the same company might wish to see much further into the future before assuming a lease for specialized manufacturing facilities, undertaking a program of management training, or developing and promoting a new product.

If a commitment appears to a manager to be for a longer period than he can foresee with reasonable accuracy and if it is not feasible to build enough flexibility at reasonable cost into a plan, the manager may decide arbitrarily to shorten his period of commitment. In many cases, particularly those involving capital expenditures, the actual recovery of cost is determined by accounting or tax practices. In these cases it is possible to decide (regardless of whether the tax authorities would agree for tax purposes) to write off an investment faster than would normally be the case. A West Coast aerospace company president was faced a few years ago with the purchase of some special-purpose machinery for performance under a government contract. The machinery would normally be written off in ten years, but, in his opinion, the contract would probably last only two years, and the machinery had no apparent use for other purposes. He argued correctly and logically (but not successfully) with government contracting officers that he should be allowed to include in his costs a two-year write-off of the machinery. By doing so, he would shorten the commitment period for a highly inflexible investment to the length of time in which he could foresee fulfillment of his commitment.

The planning period will be longer or shorter depending upon the extent to which flexibility can be built into the plan. Thus, a company might be willing to lease a factory for ten years, even though it is impracticable to plan for longer than three, because of the possibility of subleasing on a one- or two-year notice. But where there is no practicable flexibility, or where flexibility is costly, it is desirable to plan for the entire period of commitment. This almost surely explains why certain major oil companies have led the nation's business management in the excellence and length of their long-range planning, for there is probably no investment quite so fully committed as that of developing an oil field, building pipelines, and constructing refinery facilities.

Although this principle indicates that various plans call for various plan-

Figure 6.3 *Planning areas and time periods. . . . Various management decision areas typically involve planning ahead for differing periods of time. These periods also vary according to the kind of business. For instance, a large public utility may plan new power-production plants twenty-five or thirty years into the future, while a small garment manufacturer may plan new production facilities only one year ahead.*

TYPICAL KINDS OF COMMITMENTS

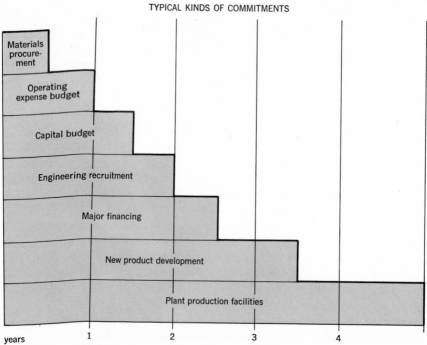

ning periods, those used are often compromises. The short range tends to be selected to conform to quarters or a year because of the practical need for making plans agree with accounting periods. The somewhat arbitrary selection of five years or so for the long range is often based on the belief that the degree of uncertainty over longer periods makes planning of questionable value.

Coordination of Short- with Long-Range Plans

Often short-range plans are made without reference to long-range plans. This is plainly a serious error. The importance of integrating the two can hardly be overemphasized, and no short-run plan should be made unless it contributes to the achievement of the relevant long-range plan. Many of the wastes of planning arise from decisions on immediate situations that fail to consider their effect on more remote objectives.

Sometimes these short-range decisions not only fail to contribute to a long-range plan but actually impede or require changes in the long-range plan. For example, if a small company accepts a large order without reckoning the effect on productive capacity or cash position, it may so hamper its future ability to finance an orderly expansion as to require a complex reorientation of its long-range program. Or, in another company, the urgency of obtaining small additions to plant may utilize vacant property so haphazardly as to thwart its longer-range use as the site for a large new plant. In other instances, the decision of a plant superintendent to discharge workers without adequate cause may interfere with the company's longer-range objective of developing a fair and successful personnel program. The short-range decision of Sewell Avery, chairman of Montgomery Ward, to curtail expansion of the business after World War II, because of his belief that a serious recession was at hand, interfered with a long-range program of enhancing the profitability of the company.

Responsible managers should continually scrutinize immediate decisions to ascertain whether they contribute to long-range programs, and subordinate managers should be regularly briefed on company long-range plans, so that they will make consistent short-range decisions. It is far easier to do this than to correct inconsistencies, especially since short-term commitments tend to engender further commitments along the same line.

FLEXIBILITY IN PLANNING

The above discussion has indicated that the commitment principle must be considered in the light of flexibility of planning. If plans can be changed to meet future requirements which either were not or could not be foreseen, the planning period can be shorter than otherwise would be the case. Because of future uncertainties and possible error in even the most expert forecast, the ideal of planning is to be flexible—the ability to change direction when forced to do so by unexpected events, without undue cost.

There are two planning principles for use in effecting the change in direction, the flexibility principle and the principle of navigational change.

The Flexibility Principle

The more that flexibility can be built into plans, the less the danger of losses incurred by unexpected events; but the cost of flexibility should be weighed against the risks involved in future commitments made.

The flexibility principle applies to the *building into* plans an ability to change direction. As noted above in the discussion of the commitment principle, Lever Brothers did actually spend some $5 million in extra construction cost in building a soap and detergent factory so that it could, if the company later decided to do so, be changed into a chemical manufacturing plant. It is not unusual, also, for companies to spend more for movable partitions than for fixed partitions in office buildings to maintain the flexibility of more easily changing space arrangements. Likewise, a company introducing a new product might use temporary tooling rather than more expensive permanent tooling, even though manufacturing costs are increased thereby, in order to avoid the risk of larger losses if the product does not succeed on the market.

To many managers, flexibility is the most important principle of planning. The ability to change a plan without undue cost or friction, to detour, to keep moving toward a goal despite changes in environment or even failure of plans, has great value. Flexibility is critical when the commitment is great and cannot be discharged in a short time (for example, in retrieving outlays for major capital facilities plus a return). But it is almost invariably true that built-in flexibility involves costs, and the most inflexible plan is likely to be the least costly if later events prove that the ability to change direction was unnecessary.

Flexibility is possible only within limits. In the first place, a decision cannot always be put off long enough to assure its rightness. This is exemplified by the decision of the General Petroleum Company to build a refinery in the Pacific Northwest. The financial point of no return was reached several years before the management could be completely certain that this would be an economic venture.

In the second place, built-in flexibility of plans may be so expensive that the benefits of hedging may not be worth the cost. Whether a company spends extra money to modify a special-purpose plant so that it can be used for other purposes, if the original program is not successful, will depend on the costs of doing so and the risks to be avoided. Some companies have felt, as apparently the top management of Montgomery Ward did for several years after World War II, that they could buy flexibility by keeping their resources in that most flexible of all assets—cash—only to have a competitor step forward with aggressive expenditures and capture much of the market.

Montgomery Ward, under the leadership of Sewell Avery, built up cash reserves exceeding 250 million dollars by 1953 but saw its share of the mail-order business fall from 40 percent in 1942 to 28 percent in 1952. Sears Roebuck, on the other hand, under the leadership of Robert E. Wood, adopted an expansionist program and increased its share of the mail-order business from approximately 50 to 66 percent in the same period. Similar differences in position existed in the retail store field for the two companies. Sears also increased its profits relative to Ward's. Although Sears stock rose during this period, that of Ward fell. Had a depression occurred during this immediate postwar period, however, Montgomery Ward would have been in an excellent position to capitalize on its liquidity, and Sears might have been in a very vulnerable position.

A third major limit to building flexibility into plans is the fact that there are often cases where flexibility either cannot be built into plans at all, or can be only with such great difficulty as to be impracticable. A special-purpose machine may only be useful to produce or package a particular product and to change it for other uses would be impracticable. An oil refinery can hardly be used for any other purpose than refining petroleum, and there is no reasonable possibility of doing anything to make it useful for any other purpose. These should be compared to a typical manufacturing plant or warehouse that might be used for a number of purposes.

The Principle of Navigational Change

The more planning decisions commit for the future, the more important it is that a manager periodically check on events and expectations and redraw plans as necessary to maintain a course toward a desired goal. This principle, unlike the flexibility principle, which applies to the adaptability built into plans themselves, applies to flexibility in the planning process. Built-in flexibility does not automatically revise plans; the manager, like the navigator, must continually check his course and redraw plans to meet a desired goal.

After two decades of intensive education, it is now fair to say that managers are becoming quite sophisticated in planning. They used to feel that a plan committed them to an invariable course of action. Now they understand that the manager manages the plan; he is not managed by it.

PLANNING INVOLVES AN OPEN-SYSTEMS APPROACH

In every aspect of managing, the practitioner must necessarily take into account interactions with his total environment. Managing is not, nor could it be, a closed-system approach to enterprise operation. This is nowhere more apparent than in the theory and practice of planning.

Objectives must obviously be set in the light of the economic, technological, social, political, and ethical elements of an enterprise environment. Planning premises represent a clear recognition that plans cannot be constructed nor decisions made in the vacuum of an internal system. The interfaces and interactions of plans with every element of the conditions and influences surrounding an enterprise are indeed many and complex. While certain scholars complain of the closed-system approach of operational management theory, they can hardly do so with an awareness of what management is. And any practicing manager with even the slightest knowledge of his task can hardly disregard the milieu in which he operates.

FOR DISCUSSION

1. "Planning is looking ahead and control is looking back." Comment.

2. If planning involves a rational approach to selected goals, how can one include goals or objectives as a type of plan?

3. Using the concepts of policies and procedures, draw up a statement of policy and devise a brief procedure which might be useful in implementing it. Are you sure your policy is not a rule?

4. If all decisions involve commitments, and if the future is always uncertain, how can a manager guard against costly mistakes?

5. Taking a planning problem which is now facing you, proceed to deal with it in accordance with the steps involved in planning outlined in this chapter.

6. Using an example of a planning decision with which you are familiar, show to what extent, and how, the principles of commitment, flexibility, and navigational change apply to it.

7. "Planning theory illustrates the open-system approach to management." Comment.

7
objectives

The ends for which people strive are variously referred to as "purposes," "missions," "objectives," "goals," or "targets." "Purpose" is often used to denote the reason for which an enterprise exists. Thus, the purpose of an enterprise might be to earn a livelihood in retail business, to educate gifted children, or to improve public health in a given area. "Mission" is a term most often used in military operations and occasionally in churches or governments. It connotes a major program objective. "Objective" is a term commonly used to indicate the end point of a management program, whether stated in general or specific terms, while the implication of a "target" or "goal" is almost invariably one of specific qualitative or quantitative aims. However, because clear distinctions are not often made in practice, these terms are generally used interchangeably in this book.

As pointed out in the first chapter of this book, every manager has, logically and morally, a "surplus" goal—to operate as a manager so that the group for which he is responsible will achieve whatever the purpose or objectives may be with the minimum of expenditure of human and material resources, or to achieve as much of a purpose as possible with the resources at his command.

This is, of course, the advantage of profit in business enterprise. It is actually a surplus of revenues over expenses in an enterprise whose purpose is the production and sale of goods and services desired by consumers. Government managers often say that they are at a disadvantage in comparison with business, that they have no profit by which to gauge their success. While it is true that government agencies, except for those in a quasi-business operation, do not have a profit objective in the conventional sense of the term, it is nonetheless true that they should have a surplus goal. In other words, whatever the purpose entrusted by society to a government agency, it is reasonable to expect that those who manage it should achieve the purpose with a minimum of resources, with as much "surplus" as possible. A chief of police, for example, has the duty to obtain as effective a police protection service as possible with the human and material means available to him.

Likewise, except for those managers who have profit responsibility for an integrated operation, managers of parts of businesses do not have responsibility for profits in the normal sense of the term. Nevertheless, each of their operations—from marketing director to machine-shop foreman—should have clear objectives and the obligation to accomplish them in a "surplus" way.

If surplus is to have any practical significance in management, the objectives of any enterprise, or of any department or section of it, must be verifiable. Otherwise, there can be no measure of effectiveness since no one can know whether he is accomplishing a vague objective. Nor can there be any measure of efficiency unless we know both output and input.

For far too many years and still for too many business firms and most nonbusiness enterprises, it has been customary to say something like: "It is our objective to make a fair profit while making and selling a quality product and being a good citizen in the community." As nice as this sounds, it is a virtually meaningless objective since no one can know whether it is being accomplished. Or one may say, as is often said, that the objective of a university is "to discover new knowledge and disseminate knowledge." This objective is likewise not very meaningful and does not make possible the operation of a surplus objective by a manager or, for that matter, by a professor.

ENTERPRISE PURPOSE AND OBJECTIVES

The surplus goal of managers still leaves open the question of what the purpose of an enterprise is and what the objectives of an enterprise and its departments are in contributing to this purpose. The purpose of business is production and marketing of economic goods and services; of government, the fulfillment of such social needs as security and welfare; of a university, research and teaching; of a church, administering to religious needs; and so on. But to accomplish these purposes, a number of enterprise objectives may be necessary and, in turn, a number of supporting goals by departments and sections.

Objectives Have Hierarchy

It can thus be seen that objectives have hierarchy. The purpose of a business may be the production and marketing of automobiles. But this, in turn, requires objectives to produce cars of a certain type and for certain markets. At the next level, there would exist objectives with respect to such major areas of operation as research and development, marketing, production, pricing, and financial arrangements. Ultimately, the objective of an assembly line foreman might be to produce a certain quantity per 1,000 man-hours or to reduce rejects or rework to a certain percentage.

Objectives Form a Network

Both objectives and planning programs normally form a network of desired results and events. A company or other enterprise is a system. If goals are not interconnected and mutually supportive, people very often pursue paths that

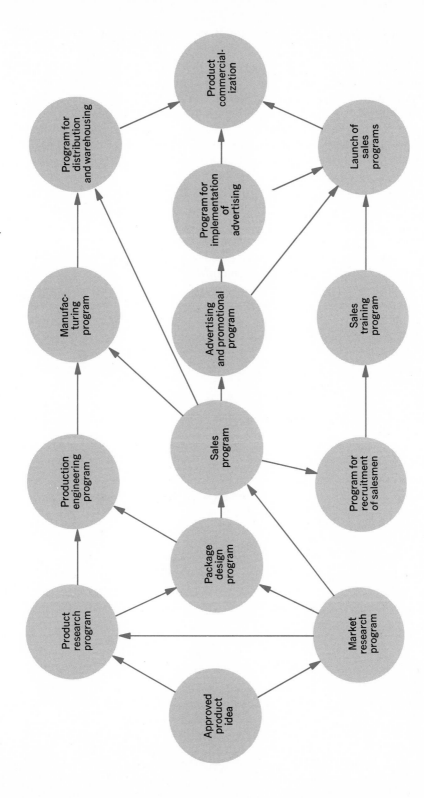

Figure 7.1 *Network of programs constituting a typical new-product program.*

may seem good for their own function but may be detrimental to the company as a whole.

In considering goals and plans as a network, it is sometimes overlooked that they are seldom linear, that is, where one objective is accomplished, followed by another, and so on. It is almost universal that goals and programs are interlocking in a network fashion. Figure 7.1 depicts the interlocking network of contributory programs (each of which has appropriate objectives) that constitute a total new-product program. Moreover, as can be readily appreciated, each of the interconnected programs shown could itself be broken down into an interlocking network. Thus the product research program shown in Figure 7.1 as a single event might involve within it a network of such subsidiary goals and programs as development of preliminary schematic design, development of a breadboard model, simplifying electronic and mechanical elements, packaging of the design, and other events.

As can be seen, the network of goals and programs places a heavy burden on managers in making sure that the components fit each other. Fitting is not only a matter of having the various programs performed, but also of timing their completion, since undertaking one program often depends upon completion of another.

It is easy for one department of a company to set goals that may seem entirely appropriate for it, only to be operating at cross-purposes with another. The manufacturing department may find its goals best served by long production runs, but this might interfere with the marketing department's desire to have all products in the line readily available, or the finance department's goal to maintain investment in inventory at a certain level.

The problem of making a network effective is difficult enough in itself. But it is compounded by the necessities of organization structure and such other factors as personality considerations. While we may try to organize units in an enterprise around key result areas, this may not always be possible. Other factors might be controlling, such as technology—an oil company simply cannot have an integrated gasoline division separate from motor oils or asphalt; or personnel attitudes—a research engineer seldom likes to see himself as a part of the marketing organization.

It is bad enough when goals do not support and interlock with each other. It is tragic when they interfere with each other. What is needed, as one company described it, is a "matrix of mutually supportive goals."

Multiplicity of Objectives

Objectives are, of course, many. Even major enterprise objectives are normally multiple. A business might include among its over-all objectives a certain rate of profit and return on investment; emphasis on research to develop a continuing flow of proprietary products; developing publicly held stock ownership; financing primarily by earnings plow-back and bank debt; distributing products in foreign markets; assuring competitive prices for superior products; achieving a dominant position in an industry; adhering, in all respects, to the values of our society.

Similarly, to say that the objective of a university is research and education is not enough. It would be much more accurate to state its objectives in the areas of attracting highly qualified students; offering basic training in the liberal arts and sciences as well as in certain professional fields; granting the Ph.D. degree to qualified candidates; attracting a highly regarded faculty; discovering and organizing new knowledge through research; operating as a private school principally supported through tuition and gifts of alumni and friends.

Likewise, at every level in the hierarchy of objectives, goals are likely to be multiple. It is exactly this fact that has caused some management specialists concern. It is believed by some that a manager cannot pursue effectively more than a few objectives. Schleh, for example, has stated that "no position should have more than two to five objectives" at one time.[1] His argument is that too many objectives before a manager tend to take the drive out of their accomplishment and may unduly highlight minor objectives to the detriment of major ones.

There is something to what Schleh says, but his number seems too arbitrary and too few. It is true that minor goals should not be given the status of important objectives unless we are dealing with a low-level job. It would hardly be useful for an upper-level manager to make much of such lesser objectives as meeting callers, attending meetings, or answering correspondence. There are certain things which any manager is expected to do and these need not be made into specific and special objectives. Goals are not conceived of as dealing with every facet of a person's job. They should not be confused with activities.

Even if routine matters are excluded, it seems that there is not any maximum number of objectives. To be sure, if there are so many that none commands adequate attention, planning will be ineffective. At the same time, it does seem possible that a manager might pursue simultaneously as many as ten or fifteen significant objectives. This depends in turn on how much he does himself and how much he can assign, thereby limiting his role to one of assigning, supervising, and controlling.

Long- and Short-range Objectives

If planning is to be effective, there must be an integral relationship between short-range and long-range objectives.

Long-range plans, drawn to specifications of objectives, are notably more speculative for distant years than for the immediate future. This means that plans for the fifth year of a five-year plan are much more uncertain than those for the first, less certain than those for the fourth, and so forth. Short-range objectives, usually to be realized in the first year of a long-range plan, are likely to be both comprehensive and specific. The approach should always be from the distant (fifth) year to the present and not vice versa, because what is to be done the first year must provide a foundation for what is to be done each

---

[1] *Management by Results* (New York: McGraw-Hill Book Company, 1961), p. 22.

successive year, and this can only be guaranteed if short-range plans are part of the long-range plan.

The selection of short-range objectives proceeds from an evaluation of priorities relating to long-range objectives. Some things simply need to be done first, either because they are a prerequisite to doing other things or because of lead-time considerations. For instance, as a new firm is established, raising capital for fixed and operating expenses is likely to be a prime objective and may be the sole short-run objective. If so, short-range objectives visualized for succeeding periods might be hiring managers for engineering, production, and sales; leasing space and equipment; and manning the organization. At the same time, if a long lead time is necessary, say, for installing a piece of specialized equipment, then writing specifications and placing the order would also be a short-range objective.

Thus, for short-range objectives to help achieve intermediate and long-range objectives, it is necessary to draw a plan for accomplishing each objective and to combine these into a master plan for review in terms of logic, consistency, and practicality.

RECENT EMPHASIS ON MANAGING BY OBJECTIVES

One of the most interesting developments that has swept across the management scene in the past decade has been the inauguration of programs of managing by objectives, or results.[2] As basic as objectives are to planning and to all managing, it is one of the remarkable phenomena of human history that only in recent years have a significant number of those responsible for managing our various enterprises come to realize the simple truth that if objectives are to be actionable, they must be clear and verifiable to those who pursue them.

No one can accomplish an ambiguous goal. He must know what his goals are, what actions contribute to their attainment, and when they have been accomplished. As basic as developing and accomplishing verifiable goals are, it is nonetheless difficult in practice. Too few managers who speak of managing by objectives are really doing so effectively, and it is an exceedingly rare nonbusiness operation that is even attempting to do so.

It is not strictly accurate to identify any one person as the originator of an approach that emphasizes objectives because common sense has told people for many centuries that groups and individuals expect to accomplish some end results. However, there have been certain individuals who have long placed emphasis on management by objectives and, by doing so, have given impetus to its development as a system.

One of these is Peter Drucker. In 1954, he acted as a catalyst by emphasizing that "objectives are needed in every area where performance and results directly and vitally affect the survival and prosperity of the business" and "the performance that is expected of the manager must be derived from the

---

[2] Much of the material on objectives in the following sections is drawn from Harold Koontz, *Appraising Managers as Managers* (New York: McGraw-Hill Book Company, 1971), chaps. 3 and 4.

performance goals of the business, his results must be measured by the contribution they make to the success of the enterprise."[3] This in turn requires "management by objectives" and "control by self-control."

At the same time, if not indeed earlier than Drucker, the General Electric Company laid out the elements of managing by objectives in its extensive planning for reorganization in 1954.[4] The company pointed out at that time:

Decentralization of managerial decision-making requires that objective goals and objective measurements of progress toward these goals be substituted for subjective appraisals and personal supervision. Through a program of objective measurements, managers will be equipped to focus attention on the relevant, the trends, and on the future. To the extent, therefore, that we are able to develop sound, objective measurements of business performance, our philosophy of decentralizing authority and responsibility will be rendered more effective. (p. 113)

The company implemented this philosophy of appraisal by identifying key result areas and undertaking considerable research on their measurement. However, there is no evidence that it was actually placed in operation by a program of appraising performance against verifiable objectives as we know it today. Nonetheless, the report reflects a pioneering approach to the problem.

Likewise, too, in 1957 Douglas McGregor, in his classic paper criticizing trait-appraisal systems as requiring "the manager to pass judgment on the personal worth of subordinates" thereby "playing God," made a strong plea for appraising on the basis of preset objectives.[5] McGregor's concern was with the then (and largely now) conventional appraisal methods which emphasized personal characteristics. He saw in appraisal against objectives a means of making evaluations constructive and placing the emphasis where it ought to be, on performance rather than on personality. Its main advantage, according to McGregor, would be to stimulate development of subordinates and give them means for greater motivation.

Considerable impetus toward emphasizing objectives was also given by Edward Schleh's stimulating book *Management by Results*.[6] He suggested that "management objectives state the specific accomplishment expected of each individual in a specific period of time so that the work of the whole management group is soundly blended at a particular moment of time" and that "objectives should be set for personnel all the way down to each foreman and salesman and, in addition, to staff people such as accountants, industrial engineers, chemists, etc."[7] Schleh recommended that delegation be by results expected and appraisals geared to the same standard.

---

[3] *The Practice of Management* (New York: Harper & Brothers, 1954) pp. 63, 101.

[4] See especially *Professional Management in General Electric* (New York: The General Electric Company, 1954), book Three, "The Work of the Professional Manager," pp. 24–28, 38–42, 113–132.

[5] "An Uneasy Look at Performance Appraisal," *Harvard Business Review*, vol. 35, no. 3, pp. 89–94 (May–June, 1957).

[6] *Op. cit.*

[7] *Ibid.*, pp. 18–19.

Singling out the basic contributions of Drucker, General Electric, Mc-Gregor, and Schleh may be unfair to their many predecessors and successors. Henri Fayol emphasized objectives, Lyndall Urwick built much of his management writing around accomplishment of objectives, and Chester Barnard made purpose the distinguishing feature of formal organizations—all of these men—and many others of the so-called classicists—many years before 1954. However, much of the early emphasis on objectives and on management by objectives in the many books and articles published in the 1960s and much of the practice then and now have failed to refine the concept to require a network of *verifiable* objectives.

It is true that interest in developing a more objective and performance-oriented system of appraising managers gave major impetus to the modern growth of total management by objectives. As interest in appraisal shifted from personality to performance and the search for objectivity in appraisal grew, it was natural and normal that attempts should be made to develop more verifiable objectives throughout the enterprise structure.

THE NATURE OF MANAGEMENT BY VERIFIABLE OBJECTIVES

As is eminently clear, a system of managing, or appraising managers, by verifiable objectives, is a reflection of the purpose of managing itself. Without clear objectives, managing is haphazard and random, and no individual, no group can expect to perform effectively or efficiently unless a clear goal is sought.

Quantitative Objectives

It has been noted that to be meaningful, objectives must be verifiable. The easiest way to get verifiability is to put goals in quantitative terms. Instead of saying a goal is to make a profit, we must say that it is to make $10 million in profit after taxes in 1972 by selling $200 million of products—with $40 million in product line A, $60 million in product line B, $20 million in product line C, and $80 million in product line D—at a gross profit margin of 33 percent, a net profit before taxes of 10 percent, and a return on stockholders' equity of 18 percent.

For a manufacturing manager, his goals might be to produce 2 million items at a total direct cost of $100 million and period costs[8] not to exceed $33 million, to reduce scrap from 2.5 to 2.0 percent, to keep factory labor turnover under 4 percent per month, or to purchase and install a given type of plant equipment at a cost not to exceed $3 million by December 15, 1972.

Similar quantitative goals could be made for other positions on down the line. Even a packaging line foreman in a given month might have goals to package 500 cases of product per hour, with a labor cost not to exceed 5 cents per case, and with a scrap loss not in excess of 1 percent. The district sales manager

---

[8] Under modern direct cost accounting, costs that vary in some way with volume are referred to as "direct" costs; those that vary with time are called "period" costs.

might have objectives of selling in his district 25,000 cases of merchandise in a month with a sales volume of $250,000 and to have his sales force make an average of six calls per man per day. Or, a personnel manager might have a department goal to recruit 100 persons of various specific qualifications each month, to hold exit interviews with each departing employee within one day of his separation, and to reduce clerical costs in his department by 4 percent.

Qualitative Objectives

Unfortunately, many goals cannot be quantified. In fact, there is danger in attempting to push numbers too far since the specious accuracy of numbers in many areas can lead managers astray. There is the danger that numbers and mathematics may even tend to replace managing. Moreover, there are too many worthwhile goals that are not quantitative; and the higher one goes in the management structure, the more objectives are likely to be qualitative.

Qualitative goals can, for the most part, be made verifiable, although admittedly not with the complete degree of accuracy possible in quantitatively stated objectives. For example, a training manager may have a goal to develop and implement a certain new program of training with specified characteristics by a certain date. Or a company controller may be charged with devising, with the cooperation of affected line managers, a program of variable budgeting by a certain date, with expense variations spread over volumes of sales outputs from $350,000 to $650,000 per month. The manufacturing manager might have, as one of his objectives, the development and installation of a certain program of equipment realignment by a given date. Likewise, the head of research and development might have an objective of completing the design of a new product with certain specifications by a certain date.

Sometimes it is said that qualitative objectives are gauged by the standard of "how well" and quantitative objectives by "how much." To some extent this is true, but the authors' experience is that any qualitative goal can be made highly verifiable by spelling out the characteristics of the program or other objective sought and a date of accomplishment. If it can be said, for example, that an objective is "to make more effective use of personnel recruitment services," it can almost as easily be said "to make more effective use of personnel recruitment services by (1) requiring all unfilled positions below a certain level to be submitted to the personnel department; (2) having the personnel department develop a program (with certain specified characteristics) for publicizing its approaches and services within the company by June 30; and (3) having the personnel department develop and implement a program of regular follow-up on candidates recommended to line managers by May 1."

Verifiability Is the Key

It should be abundantly clear at this point that verifiability is the key to useful objectives.

One of the interesting experiences one of the authors has had was in working with a government agency to install a program of management by verifiable objectives. In this rare and admirable case, many of the department heads' objectives were qualitative. In asking, as a first step, that these managers come up with objectives, it was not surprising to find many like the following:

Informing more people of available health services.
Utilization of personnel methods designed to secure and retain high caliber public employees.
Select and organize a staff in such a way as to best accomplish the departmental objective.
Eliminate all possible time now wasted in unproductive action.
Refine and manage the work program.
Establish an ongoing program for data-processing personnel.

One must recognize that, particularly in some departments of typical government agencies, setting verifiable objectives is extremely difficult. Nevertheless, as each department manager was asked the simple question, At the end of the year how will you know whether this objective has been accomplished? or How will your subordinates know when they are accomplishing an objective?, a little thought made it possible to develop highly verifiable objectives. For example, the general objective on health services became one "to increase the utilization of public health services during the fiscal year by 15 percent (as measured by the number of persons using the services) through specific programs of (1) developing three decentralized medical clinics; (2) establishing night clinics in two locations; and (3) geographically consolidating various preventive health services." Each program included enough specific characteristics and even quantitative data so that the objectives became highly verifiable and meaningful to the department manager and his subordinates.

Budgetary Objectives and Other Objectives

It is sometimes argued that all a manager really needs is a well planned and constructed budget, and this will furnish all the objectives required. The argument is that, if a budget is based on sound planning premises, including especially a credible sales forecast and an acceptable level of profit, all the department managers need to do is to meet the budget, item by item.

It is true that a good budget, like a clear and accurate profit and loss statement and balance sheet, is a summary, in numerical terms, of what a business does. It is true, too, that any well-constructed financial summary can be a "window" through which the plans and activities of managers can be seen if the observer looks far enough.

But more is needed in practice. Budget figures are resultants of plans and expected performance. They only have meaning when backed by actionable plans and programs. The end points of each plan must be some goal toward which actions are aimed.

Thus a marketing department might have a goal to accomplish sales of $20 million in a given year. To do this, however, programs must be made for pinpointed market research, for developing sales promotions with certain characteristics by a certain time, for launching advertising programs with certain features during a given period, and for specific deployment and preparation of the field sales force. In each of these areas, too, the organizational subcomponents should have plans and objectives to contribute toward the accomplishment of the various programs. In addition, the marketing area plans and objectives normally need to be supported by coordinate supporting programs in such areas as new-product development, purchasing, production, shipping, warehousing, costing, and pricing.

Without a workable network of plans and objectives, budget figures themselves tend to be wishes or guesses. Yet, no one would exclude the meeting of budget commitments from a manager's set of objectives.

THE PROCESS OF MANAGING BY OBJECTIVES

The practical importance of objectives in management can perhaps be seen best by summarizing how managing by objectives works in practice. The ideal is a system that starts at the top of an enterprise, has the active support of the chief executive, and verifiable goals are even set for him. While objective setting should start at the top, it is not imperative that it do so. It can start at a division level, at a marketing manager level, or even lower. This has happened. For example, in one company the system was first started in a division where it was carried down to the lowest level of supervision with an interlocking network of goals. Under the personal leadership and tutelage of the division general manager, it succeeded in areas of profitability, cost reduction, and improved operations. Soon, some other division managers and the chief executive became interested in and attempted to implement similar programs. In another case, the head of an accounting section started to develop a system for his group; his success not only gave him recognition (and promotion) but served as an entrance point for the entire company to embark on a program.

As in all planning, one of the critical needs is the development and dissemination of consistent planning premises. No manager can be asked to set goals or establish plans and budgets without guidelines.

Preliminary Setting of Objectives at the Top

Given appropriate planning premises, the first step in setting objectives is for the top manager concerned to determine what he perceives to be the more important goals he wants his enterprise to achieve in a given period ahead. These can be set for any period—a quarter, a year, or for five years—whatever is felt desirable in given circumstances. In most instances they are set to coincide with the annual budget. But this is not necessary and often not desirable. Certain goals should be scheduled for accomplishment in a much shorter period and others for a much longer period. Also, particularly as one goes down the line in an organization, goal accomplishment of managers tends to have a shorter time span. It is seldom feasible or wise for a first-line supervisor, for example, to set many annual goals since his goal span on most operating matters, such as cost or scrap reduction, rearrangement of facilities, or instituting of special personnel programs, is short and may be accomplished in weeks or months.

The goals first set by the top manager must be looked upon as being preliminary, based on his analysis and judgment of what can and should be accomplished by his organization in a period of time, and taking into account its strengths and weaknesses, in the light of opportunities facing him. They must be regarded as tentative and subject to modification as the entire chain of verifiable objectives is worked out by his organization. It is foolish to push top-management dictated objectives down the throats of subordinates since forced objectives can hardly induce an indispensable sense of subordinate commitment. Most managers also find in the process of working out goals with subordinates both problems to be dealt with and opportunities they could not have previously known.

In the setting of objectives, the manager also establishes measures of what will indicate goal accomplishment. If verifiable objectives are developed, these measures, whether in dollars of sales or profits, percentages, cost levels, or program execution, will normally be built into the objectives.

Clarification of the Organizational Roles

Often overlooked in installing and operating programs of management by objectives is the relationship between results expected and the location of responsibility to attain them. Ideally, every goal and subgoal should be some one person's clear responsibility. Analysis of the organization structure in terms of results expected will often show areas of fuzziness where clarification or reorganization is called for. Sometimes it is impossible to mold an organization so that a given objective is some one person's organization unit's responsibility. In setting goals for launching a new product, for example, careful coordination will normally be required of the managers of research, marketing, and production. These separate functions can be largely centralized by putting a product manager in charge. But, if this is not desirable, at least the specific parts of each coordinating manager's contribution to the total program goal can and should be clearly identified.

Setting of Subordinates' Objectives

After making sure that pertinent general objectives, strategies, and planning premises are disseminated to the subordinate manager concerned, the superior can then proceed to work with him in setting his objectives. The superior will normally give his subordinate his *preliminary* thinking on the goals he believes feasible for the company or department he manages. At this point, and preferably before he meets with his subordinate, the superior will ask what goals the subordinate believes he can accomplish, and in what time period, and with what resources.

The superior's role at this point is extremely important. Questions he should ask include: What can you do? How can we improve your operation to help me improve mine? What stands in the way, what obstructions keep you from a higher level of performance? What changes can we make? How can I help? It is amazing how many things can be found that obstruct performance and can be removed, and how many diamonds of constructive ideas can be dredged from the experience and knowledge of subordinates.

The superior must also be a patient counselor, helping his subordinate to develop consistent and supportive objectives and watching to see that he does not set goals impossible or highly improbable of attainment. Human nature tends to be the same. Anything can be accomplished a year hence, but much less by tomorrow. And one of the things that can kill a program of managing by objectives is to allow managers to set up "blue sky" objectives that they cannot reasonably be expected to accomplish.

At the same time, goal setting by subordinates does not represent the same principles as "progressive education"—where people do whatever they want to do. The superior must listen and work with his subordinate, but, in the end, he must take responsibility for approving goals for his subordinates. His judgment and final approval must be based upon what is reasonably attainable with "stretch" and "pull," what is fully supportive of upper-level objectives, what is consistent with goals of other managers in other functions, and what goals will not be inconsistent with the longer-run objectives and interests of the department and company.

Goals and Resources

One of the major advantages of setting up a careful network of verifiable goals and a requirement for doing it effectively is to tie in the need for capital, material, and human resources at the same time. Any manager at any level requires these resources to accomplish his goals. By relating these to the goals themselves, superiors are better able to see the need and economics of allocating them. It helps to avoid the bane of any upper-level manager's existence— the "nickel and diming" by subordinates who need "one more technician" or "engineer" or "one more piece of equipment" which, in isolation, is easy for them to sell to their boss and difficult for the superior to refuse.

Recycling Objectives

As indicated, setting objectives can hardly be done by starting at the top and dividing them up. Nor should they be started from the bottom. What is required is a degree of recycling. The top manager may have an idea as to what his subordinates should set as objectives, and those who report to him for their subordinates, but the process of goal setting as outlined above will almost certainly change these preconceived goals as the contributions of subordinates come into focus. Thus, objectives setting is not only a joint process but also one of interaction which will require recycling.

This process is worth the time. People involved will have a better understanding of their targets and how they fit, they cannot help but have a better feeling of commitment to meet them, the structure of objectives is likely to be characterized by a better fit, and the people involved are more likely to meet their targets.

OBJECTIVES FOR STAFF POSITIONS

It is sometimes believed that meaningful objectives can only be established for line managers since they have direct responsibility for some phase of operating results. If we consider staff positions, wherein the responsibility is to advise and counsel line managers, the question may be asked whether objectives can be set for them since the staff's primary job is to help a person in a line position succeed in his job.

The authors believe that objectives can be set for any position in an enterprise. As a matter of fact, in some cases, this has been done. In the Radio Corporation of America, for instance, an active program has been applied to staff personnel for a decade.[9] While most staff objectives in this company could not be placed in quantitative terms, staff projects (even though advisory) were established in qualitative terms, indicating characteristics and target completion dates. Many involved "developing a method" or "conducting a study," or "finding the cause of" some problem. Thus, most staff objectives, while verifiable, were qualitative.

The experience at RCA showed that some staff men even stated many quantitative objectives, such as "In 1968, I will save the company $___ through evaluation of new materials" or "Develop a cost reduction program that will reduce plant operating expenses by $___." To be sure, none of these staff individuals had the authority to implement any of these programs. They did, however, take the position that they had failed to meet an objective if the program they recommended to operating managers was not good enough to be implemented and result in targeted savings.

An objective approach to staff work is important. It should not be forgotten that the traditional definitional differentiation between line—as those people contributing directly to the attainment of enterprise objectives—and staff—as other people who help the line—has unfortunate overtones. People in a company should not be divided between those who accomplish objectives and others. Certainly no company interested in efficiency and effectiveness should tolerate anyone on its payroll who does not contribute to attainment of enterprise objectives. Developing an ongoing program of staff work by verifiable objectives is a step in the direction of making clear what staff people can and should do.

---

[9] As reported in W. S. Wikstrom, "Setting Targets for Staff," *The Conference Board Record*, vol. 1, no. 10., pp. 32–34 (October, 1964).

BENEFITS OF MANAGING BY OBJECTIVES

Because managing by objectives has excited the interest of managers through-out the world, particularly in business enterprises, and because there has been far more talk than effective action, it might be helpful to summarize the major benefits and weaknesses of the system. The potential of managing and ap-praising managers by objectives is very great. But there is the danger that, through misapplication, the system might degenerate into a management fad or gimmick.

Better Managing

One could summarize all the advantages of formalizing managing by objectives by saying that it results in much improved managing. Actionable objectives cannot be established without planning, and results-oriented planning is the only kind that makes sense. It forces managers to think of planning for *results*, rather than merely planning *activities* or *work*. To assure that objectives are realistic, it also requires the manager to think of the way he will accomplish given results, the organization and personnel he will need to do it, and the resources and assistance he will require. Also, there is no better incentive for control and no better way to know the standard for control than a set of clear goals.

Clarifies Organization

Another major benefit of managing by objectives is that it tends to force clari-fication of organizational roles and structures. To the extent possible, key re-sult areas should be translated into positions that carry responsibility for goal accomplishment.

Companies that have effectively embarked on these programs have often discovered organizational deficiencies. The most common is finding that results accomplishment requires giving major consideration to the first princi-ple of delegation of authority—delegation by results expected. As an executive of Honeywell is reported to have said: "There are two things that might also be considered fundamental creed at Honeywell: decentralized management is needed to make Honeywell work and management by objectives is needed to make decentralization work."

Elicits Commitment

One of the great advantages of managing by objectives is that it elicits commit-ment for performance. No longer is a man just doing work, following instruc-tions, waiting for guidance and decisions; he is now an individual with clearly defined purposes. He also has had a part in actually setting his objectives, has had an opportunity to put his ideas into planning programs, now understands his area of discretion—his authority, and has, it is hoped, been able to get positive help from his superiors to assure that he can accomplish his goals.

These are the elements that make for a feeling of commitment. A man becomes a willing and enthusiastic master of his own fate.

Helps Develop Effective Controls

In the same way that managing by objectives sparks more effective planning, it also aids in developing effective controls. Control, it will be recalled, is measuring activities and taking action to correct deviations from plans in order to assure desired accomplishment. As will be pointed out in later discussion of management control, one of the major problems is knowing what to watch. A clear set of verifiable goals is the best guide to knowing.

WEAKNESSES IN MANAGING BY OBJECTIVES

With all its advantages, a system of managing by objectives has a number of weaknesses and shortcomings. Some are found in the system. Others are due to shortcomings in applying it.

Failure to Teach the Philosophy

As simple as managing by objectives may seem, there is much to be understood and appreciated by managers who would put it into practice. This requires patient explanation of the entire program, what it is, how it works, why it is being done, what part it will play in appraising managerial performance, and above all, how participants can benefit.

Failure to Give Goal Setters Guidelines

Managing by objectives, like any other kind of planning, cannot be expected to work if those who are expected to set goals are not given needed guidelines. A manager must know what corporate goals are and how his activity fits in with them. If corporate goals are fuzzy, unreal, or inconsistent, it is virtually impossible for a manager to tune in on them.

He also needs planning premises and a knowledge of controlling enterprise policies. People must have some assumptions as to the future, some understanding of enterprise policies affecting their area of operation, and awareness of the nature of objectives and programs with which their goals interlock in order to plan effectively. Failure to fill these needs can result in a fatal vacuum in planning.

Goals Are Difficult to Set

It should not be overlooked that truly verifiable goals are difficult to set, particularly if they are to have the right degree of "stretch" or "pull," quarter in and quarter out, year in and year out. This may not be much more difficult than any kind of effective planning although it will probably take more study and work to establish verifiable objectives that are formidable but attainable than to develop most plans, most of which tend only to lay out work to be done.

Tendency of Goals to Be Short Run

In almost all systems of operating under management by objectives, goals are set for the short term, seldom for more than a year, and often for a quarter or less. There is clearly the danger of emphasizing the short run, perhaps at the expense of the longer range. This means, of course, that superiors must always assure themselves that current objectives, like any other short-run plan, are designed to serve longer-range goals.

The Dangers of Inflexibility

As has happened with other types of plans, and budgets particularly, managers often hesitate to change objectives during a period of time, normally a year. While goals may cease to be meaningful if they are changed too often and do not represent a well thought-out and planned result, it is nonetheless foolish to expect a manager to strive for a goal that has been made obsolete by revised corporate objectives, changed premises, or modified policies.

Other Dangers

There are many other dangers and difficulties in managing by objectives. In the desire for verifiability people may overuse quantitative goals and attempt to force numbers in areas where they are not applicable, or downgrade important qualitative goals. Sometimes managers fail to use objectives as a constructive force with the ample participation and needed assistance of the superior. There is also the danger of forgetting that there is more to managing than goal setting.

But with all the difficulties and dangers of managing by objectives, the fact is that this system emphasizes in practice the setting of goals as the logic of planning and managing has long recognized it should be.

FOR DISCUSSION

1. To what extent do you believe that managers you have known have a clear understanding of their objectives? If, in your opinion, they do not, how would you suggest that they go about setting them?
2. Make a list of goals you wish to achieve in the next five years. Are they verifiable? Are they attainable?
3. Some people object to defining long-term goals because they think it impossible to know what will happen during the long run. Do you believe that this is an intelligent position to take?
4. Take any program of any kind that you would like to see accomplished and draw a network of contributing programs and goals necessary for its accomplishment.

5. If goals of a company are multiple, how can all of them be optimized?
6. "The only planning tool we need in this company is the budget. If everyone meets his budget, we need nothing else, and management by objectives would be an unnecessary frill." Comment
7. Why do you suspect that so many business enterprises talk about and introduce programs of management by objectives, but the actual record of performance under these has been so poor?

8
planning premises

One of the essential and often overlooked steps in effective and coordinated planning is premising—the establishment of and agreement by planners to utilize consistent premises critical to plans under consideration. Planning premises, it will be recalled, are the anticipated environment in which plans are expected to operate. They include assumptions or forecasts of the future and known conditions that will affect the course of plans, such as prevailing policies and existing company plans that control the basic nature of supporting plans.

A distinction should immediately be drawn between forecasts that are planning premises and forecasts that are translated into future expectancies, usually in financial terms, from actual plans developed. For example, a forecast to determine future business conditions, sales volume, or political environment furnishes premises on which to develop plans. However, a forecast of the costs or revenues from a new capital investment translates a planning program into future expectations. In the first case, the forecast is a prerequisite of planning; in the second, the forecast is a result of planning.

At the same time, plans themselves and forecasts of their future effects often become premises for other plans. The decision by an electric utility to construct a steam-generating plant, for example, creates conditions that give rise to premises for transmission-line plans, power-sales promotion programs, and other plans necessarily dependent upon the generating plant being built.

PREMISING: THE ENVIRONMENT OF PLANS

Premising is the recognition that plans operate in an environment, both internal to the enterprise and external. It thus emphasizes the long-known fact that management is an open-system approach to organized activities. While it is true that until fairly recently businesses and other enterprises may have given primary attention to economic and demographic factors in their environment and too little to technological, political, and ethical, every alert and perceptive

155

manager now is aware of all elements of the environment that might affect the operation of his plans.

It is not enough to be responsive to the present environment. Plans operate in the future. Therefore, the effective manager anticipates the environment in which his plans *will* operate. This means, of course, that it is necessary to forecast what those elements in the environment affecting any given plans will be. As is sometimes said, the successful manager is not one who just responds to changes as they occur but one who will, rather, forecast change. Clearly, those who foresee the critical changes that will affect given plans have a far better chance of being successful than those who either cannot or will not.

This does not mean that everything can be predicted, nor does it mean that prediction is an infallible science. In fact, many scientists shy away from predicting the future on the basis that this is not dealing with what is known. Many things that affect a future are known—a plan already made that requires derivative plans, the vast array of organized knowledge of an imperishable nature, and some of the implications of current world forces. But these are not enough. There are in addition short- and long-range economic, technological, social, political, and even ethical changes that will affect what will or can be done in a near or far future.

Some of these are quite predictable, such as population growth and Gross National Product changes. Some are credibly predictable, such as price levels, population shifts, and certain technological developments. Others may not be reasonably predictable, such as the Six-Day War in the Middle East in 1967, the discovery of penicillin, or the length and extent of American involvement in the Vietnam conflict.

Increasing awareness of the impact of the future environment has led to a developing science referred to as "futurism"—the attempt to forecast changes in the various elements of the environment with skill and perceptiveness through the use of the most sophisticated available techniques. In a real way, this approach represents an extension of the much earlier attempts to base future population growth on science rather than on hunches and on the developments of national economic predictions that have come so far in the past three decades. More recently, futurism has made strides in technological forecasting and is moving on to the social and political elements of the environmental spectrum.

TYPES OF PREMISES

Planning premises may be classified as those that are external and those that are internal to the enterprise; or they may be regarded as those that are tangible and those that are intangible. In addition, premises differ in the degree that they are within the control of an enterprise.

External and Internal Premises

One is likely to think of most premises as those arising from the outside world, because they usually cause the most difficulty. External premises may be classified into three groups: the general environment, which includes economic, technological, political, social, and ethical conditions; the product market, which includes conditions influencing demand for product and services; and the factor market, which has to do with land, location, labor (not the least of which are labor unions), materials, parts, and capital. As can be seen, these groups are not completely separable, since there are interactions between them.

Internal premises include such things as capital investment in plant and equipment, strategies, policies, major programs already decided, the developed and approved sales forecast, a given organization structure that is unlikely to change, and the many other elements that will influence the nature of plans. Not the least important among these internal premises are the beliefs, behavior, strong points, and weaknesses of the top executives, of those who control them (shareholders, electors, trustees, or government agencies), and, often, of their subordinates.

Tangible and Intangible

Occasionally, managers forget that planning premises may be intangible, as well as tangible. They are referred to as "tangible" when they can be quantified, whether in dollars, labor hours, square feet of space, machine hours, or units of product.

Of equal importance are the many intangible factors normally encountered. These cannot be expressed numerically, but they are significant elements in the planning scene. Among the many examples are prestige in a product line (which might eventually have a tangible effect on sales and profits), local opinion of a certain plant as a desirable or undesirable neighbor, political stability or attitude of a city or state toward taxes, emotional impact of a certain personnel policy among employees, or the receptivity of style factors by potential customers. There are many, many areas of a manager's environment that even the best market, attitudinal, or other kinds of research cannot make tangible.

Degree of Controllability

Premises may also be classified by the degree to which they are controllable by an enterprise. There are noncontrollable premises, such as population growth, future price levels, political environment, tax rates and policies, and business cycles. There are semicontrollable premises, such as a firm's assumptions as to its share of the market, the character of labor turnover, labor efficiency, company price policy, and even industry legislative policy. And, finally, there are controllable premises, largely decided by company management and involving policies and programs such as expansion into new markets, the adoption of an aggressive research program, or the site for headquarters offices.

ENVIRONMENTAL FORECASTING: KEY TO PREMISING

As the influence on plans of the entire environment outside the firm or enterprise has come increasingly to be recognized, forecasting of the environment has risen in importance. As mentioned above, this has given rise to an embryonic science referred to as "futurism."

If the future could be forecast with accuracy, planning would be relatively simple. The manager would need only to take into account his human and material resources, compute the optimum method of reaching his objective, and proceed with a high degree of certainty toward it.

Fayol speaks of *prévoyance* as the essence of management.[1] This looking ahead, according to Fayol, includes both assessing the future and making provision for it.

As a matter of fact, a half century ago Fayol referred to plans as syntheses of various forecasts, whether short- or long-term, special, or otherwise.[2] It is interesting, in this connection, that Fayol recommended yearly forecasts and ten-year forecasts, the latter being revised at least each five years and oftener if proved necessary by the yearly ones. Furthermore, each forecast was to include a wide variety of subsidiary or elemental forecasts, composed of such data as capital, output, production costs, sales, selling price, and other factors.

In practice, forecasts vary considerably in length, breadth of coverage, and quality, from little more than a manager's hunch to a detailed analysis of the future made by a competent staff. Some enterprises need forecasts of long periods, and others may be able to operate effectively with very short forecasts. Furthermore, some who need expert forecasts may be unable to afford more than the information that grows out of a manager's reading of economic and other predictions in numerous journals plus his own judgment of the situation.

Values of Forecasting

The need for adequate forecasting is apparent from the key role it plays in planning. But it has values aside from this use. In the first place, the making of forecasts and their review by managers compel thinking ahead, looking to the future, and providing for it. Also, the very act of forecasting may disclose areas where necessary control is lacking. For example, in a report submitting the results of a pessimistic forecast to his key executives, a president of a large company said: "The declining profit in this forecast is disappointing, but it is my impression that every forecast extending beyond a year has shown profits less than we have been able to procure as the result of determined efforts by all members of our management team. This picture should not dishearten us but should stimulate our efforts to improve it."

Forecasting, especially where participated in throughout the organization, may help to unify and coordinate plans. By focusing attention on the future, it assists in bringing a singleness of purpose to planning.

---

[1] Henri Fayol, *General and Industrial Management* (New York: Pitman Publishing Corporation, 1949), p. 43. In this translation, the term is translated as "foreseeing."

[2] Fayol emphasized this usage in an interview published in the *Chronique Sociale de France* in January, 1925, quoted in Urwick's foreword to *General and Industrial Management*, p. xi.

Even though much emphasis is placed on forecasting, it must be recognized that all forecasts are subject to a degree of error, since the best analyses or judgments cannot result in true clairvoyance. Guesswork can never be omitted from forecasts, although it can often be reduced to a minimum. Managers often expect too much from forecasts and fail to recognize the unavoidable margin of error which must exist in any prophecy. They also occasionally neglect to examine the underlying assumptions of a forecast to determine whether these are supported by facts, reasonable estimates, or accurate reflection of policies and plans.

Informed and intelligent "guesstimates" made by experienced business executives and technicians are often extraordinarily prophetic. A clairvoyant quality is a rare gift, but many experienced managers have developed it, and where it exists, it is an excellent supplement to the work of the forecaster. However, what may appear to be a clairvoyant quality may really be the conceptual and computing ability of an exceptional mind.

Economic Forecasting

Fairly reliable economic premises can be obtained from the well-considered forecasts of employment, productivity, national income, and gross national product that have been available to planners for a number of years. Among the more prominent of these are those made regularly by the President's Council of Economic Advisers, the National Planning Association, the Wharton School (University of Pennsylvania) Econometric Model, the U.C.L.A. Forecasting Project, the coordinative work of the National Industrial Conference Board, and the many forecasts of university and bank economists. In fact, there is no shortage of national and even regional economic forecasts. The major problem the planner has is which to use, although, as a matter of fact, the better-known forecasts do have a record of surprising consistency and accuracy.

Most economic forecasts are derived from calculating gross national product, the total of which is not difficult to estimate if acceptable forecasts of population, productivity increases, unemployment percentage, and average work week are available. But problems do occur in estimating such components of gross national product as government purchases, personal consumption expenditures, business fixed and inventory investment, residential construction, and other investments. Greater difficulties occur as each of the elements is further broken down. In addition, of course, forecasts of gross national product need to take into account price level changes which, with persistent inflation over the years, can be very important to the planner.

After studying broad forecasts of national and regional economic trends, a company should translate them into their impact on its industry and on itself. This requires two basic estimating procedures. In one, the analyst moves downward from national data to industry group forecasts and perhaps to individual industries. In the other, referred to as a "bottom up" approach, the analyst moves upward from individual company data and summaries of industry plans to the national economic forecast.

As broad as typical national and regional economic forecasts are, it is interesting how many companies have found that their business relates fairly well, sometimes with a lag or lead-time correction, to national data. A medium-sized company for example, whose business was closely associated with the home construction industry, found a highly reliable correlation of its sales with housing starts, adjusted for an eight months' lag from starts to sales. A pharmaceutical company, after studying forecasting techniques and indicators of all kinds, found somewhat to its surprise that national consumers' disposable expenditures correlated very well with its sales pattern.

What has been needed is refined breakdowns of basic economic data that serve to forecast better the markets in which a company is operating. One of the most promising approaches is the development of input-output tables. These show the relationships of industries to one another and their sharing of gross national product by calculating the purchases and sales made between industries. While some work on input-output analysis has been done by industrial and regional specialists, these lack the accuracy and usefulness of an analysis on a national scale.

Developed by Professor Wassily W. Leontief of Harvard, input-output tables were first roughly utilized by him in 1945 and served to forecast the impending large demand in the postwar period for steel and other raw materials. The federal government issued input-output tables for 1947 several years later. Unfortunately, because of lack of government appropriation, no analyses were again available until 1964. At that time, input-output tables for the year 1958 were published and, shortly thereafter, were updated to 1961 and 1963.[3] The availability of this powerful tool for forecasting is an encouraging development for business which now can have the derivative effects of national production and income factors reflected in their impact on a given industry.

There are, nonetheless, a tremendous number of industry studies available through government and industry sources, both of a forecast and a historical nature. Most federal government departments with a business interest publish economic material useful for forecasting, as do trade associations, trade publications, banks, private research organizations, and professional associations. Certainly, in most industries, the manager who wants industry data can tap many sources.[4]

Technological Forecasting

One of the more interesting aspects of premising has been the rapid increase of interest in recent years in technological forecasting. Since the pace of technological change is so rapid and since new products and processes may be keys to a company's future plans, an increasing number of companies are

---

[3] Wassily W. Leontief, "Proposal for Better Business Forecasting," *Harvard Business Review*, vol. 42, no. 6, pp. 166–182 (November–December, 1964).

[4] An excellent bibliography for sources of market and economic forecasting information is R. N. Carpenter, *Guidelist for Marketing Research and Economic Forecasting*, Research Study No. 50 (New York: American Management Association, 1961). Also, see R. S. Reichard, *Practical Techniques of Sales Forecasting* (New York: McGraw-Hill Book Company, 1966), pp. 103–110. Reichard reports that the federal government spends over 100 million dollars each year on statistical data collection.

emphasizing regular and complete technological forecasts affecting their industry. In fact, developing premises from such forecasts may be as important to the company's planning and its future as are political, economic, or social premises.

Most companies that have gone far in developing planning premises from their technological forecasts have tended to be high technology enterprises. What has been done in these instances is to encourage members of their technical staffs to be alert to future developments; to make frequent contacts with suppliers and customers with development staffs; to think in terms of the impact of current scientific developments on the future state of technology; and to develop orderly forecasts of how these developments affect the company's products, processes, or markets. Executives who have asked their research and development staffs to undertake such an assignment have been pleasantly surprised at the enthusiasm with which these forecasts were prepared and presented. They have apparently found that scientists and engineers like to be a part of, and contribute to, basic company planning. These executives have also reported, not at all surprisingly, that these forecasts have been extraordinarily helpful in improving company planning.

Even smaller companies, without research and development staffs, can successfully make such a forecast and include the future technological environment in their planning premises. A few scientists or engineers in a company, if encouraged, can do much to present an orderly picture of the company's technological environment. And many nontechnically qualified people, as well as those with special technical qualifications, can understand much of the technical literature in a periodical or report in the company's field. Moreover, suppliers especially and often major customers are willing to pass on to the discerning small businessman the results of their research and engineering ideas, if by doing so he becomes a larger-volume customer or a more alert supplier.

One of the attempts to make technological forecasting more accurate and meaningful is the use of what is known as the Delphi technique, named after the oracle at Delphi in ancient Greece. While it smacks somewhat of hunch and judgment, or the brainstorming fad of a few years ago, it is much more. And having been developed by Olaf Helmer, prominent Rand Corporation mathematician, and his colleagues, it has a degree of scientific respectability and acceptance not enjoyed by other judgment approaches.

The Delphi technique involves several steps. First, a panel of experts on a particular problem area is selected, usually from both inside and outside an organization's ranks. Each expert is asked—anonymously, so that he will not be influenced by others—to make a forecast as to what he thinks will happen, and when, in various areas of new discoveries or developments. For example, the panel may be asked when reliable weather forecasts will be available, when a cancer cure will be accomplished, or when and how economically feasible desalination of seawater will occur. Then, the answers are compiled and the composite results are fed back to the panel members. With this information at hand, but still with individual anonymity, further estimates of the future are made, and this process may be repeated several times. When a convergence of opinion begins to occur, the results are then used as an acceptable forecast.[5] Note that the purpose of the successive opinions and feedback is not to force the experts to compromise, but rather by bringing additional informational inputs to bear, to make opinions more informed. It is thus hoped, and experience has verified this hope, that an informed consensus among experts will be arrived at.

There are, of course, other methods used to forecast the state of technology. One, referred to as "opportunity-oriented," looks at the future and raises the question as to whether a certain product may be made obsolete by a new development and, if so, what; or whether there is any technological breakthrough that might be expected which would solve a problem seen to exist in the development of a certain product. For example, the opportunity-oriented forecast might look at the possible development of an atomic power plant for an automobile and ask the question as to whether certain known limitations will probably be solved and when. Or one might forecast when economic desalination of seawater will occur.

Another approach has been referred to as the "goal-oriented" forecast. In this case, a decision is made to reach a certain goal, the technological needs for accomplishing it are identified, and analysis is made as to when, and perhaps how, these might be accomplished. Thus, after a decision was made to put a man on the moon by 1970, the technological requirements of so doing were identified, and time and resource estimates were made as to how and when each could be solved.

Still other techniques of technological forecasting follow time-honored hypotheses that knowledge expands exponentially, and it is possible to project in areas of technology when a certain technological development is likely to occur. For example, in illumination technology one can plot the growth of lumens per watt on a logarithmic scale from Edison's first lamp in 1880 to the fluorescent lamp in 1940 in almost a straight line.

The important thing is not necessarily the methods and approaches to technological forecasting. It is rather the fact that its need is widely perceived, and serious and useful attempts are being made to predict the state of the art in an increasing number of fields. This can certainly lead to planning premises of an important and useful nature.

Social and Political Forecasting

Except for the long experience with demographic forecasting, there has not been much attention paid to forecasting social, political, and ethical trends in society, despite the fact that these are extremely important areas of premising. To be sure, a few companies have done meaningful work in this area. A major oil company over two decades ago was regularly making forecasts of political environments in the foreign countries where they were planning for oil exploration. Another company concerned with world-wide transportation potentials found that, particularly for certain parts of the world, such as

[5] For a good example of the reporting of an actual Delphi technique forecast, see H. Q. North and D. L. Pyke, "'Probes' of the Technological Future," *Harvard Business Review*, vol. 47, no. 3, pp. 69–81 (May–June, 1969).

India or central Africa, they really had to make cultural forecasts because needs for transportation facilities were found to be responsive to various cultural levels. A few companies have come to the authors' attention where continuing and formalized studies and analyses have been made of the combined social, political, and ethical environments expected in areas where they produce or market.

This important area has not received the attention it should. However, there are increasing signs that it will. The problems of pollution, of belligerent students, of lawlessness and crime, and of highway safety have burst on the world's consciousness with almost surprising pressures. Surely, a reasonable man cannot really blame the automobile manufacturers for smog, but he might criticize them for not anticipating social pressures for eliminating pollution and for not, therefore, being more ready with technological solutions of the auto's contribution to air pollution.

Experience with technological forecasting has certainly opened the door to a wider spectrum of prediction of the social and political elements of the environment. One might well expect some of the same techniques that have been useful in technological prediction to be applicable to forecasting these other areas. An indication of what may be in store is given by the establishment of the Institute for the Future in 1969, a tax-exempt, nonprofit, nonmilitary research organization supported by a number of major business corporations and by the National Industrial Conference Board in particular. Its purpose is environmental forecasting in all its aspects so that business may be able to anticipate future events with more confidence and include them in its planning premises.

THE SALES FORECAST: KEY PLAN AND PREMISE

One of the major planning premises in the typical business enterprise is the sales forecast. To a considerable extent it underlies various new-product, production, and marketing plans, and it also reflects conditions of the marketplace which are external to the firm. Because it sets the framework on which most internal plans are constructed, it must be regarded as the dominant planning premise of an enterprise. Even though its use has been noteworthy in business, the idea of basing planning on a forecast of the market has much in common with nonbusiness enterprises. Certainly a university must be concerned in its planning with its student "market"; a government welfare department must gear its plans to meet expected caseloads; and church plans must be influenced by the number of communicants expected in an area.

Nature and Use

The sales forecast is a prediction of expected sales, by product and price, for a number of months or years. It is, then, a kind of pro forma sales portion of the traditional income statement for the future. With a sales forecast over a long enough period in which it has some confidence, management can usually do a good job in forecasting profits and cash flow. The revenue side of the future is usually the most difficult to forecast and the least subject to positive control by the firm. Given the revenue outlook, the firm can at least decide what it can afford to spend for operations. Moreover, since most operating expenses are within the control of managers to a major degree, the forecast of expenses can be more accurate than a forecast of revenues.

In any case, it is the sales forecast that is the key to internal planning. Business and capital outlays and policies of all kinds are made for the purpose of maximizing profits from expected sales. Although there are some enterprises that need to pay little attention to sales (for example, the small-city water company or the government defense contractor with a long-term order that has little chance of being canceled or modified), it is a rare business that can overlook the market for long. Even the farmer who, operating under support prices, may have a guaranteed market for a certain product for a coming year, can hardly ignore market influences as they affect succeeding years or alternative crops.

Since the sales forecast is so important a tool, there is scarcely a company that should not take the time and trouble to make the best one its resources will permit. Even the company with a fairly large backlog of orders for custom-made goods that need not go on the shelf as inventory requires such a forecast. One of the authors recalls a company that simply measured its future sales by the size of the total sales backlog. Although this backlog remained high, the managers were surprised to find one day that it was for a limited number of products for delivery over so long a period that the total dollar amount of the backlog would not permit capacity operation of the machinery and manpower then being employed.

Smaller companies often make the mistake of believing that sales forecasts are too expensive and of overlooking the variety of sources of data available at little or no cost. The purchasing agent, members of the sales staff, the treasurer, and the production manager are among those who may possess bits and pieces of information, which, gathered together, could make an acceptable forecast. Moreover, the wide range of information available from government and industry sources is neither difficult nor expensive to obtain.

An indicator of the increasing importance being given planning is the rapid rise of sales forecasting in the past two decades. Although better-managed companies long realized the value of good sales forecasting, the experience of World War II and the shortage years that followed led most managers to plan on the basis of maximum production rather than on the requirements of the market. With the return of normal business and strong competition, along with greater attention to the managerial job itself, managers have found that planning success depends largely upon the ability to forecast sales.

There has been a real swing away from the less formal methods, such as the managerial hunch, to more formal methods. Some few years ago, a survey by the American Management Association of 297 firms showed a strong movement toward scientific sales forecasting.[6] This study indicated that more than one-sixth of the companies surveyed, many of which were rather large, had

[6] *Sales Forecasting: Uses, Techniques, and Trends*, Special Report No. 16 (New York: American Management Association, 1956), appendix, "Survey of Sales-forecasting Practices," pp. 143–145.

embarked upon organized programs of sales forecasting only in the previous five years and that the number of companies centralizing primary responsibility for this forecasting had increased by 60 percent in the same period. Another study, made for the Controllership Foundation by Sord and Welsch in 1958, found that, of 424 companies selected for a better-than-average quality of management, 93 percent developed sales forecasts, 53 percent estimated the company's share of the market, and 42 percent developed forecasts of general economic conditions.[7] The publication of studies on sales forecasting since 1955 is an index of this trend.[8]

Methods of Sales Forecasting

Methods utilized in sales forecasting may generally be classified as the jury of executive opinion method, the sales force composite method, users' expectation method, statistical methods, and deductive methods.[9]

Jury of executive opinion method   The jury of executive opinion method is perhaps the oldest and simplest method of making sales forecasts, since it merely combines and averages the views, many of which may be little more than hunch, of top managers. In most cases, the final estimate is an opinion of the president, based upon his consideration of the opinions of other officers; in other cases, the poll of opinion leads to a rough kind of average estimate. In some cases, the process amounts to little more than group guessing; in other cases, it involves the careful judgment of experienced executives who have studied the underlying factors that influence their company's sales.

This method has the advantage of ease and simplicity; it allows for pooling of experience and judgment; and it need not require the preparation of

---

[7] B. H. Sord and G. A. Welsch, *Business Budgeting* (New York: Controllership Foundation, Inc., 1958), p. 133.

[8] In addition to the American Management Association and Controllership Foundation reports cited, attention should be drawn to the following reports: American Management Association, *Company Organization for Economic Forecasting*, Research Report No. 28 (New York: American Management Association, 1957); National Industrial Conference Board, *Forecasting in Industry*, Studies in Business Policy No. 77 (New York: National Industrial Conference Board, Inc., 1956); the special report on "Business Forecasting" by *Business Week*, pp. 90–102 (Sept. 24, 1955); and the detailed analysis by the National Industrial Conference Board in *Forecasting Sales*, Studies in Business Policy No. 106 (New York: National Industrial Conference Board, Inc., 1963); and *Sales Forecasting Practices: An Appraisal*, Experiences in Marketing Management No. 25 (New York: National Industrial Conference Board, 1970).

[9] It is interesting to compare this classification of methods with those used by *Business Week* in its special report (Sept. 24, 1955, pp. 90–122). The *Business Week* report classifies forecasting techniques as "loaded deck" (in which the forecaster is working from known data, such as backlogs or inside information on customer plans), "oaks from acorns" (in which the forecaster operates on the premise that, although the future is not identical with the past, it is an outgrowth of it), and "test tube" (in which the future is forecast by studying the natural world, finding fundamental truths, and using them to predict behavior in the world of the future). A variant of the test tube, or systematic, technique of forecasting has been dubbed the "lost-horse" technique. This technique, credited to Sidney Alexander of the Columbia Broadcasting System, is based upon the old gag about the best way to find a lost horse: go where the horse was last seen and ask yourself where you would go if you were a horse. This technique is dealt with under the deductive methods outlined by the authors.

elaborate economic studies and statistics. An advantage not often cited is that, by forcing top managers to make an estimate, it may put pressure on them to develop pertinent data. On the other hand, such a method has serious drawbacks; forecasts are based on opinion rather than on facts and analyses; averaging opinions reduces responsibility for accurate forecasting; and forecasts are not usually broken down into products, time periods, or organizational units.

Sales force composite method   One of the most commonly used methods of sales forecasting is to obtain from line salesmen and sales managers their combined view as to expected sales. The usual technique is to ask salesmen to forecast sales for their districts and have these estimates reviewed by the regional sales manager and then by the head-office sales manager. Sometimes salesmen are given guides in the form of company planning premises as to business conditions generally, and often the salesmen's estimates are reviewed by the product specialists, such as the company brand, sales, and advertising managers.

This method is based on the belief that those closest to the sales picture have the best knowledge of the market. Other advantages ascribed to this method are that it places forecasting, initially at least, in the hands of those who must make good on the forecast; it gives a broad sample that makes the total forecast more valid; and it allows an easy breakdown by product customer, or territory.

On the other hand, the sales force composite method suffers from the fact that salesmen, and often even sales executives, are apt to be poor forecasters for any period except the immediate future, since they tend to give primary weight to present conditions. Where forecasts are desired for more than the short range, sales personnel normally are at a loss to make sound forecasts because of lack of knowledge of basic social, political, and economic trends. Moreover, under certain conditions—particularly where the forecasts are used for quota purposes—sales personnel incline to pessimism, while in other instances—especially when salesmen want more liberal allowances for expenses, promotion, or advertising—they are inclined to be rather optimistic. Furthermore, since sales forecasting is not their primary responsibility, sales personnel may neither be adept at it nor give it the time and thought necessary.

At the same time, most companies have found that forecasts submitted by the sales organization are useful and valuable inputs into the company forecasting effort. It has been found that, when the sales force composite method is properly cross-checked by various other methods, such as review by head-office marketing and sales experts and constant check by salesmen of their estimates of past performance against actual results, it has furnished surprisingly good forecasts.

Users' expectation method   Many companies, particularly those serving industrial customers in industries composed of a small number of companies or where a few large companies are dominant, find it useful to base their forecasts on expected purchases by these customers. Clearly, if a company can obtain an adequate and reliable information sample of what its customers will buy, even though the actual orders are not in hand, it will have a good basis upon which to develop a sales forecast.

The users' expectation method has clear advantages where other ways of forecasting are inadequate or where the company cannot make a systematic forecast on its own, such as in small companies with limited resources for forecasting; in cases of new products where the market is known; or instances where a supplier is dependent on plans of major customers. This method is obviously difficult to use in cases where customers are numerous, or not easily located, or uncooperative. It is also subject to the difficulty of being able accurately to assess customer expectations, since the best of these are usually estimates of needs, and not commitments.

Statistical methods   The most generally relied upon approach to sales forecasting is the application of various statistical methods. As mathematical techniques have improved and the electronic computing machine has come into wider use, so have statistics. These statistical methods may be divided into trend and cycle, correlation analysis, and mathematical formula or model.

In approaching forecasting through an analysis of trends and cycles, the analyst summarizes a pertinent series of data that reflect dollar or unit sales, units per thousand population, or other basic indicators of sales volume. On the basis of his findings, he simply projects by extrapolation the directions indicated. This analysis is based on the assumption that "what is past is prologue" and that a trend will continue unless something happens to it. It is then up to the analyst to judge whether that "something" will happen. In fact, it is important to the user of a forecast to know whether it represents a mere projection of past trends or a real forecast of what the forecaster expects *will* happen.

The statistical method most widely used is correlation analysis, the measurement of the relationship between company sales and one or more other factors. What is usually desired is a close correlation between sales and some broad national index that can be used with a reasonable degree of accuracy, such as gross national product, national income, or consumers' disposable income. Such correlation, either directly or with a lag or lead of a given time period, can give a company a useful and highly reliable basis for sales forecasting.

Virtually every forecaster has found some accurate correlations in using this method. Many companies have found that *their* sales, aside from industry sales, bear a close relationship to some national index. The problem for the forecaster is, of course, to study the various relationships, with their leads and lags, to find one or more which serve as indicators of the company's sales.

The third statistical method, one which usually grows out of finding either a trend or correlation analysis relationship, is to develop a mathematical formula to depict the relationship of a number of variables to the company's sales. Often, sales for an individual company are subject to a number of variables. If the relationship of these can be ascertained with reasonable accuracy or if credible assumptions can be made to fill in statistical gaps, a mathematical model very useful to the forecaster can be constructed. Thus, the B. F. Goodrich Company found that total replacement passenger-car tire sales was given by taking the number of cars in use over two years, multiplying by four, correcting for the amount of wear tires receive, and further correcting by a factor giving effect to improved tire quality (1 percent per year in the twenty-year period 1933–1953).

Although statistical methods are good for sales forecasting from the standpoint of reliability, they are often subject to certain drawbacks. They require research and the use of statistically trained help, which may be costly. It is not always possible to find reliable trends, correlations, or mathematical relationships. Many defense subcontractors have found, for example, that their sales potential is closely related to such vague factors as defense strategy, the course of a conflict, individual program expenditure level, and advances in the art of the industry, none of which bears a reliable correlation with predictable national or industry data. There is also a danger that managers may rely too heavily on statistical relationships and the results implied and thereby miss significant changes which intelligent judgment would have appraised. In any statistical method, it must be realized that the past is used only as a *basis* for prediction and that the future does not necessarily reflect the past.

Deductive methods   No forecaster should overlook applying judgment and intelligent deduction from facts and relationships. Although this method bears certain similarities to the "lost-horse" technique mentioned on page 165, footnote 9, it has much validity. Generally, what is involved is to find out what the present situation is, where the sales are, and why, and then to analyze deductively, by resort to both objective factors and subjective judgments, the factors underlying sales. Although the indications so developed may be put into a mathematical model or merely left as an imprecisely correlated conglomeration of facts and value judgments, they are often a useful check on results arrived at through more scientific methods. After all, the state of the art of forecasting is such that independent, and often apparently intuitive, appraisal of the sales picture by an intelligent and experienced brain is still an input that no forecaster should overlook.

Combination of Methods

In practice, there is a tendency to combine sales forecasting methods. This is as it should be. The importance of the final forecast for all aspects of company planning makes desirable a forecast system in which every possible input can be utilized. What warms the forecaster's heart and gives him a feeling of reliability is when several different forecast indicators, based upon independent approaches and data, all point to the same result. And, even if they do not, the disparity may serve as a warning that a single approach may have over-- looked an essential factor.

Sales Forecasting in Practice

To understand sales forecasting techniques, one might examine some typical examples of what companies do.

One large company approaches forecasting by having a staff prepare a forecast of general business conditions referred to as an "assumption about the future." From this premise of the external business environment is projected a forecast of product sales. The staff takes into account the various factors, both external and internal, that might bear upon sales—such as prices, production capacities, markets, technological changes, competition, and sales promotion plans—and combines them to bring about the forecast.

The basic assumptions for the future are arrived at by the staff after consideration, with upper managers, of levels of gross national product, disposable income, price indexes, and other basic economic conditions. Then, before the forecast is finished, a series of meetings is held with sales and other company personnel, to make sure that all factors have been properly considered. Conferences are also held with staff specialists in production, advertising, research, costs, and pricing. After the forecast weathers these discussions, it goes to the finished products committee of the company, which includes several vice-presidents. When this committee has approved or modified the sales forecast, it then becomes a guide for all managers in planning their budgets and operations.

In another typical case, the initial forecast is made by the salesmen in the field for each of their territories and then modified by the product managers and the sales vice-president to correct for known optimism or pessimism of certain salesmen. A second forecast is prepared by the company's economists after careful study of economic and market statistics, based on a combination of historical series and judgment of future conditions as they might affect the company's sales. Supplementing these two forecasts, sampling techniques are used to determine actual markets for their products, as disclosed by plans and practices of industrial and other customers. With these three forecasts, prepared independently, top management holds a conference at which the various predictions are appraised and modified. The resulting forecast becomes the basis for company planning and operations.

Another variant found in practice is for the company, as in the previous example, to have three sets of sales forecasts prepared. One set is prepared by industry specialists in home-office sales departments, another set by the commercial research department, and still another by the salesmen in the field. These sets are submitted to the sales manager, who presents all three, plus a forecast that reconciles differences, to the sales vice-president, who, in turn, checks or modifies the reconciled forecast and submits his approved forecast as the planning basis for company operations.

This procedure can probably better be shown in Figure 8.1.

MAKING PREMISING EFFECTIVE

Since so many failures occur in planning and planning coordination through poor premising, special attention should be given to this step in planning. It is difficult enough to identify the factors in a future environment that will affect a manager's plans. But it is also difficult, once these have been identified, to get consistent and meaningful planning premises actually used in practice.

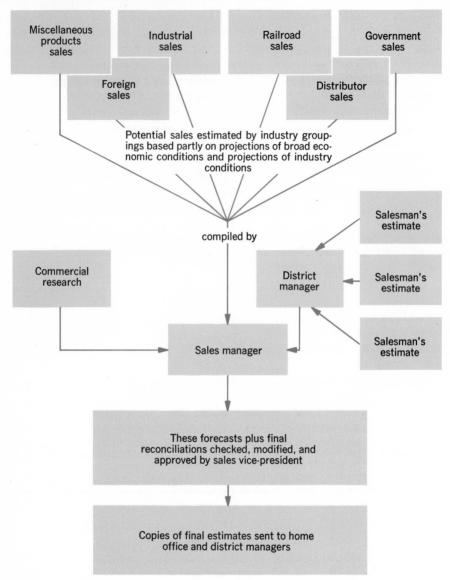

Figure 8.1   *A procedure for sales forecasting.*

Selecting Premises

Simply because a manager cannot identify and keep in mind all the factors in the future that might affect the course of plans, he limits himself to those premises that are critical or strategic for him. In making this selection he considers those that bear materially on his programs. For most enterprises and their managers, these are likely to include national and regional gross product and income and their various elements, such as defense spending, housing and other construction, savings, and consumers' disposable income. In most businesses at least, the movement of the business cycle is a critical factor, and it is difficult to see how price movements can fail to be a significant premise for almost all enterprises. Likewise, population growth and movement have virtually universal importance.

On the other hand, there are many premises of strategic importance to one enterprise and not to another. For an airline the availability of certain types of aircraft has specific importance. To a steel company, the trends of commercial construction or automobile production may be especially significant, but they may not be an important premise to a toy company. Likewise, in a closely regulated industry such as the airlines or railroads, the policies of regulatory commissions are strategic, while a toothpaste manufacturer may only be concerned with fair trade regulation.

The top managers of every enterprise, and to a certain extent every manager within it, should select their own premises. The basic question should be asked and answered—what factors in the environment, whether external or internal, will influence most the course of plans for which I am responsible?

Alternative Premises for Contingencies

Because the future cannot be foreseen with accuracy, it is usually good planning to have alternative sets of premises and plans based upon contingencies so widely varying that no single plan can encompass them all—alternative plans based on such widely varying assumptions as war, peace, peace with large defense spending, full employment, prosperity, depression, recession, rising prices, falling prices, or other major political or economic events. In ideal business planning, alternative plans should be ready whenever basic premises change materially. However, at one time or another decisions that make planning less flexible must be made. A time comes when the manager can no longer wait to order construction of a new plant, hire and train a new staff of specialists, or embark upon a sales promotion campaign. When such decisions are made, the range of alternative plans narrows, as do the premises upon which they are based.

Assuring Consistent Premises

While there can be no doubt of the desirability of consistent premises if plans are to fit each other and contribute most effectively to desired objectives, assuring that premises are consistent is not easy. Perhaps the best way of making sure is to have the planning staff at headquarters and divisional levels recommend critical planning premises applicable to an enterprise or a division to the appropriate top executive. By having a staff with this responsibility, there can be a fair assurance that the premises will represent study and analysis and that they will be internally consistent. By having the top executive approve these premises, usually after consultation with his lieutenants, there will be assurance that the assumptions selected and formulated will be the ones on which the enterprise or division is willing to stake its future.

Communicating Premises

Even after planning premises have been carefully developed and approved, there is always the question of how to communicate them to the number of persons who, by their decision-making authority, participate in the planning process. Like all communications problems, this is difficult. But at least with something to communicate, the problem is easier. A problem arises, too, from the fact that many premises, especially those based on strategy or major programs of competitive impact, may understandably be regarded as confidential.

One of the first requirements of effective premise communication is to analyze every manager's "need to know," interpret this broadly rather than narrowly, and make sure that premises important for his planning are made available to him. There may be a risk of leaks in confidential information, but it is normally better to take this risk than to have an uninformed subordinate making planning decisions. What often happens is that the competitor knows a company's strategy and major programs, but its own subordinate managers charged with effectuating this strategy or developing supportive plans do not.

Some companies have found it wise to develop and disseminate to those who need it a manual of planning premises, incorporating assumptions with wide application to planning. These will, of course, be kept current as premises change. They should also be supplemented by the practice of having superiors develop and distribute supplementary planning premises of special concern for managers reporting to them whenever a budget proposal or program recommendation is requested and whenever a major program assignment is made. It is fatal for a manager to assume that premising is no longer necessary after a program has been approved or a major decision made. The fact is that, until one gets down to the nuts and bolts of actions, decisions have to be made, and better decisions will be made if the person responsible has a clear picture of the environment in which the decision is expected to operate.

FOR DISCUSSION

1. Take a major decision problem facing you and outline the more critical planning premises surrounding it. How many of these are matters of knowledge and how many are matters of forecast? How many are intangible and how many are tangible? How many are within your control?
2. A sales forecast is often regarded both as a plan and as a premise. Comment.
3. Can objectives, policies, and procedures be premises in planning?
4. Examine how uniform premises aid in coordination of plans.
5. How should premises be developed and communicated?
6. Exactly how would you apply the Delphi technique to premising the air and water pollution problems of a company?

9

decision making

Decision making—the selection from among alternatives of a course of action—is at the core of planning. Managers sometimes see it as their central job because they must constantly choose what is to be done; who is to do it; when, where, and occasionally even how. It is, however, only a step in planning, even when done quickly and with little thought or when it influences action for only a few minutes. It is also part of everyone's daily living. Planning occurs in managing or in personal life whenever choices are made in order to gain a goal in the face of such limitations as time, money, and the desires of other people.

Moreover, a course of action can seldom be judged alone, because virtually every decision must be geared in with other plans of the firm. The stereotype of the finger-snapping, button-pushing managerial mogul fades as the requirements of systematic research and analysis come into focus.

RATIONALITY AND DECISION MAKING

Effective decision making requires a *rational* selection of a course of action. But what is rationality? When is a person thinking or deciding rationally? It is often thought to be problem solving, and a problem has sometimes been defined as a state of confusion, uncertainty, or chaos. However, if a person's *goal* is confusion, uncertainty, or chaos in a situation, obviously no problem exists and no need for a decision would arise.

It can be seen, therefore, for anyone to act or decide rationally requires certain conditions. In the first place, he must be attempting to reach some goal that could not be attained without positive action. Second, he must have a clear understanding of courses by which a goal could be reached under existing circumstances and limitations. Third, the rationalist must have the ability to analyze and evaluate alternatives in the light of the goal sought. And, finally, he must have a desire to optimize by selecting the alternative that best satisfies goal achievement.

Complete rationality can seldom be achieved, particularly in the area of managing. In the first place, since no one can make decisions for the past, decisions must operate for the future and the future almost invariably involves uncertainties. In the second place, all the alternatives that might be followed to reach a goal can hardly be recognized; this is particularly true when decision making involves seeing opportunities to do something that has not been done before. Moreover, alternatives cannot all be analyzed in most instances, even with the newest available analytical techniques and computational facilities.

What a manager must settle for is limited rationality, or what has been called "bounded" rationality. In view of the very great limits to complete rationality in practice, it is not surprising that managers sometimes will allow their aversion to risk—the desire to "play it safe"—to interfere even with the desire to reach an optimum solution. This was referred to by Herbert Simon as "satisficing," picking a course of action that is satisfactory or "good enough" under the circumstances. While it is true that many managerial decisions are made with a desire to "get by" as safely as possible, it is believed that most managers do attempt to make the best decisions they can within the limits of rationality and in the light of the size and nature of risks involved in uncertainty.

DEVELOPING ALTERNATIVES

Assuming known goals and clear planning premises, the first step of decision making is the development of alternatives. It is rare for alternatives to be lacking for any course of action; indeed, perhaps a sound adage for the manager is that if there seems to be only one way of doing a thing, that way is probably wrong. What the manager has probably not done is force himself to consider other ways; unless he does so, he cannot know if his decision is the best possible.

One of the authors was with a firm that desperately needed certain capital equipment to build up its production to where reduced costs and expanded markets would turn losses into profits. Losses had so depleted the company's capital and credit that the equipment desired apparently could not be financed. The single available course of action seemed to be to do nothing, but this would assure bankruptcy. The officers of the company therefore sought out alternatives. A manufacturer was found who had the needed equipment, which he had not been able to sell and which had been financed by some banks. Inquiry of the banks disclosed that they would let the manufacturer sell the equipment without down payment and accept two-name paper instead of the single-name notes they then held. In addition, a competitor of the firm needing equipment had new equipment on order and offered to sell, on a no-down-payment basis, his older machines. Hence, in an apparently hopeless situation two alternatives were found.

The ability to develop alternatives is often as important as selecting correctly from among them. On the other hand, ingenuity, research, and perspicacity will often unearth so many choices that they cannot be adequately evaluated. The manager needs help in this situation, and this, as well as assistance in choosing the best alternative, is found in the concept of the limiting or strategic factor.

The Principle of the Limiting Factor

A limiting factor is one which stands in the way of accomplishing a desired objective. If these factors are clearly recognized, the manager will confine his search for alternatives to those which will overcome the limiting factors. For instance, in the above example of the manufacturing enterprise, the objective was to turn a loss into a profit. The means for doing this was to acquire some capital equipment. The limiting factor was the lack of cash and credit. Consequently, the manager's alternatives were confined to those which would overcome the limiting factor. His search was unerring, direct, and successful.

From the consideration of this and numerous similar examples there emerges the principle of the limiting factor: *In choosing from among alternatives, the more an individual can recognize and solve for those factors that are limiting or critical to the attainment of the desired goal, the more clearly and accurately he can select the most favorable alternative.*

Chester I. Barnard recognized the importance of this principle when he pointed out:[1]

The analysis required for decision is in effect a search for the "strategic factors." . . . The theory of the strategic factor is necessary to an appreciation of the process of decision, and therefore to the understanding of organization and the executive functions as well as, perhaps, individual purposive conduct. As generally as I can state it, this theory is as follows:

If we take any system, or set of conditions, or conglomeration of circumstances existing at a given time, we recognize that it consists of elements, or parts, or factors, which together make up the whole system, set of conditions, or circumstances. Now if we approach this system or set of circumstances with a view to the accomplishment of a purpose, and only when we so approach it, the elements or parts become distinguished into two classes: those which if absent or changed would accomplish the desired purpose, provided the others remain unchanged, and these others. The first kind are called limiting factors, the second, complementary factors.

The discovery of the limiting factor or factors may not be easy, since these are often obscure. For example, if a company were considering a profit-

---

[1] C. I. Barnard, *The Functions of the Executive* (Cambridge, Mass.: Harvard University Press, 1938), pp. 202–203. Note that Barnard states that he has borrowed the term "strategic factor" from John R. Commons. As one of the authors' students put it, when his automobile fails to operate, he has two basic choices. He might disassemble it part by part, lay all the parts out on a canvas, check each part, replace doubtful parts, reassemble it in accordance with manufacturer's specifications and prints, put gasoline and oil in it, and it would run. Or, he might try to locate the limiting factor and replace an ignition wire. As homely as this example is, it emphasizes the fact that many problem solvers, often very intelligent individuals, tend to be "automobile disassemblers" in their attempt to solve a problem.

sharing program, the limiting factors might be tax deductibility and the attitude of employees toward the plan. In deciding whether to expand operations, one company might find its limiting factor to be availability of capital, the diseconomies of size, or the attitude of the government antitrust authorities.

The search for and recognition of limiting factors in planning never ends. For one program at one time, a certain factor may be critical to the decision; but, at a later time and for a similar decision, the limiting factor may be something relatively unimportant in the earlier planning. Thus, a company might decide to acquire new equipment when the limiting factor was capital availability, only to have the limiting factor become delivery or, later, the training of operatives.

THE BASIC PROCESS OF EVALUATION

Once appropriate alternatives have been isolated, the next step in planning is to evaluate them and select the one that will best contribute to the goal. This is the point of ultimate decision making, although decisions must also be made in the other steps of planning—in selecting goals, in choosing critical premises, and even in selecting alternatives.

Tangible and Intangible Factors

As one approaches the problem of comparing alternative plans for achieving an objective, he is likely to think exclusively of the tangible factors. These consist of things which can be measured, such as various types of fixed and operating costs, time and cost of ancillary services. No one would question the importance of this analysis, but it would be dangerous to the success of the venture if intangible factors in the situation were ignored. These are the unmeasurable elements such as the quality of labor relations, the risk of technological change, or the international political climate. There are all too many instances where the best of quantitative plans were destroyed by an unforeseen war, a fine marketing plan was made inoperable by a long transportation strike, or a rational tax plan was hampered by an economic recession. These illustrations point up the importance of giving equal attention to tangible and intangible factors in the comparison of alternatives.

To evaluate and compare the intangible factors in a planning problem and make decisions from them, the analyst must first recognize them, then determine whether a reasonable quantitative measurement can be given them. If not, he should then find out what he can about them, perhaps rate them in terms of their importance, compare their probable influence with the results disclosed from evaluation of the tangible factors, and then come to a decision. This decision may give predominant weight to a single intangible.

Such a procedure is, in effect, deciding upon the weight of the total evidence. Although it involves fallible personal judgments, few business decisions can be so accurately quantified that judgment is unnecessary. Decision making is seldom so simple. It is not without some justification that the successful executive has been cynically described as a person who guesses right.

Evaluating Alternatives: Marginal Analysis

The evaluation of alternatives may utilize the techniques of marginal analysis, wherein the additional revenues from additional costs are compared. Thus, where the objective is to maximize profits, this goal will be reached when the additional revenues and additional costs are equal.

Marginal analysis can be used in comparing factors other than costs and revenues. For example, to find the optimum output of a machine, one could vary inputs against outputs until the *additional* input equals the *additional* output. This would then be the point of maximum efficiency of the machine. Or the number of subordinates reporting to a manager might conceivably be increased to the point where incremental savings in costs, better communication and morale, and other factors equal incremental losses in effectiveness of control, direction, and similar factors.

Perhaps the real usefulness of the marginal approach to evaluation is that it accentuates the variables in a situation and deemphasizes averages and constants. Whether the objective is optimum profits, stability, or durability, marginal analysis will show the way.

Evaluating Alternatives: Cost-effectiveness Analysis

An improvement or variant on traditional marginal analysis is cost-effectiveness, or cost-benefit, analysis. It is a technique of weighing alternatives where the optimum solution cannot be conveniently reduced to dollars or some other specific measure as in the case of marginal analysis which is, in actuality, a traditional form of cost-benefit analysis. Special attention was drawn to it in deciding upon programs in the Department of Defense under Robert McNamara, who drew from the work of the Rand Corporation on the economics of defense projects.[2]

In its simplest terms, cost-effectiveness is a technique for choosing from among alternatives to identify a preferred choice when objectives are far less specific than those expressed by such clear quantities as sales, costs, or profits. For example, defense objectives may be so unspecific as those to deter or repel enemy attack; social objectives may be to reduce air pollution or retrain the unemployed; and business objectives may be to participate in these social objectives through a program of training unemployables.

This does not mean that objectives may not be given some fairly specific measures of effectiveness. In a program with the general objective of improving employee morale, for example, effectiveness may be measured by such verifiable factors as turnover, absenteeism, or volume of grievances and also supplemented by such subjective inputs as the judgment of qualified experts. Or a program for selecting a military airplane may be verifiably quantified in part by considering bomb carrying load, speed, maneuverability, but supplemented by judgment of military strategists on how effective it might be in meeting tactical requirements in combat.

[2] See C. J. Hitch and R. N. McKean, *Economics of Defense in the Nuclear Age* (Cambridge: Harvard University Press, 1960).

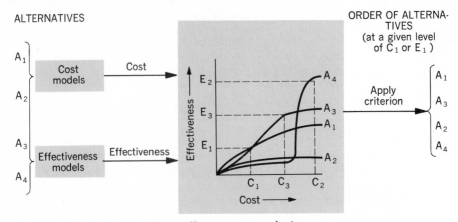

Figure 9.1 *The structure of cost-effectiveness analysis.*

The major features of cost-effectiveness are concentration on output from a program or system, weighing the contribution of each alternative against its effectiveness in serving desired objectives, and comparison of costs of each in terms of its effectiveness. This was the reasoning that apparently led to the selection of the F-111 combat airplane some years ago for both the Navy and the Air Force. As erroneous as some may believe this decision to have been and while the Defense Department clearly recognized that the airplane was not optimum for either service, its effectiveness, compared to estimated costs of undertaking two combat aircraft programs, especially when resources were needed for other defense requirements, was thought to be such as to justify the single aircraft program.

Although it involves the same steps as any planning decision, the major features that distinguish cost-effectiveness are (1) objectives are normally output or end-result oriented and usually imprecise; (2) alternatives ordinarily represent total systems, programs, or strategies for meeting objectives; (3) the measures of effectiveness must be relevant to objectives and set in as precise terms as possible although some may not be subject to quantification; (4) cost estimates are usually traditional and normal but may include nonmonetary as well as monetary costs, even though the former may be eliminated by expressing them as negative factors of effectiveness; and (5) decision criteria, while definite but not usually as specific as cost or profit, may include achieving a given objective at least cost, or attaining it with resources available, or providing for a trade-off of cost for effectiveness, particularly in the light of the claims of other objectives.

Cost-effectiveness can be made most systematic through the use of models and other operations research techniques, to be described presently. Cost models may be developed to show cost estimates for each alternative, and effectiveness models to show the relationship between each alternative and its effectiveness. Then, synthesizing models, combining these results, may be made to show the relationships of costs and effectiveness for each alternative. As illustrated in Figure 9.1, this can show how much effectiveness can be bought for a certain cost for each alternative and how much effectiveness can be had for any alternative for any given cost.

Planning under Dynamic Conditions

Analysis of economic forces under static conditions is useful only to isolate the effects of uncertainty and thereby develop further tools for analysis. Static conditions do not exist in practice, and planning is, therefore, undertaken under conditions of change and uncertainty. It is this dynamic character of the environment that makes planning difficult.

The central problem under dynamic conditions is the accuracy of a planner's estimate of the future. Since the future is uncertain—although the degree may vary widely as between products, markets, geographical and political area, and times—when a manager estimates a future situation, he necessarily makes certain assumptions as to what will happen. As he weighs his contingencies in one way or another, he obtains different results. Suppose, for example, that a manager were planning a new plant and felt that he needed ten years to recover his costs. He might estimate the future with respect to markets, prices, labor costs, material costs, utilization of plant, labor efficiency, taxes, and other factors. Suppose further that he estimated six possible situations as being most likely to occur, created out of different sets of assumptions as to the future. These might bring completely different estimates of net profits, as shown in Figure 9.2.

As might be expected, all estimates for the first year or two are fairly close together, since the manager can be more certain of short-term than long-term results. But as the planning period is extended, this or that contingency makes the estimates of accumulated profits vary from high, as in forecast A, through bare break-even (E), to projected loss (F).

Several observations may be made concerning this simplified model of planning under conditions of change and uncertainty. In the first place, the tools of marginal analysis are useful in arriving at these various estimates of possible situations. In each set of contingencies assumed, the planner would attempt to maximize profits by assuring himself that additional costs are com-

Figure 9.2   *Accumulated profits from new plant on basis of six estimates of future.*

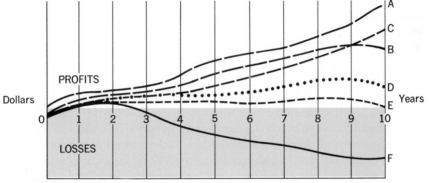

pensated for by additional revenues and that, within the limits of divisibility of units of production, no opportunity for maximizing profits by increasing or reducing costs or revenues has been neglected.

In the second place, Figure 9.2 emphasizes the fact that the uncertainties over time, plus the alternatives available to accomplish results under each set of uncertainties, give alternative possibilities astronomical in number. A manager must have some means of limiting his analysis to probable situations. In most cases, this is done by judgment and test. If he can calculate his profits on basic estimates of what is most likely to occur, he will limit the alternative projections to a few most probable ones. At this point, a decision is likely to be based upon a weighing of the risks and benefits to be expected from these few probabilities, in the light of underlying uncertainties, the resources of the firm, and the ability and willingness to assume the risks involved.

BASES FOR SELECTION AMONG ALTERNATIVES

In selecting from among alternatives, three bases for decision are open to the manager—experience, experimentation, and research and analysis.

Experience

Reliance on past experience probably plays a larger part than it deserves in decision making. The experienced manager usually believes, often without realizing it, that the things he has accomplished and the mistakes he has made furnish an almost infallible guide to the future. This attitude is likely to be more pronounced the longer his experience and the higher in an organization a manager has risen.

To some extent, the attitude that experience is the best teacher is justifiable. The very fact that the manager has reached his position appears to justify his decisions. Moreover, the reasoning process of thinking problems through, making decisions, and seeing programs succeed or fail, does make for a degree of good judgment (at times bordering on the intuitive). Many people, however, do not profit by their errors, and there are managers who seem never to gain the seasoned judgment required by modern enterprise.

There is danger, however, in relying on one's past experience as a guide for future action. In the first place, it is an unusual human being who recognizes the underlying reasons for his mistakes or failures. In the second place, the lessons of experience may be entirely unsuitable to new problems. Good decisions must be evaluated against future events, while experience belongs to the past.

On the other hand, if experience is carefully analyzed rather than blindly followed, and if the *fundamental* reasons for success or failure are distilled from it, it can be useful as a basis for decision analysis. A successful program, a well-managed company, a profitable product promotion, or any other decision that turns out well may furnish useful data for such distillation. Just as no scientist hesitates to build upon the research of others and would be foolish indeed to duplicate it, a manager can learn much from others.

Experimentation

An obvious way to decide upon alternatives is to try them and see what happens. Such experimentation is used in scientific inquiry. It is frequently argued that it should be employed more often in enterprise and that the only way a manager can make sure his plan is right—especially in view of the intangible factors—is to try the various alternatives to see which is best.

However, as Newman[3] has pointed out, "The experimental technique . . . should be utilized as a last resort after other planning techniques have been tried." It is clearly the most expensive of all techniques, especially where heavy expenditures in capital and personnel are necessary to try a program and where the firm cannot afford to prosecute vigorously several alternatives. Besides, there may be doubt, after an experiment has been tried, as to what it proved, since the future may not duplicate the past.

On the other hand, there are many decisions which cannot be made until the best course of action can be ascertained with experiment. Even reflections on experience or the most careful research may not assure the manager of a correct decision. This is nowhere better illustrated than in planning a new airplane. The manufacturer may assiduously draw from his own experience and that of other plane manufacturers and of new plane users. His engineers and economists may make extensive studies of stresses, vibrations, fuel consumption, speed, space allocations, and other factors. But all these studies do not give every answer to questions about the flying characteristics and economics of a successful plane; therefore, some experimentation is almost always involved in the process of selecting from alternatives. Ordinarily, a prototype airplane is constructed and tested, and, on the basis of these tests, production airplanes are later designed and made.

Experimentation is used in other ways. A firm may test a new product in a certain market before expanding its sale nationwide. Organizational techniques are often tried in a branch office or plant before being applied over an entire company. A candidate for a management job may be tested in the job during the incumbent's vacation.

Research and Analysis

The most generally used and certainly a most effective technique for selecting alternatives, when major decisions are involved, is research and analysis. This approach entails solving a problem by, first, comprehending it. It thus involves a search for relationships between the more critical variables, constraints, and premises that bear upon the goal sought. In a real sense it is the pencil and paper (or, better, the computer and printout) approach to decision making It has many advantages for weighing alternative courses of action.

In the second place, the solution of a planning problem requires that it be broken into its component parts and the various tangible and intangible factors studied. Study and analysis are likely to be far cheaper than experimentation. Hours of analytical time and reams of paper usually cost much less than

[3] W. H. Newman, *Business Policies and Management*, 2d ed. (Cincinnati: South-Western Publishing Company, 1949), p. 601.

trying the various alternatives in practice. In the example of building airplanes mentioned above, if careful research did not precede the building and testing of prototype subassemblies and the final assembly, one can hardly imagine the costs that would result.

A major characteristic of the research and analysis technique is seeing a problem and its relationship in mathematical terms. Being able to conceptualize a problem is a major step toward its solution. The physical sciences have long relied on mathematics, and it is encouraging to see the mathematical methodology being brought into the area of managerial decision making.

OPERATIONS RESEARCH AND PLANNING

One of the most comprehensive research and analysis approaches to decision making is operations research or, as it is sometimes called, operations analysis or "management science." These terms, although sometimes given an aura of mystery by their mathematically inclined proponents, apply to the growing practice of applying the systems methodology of the physical sciences to management decision making.

To a considerable extent, operations research is a product of World War II, although its antecedents in scientific method, higher mathematics, and such tools as probability theory go back far beyond that period. The accelerated growth of operations research in recent years has followed the whole trend of applying the methods of the physical scientist and the engineer to economic and political problems. It has also been made possible by the development of rapid computing machines, particularly those using electronics, since much of the advantage of operations research depends upon the economical and feasible application of involved mathematical formulas and the use of data with complex relationships.

The Concept

There are almost as many definitions of operations research as there are writers on the subject. As applied to decision making, where the term was originally used, the most acceptable definition is: the application of scientific method to the study of alternatives in a problem situation, with a view to providing a quantitative basis for arriving at an optimum solution in terms of the goals sought. Thus, the emphasis is on scientific method, on the use of quantitative data, on goals, and on the determination of the optimum means of reaching the goal. In other words, operations research might be called "quantitative common sense."

Operations research, like accounting analyses or correlation analyses, does not provide decisions but develops quantitative data to help the manager make decisions. In most business situations, analyses cannot be so complete or conclusive that they constitute the decision. However, in a production planning or transportation problem, the goals may be so clear, the input data so definite, and the conclusions so workable as to point positively to the optimum solution.

Some operations researchers insist that with this tool the activities of an enterprise must be viewed as *a total system* in contrast to the usual attempts to solve isolated problems. In addition, it is often claimed that operations research requires the team approach in the solution of problems, that is, the use of a variety of talents, such as those of the mathematician, the business specialist, the psychologist, the engineer, and the accountant. Although these conditions may be desirable, neither seems to be essential to operations research.

Any top manager would appreciate having a problem area completely analyzed and its solution related to every other problem in his operation, but he recognizes the practical difficulties, if not the impossibility, of doing so. It does not seem realistic for the operations research experts to overlook the usefulness of their techniques in solving limited problems within a larger enterprise system. Even a total enterprise is a subsystem of a larger system. And suboptimization within an enterprise may be better than no system optimization. Also, the use of a team of experts with various outlooks on a problem, while often useful, cannot be said to be essential in all cases.

The Essentials

Attempts have long been made to solve management problems scientifically, but operations researchers have supplied an element of novelty in the orderliness and completeness of their approach. They have emphasized defining the problem and goals, carefully collecting and evaluating facts, developing and testing hypotheses, determining relationships between facts, developing and checking predictions based on hypotheses, and devising measures to evaluate the effectiveness of a course of action.

Thus, the essential methods of operations research as applied to decision making may be summarized as follows:

1. The emphasis on models—the logical representation of a reality or problem. These may, of course, be simple or complex. For example, the accounting formula "assets minus liabilities equals proprietorship" is a model, since it represents an idea and, within the limits of the terms used, symbolizes the relationship among the variables involved.
2. The emphasis on goals in a problem area and the development of measures of effectiveness in determining whether a given solution shows promise of attaining the goal. For example, if the goal is profit, the measure of effectiveness may be the rate of return on investment, and every proposed solution will arrange the variables so that the end result can be weighed against this measure. Some variables may be subject to control by the manager; others may represent uncontrollable factors in the system.
3. The attempt to incorporate in a model the variables in a problem, or at least those which appear to be important to its solution.
4. Putting the model with its variables, constraints, and goals in mathematical terms so that it may be clearly perceived, subjected to mathematical simplification, and readily utilized for calculation by substitution of quantities for symbols.
5. The attempt to quantify the variables in a problem to the extent possible,

since only quantifiable data can be inserted into a model to yield a finite result.

6. The attempt to supplement quantifiable data with such usable mathematical and statistical devices as the probabilities in a situation, thus making the mathematical and computing problem under uncertainty workable within a small and relatively insignificant margin of error.

Of all these methods, perhaps the basic tool and major contribution of operations research has been the construction and use of conceptual models for decision making. There are many types of these. Some assert logical relationships between variables. Models may be referred to as "simulative" or "descriptive" if they are designed only to describe the relationship of elements in a situation. The models useful for planning are referred to as "decision" or "optimizing" models, designed to lead to the selection of a course of optimum action among available alternatives.

In order to construct a decision model, it is necessary to express in some kind of terms the goals sought, to set forth the relationships of the variables as they influence these goals, and then to express these mathematically to determine the optimum relationship of the factors in terms of goals.

In typical management problems, there are usually a large number of variables. In fact, in some problems the variables are so numerous and their relationships so complex as to defy mathematical expression. The use of a model is illustrated in the determination of the economic quantity of a product for a company to produce.[4] The major variables here are the requirements for the product for a year, the unit cost, the inventory carrying cost, the setup cost per order, and the order quantity. The model so derived, expressed in terms of the measure of effectiveness—economic order quantity—is as follows:

$$Qe = \sqrt{\frac{2RS}{I}}$$

where

Qe = economic order quantity
R = total yearly requirements
S = setup costs
I = inventory carrying cost per item

The experienced business planning analyst will recognize the ingredients of a decision model as those considerations he has long applied in coming to a recommendation for a course of action. He knows that in the process of evaluation, the various courses of action are weighed against the objectives sought. In fact, long before the term "operations research" came into use, the planning analyst constructed a model in the form of forecasts of costs, reve-

---

[4] For illustration of a large number of models and an explanation of model construction, see C. W. Churchman, R. L. Ackoff, and E. L. Arnoff, *Introduction to Operations Research* (New York: John Wiley & Sons, Inc., 1957).

nues, and profits. Even though he did not develop a mathematical formula and hence probably restricted his analysis to a small number of most attractive alternatives, he tested for profitability. He was also aware that, whatever the results of his quantitative tests, he had to temper his recommendations with consideration of intangibles. Indeed, this is the difficulty with many operations researchers. In order to make their model useful (to them), they may leave out certain critical intangible variables. This practice, especially if the omissions are not called to the attention of the practicing manager, has often led to distrust of the technique.

Procedure

Applying operations research involves six steps similar to those discussed in Chapter 6 on planning (see pp. 125–128).[5]

1. Formulate the problem   As in any planning problem, the operations researcher must analyze the goals and the system in which the solution must operate. That complex of interrelated components in a problem area, referred to by operations researchers as a "system," will be recognized as comprising mostly the environment of a decision and representing planning premises. This system may comprehend an entire business operation or be limited to planning production for presses and lathes. It is still, however, an interconnected complex of functionally related human or material components. Obviously, unless the problem is greatly simplified by rigorous application of the principle of the limiting factor, the more comprehensive the system, the more complex the problem.

Since the purpose of formulating the problem is to determine the optimum course of action from among various alternatives, measures of effectiveness, as well as goals, must be clearly defined. Moreover, in the typical operations research problem, it is desirable to take into account as many goals as necessary and feasible. For example, in a production and distribution planning problem, the decision maker will probably wish to minimize operating costs, minimize investment in inventory, satisfy a level of consumer service, and optimize the use of capital investments. To measure effectiveness in reaching these goals and to formulate the problem so that multiple objectives can be satisfied on a balanced optimum basis—particularly in the light of a variety of inputs—can become a very complex conceptual and computational matter. The simplest approach is to use certain goals as constraints by saying, for example, the goal is minimum costs while maintaining a certain fixed level of inventory or customer service.

2. Construct a mathematical model   The next step is to formulate the problem as a system of relationships in a mathematical model. For a single goal, where at least some variables are subject to control, the general form of the operations research model may be stated as follows:

[5] Churchman, Ackoff, and Arnoff, *op. cit.*, pp. 12–15. The authors have drawn much of their material for this section from this excellent book.

$$E = f(x_i, y_j)$$

where

E = measure of effectiveness of system
x_i = controllable variables
y_j = variables beyond control

The above model may be classified either as an optimizing model or a simulation model. When using it as an optimizing model, values inserted for the uncontrollable variables (y_j) and the controllable variables (x_i) are manipulated to optimize the measure of effectiveness (E). For example, suppose that a marketing manager wishes to optimize total sales dollars. His model to do so might include such uncontrollable variables as competitors' prices, gross national product, or price level changes; and his controllable variables might be comprised of such variables as number of salesmen, commissions allowed, his product prices, and advertising expenditures.

Although all models are intended to simulate reality, what are usually called simulation models are those where the user gives the model a set of values for the controllable variables and assumes a set of values for the uncontrollable variables. By using one or more sets of values for the uncontrollable variables (because often he cannot know them), he can compute various E's until he finds one that he believes to be satisfactory. In this event, of course, there is no way of knowing whether an *optimum* solution has been found. However, the visibility obtained can be very important. Often an optimizing model cannot be used because of lack of known input data, the difficulty of accurately simulating reality (at least the important elements of reality), and the fact that it may be very complex and difficult to build.

3. Derive a solution from the model   In arriving at a solution, there are two basic procedures. In the analytical procedure, the researcher employs mathematical deduction in order to reach, as nearly as possible, a mathematical solution before inserting quantities to get a numerical solution. This can be an exceedingly important contribution to complex decision making. Variables may be reduced or restated in terms of common variables. Certain variables (for example, sales) may appear in a number of places in a model and may be factored out or reduced. In other cases, a series of mathematical equations may be consolidated and simplified. The result of this analytical procedure is to place a complex series of relationships into as simple a mathematical form as possible. In addition, this analysis may disclose, mathematically, that certain variables are unimportant to a reasonable solution and may be dropped from consideration.

The second procedure is referred to as "numerical." In this, the analyst simply "tries" various values for the variables subject to control to see what the results will be and from this develops a set of values which seems to give the best solution. The numerical procedure varies from pure trial and error to complex iteration. In iteration, the analyst undertakes successive trial runs to approach an optimum solution. In some complex cases, such as the iterative procedures used in linear programming, rules have been developed to help the analyst more quickly undertake his trials and identify the optimum solution when it is reached.[6]

4. Test the model   Because a model, by its very nature, is only a representation of reality and it is seldom possible to include all the variables, models should usually be tested. This may be done by using the model to solve a problem and comparing the results so obtained with what actually happens. These tests may be carried out by using past data, or by trying the model out in practice to see how it measures up with reality.

5. Provide controls for the model and solution   Because a model, once accurate, may cease to represent reality, or the variables believed to be beyond control may change in value, or the relationships of variables may change, provision must be made for control of the model and the solution. This is done in the same way any control is undertaken, by providing means for feedback so that significant deviations can be detected and changes made. In many complex models, such as those used for production or distribution planning, the effect of the deviations must be weighed against the cost of feeding in the correction or against the usually greater cost of revising the entire program. As a result, the researcher may decide not to correct the model or the inputs.

6. Put the solution into effect   The final step is to make the model and the inputs operable. In anything but the simpler programs, this will involve revision and clarification of procedures so that the inputs (including control feedback information) are available in an orderly fashion, and this, in turn, often requires reorganization of an enterprise's available information. What many users of operations research have found as a major stumbling block is that no one is willing to undertake the hard work of revising the nature of basic information. Accounting and other data normally available in a company are often not adequate to the requirements of successful operations research. Many managers, intrigued with the possibilities of operations research, wish that some of the research effort of experts, now so widely employed in constructing elegant models, could be channeled toward information reorganization.

Other problems in putting the solution into effect involve getting people to understand, appreciate, and use the techniques of operations research; deciding such questions as what computing facilities to use and how, and how the information outputs are to be made useful and understandable to those responsible for decisions. In this connection, operations researchers would do the manager a real favor by frankly admitting the type and margin of uncertainty in their solution.

All this is to say that the operations researcher is not nearly done with his task when his model is reduced to paper and tested. Mathematical gymnastics may be interesting to the pure philosopher, but the manager must

[6] For a clear application of this procedure, as applied to the simplex technique in linear programming, see the explanation in *ibid.*, pp. 304–316.

make a responsible decision, and the operations researcher who would be useful to the manager must be more than a mathematical gymnast.

Operations Research and Simulation

Simulation through the use of models is sometimes regarded as one of the most powerful tools available for effective management planning and control. Not that simulation itself is new. Managers have long used it in training through role playing, teaching business policy through cases, and testing airplane models in a wind tunnel. War games long used by the military and the more recently popular business games are instances where individuals are given a kind of experience through simulating reality.

The technique of simulation through use of mathematical models and the computer not only is relatively new but has interesting promise for the decision maker. To the extent that a management problem can be reasonably simulated by the construction of a model, a manager can test the results of any proposed individual course of action that much better. As a consequence, no modern manager, faced with a difficult or complex decision, should overlook the possibility of simulation. Even with its limitations, it might show results of a decision which a manager had not anticipated, and this may be a great deal less costly way to experiment than through making decisions which are found later to have been monumental mistakes.

As in the case of any model, a simulation need not be mathematical. But, in the typical business problem, the important variables and constraints are usually so numerous and the relationships so complex that mathematics and the computer are normally necessary. The number of cases where simulation can pay off through inexpensive experimentation are numerous. To mention a few, it is relatively easy to test a program for inventory control, to experiment with proposed programs of quantity discounts, or to simulate a new production line. While active use of simulation appears to be only in its infancy, the advantages appear to be very great. Even if there are considerable uncertainties, intelligent simulation of a course of action can at least give a manager some visibility of the size and nature of risks entailed in his decision.

Special Tools

Although the construction of decision models is perhaps the central tool of operations research, it has been interesting that various mathematical and scientific techniques, generally developed in the study of the physical sciences, have had applications to the study of management problems.

Probability theory   This important statistical device is based upon the inference from experience that certain things are likely to happen in accordance with a predictable pattern. Thus, if a coin is tossed a hundred times, it is probable, although by no means certain, that it will fall heads fifty times. However, the deviations from such a probability are within a fairly predictable margin, and consequently the probability becomes a workable substitute for data otherwise unknown. In an enterprise problem, where probabilities can be substituted for unknowns, the margin of error in the solution, although not removed, is limited.

Game theory   Although far too complicated to describe here, this tool is based upon the premise that a man seeks to maximize his gain and minimize his loss, that he acts rationally, and that an opponent will be similarly motivated. Under these circumstances, game theory attempts to work out an optimum solution in which an individual in a certain situation can develop a strategy which, regardless of what his adversary does, will maximize his gains or minimize his losses. Even though the mathematical development of game theory has not proceeded beyond the stage of the most simple competitive situations and there is little evidence that it has been very useful in actual planning, future development of this theory may have a remarkable impact on the scientific approach to strategic planning in competitive situations.[7]

Queuing, or waiting-line, theory[8]   This theory uses mathematical techniques to balance the costs of waiting lines versus the costs of preventing waiting lines by increased service. It is based on the premise that, although delays are costly, the cost of eliminating them may be even more costly. One of its interesting applications, often used as an example, was the case of the New York Port Authority, which used queuing theory to solve a problem involving the number of toll stations at the entrance to bridges and tunnels.

---

[7] One of the most interesting and elementary expositions of game theory may be found in J. D. Williams, *The Compleat Strategyst* (New York: McGraw-Hill Book Company, 1954).

[8] For example, in the simplest example of a queuing system with one queue and one servicing station and where arrivals are random and reasonably described by the Poisson distribution, there exists a constant λ (independent of queue length, time, or any other property of the queue) such that the probability of an arrival during an interval Δt (where Δt is very small) is given by $\lambda \Delta t$. Or

Probability {arrival between time t and $t + \Delta t$} $= \lambda \Delta t$

If n is a discrete random variable representing the number of arrivals in a fixed interval of time T, the frequency distribution of n is described by:

$$\int T(n) = \text{probability } \{n \text{ arrivals in time } T\} = \frac{(\lambda T)_e^{n - \lambda T}}{n!}$$

Therefore, if T were to represent the distribution of intervals between arrivals (also a random variable), the density function for T or $g(T)$ would be an exponential distribution of:

$$g(T) = \lambda e^{-\lambda T}$$

Similarly, the probability of turning out a finished unit (*i.e.*, completing service at the station) in the interval Δt (where Δt is small) is given by the formula:

Probability {service completed between t and $t + \Delta t$} $= \mu \Delta t$

Where μ is a constant, then the random variable s, representing the time it takes to complete service in a unit, can be defined by the probability function

$$g(s) = \mu e^{-\mu s}$$

Through the application of this operations research device, the Authority found it could reduce waiting lines and, at the same time, reduce the number of toll stations.

Linear programming[9]   A technique for determining the optimum combination of limited resources to obtain a desired goal, linear programming is one of the most successful applications of operations research. It is based upon the assumption that a linear or straight-line relationship exists between variables and that the limits of variations can be determined. For example, in a production shop, the variables may be units of output per machine in a given time, direct labor costs or material costs per unit of output, number of operations per unit, and so forth. Most or all of these may have linear relationships, within certain limits, and by solving linear equations, the optimum in terms of cost, time, machine utilization, or other objectives can be established. Thus, this technique is especially useful where input data can be quantified and objectives are subject to definite measurement. As one might expect, the technique has had its most promising use in such problem areas as production planning, shipping rates and routes, and the utilization of production and warehouse facilities to achieve lowest over-all costs, including transportation costs. Because it depends on linear relationships and many decisions do not involve these or cannot be accurately enough simulated, newer and more complex systems of nonlinear programming have come into use.

Servo theory   This is another important contribution of operations research to management problems. Originally used in the design of automatic

---

For this simple single station, single queue model with Poisson arrivals (mean arrival rate λ) and exponential service times (mean service time μ), the probability of having n units in the system (i.e., in queue and being serviced) at any one time is given by

$$P_n = \left(1 - \frac{\lambda}{\mu}\right)\left(\frac{\lambda}{\mu}\right)^n$$

where $n \geqq 0$ and $\mu > \lambda$

A simple explanation of queuing theory may be found in many books. See, for example, M. Sasieni, A. Yaspan, and L. Friedman, *Operations Research: Methods and Problems* (New York: John Wiley & Sons, Inc., 1959), chap. 6.

[9] A linear program, in its general form, can be expressed as follows:
Objective function

$$P = C_1X_1 + C_2X_2 + C_3X_3 + \cdots C_nX_n = \text{Max}$$

Subject to

$$a_{11}X_1 + a_{12}X_2 + a_{13}X_3 + \cdots a_{1n}X_n = b_1$$

$$a_{21}X_1 + a_{22}X_2 + a_{23}X_3 + \cdots a_{2n}X_n = b_2$$

$$a_{31}X_1 + a_{32}X_2 + a_{33}X_3 + \cdots a_{3n}X_n = b_3$$

$$\vdots$$

$$a_{m1}X_1 + a_{m2}X_2 + a_{m3}X_3 + \cdots a_{mn}X_n = b_m$$

where $X_i \geq 0, i = 1, 2, \ldots n$

or remotely controlled systems (for example, the thermostat), the feedback principle, by which information is fed back to correct for deviations, has become an important aspect of control. The dynamic characteristics of problems emphasize the necessity for correcting for changes in the inputs in a mathematical model. The servo theory has important implications for managerial control.

Other Tools

There are, of course, many other tools of operations research. *Symbolic logic,* by which symbols are substituted for propositions or even programs, has led to a sharper analysis of complicated and sometimes ambiguous problems. *Information theory* has sharpened the evaluation of the information flow within a given system. *Value theory* assigns numerical significance to the value of alternative tangible choices. *Monte Carlo methods* put random occurrence in models, to simulate such occurrences as machine breakdown or customer arrivals.

Limitations

In the enthusiasm for the potentialities of operations research, its limitations should not be overlooked. So far, it has been used to solve only a fairly limited number of problems.

In the first place, one is faced with the sheer magnitude of the mathematical and computing aspects. The number of variables and interrelationships in many problems, plus the complexities of human relationships and reactions, apparently call for a higher order of mathematics than does nuclear physics. The late mathematical genius John von Neumann found, in his development of the theory of games, that his mathematical abilities soon reached their limit in a relatively simple strategic problem. However, it can also be said that managers are a long way from using the mathematics now available.

In the second place, although probabilities and approximations are being substituted for unknown quantities and scientific method is quantifying factors heretofore believed to be impossible to quantify, a major portion of important managerial decisions involve intangible factors. Until these can be quantified, operations research will have limited usefulness in these areas, and selections between alternatives will continue to be based on nonquantitative judgments.

Related to the fact that many management decisions involve unmeasurable factors is the lack of information inputs to make this tool useful in practice, even though the information desired might be obtained. By conceptualizing a problem area and constructing a mathematical model to represent it, variables are disclosed on which information, not now available, is required. What is needed is far more emphasis by those interested in the practical applications of operations research toward developing this needed information. At times it appears that if the same intelligence now devoted to the building of models and their mathematical manipulation were applied by specialists to developing information inputs, the application of operations research would be greatly accelerated.

Still another limitation concerns bridging the gap between manager and trained operations researcher. Managers in general lack a knowledge and appreciation of mathematics, as the mathematician lacks comprehension of managerial problems. This is being dealt with, to an increasing extent, by the business schools and, more often, by business firms that team up managers with operations researchers. But it is still the major cause of slowness in using operation research.

One of the outstanding specialists in operations research reported a few years ago in a rather pessimistic tone concerning the actual use of this important tool.[10] He had his graduate students write the authors of cases reported in the journal *Operations Research* over the first six years of its publication with a view to determining the extent to which recommendations of the studies had been carried out by practicing managers. He reported that there was not sufficient evidence in any case that the recommendations had been accepted. However, in recent years much more, but still fairly small, use is being made of this technique.

A final serious drawback of operations research—at least in its application to complex problems—is that analyses and the use of electronic computers are expensive, and many problems are not important enough to justify this cost.

Future Possibilities

The future of operations research applied to management decisions warrants enthusiasm. By introducing more effectively than heretofore the methods of the physical sciences into managerial decision making, operations research concentrates attention on goals, recognition of variables, search for relationships and underlying principles, and—through use of the model, advanced mathematics, and computation—on optimum solutions from many more alternatives than ever before possible. The analyst of a few years ago ordinarily could study only a few alternatives because of the sheer size of the analytical task. With operations research techniques and the high-speed electronic computer, he can analyze the probable results of thousands or millions of alternatives.

This implies a revolution in the planning activities of the future decision maker. The ultimate goal of operations researchers is to be able to formulate such complete policy or decision models that every aspect of a problem, every significant variable, every probability, and every related decision made or likely to be made will be included. It is even hoped by some that this will extend to important decisions at all levels in the enterprise.

This cursory examination of operations research indicates that it will continue to influence managerial decision making. By improving the quality of planning, it should likewise improve the quality of managerial control. In

[10] C. W. Churchman, "Managerial Acceptance of Scientific Recommendations," *California Management Review*, vol. 7, no. 1, pp. 31–38, at p. 33 (Fall, 1964).

fact, an increasing number of promising applications to planning and control systems are appearing. Some of these will be dealt with in Chapter 30. In the decades to come, managers cannot overlook this technique and the scientific attitude behind it, if they want to stay ahead in the competitive race.

On the other hand, it would be fatuous to believe that this means a new kind of management, a sort of management by mathematics and the machine. The limitations of operations research pointed out above must ever be borne in mind. It is a tool of management showing the way to decisions rather than making them and, like any other tool, an aid to, rather than a replacement for, managers.

NEWER APPROACHES TO DECISION MAKING UNDER UNCERTAINTY

Supplementing the systematic analysis of operations research in analyzing problems, a number of newer techniques have come into use to improve the quality of decision making under the normal conditions of uncertainty. Among the most important of these are risk analysis, decision trees, and preference theory.

Risk Analysis

Every intelligent decision maker dealing with uncertainty likes to know the size and nature of the risk he is taking in choosing a course of action. This is one of the deficiencies in using the traditional approaches of operations research for problem solving. Many of the inputs into a model are merely estimates, and others are based upon probabilities. The ordinary practice is for staff specialists to come up with "best estimates." But these might be like saying that the best estimate is that, on a given roll of the dice, the number 7 is more likely to come up than any other number, even though there is only a 1 in 6 chance that it will. Consequently, to give a more precise view of risk, new techniques have been developed.

Virtually every decision is based on the interaction of a number of critical variables, many of which have an element of uncertainty but, perhaps, a fairly high degree of probability. Thus, the wisdom of undertaking the launch of a new product might depend upon the critical variables of expense of introduction, cost of production, capital investment required, price obtainable, total market for the product, and share of market obtainable by it. A best estimate might be made that the new product has a high (say, 80 percent) chance of yielding a return of 30 percent on the total investment made in it.

But, suppose that further analysis of each critical variable shows that the introduction, operating, and investment costs each have a 90 percent probability of being accurate, the price estimate a 70 percent chance of being correct, and the market quantity estimate a 60 percent probability of being correct. In this case, the calculated probability of the entire program estimate being right would almost certainly be less than 80 percent; exactly how much less would depend upon the values of each variable and the extent to which probabilities less or more than 80 percent would affect costs or revenues. It can be said, however, that the probability of *all* the estimates of the various critical variables being correct is only 30.6 percent (.90 × .90 × .90 × .70 × .60).

Risk analysis attempts to develop for every critical variable in a decision problem a probability distribution curve. Usable ones can be derived by asking each specialist who estimated a variable to gauge what the range and probability of each variable is. For example, the sales manager might be asked to estimate what the probability would be of a selling price exceeding or falling below the best estimate, and by how much. No matter how judgmental these estimates might be, a range of values and probabilities will be better than a single "best estimate." With the aid of computer programs that have been developed, a range of expectancies for the "rightness" of any total estimate can be made.[11]

In the example of the new-product investment program noted above, the range of probabilities for a return on investment might turn out as follows:

Rate of return (percent)	Probability of achieving at least rate shown
0	.90
10	.80
15	.70
20	.65
25	.60
30	.50
35	.40
40	.30

Given such data as these, a manager is better able to assess the probability of accomplishing a "best estimate" and can see the chances that he might have if he is satisfied with a lesser return. He can also see that he has a 10 percent chance of even losing on his original investment and other costs on the project. Had the risk analysis shown a 50 percent chance of making the 30 percent return on investment, but a 25 percent probability of losing a considerable amount, he might even decide that undertaking the project would not be worth the risk.

Decision Trees

One of the best ways to analyze a decision, by seeing the possible directions that actions might take from various decision points, and the decision points relating to it in the future, is the use of what has been called "decision trees." Obviously useful because adequate information is seldom available to make a confidently accurate decision at a given time, the tree depicts future decision points and possible chance events, usually with a notation of the probabilities of the various uncertain events happening.

For example, one of the common problems that occurs in business is to decide, when a new product is introduced, whether to tool up for it in a major way so as to assure production at the lowest possible cost, or to undertake

[11] As an example of how this works out with investment analysis, see D. W. Hertz, "Risk Analysis in Capital Investment," *Harvard Business Review*, vol. 42, no. 1, pp. 95–106 (January–February, 1964).

cheaper temporary tooling involving a higher manufacturing cost but lower capital losses if the product does not sell as well as estimated. In its simplest way, a tree showing the decision a manager faces in this situation might be similar to that in Figure 9.3.

As can be seen, the tree shows the manager in what direction his chance events are and what their values in terms of profits and losses are for each of the two tooling alternatives. But it is not enough to give him the visibility he would like to have in order to decide between going for permanent tooling or more conservative temporary tooling. What is needed is an assessment of the probabilities of each course of possible events. If the probability that product sales will be as much as estimated is 60 percent, that they will be slow is 20 percent, and that the product may fail to sell is 20 percent, his decision can be greatly helped. Using these probabilities, we can see that there is a 60 percent chance that an investment of $2 million will yield $1 million per year for the assumed product life of five years and a similar chance that an investment of $100,000 will yield $300,000 per year. Taking into account these probabilities, the $2 million investment has a predicted worth of $600,000 per year for the five years of product life assumed and the $100,000 temporary tooling alternative a worth of $180,000 per year for five years. On considerations of rate of return on investment, only, the temporary tooling approach would seem to be preferable. But, depending on the availability of capital, a 30 percent return on $2 million over five years would normally be regarded as greatly preferable to a 120 percent return on $100,000 over the same years.

Figure 9.3 *Decision tree without probabilities.*

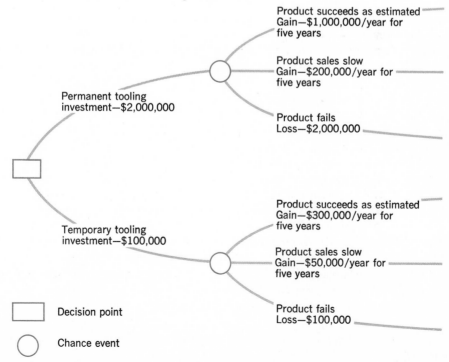

There is also the possibility that if we drew a decision tree for a longer period and took into account a further chance event such as that one or more competitors would enter the market, thus putting a squeeze on prices and volume, the larger investment would look ever so much better. With the same basic probabilities mentioned and the further probability that a vigorous competitor would enter the field, a more far-sighted and complete decision tree might look like that in Figure 9.4.

As can be seen, by calculating the value of each probability over a five-year assumed product life (and disregarding the cost of interest and the discounting of future income), the total probability-modified return on the permanent tooling would be $1,918,000 and on the temporary tooling $360,000. While on percentage return on investment the temporary tooling approach still looks better, the higher total profits expected plus the possibility of a product life exceeding five years and considerations of better meeting competition might indicate that the permanent tooling program would probably be preferred. Whether this course is taken, however, would depend in large part on the extent to which the decision maker might prefer to avoid the risk of investing $2 million before a product proved itself on the market.

As can be seen, as chance events increase, the decision tree becomes more complicated and the compounding of various probabilities makes the solution much more difficult. In many real life cases a computer may even be necessary to calculate them. Also, in real life, the tree would show various decision points in the future. For example, the firm might have open the option, in case it initially followed the temporary tooling approach, to invest later in permanent tooling (at the loss of the $100,000 for temporary tooling) if product demand justified doing so. Also, it might make a decision later to reduce price, adopt a new marketing strategy, or develop a substitute improved product.

What is significant about the decision tree approach is that it does several things for the alert and intelligent decision maker. In the first place, it makes possible seeing at least the major alternatives open to him and the fact that subsequent decisions may depend upon events of the future. In the second place, by incorporating probabilities of various events in the tree, it is possible to comprehend the true probability of a decision leading to results desired. The "best estimate" may really turn out to be quite risky.

According to a recent study, a fairly significant number of managers and companies have become interested in and have explored potential applications of decision trees.[12] However, only a few companies have apparently used this approach to any important extent for very long. Nevertheless, growing interest in it in recent years leads some to believe that its probable use presages a new era of sharper decision making. One thing is certain. Decision trees and similar decision techniques do force replacement of broad areas of judgment with focus on the critical elements in a decision, thrust into the open premises often hidden in judgment, and disclose the steps in reasoning by which decisions under uncertainty are made. Some executives, long accustomed to using broad judgment, even resent these methods because they do these very things.

[12] R. V. Brown, "Do Managers Find Decision Theory Useful?" *Harvard Business Review*, vol. 48, no. 2, pp. 78–89 (May–June, 1970).

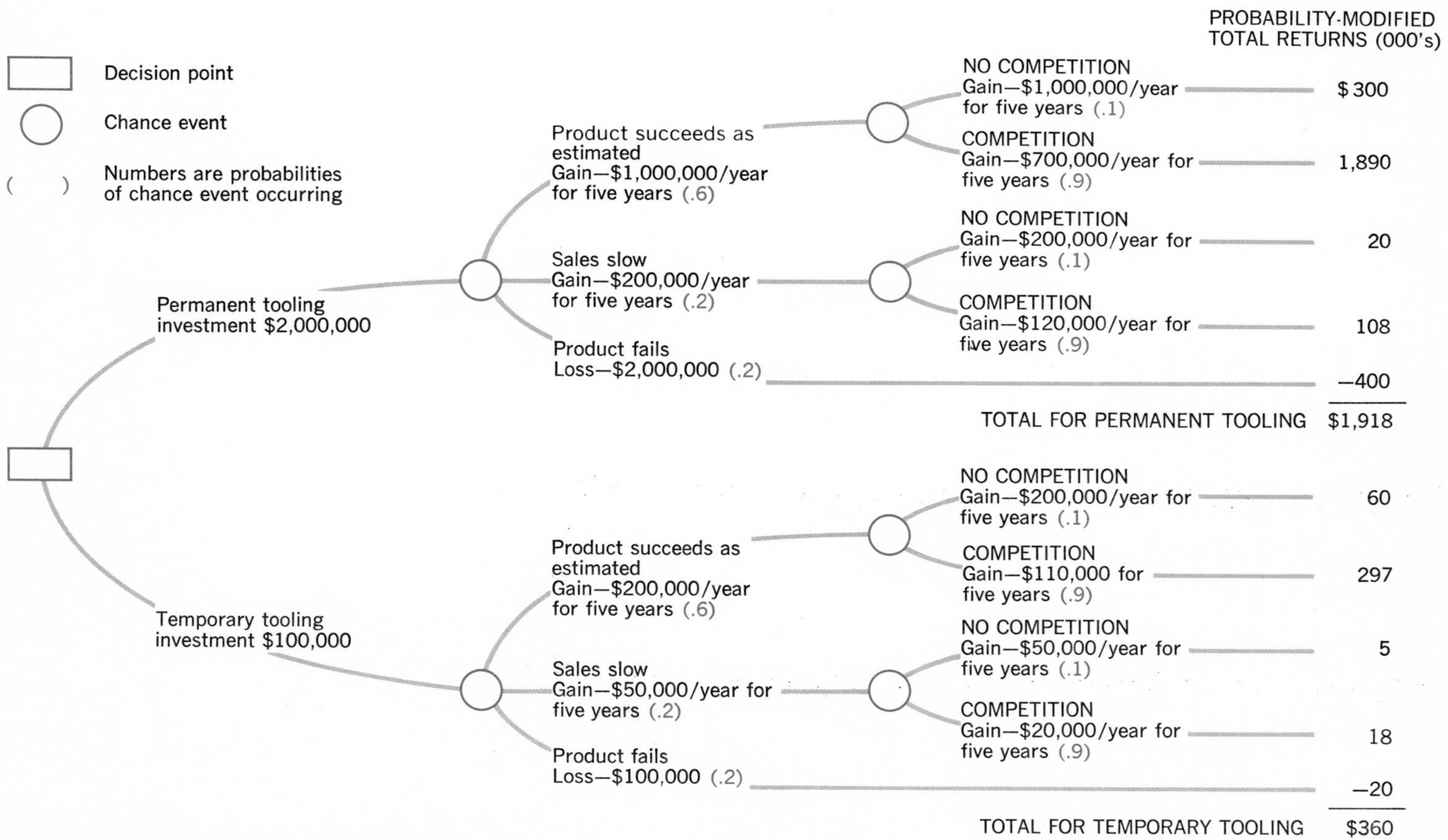

PROBABILITY-MODIFIED
TOTAL RETURNS (000's)

Decision point

Chance event

( ) Numbers are probabilities
of chance event occurring

Permanent tooling
investment $2,000,000

Product succeeds as
estimated
Gain—$1,000,000/year
for five years (.6)

NO COMPETITION
Gain—$1,000,000/year
for five years (.1) ——— $ 300

COMPETITION
Gain—$700,000/year for
five years (.9) ——— 1,890

Sales slow
Gain—$200,000/year
for five years (.2)

NO COMPETITION
Gain—$200,000/year for
five years (.1) ——— 20

COMPETITION
Gain—$120,000/year for
five years (.9) ——— 108

Product fails
Loss—$2,000,000 (.2) ——— −400

TOTAL FOR PERMANENT TOOLING $1,918

Temporary tooling
investment $100,000

Product succeeds as
estimated
Gain—$200,000/year
for five years (.6)

NO COMPETITION
Gain—$200,000/year for
five years (.1) ——— 60

COMPETITION
Gain—$110,000 for
five years (.9) ——— 297

Sales slow
Gain—$50,000/year for
five years (.2)

NO COMPETITION
Gain—$50,000/year for
five years (.1) ——— 5

COMPETITION
Gain—$20,000/year for
five years (.9) ——— 18

Product fails
Loss—$100,000 (.2) ——— −20

TOTAL FOR TEMPORARY TOOLING $360

Figure 9.4 *Decision tree with probabilities.*

Preference Theory

One of the interesting and practical supplements of modern decision theory is the work that has been done and the techniques developed to supplement statistical probabilities with analysis of individual preferences in the assumption or avoidance of risk. While referred to here as "preference theory," it is more classically denoted "utility theory." Purely statistical probabilities, as applied to decision making, rest upon the questionable assumption that decision makers will follow them. It might seem reasonable that if a person had a 60 percent chance of a decision being the right one, he would take it. But this is not necessarily true, since the risk of being wrong is 40 percent and a manager might not wish to take this risk, particularly if the penalty for being wrong is severe, whether in terms of monetary losses, reputation, or job security. If anyone doubts this, he might ask himself whether he would risk, say, $40,000, on the 60 percent chance that he might make $100,000. He might readily risk $4 on a chance of making $10, and gamblers have been known to risk much more on a lesser chance of success.

Therefore, in order to give probabilities practical meaning in decision making, we need better understanding of the individual decision maker's aversion to or acceptance of risk. This not only varies with people, but it also varies with the size of the risk, the level of managers in an organization, and whether the funds involved are personal or belong to a company.

Higher-level managers are accustomed to taking larger risks than lower-level managers, and their decision areas tend to involve larger elements of risk. A company president may have to take risks of great size in launching a new product, in selecting an advertising program, or in selecting a vice-president, while a first-level supervisor may have his risk taking limited to hiring or promotion of low-skilled workers or approving vacation times for his subordinates.

Also, it can hardly be denied that the same top managers who may make a decision involving risks of millions of dollars for a company in a given program with a chance of success of, say, 75 percent, would not be likely to do that with their own personal fortune, at least unless it were very large. Moreover, the same manager willing to opt for a 75 percent risk in one case might not do so in another. Furthermore, a top executive may go for a large advertising program where the chances of success are 70 percent, but might not decide in favor of an investment in plant and equipment unless the probabilities for success were higher. In other words, attitudes toward risk vary with events, as well as with people and positions.

While we do not know much about attitudes toward risk, we do know that some people are risk averters in some situations and gamblers in others, and that some people have by nature a high aversion to risk and others a low one. The typical risk or preference curve may be drawn as in Figure 9.5. This set of curves shows both risk averter's and gambler's curves as well as what is referred to as a "personal" curve. The latter, of course, implies that most of us are gamblers when small stakes are involved but soon take on the role of risk averters when the stakes rise.

Since most managers, understandably influenced by the dangers of failure, tend to be, to some extent, risk averters and do not, in fact, play the aver-

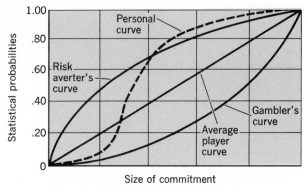

Figure 9.5 *Typical preference curves.*

ages, it can be readily seen that statistical probabilities are not good enough for practical decision making. Indeed, as one researcher pointed out after having studied business executives' attitudes toward risk, "Our managers are not the takers of risk so often alluded to in the classical defense of the capitalistic system."[13]

Although it may be true that too many managers are risk averters and thereby miss opportunities, the fact is that few are players of pure statistical averages, at least in important decisions. Therefore, risk preference curves should be substituted for statistical probabilities in decision trees. This can be done, at least roughly, by assessing a manager's willingness to take risks in a variety of real or hypothetical situations and by developing a preference curve for him. But even if this is not done systematically, there is certainly an important advantage for those who recommend a course of action to their superior to be aware of the effect of his attitude toward risk in his decisions.

EVALUATING THE DECISION'S IMPORTANCE

Since the manager must not only make correct decisions but must make them as needed and as economically as possible, and since he must do this often, guidelines to the relative importance of decisions are useful. Decisions of lesser importance need not require thorough analysis and research, and they may even safely be delegated without endangering an individual manager's basic responsibility. The importance of a decision also depends upon the extent of responsibility, so that what may be of practically no importance to a corporation president may be of some importance to a section head.

Size or Length of Commitment

If a decision commits the enterprise to heavy expenditure of funds or to an important personnel program, such as a program for management appraisal

---

[13]R. O. Swalm, "Utility Theory—Insights Into Risk Taking," *Harvard Business Review*, vol. 44, no. 6, pp. 123–136 (November–December, 1966).

and training, or if the commitment can be fulfilled only over a long period, it should be subjected to suitable attention at an upper level of management.

Flexibility of Plans

Some plans can be easily changed; some have built into them the easy possibility of a future change of direction; and others involve action difficult to change. Clearly, decisions involving inflexible courses of action must carry a priority over those easily changed.

Certainty of Goals and Premises

If goals and premises are fairly certain, a decision resting on them tends to be less difficult than where they are highly uncertain.

Quantifiability of Variables

Where the goals and inputs, parameters and variables can be accurately quantified, as with definite inputs in a production machine shop, the importance of the decision, other things remaining the same, tends to be less than where the inputs are difficult to quantify, as in pricing a new consumer product or deciding on its style.

Human Impact

Where the human impact of a decision is great, its importance is high. The decision should be rated up in terms of importance, since no action contemplated for a group of people can afford to overlook its acceptance by the group.

THE POLITICS OF DECISION MAKING

Politics has been defined as the art of the possible. A good manager must be sensitive in his decision making to what he *can* do. It is not enough that a decision be logical and point to the best way of reaching a goal. The beliefs, attitudes, and prejudices of people must often be taken into account.

A few years ago, in one of the nation's major defense companies, the top management approved a commercial research project, largely to assuage the feeling of key scientific and engineering personnel that weapons development was unsocial and offered little long-range security to the enterprise. Further study disclosed both lack of resources to complete the project and a large commercial company already entrenched in the field. Faced by these facts, the board of directors decided to abandon the project but the president considered abandonment unthinkable without adequately preparing the people involved. Following a program for providing complete information on the project and on the available alternatives to a committee of the key people involved, the president was able to obtain their unanimous support for abandoning the project, when *they too* saw the practical logic of doing so.

The political environment of decisions thus rests largely on communication and is favorable when everyone is well informed about his particular planning area. While the "need to know" has limits, the limits should be set as broadly as company or national security and the costs of information will permit. Much carping at the "stupidity" of decisions is eliminated when they are explained to people affected by them. Furthermore, such information helps the subordinate manager make implementing decisions.

Political problems of decision making often disappear with widespread participation in planning. The widest possible participation—whether in the form of consultation, contribution of analyses, or whatever—is the best assurance that good decisions will be reached and plans intelligently and enthusiastically administered.

FOR DISCUSSION

1. Why is experience often referred to not only as an expensive basis for decision making but also a dangerous one? How can a manager make best use of experience?
2. In a decision problem you now know of, how and where would you apply the principle of the limiting factor?
3. Taking the above decision problem, whether the variables are quantifiable or not, apply operations research methodology to it in as simple form as you can. What does this do for your understanding of the problem? Does it help you solve it?
4. Take the decision problem and draw a decision tree for it.
5. Could you conceptualize an operations research problem in broad terms without the use of mathematics?
6. "Decision making is the primary task of the manager." Comment.
7. How does risk aversion affect your own life? Given a situation, can you draw your preference curve?

10
strategies and policies

It is ever the history of a burgeoning science that no sooner has it begun to clarify the principles and concepts that rest upon a generally accepted theory than new theory is introduced. In the end, fortunately, the science is the beneficiary. This process is currently characteristic of planning theory. For some years, and after much travail, the term "policy" was fairly well understood. Then, the game theorists began to use the term "strategy," with the result that management literature now is thoroughly confused about its meaning and its relationship to policy.[1]

There is, of course, no reason to modify the definition of policy. It remains a guide to the thinking and action of those who make decisions. It does not actively require action, but is passively present to guide managers when they are faced with future decisions. As will be recalled, the essence of policy is the existence of discretion. Strategy, on the other hand, concerns the direction in which human and physical resources will be deployed and applied in order to maximize the chance of achieving a selected objective in the face of difficulties. Thus, the authors of this book see a strategy as a decision about how to use available resources to secure a major objective in the face of obstruction. The obstruction is usually thought of as competitors, but it may be public opinion, legal status, taboos, and similar forces; therefore these barriers apply to monopolies and governments as well as competitive enterprises. Strategy also implies action and guides decision making, but, unlike a policy, it spells out directions that will be taken.

Strategy may exist without a policy. For example, a college president may have a policy of enforcing disciplinary regulations, but his strategy is to wait until enforcement is demanded by taxpayers. The waiting strategy is not likely to be embodied in policy (it is much too specific and perhaps short-run in ap-

[1] Cf. George A. Steiner, *Top Management Planning* (New York: The Macmillan Company, 1969), pp. 237–239.

plication). Policy and strategy may be coextensive. For instance, a business policy may be to distribute through retailers. The strategy is the same, but it implies that action involving resource allocation to implement policy will be taken when the timing is right.

Seen in this light, policies and strategies furnish the framework for plans by channelling decisions and often predeciding them. The more *strategies and policies are clearly understood, the more consistent and effective will be the framework of enterprise plans.* If this principle were really followed in practice, consistency in action and efficiency in the employment of resources would replace much conflict and dissipation of resources. A company, for example, that has a major policy of developing only new products that fit its marketing organization will avoid having energies and resources applied by people working on new products that do not meet this test.

It is sometimes said that there is a policy level of management and an administrative or operating level. This is not strictly true. Policy making is not reserved for top management. To be sure, the higher a manager is in the organization structure, the more important his role in policy making is likely to be. This is understandable since the purpose of policies is to guide subordinates' decision making. Even though managers at lower levels mainly carry out policies furnished by their upper-level superiors, they may also make policies, however limited they may be, to guide themselves and their subordinates.

SOURCES OF POLICIES AND STRATEGIES

To understand the nature of policies and strategies, it may be useful to analyze their sources. These may be classified as originated, appealed, implied, and externally imposed.

Originated

The most logical source of policy or strategy is that originated by top management for the express purpose of guiding subordinates in their operations. Originated policy or strategy flows basically from the objectives of the enterprise, as these are defined by the top executive authority. These may be broad in scope, allowing key subordinates to give them clearer definition, or they may be promulgated so completely as to leave little room for definition and interpretation. The extent to which they are centralized or decentralized is obviously dependent upon the extent to which authority is concentrated or dispersed.

Characterizing a policy, or strategy, as originated does not necessarily imply that it is imposed by command. Many are the adroit managers who originate policy and obtain compliance by making unobtrusive suggestions. In fact, some skillful managers originate policy and secure compliance by allowing a subordinate manager to leave a conference believing that he himself originated it. But often a policy or strategy is imposed upon subordinates with a force and clarity that permit no deviation. Thus, a company president might originate a policy of using sales agents on a commission basis, rather than full-time salesmen, by merely making indirect suggestions along this line to his sales manager; or, in another instance, he might be positive and blunt in stating a policy that the company will not engage in sharp dealings to make a sale.

Appealed

In practice, perhaps most policy and even some strategies stem from appeal of exceptional cases up the hierarchy of managerial authority. If an occasion for decision arises for an executive who does not know whether he has sufficient authority or how this matter should be handled, he may appeal to his superior. As appeals are taken upward and decisions made on them, a kind of common law is established. Precedents develop and become guides for future managerial action.

Policies or strategies developed from appeals are sometimes incomplete, uncoordinated, and confused. If decisions are made on a given set of facts, without regard for their possible effects on other aspects of the operation, or if unintended precedents develop from them, the resulting policies may not guide the thought and action of subordinates as really desired by top managers. Moreover, policies, or even strategies, about which the top executives do not even know may be formulated.

The aimless formulation of policy or strategy arising from appeals explains in part why it is usually so difficult to know exactly what ones exist. As analysts have come to find out in attempting to compile policy manuals, many managers simply do not know company policy in many areas. This arises partly because policy formulation is by nature complex, but it also arises because many managers dislike to meet issues until forced to do so and thereby delay policy making until a body of precedent from individual decisions accumulates.

Appealed policy may be foresighted and internally consistent, especially if the manager realizes that his decision constitutes policy. However, when he finds himself constantly making policy by appeal, he might well ask himself whether he has left too large an area of policy making to chance and whether his subordinates have understood the policy he has formulated.

Implied

It is not unusual for policy and even strategy to develop from actions which people see about them and believe to constitute policy. Employees will readily understand what is real policy if they work for an enterprise that may have published policies to produce high-quality goods, to maintain plant cleanliness, or to promote from within, and yet permits the contrary action. Its real policies, or the lack of them, are implied.

Different circumstances account for the development of implied policy. It may be that stated policy is simply not enforced. It may be that the enterprise states a certain policy in order to create a desired image but is unable or unwilling to enforce it. It is suspected that in most cases implied policies develop where no clear policy exists. Decision makers will adopt their own guidelines as they interpret the actions of their superiors.

For example, the top managers of a company earnestly solicited new product ideas, especially from its marketing and engineering groups. The response was generous. Each idea was subjected to complex investigatory procedures and judged by conservative standards. Most were rejected and no explanations were made. Even key people in the firm came to believe that it was company policy to confine new products to low-risk items. This imputed policy, which was quite contrary to what the firm really wanted, became the guideline for new product decisions.

Externally Imposed

To a rapidly increasing extent, policy or strategy is being externally imposed by government, trade unions, and trade associations. Whether in the form of direct regulation, or the competition of government-owned or government-supported business, or the many conditions for accepting government aids or contracts, the result is to circumscribe and dictate many aspects of policy. Strong national unions, operating through collective bargaining and detailed labor contracts, have also imposed policy upon the manager. Besides, thousands of local, regional, and national associations have their effect in varying degrees on policy. Other social groups—such as church, school, fraternal, social, and charitable organizations—also mold or dictate policy.

DEVELOPING STRATEGIES

In order to develop practical and useful strategies, a business or other enterprise should engage in a thorough self-appraisal. A business, for example, should recognize its strengths and also know its weaknesses. It should first ask what kind of company it is. Is it a single product or product-line company, such as automobiles, shoes, or furniture? Or is it a process company, such as certain chemical and electronic companies? Or is it an end-use company, such as transportation, communications, or defense? Just what kind of company is it? This is not the easiest question to answer, as the glass bottle manufacturers found a few years ago when they awakened to find themselves in the broader liquid container field, or as the steel companies have only recently learned (or at least some of them) that they are in the structural materials industry.

A corporate self-appraisal will, of course, take into account products, markets, and technology. But it cannot overlook also the values, aspirations, and prejudices of those top managers who control it. What do these men want? Growth? Security? Increase in stock prices? Status?

After an objective self-appraisal, the next questions that should be asked have to do with the company's opportunities in the market it has before it and whether it can shore up its weaknesses by hiring certain new executives, by acquiring other firms, or otherwise. One company with limited capital and with a sales volume of less than 1/25 of that of any of its three competitors in a highly competitive commercial field saw that the chink in the armor of its much larger competitors was their reliance on a marketing strategy that required preselling through heavy advertising expenditures. This much smaller company developed a counterstrategy of selling equally high quality products at a much lower price and with higher profit margins to retailers, but with very low sales promotion and advertising expenses. It succeeded because it recognized its own weakness, saw an opportunity growing out of the strengths of its much larger competitors, and took vigorous action.

Self-appraisal involves, then, asking the right questions. Effective strategy is knowing and capitalizing on one's strengths, while avoiding weaknesses, then attempting to match these appropriately with opportunities.

Even some very intelligently managed companies fail in this area. An interesting case was the Elgin National Watch Company in the 1950s. Seeing their watch business increasingly fall to Swiss imports, they naturally looked for opportunities for diversification. They identified their company's strengths as precision, quality, and integrity and made attempts to diversify into the high-precision industrial instrument and electronics fields. But they overlooked their greatest strength of all—a nation-wide direct marketing organization leading into every jewelry and department store in the country—and underestimated their inability to market instruments and electronics in a fast-growing field with which they were unfamiliar. While their idea of diversification was sound, the product strategy underlying it was doomed to failure, mainly because of a failure to diagnose correctly their strengths and weaknesses.

It is interesting and somewhat ironic that, while Elgin was fighting a losing battle in its ill-conceived diversification, U.S. Time Corporation made a huge success in the watch business. It did so with a new product and marketing strategy, the introduction of Timex, a low-priced throw-away watch!

STRATEGIES AND POLICIES: PRODUCT

To illustrate the nature and impact of strategies and policies, a few major areas applicable to the typical business firm have been selected. Among these are strategies and policies having to do with: (1) product, including not only the selection and development of product but also its pricing and marketing; (2) production; (3) finance; and (4) personnel and public relations. While all may be referred to as policies, the reader will be able to see that some, such as the type of product or product line and marketing, have elements that justify classifying them also as strategies.

Obviously, one of the major strategy and policy areas is that having to do with management. The extent to which a company successfully decentralizes authority, its strategy on management development or compensation, the extent of participation in decision making, or the formality and thoroughness with which planning is done are all important strategy and policy areas. But because they are really the subject of this book they are not dealt with separately here.

Product Expansion Strategy

The strategy a company develops for its product expansion can be critical to planning. One company may develop an intensive strategy, not going beyond its basic product line but either attempting to get more of a market share or developing new markets that it had not been in, such as Reynolds Aluminum did when it went aggressively into the consumer field. Or a company might follow an intensive strategy by changing its present products to fit different markets, as has been done by the automobile manufacturers and the soap and detergent companies.

Another basic direction a firm might take is an extensive product strategy. This could involve going into more vertical integration through making more of its parts and components or expanding into retailing. Another prominent kind of extensive strategy is to go into products using existing skills, capacities, or strengths. Lever Brothers, for example, has followed this kind of strategy to a considerable extent by developing products that fit its established competence of marketing to grocery stores.

Still other companies have followed conglomerate diversification by going into products not necessarily related. In some cases, such as Boise Cascade, the products have some relationship by being largely aimed at the broad housing and home market. In others there has seemed to be no perceptible product strategy.

Product Selection and Development

This is perhaps the most important single area of a company's strategy and policy. Its part in decision making largely determines the kind of production facilities and organization required, greatly influences and is influenced by marketing, gives shape to the financial problems involved in a company, and has much to do with many other policy areas.

Product policy and strategy have to do with (1) selecting items and product lines, (2) developing and producing the items and lines, or services, (3) determining pricing, and (4) selecting marketing strategy. Of course, there are many attendant considerations, such as those dealing with the availability of financing, the effect of the product on the organization, hiring and training of necessary labor, purchasing of material, and acquisition of facilities. Also included in this area are policies dealing with expected profits, fitting the product into product-line strategy, and the compatibility of the product with the firm's know-how, facilities, material sources, and distribution channels. Even though prospective profit may be of primary concern, these other factors cannot be overlooked.

Because of recognition that products must be developed to supply a market and product design and engineering are part of this, a company will usually insist that its scientists and engineers develop products to fit a certain market, and this may require the product to be designed to a certain price or quality objective. Or, product development policy might extend to organization, requiring—as many military contracts do—product engineering to be set

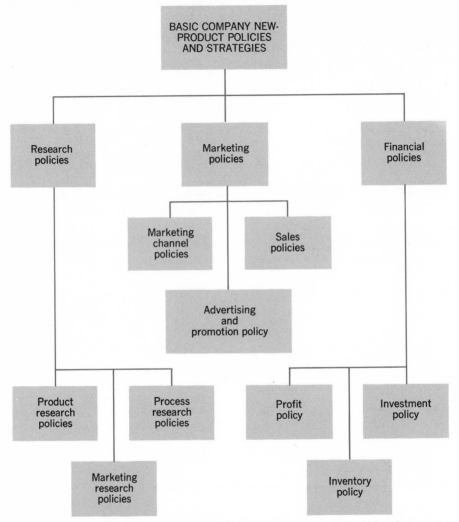

Figure 10.1 *The hierarchy of policy and strategy in new-product development . . .
Policy generally exists in layers. For instance, basic company new-product policies
or strategies are most often determined by top management. These, in turn, may affect or generate research policies, marketing policies, and financial policies. If top
management does not itself generate derivative policy, managers at lower levels may
develop policies governing product research, marketing research, advertising, and
so forth. Basic company policy must be so logical and clear that derivative policy
can be easily formulated.*

up under a project manager with authority and budget necessary to oversee the product from original concept, through preliminary design, to final
engineering.

Other policies may require a development group to work closely with
materials suppliers, to obtain engineering help from them; or they may require close liaison between development engineers within a company and

production engineers, to assure the utmost of economic production potential in the final design. Or—as with General Motors' profit-oriented concept of a "family of cars"—styling policy may dictate that the product developed—in this case, cars—emphasize commonality of parts and tooling between different makes. Except for the relatively few cases of basic research where only the most general of guidelines are given, technical developments tend more and more to be placed under policies that will assure low costs and market acceptability for the new product. Pouring money into research and development without practical guidance is no longer countenanced in the effective development of products.

Pricing

Pricing policy includes not only determination of base prices but also schedules of discounts and price differentials between products in a line. With product differentiation, pricing policy has become a key instrument of sales policy. However, even in these cases and despite the existence of price leeway, the pressure of competition is such that prices even of differentiated products must bear a close relationship. Despite imperfections in competition, there are few companies that do not feel in formulating pricing policy the aggressiveness of existing or potential competitors.

Price policies vary in many ways. One company may have a policy of never undercutting competition; another may have a policy of always selling below competition. One company may have a policy of selling at fixed price; another may have a policy of selling on a cost plus basis; other companies may have both policies, applying one to a given line of products and another to a second line, the applications depending upon such environmental factors as the market and the risk involved in design and production. One company may have a policy of distributing nationally at one price; another may have a policy of varying prices between regions, depending on costs of delivery and regional competition. One company may have a policy of giving the utmost in quantity discounts; another may have a policy opposing such discounts. But virtually all companies have considerable policy imposed on them by the rigorous application of price discrimination laws of the federal and state governments.

Moreover, pricing is often an instrument of sales promotion. If a firm's policy is to appeal to the mass market, price structure can make customers see the firm as a low-price source of goods and services. But the firm whose policy is to appeal to the prestige market will use price to enhance this appeal. Thus, a certain retailer handling high-grade men's clothing has a policy of selling suits at $100 or $150 and not at $99.95 or $149.95.

Sales Promotion

Promotion policies may have to do with pricing, or with advertising, packaging, distribution, grading, sampling, or many other activities. But promotion goes far beyond the more obvious methods of selling.

A company's reputation for a good product, good service, or fair dealing may be sales promotion considerations. In the oil-drilling business, for example, it is well known that the availability of materials and supplies is more decisive than price, for a rig idled for lack of pipe or a drilling bit is very costly. As a result, supply houses and equipment manufacturers offering adequate field service and inventories get the business, regardless of small differences in price. Likewise, such apparently remote factors as a good market for resale materially affect sales, as indicated in the passenger automobile business.

Distribution Channels

In industries such as drug manufacturing, distribution channels are fairly clear-cut. In other industries, the use of jobbers, wholesalers, and retailers with fixed discounts is so standardized that little question of policy arises, aside from which distributors to select and how to sell them. But to many businesses, the selection of distribution channels presents difficult policy decisions. For example, a small laboratory equipment manufacturer had the choice of distributing by way of direct customer inquiry, field salesmen, manufacturers' agents, or established jobbers.

Policy on distribution channels is sometimes hard to change, once established. It is not easy to expect a very great change in practices affecting use of dealers to distribute automobiles, or advertising to sell proprietary drugs, or many other long-standing methods of doing business. On the other hand, certain types of enterprise—among them the chain stores, the supermarkets, many of the farm cooperatives, and the discount houses—have revolutionized distribution channels and methods.

STRATEGIES AND POLICIES: PRODUCTION

As with product, there are many strategy and policy considerations connected with production, major examples of which follow.

To Buy or to Make

A policy question continually facing management is whether to buy or make a product or component of a product. Not only the small firm but many larger ones decide to buy a product or component rather than to tool up their own facilities for making it; in some cases, this decision is based on the specialized nature of the facilities or know-how required. Many of the larger firms do not, for example, do their own casting; others farm out their forgings; and many contract their screw-machine work. Furthermore, items that typically go into many products—such as steel and aluminum shapes, electric motors, wire, transistors, gears, bearings, and many others are ordinarily purchased from companies specializing in them.

What would guide a company in the direction of buying rather than making its product? Obvious answers include lack of facilities or technique or lack of capital to expand into a particular new field. Other answers include timing, since a company might not be able to engineer a product, remove the "bugs," and get into production in time to take advantage of a market. Or a company might not wish to make a heavy commitment of capital and labor until it had amply tested the market. Furthermore, there are many products which a specialized or smaller company can make more efficiently than a more integrated larger company. In addition, especially as businessmen mistrust the stability of boom conditions, they may prefer not to have their capital so heavily committed. They may buy flexibility in planning, with a policy of buying rather than making.

Size of Run

The size of the production run, where a company has an adequate backlog of orders, will normally be dictated by the economics of producing at capacity. But where, as is more usually the case, the company must produce on speculation for future sale, efficiency through large-volume operation runs the risk of creating an inventory too large either to finance or warehouse. Thus, the costs of tooling up for a run must be set against the risks of overstocking. At this point, of course, a reliable sales forecast can be the determining factor, although often competitive forces and the economics of volume production require a company to take the risk of overstocking in order for costs and prices to be low enough to meet competition profitably.

Production Stabilization

Difficult policy decisions also arise in connection with timing production to market demands without upsetting stabilization of operations. The demand for many products is highly seasonal, and almost every product is subject to some demand variability. Some companies deal with this by merely producing to order. Other companies assume the risks of changing demands and price levels by producing for inventory. Still other companies make fill-in products, perhaps less profitable ones, to take up the slack of off-season facilities or labor.

In service companies, such as transportation businesses, however, cyclical demands have a serious effect on costs. An unfilled boxcar or passenger seat is a perishable product and cannot be carried in inventory, with the result that operational stability and cost saving cannot be obtained by inventorying product. In such companies, there is usually no choice but to operate at times with unfilled or idle equipment and unused labor and at other times with unfilled or deferred demands. These peaks and valleys have been reduced somewhat by policy decisions in other areas, such as the sales policy of offering reduced family fares by air, or off-season fares, or encouraging people to take off-season vacations.

Inventory

Many production policies tie closely to inventory policy, and planning the economical level of inventories is one of the key decision areas of business.

Inventories must be high enough to make products available as needed by the customer and as required by competition. And yet, too high inventories increase the cost of doing business and greatly magnify the risk of loss from price declines, or from changes in style, technology, or demand. Inventory size may also be influenced by the economics of production runs and will necessarily be limited by the financial capacity of the company.

Although the general principles governing inventory policy are fairly clear, the actual policy of a given company at a given time is not so simple. In one business, the time required to procure or make products may be a month, while in another it may be a year or, as with airplanes, three to five years. In one business, the customer may be willing to wait for months for a product, while in another, if the product is not immediately available, the sale will be lost. In one business, the market may be stable in terms of both demand and price; in another, both demand and price level may be mercurial. In one business, the inventory may be highly perishable; in another, everlasting.

STRATEGIES AND POLICIES: FINANCE

The controlling importance of the financial aspects of business enterprise is recognized at many points in this book. A company's capital, whether furnished by its owners or borrowed, sets the limits to expansion and provides the means for obtaining those assets necessary to business operation. As with sales and production, policy making is much involved with financial considerations.

Capital Procurement

Policies dealing with capital procurement depend to a very great extent upon the size of the business and the willingness of its owners to draw upon outside capital. In developing policy for the procurement of capital, owners of a business must resolve a number of issues. Assuming that a realistic estimate of future capital requirements is available, policy questions arise as to the extent to which equity capital will be solicited from the public or from sources outside the principal owners. This raises questions, particularly for the small enterprise, about danger in the loss of control.

Furthermore, since a large portion of the ordinary company's funds comes from reinvesting profits, a policy question arises as to the extent to which profits should be retained or disbursed. This, in turn, raises numerous questions of dividend policy. The question of borrowing also requires decision. Should the firm's assets be mortgaged or otherwise pledged against loans? If so, upon what basis, with what kind of lender (bank, private lender, insurance company, factoring company, or other), for what term, with what provision for repayment, at what interest rate, and with what restrictions on operating and financial practices?

For smaller corporate enterprises of all kinds, there is normally little room for decision as to capital structure. Long-term borrowing is usually out of the question, and the owner of the small business is generally limited in his capital expansion to obtaining funds through resources of himself and friends (and this seldom goes far, for even friends, investing any sizable amount of equity capital, want control commensurate with their investment) and through such working capital borrowing as may be obtained through commercial banks or factoring companies.

Cash and Depreciation Allowances

Perhaps the largest single source of cash for going enterprises in recent years is the funds held in the business through depreciation reserve accounting. Although it is customary in business to speak of spending depreciation cash, every accountant realizes that depreciation charges do not *make* cash. A depreciation charge is a noncash expense, unlike most other expenses, and cash expenses are, therefore, overstated to the extent that depreciation (in addition to certain other noncash expenses) is charged. In other words, depreciation is a proper charge against earnings and is a real expense, but, because it is merely a write-down of asset values, it requires no cash outlays. Obviously, if the company takes in no cash beyond that for cash expenses, neither depreciation allowances nor book profits will give rise to cash. However, in most businesses, it is both accurate and customary to conclude that cash available from operations, even though used to finance such assets as receivables and inventories, is equal to book profits plus noncash expenses, notably depreciation.

The extent to which companies depend on cash "generated" through depreciation charges is indicated by the fact that many firms have relied on this source for a major portion of their capital expenditures. Consequently, in any policy having to do with capital sources, the reinvestment of funds arising because of depreciation charges plays a major role. Because of special tax dispensations in recent years, which have allowed accelerated depreciation, and because most businesses are anxious to accrue depreciation allowances as fast as possible, depreciation policy questions strike at the heart of capital planning.

Working Capital

Working capital is generally defined as the excess of current assets over current liabilities and is thus that portion of current assets which has been supplied by the permanent investors of the business. Since assets are regarded as current if it is expected that they will be converted into cash in the normal course of the business (usually defined by accountants as within one year), and since liabilities are current if they will be liquidated in the same period, working capital becomes a measure of the ability of the business to meet its obligations. Adequate working capital, particularly that portion available in cash, is thus the first requirement for maintaining credit, meeting obligations promptly, and avoiding bankruptcy. It is the ability of the firm to pay its bills when they are due that assures continuance as a going enterprise, and not the size of the firm's surplus account, as many businesses have come to find out when a lack of liquid assets forced them to the wall.

Working capital requirements and policies vary between companies. The electric utility company with regular cash collection needs less working capital than the manufacturer of expensive specialized machines. The company operating on a strictly cash basis will require less than a similar enterprise with predominantly credit sales. The company with the short-production cycle will need less than a similar company with a long-production cycle. These and other differences, then, affect seriously working capital policies.

Among the working capital problems that firms face are the extent to which current assets should be held in cash or easily marketable securities, the nature and liquidity of receivables and inventories, the nature and immediacy of current liabilities, creditor discounts, and other questions. Of course, of paramount significance are the size and adequacy of working capital and its variability as business operations expand or contract and as collections vary. Working capital policy understandably has a strong relationship to the firm's policy on credits and collections.

Working capital policies are also closely related to policies concerned with bank borrowing and the maintenance of a line of credit. The amount of credit line will reflect business variations, and the adequacy of invested working capital will be an important consideration in planning for periods when the firm can "clean up" its bank borrowings. Banks usually like to see credit used only for cyclical swings in working capital needs and not as a permanent source of these funds.

Profit Disposition

Every firm must make policy decisions in connection with the disposition of profits. In the closely held company, this may be no problem, since the requirements of expansion and the desire to reinvest earnings, as well as the tax advantage of not paying dividends to well-salaried insiders, may make the policy choice clearly one of maintaining profits in the business. But in the typical large enterprise whose stock is widely held, difficult questions may arise. If the company wishes to develop an investment reputation for its stock, it may favor regular dividend payments. Even in this case questions arise as to how high dividends should be or what portion of earnings should be distributed in dividends. Or if a company prefers to rely on growth to make its stock attractive in the market, it will favor a policy of reinvestment of profits and the distribution of little or no earnings. Some investors even regard cash dividends as a sign of weakness in a "growth" company, an indication that it cannot profitably use its cash in the business. Clearly, the desirability of one policy or another will depend upon a number of factors, including (1) the desires of the stockholders, (2) the company's plan, if any, to raise additional funds through further stock flotations, (3) other available sources for obtaining capital, (4) the urgency of the need for additional capital, and (5) the profits possible from reinvesting the company's earnings.

STRATEGIES AND POLICIES: PERSONNEL AND PUBLIC RELATIONS

Company management must strive for loyal, intelligent, competent, and enthusiastic subordinate managers and employees. Therefore, in most companies, the largest group of policies is concerned with personnel. In addition, since the company must live and prosper within a community and since what the community thinks of it may greatly affect its success, it must develop a careful policy of public relations.

Personnel Selection and Training

Selection and training are at the base of personnel policies. They involve a number of policy questions such as the following: In filling vacancies at the lowest rank, how much testing, interviewing, and other measurement should be taken of the prospective employee? Or should selection be rather casual, with a policy of ruthlessly weeding out the unfit after a short probationary period? What shall be the minimum educational requirements? How much experience or training should be required of an applicant, or should the company do its own training? Should company training be extensive, and, if so, through classroom procedures, conferences, committees, on-the-job coaching, or rotation through jobs? To fill positions of higher rank, should the firm adopt an ironclad policy of promotion from within or one of open competition from within and outside? What should be the policy on hiring relatives of present employees? Should religious, geographical, marital, or other personal factors be weighed in the selection or promotion of employees?

Compensation

Personnel policy gives rise to serious questions involving compensation, whether in terms of wages, profit sharing, bonuses, or other types of financial remuneration. These questions arise not only in connection with the absolute amount of the compensation, but also with the comparative amounts paid on jobs on the same general level, and with the relation of this compensation to pay scales vertically throughout the organization. Other questions arise as to the method of arriving at the compensation and the method of paying it.

Most companies adopt the policy of paying competitive wages and salaries, that is, equal to those paid by other companies employing the same skills in the same community. In the first place, such payments will probably attract the necessary personnel. In the second place, by not paying more, costs can remain competitive. Furthermore, as labor organizations have gained power and contracts are concluded with large national unions, wage scales among nonmanagerial employees approach uniformity in given industries. However, many companies purposely adopt other policies when union or industry pressures permit them to do so. Some companies have adopted high pay policies to attract more competent workers, to lower costs by reducing turnover and increasing morale and efficiency, or to thwart union organization.

Employee Benefits and Morale

Personnel policy includes many decisions regarding employee benefits and other devices for improving morale: questions on vacations, sick leaves, leaves of absence, retirement pay, company cafeterias, and working conditions. In addition, most companies face policy questions of the extent and nature of recreational and social activities they should furnish, the kinds of insurance they should offer and how much the employee should pay, the kind of medical services they should offer, and the nature of employee publications. These questions require not only basic policy decisions on the extent to which the company should develop and support each program, but also detailed policy decisions on the nature of each portion of the program. Since many employees dislike the paternalistic approach in personnel programs—especially when they believe that the costs replace wages to which they might otherwise be entitled—intelligent top management should carefully guide policy in these areas.

Union Relations

Since the rise of national unionism, under the protection of the National Labor Relations Act of 1935, many policy considerations are beyond a manager's discretion. But there still exist some policy questions in union relations. A basic question has to do with the attitude of the company toward its labor organizations. In most cases, management has decided that a cooperative attitude saves trouble and money. In some cases, management has all but abdicated its leadership role, relying on union organization to serve as the primary channel of communication between the workers and the managers. But in most cases where employees are organized, the company has insisted, as a matter of policy and practice, on continuing an effective communication with employees.

In handling grievances, some companies adopt a policy of allowing almost any grievance to go through all established channels to an impartial arbitrator set up by the company-union contract. In these cases, the managers through whose hands the grievances go do little more than hear them and keep records. In other companies, however, there has been a fairly effective policy of encouraging managers at the very lowest levels to settle grievances, so that the grievance machinery is used only in the truly exceptional case. Of course, company policy in handling grievances is affected by union policy. Some unions seem to prefer pressing grievances to the utmost, while others obtain settlement at the lowest organizational level possible.

Public Relations

Public relations policy making has become one of the major preoccupations of the typical chief executive. From a bygone attitude of secrecy and reticence, modern business policy has become one of aggressively informing the public.

This policy has been furthered by another, that of news releases, speeches, and participation in outside functions by managerial personnel. Such control is designed to obtain a unified public relations program to ensure that the company presents the public image it desires.

In general, public relations policies of recent years have had certain definite manifestations. More complete and accurate financial and other information have been published. Businesses have taken a lead in supporting local and national charitable, educational, and other organizations. Management personnel has been encouraged to participate in community affairs and even to take governmental posts or run for political office. In more and more ways, business management has properly come to regard its job not only as that of offering a good product or service at a fair and profitable price, but also as that of making the public understand the importance of business to the community.

GUIDELINES FOR EFFECTIVE STRATEGIES AND POLICIES

All companies have strategies and policies, whether they are written or unwritten, sound or unsound, followed or not followed, understood or not understood, complete or incomplete. It is virtually impossible to delegate authority without the existence of policy, since a subordinate manager cannot make decisions without some kind of guidelines.

It is surprising that so many companies neglect this powerful tool of management. Many companies do not have policy manuals, and of the increasing number of companies that do, many manuals are not kept up-to-date and the majority of them contain a mixture of policies, rules, and procedures. On the basis of analysis of a considerable number of policy manuals issued by well-managed companies, the authors have not been impressed with their quality or usefulness. And in companies without manuals, the fact that policy has not even been published is probably evidence that its formulation and use have serious shortcomings.

There is not space here to describe all the ways of making strategies and policies effective, but certain guidelines can be set down.

Strategies and Policies Should Contribute to Objectives and Plans

If strategy or policy does not further plans or make enterprise objectives more attainable, it has not done its job. No manager should ever be able to say: "There's no good reason why we do it, it is just our policy!"

Strategies and Policies Should Be Consistent

An obvious point, true, but often violated in practice. For instance, an ineffective sales program would surely result if the promotion for a product were based upon both a strategy of product differentiation through heavy advertising and a strategy of vigorous price cutting.

Strategies and Policies Should Be Flexible

While many policies and some strategies are, in effect, permanent, it should never be assumed that they represent natural laws engraved on stone. If goals, premises, or major plans change, strategies and policies should be reconsidered to meet the new situation.

To be flexible as the situation changes is not to be casual in application. Strategies and policies should not be regarded lightly and disregarded on slight pretext. This does not mean that exceptions should never be made. It is sometimes impossible to make them cover all conditions. But if either a strategy or a policy must be disregarded often, there is indication that it is not sound, is not applicable, or too tightly circumscribes a manager's area of discretion.

Policies Should Be Distinguished from Rules and Procedures

Careful distinction should be made between policies, rules, and procedures. This is not recommended to be petty in the semantics of management but because the understanding of this distinction is important to managerial functioning. The major criticism the authors have of company so-called policy manuals is that they are often a mishmash of policies, rules, and procedures.

Some policies are rules and not recognized as such; other so-called policies are really procedures designed to channel action, not thinking. The correct separation of these three types of guidelines is important to good planning, workable delegation of authority, and even good human relations, and it can be accomplished.

Policies Should Be in Writing

Managers sometimes fear that written policies will lead to rigidity and lack of creative aggressiveness and will spoil a feeling of free teamwork. Other managers feel that policies must be so general or vague that they cannot be written. In companies without written policies, the position has often been that memoranda and bulletins which incorporate policy make formalized written policy unnecessary. While some top managers still oppose written policies, the attitude toward them has changed considerably in recent years.

If policies are to be used, they should be written. Putting a policy in writing does not make it clear, but a policy that cannot be put in writing is, at best, an unclear one. The difficulty of communicating intentions and desires is reduced by more precise communication in writing. Furthermore, the very act of writing policies has a way of eliminating fuzziness and inconsistency. As one major management consulting firm has summarized the importance of writing policies:[2]

---

[2] As stated by Booz Allen and Hamilton, Inc., and quoted by Louis Cassels and Raymond L. Randall in "Written Policies Help Nine Ways," *Nation's Business*, vol. 47, no. 12, pp. 84–87 (December, 1959).

It builds on proved decisions of the past, conserving executive energy for new decisions; it creates an atmosphere in which individual actions may be taken with confidence; it speeds administration by reducing repetition to routine; it supports consistency of endeavor across a large group through the years. It stabilizes the enterprise. It frees top management so that more creative consideration can be given to the problems of today and the new programs of tomorrow.

In other words, putting policies in writing is the best way of putting them to work.

Policies Should Be Taught

Written policies must be explained, interpreted, and taught. What people do not understand they cannot use correctly and are likely to distrust. No top manager may assume that the issuance of a written policy is enough. He must see that questions regarding it are answered and that subordinates comprehend its goal and why it has developed.

Strategies and Policies Should Be Controlled

Because strategies and policies have a way of becoming obsolete and because they may be misinterpreted or may not accomplish their purpose, they must be controlled. To undertake this kind of control takes talent that companies are often unwilling to assign to the task. It is truly a top-management job. Administrative assistants and other staff personnel, unless on a high level in the company, cannot be expected to do it. One of the best programs of strategy and policy formulation and control that the authors have seen was carried out by a vigorous senior executive, nearing retirement. Not only did he have skill in writing and in teaching subordinates, but he was also thoroughly familiar with the company's operations and history and had the valuable experience and connection of having served on its executive committee. His qualifications give an idea of what it takes to properly assess, express, teach, and control strategies and policies.

FOR DISCUSSION

1. Select a policy in an enterprise with which you are familiar and, after determining that it is a policy, attempt to trace how it originated.
2. It has been found that most middle managers are anxious for a business firm to develop and publish clear policies. Can you see any reasons why this should be the case?
3. Should policies be permanent or subject to ready change?
4. Is policy making properly only the task of top managers in an enterprise?
5. How would you go about formulating a company's strategies or policies?
6. Are strategies and policies as important in nonbusiness organizations as in business enterprises?

11

making planning effective

When a plan is complete—with proper assignments made and understood—and it enters the phase in which the manager checks on actual execution, the function of the manager becomes one of control. But, as has been repeatedly emphasized, in practice these managerial functions blend into a single whole. The shift to control may be imperceptible, as exemplified in budgeting. Budget making is planning, while budget administration—the follow-up of planning—is control. Even in the course of planning, some follow-up is necessary; managers on each level of organization must make sure that their subordinates make and integrate derivative plans. Obviously, coordination of plans must precede their proper execution.

COORDINATION OF THE PLANNING PROGRAM

To coordinate plans, the manager must make sure that derivative plans are consistent with and timed properly to support objectives and other decisions involved in a major plan. He must also set clear goals and clearly delegate authority, because people can only perform when they know what is expected of them and what their area of discretion is.

Even so simple a plan as that to select a new piece of factory machinery may require many subsidiary, or derivative, plans. Arrangements must be made for its purchase, its shipment, and its payment; for the receipt, unpacking, inspection, installation, use, and maintenance; plans have to be ready so that it will be properly located and have the necessary power supply; production schedules must be modified, cost standards changed, and probably still other things must be done in connection with the installation and operation of the machine.

Managers seem often to forget how complex derivative planning is and how many delegations of authority must be geared into its making and execution. A great advantage of some of the new planning and control systems is that they force managers to consider these intricacies. Some of these new systems are discussed in Chapter 30 in connection with control. While such programs as PERT (Program Evaluation Review Technique) are often thought of as control programs, their real significance is in connection with planning, for they reflect basic principles of planning. For example, in one fairly simple project that one of the authors observed, the complex of derivative plans was so intricate that the project manager could not carry them in his head; the relatively simple problem of installation of a machine to make plastic bottles involved thirty-two distinct but closely related decisions necessary to coordinate derivative plans.

Timing

Since the planning process is a complex of many major and derivative plans, and since plans are necessarily related to one another, it is important that they fit together, not only in terms of content and action but also in terms of timing. The principle of timing, then, reflects the fundamental truth that *the more plans are structured to provide an appropriately timed, intermeshed network of derivative and supporting programs, the more effectively and efficiently they will contribute to the attainment of enterprise objectives.* Part of the importance of planning premises is to assure proper timing in fitting plans together. What is sometimes overlooked in planning is that timing is horizontal as well as vertical. Thus, a retirement plan must be timed vertically by properly meshing with requirements for funding, insurance reserves, calculating benefits, and giving effect to past service. The plan must also be timed horizontally by being coordinated with plans for financing, for layoffs and leaves of absence, and for profit sharing.

Timing is one of the most difficult problems of business planning, especially in assembly-line operations, where an entire operation may be held up for lack of a single small part. Sometimes, the need for timing is not apparent—as in working out an organization plan, initiating a personnel program, or planning a sales strategy—yet the costs of poor timing even in these areas may be considerable.

PLANNING COMMUNICATION

The often-encountered failure to plan by managers at all levels is frequently not caused by inability or unwillingness to plan but rather by lack of knowledge concerning the firm's objectives, its planning premises, its major policies, and those plans made at higher levels in the organization structure which necessarily affect a subordinate's area of planning. An uninformed manager or employee is almost sure to be an ineffective one, no matter how sincere his wish to play well his position on the team. One reason production planning has been so well done in most American firms is that factory supervisors and their employees understand clearly what they are required to do.

The Planning Gap

Because of the practical difficulties of furnishing adequate information, because many managers do not understand the importance of planning communication, and because internal security is often necessary, the typical enterprise develops what might be called a planning gap. The top executives understand the company's goals and policies, and the workers in the shop understand what they are expected to accomplish in a day's work, but there exists a gap between the top and bottom in which managers do not understand how their departmental goals and policies tie in with those of the enterprise as a whole. In one large, well-managed company, a survey of the top fifty executives immediately under the vice-presidential level disclosed that their most pressing need was for knowledge of top-management plans. If this gap was that bad in the second level of command, one wonders how serious it was at lower levels.

Planning Communication

The best planning occurs when everyone has access to complete information affecting the area for whose planning he is responsible. This implies that objectives, premises, policies, plans of others—whether superiors or colleagues—and other pertinent information which clearly affect their planning should ideally be available to all managers concerned.

Information should be as specific and thorough as possible. The person executing a plan will do his best if he understands his own assignment and the plan in its entirety—including its objective, the general and specific means of attaining it, and the jobs others are expected to do. In many cases, however, this is clearly impossible. The foreman in a large chemical plant can hardly expect to know top-management strategy in developing a new synthetic, the chemical engineering involved, how the finance department is making available capital funds, the tax planning, or the accounting procedures. There are limits to the information any manager or employee can gain concerning a specific plan. But the existence of limits in relation to time, capacity to absorb knowledge, requirements of security, or other factors should not prevent top management from providing as much information as possible to help managers plan well. They should know, if at all possible, how their decisions contribute to major goals and plans.

Another problem of communication lies with the manager who interprets and explains plans to his subordinates. Often, halfhearted or even belligerent conformity to a management policy or program by employees results from their lack of understanding. Much of the carping at the stupidity of the "brass" for a given policy or program might be eliminated by supplying employees with adequate information. Experience in many companies has shown that the gain of having a well-informed group of managers and employees offsets any losses —often greatly exaggerated—caused by a competitor's learning details of a plan. On the contrary, the authors have seen many cases where the competition knew a company's "secrets" but its employees charged with accomplishing a plan were uninformed.

PLANNING PARTICIPATION

The best planning is done when managers are given an opportunity to contribute to plans affecting the areas over which they have authority. A good way of assuring adequate knowledge of plans, with the extra dividend of loyalty to them, is to have as many managers as possible participate in planning. Plans are more likely to be enthusiastically and intelligently executed under these circumstances.

Extent of Participation

The informed manager should be encouraged to contribute suggestions which may be valuable to his superior. Another kind of participation sometimes possible to effect is that of consulting with managers in advance about plans they are to execute. Clearly, also, each manager participates by making the plans necessary for his department. This is especially true in setting the objectives for which he is responsible.

Participation in all planning affecting a manager's area of authority, through his being informed, contributing suggestions, and being consulted, leads to good planning, loyalty, and managerial effectiveness. Yet one may ask how, in a large plant, the hundreds of foremen and superintendents, sales and other managers *can* be consulted. One cannot imagine the top managers of the Ford Motor Company, for instance, consulting with their thousands of subordinate managers on plans for a new line of cars.

Means

Even so, there are means for wider participation by subordinate managers in planning for their departments. As was pointed out in the earlier discussion of management by objectives, participation of subordinates with superiors is a key element in making this program work. Not only does this improve the quality of objectives and their contribution to the superior's goals, but it also elicits clarity in planning and a sense of commitment in the subordinate. A planning staff, which spends time with key subordinate managers in developing plans and encourages these managers to discuss the plans with their subordinates, is another means of increased participation. In some companies, this practice has produced excellent results.

Planning committees are a further means. Although committees have limited administrative use, their appropriate establishment at various levels and points of the organization structure can improve communication by transmitting planning information, by eliciting suggestions, and by encouraging participation. They must be skillfully handled to avoid wasting time, but they can pay handsome dividends in helpful advice, improved understanding of objectives and programs, and loyalty.

Another means of increasing participation is what has been called "grass roots" budgeting. Instead of a budget for operations or capital expenditures being prepared at the top or departmental level, the smallest organization units prepare their budgets and submit them upward. Naturally, to be effective, these units must be aware of objectives, policies, and programs which affect their operations, must above all be given clear planning premises, and be furnished factors enabling them to convert work load into requirements for men, material, and money. If these budget requests are reviewed and coordinated by departmental management, and if the budget makers are required to defend their budgets, this means of planning participation becomes real and purposeful. There probably exist no greater incentive to planning and no stronger sense of participation than those created in developing, defending, and selling a course of action over which the manager has control and for which he bears responsibility.

Still another helpful means employed successfully in some companies is the management club, an organization of all members of management, from the president to the foreman, which, in a large company, may be broken up into divisional or territorial clubs. At a specified number of meetings during the year the company president or a team of top managers conducts a meeting at which the planning and thinking of this top echelon are candidly reported to the club, and questions answered. The authors have noted that in several companies where this device has been tried, the lower-management group has responded avidly and gained a strong feeling of unity with top management. Even the dullest financial matters thus become vital, and the most complicated plan interesting. What many top managers overlook is the simple fact that the rank and file of managers have a strong interest in enterprise planning, because their work is of paramount importance in their lives.

No means of encouraging participation in planning will replace managerial deficiencies in other directions. The strength of top leadership, the example given to subordinate managers, clear delegations of authority, careful job descriptions, proper training, and competent direction and control cannot be replaced by any system of communication and participation.

LIMITS TO PLANNING

Limits to planning are not so great as to reduce seriously the possibility of making complete and adequate plans and should not interfere with bending every effort to plan. Nevertheless, awareness of them can remove many of the frustrations and inefficiencies of planning.

Difficulty of Accurate Premising

A limiting factor in planning is the difficulty of formulating accurate premises. Since the future cannot be known with accuracy, premising must be subject to a margin of error. Fortunately, this disability can be narrowed as forecasting techniques advance and as an enterprise gives more attention to the total environment of plans.

One way of reducing the risks involved in future uncertainties is to have alternative sets of premises and alternative plans based on them, so that unexpected circumstances can be readily reflected in action. Another is to be ready with detours in planning to allow for unforeseeable events. The latter provides flexibility which may take the form of utilizing plant facilities for an operation not originally intended, such as shifting an advertising program in accordance with a revised sales policy, or changing radically a product line.

Such flexibility is, however, possible only within limits. In the first place, an enterprise cannot always put off a decision long enough to make sure of its rightness. In the second place, built-in flexibility may be so costly that the probable benefits are not worth the expense. Or, a company may keep so financially liquid in preparing for the right opportunity that the advantages may be in substantial measure offset by missing opportunities for expansion.

Problem of Rapid Change

Another limiting factor in planning arises from social dynamics. In a complex and rapidly changing industry, the succession of new problems is often magnified by complications that make planning most difficult. The planning problem in the first few years of expansion in the aircraft industry during World War II—when the growth of the industry from that of a few small businesses to that of very large companies was coupled with an exceptionally complex and rapidly changing product—was almost beyond comprehension.

Essentially the same kind of difficulty has existed in many other enterprises. The growth of the electronics industry after 1948, the space program expansion in the 1960s, and the space and defense slowdown in the 1970s are noteworthy examples of highly dynamic situations in which planning has been exceedingly difficult. One might contrast planning in these areas with that of such stable businesses as a local water utility in New England or a flour mill in Minneapolis. Although all businesses are subject to some change, the degree of instability and complexity caused by social dynamics varies considerably from industry to industry and among firms within an industry.

Even in a dynamic industry, however, many problems are of a recurring nature. In every new problem, there may be the same elements, and a well-developed pricing formula may apply to widely different situations. Likewise, problems of manufacture and utilization of plant and machinery may have common elements despite differences in product. If the *common elements* in problems are sought out and separated, planning in a dynamic situation can be simplified.

Internal Inflexibilities

Major internal inflexibilities that may limit planning are related to human psychology, policies and procedures, and capital investment.

Psychological inflexibility   One of the important internal inflexibilities is psychological. Managers and employees may develop patterns of thought and behavior sometimes hard to change. A company may be so imbued with a tradition for operating flamboyantly or expensively that a program of retrenchment is difficult. For example, necessity for production at any cost in many war plants developed a psychological point of view difficult to over-

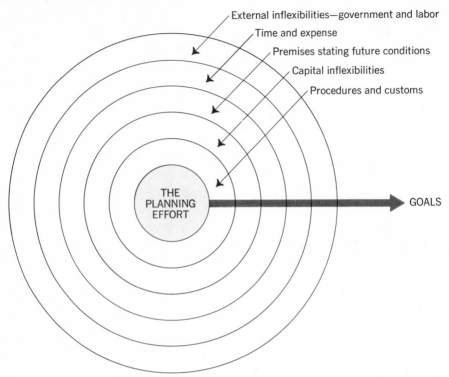

External inflexibilities—government and labor
Time and expense
Premises stating future conditions
Capital inflexibilities
Procedures and customs

THE
PLANNING
EFFORT

GOALS

Figure 11.1 *Limitations on planning effort. . . . A manager's plans are directed at achieving goals. But a planning effort usually encounters limitations, hemming in the planning effort. Procedural inflexibilities within the enterprise often make it difficult to plan efficiently. Investment in fixed capital tends to limit a manager's area of choice. Premises usually present a whole series of limitations. Time and expense required for effective planning are also limiting elements. And there are many limitations imposed on managers by external factors such as government regulations and labor rules.*

come in the more cost-conscious eras. Also, the attitude engendered by excess-profits taxes—that a dollar of expense was really only eighteen cents—became a serious threat to the efficient operation of many businesses.

In other cases, particularly in old, established businesses, people develop patterns of thought resistant to change. Managers and employees may eschew new methods, new products, and organization changes. Or, close government regulation may bring about an attitude of running the business so as to avoid breaking the law rather than to seek efficiency.

Managers are often frustrated in instituting a new plan simply by the unwillingness or inability of people to accept the condition of change. This is a difficult planning limitation to overcome. To do so requires patient selling of ideas, careful dissemination of information, aggressive leadership, and intentional development of a tradition of change among the members of the organization.

Policy and procedural inflexibility   Closely allied to psychological inflexibilities are those inherent in policies and procedures. Once established, these become ingrained in the enterprise, and changing them becomes difficult. A way of doing things, a chain of reports or invoices, or the routine of employees in following out procedure may often be hard to modify. During World War II, an aircraft company developed from a small operation to one of fourteen divisions and some 200,000 people. Procedures, paper work, and controls were developed for this large, far-flung operation. When the war ended and the company shrank to two divisions and 25,000 people, the wartime procedures lingered on. So drastic was the change in scale that a complete revamping of procedures was needed for guiding research and development, manufacture, and servicing of customers. Yet this would have required major overhaul of many aspects of operations and was believed to be impracticable.

One of the most convincing evidences of bureaucracy, whether in business or government, is the existence of complicated procedures designed to avoid mistakes. Progressive planning requires an environment of change, with some reasonable degree of freedom and willingness to assume the risks of mistakes; this is prevented in an enterprise bound by the strait jacket of policy and procedural inflexibilities.

Capital investment   In most cases, once capital is invested in a fixed asset, the ability to switch courses of future action becomes limited, and the investment itself becomes a planning premise. Similar inflexibilities also exist where investment is sunk in items other than what is normally regarded as fixed assets. An investment in training of a particular kind or in building up a certain customer reaction to a product—through advertising, packaging, or otherwise—may become sunk. Unless the company can reasonably liquidate its investment or change its course of action or unless it can afford to write off the investment, these irretrievable costs may block the way of change. Although it may be a good axiom to disregard sunk costs in planning, their existence does influence planning.

External Inflexibilities

The manager has little or no control over external inflexibilities, because they are related to the social, technological, geographic, and economic environment. Whether these are subject to fast or slow change, they do stand in the way of planning. Three major external inflexibilities are briefly described below.

Political climate   Every enterprise, to a greater or lesser degree, is faced with inflexibilities of the political climate existing at a given time. If the local, state, or national government actively regulates business, or if the national government adopts a high tariff or otherwise restricts trade, this must be taken into account in planning. Tax, antitrust, and fair trade policies also cause inflexibilities. Moreover, the basic attitude of government, as reflected in investigations of business practices, has significant effects. Furthermore, now that government has become business's largest customer, the procurement policies and programs of government agencies may cause rigidities in planning.

Labor organization   The existence of strong unions, particularly those organized on a national basis, tends to restrict freedom of planning. The numerous wage- and working-condition provisions of union contracts and the influence of union policies on employee productivity and attitudes must be taken into account. In addition to being important environmental influences, they often give rise to definite inflexibilities. In the railroad industry, for example, management and unions entered into agreements in 1936, providing specific restrictions in the form of dismissal compensation and preservation of job rights. These agreements have been given the standing of law by the policy of the Interstate Commerce Commission of requiring such labor safeguards as a condition for approval of combinations or abandonments. The more recent resistance of the railroad brotherhoods to elimination of unneeded firemen and changing obsolete rules is also a case in point.

Technological change   The rate and nature of technological change also present external limitations upon planning. There are perhaps few things as unyielding as the state of technological development. Not that technology does not change. It, of course, changes rapidly, and one new development begets another. But at any given time, the status of technical progress is relatively inflexible. The full use of the solution to a technical problem that has been solved may depend upon solution of a problem that has not been solved. In developing an electronic fire-control system, for example, guiding a projectile toward a target may be well understood and it may be possible to engineer the necessary circuits, but inadequate development of a single component may delay accomplishment of the entire plan.

Time and Expense

The effort that could be spent on forecasting, evaluation of alternatives, development of derivative plans, or other aspects of planning is almost limitless, the only effective brake being the cost to the firm and the time available to the manager.

From the standpoint of expense, the underlying principle applicable to planning is simple: no firm should spend more on planning than the value of the expected benefits. But the application of this principle is more complex, for a manager cannot easily know how much planning will be worth its cost. There are useful guides to planning expense, however.

In the first place, a large firm can almost certainly engage in more thorough planning than a small one, because the ratio of planning expense to operating expenses or to capital resources will be small.

In the second place, the more detailed planning becomes, the more expensive it will surely be. In modern engineering and production planning, a small project may receive the same attention as a large one. One of the authors recalls a project, undertaken by a large aircraft manufacturer, in which a minor modification of an airplane took some 3,000 man-hours of engineering and production planning for a job requiring 50 direct man-hours, when, had the job been done on a relatively unplanned basis, the planning time could have been reduced to some 30 man-hours, with only a doubling of the direct man-hours involved.

In the third place, the further into the future plans are projected, the more costly they are likely to be. If long-term forecasts are to be more than informed guesses and if long-term plans are to be worked out more than in outline form, the cost of investigation and of fitting plans together, with a tolerable margin of error, is likely to be high.

In addition to the restriction placed on planning by sheer expense, available time is a limiting factor. There comes a time when a decision must be taken, a course selected, and plans translated into action. Whether ready or not, the management may be forced to move. However, adequate planning done well in advance reduces the occasions when the manager may be forced into snap decisions under the pressure of crises or the necessity for fighting business fires.

ESTABLISHING A CLIMATE

In a period of change and world-wide rivalry, planning becomes a matter of great urgency for those who manage the resources of an enterprise or a nation. It is critical that every manager establish a climate for planning.

Planning Must Not Be Left to Chance

Every superior manager should remove obstacles to planning and try to establish a climate in which his subordinates must plan. This involves, at each level of management, setting goals; establishing and publicizing applicable significant planning premises; involving all managers in the planning process; reviewing subordinate plans and their performance; assuring appropriate staff assistance and information. All this adds up to recognizing that planning will not occur unless it is forced and the facilities to undertake it are made available.

Planning Should Start at the Top

Logically, basic goals from which others stem must be company-wide and, therefore, these must be set at the top-management level. The example and drive of top management is the most important single force in planning. When it rigorously reviews subordinates' programs, it naturally stimulates planning interest throughout an enterprise.

While the most effective planning should start at the top and receive the support of managers at that level, this does not mean that subordinates can do nothing. There is something to encouraging an "upward push" as well as a "downward press"; superiors may be pushed into setting goals and premises and approving plans, if a well-reasoned program is presented to them. Top managers often *want* to make decisions and guide planning but simply have not sufficient knowledge, or assistance from their subordinates, to do so. Top managers have wistfully pointed out to the authors that they would like more subordinates to present solutions rather than problems. Certainly, no subordinate should be unduly critical of his superior without having come up with his program, recommended it, pressed for it, and been able to defend it.

Planning Must Be Organized

Good organization structure—through appropriate grouping of activities and clear delegation of authority—establishes an environment for performance. Managers must be held responsible for planning within their area of authority. What is sometimes neglected is sufficient staff assistance. While no manager can delegate to a staff his responsibility for decisions, most managers could improve their planning if they had help in gathering information and in its analysis.

Good planning organization, then, implies that planning and doing cannot be separated. In other words, there is no practicable way that a manager can make decisions without taking part in planning since decision making is central to the planning process. Yet, one often sees in all types of enterprises special planning staffs working to develop programs which never become operative simply because those responsible for decisions make commitments without regard to such planning proposals. A planning staff is just that. Its task is to advise and assist those in an operating-line position to make formal plans.

To avoid the error of separating planning from doing, it would seem wise for the manager to consult his planning staff by putting proposed decisions of any importance before it for the staff's analysis and recommendations—*before* he makes a decision. Also, the planning staff should be required to be knowledgeable of the realities of the situation on which its advice is sought. This means close informational contact with those who actively operate an enterprise in place of the ivory tower situation one often finds with such staffs. If staff advice in planning can be intermeshed with staff contact with reality, and if there is a clear recognition that decision making itself is central to planning and a plan is only a study or proposal until a decision has been made, the dangerous tendency in practice to separate planning from doing can be avoided.

Planning Must Be Definite

Although some planning cannot be entirely definite, it need not even then represent little more than wishing. The need for verifiable goals has been repeatedly emphasized in this book, as has the requirement for a network of derivative goals throughout the structure of programs and organization. Also, the critical premises against which to make planning decisions must be definite, and vague or nonexistent policies are an invitation to unstructured, uncoordinated planning. Plans can eventually be made definite, include specific steps of action, and be translatable into needs for men, materials, and money. As has been indicated, the budget, by quantifying plans, may force this kind of definiteness. There are few areas of planning in which—if the larger problem can be divided into steps or component parts—a manager cannot see what he must do, how long it should take, and how much it should cost. Recent experience in planning research and development projects, by breaking them down into a series of definite interrelated parts, has resulted in a marked increase in definite and meaningful planning.

Goals, Premises, and Policies Must Be Communicated

Perhaps the greatest single cause for uncoordinated planning is the manager's lack of understanding of his goals and of the critical planning premises which affect his areas of planning. Likewise, high on the list of basic causes of planning failures is the lack of understanding of company policies in the area where a manager makes his decisions. Where these situations exist, no amount of logical ability or analysis will lead him to a decision which supports and coordinates with the other plans of the enterprise.

Yet communication is a difficult process. But it is most difficult either when there is nothing to communicate or when what is available is general, fuzzy, or inapplicable to a manager's planning problems. Until enterprise managers have attempted to make sure that clear goals, premises, and policies are communicated to those who must have them, they are not doing what they can and should do to establish an environment for effective planning.

Long-range Planning Must Be Integrated with Short-range

Managers often focus attention on very short-range ("tomorrow") planning, if they plan at all, and regard long-range planning as not affecting this area of responsibility. Part of this difficulty stems from a lack of appreciation of what long-range decisions should cover. The commitment principle gives a practical guide to this problem. As applied to the usual business enterprise, those areas which are likely to involve long-range decisions are (1) new-product selection and development; (2) marketing channels and strategies; (3) facilities, particularly major capital facilities; (4) cash, particularly in a growing business; and (5) people and organization. Obviously, there are few day-to-day decisions not concerned with at least one of these, and successful planning cannot exist when short-range plans and decisions do not contribute to or fit in with longer-range planning.

Planning Must Include Awareness and Acceptance of Change

Change is always necessary for enterprise survival. Yet, since people resist change, it must be an objective of the manager to build in his organization an awareness of change and an ability to forecast it, and to cultivate an attitude of welcoming change.

The distilled experience of the president of a large American company sheds light on this subject.[1]

Change is more acceptable when it is understood than when it is not.

Change is more acceptable when it does not threaten security than when it does.

Change is more acceptable when those affected have helped create it than when it has been externally imposed.

Change is more acceptable when it results from an application of previously established impersonal principles than it is when it is dictated by personal order.

Change is more acceptable when it follows a series of successful changes than when it follows a series of failures.

Change is more acceptable when it is inaugurated after prior change has been assimilated than when it is inaugurated during the confusion of other major change.

Change is more acceptable if it has been planned than if it is experimental.

Change is more acceptable to people new on the job than to people old on the job.

Change is more acceptable to people who share in the benefits of change than to those who do not.

Change is more acceptable if the organization has been trained to accept change.

SUMMARY OF MAJOR PLANNING PRINCIPLES

Although a complete set of empirically proved, interrelated principles has not been discovered and codified, experience and observation of planning indicate certain fundamental planning principles.[2] As has been indicated earlier, management cannot progress as a science without a systematic theory. This, in turn, requires a conceptual scheme in which to arrange principles, not only for the benefit of the manager, but also as indicators of research areas. After all, one of the values of a conceptual scheme is that it makes visible what might otherwise remain unseen.

Major planning principles can be grouped around those dealing with (1) the purpose and nature of planning, (2) the structure of plans, and (3) the process of planning.

The Purpose and Nature of Planning

The purpose and nature of planning might be summarized by reference to the following principles:

Principle of contribution to objectives   The purpose of every plan and all derivative plans is to facilitate the accomplishment of enterprise objectives.

[1] R. M. Besse, "Company Planning Must Be Planned," *Dun's Review and Modern Industry,* vol. 74, no. 4, pp. 62–63 (April, 1957).

[2] Drawn from H. Koontz, "A Preliminary Statement of Principles of Planning and Control," *Journal of Academy of Management,* vol. 1, no. 1, pp. 45–61 (April, 1958). This original formulation of principles was first presented to the Academy of Management in 1956.

Principle of efficiency of plans   The efficiency of a plan is measured by the amount it contributes to objectives offset by the costs and other unsought consequences required to formulate and operate it.

Principle of primacy of planning   Planning logically precedes the execution of all other managerial functions.

The principle of contribution to objectives derives from the raison d'être of organized enterprise. The principle of efficiency of plans indicates the attempt to assure economical expenditure of resources to reach group goals. The principle of primacy of planning emphasizes that a manager can hardly undertake organizing, staffing, directing, or controlling without plans to guide him.

The Structure of Plans

Three major principles dealing with the structure of plans can go far in tying plans together, making derivative plans contribute to major plans, and assuring that plans in one department harmonize with those in another.

Principle of planning premises   The more individuals charged with planning understand and agree to utilize consistent planning premises, the more coordinated enterprise planning will be.

Principle of strategy and policy framework   The more strategies and policies are clearly understood, the more consistent and effective will be the framework of enterprise plans.

Principle of timing   The more plans are structured to provide an appropriately timed, intermeshed network of derivative and supporting programs, the more effectively and efficiently they will contribute to the attainment of enterprise objectives.

These principles indicate that guided knowledge is the key to a sound structure of plans. All who plan in an enterprise must proceed from understood goals and uniform premises, and the decisions which lead to plans cannot be accurately focused toward the enterprise objectives without a framework of policy. Both premises and policies are useless without proper timing; and information with respect to premises, policies, timing, and other factors is essential to the manager.

The Process of Planning

Within the process of planning, there are four principles, the understanding of which can help develop a science of planning.

Principle of the limiting factor   In choosing from among alternatives, the more an individual can recognize and solve for those factors that are limiting or critical to the attainment of the desired goal, the more clearly and accurately he can select the most favorable alternative.

The principle of the limiting factor is the essence of decision making. The key to decision making is to solve the problem posed by alternatives, if possible, by seeking out and solving for the limiting, or strategic, factor. To do otherwise is not only to sacrifice time and expense in examining every facet of a problem but also to risk giving too much weight to factors not critical to the decision.

The commitment principle   Logical planning covers a period of time in the future necessary to foresee, through a series of actions, the fulfillment of commitments involved in a decision.

Principle of flexibility   The more that flexibility can be built into plans, the less the danger of losses incurred through unexpected events, but the cost of flexibility should be weighed against its advantages.

Principle of navigational change   The more planning decisions commit for the future, the more important it is that the manager periodically check on events and expectations and redraw plans as necessary to maintain a course toward a desired goal.

The commitment principle and the principles of flexibility and navigational change are all closely related. Although it makes sense to forecast and draw plans far enough into the future to make reasonably sure of meeting commitments, often either it is impossible to do so or the future is so uncertain as to make the fulfillment of commitments subject to undue risk.

The principle of flexibility deals with that ability to change which is built into plans. The principle of navigational change, on the other hand, implies reviewing plans from time to time and redrawing them if that is indicated by changed events and expectations. As is apparent, unless plans have built-in flexibility, navigational change is difficult or costly.

FOR DISCUSSION

1. If you were asked to take steps to make sure that adequate planning was accomplished in a company, what would you do?
2. How can a company plan in an orderly way for "business as usual" and at the same time for a contingency such as a major fire or the outbreak of war?
3. In organizing for long-range planning, the typical corporation has a central long-range planning staff. But it is generally recognized that planning is the task of each operating manager and that he must take responsibility for his plans and their execution. Can these kinds of approaches be reconciled in practice?

4. The job of good planning is to meet change successfully. How would you undertake to meet this problem in the light of the many inflexibilities and uncertainties involved in planning?

5. Show in what ways application of the major principles of planning clarifies the methods and approaches used in planning.

part three
ORGANIZING

In order to make it possible for people to work effectively toward accomplishing goals, an intentional structure of roles must be designed and maintained. This is the purpose of the managerial function of organizing. For a meaningful role to exist, it will be recalled, it should incorporate verifiable objectives, an understood area of authority or discretion, a clear concept of the major activities or duties involved, and a clear understanding of the relationships of that role with others where coordination is required. To make a role fully operational, these structural requirements must be additionally provided with needed information wherever and however it may be obtained.

In this part the authors are concerned with theory underlying organization structure. Chapter 12 deals with the nature and purpose of organizing. Although emphasis is placed on structure of roles, this does not imply that a manager disregards people. Quite the contrary. Roles are designed for people to fill. The practical organizer is often faced with situations in which he must allow for the limitations, strengths, availability, and interests of people. Moreover, as will be seen in the analysis of the functions of staffing and directing, people are central to these two functions of managing. Furthermore, in speaking of role structuring there is no implication that any role need be restrictive. It may be as narrow as the defined task of an assembly-line worker or a bank teller, or it can be as broad, with a considerable area of discretion, as that of a company president or research scientist.

Although people operate in groups primarily to accomplish objectives that they cannot attain acting alone, the real cause of formal organization, as is pointed out in Chapter 13, is the limitations of the span of management. Even though there is no definite and universally acceptable number of persons that a manager can effectively supervise, we do know that there is a limit to the number in individual cases. This limit, known as the span of management, is what makes levels of organization necessary and problems of delegation and

237

policy making so important. In any given situation there are many underlying factors that determine the number of persons a manager can supervise.

Chapter 14, "Basic Departmentation," and Chapter 15, "The Assignment of Activities," deal with activity grouping in organization structures. To understand the material presented in these chapters quickly and with the least effort, it is important to recall that grouping has two aspects. One has to do with basic forms of departmentation which experience and logic have found useful. These forms and the advantages and disadvantages of each, along with their special uses in practice, are discussed in Chapter 14. The second aspect has to do with guides for assigning activities to existing departments within a structure. This is dealt with in Chapter 15. While most tasks are assigned on the basis of similarity to those in an existing department, others are assigned according to a variety of guides which experience and logic have found to be useful and important.

Chapter 16, "Line and Staff Authority Relationships," discusses two basic kinds of formal relationships that may exist in an organizational role. The material in the chapter differentiates between the two and points out reasons for confusion. If the reader remembers that a person in a line capacity is one who bears responsibility for the performance of those who report to him and that a person in a staff role may only make recommendations or offer advice, he need not be disturbed by the complex reasoning behind this concept. This applies even to those hybrid functional authority positions which have some staff characteristics and some line characteristics.

Chapter 17 deals with service departments. A point of possible confusion here arises from the fact that service departmentation itself has nothing directly to do with the question of line and staff relationships, although most service departments act in a staff capacity. Service departments are merely groupings of activities, usually quite specialized, which are concentrated in a given department for purposes of economy or control. For instance, a specialized typing and clerical service pool attached to the controller's department is a typical service grouping. In modern complex enterprises, service departments tend to proliferate. But as they have grown, operating problems have increased. In this chapter, special effort is given to presenting material on efficient operation of service departments.

Chapter 18 analyzes the problem of delegation and degree of authority dispersion in an enterprise. As management has become better understood and as enterprises have grown, it has become almost fashionable to "decentralize" authority. While authority must be dispersed in an organization structure, the degree and kind of decentralization are a source of difficulty and misunderstanding. The chapter undertakes to analyze the principles and art of delegation and the factors behind proper decentralization or centralization, with a view to developing some theoretical and practical bases for this important organizational area. The authors believe that centralization or decentralization should not be regarded as desirable or undesirable trends in and of themselves, but that the actions of an enterprise in this area must be determined by studying actual circumstances and needs in every case. Centralization and decentralization are, after all, simply means of structuring roles for achieving desired goals.

The committee form of organization is given special attention in Chapter 19. Uses and abuses and advantages and disadvantages are discussed with emphasis on methods of making the committee more effective.

In the final chapter, organization practice is analyzed from an over-all point of view. This chapter puts special emphasis on applying organizational principles.

12

nature and purpose of organizing

It is often said that good people can make any organization pattern work. It has even been said that ambiguity in organization is a good thing in that it forces teamwork since people know that they must cooperate to get anything done. However, there can be no doubt that good people and those who want to cooperate will work together most effectively if they know the part they are to play in any collaborative endeavor and how their roles relate to each other. This is as true in business or government as it is in football or baseball. To design and maintain these systems of roles is basically the managerial function of organizing.

For an organizational role to exist and to be meaningful to people, it must incorporate (1) verifiable objectives which, as already indicated in the previous part, are the task of planning; (2) a clear concept of the major duties or activities involved; and (3) an understood area of discretion, or authority, so that the person filling it knows what he can do to accomplish results. In addition, to make a role operational, provision should be made for needed information and where and how it may be obtained.

It is in the sense of a structure of roles that formal organization is conceived. It is within this connotation that we think of organizing as the grouping of activities necessary to attain objectives, the assignment of each grouping to a manager with authority necessary to supervise it, and the provision for coordination horizontally and vertically in the enterprise structure. An organization structure should be designed to clarify the environment so that everyone knows who is to do what and who is responsible for what results; obstacles to performance caused by confusion and uncertainty of assignment are removed; and there is furnished a decision-making communications network reflecting and supporting enterprise objectives.

Essentially, organization grows out of the human need for cooperation. As Barnard emphasized,[1] human beings are forced to cooperate to achieve

---

[1] *The Functions of the Executive* (Cambridge, Mass.: Harvard University Press, 1938), chap. 6, 7, 9.

personal goals because of physical, biological, psychological, and social limitations. Cooperation can be more productive and less costly, in most instances, with some kind of organization structure.

It should be noted that "organization" is a loosely used word with many management theorists. Some would say it "includes *all* the behavior of *all* participants."[2] Others would equate it with the total system of social and cultural relationships. Still others refer to an enterprise, such as the United States Steel Corporation or the Department of Defense, as an "organization." But for most practicing managers, the term implies a formalized intentional structure of roles or positions. It is used that way in this book. Certainly most managers believe they are organizing when they establish such a structure.

FORMAL AND INFORMAL ORGANIZATION

Taking the lead from Barnard and from the discoveries of the Hawthorne experiments,[3] many management people distinguish between formal and informal organization.

Formal

People, their behavior, and their association belong to a large system of social relationships of which a single formally organized enterprise is but a subsystem. Barnard referred to an organization as "formal" when the activities of two or more persons were *consciously* coordinated toward a given objective. He found that the essence of formal organization is conscious common purpose and that formal organization comes into being when persons (1) are able to communicate with each other, (2) are willing to act, and (3) share a purpose. This definition is far broader than that used in this book, and few managers adopt it. In the first place, it covers any kind of group action with a common purpose and could apply to activities such as a card game or car pool, which are certainly not regarded by practitioners as formal organizations. In the second place, it goes beyond our goal-activity-authority concept. No formal organization, as typically designed, can cover *all* human enterprise relationships. If role definition and authority lines map the course of responsible action and decision making, they are doing all that was ever intended.

As Wilfred Brown has declared, after managerial experience of many years and after participating in one of the most thorough research projects on organizational life ever undertaken:[4]

---

[2] C. Argyris, *Personality and Organization* (New York: Harper & Row, Publishers, Incorporated, 1957), p. 239.

[3] The importance of human behavior independent of the structural considerations of formal enterprise organization was brought out by the researches of Elton Mayo and F. J. Roethlisberger at the Hawthorne Works of the Western Electric Company, beginning in 1927. For a comprehensive account of the experiments, see F. J. Roethlisberger and W. J. Dickson, *Management and the Worker* (Cambridge, Mass.: Harvard University Press, 1939).

[4] "What Is Work?" *Harvard Business Review*, vol. 40, no. 5, p. 127 (September–October, 1962). The research referred to is that undertaken first by the Tavistock Institute of Human Rela-

Thus, I personally believe that the more formalization that exists, the more clearly we will know the bounds of discretion which we are authorized to use, and will be held responsible for, and [that] prescribed policies make clear to people the area in which they have freedom to act. Without a clearly defined area of freedom there is no freedom. This, in fact, is a very old story reaching down through the history of mankind: there is no real freedom without laws.

Unquestionably, some of the concern about the restrictive dangers in formal organization arises from poor organization practice. There should be room for discretion, for taking advantage of creative talents, and recognition of individual likes and capacities in the most formal of organizations. Yet, to assume that individual effort in a group situation can be unchanneled is to overlook the basic realities of any group activity.

There is nothing inherently inflexible about formal organization. On the contrary, if the manager is to organize well, structure must furnish an environment in which individual performance, both present and future, contributes to group goals.

Although the attainment of goals must be the reason for any cooperative activity, we must look further for principles to guide the establishment of effective formal organization.

Principle of unity of objective   *An organization structure is effective if it facilitates the contribution of individuals in the attainment of enterprise objectives.*[5] The application of the principle of unity of objective implies, of course, the existence of formulated and understood enterprise objectives. If the objective is to make a profit over a period of time, then the organization pattern that helps to accomplish this conforms to the principle of unity of objective. Whatever the goals, or derivative goals, organization structure and action must be measured against the criterion of effectiveness in meeting them.

Principle of efficiency   *An organization structure is efficient if it facilitates accomplishment of objectives by people* (that is, is effective) *with the minimum unsought consequences or costs* (going beyond the usual thinking of costs entirely in such measurable items as dollars or man-hours). Even though financial or material unit costs are important in measuring organizational efficiency, the principle of efficiency as employed here encompasses such matters as individual and group satisfactions. To an employee, an efficient organization structure is likely to be one that operates without waste or carelessness and makes for work satisfaction, has clear-cut lines of authority

---

tions, London, in cooperation with Brown's Glacier Metal Company, Ltd. and after a few years by the company alone. This research project, started in 1948, is reported in Wilfred Brown, *Exploration in Management* (New York: John Wiley & Sons, Inc., 1960).

[5]Urwick referred to this as "the principle of objective," one of ten principles of organization. See also his *Notes on the Theory of Organization* (New York: American Management Association, 1952), pp. 18ff. Barnard (*op. cit.*, pp. 19ff.) refers to this principle as a matter of "effectiveness" or organization, making the point that an organization is effective, although not necessarily efficient, when it gains its objective.

and proper exaction of responsibility, allows appropriate participation in problem solving, gives provision for security and status, and furnishes an opportunity for personal development and reasonably adequate pay rates.

The principle of efficiency must be applied judiciously. Too often, in establishing an organization structure, managers see the savings possible in setting up a service department, without ascertaining the complementary costs outside the department. For example, all activities dealing with the compilation of statistics may be assigned to a central department; although this may produce statistics at low cost, their value may decline even more because they do not suit the needs of managers. Also, a customary way for the inexperienced efficiency engineer to save money is to establish secretarial pools. While these sometimes work efficiently, there are many occasions where efficient secretarial work is done at the cost of hours of executive time waiting for needed stenographic work to be done.

Efficiency may become a vague and variable criterion. One manager may measure efficiency by profit, while others may measure it in terms of survival, business status, public service, or business expansion. Or a company president may impatiently drive toward cost, market, and profit goals by tactics that create morale problems for subordinates and eventual losses for the business.

However the standards of efficiency are applied, the principle of efficiency underlies the measurement of any organization structure. Difficulties may be encountered in selecting an appropriate standard. Thus, one person may criticize the overlapping of activities in certain government departments, while another may feel that this overlapping is a necessary cost of gaining protection against the danger inherent in concentration of power. A president of a business may be criticized as inefficient in pressing too slowly for organizational changes, when this slowness may be justified by the benefits of having subordinates learn for themselves the advantages of such changes and voluntarily embrace them more completely.

Informal

Barnard regarded as informal organization any joint personal activity without conscious joint purpose, even though possibly contributing to joint results. As thus defined, all manner of groups fall within the sphere of informal organization, including an airplane load of passengers, or people walking down a street. Pursuing this thinking, informal organizations—relationships not appearing on an organization chart—might include the machine-shop group, the water-cooler clique, the production-engineering group, the sixth-floor crowd, the Friday-evening bowling gang, and the morning-coffee "regulars."

An inquiry into why and how these informal organizations exist is a special study in social psychology. The manager knows that these interpersonal relationships are important for his managing. If it were not for the fact that they are so dynamic in terms of the nature of the group, the number in the group, the actual personnel involved, what the group is concerned with, its changing leadership, and the continuing process of formation and dissolution, the manager might be tempted more consciously and specifically to take informal organizations into account as he formally organizes or changes the organization. This, however, he cannot do. He is reduced to keeping himself aware of the informal organization, avoiding antagonizing it, and using it as he directs his subordinates. How he does these things is considered in Chapter 28.

THE TERM "DEPARTMENT"

"Department" designates a distinct area, division, or branch of an enterprise over which a manager has authority for the performance of specified activities. A department, as the term is generally used, may be the production division, the sales department, the West Coast branch, the market research section, or the accounts receivable unit. In some enterprises, departmental terminology is loosely applied; in others, especially larger ones, a stricter terminology indicates hierarchical relationships. Thus, a vice-president may head a division; a director, a department; a manager, a branch; and a chief, a section. This relationship of terminology to status is often found in the federal government, where, in the typical executive department, the hierarchy runs from office or bureau to divisions, branches, sections, units, and subunits.

Indeed, in an enterprise requiring successive subordinate groupings, exact definitions may become imperative, since certain designations carry connotations of authority, prestige, and salary. If the vice-president of production heads a *division*, the vice-president in charge of sales will hardly be satisfied to head a *department*. Some large organizations tend to run out of appropriate designations; then they invent such terms as "group," "activity," or "component."

ORGANIZING AS A PROCESS

In looking at organizing as a process, it is apparent that several fundamental inputs must be considered. In the first place, the structure must reflect objectives and plans, because enterprise activities derive from these. In the second place, the structure must reflect the authority available to enterprise management; this depends upon such social institutions as private property, representative government, and the host of customs, codes, and laws that both restrict and sanction individuals in operating a business, a church, a university, or any group venture. Authority in a given organization is, then, a socially determined right to exercise discretion; as such, it is subject to change.

In the third place, organization structure, like any plan, must reflect its environment. Just as the premises of a plan may be economic, technological, political, social, or ethical, so may be those of an organization structure. The structure must be designed to work, to permit contributions by members of a group, and to help people gain objectives efficiently in a changing future. In this sense, a workable organization structure can never be either mechanistic or static.

Fourth, the organization must be manned with people. Obviously, the activity groupings and authority provisions of an organization structure must take into account people's limitations and customs. This is not to say that the structure must be designed around individuals instead of around goals and accompanying activities. But an important consideration—often a constraining factor for the organization architect—is the kind of people who are to man it. Just as the engineer considers the performance strength and weaknesses of materials going into his projects, so must the organizer consider his materials—people.

By Logic

There is a fundamental logic to organizing. Application of logical method to this process, in the light of the inputs outlined above, indicates the following steps: (1) establishment of enterprise objectives; (2) formulation of derivative objectives, policies, and plans; (3) identification and classification of activities necessary to accomplish these; (4) grouping these activities in the light of human and material resources available and the best way of using them; (5) delegating to the head of each group the authority necessary to perform the activities; and (6) tying these groupings together horizontally and vertically, through authority relationships and information systems.

This logical process does not imply—as so many critics have declared it does—extreme occupational specialization, which in many instances makes labor uninteresting, tedious, and unduly restrictive. There is *nothing* in organization itself that dictates this. To say that tasks should be specific is not to say they must be limited and mechanical. Whether or not they should be broken down into minute parts—as on a typical assembly line—or be broad enough to encompass the design, production, and sale of a machine, is for the organizer to consider in light of the total results desired. In any organization, jobs can be defined to allow little or no personal discretion or the widest possible area of discretion, as a pure detail of operation or as the most creative of activity.

In Practice

The logical pattern of organizing conforms to the usual practice of developing departmentation. The owner or promoter of a new, small business hires men as the size of his business requires. When the point is reached beyond which he is unable to employ, train, supervise, and control additional employees, subordinates are grouped into one or more sections, with a supervisor or manager appointed for each. Two organizational levels then exist. Further expansion of the labor force would give rise to more sections. When the chief executive can no longer properly manage the increasing number of subordinate managers, he will group them into departments and appoint a manager for each. Thus, three organization levels would be created, and the chief executive would be removed one step further from the nonmanagers. Of course, in a going concern, the question of whether to build from the top down or from the bottom up does not arise. The organizing process is continuous, and the activities themselves and their grouping are simultaneously under consideration at all levels, in order to maintain the enterprise in line with tested guides of association and assignment.

According to Drucker

In both logic and practice, the organizing process outlined here is similar to that emphasized by Peter Drucker,[6] who finds three ways to determine the kind of structure needed in a specific enterprise: activities analysis, decision analysis, and relations analysis. Drucker believes in finding out what an enterprise actually does—in terms of concrete activities necessary to attain objectives, rather than under such preconceived general headings as "engineering" or "selling."

Drucker points out that only by rigorous activities analysis can managers find out what work has to be performed, what work belongs together, and how each activity should be emphasized in the organization structure. His decision analysis determines what kinds of decisions are needed, where in the organization structure they should be made, and how each manager should be involved in them. By relations analysis Drucker means knowing the contribution to programs that each manager must make, with whom he is to work, and what contribution other managers must make to him. His approach, then, is in accordance with what sound management practice has long recognized as logical and practical.

Organizing is, then, a process by which the manager brings order out of chaos, removes conflicts between people over work or responsibility, and establishes an environment suitable for teamwork. Implicit also is recognition of the human factor—that jobs must be designed to fit people, with all their strengths and weaknesses, and that people must be motivated.

BASIC QUESTIONS

In this book, the authors have found it useful to analyze the managerial function of organizing by answering, in succeeding chapters, the following questions:

1. What determines the span of management and hence the levels of organization?
2. What determines the basic framework of departmentation, and what are the strengths and weaknesses in the basic forms?
3. What determines whether activities should be assigned to a given department in this basic framework?
4. What kinds of authority relationships exist in organization?

---

[6] See *The Practice of Management* (New York: Harper & Row, Publishers, Incorporated, 1954), pp. 194–201.

5. How should authority be dispersed throughout the organization structure, and what determines the extent of this dispersion?
6. What place do committees have in organization?
7. How should the manager make organization theory work in practice?

The answers to these questions form a basis for a theory of organizing. When considered along with similar analyses of planning, staffing, directing, and controlling, they are offered as an operational approach to management.

FOR DISCUSSION

1. Since people must occupy organization positions and an effective organization depends on people, it is often said that the best organization arises when a manager hires good people and lets them do a job in their own way. Comment.
2. A formal organization is often conceived of as a communications system. Is it? How?
3. Construct a diagram depicting the formal organization of some enterprise or activity with which you are familiar. How does this help or hinder the establishment of an environment for performance?
4. Using the same enterprise or activity as in the above question, chart the informal organization. Does it help or hinder the formal organization? Why?

13

span of management

That the problem of span of management[1] is as old as organization itself is apparent from the passages of the Bible dealing with Moses organizing the exodus of the Israelites. The difficulties that Moses met and the departmentation he employed to meet them are recounted in Exodus 18:17–26, in which it is recorded that Moses' father-in-law, noting that Moses was spending so much time giving counsel to so many individuals, advised him as follows:

The thing thou doest is not good. Thou wilt surely wear away, both thou and this people that is with thee: for this thing is too heavy for thee; thou art not able to perform it thyself alone. Hearken now unto my voice, I will give thee counsel. . . . Thou shalt provide out of the people able men . . . and place such over them [the people], to be rulers of thousands, and rulers of hundreds, rulers of fifties, and rulers of tens. And let them judge the people at all seasons; and it shall be, that every great matter they shall bring unto thee, but every small matter they shall judge: so shall it be easier for thyself, and they shall bear the burden with thee. If thou shalt do this thing, and God command thee so, then thou shall be able to endure, and all this people shall also go to their place in peace.

Moses thereupon followed his father-in-law's advice, with the result that he:

. . . chose able men out of all Israel, and made them heads over the people, rulers of thousands, rulers of hundreds, rulers of fifties and rulers of tens. And they judged the people at all seasons: the hard causes they brought unto Moses, but every small matter they judged themselves.

[1] In much of the literature of management, this is referred to as the "span of control." Despite the widespread use of this term, the authors have preferred since the first edition of this book in 1955 to use "span of management," since the span is one of management and not merely of control, which is only one aspect of the managing practice.

HOW WIDE A SPAN?

In every organization it must be decided how many subordinates a superior can manage. Students of management have found that this number is usually four to eight subordinates at the upper levels of organization and eight to fifteen or more at the lower levels. For example, the prominent British consultant Lyndall Urwick[2] found "the ideal number of subordinates for all superior authorities . . . to be four," and "at the lowest level of organization, where what is delegated is responsibility for the performance of specific tasks and not for the supervision of others, the number may be eight or twelve." An experienced military observer has stated that he believes the proper number to range between three and six, with three likely to be best near the top of an organization and six near the bottom.[3] Others find that a manager may be able to manage as many as twenty to thirty subordinates.[4]

In actual experience, one finds a wide variety of practices, even among admittedly well-managed enterprises. General of the Army Dwight D. Eisenhower had three immediate line subordinates when he was Supreme Commander of the Allied Expeditionary Forces in World War II, and none of these had more than four line subordinates. Yet, at the same time, the Army Chief of Staff had reporting to him and his deputies at least fifteen major line and staff officers. In the General Motors Corporation in 1970, the president had reporting to him three executive vice-presidents, but one group vice-president had fifteen reporting to him. The president of a railroad generally regarded as one of the best managed in the industry had in 1970 ten top executives reporting to him, and one of these had eleven subordinates. Yet the head of another large carrier, not regarded as so well managed, had only seven major subordinates. The president of one well-managed department store had four key executives, none of whom had more than five subordinates, while an equally large and successful store showed twelve key executives reporting to the president and an equally large number of subordinates reporting to most of them.

In a survey of a hundred large companies made by the American Management Association in 1951,[5] the number of executives reporting to the

---

[2] Lyndall Urwick, "Axioms of Organization," *Public Administration Magazine* (London), pp. 348–349 (October, 1955). However, in other writings, Urwick modified this position by saying that "no person should supervise more than five, or at the most, six, direct subordinates *whose work interlocks.*" See *Notes on The Theory of Organization* (New York: American Management Association, 1952), p. 53 (emphasis in quotation added).

[3] Sir Ian Hamilton, *The Soul and Body of an Army* [London: Edward Arnold (Publishers) Ltd., 1921], p. 229.

[4] J. C. Worthy, "Men, Management, and Organization," *Proceedings, Fifth Personnel Management and Industrial Relations Seminar* (Los Angeles: University of California at Los Angeles, Oct. 30, 1951; mimeographed). The term "subordinates" referred to in this section excludes personnel such as staff or administrative assistants, secretaries, clerks, and stenographers.

[5] As summarized in *Business Week*, pp. 102–103 (Aug. 18, 1951). Healey found similar variations in his study of 409 manufacturing companies in Ohio, although the median was six subordinates. See J. H. Healey, *Executive Co-ordination and Control* (Columbus, Ohio: Ohio State University Press, 1956), p. 66.

presidents varied from one to twenty-four, and only twenty-six presidents had as few as six or less subordinates. The median number was nine. In forty-one smaller companies surveyed, twenty-five of the presidents supervised seven or more subordinates, and the median was eight. Comparable results were found by White in 1963 in a study of sixty-six companies.[6] In a much more narrowly based study, using a random sample, Fisch, on the other hand, discovered in 1962 a tendency among very large companies (those with over 1 billion dollars of sales) for a span of management at the top to be more than twelve, with the span tending to be smaller as the company size decreases.[7]

In a very real sense, none of these studies is truly indicative of the span of management actually practiced. For one thing, they measure the span only at or near the top of an enterprise. This is hardly typical of what the span may be throughout the enterprise, particularly since every organizer has experienced the tremendous pressure for a large number of the functions of an enterprise to report to the top executive. It is probable that spans below the top executive are much narrower. Indeed, analysis of more than 100 companies of all sizes made by one of the authors discloses a much narrower span in the middle levels of management than at the top.

In addition, the fact that apparently well-managed companies have, between them and certainly within them, widely varying spans indicates that merely counting what is actually done is not enough to establish what a span ought to be. And this is true even if it could be assumed that, through trial and error, each company has reached an optimum. It may only prove that underlying conditions vary.

PROBLEMS WITH LEVELS

There is a tendency to regard organization and departmentation as an end in themselves and to gauge the effectiveness of organization structures in terms of clarity and completeness of departments and department levels. Division of activities into departments and hierarchical organization and the creation of multiple levels are not completely desirable in themselves.

In the first place, levels are expensive. As they increase, more and more effort and money are devoted to managing, because of the additional managers, staffs to assist them, and the necessity of coordinating departmental activities, plus the costs of facilities for such personnel. Accountants refer to such costs as "overhead," or "burden," or "general and administrative," in contrast to so-called direct costs. Real production is accomplished by factory, engineering, or sales employees, who are or could logically be accounted for as direct labor. Levels above the "firing line" are predominantly staffed with managers who

---

[6] K. K. White, *Understanding the Company Organization Chart* (New York: American Management Association, 1963), pp. 60–61.

[7] G. G. Fisch, "Stretching the Span of Management," *Harvard Business Review*, vol. 41, no. 5, pp. 80–81 (September–October, 1962).

are not directly productive and whose cost it would be desirable to eliminate, *if that were possible.*

In the second place, departmental levels complicate communication. An enterprise with many levels has greater difficulty communicating objectives, plans, and policies through the organization structure than does the firm in which the top manager communicates directly with employees. Omissions and misinterpretations occur as information passes down the scalar chain. Levels also complicate communication from the "firing line" to the commanding superiors, which is every bit as important as downward communication.

Finally, departments and numerous levels complicate planning and control. The plan that may be definite and complete at the top level as it is subdivided and elaborated at lower levels loses coordination and clarity. Control becomes more difficult as levels and managers are added, while at the same time the complexities of planning and difficulties of communication make this control more important.

OPERATIONAL SCHOOL POSITION

The so-called classical school approach to the span of management has tended to deal with generalizations embodying specific numbers of subordinates for an effective span. Empirical data do give support to the classical school consensus of an upper- and top-level span from three to seven or eight subordinates.[8] However, more recent operational management theorists have taken the position that there are too many underlying variables in a management situation to conclude that there is any particular number of subordinates which a manager can effectively supervise.[9] It is concluded that there is a limit to the number of subordinates a manager can effectively supervise, but the exact number will depend upon underlying factors, all of which affect the difficulty and time requirements of managing.

In other words, the dominant current view is to look for the causes of limited span in individual situations, rather than to assume that there is a widely applicable numerical limit. If one can look at what it is that consumes the time of a manager in his handling of his superior-subordinate relationships, and also ascertain what devices can be used to reduce these time pressures, the analyst has an approach helpful in determining the optimum span in individual cases. He also has a powerful tool for finding out what can be done to extend the span without destroying effective supervision. There can be no argument that the costs of levels in supervision are such as to make it highly desirable for every individual manager to have as many subordinates as he can *effectively* supervise.

[8] A consensus as found by Healey, *op. cit.,* pp. 11–14.

[9] The authors of this book have taken this position since its first edition. Also see H. Stieglitz, *Corporate Organization Structures,* Studies in Personnel Policy No. 183 (New York: National Industrial Conference Board, Inc., 1961), p. 8.

GRAICUNAS'S THEORY OF SUBORDINATE-SUPERIOR RELATIONSHIPS

In a paper first published in 1933, French management consultant V. A. Graicunas[10] analyzed subordinate-superior relationships and developed a mathematical formula based on the geometric increase in complexities of managing as the number of subordinates increases. Although the formula may not be applicable to a given case, it focuses attention upon the central underlying problems of the span of management perhaps better than any other device. Graicunas's theory identifies three types of subordinate-superior relationships: (1) direct single relationships, (2) direct group relationships, and (3) cross relationships.

The direct single relationships, easily understood and recognized, relate the superior directly and individually with his immediate subordinates. Thus, if A has three subordinates—B, C, and D—there are three direct single relationships.

The direct group relations exist between the superior and each possible combination of subordinates. Thus, a superior might consult with one of his subordinates with a second in attendance, or with all his subordinates, or with various combinations of them. If A has three subordinates, these relationships include:

B with C
B with D
C with B
C with D
D with B
D with C
B with C and D
C with B and D
D with C and B

Although it may be objected that the relationship when A deals with B, with C in attendance, is no different from that when A works with C, with B in attendance, Graicunas implies a difference. In any case, three additional direct group relationships could have been included, as when A consults equally with BC, BD, and BCD, furnishing a different psychological situation from any of those noted above.

Cross relationships are created when subordinates must consult with one another. For B, C, and D, Graicunas gave six cross relationships:

B to C
B to D
C to B

---

[10] V. A. Graicunas, "Relationship in Organization," *Bulletin of the International Management Institute* (Geneva: International Labour Office, 1933), in L. Gulick and L. Urwick (eds.), *Papers on the Science of Administration* (New York: Institute of Public Administration, 1937), pp. 181–187.

C to D
D to B
D to C

From this analysis of direct single, direct group, and cross relationships, Graicunas developed the following formula to give the number of all possible types of subordinate-superior relationships requiring managerial attention. Where n equals the number of subordinates, the number of all kinds of relationships will be represented by

$$n(2^n/2 + n - 1) \quad \text{or} \quad n[2^{n-1} + (n - 1)]$$

The results of this formula are shown in Table 13.1.

Significance of the Formula

The rapid rise in the number of relationships with the increase in number of subordinates is startling. Mathematically, but as will be seen below not necessarily in practice, an executive with four subordinates, by adding a fifth, increases the *possible* relationships for which he is responsible by 127 percent (from 44 to 100). Clearly, an executive must think twice before he increases the number of his subordinates, even though this mathematical truism does not prove he should not do so.

The usefulness of the formula is weakened because it does not deal with frequency or severity (in terms of time demands) of relationships. Their total possible number is probably less important to a manager (as Graicunas recognized) than their frequency and their demands on his time.

The Graicunas theory emphasizes the complexity of managing more than a few subordinates. Yet any managerial action that will reduce the num-

TABLE 13.1. POSSIBLE RELATIONSHIPS WITH VARIABLE NUMBER OF SUBORDINATES

Number of subordinates	Number of relationships
1	1
2	6
3	18
4	44
5	100
6	222
7	490
8	1,080
9	2,376
10	5,210
11	11,374
12	24,708
18	2,359,602

ber and frequency of relationships requiring the manager's attention will increase his span of management and thereby reduce the costs and inefficiencies of an undue number of departments.

FACTORS DETERMINING FREQUENCY AND TIME-IMPACT OF RELATIONSHIPS

In searching for the answer as to how many subordinates a manager can effectively control, one discovers that—aside from such personal capacities as comprehending quickly, getting along with people, and commanding loyalty and respect—the most important determinant is the manager's ability to reduce the frequency and time impact of superior-subordinate relationships. This ability naturally varies with managers and their jobs, but seven general factors materially influence the number and frequency of such relationships.[11]

Subordinate Training

The better the training of subordinates, the less the impact of necessary superior-subordinate relationships. A well-trained subordinate requires not only less time of the manager, but also fewer contacts with his superior.

Training problems increase in new and more complex industries. Managers in the railroad industry, for example, would—after a long development of railroad technology—tend to be more completely trained than those in the aerospace industry. Similarly, the rapid changes in policy and procedures in the complex electronics and missile industries would increase training problems.

Delegation of Authority

Although training procedures enable managers to reduce the frequency and severity of time-consuming relationships, the principal cause of the heavy time burdens of such relationships is to be found in poorly conceived and confused organization. The most serious symptom of poor organization affecting the span of management is inadequate or unclear authority delegation. If a manager clearly delegates authority to undertake a well-defined task, a well-trained subordinate can get it done with a minimum of the superior's time and attention. But if the subordinate's task is not one he can do, or if it is not clearly defined, or if he does not have the authority to undertake it effectively, he will either fail to perform it or take a disproportionate amount of the manager's time in supervising and guiding his efforts.

---

[11] One study found that nearly half of a top-level executive's time is spent in committees and direct personal conferences with subordinates. See Fred E. Case, "The Executive Day," *California Management Review*, vol. 5, no. 1, p. 68 (Fall, 1962).

Planning

Much of the character of a subordinate's job is defined by the plans he is expected to put into effect. If these plans are well defined, if they are workable within his framework of operations, if he has the authority to undertake them, and if he understands what is expected, he will require little of his superior's time. Such is often the case of production foremen responsible for largely repetitive operations. Thus, in one volume workclothing manufacturer's plan, production foremen operated satisfactorily with as many as sixty or seventy subordinates.

On the other hand, where plans cannot be drawn accurately and where the subordinate must do much of his own planning, his decisions may require considerable guidance. However, if his superior has set up clear policies to guide his decisions and made sure they are consistent with the operations and goals of the department, and if the subordinate understands them, there will certainly be fewer demands on the superior's time than if these policies are indefinite, incomplete, or not understood.

Rate of Change

Obviously, certain enterprises change much more rapidly than others. The rate of change is important in determining the degree to which policies can be formulated and the stability of formulated policies maintained. It may, indeed, explain the organization structure of companies—railroad, banking, and public utility companies, for example—operating with wide spans of management or, on the other hand, the very narrow span of management used by General Eisenhower during World War II.

The effect of slow change on policy formulation and on subordinate training is dramatically shown in the organization of the Roman Catholic Church. This organization, in terms of durability and stability, can probably be regarded as the most successful in the history of Western civilization. Yet the organization levels are few: in most cases, bishops report directly to the Pope, and parish priests to bishops, although in a few instances bishops report to archbishops. Thus, there are generally only three levels in this world-wide organization and a consequent wide span of management at the top. Even though it is unquestionably too broad, this extraordinarily wide span is apparently tolerable, partly because of the degree of training possessed by the bishops and even more because the rate of change in the Church has been exceedingly slow. Changes in procedures or policies are developments of decades, and objectives have remained the same over almost two millennia.

Use of Objective Standards

A manager must find out, by either personal observation or use of objective standards, whether subordinates are following plans. Obviously, good objective standards, revealing with ease any deviations from plans, enable the manager to avoid many time-consuming relationships and to direct his attention to exceptions at points strategic to the successful execution plans.

Communication Techniques

The effectiveness with which communication techniques are used also influences the span of management. Objective standards of control are a kind of communications device, but many other techniques reduce the frequency of superior-subordinate relationships.

If every plan, instruction, order, or direction has to be communicated by personal contact and every organization change or staffing problem handled orally, the manager's time will obviously be heavily burdened. Some executives use "assistant-to" positions or administrative staff personnel as a communications device in helping to solve their problems with key subordinates. Written recommendations by subordinates, summarizing pertinent considerations, frequently expedite decision making. The authors have seen busy top executives widen their span of management by insisting upon summary presentation of written recommendations, even when these involved enormously important decisions. A carefully reasoned and presented recommendation helps the executive reach a considered decision in minutes, when even the most efficient conference would require an hour.

An executive's ability to communicate plans and instructions clearly and concisely also tends to increase a manager's span. The subordinate who, after leaving his superior's desk or receiving his memorandum of instructions, is still in doubt as to what is wanted or what has been said is sure to increase the relationships that will sooner or later require the manager's attention. One of the pleasures of being a subordinate is to have a superior who can express himself well. A manager's casual, easy style may please subordinates, but where this easiness degenerates into confusion and wasted time, the effect is sharply to reduce the effective span of management and often morale as well.

Modern communication techniques are of considerable variety. Some are mechanical and some are electrical, like the telephone, the dictating machine, and the buzzer. The electronic data-computing machine has made communications more expeditious, exact, and complete, and, if properly used, may considerably affect the span of management. Whatever techniques are used are subject to invention and discovery, so that what may be a limited span for a manager today may be less limited tomorrow.

Amount of Personal Contact

In many instances in management, face-to-face relationships are necessary. Many situations cannot be completely handled by written reports, memoranda, policy statements, planning documents, or other communications not calling for personal contact. The executive may find it valuable to him and stimulating to his subordinates to meet and discuss problems in the give-and-take of a conference. There may also be problems of such political delicacy that they can only be handled in face-to-face meetings. This is also true when it comes to appraising people's performance and discussing it with them. And there are other situations where the best way of communicating a problem, instructing a subordinate, or getting a direct "feel" as to how people really think on some matter is to spend time in slow personal contact.

One wonders, however, whether the high percentage of executive time spent in conferences and committees might be reduced somewhat by better training, better policy making and planning, clearer delegation, more thorough staff work, better control systems and objective standards, and, in general, better application of sound principles of management. One wonders, also, whether much of the time spent in personal contact might not be much better spent in thought and study.

At the other extreme of management, many companies seem somewhat unaware of how newer personnel techniques affect first-line supervisers, many of whom appear to have spans far beyond their abilities to handle. Merit rating, insurance programs, grievance procedures, and other personnel matters now requiring the foreman's time in face-to-face relationships have perhaps reduced his traditionally wide span of management. This is not to say that these innovations are not worth their cost, but the span of management limitations must be evaluated in the light of these factors.

WIDE VERSUS NARROW SPANS

Limitations affecting the span of management are what create levels in organization: the larger the enterprise or the narrower the spans, the greater the number of levels.

Organization structure laden with departments and levels causes complexity and losses. Experience with large organizations proves to anyone the frustrations of "layering," whereby authority, suggestions, questions, and instructions must flow up and down the chain of command. Although some of this may be allayed by understanding that requests for information need not follow the line of command, decision making—in which authority is required and used—does need to.

The Sears, Roebuck Studies

An interesting study of the effect of organization levels on enterprise efficiency was made some years ago by Sears, Roebuck and Company.[12] In the course of this study, the operations of two groups of B stores (150 to 175 employees) in towns of approximately the same size were analyzed. In one group the managers had organized their stores with an assistant manager and some thirty merchandise managers in charge of departments. In the other group the stores were organized with an extra level of management between store managers

---

[12] J. C. Worthy, "Organization Structure and Employee Morale," *American Sociological Review*, vol. 15, pp. 169–179 (April, 1950).

and department heads. Analyses of sales volume, profit, morale, and lower-management competence all indicated that the stores with the "flat" type of organization were superior on all scores to those more conventionally organized.

The results—clearly violating the traditional numerical limitations of span of management—were traced to several factors. The principal one appeared to be that managers having a large number of subordinate managers reporting to them had no alternative but to delegate adequate authority to these subordinates, who were thereby enabled to make important decisions. This not only improved their morale, but, because of the pressure placed on them to perform, actually improved the quality of their performance. By being forced to manage, they learned to manage. By the same token, the store manager, knowing that he had to delegate considerable authority, took greater care in selecting, guiding, and training his subordinates and also adopted efficient methods of objective control. In addition, the Sears study revealed that reducing the length of channels vastly improved communication between managers and subordinates, despite the large number of subordinates.

Flat versus Tall Structures

The question of desirable spans of management and their effect on flat versus tall organization structures has been subjected to continued research by various behavioral scientists and has raised questions concerning the desirability of the wide spans indicated by the Sears, Roebuck studies.[13] In general, these later studies show no greatly significant performance difference between flat and tall structures. It appears that, in experimental work, the advantages of flat structures, such as faster information flow and individual satisfaction, were often offset by the advantages of narrower spans in faster and more effective problem resolution.[14]

However, the experimental study of Carzo and Yanouzas showed that groups operating under a relatively tall organization structure showed "significantly better performance than groups operating under the flat structure.[15] This was believed to be due to the fact that, with narrower spans, group members were able to evaluate decisions more frequently and a more orderly decision process was possible.

These studies support conclusions of the authors in this book. It is difficult to generalize on wide or narrow spans of management since there are so many underlying variables to be considered. There are advantages to one and advantages to another. The result is that the practitioner must seek balance,

---

[13] The considerable volume of research is well summarized in R. Carzo and J. N. Yanouzas, "Effects of Flat and Tall Organization Structures," *Administrative Science Quarterly*, vol. 14, no. 2, pp. 178–191 (June, 1969).

[14] Although, in one study, the time required to make decisions was found to be better in somewhat flatter organization structures. See H. R. Jones, Jr., "A Study of Organization Performance for Experimental Structures of Two, Three and Four Levels," *Academy of Management Journal*, vol. 12, no. 3, pp. 351–365 (September, 1969).

[15] Carzo and Yanouzas, *op. cit.*, p. 191.

or compromise, to obtain the best total results in the light of the realities of a given situation.

Small-Group Research and the Span

There has been a considerable volume of research by those behavioral scientists interested in the operation of small groups.[16] Although this research is interested in the operation of small groups, whether formally organized or not, and in such considerations as group cohesiveness, individual satisfaction, performance, and leadership, it does have some relevance to the problem of span of management. In a very real sense, a manager and his immediate subordinates represent a small group. It is therefore interesting to see what light this research casts on the problem of span.

A number of interesting findings have come from these studies. In general, it has been found that group cohesiveness is best with approximately five members; fewer members do not provide enough interaction for cohesiveness, and many more than five tend to result in the breakdown of the groups into subgroups, or cliques. As might be expected, smaller groups tend to generate more individual satisfaction than larger ones, largely because of the greater opportunities for participation and the better chance of understanding group goals. Likewise in decision making, it has been shown that groups of five take less time than larger groups. However, studies have shown that a larger group may be able to solve a greater variety and a greater complexity of problems because of the probability of a greater variety of skills being available. On the other hand, these same studies have indicated that as group size increases, the problems of coordination and reaching a consensus become more difficult, particularly where a problem solution sought has no clear or objective answer. Furthermore, small group studies have shown that as groups become larger, the demands on the leader become more exacting and complex, and the group soon welcomes having more directive and highly structured leadership.

A review of small-group research and other behavioral investigations led House and Miner to conclude:[17]

The implications for the span of control seem to be that (1) under most circumstances the optimal span is likely to be in the range of 5 through 10; (2) the larger spans, say 8 through 10, are most appropriate at the highest, policy-making levels of an organization, where greater resources for diversified problem-solving appear to be needed (although diversified problem-solving without larger spans may well be possible); (3) the breadth of effective spans of first line supervisors is contingent on the technology of the organization; and (4) in prescribing the span of control for specific situations, consideration must be given to a host of local factors such as desirability of high group cohesiveness, the performance demands of the task, the degree of stress in the environ-

---

[16]This research is well summarized in R. J. House and J. B. Miner, "Merging Management and Behavioral Theory: The Interaction Between Span of Control and Group Size," *Administrative Science Quarterly*, vol. 14, no. 3, pp. 451–464 (September, 1969).

[17]*Ibid.*, pp. 461–462.

ment, task interdependencies, the need for member satisfaction, and the leadership skills available to the organization.

OPERATIONAL APPLICATION OF UNDERLYING-VARIABLES APPROACH

If, as the authors of this book believe, the number of subordinates that a manager can effectively supervise is not an exact number applicable generally but depends on underlying variables, it follows that managers should look at these variables for an answer to the span problem. Fortunately, such an experiment was undertaken a few years ago by the Lockheed Missiles and Space Company.[18]

The Underlying Variables

In the Lockheed program, the company identified a number of critical variables underlying the span of management. While the program was designed only to apply to the middle-management group where spans were found to be quite narrow (three to five), and while the underlying variables are not the same as those outlined by the authors above, there are many similarities. The company utilized for its analysis the following variables:

1. Similarity of functions. This factor referred to the degree to which functions performed by the various components or personnel reporting to a manager were alike or different.
2. Geographic contiguity. This factor referred to the physical locations of units of personnel reporting to a superior.
3. Complexity of functions. This factor referred to the nature of the task done and the department managed.
4. Direction and control. This factor referred to the nature of personnel reporting to a superior, the amount of training required, the extent to which authority could be delegated, and the personal attention needed.
5. Coordination. This factor was related to time requirements of keeping an organizational unit keyed in with other divisional or companywide activities.
6. Planning. This factor was designed to reflect the importance, complexity, and time requirements of the planning functions of the manager and his organizational unit.

Degree of Supervisory Burden within Span Factors

After identifying the underlying variables related to the span of management, the company spread each of them over a spectrum of five degrees of difficulty.

[18]For a report on this program see H. Koontz, "Making Theory Operational: The Span of Management," *The Journal of Management Studies*, vol. 3, no. 3, pp. 229–243 (October, 1966). See also, on the same problem, H. Stieglitz, "Optimizing the Span of Control," *Management Record*, vol. 24, no. 9, pp. 25–29 (September, 1962), and C. W. Barkdull, "Span of Control: A Method of Evaluation," *Michigan Business Review*, vol. 15, no. 3, pp. 25–32 (May, 1963).

For each span factor, also, weightings were given to reflect relative importance. The degrees and weights of the span factors are shown in Table 13.2.

It is worth noting that the weight values in these span factors were based on an analysis of 150 cases at the middle-management and department-director levels. They were also checked against a number of comparative cases, the measuring standard being those organizational units which were regarded on the score of both reputation and performance as being well managed. Even though the weightings and values applied can be criticized as representing pseudo-science, there is evidence that they were developed with care. Moreover, as in so many measurements applied to life, the breaking down of factors and assigning values to them did help in clarifying issues and giving visibility to the problem being analyzed.

Correction for Organizational Assistance

After each position had been evaluated and the total of values from factor weightings had been added, corrections were then made by application of a reducing factor to each score to take into account the amount of organizational assistance that a manager had. Thus, a direct-line assistant with responsibility

TABLE 13.2.   DEGREES OF SUPERVISORY BURDEN WITHIN SPAN FACTORS (numbers show relative weighting)

Span factor				
Similarity of functions	Identical	Essentially alike	Similar	Inherently different	Fundamentally distinct
	1	2	3	4	5
Geographic contiguity	All together	All in one building	Separate building, 1 plant location	Separate locations, 1 geographic area	Dispersed geographic areas
	1	2	3	4	5
Complexity of functions	Simple repetitive	Routine	Some complexity	Complex, varied	Highly complex, varied
	2	4	6	8	10
Direction and control	Minimum supervision and training	Limited supervision	Moderate periodic supervision	Frequent continuing supervision	Constant close supervision
	3	6	9	12	15
Coordination	Minimum relation with others	Relationships limited to defined courses	Moderate relationships easily controlled	Considerable close relationship	Extensive mutual non-recurring relationships
	2	4	6	8	10
Planning	Minimum scope and complexity	Limited scope and complexity	Moderate scope and complexity	Considerable effort required guided only by broad policies	Extensive effort required; areas and policies not charted
	2	4	6	8	10

for certain portions of a manager's operations resulted in the application of a factor of 0.70, and a staff assistant in administering, planning, or controlling resulted in the application of a reducing factor of 0.75 or 0.85. A first-line supervisor with four lead men would have a factor of 0.40 applied to his score.

The Supervisory Index

After scores for a given manager's position had been calculated and had been corrected by the organizational-assistance factor, they were compared with a standard. The suggested supervisory indexes are shown in Table 13.3. These were developed by using as a standard the cases of organizational units with wider spans which were generally considered to be effectively organized and managed. Thus, an individual manager could compare his own span factor ratings with the suggested standard span to determine whether he was below or above standard.

Results

Results from this experimental program were interesting. Even though the program was not completely adopted in the company and was not too strongly pressed, there is evidence that it did lead to a widening of the span of management in the middle-management area and to elimination of one complete level of supervision, with a consequent reduction in supervisory costs. Despite the rather crude methods necessarily used, by identification of the problem through looking at underlying variables and making personnel in managerial posts aware of these, significant results were attained. The program thus indicates that material rewards in practice can follow the application of theory to real problems, even where methods are not completely proved and basic data are inexact.

The Need for Balance

There can be no doubt that, despite the desirability of flattening organization structures, the span of management is limited by real and important restrictions. A manager may have more subordinates than he can manage, even

TABLE 13.3.   SUGGESTED SUPERVISORY INDEX

Total span factor weightings	Suggested standard span
40–42	4–5
37–39	4–6
34–36	4–7
31–33	5–8
28–30	6–9
25–27	7–10
22–24	8–11

though he delegates authority, carries on training, formulates plans and policies clearly, and adopts efficient control and communication techniques. It is equally true that, as an enterprise grows, the span-of-management limitations force an increase in organization levels.

What is required, of course, is a more precise balancing, in a given situation, of all pertinent factors. Widening spans and reducing levels may be the answer in some cases; the reverse may be true in others. One must balance *all* the costs of adopting one course or the other—not only the financial costs but costs in morale, personal development, and the attainment of enterprise objectives—in short, all the advantages and disadvantages. In military organization, perhaps the attainment of objectives quickly and without error would be most important; in department store operation, on the other hand, the long-run objective of profit may be best served by forcing initiative and personal development at the lower levels of the organization.

Much misunderstanding concerning the span of management has arisen from confusion. There is a tendency to regard the "theoretical" limits of effective span as being a fixed number of approximately three to seven or eight subordinates.[19]

The correct principle of span of management is that *there is a limit in each managerial position to the number of persons an individual can effectively manage, but the exact number in each case will vary in accordance with the effect of underlying variables and their impact on the time requirements of effective managing.* This basic principle does exist, has not been superseded, and is useful in guiding managers toward ably managing more subordinates and simplifying organization.

FOR DISCUSSION

1. Some 750 line bishops and some 1,200 other persons report directly to the Pope. Urwick and other writers seem to say that at top levels the number should not exceed six. At one time in the Bank of America organization over 600 bank managers reported to the chief executive officer. How do you fit these facts with the idea that there is a limit to the number of subordinates a manager can supervise?
2. At Lockheed Missiles and Space Company an attempt has been made to determine the span of managers by an arithmetic formula. Do you think this approach can be adopted in other enterprises? How?
3. When you become a manager, what criteria will you favor to determine your span?
4. How would you determine the optimum span of management in a given situation?
5. Does the application of principles recommend, as many critics insist, a "tall" organization structure with a limited span of management?

---

[19] For a summary of the opinions of various authorities, see Healey, *op. cit.*, pp. 11–15.

14

basic departmentation

The limitation on the number of subordinates that can be directly managed would restrict the size of enterprises if it were not for the device of departmentation. Grouping activities and employees into departments makes it possible to expand organizations to an indefinite degree. Departments, however, differ with respect to the basic patterns used to group activities. The nature of these patterns, developed out of practice, and their relative merits are dealt with in the following sections.

DEPARTMENTATION BY SIMPLE NUMBERS

Departmentation by simple numbers was once an important method in the organization of tribes, clans, and armies. Although it is rapidly falling into disuse, it still has certain applications in modern society.

The simple-numbers method of departmentizing is achieved by tolling off undifferentiated persons who are to perform certain duties at the direction of a manager. The essential fact is not what these people do, where they work, or what they work with but that the success of the undertaking depends only upon manpower.

In armies, portions of the infantry division are sometimes still organized upon the basis of numbers of men. Ground keepers for municipalities, universities, and large estates may be organized on this basis, as are house-to-house sales crews, collectors for community funds and membership drives, and common-labor crews.

Even though a cursory examination may impress an investigator with the number of people departmentized on a manpower basis, the usefulness of this organizational device has declined with each passing century. For one thing, labor skills have increased. In America the last stronghold of common labor is agriculture, and even here it is restricted more and more to the harvesting of fewer and fewer crops.

A second reason for the decline of the manpower basis of departmentizing is that groups composed of specialized personnel are frequently more efficient than those based on mere numbers. The reorganization of the defense forces of the United States on this basis is a case in point. Many ways have been found to combine men skilled in the use of different types of weapons into single units. For instance, the addition of artillery and tactical air support to the traditional infantry division makes it a much more formidable fighting unit than when each was organized separately.

A third and long-standing reason for the decline of departmentation by numbers is that it is only useful at the lowest level of the organization structure. At the middle- and higher-management levels activities tend to be grouped on a basis other than similarity. As soon as any other factor besides pure manpower becomes important, the simple-numbers basis of departmentation fails to produce good results.

DEPARTMENTATION BY TIME

One of the oldest forms of departmentation, normally used at lower levels of organization, is to group activities on the basis of time. The use of shifts is common in many enterprises where for economic or technological reasons the normal workday will not satisfy needs. Except for problems of supervision and the question of efficiency and cost of "swing" and "graveyard" shifts, this form causes few managerial problems.

DEPARTMENTATION BY ENTERPRISE FUNCTION

The grouping of activities in accordance with the functions of the enterprise is a widely accepted practice. It embodies what enterprises typically do. Since all undertakings involve the creation of utility and since this occurs in an exchange economy, the basic enterprise functions consist of production (creating utility or adding utility to a good or service), selling (finding customers, patients, clients, students, or communicants who will agree to accept the good or service at a price), and financing (raising and collecting, safeguarding, and expending the funds of the enterprise). It has been logical to group these activities into such typical departments as production, sales, and finance.

Often, these particular terms do not appear in the organization chart. First, there is no generally accepted terminology: manufacturing enterprises employ the terms "production," "sales," and "finance"; a wholesaler will speak of his activities as "buying," "selling," and "finance"; and a railroad, as "operations," "traffic," and "finance."

A second reason for variance of terms is that basic activities differ in importance: hospitals have no selling departments; churches, no production departments. This does not mean that these activities are not undertaken but merely that they are unspecialized or of such minor importance that they are combined with other activities.

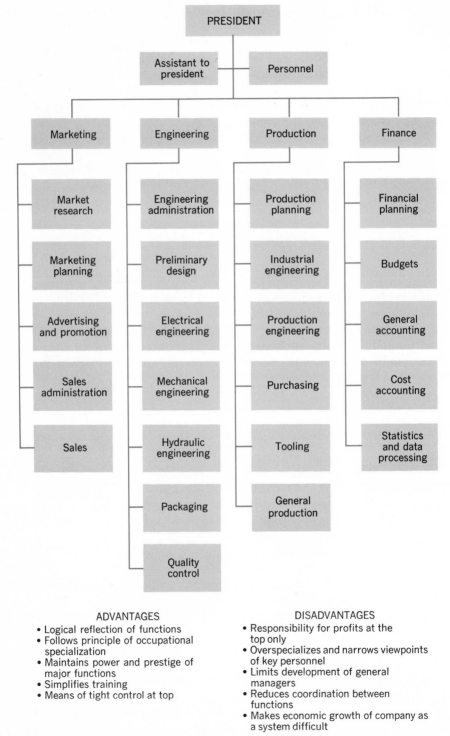

Figure 14.1 *Typical functional organization grouping (manufacturing company).*

A third reason for the absence of sales, production, or finance departments on many organization charts is that other methods of departmentation may have been deliberately selected, the functional basis being, after all, merely one way to organize. Those responsible for the enterprise may decide upon a product, customer, territorial, or marketing channel basis.

Functional departmentation is the most widely employed basis for organizing activities and is present in almost every enterprise at some level in the organization structure. When it is partially used, one function may be found—usually the finance department—beside or above a department based upon product, customer, or territory.

The characteristics of the selling, production, and finance functions of enterprise are so widely recognized and thoroughly understood that they are the basis not only of departmental organization but most often of primary departmentation. The primary level is the first level in the organization structure below the chief executive. The designation is made without consideration of the major or minor nature of the departments or the basis for grouping enterprise activities. Whenever activities are grouped into major functional departments, they will naturally be located in the organization structure at the primary level, while minor functional departments may be found almost anywhere below the first echelon.

Minor Functional Departments

In minor functional departments are grouped those activities which, although important to the enterprise, nevertheless lack the supremacy of major departments. What may be major in one enterprise, or at one time, may be minor at another. For example, in many enterprises during World War II, sales departments suddenly sank from major to minor importance because the firms had no sales problems other than that of rationing.

The choice of customer, territory, or product departmentation does not eliminate functional activities, but it diffuses and subordinates them. The structure may then be likened to the roots of a plant. Each root performs an essential function, but each, regarded singly, is subordinate in that its loss would not endanger the life of the plant. However, all the roots, combined, are of major importance.

Major Functional Departments

The term "major" may be used by various writers to identify departments with large budgets, many employees, or an importance related to the very existence of the enterprise. Large budgets and many employees are obviously independent of the causes of departmentation. The major functional departments in any organization structure are those which carry on its *characteristic activities*.

Without exception, every organization is engaged in creating utility in goods or services, exchanging this wealth at a price for purchasing power, and managing the cash flow which is entailed in the operation. This means that every organization has a production, sales, and financing function. Of course, everyone may not use these terms. A university produces educational services, it attracts students, and it finances its operations; a religious organization provides services, it attracts worshippers, and it also finances its operation. A lawyer offers services to his clientele for a price; a public accountant likewise proffers services to clients for a fee.

In each case, the services proffered are often divided between major departments. A university will offer services within groups of activities that may be called liberal arts, engineering, law, medicine, and business. A church may divide its services under such heads as general, Sunday school, missions, etc. If special departments covering any of these activities are not organized, it may mean that the state of the market does not require the exertion of maximum effort.

Derivative Functional Departments

Derivative functional departments are established when the manager of any functional division feels that his span of management is too broad. For instance, when an enterprise is small, the production manager may have only workers reporting to him. With the expansion of activities it may be necessary to split off the buying function and place a purchasing agent in charge. The new purchasing unit is a derivative functional department; it would appear on an organization chart at the second level, if production is a primary division. A typical grouping of functional activities into derivative departments is suggested in Table 14.1.

There are several points of interest here. First, the titles assigned to activities are not intended to represent standard practice, for none exists. They do, however, conform to rather widespread custom. Second, the suggested departmentation does not follow the practice of any single firm, since the stage of departmentation depends upon the span of management peculiar to each. A third point is that some types of enterprises, such as department stores, do not organize all primary functional departments directly into subordinate functional groups. The merchandise manager is in charge of the total buying and selling activity of the store, but the people who report to him are product-line buyers, who, in turn, do organize their activities into derivative functional groups. Some derivative functional departments, finally, are in turn subdivided into a second derivative functional grouping.

Advantages

The most important advantage of functional departmentation is that it is a logical and time-proved method. It is also the best way of making certain that the power and prestige of the basic activities of the enterprise will be defended by the top managers. This is an important consideration among functional managers, for they see on every side the encroachments of staff and service

TABLE 14.1. DERIVATIVE FUNCTIONAL DEPARTMENTS OF TYPICAL ORGANIZATION STRUCTURES

Primary functional department	*Derivative functional departments*

In a manufacturing organization

Production	Manufacturing:
	Fabrication
	Assembly
	Tooling
	Purchasing
	Production control:
	Scheduling
	Materials control
	Quality control
Sales	Selling:
	Selection
	Training
	Operation
	Advertising
	Sales promotion
Finance	Capital requirements
	Fund control
	Disbursements
	Credit
	Accounting

In a department-store operation

Publicity	Advertising
	Display
	Media public relations
Merchandising	Buying (organized by product line):
	Budgeting
	Merchandise control
	Sales promotion
	Sales force
General superintendent	Supplies
	Customer service
	Store protection
	Warehousing
	Receiving, marking, delivery
Finance	Financial management:
	Cash control
	Credit
	Accounting

In a wholesale organization

Sales	Buying (organized by product line):
	Budgeting
	Merchandise control
	Sales promotion
	Sales force

TABLE   14.1 *(continued)*

Primary functional department	Derivative functional departments

General superintendent	Warehousing:
	  Receiving
	  Will call
	  Shipping
	  Stockroom

Finance	Money management Credit and collections Accounting
In a service organization (airline)	

Operations	Engineering:
	  New equipment
	  Modification of equipment
	  Communications engineering
	Maintenance:
	  Line maintenance
	  Overhaul
	Ground operations:
	  Station management
	  Food and commissary
	Flight operations:
	  Flying
	  Communications
	  Dispatching

Traffic or sales	Administration:
	  Reservations
	  Schedules
	  Tariffs
	Sales:
	  Passenger sales
	  Cargo sales
	  Sales promotion
	Advertising:
	  Direct mail
	  Newspaper and periodical
	  Radio and television

Finance	Financial management:
	  Cash control
	  New financing
	  Foreign exchange
	Accounting:
	  Revenue
	  Disbursements
	  General ledger

groups, which sometimes threaten the security of the principal line executives. A third advantage is that functional departmentation follows the principle of occupational specialization, thereby making for efficiency in the utilization of manpower. Still other advantages are that it simplifies training and, because the top managers have end-result responsibility, it furnishes a means of tight control at the top.

Disadvantages

In spite of the advantages of functional departmentation, there are times when the claims of other methods seem even stronger. The size of the geographical area over which an enterprise operates may call for territorial grouping of activities; the production or purchase of numerous product lines, or of products designed for certain buyer classifications, may call for grouping along product or customer lines. In addition, functional departmentation may tend to de-emphasize the enterprise objectives as a whole. Accountants, production experts, and salesmen, growing up in specialized departments, often have difficulty seeing the business as a whole, and coordination between them is frequently difficult to achieve. Another disadvantage is that only the chief executive officer can be held responsible for profits. In small firms, this is as it should be, but in large firms the burden becomes too heavy for one man to bear.[1] What is perhaps most important is that, since the first *general* managerial position is that of the president or the executive vice-president, the functionally organized company is not the best training ground for promotable top managerial manpower.

DEPARTMENTATION BY TERRITORY

Departmentation based on geographical areas is a rather common method for physically dispersed enterprises. The principle is that all activities in a given area or territory should be grouped and assigned to a manager.

Extent of Use

Territorial departmentation is especially attractive to large-scale enterprises or other enterprises whose activities are physically or geographically spread. A plant may, however, be local in its activities and still assign the guards in its protection department on a territorial basis, placing two men, for instance, at each of the south and west gates. Department stores assign floor-walkers on this basis, and it is a common way to assign janitors, window washers, and the like. Business firms resort to this method when similar operations are undertaken in different geographic areas, as in automobile assembly, chain retailing and wholesaling, and oil refining. Many government agencies—the Internal Revenue Service, the Federal Reserve Board, the federal courts, and the Postal Service, for example—adopt this basis of organization in their efforts to provide like services simultaneously across the nation.

Reasons for Use

Although it is important for the enterprise considering territorial departmentation to base its decision on the right reasons, frequently the choice is made for the wrong reasons.

---

[1] See Cyril O'Donnell, "Gladding, McBean & Company," in *Cases in General Management* (Homewood, Ill.: Richard D. Irwin, Inc., 1961).

The wrong reasons   Poor communication facilities are often advanced as a reason for territorial departmentation. At one time, this reason was good, and in many parts of the world it still is. In general, communication is now so easy that this reason is less forceful. With telephone, telegraph, and television, an associate many miles away can sometimes be reached more quickly than can the man in the next office.

The need for taking prompt action in a given area is also cited as a good reason for territorial departmentation. The assumption is that the local officer will be prompt, but he may not be. Nor is so-called ease of coordination and control on a local basis sufficient reason for territorial grouping. Fumbling will give poor results, whether perpetrated by local officers or by central office managers.

Further, those who advocate area grouping for the above reasons miss the point, developed in the next section, that not all the enterprise activities are actually associated on a territorial basis anyway. Concentrating attention on those which are locally grouped overlooks the serious management problems created when different organizational methods are employed simultaneously.

The right reasons   Territorial departmentation is proper when its purpose is to encourage local participation in decision making and to take advantage of certain economies of localized operation. Many enterprises, as a matter of policy, avoid local participation in some or all phases of their activities. On the other hand, the managers of many firms, with great or little fanfare, do their very best to encourage it.

The firm that makes allowances for local elements in a situation will find many opportunities to do so. Those which can tie in their product with such local phenomena as fishing facilities, skiing opportunities, sunbathing, or the occurrence of smog can use local appeals in their advertising. Sometimes supplies are ordered on a local basis, as when managers of chain retail stores tie in with local businesses for construction, supplies, and services.

Sales managers look with favor upon the local recruitment of salesmen. Familiar with area factors that outsiders would have to learn, such men are not required to uproot their families and are presumed to know how to deal with area customers. Men recruited elsewhere may be better men, but they will require adjustment to local factors.

Although the great improvements in communication have largely eradicated differences in custom, style, and product preferences, many enterprises still consider these differences important enough to treat on a local basis. If it is enterprise policy to heed local factors, territorial departmentation can provide the area with a manager who has the prestige essential for getting results. Middle- and high-level managers may not be ready to listen to the bleat of a distant salesman, but they will listen to the representations of a regional executive. Finally, good as mechanical and electronic communication is becoming, there is really nothing that takes the place of face-to-face discussion. A deeper and fuller understanding is achieved, both about the person and the subject matter being discussed.

The economic reasons for selecting territorial departmentation concern the cost of getting things done. Plants for the manufacture and assembly of parts may be located so as to reduce transportation costs. The proper location of warehouse facilities will reduce the time required for delivery, a factor that may affect booking the order. Any arrangement of salesmen's routes to reduce traveling during their best hours for sales will likewise reduce the expense of distribution.

The district, region, or branch has long been recognized as an excellent training ground for managers. It is made to order for giving them essential experience at a place in the organization structure and at a time in their careers most valuable to them and least risky for the firm. This is not to say that a firm should organize territorially in order to permit subordinate managers to gain essential experience, but it is a factor to consider in deciding upon the type of departmentation.

Application in Functional Areas

The reasons for departmentation on a territorial basis do not apply with equal force to all enterprise activities. Neither are they applicable at the same organization levels within different departments. The place and the point in an organization structure at which the strength of these reasons overpowers other considerations are so highly variable that there are few rules to guide the organizer.

Advantages

Each of the three primary functional areas of enterprise activity may now be analyzed from the point of view of the proper reasons for regional grouping. In the production department, the proposal for organizing on a regional basis would mean the establishing of plants, to be engaged in manufacturing, mining, refining, or assembling the *same* product, in various areas. By catering to local factors, the production activity would gain certain advantages: the good will produced by providing jobs for local labor, for instance. But the chief gains would be economic: lower freight rates, and perhaps lower rent, and lower labor costs.

The advantages of territorial organization of sales activity are primarily economy and effectiveness. Sales personnel with a localized territory can spend more of their time in sales and less in travel. Also, they can be closer to customers and get to know their needs better, and in so doing serve customers better. By being closer, they can know what the market is, what its preferences are, and what marketing strategy is most likely to succeed. Perhaps of all enterprise activities, sales is most likely to be organized on a territorial basis.

The span of management is also an important factor in such practices. The grouping of activities on an area basis may mean establishing a thousand districts, the managers of which cannot report directly to the general sales manager. Since his span of management may be limited to eight or ten sub-

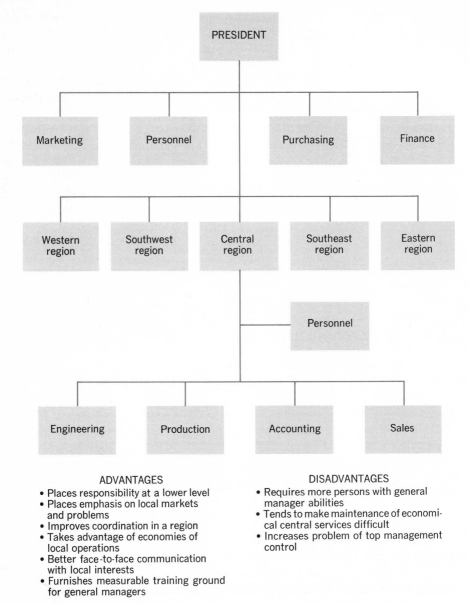

ADVANTAGES
- Places responsibility at a lower level
- Places emphasis on local markets and problems
- Improves coordination in a region
- Takes advantage of economies of local operations
- Better face-to-face communication with local interests
- Furnishes measurable training ground for general managers

DISADVANTAGES
- Requires more persons with general manager abilities
- Tends to make maintenance of economical central services difficult
- Increases problem of top management control

Figure 14.2 *Typical territorial organization grouping (manufacturing company).*

ordinates, he would have to have the thousand managers report to about a hundred superiors at the branch level, who would in turn report to ten or so regional managers. Three territorial *levels* within the sales department would thus be established.

The reasons for area departmentation apply with little or no force to the finance function of enterprise. The development of sources of funds, their safety, disbursement, and control—typical activities of a finance department— enjoy few gains from catering to local factors. On the other hand, the economies of centralization of these activities are so pronounced that virtually all enterprises strive for them.

Neither is there a general rule relating to the level within the department at which territorializing should be considered. Decisions depend upon the facts in each case. It would be purely a coincidence if both the sales and the production activities would reap net advantages from area grouping at the same levels. Also, the likelihood that all derivative functional departments should be departmentized on an area basis is extremely remote.

Disadvantages

There are, however, definite disadvantages in organizing territorially. Most of them are the same as those found with product departmentation. Geographic departmentation requires more persons with general managerial abilities, clearly increases the problem of headquarters control, and tends to lead to duplication of many services which could be performed centrally in a functional organization.

Especially at the top level, the general manager of a territorial division understandably wants to have his own purchasing, personnel, accounting, and other services so that he can be truly responsible for profitable operations. This is also likely to be true of territorial departmentation of a sales or production activity. The district sales manager or the Midwest manufacturing manager is not unreasonable in preferring not to rely on central services at headquarters. Sometimes, it is feared, headquarters managers worry unduly about this apparent duplication of service functions and are concerned more with what they cost than with how they help a territorial manager to perform more effectively.

DEPARTMENTATION BY PRODUCT

The grouping of activities on the basis of product or product lines has long been growing in importance in multiline large-scale enterprises. It has been an evolutionary process. Typically, the enterprises adopting this form were originally organized functionally. With the growth of the firm, production managers, sales and service managers, and engineering executives encountered problems of size. The managerial job became intolerably complex, and the span of management limited their ability to increase the number of immediate subordinate managers. At this point, reorganization on a product division basis was indicated. This strategy permits top management to delegate a division executive extensive authority over the manufacturing, sales, service, and engineering functions that relate to a given product or product line and to exact a considerable degree of profit responsibility from him.

Advantages

Product or product line is an important basis for departmentation because it facilitates the employment of specialized capital, makes easier a certain type of coordination, and permits the maximum use of personal skills and specialized knowledge. For instance, the sales effort of a particular man may be most effective when confined to lubricants, or conveyors, or power plants, each of which is best sold by the expert thoroughly familiar with his product. Where the potential volume of business is high enough to employ fully such a salesman, the advantages of product departmentation are significant.

This basis of grouping activities also permits, although not exclusively,

Figure 14.3 *Typical product organization grouping (manufacturing company).*

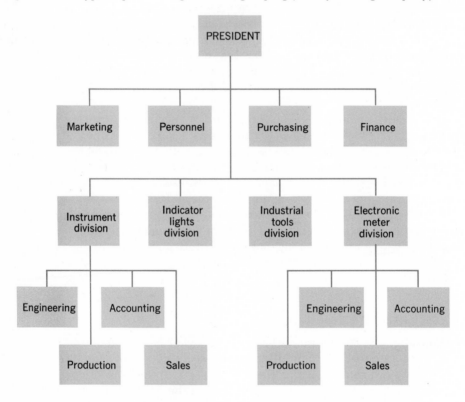

ADVANTAGES
- Places attention and effort on product line
- Places responsibility for profits at the division level
- Improves coordination of functional activities
- Furnishes measurable training ground for general managers
- Permits growth and diversity of products and services

DISADVANTAGES
- Requires more persons with general manager abilities
- Tends to make maintenance of economical central services difficult
- Presents increased problem of top management control

the employment of specialized capital goods. If production of an item, or closely related items, is sufficiently large to employ specialized facilities fully, strong pressure will be felt for product departmentation, in order to realize economic advantages in manufacturing, assembly, or handling.

If it is important for activities relating to a particular product to be co-ordinated, then product departmentation may be preferred. Better timing and customer service can thus sometimes be provided. If sales and engineering effort also emanates from the plant, cooperation with production can be exceptionally good. Other factors that may reduce this advantage will be considered presently.

Finally, profit responsibility can be exacted from product department managers. Where they supervise the sales, production, engineering, service, and cost functions, they may be required to achieve predetermined profit goals. They share the responsibility of producing a profit along with other similarly organized groups and thus enable a general manager to evaluate more intelligently the contribution of each product line to total profit.

In considering this advantage, however, care is essential if oversimplification is to be avoided. Even product-line managers may be saddled with heavy overhead costs, allocated from the expense of operating the general office, perhaps a research division, and frequently many service divisions.

Accountants will recognize the similarity of these problems with those attendant upon establishing profit centers within primary functional departments, or with those accounting procedures designed to identify the responsibility of product lines within functional divisions for generating costs. In these cases the amount of guesswork in making allocations is simply greater than is the case in true product departmentation.

Employment in Functional Areas

The product basis for grouping activities can be successful in all functional areas except industrial relations and finance. In the former, where the enterprise must deal with a single national union, and especially with its national officers, it is usually essential that administration be centralized. This permits the employment of skilled managers to negotiate with unions and to make authoritative interpretations of the company-wide agreement. The centralization of authority over finance enables top managers to economize in the use of a very scarce resource and, by this means, hold the enterprise together.

All other functions can be successfully organized on a product basis. Such a well-known grouping as Buick, Cadillac, Chevrolet, and other divisions of General Motors rests upon the product basis. The buyers who report to the merchandise manager of a department store are known by their product lines. Hospitals departmentalize on the basis of such services as surgery and radiology, and relief organizations include such "product" departments as food, clothing, shelter, and medical care.

Sales managers of enterprises that manufacture numerous items group them on the basis of their similarity. Wholesalers do the same thing. Examples: a linen department; a period-furniture grouping; an electronics department, including condensers, capacitors, transistors, and similar items. This departmental structure permits the salesmen to gain a broad and deep product knowledge. A commercial bank, too, is quite likely to subdivide its loan activities into commercial, industrial, and personal loans, and its investment activities into securities, real estate, and trusts.

Disadvantages

The disadvantages of product departmentation are virtually identical with those encountered in territorial departmentation. They include the necessity of having more persons with general managerial abilities available, the dangers of increased cost through duplication of central service and staff activities, and the problem of maintaining top-management control. The latter becomes especially important because a product division manager is, to a very great extent, in the same position as the chief executive of a single product-line company. Enterprises that operate with product divisions take care, as the General Motors Company has, to place enough decision making and control at the headquarters level so that the entire enterprise does not disintegrate.

CUSTOMER DEPARTMENTATION

The grouping of activities to reflect a paramount interest in the customer is commonly found in a variety of enterprises. The customer is the key to the way activities are grouped when the things an enterprise does for him are managed by one department head. The industrial sales department of a wholesaler who also sells to retailers is a case in point.

There are close decisions to be made in separating some types of customer departments from product departments. For instance, in the great central cash markets for agricultural products, the loan officers of commercial banks frequently specialize in fruit, vegetables, and grain, and even to such a point that they will make loans only on wheat or oranges. This is a clear case of customer departmentation, because loan service is provided by type of customer. On the other hand, a grouping such as sales, manufacturing, engineering, and cost accounting, all of which are concerned with serving a single customer type, such as public utilities, would be likely to be called "functional departmentation" even though the special customer is identifiable.

Extent of Use

Customer departmentation is utilized in many types of enterprises. Businessmen frequently arrange activities on this basis to cater to the requirements of clearly defined customer groups; and educational institutions offer regular and extension courses to serve different groups of students.

Reasons for Use

The special and widely varied needs of customers for clearly defined service impel many suppliers to departmentize on this basis. The manufacturer who

TABLE 14.2   DERIVATIVE PRODUCT DEPARTMENTS OF TYPICAL ORGANIZATION STRUCTURES

Primary product department	Derivative product departments
A meat packer (production department)	
Dairy and poultry	Butter, cheese, hatcheries, ice cream, eggs, poultry, dried milk
Beef, lamb, and veal	Calf buying, cattle buying, lamb buying, hides and skins, wools
Branch-house provision (functional department)	Casing, hog buying
By-products	Hides and fats, cleanser, gelatin, glue, industrial oils, soap and glycerine, tallow
Plant food	Insecticides and fungicides, phosphate rock
Agricultural research	Canned foods, margarine, table-ready meats, vegetable oil, dog and cat food
A container manufacturer (sales department)	
Food industries	Processed food, prepared food, coffee, dairy
Drug and chemical	Pharmaceutical and proprietary, household and chemical, prescription
Closure and plastics	
Beverage industries	Beverage, brewery, liquor
An insurance company (finance department)	
Investment (a functional derivative)	Mortgages, private placements, public utility, transportation, industrial, government

sells to both wholesalers and industrial buyers frequently finds that the needs of the two outlets can best be met by specialized salesmen. The wholesaler requires a product of dependable quality, available on a continuous reorder basis, and suited to the ultimate consumer. The industrial buyer wants a product that will save money, which frequently calls for high quality, plus a service that includes survey of needs, installation and repair of the product, and the specific training of employees.

Nonbusiness groups follow similar practices. The extension work of universities is arranged, with respect to time, subject matter, and sometimes instructors, to appeal to an entirely different group of students from those who attend on a full-time day basis. The operations of a Community Chest drive are arranged on the basis of different "customer" classifications. And departments of the federal government are set up to care particularly for farmers, businessmen, industrial workers, old people, and others.

Employment in Functional Departments

Customer departmentation is often found useful for grouping the sales activity of those firms that cater to different classes of customers. For instance, it is not unusual for a manufacturer with only an industrial market to divide his customers into large and small accounts. On the other hand, manufacturers may not develop derivative customer departments in their production function.

A manufacturer of typewriters does not specialize his production facilities in terms of university students and insurance-company customers. Even when separating the manufacture of standard and electric typewriters, the resulting departmentation is on a product and not on a customer basis.

Independent wholesalers and retailers combine their sales and production functions and then subdepartmentize them according to product. Sometimes, however, they organize customer departments. For instance, department stores often carry similar merchandise in the bargain basement and on an upper floor, organizing the two departments under two buyers. This is customer departmentation, since it assumes that different income groups patronize the two areas.

The finance departments of manufacturers, wholesalers, and retailers have no need for customer departmentation, since they are operated with a view to the welfare of the enterprise rather than to the needs of customers.

Disadvantages

Customer departmentation is not enjoyed without certain drawbacks. There is, for instance, the difficulty of coordination between this type of department and those organized on other bases, with constant pressure from the managers of customer departments for special treatment.

Another disadvantage is the possibility of underemployment of facilities and manpower specialized in terms of customer groups. In periods of recession some customer groups may all but disappear, for example, machine-tool manufacturers; in periods of expansion the unequal development of customer groups is characteristic.

MARKETING CHANNEL DEPARTMENTATION

One of the newer forms of basic departmentation is to organize an enterprise around channels of marketing. It is not uncommon for the same product to be marketed through widely different marketing channels.

This may appear to be customer departmentation, and it is similar. However, the essential consideration in departmentation is the marketing channel used and not the customer himself.

For example, the Purex Corporation found some years ago, when it moved from a functional to a divisional organization, that neither product nor territorial departmentation patterns would work. Various soaps and detergents moved to the ultimate customer through the grocery supermarkets as well as through drug stores and drug chains. On investigating these channels it was found that the ways of doing business, the kinds of buyers, and the methods of sales and promotion were so different in grocery markets and in drug chains and stores that it was wise to establish a grocery products division and a drug and toiletries division. While this may sound like product departmentation, it was not. The grocery products division made the various soap and detergent items that were marketed through the drug and toiletries division.

This innovation in basic departmentation is, in a way, not surprising. As industry has moved into an era of supercompetition, one could expect that marketing considerations would be dominant in setting up an organization structure. Where these fit with product or territorial departmentation, such more traditional forms will work. But, to a very great extent, product divisisionalization has been based on technical production factors and not on marketing. The du Pont Company found this some years ago when marketing considerations led the company to consolidate their Orlon, Nylon, and Dacron Divisions into one Textile Fibers Division. Likewise with the reorganization of Westinghouse in recent years, Chairman Burnham has methodically not organized primarily around products but around marketing channels. As in the case of the Purex Corporation, where a given product is best marketed through different marketing channels and it has seemed wise to divisionalize around these channels, the decision is then made on which division will manufacture a given product for another division.

It is reasonable to expect that basic departmentation around marketing channels may increase as time goes by. Like all types of organization patterns, the purpose of any grouping of activities must be to facilitate successful operation, to create an environment for effective performance.

PROCESS OR EQUIPMENT DEPARTMENTATION

The grouping of enterprise activities about a process or a type of equipment is often employed by manufacturing establishments. Such a basis of departmentation is illustrated in a paint or electrolytic-process grouping or in the arrangement in one plant area of punch presses or automatic screw machines. Manpower and materials are brought together in such a department in order to carry out a particular operation.

One of the common examples of equipment departmentation is the existence of electronic data-processing departments. As such installations become more expensive and complex and have ever-increasing capacities, they have tended to be isolated in a separate department. While it has become a rare medium-sized and even smaller company that does not have such a department, and virtually all major divisions of larger companies have such installations, changes in technology have, to some extent, given rise to a degree of decentralization. Computer stations connected to an enterprise's central computer or an outside one under a time-sharing or leasing basis, minicomputers, and electronic desk computers have tended to slow the proliferation of centralized computer departments. However, the major data-processing departments will unquestionably continue to exist and to be placed fairly high in the organization structure.

The purpose of such departmentation is to achieve economic advantages, although it may also be required by the nature of the equipment involved. For instance, a large computer requires heavy specialized capital, since it may not be possible to utilize economically small units of this apparatus.

MATRIX ORGANIZATION

One of the interesting and increasingly used forms of organization is variously referred to as "matrix" or "grid" organization, or "project" or "product management" although, as will be noted presently, pure project management need not imply a grid or matrix. The essence of matrix management, as one normally finds it, is the combining of functional and product forms of departmentation in the same organization structure. As is shown in Figure 14.4, depicting matrix organization in an engineering department, there are functional managers in charge of engineering functions with an overlay of project managers responsible for the end product—a project. While this form has been common in engineering and research and development, it has also been widely used, although seldom drawn with a matrix, in product marketing management.

Why Matrix Management Is Used

Matrix management really represents a compromise between functional and product departmentation. As companies and customers have become increasingly interested in end results, that is, the final product or completed project, there has been pressure to establish responsibility in someone to assure such end results. Of course, this could be accomplished by organizing along traditional product departmentation lines. This is often done, even in engineering where a project manager is put in charge of all the engineering and support personnel to accomplish an entire project. This kind of organization is depicted in Figure 14.5.

But full project organization may not be feasible for a number of reasons. In engineering, for example, the project may not be able to utilize certain specialized personnel or equipment full time; a solid state physicist may only be needed occasionally and the project might only need part-time use of an expensive environmental test laboratory or a prototype shop. Also, the project might be of relatively short duration. While there is no *logical* reason why an organization structure should not be changed daily or monthly, there is the practical reason that people, particularly highly trained professionals, simply will not tolerate the insecurity of frequent organization change. Another reason why pure project organization may not be feasible is that highly trained professionals (and some that are not so highly trained) generally prefer to be allied organizationally with their professional group. They feel more at home; they feel that their professional reputation and advancement will be better served by belonging to such a group than by being allied with a project; and they believe that if their superior is a professional in the same field, he will be more likely to appreciate their expertise at times of salary advances, promotions, or layoffs. This is not only true of engineers and scientists; one finds it also with lawyers, accountants, and university professors.[2]

The reasons for existence of a matrix organization in commercial or in-

---

[2] Very few professors, for example, want to be known as members of the undergraduate, M.B.A., or Ph.D. faculties; they would rather be known as members of the accounting, finance, or management theory departments.

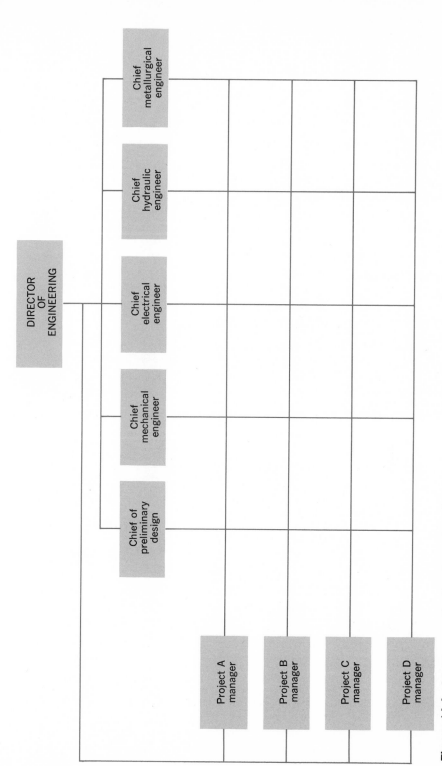

Figure 14.4 *Matrix organization in engineering.*

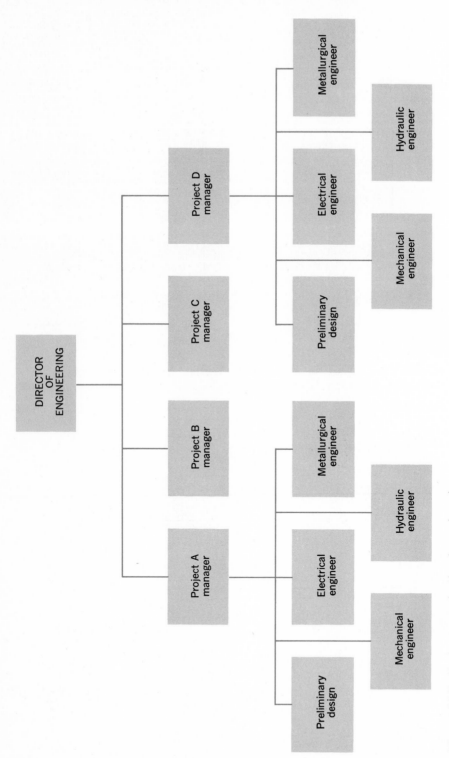

Figure 14.5 *Project organization in engineering.*

dustrial product management may be somewhat different. In a soap and detergent company, for example, the top management may want individual responsibility for profit to exist for a given product or brand. If the company had only one product or brand, there would obviously be no problem; the chief executive would have profit responsibility. If the company could organize through the use of an integrated (research, marketing, manufacturing) product division, then the division manager would have profit responsibility. But where, as in a multiproduct soap and detergent company, technology and economics dictate that the company will not have separate manufacturing facilities or sales forces for each product, the only way to get a degree of profit responsibility is to overlay, in some way, a product manager with responsibility for profit for a given brand or product.

Variations in Practice

There are many variations of the project or product manager in practice, in addition to the pure product department. In some cases, the project or product manager has no authority to tell any functional department to do anything. In these cases, he may be only an information gatherer on how his project or product is proceeding, reporting to a top executive when significant deviations from plans occur. His role might be that of a persuader, using his knowledge and personality to get results. Obviously, these roles have some very serious drawbacks, particularly if the manager without any organization power whatsoever is actually held responsible for end results. There can be no wonder that turnover among such position holders has been high.

Another variation in practice is to simply draw the grid or matrix, showing certain managers in charge of functional departments and others in charge of projects or products. This is usually intended to convey a pure case of dual command. The results, as experience has shown, are predictable. If something goes wrong with a project or product, it is often difficult for a top superior to know whose fault it is and where the difficulties really lie. A superior faced with this kind of situation would do just as well not to know that the deviation exists since, if he cannot trace responsibility, there is little he can do to correct it. Also, in such cases, there tend to arise the usual friction, buck-passing, and confusion one would expect from disunity of command.[3]

Solution in Engineering and Research and Development

The more sophisticated companies in high technology industries, that have found no alternative to matrix management, have largely solved the problem by clarification of the authorities and responsibilities of the functional and project managers. The project manager is normally given authority over the integrity of a total design; he usually has the interface with the customer, al-

---

[3] For interesting research on problems in project management, see C. Reeser, "Human Problems of the Project Form of Organization," *Academy of Management Journal*, vol. 12, no. 4, pp. 459–467 (December, 1969).

though in many instances this will be passed on to the marketing department; he is given authority over budget and in this case becomes essentially a buyer of services from the functional managers; and he is given the authority to work out schedules and priorities for his project with the functional departments. On the latter point, if he cannot work out priorities on his project because of the claims of another project manager and if he and the other project manager cannot compromise these, then the matter of priorities goes to a higher authority, usually the manager who has primary responsibility for relationships with all customers.

Under this system of clarification, the functional manager is given authority over the people in his area and over the integrity of engineering or research work done in his function. Thus, between the project manager and the functional manager, much of the problem of disunity of command is eliminated, although there still may be a degree of conflict and fuzziness in such borderline areas as total project design accuracy and integrity.

Solution in Product Management

Although the Procter & Gamble Company and Libby, McNeil & Libby have successfully used product management in the marketing of their products for over forty years, and other prominent companies like Lever Brothers and General Foods have used it for many years, most of the development of its use has occurred in the past two decades.[4]

There are, as might be expected, a very large number of uses of the term "product manager," varying all the way from applying it to the general manager of an integrated product division to applying it to little more than a staff assistant in the marketing head's organization who gathers information and makes recommendations. But a matrix form of organization does not occur until the product manager has some degree of authority over functional departments that do not report to him.

Research on the degree of authority held by product managers shows that in most companies he may be held, to some degree, responsible for the success of the brands of products assigned to him, but he has been given either little or no authority to accomplish these results, or an ambiguous one of being a charming persuader.[5] It is an interesting thing that this promising organizational device, aiming as it does in a functionally organized company toward giving someone responsibility for end results, should follow the history of ambiguity and lack of authority experienced for years in engineering.

However, there are a number of companies that have begun to solve this problem of authority in a way to make this a real and reasonably workable

---

[4] See R. M. Fulmer, "Product Management: Panacea or Pandora's Box?" *California Management Review*, vol. 7, no. 4, pp. 63–74 (Summer, 1965).

[5] See, for example, Fulmer, *op. cit.*; G. H. Evans, *The Product Manager's Job* (New York: American Management Association, 1964); B. C. Ames, "Payoff from Product Management," *Harvard Business Review*, vol. 41, no. 6, pp. 141–152 (November–December, 1963); D. J. Luck and T. Nowack, "Product Management—Vision Unfulfilled," *Harvard Business Review*, vol. 43, no. 3, pp. 143–157 (May–June, 1965).

matrix organization. One of the best solutions is that used by Proctor & Gamble for many years. In this company a brand manager (located in the advertising department since the company has long had a policy of preselling through advertising and promotion) derives his authority in an interesting way. He develops the plan for his brand, covering not only advertising but also use of the field sales force, research assistance, packaging, and manufacturing programs, and he negotiates with the various functional departments for the part they will play in the program and the costs involved. After such a comprehensive brand program is developed, it goes up the line in the company until it and other brand programs are finally approved by the chief executive. Then, armed with such an approved plan, the brand manager hardly needs any other authority. While the organization chart would not show a grid, the fact is that one exists through plans approved at the top.

Matrix Organization and the Future

With increased emphasis on end results and in goal accomplishment, there can hardly be any doubt that increasing use will be made of some form of matrix organization, especially since it is often not possible to give a manager direct line authority over all the activities necessary to accomplish major end results. This trend is also a recognition of the fact that programs represent interacting networks and systems.

But if modern managers are to meet the challenge involved in matrix organization and get the results desired, they must step up better than they have to the task of clarifying authorities. As noted earlier, good people may make an ambiguous structure work, but they can certainly work better where roles are clarified.

TEMPORARY DEPARTMENTATION

This classification may sound a bit odd, but it does convey the chief attribute of certain organizational devices. Among those of widest application and usefulness are the temporary product division and the task force.

Temporary Product Division

This type of structure is identical with the product department organization discussed above. It is distinguished only in the fact that it has a predetermined lifetime. The best example comes from the defense industry. A firm may win a production contract for a given number of a specific missile. The production schedule covers an intermediate period of time, such as three years. Instead of integrating this production with its other products, a firm may decide that a separate division should be organized to undertake the effort, with the full intention of dismantling the division as soon as the contract is completed.

There are several advantages of departmentizing in this way. Costing is facilitated. The production is not expected to recur, and the facilities are not integrated with others which are normally required. The whole operation is looked upon as supplemental to the normal effort of the firm, and there is no implication that either facilities, leases, capital or employees will be absorbed by the firm at the conclusion of the contract.

The major disadvantage in operating in this way concerns the employees. They are sometimes not covered by all the corporate fringe benefits enjoyed by the permanent cadre. They know they are temporary in the sense that the job is predetermined in time. For these reasons morale problems are a major consideration, even though any firm will try to persuade those employees it highly regards that they will have an opportunity to transfer to the more permanent parts of the enterprise.

Task Force

As the name implies, although it is sometimes referred to as a composite or interdisciplinary team, this is a temporary organization whose objective is to investigate and recommend a solution for a problem or a proposal. Instead of breaking a problem down into its parts, assigning them to various departments, and relying on coordination between them, a group with appropriate expertise is assembled to solve the problem as a joint effort. Each member of the force is selected for his expertise; he typically reports administratively to his regular manager; he is detailed full- or part-time to the force; and the group is chaired by a person to whom is delegated the authority essential to accomplish the task.

This approach to problem solving is an effective way to get a solution for situations beyond the power of one manager to settle. Because it is assigned nonrecurring yet difficult problems, there is no need for a permanent group to be established. The members of the force are specialists detailed from anywhere in the total organization. A quick recommendation is provided and the group can then be disbanded. And it is often much more economical and effective than outside consulting services.

There are several disadvantages in using this form. The enterprise may not have the required specialists on its payroll. Even if it does, it is entirely possible that they cannot be spared, even part-time, from their regular duties. On the other hand, if the specialist can be spared for such a temporary assignment, he may be reluctant to serve for fear of losing contact with his regular position. Another drawback is that the task-force manager is seldom given administrative authority over his team members and may encounter difficulty in getting their active cooperation to accomplish the task on schedule. On the other hand, where a task is regarded as important in an enterprise and where it is challenging to the team members, motivation is not normally a difficulty.

EVALUATION OF ALTERNATIVES IN SELECTING DEPARTMENTATION

Departmentation is not an end in itself but is simply a method of arranging activities to facilitate the accomplishment of enterprise objectives. It is not even an unmixed good, for the separation of activities on any basis creates problems of coordination difficult to solve. Each method has its advantages and disadvantages. Consequently, the process of selection involves a consideration of the relative advantages of each type at each level in the organization structure. In all cases the *central question* concerns the type of environment that the manager wishes to design.

Primary Departmentation

At the primary level the claims of the functional basis of departmentation are especially strong. This method most closely conforms to the basic activities of every enterprise, and it permits the coordination by one person of each function. With all production activity under one person, sales under someone else, and finance under another, the chief general officer can concentrate on the coordination of staff and service departments with functional areas without being himself involved in the internal affairs of production, sales, and finance.

Exceptions to functional departmentation at the primary level are usually difficult to justify except in multiproduct firms or enterprises selling or servicing widespread geographic areas. Even here, coordination along functional lines is often provided for by staff executives. On the other hand, there should be no hesitancy in employing any basis if a legitimate case can be made for it.

Although there may be occasions when functional sales and production departments will not be organized at the primary level, there are almost never circumstances that justify a similar abandonment of the functional finance department. Indeed, the finance division occupies a unique place in enterprise. As a function, finance must be represented at the primary level, because the corporate handling of and accounting for funds must be coincident with the general management of the corporation. This is not to say that all financial and accounting activities must be carried on in a functional finance department reporting at a primary level, but rather that there must be such a central function summarizing and controlling the accounting for those activities on an over-all corporate basis.

Intermediate Departmentation

Intermediate departmentation includes all the grouped activities that appear in the organization structure between the primary departments at the top and the departments at the bottom of the hierarchy. It is in the choice of bases for departmentation at such levels that managers find decision making most difficult. There are no general rules. It is certain, however, that below the primary functional departmentation the claims of most of the other methods of grouping activities become more insistent. And it is probable that at secondary and lower levels these claims may best be satisfied.

In the production function the claims of product departmentation exert heavy pressure at the secondary level whenever there is marked diversity of product or of product lines or a geographic dispersion of operations. The functional production manager of a firm manufacturing various electronic components normally will establish product-line departments. But if only condensers were made, no product departmentation would take place. Consideration might then be given to the claims for territorial departmentation at the secondary level.

Sometimes it is possible to secure advantages of two or more methods at the same level, as when the establishment of a secondary-level product department permits a firm to locate the plant where it can also reap the economies of territorial departmentation.

The functional sales manager is usually faced with strong reasons for territorial departments at the secondary level. This is true even of firms that narrowly confine their distribution. City department stores open branches to serve suburban territories; salesmen's territories are commonly established even within cities. Where the product basis has strong appeal, the coordination of activities is greatly facilitated if this departmentation is organized at the secondary level. Similarly, customer departmentation usually occurs at the secondary level.

There is no virtue in attempting to maintain a mechanical similarity in choosing the bases of departmentation. Although strong claims of functional departmentation may result in functional grouping at the primary level, the secondary level in a sales department may be composed of a territorial or customer grouping, the production department may have a product classification, and the finance department may utilize derivative functional groupings. It is on the ground of net advantage to the functional department executive, not of parallelism, that the basis is selected.

MIXING DEPARTMENTATION

In the evaluation of the alternative methods of departmentation it was made clear that each method yields certain gains, and that the achievement of parallelism in the intermediate departmentation of the functional divisions is not a proper organizational objective.

Another point to be highlighted concerns the mixing of departmentation within a functional area. For instance, a wholesale drug firm has grouped the buying and selling activities relating to beverages in one product department but has grouped, on the same level, all other selling activities on a territorial basis. A manufacturer of plastic goods has territorialized both the production and sale of all of its products except dinnerware, which is a product department. A functional department manager may, in other words, employ two or more bases for grouping activities on the same organizational levels. Such practices may be justified on logical grounds, because the objective of departmentation is not to build a rigid structure, balanced in terms of levels and characterized by consistency and identical bases. The purpose is to group activities in the manner which will best contribute to achieving enterprise objectives. If variety of bases does this, there is no reason why any manager should not take advantage of the alternatives before him.

The logic of this view is frequently ignored by the heads of organization service or staff departments in large-scale enterprises whether of a public or a private nature. For some reason, possibly aesthetics or control, it is often insisted that all departmentized activities below the primary level of organization be grouped in exactly the same manner. For instance, the organization structure of the Internal Revenue Service at the regional and district levels is exactly the same despite tremendous variation in district sizes. Firms with multiplants often organize them in the same way; thus, the same departments will be found in virtually all stores of Sears, Roebuck and Company.

The aesthetic reason for identical organization structure of similar enterprise groupings is really not at all persuasive. The organization planner may think it "looks better," but this is a poor reason for organizing in a particular way. The control reason, however, is quite different. There may be very important reasons for comparing the operation of similarly organized plants, stores, and agencies. They all may be comparable profit centers; their managers can be more readily compared within this organization structure. Even though these, and others, are important arguments for similarity of organization structure, it must be remembered that no one organizes to control; he organizes to produce efficiently and effectively. If the latter purpose is sacrificed for the former, the cost of control is too great to bear.

The Principle of Division of Work

The mixing of departmentation in practice is, then, merely a reflection of the operation of the principle of division of work. Originally noted by Fayol as the first of his fourteen principles of management,[6] his principle might be stated as follows: *the more an organization structure reflects the tasks or activities necessary to attain goals and assists in their coordination, and the more roles are designed to fit the capabilities and motivations of people available to fill them, the more effective and efficient an organization structure will be.* It concerns what has been called the primary step in organization, the determination and establishment of "the smallest number of dissimilar functions into which the work of an institution may be divided."[7] As Fayol indicated, this is the principle of specialization; it is the "division of work to produce more and better work with the same effort."[8]

It should be emphasized that division of work—in the sense of occupational specialization—is an *economic* principle and *not* a management principle. In other words, it has been found in many cases that when work is specialized, people learn the task more easily and perform it more efficiently. It

[6]Henri Fayol, *General and Industrial Administration* (New York: Pitman Publishing Corporation, 1949), p. 20. It should be pointed out that the authors' list of principles of organization vary from those of Fayol. A number of them are essentially the same, such as Fayol's principles of division of work, authority and responsibility, unity of command, unity of direction, centralization (balance), and scalar chain. Other Fayol principles apply to such managerial functions as direction. Still other principles expressed by Fayol, such as equity, initiative, and *esprit de corps.* seem to refer only to problems of leadership or characteristics of planning, control, or direction and are therefore not included in the authors' list.

[7]H. A. Hopf, *Organization, Executive Capacity, and Progress* (Ossining, N.Y.: Hopf Institute of Management, 1945), p. 4.

[8]Fayol, *op. cit.,* p. 20.

may well be that in many cases work has been over-specialized, with resultant loss of both motivation and a sense of accomplishment. Job enlargement may often be a highly desirable thing. But the organization designer has to work within certain economies and other conditions. Given these, his primary task is to design a structure of roles which will help individuals contribute to objectives. Not that he should remain silent if he feels that other considerations, such as occupational specialization, force an unworkable organization structure from the standpoint of manning it. But the *management organization* principle of division of work implies that: given a system of tasks or activities required economically to attain enterprise goals, the better an organization structure reflects a classification of these tasks and assists in their coordination through creating a system of interrelated roles, and the more these roles are designed to fit the capabilities and motivations of people available to fill them, the more effective and efficient it will be.

FOR DISCUSSION

1. Sociologists tell us that organization is a social invention. What do you think they mean? Do they imply that there is a "right" and "wrong" way to organize? What test would you prefer?
2. Some managers feel that a firm should not "mix up" its basic departmental forms. Would you agree with them? What is your opinion of an organizational philsophy of requiring all activities to be organized in the same manner?
3. Some managers are not satisfied with the alternatives they have in basic departmentation. Propose some additional ideas for them to consider.
4. Take as an example the organization of a typical engineering or research and development department. How is it organized? Why?

15
assignment of activities

In the preceding chapter two subjects were considered: the alternative methods of grouping organizational activities and the factors that influence a manager's decision to choose one or another. Now, there is a need to examine how a manager determines where to assign a new activity or where to shift an old one. The principles of basic departmentation do not answer such questions as whether all accounting should be done in an accounting department, whether handling customer claims should be a matter for the legal department, or whether service activities should be decentralized among primary departments.

Problems of this nature do not stay settled. All enterprises change to better meet dynamic conditions in the economic and social system, in technology, in consumer needs. Part of the problem of meeting change successfully is to group activities in such a way as to facilitate coordination and be prepared to change the grouping through time.

THREE ISSUES IN ASSIGNING ACTIVITIES

There are three fundamental issues involved in assigning activities to a particular department.[1] First is the need to identify and determine whether to recognize the activity. Second is the decision to combine the recognized activities. Third is the need for guides to the assignment of activities.

Recognition of Activities

Though often overlooked, the problem of deciding just what activities should be undertaken within the enterprise can be very stubborn. Should a church

[1] The original systematic examination of the issues involved in assigning activities was made by the late L. C. Sorrell, "Organization of Transportation and Traffic Activities," *Traffic World*, vol. 46, nos. 24–25 (November–December, 1930). The authors have followed Dr. Sorrell's approach.

conduct games, a university engage in politics, the State Department operate a business? Should a business operate a fleet of trucks, use independent computer services, employ programmers, have a planning staff, or engage in plating? A method of analysis is required in order to recognize those activities which are essential to the realization of the enterprise objective.

Essentiality is a matter of degree, and this characteristic is a matter of considerable importance. A university needs classrooms, but does it require a football stadium? A city needs personnel to conduct its business, but does it need a garage to service automobiles? A business needs to manufacture products geared to the market, but does it need a private airplane? It can be recognized that here is a never-never land where the marginally essential grows more "essential" as affluence, or budget, or taxes permit. Cost-effectiveness is the route to evaluation, but it is often considered uncivil to propose it.

One approach to identifying the activities to be recognized is to discover what is being done. This might be accomplished by counting the number of people having identifiable skills, such as thirteen chemists or eleven process engineers, and assuming that because they exist their services are needed. Another approach would be to ask employees what they are doing, and still another is to observe what is being done. All these approaches assume that what is being done should be done. This might very well be true; but on the other hand, it might not be. Can one always be sure?

The investigator may choose an alternative procedure. He could discover the goals of the enterprise, deduce the primary functions required to achieve them, and analyze in like manner those activities required to meet goals. This method has two important advantages: it establishes a classification system for all the activities essential for goal achievement, and it guards against the inclusion of activities unrelated to enterprise objectives. This is actually the common technique used in organizing new enterprises, and it is a good diagnostic technique for auditing ongoing structures.

Need for Combining Activities

Whether to departmentize recognized activities is not always a simple question to answer. The case for primary and secondary levels of departments is often easy to settle. The case for certain activities, especially those lower in the organization structure, is less clear. For instance, should individual salesmen take care of the complaints of their own customers, or should a customer complaint department be established? Should the Internal Revenue Service have a primary department whose function it is to encourage people to pay their taxes voluntarily, or should every employee shoulder this burden? Should the financing of a church be left to the individual membership, or should it be departmentized in a finance committee? Should the achievement of academic freedom in teaching be policed by a committee on ethics, or should it be left to the vagaries of the individual? Should an enterprise departmentize stenographic services, or assign stenographers to individuals? Merely raising these issues focuses attention on the fact that some are relatively easy to answer and some are not. Such questions are most frequently resolved in terms of the major thrust of the enterprise, whether this be efficiency, prestige for the membership, employment of large numbers of people (uneconomic though this may be), or bureaucratic maintenance.

Need for Guides

The third issue in the problem of assigning activities, and the one with which the following material is concerned, involves the considerations in response to which activities are combined. It is one thing to recognize the activity of receiving shipments; it is quite another to know where to locate it in the departmental structure. The guides useful in this respect relate to similar activities and intimate association of activities.

ASSIGNMENT BY SIMILARITY OF ACTIVITY

The practice of grouping together similar activities is both apparent and logical. Its wide usage emphasizes the need for understanding its advantages and the bases upon which it rests.

The search for a basis of classifying activities that leads to the association of those which are similar eventually brings the organizer to the skills of people. At first, he may be persuaded that the important element is the object to which labor is applied. But that which results from labor depends upon the skills applied to it. After determining what needs to be done and what skills are required, the organizer can then group them under such heads as typing, chemical analysis, process engineering, and accounting. In this way people who perform similar activities can be grouped in one department, and the advantages of occupational specialization realized.

Several illustrations of this procedure may be cited. Research engineers, salesmen, file clerks, and machine schedulers are commonly grouped in the research and development department, sales department, general office, and production control department, respectively. Sometimes it is also convenient to group together people who operate similar equipment or who undertake the assembly of a product. However, the fact that similar activities are not always combined suggests that there are some limitations in practice. We find that diversity as well as similarity may be grounds for grouping activities.

GUIDES FOR ASSIGNMENT BY INTIMATE ASSOCIATION

The association of activities merely on the ground that they are diverse would, of course, be foolish. The diversity must be of a particular kind, and there must be very good reasons for using it as a basis for grouping. Such reasons are found in the guides for assignment by intimate association, which occurs when diverse activities are so closely related in the achievement of departmental purposes that they are carried out most effectively when grouped in the same organizational unit.

Most Use

This guide suggests that an activity for which a manager has the most use should normally be assigned to him. Such functions as traffic, process engineering, and purchasing are sometimes located in the production departments. For example, in manufacturing establishments, the traffic function, which includes such activities as the purchase of transportation services, the use of equipment for transporting materials to the plant, in-plant movement of materials, and warehousing, may be assigned to the production manager. Since his department uses traffic services much more than do others, he would endeavor to manage them efficiently. Other departments are not thereby deprived of the service, for the production manager can operate it for the benefit of all departments.

Cost accounting may be assigned to the manufacturing department rather than to the accounting department, on the grounds that it is most used there. Likewise, computer operations are often assigned to the controller's department on the basis that much of their time is devoted to processing accounting information.

Executive Interest

An activity may be assigned to a particular manager if he is especially interested in it and has the capacity to direct it intelligently. In many manufacturing and service enterprises, for example, real estate activities are assigned to the general counsel's office. A manufacturing company may have many real estate leases and a fair number of real estate sales and purchases. These are often not important enough to justify establishing a separate functional department nor do they logically belong in any existing department. The problem is solved by assigning them to that executive who has an interest in them—most likely, because of the extensive legal and contractual work involved, the chief legal officer.

Observation of practice shows other interesting examples. In a small company, the personnel activity was given to the controller, not because it fitted in with his accounting activities, but he was both interested in the field and was regarded as available to handle it. In another company, stockholder relations were separated from public relations and assigned to the chairman of the board because of his great interest in the area. In still another case, the chairman was assigned the task of developing international operations for the same reason.

Competition

Often a desired activity does not flourish because various executives fear it, because its possibilities are not recognized, or because it fails to receive vigorous direction. The cure for a wilting activity is sometimes the application of the guide of competition. For instance, American universities attempted, in the early 1920s, to meet the growing demand for business instruction by offering a few courses such as corporation finance, marketing, and accounting in the department of economics. Since there were few economists with much interest in or knowledge of the subject matter, there was definite hostility in their departments against such instruction. The insistent demand was met by splitting off business from economics courses and establishing a competitive department. Since then, departments of business administration have achieved equal stature and have surpassed the parent department in numbers of students, facilities, and budgets.

Encouraging competition between departments, divisions, and other units enables the firm to make comparisons that greatly aid in control. For instance, similar measures of efficiency can be applied to the domestic and foreign sales departments of a multinational company. From such records as costs of sales, gross profit per net sales dollar, and sales per dollar of effort, the president is able to compare the relative efficiency of managers operating similar and somewhat competitive divisions.

Suppressed Competition

As its title implies, this guide is the exact reverse of the one that encourages competition and, naturally, is applicable under a different set of conditions. As the advantages to be reaped from competition become fully realized, the president of the firm may feel a growing need for greater coordination between two functions, for more cooperation and less competition. To achieve this, he need only change the place in the organization structure where the two activities are coordinated.

A good example of organizing along this guideline, as well as a case of departmentizing in accordance with marketing channels, was the action the du Pont Company took when it combined its Nylon, Orlon, and Dacron Divisions. It found that the competition of these three divisions for the same market was not in the best interests of the company as a whole. Many other companies with product divisions have found that where once-healthy competition turns into destructive and inefficient rivalry between parts of the same company, combination of the parts under a single manager may be the best cure.

Policy Control

Policies may be variously interpreted. General intentions—such as to compete on a price basis, not to advertise on Sunday, or never to sue a customer—rarely encounter differences of managerial opinion, but other policies, such as those relating to credit, customer claims, and returned goods, may suffer from a lack of clear specifications, permitting variations in interpretation. In such instances, it might be important that the policy be enforced by that manager who would best reflect the intention of the manager who originally adopted it.

The customer claims activity of department stores, for example, is generally recognized as necessary and important. The typical policy relating to this activity is one of fairness to the store and to the customer. But the very vagueness of what fair dealing is makes possible sincere but widely different attitudes. If customer claims are assigned to the merchandising manager, his interpretations may favor the customers because of his desire to keep their good will and continued patronage; furthermore, he is in a position to shift any blame for the cost of the activity to department buyers. If the activity is placed in the several departments, however, the buyers will be torn between pleasing the customer and taking the blame for buying the unsatisfactory product in the first place, and there may be as many interpretations of policy as there are buyers. The accounting department, finally, might administer the activity on a coldly factual basis that would alienate both customers and department buyers. All these alternatives have been tried in independent department-store operations. Since each might endanger the original policy, it is a growing practice to assign the activity to the general superintendent, the official in charge of the store building, receiving and delivery, warehousing, and safety. Many store executives feel that this manager is in the best position to execute the claims policy in the way it was originally designed.

The administration of credit policy also causes considerable difficulty because of the impossibility of establishing objective rules for time purchases. Credit managers rightly insist that every such rule needs to be interpreted on an individual basis. But to whom should a credit manager report? A sales manager would prefer a liberal interpretation in order to facilitate selling. It is likewise beyond the proper scope of accounting. Credit really belongs in the treasurer's department because of its effect upon working capital and the financial safety of the enterprise.

The important point is that activities should be assigned to that manager who will interpret policy in a way satisfactory to those drafting it. It is their *intention* which needs to be reflected in policy applications. So important are the virtues of accuracy and consistency that policy control often can be vital to enterprise welfare.

Lack of a Clean Break

Sometimes difficulties are encountered in assigning activities that would logically be placed in separate departments but are, for some conflicting practical reason, best undertaken together. In a sense, this is a perennial problem that arises the moment an enterprise is organized.

Students of independent department-store operations are frequently surprised to learn that a department manager, called the "buyer," is responsible for *both* purchasing and selling merchandise. The assignment of both activities to the buyer results from the close relationship of sales volume to what is bought for resale, and when one manager is assigned both activities, it is easy to fix responsibility for results.

In the responsibility for operations of an airline at an airport, similar problems exist. People at the counter sell tickets and deal with customers— a task that logically belongs to the sales department. But they also check baggage—a task that belongs to the ground service or operations department. It would obviously be difficult to separate these functions organizationally, with a result that they are usually combined under the airline's station manager who normally reports to the operating department.

These illustrations emphasize the fact that arbitrary decisions to divide control of an activity may be impractical, resulting in unworkable assignments of parts of functions to several managers. If for any reason the activities in question refuse to break clean, even though their nature may make it appear logical to do so, the appropriate guide is to avoid forceful separation.

Separation

The successful operation of enterprises of all types requires that certain activities be undertaken purely as a check upon the effectiveness and propriety with which functions are carried out. They should almost invariably be assigned to a manager independent of the executive whose work is being evaluated.

Manufacturing firms, for example, commonly provide for quality control of purchased materials and goods in various stages of production. This activity could clearly be subverted if its personnel were responsible to the purchasing agent or the plant superintendent.

Similar issues are involved in the employment of an outside auditor and in the separation of accounting from the finance function. The certification of financial records could hardly be made by a subordinate in the finance department. And since accounting activities are useful checks upon the treasurer, who controls the enterprise funds, it is not good practice to have the chief accountant reporting to the treasurer, or vice versa.

The principle of separation—that if an activity is designed as a check on another activity, the individual charged with the former cannot report to the department whose activity he is expected to evaluate—is a valuable and invariable rule.

Functional Interest

Functional interest, although it does not have the general applicability of other guides is useful in grouping activities that are closely related in terms of purpose. For instance, a publicity manager may have such functions as institutional advertising and publicity assigned to him. These are functionally related because both concern the impact on the general public of the firm, its policies, practices, and personnel. In the General Motors Corporation for example, it is interesting that the Motors Holding Division, a division whose responsibility is handling new dealer financing, is attached to the marketing staff, rather than the financial staff, for the obvious reason that marketing has a strong functional interest in the area. Likewise, one often finds the company cafeteria a responsibility of the personnel department.

APPLICATION OF THE GUIDES FOR ASSIGNMENT OF ACTIVITY

The application of the guides for assigning activities presents many problems to the organizer. They cannot be followed like directions for assembling a toy because they present alternatives, the selection and use of which require good judgment. Nevertheless, a conscientious effort to follow the guides is part of good management practice, and many problems are simplified, if not eliminated, by this means.

Similarity and Intimate Association as Alternatives

Perhaps the first choice that the organizer faces is that between the similarity of activity and the intimate association guides. The advantage of grouping assignments by similarity of function lies in economy. Assignment by intimate association, on the other hand, has the advantages of the task-force method of grouping different but closely related activities. Its employment is mandatory at the top echelon of the structure but may become less of a necessity in middle and lower levels.

Conflict in Guides

One of the difficulties in applying the guides for assignment of activities is that some of them are in open conflict. This does not mean that any is wrong but that under some circumstances in the life and growth of enterprise some of the guides are clearly inappropriate. Small firms may have difficulty in using guides for similarity of activities, because they may not be able to realize fully the economies of specialization. No firm, moreover, could encourage and discourage competition at the same time for the same activity. Consequently, in the application of guides, the organizer must keep in mind the stage of growth and the size of the enterprise, on the one hand, and the purpose to be achieved, on the other.

Jurisdictional Disputes

All enterprises experience more or less disagreement among managers in connection with the assignment of certain activities. Few top managers have not been present at discussions about assigning engineering to production, credit to accounting, public relations to personnel, or receiving to purchasing. These and similar discussions consume hours of the time of expensive personnel, and, unfortunately, most of the discussion is futile, because it is not about the *right issues.*

The guides for assigning activity are sharp weapons to use in these controversies. Attention to them avoids overtones of personal bases for decision making and focuses attention upon both the main problem and the selection of the appropriate method to solve it. In such an atmosphere few jurisdictional disputes would be permitted to cause more than a ripple of concern.

The Right to Change the Assignment of Activities

An assignment, once made, does not carry with it the sacrifice of all rights to make a subsequent change. In fact, just the opposite is true. The organizer makes the best assignment possible under the circumstances. He puts the allocation into effect with the view of letting it rest until future developments raise the question again. Enterprises, even the most static, are forever changing their emphasis, and consequently their organization structures are likely to burst at the seams unless pressure is relieved by reallocating activities. Assigned activities should be shifted in the manner dictated by purpose, time, and circumstance.

Quality of Organizing Activity

The degree to which the guides for assigning activity are appropriately applied at a given time is an index of the quality of organizing. The correctness of the guide chosen and the good judgment with which it is applied inevitably lead to good organization structure. It is, unquestionably, a fruitful way to facilitate good management.

FOR DISCUSSION

1. It has been argued that business is so dynamic that no rules for assigning activities can be applied. Do you agree?
2. Until recent years the transportation function had generally been assigned to manufacturing or to sales. It is now argued that the activities are much broader, including getting goods into the plant, moving them to storage, through the production process to shipping, and thence to warehouse or customer. Therefore, say these advocates, transportation (or physical distribution as it is now called) should be a major function reporting on a par with sales, production, finance, etc., to the executive vice-president. What guides or principles underlie these viewpoints?
3. What becomes of the guides to assigning activities if a firm "organizes around people"?
4. It has been argued that guides to the assignment of activities are conflicting and therefore inappropriate. How do you feel about this?

16

line and staff authority relationships

The reason for departmentation and the guides for assigning activities to departments have been discussed. We now consider another essential organization question: What *kind* of authority is allocated in the organization structure? The question has to do with the nature of authority relationships—the problem of line and staff.

Without coordinated allocation of authority to department heads, the various departments cannot become a smoothly working unit properly harmonized for the accomplishment of enterprise objectives. Authority relationships, whether perpendicular or horizontal, are the factors that breathe life into an organization, harness departmental activities, and bring coordination to the enterprise.

LINE AND STAFF CONCEPTS

Much confusion has arisen both in literature and among managers as to what line and staff are; as a result, there is probably no area of management which causes more difficulties, more friction, and more loss of time and effectiveness. Yet line and staff relationships are important as an organizational way of life, and the kind of authority relationship that a member of an organization has must necessarily affect his part in the operation of an enterprise.

One widely held concept of line and staff is that "line functions are those which have direct responsibility for accomplishing the objectives of the enterprise," and that staff "refers to those elements of the organization that help the line to work most effectively in accomplishing the primary objectives of the enterprise."[1] Those who hold to this view almost invariably

[1] L. A. Allen, *Improving Line and Staff Relationships,* Studies in Personnel Policy No. 153 (New York: National Industrial Conference Board, Inc., 1956), pp. 12, 20. See also similar definitions in L. A. Appley, "Staff and Line," *Management News,* vol. 29, no. 5, p. 1 (May, 1956), and R. C. Sampson, *The Staff Role in Management* (New York: Harper & Row, Publishers, Incorporated, 1955), pp. 42–44.

classify production and sales (and sometimes finance) as line functions, and purchasing, accounting, personnel, plant maintenance, and quality control as staff functions.

The confusion arising from such a concept is immediately apparent. It is argued that purchasing, for example, is auxiliary to the main goals of the business in the sense that, unlike the production departments—such as heat-treating or parts assembly—it is not directly essential. But is purchasing really any less essential to the gaining of company objectives? Could the company not store up heat-treated or assembled parts and get along without these departments as well as it could without purchasing? And could not the same question be raised as to other so-called staff departments such as accounting, personnel, and plant maintenance? Moreover, there is probably nothing that could stop satisfactory production and sale of most manufactured goods more completely than the failure of quality control.

The Nature of Line and Staff Relationships

A more precise and logically valid concept of line and staff is that they are simply a matter of relationships. In line authority, one finds a superior with a line of authority running to a subordinate. As Mooney[2] so aptly recognized, this gradation of authority is found in all organizations as an uninterrupted scale or series of steps. Hence this hierarchical arrangement has been referred to as the scalar principle in organization, which is: *the more clear the line of authority from the ultimate authority for management in an enterprise to every subordinate position, the more effective will be responsible decision making and organization communication.* In many large enterprises, the steps are long and complicated, but even in the smallest, the very act of organization introduces the scalar principle.

The nature of line authority, therefore, becomes apparent from the scalar principle as being that relationship in which a superior exercises direct supervision over a subordinate—an authority relationship in direct line or steps.

The nature of the staff relationship is advisory. As Mooney[3] has stated, staff is auxiliary, and although "it may suggest that the structure of organization is like a double-track railroad, consisting of line and staff as two coordinate functions . . . there could be no more erroneous conception." For, as he points out:[4]

The structure of organization is single track only, and can never be anything else. What is known in military organization as line is synonymous with what we have called the scalar chain, and there can be but one chain of line authority. Any duty in organization that cannot be identified as an actual link in the scalar process is an auxiliary function, adhering to the line like sidings along the main track. This means that every staff function must adhere to the line in some dependent relation, and could

---

[2] J. D. Mooney, *Principles of Organization* (New York: Harper & Row, Publishers, Incorporated, 1947), pp. 14–15.

[3] *Ibid.,* pp. 34–35.

[4] *Ibid.,* p. 35.

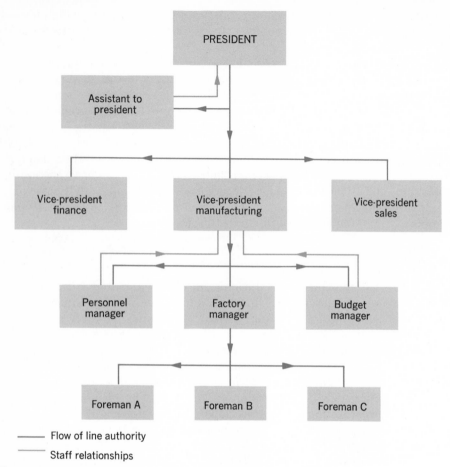

Figure 16.1 *Line and staff authority relationships.*

not otherwise exist. If we find in staff organization a counterpart of the same scalar gradations that appear in the line, this is implicit in the fact of its adherence. It must of necessity follow the gradations of that to which it adheres.

Line and Staff: Relationship or Departmentation?

Frequently, line and staff are regarded as types of departments. Although it is true that a department may stand in a predominantly line or staff position with respect to other departments, line and staff are distinguished by their authority relationships and not by what they do.

The public relations department, for example, being primarily advisory to the top executives, may be thought of as a staff department. But within the department are line relationships; the director will stand in a line authority position with respect to his immediate subordinates. On the other hand, the vice-president in charge of production may be regarded as heading a line department. His job is not *primarily* advisory to the chief executive officer. If, however, he counsels the chief executive on over-all company policy, his relationship becomes one of staff. Within the production department there may be many subordinates and among them a number having an advisory role and, therefore, having a staff relationship to the whole department or any of its parts.

When one looks at an organization structure *as a whole*, the general character of line and staff relationships for the total organization emerges. Certain departments are predominantly staff in their relationship to the entire organization. Other departments are primarily line.

Figure 16.2 portrays the skeletal organization of a manufacturing company. The activities of the director of research and the director of public relations are apt to be mainly advisory to the main stream of corporate operations and are consequently often referred to as staff activities. The finance, production, and sales departments, which have activities generally related to the main corporate functions, are ordinarily referred to as line departments.

Although it is often convenient and correct to refer to one department as a line department and another as a staff department, *their activities do not so characterize the departments*. Line and staff are characterized by relationships and not by departmental activities. Should research be a principal function of the company—as in aerospace manufacturing, where the engineering department produces ideas for sale to military and commercial customers— it will stand in an operating relationship to the organization as a whole and take on the authority characteristics of a factory department in a typical manufacturing enterprise.

Some of the tendency to regard line and staff as types of departments arises from confusing service departments with line and staff. Service departments represent grouping of *activities* for the purpose of control or economy arising from specialization. Thus, purchasing, accounting, or certain personnel activities may be separated from other departments and grouped in service departments. As service departments, they are auxiliary to the principal operations of sales or production. Because service departments are composed of specialists, their advice is usually sought by company managers, and, at such times, they stand in a staff relationship to the rest of the company. Nevertheless, the line authority within these departments is as real as that in a production or sales department.

Line and Staff: Specialization of Managerial Functions?

Although recognizing the inherent nature of line and staff as one of authority relationships, many students of management have attempted to distinguish between them on grounds that they represent a specialization of managerial functions. Some express the distinction by asserting that it is the line executive's function to *act* and the staff executive's function to *think*.[5]

---

[5] L. Gulick, "The Theory of Organization," in L. Gulick and L. Urwick (eds.), *Papers on the Science of Administration* (New York: Institute of Public Administration, 1937), p. 31. Gulick observed that "when the work of the government is subjected to the dichotomy of 'line' and 'staff' there are included in staff all those persons who devote their time exclusively to the knowing, thinking, and planning, and making suggestions to superior officers. They cannot operate otherwise. But this does not make them staff officers. Those also in the staff are *doing* something; they

The implied distinction between line and staff in terms of a division of managerial functions may possibly be traced to Frederick W. Taylor's attempt to separate planning from performance. It will be recalled that he advocated the division of the functions of foremen into eight groupings and these, in turn, into a planning level and a performance level.[6] This principle has never had wide application in industry nor been regarded as workable, for it involves division of managerial functions. The fact is that no manager can manage unless he has the authority to plan, organize, direct, staff, and control, although the degree to which he may be called upon to engage in these several functions may vary. However, as will be noted below, many instances of functional authority do have a flavor of Taylor's functional foremanship.

Staff officers do *assist* line officers in carrying out their managerial functions. They often specialize in planning assistance and may also assist in other managerial functions. On every hand, one can see departments engaged actively in planning, in examining organizational problems, in drawing up instructions or commands for the use of superiors, and in staffing studies. These are truly staff activities, not because they represent planning instead of performance but because they represent counsel and advice.

It is thus often stated that staff officers are assigned an "authority of ideas" and line officers an "authority to command."[7] Although this appraisal can be helpful in dramatizing these relationships, it must not be taken to mean a splitting of the managerial functions. The manager may benefit greatly by ideas, but he cannot delegate his job.

Importance of Understanding Line and Staff

In view of the confusion about line and staff, the distinction is sometimes assumed to be meaningless. It is argued that these are obsolete concepts, carried into industry from military organization, and that modern firms have obliterated them by new organizational devices so that they no longer have any meaning.

The distinction seems important, however, as a way of organizational life. Superior and subordinate alike must know whether they are acting in a staff or a line capacity. If in a staff capacity, their job is to advise and not

---

do not merely sit and twiddle their thumbs. But they do not organize others, they do not direct or appoint personnel, they do not issue commands, they do not take responsibility for the job. Everything they suggest is referred up, not down, and is carried out, if at all, on the responsibility and under the direction of a line officer."

[6] F. W. Taylor, *Shop Management* (New York: Harper & Brothers, 1911), p. 99. Taylor believed that efficiency would be gained if the job of the shop foreman were subdivided into the following activities and duties: (1) order of work and routing, (2) instruction, (3) time and cost, (4) gang boss, (5) speed boss, (6) repair boss, (7) inspector, and (8) disciplinarian. He thus distinguished planning and performance levels, placing the first three functions on the planning level and the remainder on the performance level.

[7] E. Petersen and E. G. Plowman, *Business Organization and Management*, rev. ed. (Homewood, Ill.: Richard D. Irwin, Inc., 1948), p. 259. A similar idea is expressed by Mooney (*op. cit.* p. 34), who notes that "the line represents the authority of *man*; the staff, the authority of *ideas.*"

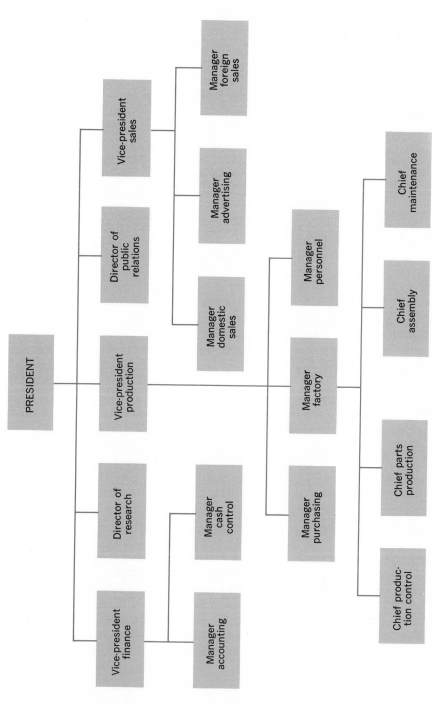

Figure 16.2 *So-called line and staff organization of a typical manufacturing company.*

command; their line superiors must make the decisions and issue instructions through the scalar chain.

A case in point is that of a competent young staff assistant, with unusual industrial experience as controller and internal auditor of several large business enterprises, who was hired by the executive vice-president of an expanding company. The assistant's charge was clear—to bring to the attention of the executive vice-president means and places for reducing costs of operations, expending scarce capital wisely, and achieving growth in orderly fashion. But some uncertainty must have existed in his mind as to whether he was limited to a staff position or whether he had line authority from the executive vice-president to see that these things were done. In any event, he gathered together many statisticians, production-efficiency experts, planners, economists, budgetary-control personnel, and organization specialists. With their help, he readily and accurately discovered numerous places where costs could be reduced, production and service improved, management bettered, and money efficiently expended; yet the entire program failed, and the executive vice-president was forced to abandon it. The reason was simple: his assistant had not understood that he was to act in a staff capacity, that he could not force his findings and policy determinations on unwilling line executives but must instead sell his ideas to them. The line executives resented the intrusion of this staff officer, as well they might, since he was, in effect, stripping from them their power to manage. The result was not only complete lack of co-operation by the line officers but their insistence that the staff position be abolished. Faced with a choice between supporting his chief line lieutenants and supporting a staff officer who had not confined his activities to investigation and recommendations, the executive vice-president could only favor the line.

Many other examples could be given of the importance of understanding line and staff relationships. Not only must the staff executive recognize that his job is to counsel, but the line executive must not confuse such counsel with the power to make decisions. Authority to manage must rest with the executive who stands in a line relationship with his subordinates. Failure to understand this is a common cause of friction.

DEVELOPMENT OF THE STAFF CONCEPT

The staff concept is probably as old as organization itself. Since organization almost certainly developed first in political and military areas of social activities, the first traces of staff are found there. Mooney found that the pure staff function of the boule of ancient Athens was to prepare measures for the consideration of the ecclesia,[8] and that the early Roman senate first exercised a pure staff function but later changed to a line function. In the age of feudalism, too, and on to the present, the importance of staff counsel has ever

---

[8]For his excellent description of organization in antiquity, see *ibid.*, chap. 7; chaps. 8–20 include other pertinent material; chaps. 14, 17, and 18 deal with the development of staff.

been recognized, even though the emphasis of early organization was clearly on the development of line relationships.

Application of the Staff Principle in the Catholic Church

Mooney finds that the use of staff provides one of the "most notable lessons" furnished by the long history of Catholic Church organization, where staff service has taken forms unknown in other areas. The most obvious instance is in the central administration of the Church, consisting of two major organizations, the Sacred College and the Roman Curia. During the entire history of these institutions, they have been regarded as advisory to the pope, who delegates none of his final authority to them and has no obligation to adopt their advice.

One of the institutionalized organization principles of the Catholic Church has been described by Mooney as "compulsory staff service." This principle operates to force the superior to *listen* to his subordinates. While the line decision rests with the superior, he cannot refuse to listen. This principle—at least as old as the Rule of St. Benedict, promulgated in the sixth century—originally required the abbot of a Benedictine monastery to consult the elder monks, even on minor matters, and is now applied to some extent throughout the Church.

Another interesting principle Mooney calls "staff independence." In Catholic organization staff advisers are often independent of superiors with respect to both tenure and position. Advice is thus unweakened by the fact of dependence. As Mooney so well reflects on the lack of this in military, civic, and business organization:[9] "The weakness of many forms of staff service is that the counselor is dependent on the man whom he counsels, and hence is subject to the danger of sinking to the level of a 'yes' man."

The Army General Staff

Although the staff concept can hardly be called a military invention, the terms "line" and "staff" appear to have had their origin in military organization. The modern concept of the army general staff is usually traced to the seventeenth century, when emphasis was placed upon a staff of experts by Gustavus Adolphus of Sweden. The Mark of Brandenburg is given credit for the evolution of the general staff organizations of the Prussian and German armies. The Prussian general staff, as organized by Scharnhorst in the early nineteenth century, was a completely organized advisory service coordinated under a single head, the chief of staff. Scharnhorst saw the dangers of separation of line and staff personnel and required that, periodically, all staff officers assume line duty and all line officers be given staff assignments.

As a result of the brilliant report of Secretary of War Elihu Root in 1902, the American army adopted the general staff device that is the basis of its or-

[9]*Ibid.*, p. 122.

ganization today. Root's report is a classic on the need for a general staff with no other duties than gathering information, presenting alternative plans, and preparing the details of selected plans.

Staffs in Business

Widespread use of staff in American business developed only in the twentieth century, particularly after the Great Depression of 1929–1932. The emphasis on planning and control, with their requirements for information, the growing complexities of labor relations, the expansion of government regulations, and the difficult legal and accounting problems arising from tax legislation have argued for staff assistance. The development has been accelerated by the growth of large business, in which the problems of managing approach those of any army and require specialized information of a breadth and complexity unknown to smaller operations.

The proliferation of staffs in business takes many forms. Few indeed are the top managers who do not have staff assistants in law, taxes, accounting, and perhaps research. Executives of large companies add staff assistants in public relations, personnel, engineering, or planning. Staff assistants are so widely used that a sales or production manager may have from one to a half dozen. In large-scale enterprises, for example, the sales managers may have staff men separately assigned to such activities as the selection and training of salesmen, sales strategy, research, quotas, budgets, traffic, and warehousing. Moreover, some large companies are reminiscent of the army general staff. In the General Motors Corporation, for example, there exists an operations staff of seven key managers—each in charge of a staff group devoted to such important activities as distribution, engineering, styling, personnel, and public relations—plus financial and legal staffs.

On the other hand, many corporation presidents studiously avoid having many staff assistants or staff departments, choosing instead to have staff men report to the managers in the major line departments. Their purpose is to place the staff assistance at the point in the line where it can best be used, and to avoid undermining the line officers by concentrating too much staff assistance at the top level.

FUNCTIONAL AUTHORITY

Functional authority is the right which an individual or department may have delegated to it over specified processes, practices, policies, or other matters relating to activities undertaken by personnel in departments other than its own. If the principle of unity of command were followed without exception, authority over these activities would be exercised by their line managers, but numerous reasons—including lack of special knowledge, lack of ability to supervise processes, and danger of diverse interpretations of policies—explain why they occasionally are not allowed to exercise this authority. In such cases, the line manager is deprived of this limited authority. It is delegated by their common superior to a staff specialist or a manager in another department.

Functional authority is not restricted to managers of a particular type of department. It may be exercised by line, service,[10] or staff department heads, more often the latter two, because they are usually composed of specialists whose knowledge becomes the basis for functional controls.

Development of Functional Authority

The successive steps by which a line manager is deprived of his authority over particular activities make an interesting study. The pure staff specialist offers advice or recommendations to his line superior, who may issue them as instructions to be filtered down the organization hierarchy. The first modification of this relationship may occur when the superior delegates authority to the staff man to transmit information, proposals, and advice directly to the former's subordinates. For example, a personnel assistant might be permitted to transmit directly to the operating department heads information and advice on the handling of labor grievances. Obviously, this saves the president time and trouble and expedites the spread of the information.

A second modification might be to allow the staff specialist to consult with operating managers and show them how the information should be used or put into effect. For instance, the personnel assistant might be asked to advise line personnel on procedures to eliminate mishandling of grievances. It will clearly be advantageous to all concerned if the staff man can instruct the persons responsible for this activity. Here, there is no question of his ordering them; the agreement of the line executive concerned is needed; should this not be forthcoming, he can appeal to his superior to issue the requisite instructions. Even with the variations outlined above, the specialist is still operating wholly in a staff capacity.

The transition to functional authority is accomplished when the assistant is delegated specific authority to *prescribe* processes, methods, or even policy to be followed in all subdivisions of either staff or operating departments. The personnel assistant, for example, who once could only advise, now may be given limited authority to supervise a special function or process of the line organization. He no longer merely advises his superior or the line organization concerning handling grievances. Now, he may issue instructions *prescribing* procedures. Or, to use another example, a corporation controller may be given authority to prescribe the kind of accounting records to be kept by the sales and manufacturing departments.

By limiting this authority to function, the factory manager—handling his labor grievances in accordance with procedures prescribed by the personnel

---

[10] Some so-called staff departments are service departments. Since the latter reflect a special grouping of activities and since the discussion here is concerned with line and staff authority relationships, the analysis of service departments as a special organizational form is postponed to Chapter 17.

manager—and the sales manager—keeping his records according to instructions of the controller—are still primarily subject to the orders, supervision, and control of their line superiors. The extent of their control by the staff officer is governed by the latter's functional authority.

Functional Authority Delegation

Functional authority can perhaps be better understood if it is regarded as a small slice of the authority of the line superior. A corporation president, for example, has complete authority to manage the corporation, subject only to limitations placed upon him by such superior authority as the board of directors, the corporate charter and bylaws, and government regulations. In the pure staff situation, his advisers on personnel, accounting, purchasing, or public relations have no part of this authority, their duty being merely to offer counsel. But when the president delegates some of his authority to these advisers to issue instructions directly to the line organization as shown in Figure 16.3, that part is called "functional authority."

As illustrated, the four staff executives have functional authority over the line organization with respect to procedures in the fields of accounting, personnel, purchasing, and public relations. What has happened is that the president, feeling it unnecessary that such specialized matters be cleared through him, has delegated his line authority to staff assistants to issue their own instructions to the operating departments. Likewise, of course, subordinate managers can use the same device, as when a factory superintendent sets up cost, production-control, and quality-control supervisors with functional authority to prescribe procedures for the foremen.

Functional Authority as Exercised by Operating Managers

Operating department heads sometimes have good reason to control some method or process of another line department. For example, the vice-president in charge of sales may be given functional authority over the manufacturing executives in scheduling customer orders, packaging, or making service parts available.

Where a company is organized along product lines, the exercise of functional authority over the product division managers by other executives is rather commonplace. All functions of sales, production, finance, or other so-called line functions (that is, "line" to the enterprise) may be placed under a division or product manager. In this case, certain top line officials in charge of a major function of the business might not have a direct line of authority over the product managers. But, to make sure that sales or financial policy is properly followed in the divisions, these officers may be given functional authority, as illustrated in Figure 16.4.

The Area of Functional Authority

Functional authority should be carefully restricted. Such authority of the purchasing manager, for example, is generally limited to the procedures to be used

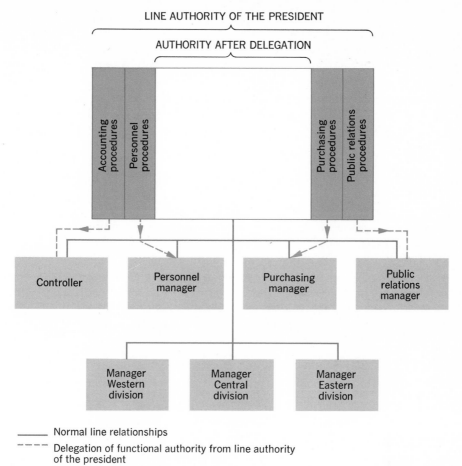

Figure 16.3 *Functional authority delegation.*

in divisional or departmental purchasing. When he *conducts* certain purchasing activities of an over-all company nature, he is acting as head of a service department. The functional authority of the personnel manager over the general line organization is likewise ordinarily limited to the prescription of procedures for handling grievances, for sharing in the administration of wage and salary programs, and for handling vacation procedures and matters of a similar nature.

Functional authority is usually limited to the area of "how" and sometimes "when" and seldom applies to "where," "what," or "who." The reason for this limitation is not found in any logical demarcation between normal line authority and functional authority, since the latter *can* be made to apply to any aspect of operations. It is rather that the functionalization of management, if carried to extremes, would destroy the manager's job. Whenever a manager loses his authority to plan, organize, staff, direct, and control the activities within his department, he can no longer manage.

To some extent, this occurs when a staff or line executive has functional authority over some part of another manager's job. Even when the personnel manager requires the factory manager to follow seniority in layoffs or to grant employees definite pay and vacation allowances, he is interfering with some of the factory manager's prerogatives. When the accounting department requires district sales managers to file their expense accounts in a certain form, it is, to some extent, interfering with the authority of the general sales manager over his subordinates.

Therefore, well-managed concerns recognize that functional authority should be used sparingly and only where a real necessity exists. This necessity comes from both outside and inside influences. On the outside are such requirements as those of government agencies and labor union contracts that must be interpreted and administered by specialists. On the inside some matters are of such importance or complexity that the best possible grade of uniform action is required, necessitating in turn that the expert be given sufficient authority to carry out desired procedures. A rather thin line sometimes divides what should be controlled by the expert and what should be under the jurisdiction of the operating manager. Where there is doubt, good practice would seem to favor limiting the area of functional authority so that the operating manager's position is not weakened.

Figure 16.4 *Functional authority of line departments.*

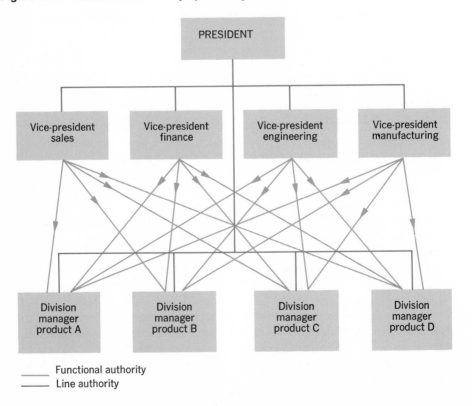

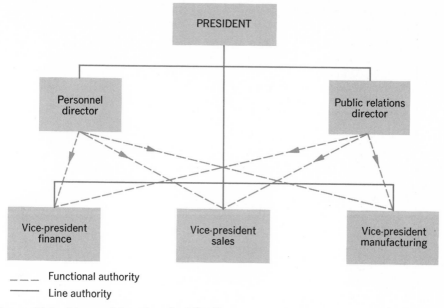

Figure 16.5 *Line and functional authority.*

Unity of Command and the Flow of Functional Authority

Limiting the area of functional authority is, then, important in preserving the integrity of the managerial position. If a company had, as some do, executives with functional authority over procedures in the fields of personnel, purchasing, accounting, traffic, budgets, engineering, public relations, law, sales policy, and real estate, the complications of authority relationships could be great indeed. A factory manager or a sales manager might have, in addition to his immediate line superior, five, ten, or even fifteen functional bosses. Although much of the multiplication of command is unavoidable because of the demands for specialist prescription in complex areas, it is obvious that it can precipitate serious, and frequently intolerable, confusion and dispersal of responsibility.

Some semblance of unity of command can be maintained by requiring that the line of functional authority shall not extend beyond the first organization level below that of the manager's own superior. Thus, in Figure 16.5 the functional authority of the personnel or public relations director should not extend beyond the level of the vice-presidents in charge of finance, sales, and manufacturing. In other words, functional authority should be concentrated at the nearest possible point in the organization structure, to preserve, as much as possible, the unity of command of the line executives.

This principle is often widely violated. Top managers with functional authority sometimes issue instructions directly to personnel throughout the organization. Where the policy or procedure determination is so important that there must be no deviation, both the prestige of the top manager and the necessity for accurate communication may make it necessary and wise to issue such instructions. Issuing them to the responsible line subordinate, as well as to the functional counterpart at the lower level, may not seem harmfully to increase the multiplicity of command. As will be noted later, there are forces of centralization of authority that may make this kind of exercise of functional authority unavoidable.

Lack of Clarification in Practice

It is surprising how many companies, even those otherwise well managed, fail to define the exact nature of the functional authority that a manager may have. Analysis by the authors of authority delegations in a large number of companies shows that adequate clarification in this area is rare. Most companies seem satisfied to say, for example, that the division managers are "administratively" responsible to the president, but "functionally responsible in accounting and similar matters" under the jurisdiction of the controller. This is an open invitation to confusion, compounded of ambiguity, lack of careful meaning and understanding, and the unsurprising tendency of specialists to see everything in a company through their own eyes. As a company controller once told one of the authors, "I realize that my authority in accounting matters throughout the company is limited; all I insist on approving is anything with a dollar sign attached."

The lack of clarification in the area of functional authority has been found in a number of studies. Studies of personnel managers, for example, have shown varying perceptions of the authority of this officer as between himself and his staff, his superior, and the various areas of the company subject to his influence.[11] Likewise, a recent study of company controllers with functional authority showed a high degree of confusion to exist between controller and noncontroller groups, and even within the controllers' departments, as to what the authority of the controller really was.[12] Other studies have shown the extensiveness of this lack of clarity and the conflict it engenders.[13]

Particularly in the light of the wide use and apparent inevitability of functional authority in all kinds of enterprises, lack of clarification is difficult to understand. It is true that many people can accommodate themselves to lack of clarity or work themselves through it by trial and error or persuasion. But if it is important to place functional authority in a position, it would appear to be a waste of time and resources not to make it clear.

[11] See, for example, W. French and D. Henning, "The Authority-Influence Role of the Functional Specialist in Management," *Journal of the Academy of Management,* vol. 9, no. 3, pp. 187–203 (September, 1966); D. E. McFarland, *Cooperation and Conflict in Personnel Administration* (New York: American Foundation for Management Research, 1963); even J. A. Belasco and J. A. Arlutto, while professing to find that line-staff relationships in this area are less severe than usually believed, did find that "there may be a high conflict over 'how' the agreed upon role is performed." See "Line and Staff Conflicts: Some Empirical Insights," *Academy of Management Journal,* vol. 12, no. 1, pp. 469–477 (December, 1969).

[12] See R. McIntire, "Functional Authority in the Controller's Position" (Ph.D. diss., University of California, Los Angeles, 1971).

[13] See, for example, R. Golembiewski, *Organizing Men and Power* (Chicago: Rand McNally & Company, 1967).

Clarifying Functional Authority

Almost certainly the best means of avoiding some of the problems, confusions, and frictions of functional authority is to make sure it is clarified. Thus, it is not enough to say that a division or plant manager is "administratively responsible" to his line superior and "functionally responsible" to the controller. If the controller, like a few the authors have known, regards his functional authority over accounting matters to extend to all expenditures of funds, there is a built-in situation for undue conflict through multiplication of command. Or if a personnel manager interprets his delegation to cover anything concerned with people, the conflict potential is obvious. Likewise, if an operating manager regards the controller as being "staff" with no authority even to prescribe the form and nature of the company's accounting system, the controller cannot discharge his responsibility.

In order to obtain clarity, it is imperative that the exact functional authority delegated to a manager or to a department be clearly spelled out. This is necessary not only from the standpoint of the bearer's use and understanding of this specialized type of authority, but also for those operating managers who are on the receiving end. An example of one company's attempt to define the authority of the vice-president–controller is the following specific delegations to that officer, which delegations were thoroughly discussed with him and his subordinates and with key operating managers and their subordinates over whom he was expected to exercise such authority.

1. Authority to prescribe the corporate chart of accounts and the division's charts of accounts so far as they are supportive to and necessary for the corporation chart of accounts; authority to direct the development and maintenance of necessary procedures to insure the integrity of the company's accounts and statements; authority to see that the company's accounting policies and procedures are followed in the divisions.
2. Authority to prescribe policies and procedures in the handling of cash, including banking arrangements, methods of handling receipts and disbursements, and the requirements for bonding throughout the company.
3. Authority to prescribe policies, standards, and procedures with respect to inventory control matters which affect the integrity of accounting records.
4. Authority to prescribe the necessary form, procedures, and timing for the preparation and submission of profit plans.
5. Authority to require from the various divisions and departments of the company financial, accounting, and statistical reports and forecasts in a form and at times believed to be necessary for proper company planning and control.
6. Authority to approve the selection of the chief financial officer of any division or affiliate.
7. Authority to prescribe and undertake a program of internal auditing of financial, cash, credit, and accounting transactions, and an audit of corporate and divisional financial and accounting policies and procedures.

LINE AND STAFF IN PRACTICE

The essential character of line and staff relationships becomes readily apparent in the study of well-managed enterprises. Although the semantics of management occasionally mislead the student (and, more often, those managing and being managed), a clear statement of authority relationships will identify the kind of authority—whether it be line, staff, or functional authority.

In one instance, one of the nation's leading management consulting firms spelled out the treasurer's authority in a fast-growing enterprise with territorial divisions for major line operations and a staff of top executives to control over-all policy as follows:[14]

The Treasurer has line authority over and is responsible for directing activities of such personnel as he requires to establish system policies and procedures for the functions under his jurisdiction and to administer system treasury and accounting functions which are reserved for his department. He has no direct line authority over the day-to-day activities of accounting personnel in the divisions and regions except as specifically delegated by the president. He is responsible for developing and interpreting budgeting, accounting, and financial policies to the divisions and regions for assisting these organizations in carrying out such policies, and for satisfying himself that such policies are correctly and ably administered in the field.

At the request of division managements, or voluntarily when system welfare is materially concerned, the Treasurer shall make recommendations concerning the employment, promotion, dismissal, or change in compensation of supervisory personnel engaged in activities within his functional responsibility. Final action on such matters shall be taken by division managements when mutual agreement has been reached with department heads concerned.

This general description of authority is supplemented by a list of duties making clear that the treasurer's major assignments are establishing budgetary policy and procedures, instituting accounting policies and procedures for maintaining division records, and such other procedures as might be necessary for the discharge of his duties. The description and list make clear the line, staff, and functional authority relationships of the treasurer: He has line authority over his own department, staff relationship to top and divisional managers, and functional authority to require the major operating departments, the divisions, to follow good budgeting and accounting procedures.

Unavoidability of Functional Authority

In virtually every large enterprise, and in many smaller enterprises, some delegation of functional authority to staff departments seems unavoidable. Even though a manager may abhor and try to avoid this hybrid combination of line and staff authority, most major staff departments have some functional authority. This practice is largely due to the necessity for expert interpretation of policy and for formulation of procedures by specialists, which, in turn, results from the need for varying degrees of uniformity in accounting, labor, public relations, and other activities.

[14] From a confidential organization report by a major management consulting firm.

Of course, the line executive could maintain the separation of line and staff authority relationships in his organization structure if he were to insist on issuing all the instructions relating to matters required by specialized staff assistance. As a matter of fact, some corporation and division executives have done so. However, in most enterprises, this either taxes unduly the line manager's span of management, or, if he automatically accepts his staff's recommendations, it makes the apparent avoidance of functional authority a meaningless pretense. It is always good practice for the person actually making decisions to be plainly identified.

STAFF AND THE SMALL BUSINESS

Since the staff type of department represents a refinement in specialization resulting from division of labor, the appearance of staffs is usually proportional to the size of the enterprise. Just how large a business firm must be before it will gain by regrouping certain activities into staff departments cannot be stated generally. However, it need not be very large before it feels the necessity for specialized assistance on such matters as taxation, government procurement, personnel policy and procedures, accounting, financing, contracts and legal matters, and even management itself. The web of government, union, and other controls and complexities in which even the small business finds itself has blurred many of the old sharp distinctions between the small and larger business.

Even without being able to develop extensive staff departments, the small company can benefit from staff assistance in many ways. Indeed, in the present economic, social, and political environment, the price of error in such matters as the determination of costs and taxes, the maintenance of labor relations, and planning and control is so great that the small firm cannot afford to do without the best possible counsel. Heads of companies of thirty or even fewer employees can frequently afford a general staff assistant. No matter how small the company, one of its essential costs is for legal and tax advice on a retainer, hourly, or job basis. Any company can receive accounting counsel at moderate cost from its auditing firm, and audit of a company's books is usually a necessity in connection with income taxes and bank loans. Other advisory services include those of bankers and those relatively untapped but available resources in universities and colleges. Just as medical schools contribute to the community—particularly that part of the community which cannot afford the services of a high-priced specialist—so can university staffs be available, at a reasonable cost, to small businesses in such areas as engineering, accounting, economics, and management. The small corporation, furthermore, can use its board of directors as a source of advice and assistance. Sitting on boards of directors has attractions for men challenged by the opportunity for interesting service and for strengthening the free enterprise system.

In the small firm managers often operate in both line and staff capacities. The production manager may be the president's chief adviser on present and future costs and even on product design. The treasurer or controller may be the counselor on taxes, prices and availability of materials, or wage levels. But this fact does not change the essential nature of line and staff relationships, which are the same in small as in large firms. However, a staff organization suitable for the General Motors Corporation would bankrupt a medium-sized company, and a staff organization suitable for the latter would be too expensive for a small firm. Thus, one of the arts of good managing is to tailor the application of the various management devices to the resources available.

LIMITATIONS IN USING STAFF

Although staff departments are necessary to an enterprise and can do much to make it successful, the nature of staff authority and the difficulty of understanding it lead to certain limitations in practice. Knowing these, both the line executive who is creating a staff and the staff personnel may be able to employ this desirable device effectively.

Danger of Undermining Line Authority

Staff personnel are usually viewed with skepticism by operating executives, who see in them a high potential for harm. Observation of the fortunes of staff departments in many enterprises gives evidence that their prestige ebbs and flows. Too frequently, a president brings in a staff executive, clothes him with authority (frequently very vague), and commands all other managers to be cooperative. The proposals of the staff man are received by the president with enthusiasm, and pressure is brought to bear upon the managers involved to put them into effect. What is actually taking place here is that the authority of the department managers is being undermined, yet, grudgingly and resentfully, the proposals will be accepted, because all will recognize the high tide of the staff's prestige. A continuation of this situation might harm or even destroy the operating departments. Capable managers, not willing to submit to indignity or wait until the tide ebbs, would be snapped up by competitors, and the operating departments would gradually fall into inept hands. The denouement would be for the board of directors to fire the president or, as is more probable, for the president to discharge the staff.

These operating departments represent the main line of the enterprise and their heads gain a degree of indispensability. If a staff adviser forgets that he is to counsel and not to order, if he overlooks the fact that his value lies in the extent to which he strengthens the line manager, and if—worse yet—he should undermine line authority, he risks becoming expendable. If there is a supernumerary in an organization, it is likely to be the staff assistant.

A personnel manager recently extended his service activities and advisory functions to encompass control over the actual staffing and much of the supervision of subordinates in line departments. For a time, the line managers welcomed his assistance with their personnel problems. But when they realized they no longer controlled their subordinates and when the personnel manager was unwilling to relinquish his control, the resultant outcry forced the president to request the resignation of the personnel manager.

Lack of Responsibility of Staff

Advisory departments only propose a plan. Others must make the decision to adopt it and put it into operation. This creates an ideal situation for recrimination and the shifting of blame. The staff will claim that it was a good plan and that it failed because the operating manager was inept, uninterested, or intent on sabotage. The manager who must make the plan work will claim that it was a poor plan hatched by inexperienced and impractical theorists.

Thinking in a Vacuum

The argument that a staff position gives the planner time to think is appealing, but it overlooks the possibility of thinking in a vacuum. The weakness of impracticality has resulted, in business and government alike, in friction, loss of morale, and sabotage.

Another weakness in the assumption that planners must be set off from line departments in order to think is the implication that operating managers are without creative ability. They may, indeed, be without specialized knowledge, but this can be furnished them by properly hired and utilized staff assistants. Good operating managers can analyze plans, see long-range applications, and spot fatal weaknesses far better than most staff assistants. An intelligent manager will not delegate his managerial functions, and it is fatal to his managership to strip away real responsibility for activities such as planning and to assign them to a staff assistant.

Management Complication

Few would deny the importance of maintaining unity of command. It is not easy for a department head to be responsible to two or three people; at the worker level it may be disastrous to attempt multiple responsibility. Some disunity in command may be unavoidable, since functional authority relationships are often unavoidable. But the manager should remain aware of the difficulties of multiple authority and should either limit them—even at the cost of some uniformity or loss of the fruits of specialization—or else carefully clarify them.

Furthermore, too much staff activity may complicate the line executive's job of direction and control. A corporation president may be so busy dealing with the recommendations of a large number of staff assistants and straightening twisted lines of authority that he may not be able to give requisite time and attention to his operating departments; or the business may be come so oriented to making policy and setting procedure that there is little time left to make shoes or give transportation service.

MAKING STAFF WORK

Observation of many business, government, educational, and other enterprises leads the authors to the belief that the line-staff problem is not only one of the most difficult that organizations face, but that it is also the source of an extraordinarily large amount of inefficiency. Solving this problem requires high managerial skill, careful attention to principles, and patient teaching of personnel.

Understanding Authority Relationships

Before the problems of line and staff can be solved, the nature of their authority relationships must be understood. So long as line and staff are regarded as groups of people or are confused with groupings of activities—as when service departments are confused with staff—this understanding is lacking. It must be recognized and emphasized that line and staff are relationships and that most managerial jobs have elements of both.

Every manager and his subordinates should understand the purpose of their tasks and whether they operate in a line or in a staff capacity. This understanding must be accompanied by inculcation of the idea that line authority means making decisions and acting on them, while staff authority implies only the right to advise and counsel. The line may tell, but the staff must sell.

Making Line Listen to Staff

If staff counsel and advice are justifiable at all, the reason must be found in the complexities of enterprise operation and the need for assistance either from experts or from those freed from more pressing duties to give such assistance. Obviously, if staff help is not used, it would be prudent to abolish it. Line managers should realize that the competent staff assistant offers suggestions to aid and not to undermine or criticize. Although most line-staff friction probably arises from ineptness or over-zealousness on the part of staff people, trouble also arises because the line executive too carefully guards his authority and resents the very assistance he needs.

Line managers should be encouraged or forced to consult with staff. Enterprises would do well to adopt the practice of compulsory staff assistance wherein the line must *listen* to staff. In General Motors, for example, the product division manager consults with the staff divisions before proposing a major program or policy to the executive committee. He may not be *required* to do so, but he is likely to find smoother sailing for his proposal if he has done so; and if he can present a united front with the staff division concerned, there will unquestionably be a better chance for its adoption.

Keeping Staff Informed

Common criticisms of staff are that specialists operate in a vacuum, fail to appreciate the complexity of the line manager's job, or overlook salient facts in making recommendations. To some extent, these criticisms are warranted because the specialist cannot be expected to know all the fine points of a manager's job. The specialist should take care that his recommendations deal only with matters within his competency; and the operating manager should not lean too heavily on a recommendation if, as is often the case, it deals only partially with a problem.

Many criticisms arise because the staff assistant is not kept informed on matters within his province. Even the best assistant cannot advise properly in such cases. If the line manager fails to inform his staff of decisions affecting its work, or if he does not pave the way—through announcements and requests for cooperation—for his staff to obtain the requisite information on specific problems, it cannot function as intended. In relieving his superior of the necessity for gathering and analyzing such information, the staff assistant largely justifies his existence.

Completed Staff Work

Many staff persons overlook the fact that to render the most and best assistance, their recommendations should be complete enough to make possible a simple positive or negative response by the line manager. The staff assistant should be a problem solver and not a problem creator. He creates problems for the manager when his advice is indecisive or obscure, when his conclusions are erroneous, when he has not taken into account all the facts or consulted the persons seriously affected by the proposed solution, or when he does not point out to the manager the pitfalls as well as the advantages in a recommended course of action.

Completed staff work implies presentation of a clear recommendation based upon full consideration of a problem, clearance with persons importantly affected, suggestions about avoiding any difficulties involved, and, often, preparation of the paper work—letters, directives, job descriptions, and specifications—so that the manager can accept or reject the proposal without further study, long conferences, or unnecessary work. Should he accept the recommendation, thorough staff work provides him with the machinery to put it into effect.

Staff Work as an Organizational Way of Life

Understanding staff authority lays the foundation for an organizational way of life. Wherever staff is used, its responsibility is to develop and maintain a climate of favorable personal relations. Essentially, the task of the staff assistant is to make the responsible line manager "look good," to help him do a better job. A staff assistant should never attempt to assume credit for his ideas. Not only is this a sure way of alienating his line colleague, but the operating manager who accepts the idea actually bears responsibility for his action.

Even under the best of circumstances, it is difficult to coordinate line and staff authority, for men must be persuaded to cooperate. The staff officer must gain and hold the confidence of his colleagues. He must keep in close touch with the operating departments, know their managers and staffs, and understand their problems. He must, through precept and example, convince his line colleagues that his prime interest is their welfare, and he must deprecate his own contributions while embellishing theirs. He will have "arrived" when line executives seek his advice and ask him to study their problems.

FOR DISCUSSION

1. Select four articles or books in which the terms "line" and "staff" are used. How are they defined? To what extent do the concepts you find agree or disagree with those in this book?

2. Why is it there has been a conflict between line and staff for so long and in so many companies? Can this conflict be removed?

3. Take as examples a number of positions in any kind of enterprise (business, church, government, or elsewhere). Classify them as line and staff.

4. If the task of a person in a purely staff position is to offer advice, how can a person receiving this advice make sure that it is competent, independent, and true?

5. How many cases of functional authority in organization have you seen? Analyzing a few, do you agree that they could have been avoided? If they could have been, would you have eliminated them? If they could not have been avoided or you would not have wanted to eliminate them, how would you remove any possible difficulties which might arise?

17
service departments

A service department is a grouping of activities that might be carried on in other departments but are brought together in a specialized department for purposes either of efficiency or control, or both. As such, it could be looked upon as a form of departmentation.

Although often referred to as "staff," the concept of a service department is distinct from that of line and staff authority relationships. Such terms as "service," "facilitating," "auxiliary," and, more simply, "support" have been employed to convey the nature of service activities. A service department is an auxiliary activity that facilitates the operation of other departments and by representing a *grouping of activities* involves performance of an operating function. A distinction between the service department and others lies in the occasion for its appearance. Although the span of management is the limitation that ordinarily makes departmentation necessary, such is not usually the case with respect to service activities.

DEVELOPMENT OF SERVICE DEPARTMENTS

Persons familiar with the large, smoothly operated service department of a large-scale business may overlook such departments in embryo form—for instance, the maintenance, accounting, or personnel departments created in a new college, bank, public utility, or department store. The *reason* for organizing activities in this way may be more clearly observed in connection with the establishment of a small enterprise and in its subsequent growth. Such a metamorphosis of service departmentation is illustrated in Figure 17.1.

Origin in Economies of Specialization

There is no question, of course, of division of labor in a one-man business, but with the addition of one or more employees the owner shifts some non-managerial duties to his subordinates. In the case of a grocery store, the clerks

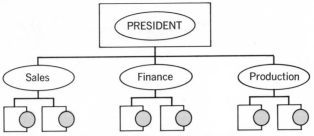

A. Organization without specialized service department.

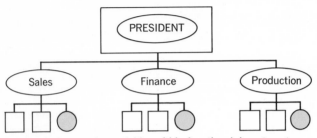

B. Independent service activities within functional departments.

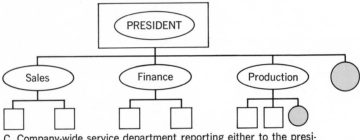

C. Company-wide service department reporting either to the president (1) which is typical of accounting or to the production manager (2) which is typical of maintenance and sometimes personnel.

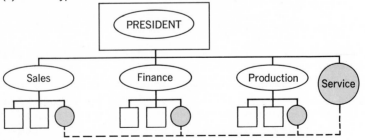

D. Specialized service department with functional authority over decentralized units reintroduced into functional departments.

⬤ Shaded areas represent a kind of service activity.

Figure 17.1 *Metamorphosis of service departmentation in a factory.*

may be expected to receive and check goods against invoice, to price and display goods on shelves, to assist customers, and to contribute to the neat appearance of the store. Continued growth, accompanied by additions to the clerical force, enables the clerks to perform specialized activities. More specific titles are then used to describe their functions, such as cashiers, janitors, stock boys, and the like. Further expansion will force the owner, in accordance with the limitations of the span of management, to organize the enterprise by grouping activities and personnel under grocery, meat, and produce department managers, who will be engaged in assigning subordinates to do paper work, maintenance activity, and line work.

Paper work—such as orders, invoices, pay records, and asset records—is typically assigned to the office of the owner, who may employ a part-time bookkeeper to undertake the accounting function. When the volume of work will support a full-time accountant, such a person will probably, though not necessarily, be hired. Similarly, the work that the part- or full-time maintenance workers perform may be accomplished more economically if it is split off from the duties of the department managers and regrouped into a single department, the head of which may report to the owner or to the grocery manager.

The bases for economy in specialization of service activities are rooted in the use of personal skills and specialized equipment, in the full employment of personnel, and in the potential improvement in the quality of service. The existence of a volume of work sufficient to occupy an employee's full time permits the employment of a skilled individual; hence, a trained accountant is ordinarily hired as soon as a full-time job exists for him. Such a situation is portrayed in Figure 17.1A, where each department services itself with the aid of a few part-time or full-time specialists.

The consolidation of the accounting or maintenance activity in line departments will often permit the economical employment of small specialized equipment, such as computing machines or floor waxers. At the same time, several part-time jobs may be consolidated into a few full-time jobs, to be undertaken by employees able to render prompt service. Centralization to this extent is illustrated in Figure 17.1B, where the departments in the sales, production, and finance divisions (shown in color) may represent grouped activities relating to recruiting and training employees.

As a firm continues to grow, further economies may be reaped in the manner suggested in Figure 17.1C. The centralization of all accounting activities into a department whose head reports directly to the chief executive can be justified on the basis of economical use of specialized personnel and equipment and the easy access to information required for developing budgets, controls, and plans. Alternatively, it is common factory practice to consolidate maintenance service in a department subordinate to the production manager, thus permitting the economical employment of specially trained labor and specialized equipment in a new service department ready to perform services for all departments.

The final stage in the development of service departmentation is illustrated in Figure 17.1D. In this instance the firm has grown to the point where a certain lack of effectiveness is felt from the degree of centralization achieved in Figure 17.1C. These drawbacks become important where mere size destroys the freedom of quick communication, or causes other problems, with a consequent deterioration in the quality of service. In response to such a situation it is not uncommon for a firm to reestablish within the important functional divisions a subdepartment whose duty it is to render specialized service. For instance, the main accounting or personnel department may, as a result of delays, misunderstanding of needs, or other problems, be forced to agree to the opening of a cost or a personnel subdepartment in the sales and production divisions, respectively. But, in doing so, they may retain functional authority over the subdepartment head—authority to specify how, but not when or where, he shall undertake his assigned duties.

Origin in Need for Control

Although service departments usually develop because of a need to realize the economic advantages of specialization, they are organized occasionally from the need for assuring control; in other cases the economies of specialization are buttressed by considerations of control. There are many modern service departments where the control influence can be seen. With complicated union agreements and extensive labor legislation requiring uniform interpretation, many companies have been forced to concentrate the handling of such matters in a personnel or industrial relations department. To be sure, economies are gained merely from having specialists work with these problems, but perhaps more important to the firm is the assurance of uniform policies, interpretations, and procedures.

A comparable situation is illustrated in the case of corporate accounting departments. The element of control, through assuring accurate accounting statements, is almost certainly as important as obtaining lower accounting costs. Likewise, one of the major considerations in establishing central purchasing departments is to control the nature and operation of this function. Control has also had an influence in the organization of a tax department in many companies, a matter requiring close and careful attention, although economies from specialization have perhaps been an equally strong motive. Moreover, companies doing much business with the armed forces, such as aerospace and electronics firms, have found it necessary, in the interest of uniform policy, to consolidate contract interpretation and surveillance into a service department.

FUNCTIONS OF SERVICE DEPARTMENTS

The functions of service departments, even those with the same titles, vary widely from time to time and from firm to firm. All personnel departments do not carry on the same activities, and wide variations in function are typical of departments of accounting, real estate, law, traffic, general office work, engineering, maintenance, and purchasing. To determine first the exact function of a particular service group, it is necessary to learn what duties have been assigned and what authority has been delegated to its manager.

Service to Other Departments

Service departments would hardly exist if they were not to perform a service for major divisions. The maintenance department, for example, may furnish for all departments heating, ventilation, repair of the business premises, installation of equipment, and janitorial service. But whether this department should also be responsible for redecorating, internal modifications of the building, the purchase of small motors and their installation, relocation of power outlets, salvage, or equipment repair depends entirely upon the exact assignment of duties. Questions of precedence of the various departments in receiving service might be determined in the same way.

One of the problems encountered in service departments is that the quality of the service performed by the several divisions within the firm may vary. It may be difficult, for example, to persuade the accounting department to provide for the sales or market research department a cost service similar to that which it offers the manufacturing division. Or the centralized stenographic department may offer ample service to a top executive but feel less inclined to be as alertly useful to a minor manager.

The organization of a department for the purpose of performing certain services for all other departments is almost always accompanied by an edict that its service must be used. This makes sense, because the cost of a service department is a burden and its underemployment results in undue cost. Many managers object to granting any department a monopoly of the service to be performed and are quick to complain of poor results and high costs. Frequently complaints result in improvement, but they can also result in the decentralization of the service activity or its abolition in favor of buying the service from independent entrepreneurs.

It is not unusual for certain advisory duties to be assigned to service groups. When these functions are undertaken, they are performed in the same manner as that in which a staff group would undertake them. A maintenance or a traffic department frequently carries out an investigation and makes a recommendation to the proper authorities for the purchase of machinery, trucks and trucking facilities, or transportation facilities at one location rather than another. A personnel department may be assigned the duty of investigating and reporting on the practices of leading business firms with respect to executive training programs. The legal department may be required to study and recommend action relating to workmen's compensation. The general office manager may be asked to make a recommendation about the best method of reproducing forms. And the real estate department may be charged with the duty of making recommendations with respect to the prospective purchase of a warehouse.

The chief difficulty arising from service departments acting in a staff capacity results from a misunderstanding of the kind of authority delegated. Service departments make decisions that facilitate the operations of other departments. A legal department will determine how the clauses in a sales contract shall read; a traffic department will establish its own routes and select its own equipment; and an engineering department will write a bill of materials. In all these areas, the authority to make the decision is delegated to the service department. But when the same departments act in a staff capacity, they do so with authority to investigate and recommend, but not to decide.

Functional Authority Relationships

In many instances it is convenient to delegate functional authority to a service department. In such cases it is given a prescriptive right over certain phases of an activity being performed in other departments. For instance, the accounting department may have the functional authority to train and assign cost men for the factory. *How* their work is done may be the responsibility of the accounting department, but in every other respect the cost men work for the plant manager, are paid by him, and conform to the same working conditions as other factory employees.

The grant of functional authority to service departments often works well, although there is one exception. This involves the problem of divided loyalties. In case of a dispute, in the above instance, between the factory and the accounting department, the cost man has a difficult time deciding where he stands. He is serving the factory in a manner that the parent service department disapproves and, consequently, may be expected to stand with the factory in matters of improving service facilities. On the other hand, his promotion may be in the hands of the service department. Smoothing out these situations is truly a job for a diplomat, although diplomacy may not have been regarded as a qualification when the man was originally employed.

PLACE IN THE ORGANIZATION STRUCTURE

So long as service activities remain undifferentiated or are scattered throughout the organization structure, questions of good organization practice in respect to them either do not arise or are relatively minor in importance. But at the point where the economies of grouped performance or the desirability of policy control begin to weigh heavily, managers need to determine not only whether to create a service department but also where to assign it in the organization structure. When the problem of servicing geographically separated units arises, a further complication ensues.

Independent versus Subsidiary Department

The practices of managers in locating a service department in the organization structure are so widely diverse that no general rule can be derived. Personnel departments are found within production divisions or at the first level of departmentation. Accounting may be found within the treasurer's division or at the level of major functional departments. Legal departments may be independent and report to the chief executive, or they may be found within the controller's office or in the finance division. Maintenance and traffic may be assigned to the production or sales departments or they may be independent of both. In the face of such varied treatment, can anything be said about the desirability of a given practice? Recourse to the guides of intimate association will aid in differentiating between good and poor practice in many cases. The following skeletonized charts, showing the major functional departmentation and the location of important service departments, illustrate good organizational structuring in important areas of enterprise activity.

The independent medium-to-large department store   The most usual departmentation of service activities in a retail store of this type includes accounting, maintenance, personnel, and customer service. Good practice would dictate the arrangement in Figure 17.2. Accounting is here shown as independent of the other functions, with the chief accountant reporting to the controller, who is normally assigned the duties of maintaining the financial records and developing information required by other managers. To the gen-

Figure 17.2   *Typical service departmentation in a department store.*

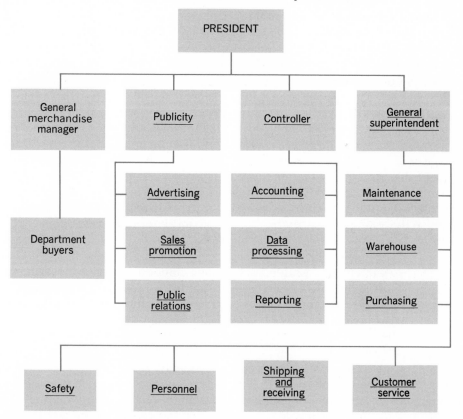

Service functions underlined

eral superintendent, an important officer in department-store structuring, fall the duties of maintaining the physical facilities of the firm, managing the warehouse, making purchases of operating supplies, and supervising store protection. It is customary to assign to him such additional service activities as personnel, shipping and receiving, and customer service. All these activities are intimately associated in the sense that they contribute to the success of the main business of the firm, that is, to sell merchandise. The inclusion of customer service is a happy solution of a difficult problem, since it lends confidence that the policy governing the return of merchandise will be carried out impartially and with justice to both the firm and the customer. The inclusion of the personnel activity reflects a decision that this function should be coordinated at a level just below that of the chief executive rather than in his office.

The independent full-service wholesaler Good organization practice for this type of enterprise, as illustrated in Figure 17.3, does not differ materially from that proposed for the independent department store, because both types of enterprise are in the business of buying for resale. Consequently, each requires the services of a merchandise manager, a controller, perhaps a treasurer, and a superintendent.

The terminology that different types of wholesale firms employ to identify the departments suggested above varies widely. The terms employed here indicate the activities normally assigned to the several departments. It is important to separate the controller from the treasurer because each is a check upon the other. Consequently, the heads of these departments should report to the same superior. The service manager is assigned those activities that relate to the smooth operation of facilities. It may be wise for the president to have the responsibility for these functions centralized. Depending upon the number of employees and whether they are unionized, the assignment of the personnel service will normally be made either to the service manager or to an independent department. The latter solution is a good one if the director also has charge of negotiations with the union and undertakes the myriad activities relating to employee welfare; if neither of these situations obtains, the personnel activity will ordinarily be the responsibility of the service manager.

The manufacturing establishment The important service departments in manufacturing establishments are accounting, industrial relations, and maintenance. Their assignment in a typical organization structure is shown in Figure 17.4. For reasons already stated, the accounting service is best separated from the activities of the treasurer. Since the heads of these departments should report to a common superior, smaller concerns coordinate them at the level of the president, but larger ones frequently install a vice-president in charge of finance to undertake this activity. The usual practice of assigning maintenance to the production manager rests on the fact that most maintenance activity is performed for his department. Since the person in charge of manufacturing has the greatest interest in making certain that maintenance is car-

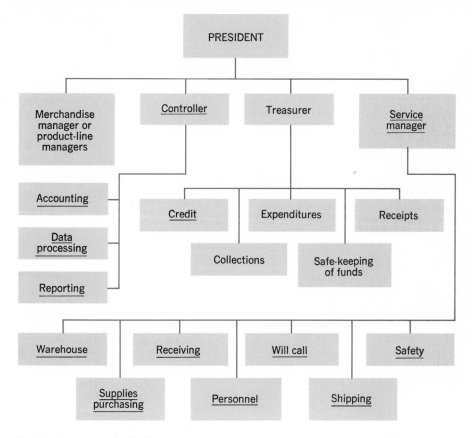

Service functions underlined

Figure 17.3 *Typical service departmentation in a wholesale enterprise.*

ried out efficiently, he is likely to give it adequate supervision; it is probable that the other department heads, for whom the maintenance group also performs service, would neglect such an activity if it were assigned to them. Manufacturing enterprises have tended, in recent years, to detach the personnel department from the factory and require its head to report to some general officer. This is particularly likely to occur if the personnel director is also assigned the duty of negotiating with trade or industrial units and handling grievances. If he is merely concerned with record keeping, recruiting of labor, employee services, and plant safety, he will still quite properly report to the production manager, for the same reasons as were suggested for the maintenance service activity. In such a case, the production manager would carry on negotiations with the union.

Decentralization of Service Departments

The same calculus that pointed strongly to the economies of specialized service departments will yield a somewhat different answer when applied to very

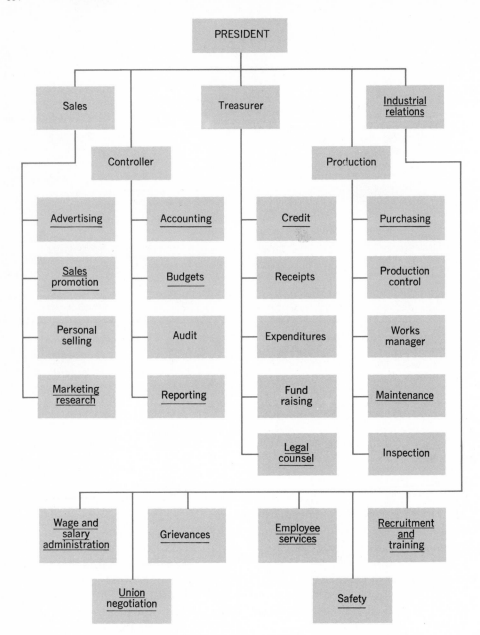

Service functions underlined

Figure 17.4 *Service departmentation in a manufacturing enterprise.*

large enterprises. As a firm grows in size, the net advantage progressively favors an increasing degree of centralization in the service activity until an optimum is reached. When line department heads, however, find themselves charged with sharply rising costs for sustaining the accounting, personnel, and maintenance services, they are likely to question their value. And if, in addition, they feel that these services are ineffective, that attention to their particular needs is lacking, or that reports required for their operations lag, pressures to decentralize the service departments arise. It is important to note, however, that throughout this period of growing criticism it is difficult to place a finger on the total cost of alternative ways to provide the necessary service. Even an accurate measure of observable costs fails to tell the complete story because of the many intangibles involved. One of the most interesting of these is the attitude of line and staff department heads toward service bureaucracies.

Businessmen are quick to recognize a striking parallel between the operating tendencies of service departments and the costly, rigid formalism in government. The private bureaucracy reaches its terrifying size not in one fell swoop, but by minute accretions of function and procedure. It is here that the "empire builder" is seen at his best. The heads of these departments are quite free to propose further "services" from time to time, each of which is viewed marginally and evaluated in terms of its particular contribution rather than in terms of the complete service the department was created to perform. Many added services can readily be created by an accounting, a personnel, an industrial engineering, or a data-processing department. The critical issue is their net help to the major departments. The basis for measuring such aid is its cost as compared with its over-all value. Viewed in this light, few bureaucracies could flower. Thus, the lack of adequate top-level supervision of service departments on an over-all basis and the lack of adequate service standards create a no-man's-land wherein he who asserts that a service is needed is rarely opposed. The executive who criticizes the cost of the service knows full well that the whole department cannot be eliminated. Since he does not know just where the cuts should be made, he is inclined to favor a type of decentralization that will give him some control over the amount and cost of the service for which he pays.

Bases for Decentralization

The bases upon which a centralized service department should be decentralized and its functions scattered among other departments are complex. Such an undertaking involves at least three areas of investigation: (1) Should a given service activity be decentralized among *all* other departments? (2) Should all the services performed be decentralized? (3) What should be the relationship between the decentralized services and the centralized service departments? One must turn to economic and management principles for a proper analysis of these issues.

Quite patently, the fragmentation of such service activities as data processing, purchasing, personnel, and maintenance among *all* departments is undesirable. The chief argument against this procedure is economic. For instance, the centralized recruitment of nonmanagerial personnel permits the economical use of advertising, the employment of skilled interviewers, and the full employment of centralized effort. The centralization of data processing permits full employment of high-cost equipment rather than the use of less desirable apparatus.

On the other hand, the assignment of decentralized service activities to *some* departments is feasible. A company that operates with a head office and two or more branch plants may have no centralized maintenance, personnel, or data-processing department. Distance, time, and variations in the labor market may point to the economy of decentralization in these instances.

The problem of discriminating between the services of a given department for the purpose of decentralizing some services but not others raises issues involving the quality, as well as the cost, of the service. Few would deny the need to establish a centralized general accounting department. This service activity involves financial and tax accounting for the firm as well as the recording and reporting of information internally useful for decision making. Financial accounting should remain centralized in view of realizable economies; the lack of direct interest in, and understanding by, the several department heads; the greater ease in achieving proper policy interpretations; and the relative ease of coordinating it with other functional areas. On the other hand, it is probable that cost accounting should be decentralized, at least to the extent of the sales and manufacturing divisions. The typical deplorable lack of production and sales cost data can often be explained by the centralization of cost accounting in a separate department, where the needs of major departments for accurate and timely information are not always understood. Although it is not unusual for some types of cost reporting to be decentralized in the production division, it is extremely rare for this to be permitted in the sales division. It is little wonder that distribution costs remain indeterminate in so many manufacturing, wholesale, retail, and service establishments.

Similar issues are resolved in favor of decentralized service when the recruitment of salesmen is undertaken by the sales division rather than by the personnel department; when the traffic department buys and services but does not control the use of automobiles for sales personnel; and when the production division trains and assigns service personnel to the sales division but does not control their activities.

Elimination of centralized service and centralization of service represent the two extremes in organization. Partial decentralization, contemplated usually with a grant of functional authority to the centralized department, is middle ground, but it is an unstable compromise, giving rise to recurrent shifts in the degrees of authority over the decentralized service.

Advantages of Partial Decentralization

The right kind and degree of partial decentralization of service activities can be attractive from several points of view. Complaints about poor service are usually forestalled. The decentralized unit comes to understand the importance of time and works with good will to provide quick service. Or, even where there is little improvement in the time factor, the operating executive can be made to understand the reasons for the delay.

However, the allocation of service department overhead to an operating division is a source of continuous irritation. Comparisons are made, frequently on a subjective basis, between the uncontrollable charge and the value of the service, much to the disadvantage of the former. Operating department heads admit the need for the service but are frustrated by lack of control over its cost. Consequently, when decentralization does take place, service personnel are in a position to emphasize their contribution to operations in a much more direct and forceful manner. And skill in doing this can result in allaying dissatisfaction with the amount of the service charge in the operating department budget.

A closely related yet distinct advantage of partial decentralization lies in the importance to the major department managers of getting control over the service function. The successive splitting off of activities which occurs in the centralizing process is viewed with grudging concern by line executives. Aside from losing power, they worry about the inevitable decline in the quality of service. When their feeling is confirmed by experience with the central service setup, the move to decentralize, even on a basis entirely different from the original one, is greeted with much satisfaction. For once again direct control over much of the activity will be established; and this way of doing things is one that operating men like.

There is still another advantage in partial decentralization. The operating manager may confidently look forward to obtaining a special pleader in the centralized service department. For instance, the frustration that production and sales managers feel toward the controller's office is proverbial. The men often fail to understand one another, and the operating man often feels that he cannot get needed information. The decentralization of the cost function often results in the "friend-at-court" situation. The cost personnel come to understand the production or distribution problems of the operating executive, evaluate the necessity for reports containing different content and better explanations of accounting practices, and become, perhaps, the best group to represent the operating department.

Dangers of Partial Decentralization

Partial decentralization of service activities is not without its disadvantages, several of which have been suggested. Functional authority relationships give rise to potential conflicts between the managers of service and operating departments. The difficulty becomes clear as soon as a service is divided. After decentralizing cost accounting, the controller may draw up instructions relating to what data to gather for corporate purposes and how and when to report them. But who appoints the cost representative? Suppose the production manager demands entirely different reporting of data, or new data? Who decides questions of pay rates and promotions of the cost representatives? And who terminates them? These matters, usually ignored when decentralization is decided upon, inevitably lead to recurring controversies.

There is also the danger that, once started, the trend toward decentralization of service will be permitted to go beyond the bounds dictated by savings in time and cost and by improvement in service. The initial exuberance in establishing division service groups may discourage careful analysis of the complete cost picture.

Finally, there is the danger that the divided loyalties of the decentralized personnel will not only lead to instability of the function but will also result in disaster for the personnel. The fact that, whenever contentions arise, such people are caught between the upper and nether stones of central service and operating division underscores the human cost of decentralization. Also, the ease or difficulty in getting pay raises and promotions must be fully considered by the employee when he decides whether to work in a service or in an operating department.

EVALUATING SERVICE DEPARTMENTS

Managers have a continuing concern with the economics of service departments. The relationship of service activities to other departments and to the total activity of the enterprise is never settled. Circumstances that favor the growth of service activities can change radically when the enterprise must trim its sails in face of the changing economies of war, defense, and peace; of the cyclical stages of business activity; of revolutionary innovations in products and their uses; and of technological and organizational changes in the economic structure.

Costs and Benefits

The manager must balance the costs of service departments against the benefits they provide and decide whether the firm stands to gain from modifying their scope and duties.

Measurable and unmeasurable costs   Although savings and costs of personnel and equipment can usually be accurately calculated, the *total* costs of operating a service department can rarely be set down in a neat row and summed. Much to the discouragement of cost analysts, many unmeasurable elements—among them poor service, poor communication, delays, failures to act, and simple arrogance—must somehow be evaluated. The separation of service from other functions inevitably leads to reduced understanding of each other's needs. A service department separated from the operating activities it is designed to serve may not know what service is required. A statistics department, for example, may not know what managers need to know to run their operations. A personnel department may not be aware of the exact training needs in an enterprise. While the service department is characteristically criticized for these deficiencies, most often they exist because the operating users of services have not made their needs clear.

A second type of service department cost involves delayed performance. Every executive is conscious of the "poor" service he receives. This feeling is induced by delays in the receipt of cost or budget reports, by failure of the personnel department to maintain an active roster of immediately available candidates, and by the frustrations of postponed installations or repairs of equipment by the maintenance department. Rarely is the *cost of these delays* actually calculated. Indeed, they may not be measurable at all, but this does not make them less costly.

A further type of unmeasurable cost involves a frequently encountered characteristic of bureaucracies—arrogance. It is unfortunate but true that personnel in service departments occasionally develop an overbearing attitude toward other activities, a result usually of the political power of the service head within the organization structure. Lordly attitudes breed suspicion and opposition which disrupt the basic activity of service to the line.

Finally, there is the measurable cost of overhead. A basic theory of service specialization is that the centralized department can perform an activity more economically than decentralized departments. But few indeed are the departments that are established *after* a careful study of relative costs.

Benefits   Since service departments may be justified on the basis of savings in cost as compared with other methods of servicing, the evaluation of benefits is exceedingly important. Benefits include skilled service, adequate attention to service, and smoothing out of fluctuating needs.

Centralization of service permits the employment of specialized skills in group activities that would otherwise be scattered through the organization structure. For instance, centralization in a personnel department brings to one place a volume of work that makes it economical to employ experts on a full-time basis. Thus it is probable, although unproved, that centralization costs less, compared with the value received, than would diffused personnel work. The benefits of centralization are nowhere more marked than in the case of electronic data processing, where the high performance characteristics of a large and expensive installation often make a degree of centralization economically unavoidable.

A strong argument can be made that by centralizing services, adequate attention can be given to an area by a group of devoted specialists. But this is not always true. Analyses of individual situations sometimes show that if an operating manager were given a similar allocation of budget, he might be able to perform the function with the same or better quality of attention, largely because he may know better exactly what kind of service is necessary. For example, in putting together statistical reports for his use, the operating manager, to whom a decentralized service reports, could better make sure that the exact report he requires is available.

Finally, the benefit received by ironing out uneven demands for certain types of service can be exceedingly valuable. The maintenance department in a factory is a good example. Seasonal changes in weather lead to changing emphasis on certain types of work. Winter calls for attention to heating, humidity, and lighting service. Summer permits an emphasis on painting, cleaning, and construction. If the same work force can be utilized to carry out both groups of activities, steady annual employment can be furnished to a given complement of men.

Evaluation   The importance of making a determined effort to weigh the costs and benefits of a given service department and its location in the organization structure cannot be stressed too much. It is usually easy to ascertain how much can be saved, in terms of such things as fewer clerks, or technicians, or better utilization of equipment. It is far less easy to measure how much is lost by an inadequate or reduced quality of service for those it is intended to serve. Just because intangible costs and benefits make accurate evaluations extremely difficult, every proposed expansion or change should be analyzed with great caution.

Purchased versus Owned Services

Up to this point, attention has been directed to the desirability and organization of service activities. Various ways of handling them have been considered, with the emphasis on tangible and intangible savings and on control. There is, however, the alternative of purchasing the service from another firm.

Analysis of savings through purchased services   In analyzing the purchase of services, there are several measurable costs to be considered. One is the savings in the direct cost of operating a service as compared with hiring another firm to operate it. Since current or projected service department expense and capital budgets are readily available, they may be directly compared with the bids of outside firms, so that there can be no room for doubt about the realizable savings, if any.

Some argue that purchased service involves heavy costs when it involves waiting time. This is particularly true where a company has a service contract for maintenance of its machinery or equipment. Sometimes the cost of downtime while waiting for the outside agency to send in its repair crew may be so considerable as to offset any possible savings from using purchased services. The proper approach is to determine whether in fact there are greater delays in purchased service than in owned service and then calculate the value of the net loss of time. Once the differential in lost time can be calculated, it is a relatively easy matter to calculate the cost of the net loss.

Another calculable cost savings between owned and purchased service lies in the frequency of the required service. For instance, legal counsel needed but a few times a year is much too expensive to provide within the firm. Or a company may only need service on its electronic data-processing equipment once every one or two months. The real test of whether such services should be maintained in-house is an analysis of cost. It may not be necessary to have enough legal work to keep a house counsel busy all the time. Because legal firms must cover overhead and profit, it might be economically feasible to have a house counsel with only enough work to keep him busy half or two-thirds of his time.

A final measurable cost concerns the burden of service expense, an overhead cost if the service is owned. The firm that purchases service is not hampered at all with this problem. The kind and amount of service are contracted for; it is an operating, and not an overhead, cost of doing business; and it can readily be dispensed with or postponed whenever indicated.

There are, on the other hand, certain unmeasurable costs of purchased service that require mention. These include the matter of divided attention of the service firm, the danger of not knowing what service to ask for, and the question of relative managerial skill. In the first place, the service available from outside firms usually does not belong to any one customer. Outside specialists necessarily have a number of clients, and it is reasonable to expect that they would, from time to time, have conflicts in priority as to who should be served first. But, of course, the same problem can arise with in-house service departments.

The second matter involves the firm not knowing what to ask a service to do. This is by no means unusual. The managers of nearly all enterprises are in a quandary at one time or another, not knowing what to expect of a data-processing, personnel, accounting, legal, traffic, or other service group. There are many instances where an enterprise will purchase outside services without clear specification of exactly what services it wishes furnished. The results are predictable in cost and quality. However, as will be recognized, the same problem can arise from owned service operations.

Third, it may be considered strange that there are differences in skill between the managers of owned and purchased service. Nevertheless, the firm that wants to provide its own service may have great difficulty in finding a manager as skilled as the managers of outside service firms. This is frequent in the case of legal, insurance, tax, data-processing, real estate, and some other services. This has been particularly true with the fast growth of internal data-processing departments. Many are the companies that have gone through hiring and replacement of several managers of these services before they found a competent person who could obtain from these expensive tools the service required.

Practical application   There are no general rules that can be summoned for a quick solution of the problem of whether to own or purchase service. It is not possible to say that any particular service should be purchased. Each instance requires individual analysis and should be decided on its merits. But the framework of the correct *procedure* is both clear and applicable to all kinds of service activities. The first step involves the careful calculation of the measurable costs of owned versus purchased services and the determination of the net savings to the firm. The second step consists of the painstaking analysis of the unmeasurable relative costs of the alternatives. The third step requires the comparison of the results of the first steps and a decision in the best interests of the firm.

In the situation where the contemplated service is *in addition to* activities currently performed by either an owned or a purchased service, the same scientific approach is essential but with a difference in the nature of the costs. The important costs here are marginal and should be calculated in terms of the added expense of each alternative. For instance, a firm with an owned personnel department may need a training service. The question arises whether to add this activity to the department or purchase it outside. On the basis of the relative costs involved, the decision may go either way.

FOR DISCUSSION

1. Very few managers distinguish between staff and service groups. What are the advantages of making the distinction?
2. Many managers feel that service departments "run the business." What faults in assigning activities and in communication may explain this situation?
3. How do you think the budget for a service department should be fixed?
4. If you were manager of electronic data processing in an enterprise, how would you make sure you had an effective and efficient service department?

18

decentralization
of authority

Whether authority should be concentrated or dispersed throughout the organization is a question not so much of *what kind* as of *how much* authority. Decentralization is a fundamental aspect of delegation; to the extent that authority is not delegated, it is centralized. Absolute centralization in one person is conceivable, but it implies no subordinate managers and therefore no structured organization. Consequently, it can be said that some decentralization characterizes all organizations. On the other hand, there cannot be absolute decentralization, for if a manager should delegate *all* his authority, his status as manager would cease; his position would be eliminated; there would, again, be no organization. Centralization and decentralization are, therefore, tendencies; they are qualities like "hot" and "cold."

As one management writer[1] has explained, the degree of decentralization is greater:

1. *The greater the number of decisions made lower down the management hierarchy.*
2. *The more important the decisions made lower down the management hierarchy. For example, the greater the sum of capital expenditure that can be approved by the plant manager without consulting anyone else, the greater the degree of decentralization in this field.*
3. *The more functions affected by decisions made at lower levels. Thus companies which permit only operational decisions to be made at separate branch plants are less decentralized than those which also permit financial and personnel decisions at branch plants.*
4. *The less checking required on the decision. Decentralization is greater when no check at all must be made; less when superiors have to be informed of the decision after it has been made; still less if superiors have to be consulted before the decision is made. The fewer people to be consulted, and the lower they are on the management hierarchy, the greater the degree of decentralization.*

[1] E. Dale, *Planning and Developing the Company Organization Structure*, Research Report No. 20 (New York: American Management Association, 1952), p. 107.

"Centralization" has been used to describe tendencies other than the dispersal of authority, as in centralization of performance (discussed below on page 358). This is a problem of geography: a business characterized by centralized performance operates in a single location or under a single roof. Centralization often refers, furthermore, to departmental activities: service divisions centralize similar or specialized activities in a single department. But when centralization is discussed as an aspect of management, it refers to withholding or delegating authority and the authority dispersal or concentration of decision making.

Although closely related to delegation of authority, decentralization is more: it reflects a philosophy of organization and management. It requires careful selection of what decisions to push down into the organization structure and what to hold at or near the top, specific policy making to guide the decision making, selection and training of people, and adequate controls. Indeed, a policy of decentralization affects all areas of management.

DELEGATION OF AUTHORITY

The primary purpose of delegation is to make organization possible.[2] Just as no one person in an enterprise can do all the tasks necessary for accomplishment of group purpose, so is it impossible, as an enterprise grows, for one person to exercise all the authority for making decisions. As was shown in Chapter 13, there is a limit to the number of persons a manager can effectively supervise and for whom he can make decisions. Once this limit is passed, authority must be delegated to subordinates who will make decisions within the area of their assigned duties.

How Authority Is Delegated

Authority is delegated when organization discretion is vested in a subordinate by a superior. Clearly, no superior can delegate authority he does not have, whether he is a board member, the president, a vice-president, or a foreman. Equally clear, a superior cannot delegate all his authority without, in effect, passing on his position to his subordinate.

The entire process of delegation involves the *determination* of results expected, the *assignment* of tasks, the *delegation* of authority for accomplishing these tasks, and the *exaction* of responsibility for their accomplishment. In practice, it is impossible to split this process, since expecting a person to accomplish goals without the authority to achieve them is meaningless, as is the delegation of authority without knowing for what end results it will be used. Moreover, since responsibility cannot be delegated, the delegant has no practical alternative but to exact responsibility from his subordinate for completing his assignment.

[2] For one of the best and most detailed treatises on the process of delegation, see Alvin Brown, *Organization of Industry* (Englewood Cliffs, N.J.: Prentice-Hall, Inc., 1947), chaps. 2–12.

Clarity of Delegation

Delegations of authority may be specific or general, written or unwritten. If the delegation is unclear, a manager may not understand the nature of his duties or the results expected. The job assignment of a company treasurer, for example, may specify such functions as accounting, credit control, cash control, financing, export-license handling, and preparation of financial statistics, and these broad functions may even be broken down into more definite duties. Or, a treasurer may be told merely that he is expected to do what treasurers generally do.

Specific written delegations of authority are extremely helpful both to the manager who receives them and to the grantor, who will thereby more easily see conflicts or overlaps with other positions. He will also be able better to isolate those things for which he can and should hold a subordinate responsible.

One top executive claims he never delegates authority but merely tells his subordinate managers to take charge of a department or plant and then holds them responsible for doing so. This particular executive is actually making an extremely broad delegation of authority—that of full discretion to operate as the subordinates see fit. However, in too many cases where such nonspecific delegations are made, the subordinate is forced to feel his way and—by testing through practice what the superior will stand—define his authority delegation by trial and error. Unless he is very familiar with top company policies and traditions, knows the personality of his boss, and exercises sound judgment, he may be placed at a disadvantage. An executive will do well to balance the costs of uncertainty against the effort to make the delegation specific.

On the other hand, there are those who argue that, especially in the upper levels of management, it is too difficult to make authority delegations specific and that the subordinate, robbed of flexibility, will be unable to develop in the best way. Sometimes, particularly for new top jobs, delegations cannot be very specific, at least at the outset. If a large company establishes for the first time a traffic manager to coordinate transportation activities at its various plants, the president may be unclear about the amount of authority called for. But this situation should be remedied as soon as possible. One of the first duties of the new appointee should be a description of the job and clearance of the description with his superior and, ideally, with those other managers on the same level whose cooperation is necessary. Otherwise, organizational frictions, unnecessary meetings and negotiations, jealousies, and numerous other disadvantages are likely to follow. Too many top executives believe they have a happy team of subordinates who do not need specific authority delegations, when, in fact, they have a dissident group of frustrated managers.

The fear that specific delegations will result in inflexibility is best met by developing a tradition of flexibility. It is true that, if authority delegations are specific, a manager may regard his job as a staked claim with a high fence around it. But this attitude can be eliminated by making necessary changes in organization structure an accepted and expected thing. Much of the inflexibility of definite delegations comes from managerial laziness and failure to reorganize often enough for the smooth accomplishment of objectives.

Splintered Authority

Splintered authority exists wherever a problem cannot be solved or a decision made without pooling the authority delegations of two or more managers. Thus, when the superintendent of plant A sees an opportunity to reduce his costs through a minor modification in procedures in plant B, his authority cannot encompass the change. But if the superintendents of the two plants can agree upon the change and if it affects no other equal or superior manager, all they need do is pool their authority and make the decision. Individually, their authority is said to be "splintered." In day-to-day operations of any company, there are many cases of splintered authority and probably many managerial conferences are held because of the necessity of pooling authority to make a decision.

As may readily be seen, such problems can be handled by merely referring the decision upward until one person can make it. In the case of the two plant superintendents, it would lie within the authority of the vice-president in charge of manufacturing. However, in many cases, the splinters of authority, although far down in the organization, exist in departments that have their common superior only in the office of the president. For example, one of the authors observed the solution of a problem involving a Western railroad with headquarters in Chicago. The problem was relatively minor, but a decision on it in Los Angeles required the consolidated authority of the traffic department, the operating department, and the public relations department. It could have been referred up the line by each of the managers to the president's office, where sufficient authority for making the decision was concentrated. But if such decisions were always to be handled by upward reference, the president's office would be swamped. In this case, the managers of the three departments in the Los Angeles office met briefly, pooled their delegated authority, and quickly made the decision.

Splintered authority cannot be wholly avoided, especially in making decisions. However, recurring decisions on the same matters may be evidence that authority delegations have not been properly made and that some reorganization is required.

Recovery of Delegated Authority

All delegations of authority are subject to recovery by the grantor. It is a characteristic of authority that the original possessor does not permanently dispossess himself of this power by delegating it. Just as, in the political area, the right of Americans to change or revoke the Constitution and thus redistribute rights is unchallenged, so, in the area of enterprise operation, the right of the superior manager to recover authority is unquestioned.

Reorganization inevitably involves some recovery and redelegation of authority. A shuffle in organization means that rights are recovered by the responsible head of the firm or a department and then redelegated to managers of new or modified departments, so that the head of a new department may receive the authority formerly held by other managers. For example, when a reorganization takes quality control away from the works manager and assigns it to a new manager of quality control reporting to the vice-president in charge of manufacturing, the vice-president has recovered some of the authority formerly delegated to the works manager and has redelegated it, with or without modification, to the new executive.

PRINCIPLES OF DELEGATION

The following principles are guides to delegation of authority. Unless carefully recognized in practice, delegation may be ineffective, organization may fail, and the managerial process may be seriously impeded.

Principle of delegation by results expected   Since authority is intended to furnish managers with a tool for so managing as to gain contributions to enterprise objectives, *authority delegated to an individual manager should be adequate to assure his ability to accomplish the results expected of him.*[3] Too many managers try to partition and define authority on the basis of the rights to be delegated or withheld, rather than looking first at the goals to be achieved and then determining how much discretion is necessary to do it. In no other way can a manager delegate authority in accordance with the responsibility exacted. Often a superior has some idea, vague or fixed, as to what he wants accomplished, but does not trouble to determine whether the subordinate has the authority to do it. Sometimes the superior does not want to admit how much discretion it takes to do a job and is likewise reluctant to define the results expected. Perhaps it is no wonder that it has become common in enterprises to speak erroneously of delegating "responsibilities."

Delegation by results expected implies that goals have been set and plans made, that these are communicated and understood, and that jobs have been set up to fit in with them. It also demonstrates that planning is a prerequisite to all the tasks of management, and that the managerial functions in practice coalesce into a single activity.

Principle of functional definition   To develop departmentation, activities must be grouped to facilitate the accomplishment of goals; and the manager of each subdivision must have authority to coordinate its activities with the organization as a whole. This gives rise to the principle of functional definition: *the more a position or a department has clear definitions of results expected, activities to be undertaken, organization authority delegated, and*

---

[3] On this subject see the excellent work of Edward C. Schleh, *Successful Executive Action* (Englewood Cliffs, N.J.: Prentice-Hall, Inc., 1955), chaps. 21 and 23, and his *Management by Results* (New York: McGraw-Hill Book Company, 1961).

authority and informational relationships with other positions understood, the more adequately individuals responsible can contribute toward accomplishing enterprise objectives. To do otherwise is to risk confusion as to what is expected of whom. This principle—which is both a principle of delegation and of departmentation—although simple in concept, is often difficult to apply. To define a job and delegate authority to do it requires, in most cases, patience, intelligence, and clarity of objectives and plans. It is obviously difficult to define a job if the superior himself does not know what he wants done.

Scalar principle　The scalar principle refers to the chain of direct authority relationships from superior to subordinate throughout the organization. Ultimate enterprise authority must always rest somewhere. The more clear the line of authority from the top manager in an enterprise to every subordinate position, the more effective will be the responsible decision making and organization communication. The scale is described by Fayol[4] as

... the chain of superiors ranging from the ultimate authority to the lowest ranks. The line of authority is the route followed—via every link in the chain—by all communications which start from or go to the ultimate authority. This path is dictated both by the need for some transmission and by the principle of unity of command, but it is not always the swiftest. It is even at times disastrously lengthy in large concerns, notably in governmental ones.

A clear understanding of the scalar principle is necessary for proper organization functioning. Every subordinate must know who delegates authority to him, and to whom matters beyond his own authority must be referred. Although the chain of command may be safely departed from for purposes of information, departure for purposes of decision making destroys authority and undermines managership itself.

Authority-level principles　Functional definition plus the scalar principle gives rise to the authority-level principle. Clearly, at some organization level authority exists for making a decision within the competence of the enterprise. Therefore, the authority-level principle derived would be: *maintenance of intended delegation requires that decisions within the authority competence of an individual be made by him and not be referred upward in the organization structure.* In other words, each manager at each level should make whatever decisions he can in the light of his authority, and only matters that authority limitations keep him from deciding should be referred to his superior.

A fairly common complaint of top executives is that, while they know the importance of delegating downward, they are concerned with the practice of subordinates delegating "upward." In other words, as chief executives have pointed out to the authors, they assign a problem only to find it in a few days or weeks back on their desks. The answer to this situation is, of course, not

[4] Henri Fayol, *General and Industrial Administration* (New York: Pitman Publishing Corporation, 1949), p. 14.

to permit these problems to come upward. If discretion to make a decision is properly delegated, the superior must resist the temptation to make it himself. Subordinates have a way of quickly detecting a boss who is willing to make decisions that should have been made by those reporting to him.

It is obvious from the authority-level principle that, if a manager wishes to make effective authority delegations and thereby to be relieved from some of the burden of decision making, he must make sure that delegations are clear and that the subordinate understands them. Moreover, he will do well to avoid the temptation to make decisions for subordinates.

Principle of unity of command   A basic management principle, often disregarded for what are believed to be compelling circumstances,[5] is that of unity of command. It may be stated: *The more completely an individual has a reporting relationship to a single superior, the less the problem of conflict in instructions and the greater the feeling of personal responsibility for results.* In discussing delegation of authority, it has been assumed that—except for the inevitable instances of splintered authority—the right of discretion over a particular activity will flow from a single superior to a subordinate. Although it is possible for a subordinate to receive authority from two or more superiors and logically possible for him to be held responsible by them, the practical difficulties of serving two or more masters are obvious. An obligation is essentially personal, and authority delegation by more than one person to an individual is likely to result in conflicts in both authority and responsibility.

The principle of unity of command is useful in the clarification of authority-responsibility relationships. A president, for example, does not normally divide sales activities among sales, manufacturing, public relations, finance, accounting, and personnel, with no single person responsible for them. Instead, since sales is a cohesive activity, he assigns it to the sales manager. Unity of command would not exist if, instead of a single sales manager, the president appointed an executive committee to run the department. To force every major subordinate in the sales department to owe his full obligation to each committee member rather than to one manager would produce confusion, buck passing, and general inefficiency. Similarly, it is undesirable to have several managers assign duties to one employee, who would then be obligated to each of the several managers.

Principle of absoluteness of responsibility   As discussed in Chapter 3, since responsibility, being an obligation owed, cannot be delegated, no superior can escape, through delegation, responsibility for the activities of subordinates, for it is he who has delegated authority and assigned duties. Likewise, *the responsibility of the subordinate to his superior for performance is absolute,* once he has accepted an assignment and the power to carry it out, *and no superior can escape responsibility for the organization activities of his subordinate.*

[5] Note in chap. 16 the case of functional authority.

Principle of parity of authority and responsibility   Since authority is the discretionary right to carry out assignments and responsibility is the obligation to accomplish them, it logically follows that the authority should correspond to the responsibility. From this rather obvious logic is derived the principle that *the responsibility for actions cannot be greater than that implied by authority delegated, nor should it be less*. This parity is not mathematical, but, rather, coextensive, because both relate to the same assignments. The president of a firm may, for example, assign duties, such as buying raw materials and machine tools and hiring subordinates in order to meet certain goals, to his manufacturing vice-president. The vice-president would be unable to perform these duties without being given enough discretion to meet his responsibility. Nor should he, on the other hand, have more authority than his responsibilities call for. Managers often try to hold subordinates responsible for duties for which they do not have the requisite authority. This is, of course, unfair. Sometimes sufficient authority is delegated, but the delegant is not held responsible for its proper use. This is, obviously, a case of poor managerial direction and control and has no bearing upon the principle of parity.

Managers are sometimes said to be given authority to do that for which they cannot be held responsible; thus, a sales manager is given authority to sell, but he cannot be responsible for making people buy. The answer to this is that the sales manager has the authority to use certain material and human resources to obtain sales wherever possible. Obviously, no one can hold him responsible for compelling people to buy. Here, parity consists of his responsibility as an executive for managing the sales force in the best possible way, equated with his authority to sell.

THE ART OF DELEGATION

Most failures in effective delegation occur not because of lack of understanding of the nature or principles of delegation, but because of inability or unwillingness to apply them in practice. Delegation is, in a way, an elementary art of managing. Yet studies made of managerial failures almost invariably find that poor or inept delegation is at or near the top of the list of causes.[6] Much of the reason for this lies in personal attitudes toward delegation.

Personal Attitudes toward Delegation

Although charting an organization and outlining managerial goals and duties will help in making delegations and knowledge of the principles of delegation will furnish a basis for it, certain personal attitudes lie back of making real delegations.

---

[6] See, for example, the study made by F. J. Gaudet of managerial failures in 200 companies, in which one of the three principal deficiencies was found to be inability to delegate authority. "The Mystery of Executive Talent," *Business Week*, pp. 43–46 (May 21, 1955).

Receptiveness   An underlying attribute of the manager who would delegate authority is a willingness to give other people's ideas a chance. Decision making always involves some discretion, and this means that a subordinate's decision is not likely to be *exactly* that which his superior would have made. The manager who knows how to delegate, must have a minimum of NIH ("not invented here") factor and must be able not only to welcome the ideas of others but to help others and to compliment them on their ingenuity.

Willingness to let go   The manager who would effectively delegate authority must be willing to release the right to make decisions to his subordinates. A great fault of managers who move up the executive ladder—or of the pioneer who has built a large business from the small beginnings of, say, a garage machine shop—is that they want to continue to make decisions for the positions they have left. The authors have seen corporate presidents and vice-presidents insist upon confirming every purchase or the appointment of every workman or secretary, not, perhaps, realizing that doing so took time and attention from far more important decisions.

Where size or complexity forces delegation of authority, managers should realize—even if their superiors must go out of their way to teach them—that there is a kind of law of comparative managerial advantage, somewhat like the law of comparative economic advantage that applies to nations. Well known to economists and logically indisputable, the law of comparative economic advantage states that a country's wealth will be enhanced if it exports what it produces most efficiently and imports what it produces least efficiently, even though it could produce such imports more cheaply than any other nation. Likewise, a manager will enhance his contribution to the firm if he concentrates on tasks that contribute most to the firm's objectives and assigns to subordinates other tasks, even though he could accomplish the latter better himself. This is hard to practice, but failure to do so defeats the very purpose of delegation.

Willingness to let others make mistakes   Although no responsible manager would sit idly by and let a subordinate make a mistake that might endanger the company or the subordinate's position in the company, continual checking on the subordinate to assure that no mistakes are ever made will make true delegation impossible. As everyone makes mistakes, a subordinate must be allowed to make them, and their cost must be charged to investment in his development.

Serious or repeated mistakes can be largely avoided without negating delegation or hindering the development of the subordinate. Patient counseling, asking leading or discerning questions, and careful explanation of objectives and policies are among the tools available to the manager who would delegate well. None of these involves discouraging the subordinate by intimidating criticism, harping on shortcomings, or hovering over him.

Willingness to trust subordinates   Closely allied to willingness to let others make mistakes is willingness to trust subordinates. Superiors have no alternative to trusting their subordinates, for delegation implies a trustful attitude between the two. This is sometimes hard to come by. The superior may put off delegation with the thought that the subordinate is not well enough seasoned, that he cannot handle men, that he has not yet developed judgment, or that he does not appreciate all the facts bearing on a situation. Sometimes these considerations are true, but then the superior should either train subordinates or else select others who are prepared to assume the responsibility. Too often, however, the boss distrusts his subordinates because he does not wish to let go, does not delegate wisely, or does not know how to set up controls to assure proper use of the authority.

Willingness to establish and use broad controls   Since a superior cannot delegate his responsibility for performance, he should not delegate authority unless he is willing to find means ("feedback") of assuring himself that the authority is being used to support enterprise or department goals and plans. As will be noted in later chapters, the establishing of effective controls is one of the more difficult arts of management. Obviously, controls cannot be established and exercised unless goals, policies, and plans are used as basic standards for judging the activities of subordinates. More often than not, reluctance to delegate and to trust subordinates lies in the planning deficiencies of the superior and his understandable fear of loss of control.

Guides for Overcoming Weak Delegation

Fuzzy delegations, partial delegations, pseudo delegations, delegations inconsistent with the results expected, and the hovering of superiors who refuse to allow subordinates to use their authority are among the many widely found weaknesses of delegation of authority.

Combine with these weaknesses untrained, inept, or weak subordinates who go to their bosses for decisions, and subordinates who won't accept responsibility, plus lack of plans, planning information, and incentives, and the failure of delegation is partly explained. But most of the responsibility for weak delegation lies with superiors and, primarily, with top managers. In overcoming these errors—and emphasizing the principles outlined above— the five following guides are practical in making delegation real:

1. Define assignments and delegate authority in the light of results expected. Or, to put it another way, grant authority to make possible the accomplishment of goal assignments.
2. Select the man in the light of the job to be done. This is the purpose of the managerial function of staffing and should be borne in mind, since the qualifications of the man influence the nature of the authority delegated. Although the good organizer will approach delegation primarily from the standpoint of the task to be accomplished, he cannot, in the final analysis, ignore the staffing angle.
3. Maintain open lines of communication. Since the superior does not delegate all authority, or abdicate his responsibility, and since, therefore,

managerial autonomy does not exist, decentralization should not lead to insulation. Because plans change and decisions must be made in the light of changing conditions, delegations tend to be fluid and to be given meaning in the light of such changes. This means that there should be a free flow of information between superior and subordinate, furnishing the subordinate information with which to make decisions and to interpret properly the authority delegated to him.

4. Establish proper controls. Because no manager can relinquish his responsibility, delegations should be accompanied by techniques to make sure the authority is properly used. But if controls are not to interfere with delegation, they must be relatively broad and designed to show deviations from plans rather than interfere with detailed actions of subordinates.

5. Reward effective delegation and successful assumption of authority. It is seldom sufficient to suggest that authority be delegated, or even to order that this be done. Managers should ever be watchful for means of rewarding both effective delegation and effective assumption of authority. Although many of these rewards will be pecuniary, the granting of greater discretion and prestige—both in a given position and in promotion to a higher position—is often even more of an incentive.

FACTORS DETERMINING THE DEGREE OF DECENTRALIZATION OF AUTHORITY

A manager cannot ordinarily be for or against decentralization of authority. He may *like* to delegate authority, or he may *like* to make all the decisions himself. A well-known despot in a certain large enterprise in this country, who would like to make all the decisions, finds that he cannot. Even the autocrat in a smaller enterprise is often forced to delegate some authority.[7]

Although the temperament of individual managers affects the extent of authority delegation, other factors also affect it. Most of these are beyond the control of the individual manager. One may resist their influence, but no successful manager can ignore them.

Costliness of the Decision

Perhaps the overriding factor determining the extent of decentralization is, as in other aspects of policy, the criterion of costliness. As a general rule, the more costly the action to be decided upon, the more probable it is that the decision will be made at the upper levels of management. Cost may be reckoned directly in dollars and cents or in such intangibles as the company's reputation, competitive position, or employee morale. Thus, an airline decision to purchase airplanes will be made at the top levels, while the decision to purchase

---

[7]*Business Week*, pp. 182–194 (Sept. 6, 1952), ran a feature story on the president of a $50,000,000-a-year rayon converter who apparently disproves "what the books say" by not delegating decision making. Yet, even though he makes a surprising number of detailed decisions, the article quotes him as disposing of callers by saying, "See my advertising manager," or "Talk to Marty."

desks may be made in the second or third echelon of an operating department. Quality control in drug manufacturing, where a mistake might endanger lives, to say nothing of the company's reputation, would normally report at a high level, while the quality inspection in toy manufacturing might report much lower.

The fact that the cost of a mistake affects decentralization is not necessarily based on the assumption that top managers make fewer mistakes than subordinates. They may make fewer mistakes, since they are probably better trained and in possession of more facts, but the controlling reason is the weight of responsibility. As already discussed, delegating authority is not delegating responsibility; therefore, the manager typically prefers not to delegate authority for crucial decisions.

On the other hand, this concept must be applied cautiously and, in large companies, sparingly. Some managers fear to delegate any authority for decision making, exaggerating the dangers and costs of mistakes by subordinates. An overburdened manager may incur greater costs from delay or indecision than he hopes to avoid by withholding decision-making rights. Although it cannot be proved statistically, experience supports the conclusion that it may cost more to centralize too much authority, thereby permitting subordinates to drift without clear-cut decisions, than it would to risk subordinates' mistakes.

The need for top control depends on the area of decision. In the typical large business, top management may reasonably feel that it cannot delegate authority over the expenditure of capital funds. In General Motors Corporation, the financial aspects of that company's operations are well centralized under an executive vice-president, who reports to the chairman or vice-chairman of the board of directors rather than to the president. This is a living example of the importance of centralization in this area.

Uniformity of Policy

Another, and somewhat related, factor favoring centralization of authority is the desire to obtain uniform policy. Those who value consistency above all are invariably in favor of centralized authority, since this is the easiest road to such a goal. They may wish to ensure that customers will be treated alike with respect to quality, price, credit, delivery, and service; that the same policies will be followed in dealing with vendors; or that public relations policies will be standardized.

Uniform policy also has certain internal advantages. For instance, standardized accounting, statistics, and financial records make it easier to compare relative efficiencies of departments and keep down costs. The administration of a union contract is facilitated through uniform policy with respect to wages, promotions, vacations, dismissals, and similar matters. Taxes and government regulation entail fewer worries and chances for mistakes with uniform policies.

Yet many enterprises go to considerable length to make sure that some policies will not be completely uniform. When a firm organizes on a product or territorial basis, it obviously prefers at least some nonuniformity in certain important policies. When a company decentralizes authority to encourage individual initiative, certain business policies may be as varied as the individual managers make them. Many companies encourage this variety in all except major matters, hoping that out of such nonuniformity may come managerial innovation, progress, competition between organizational units, improved morale and efficiency, and a supply of promotable managers.

Economic Size

The larger the firm, the more decisions to be made; and the more places in which they must be made, the more difficult it is to coordinate them. These complexities of organization may require policy questions to be passed up the line and discussed not only with many managers in the chain of command but with many managers at each level, since horizontal agreement may be as necessary as vertical clearance.

Slow decisions—slow because of the number of specialists and managers who must be consulted—are costly. To minimize this cost, authority should be decentralized wherever feasible. Indeed, the large enterprise that prides itself on the right kind of decentralization is recognizing the inevitable, although the extent and effectiveness of decentralization may differ widely among companies, depending largely upon the quality of their management.

Diseconomies of large size may be reduced by organizing the enterprise into a number of units. Considerable increases in efficiency are likely to result from making the unit small enough for *its* top executives to be near the point where decisions are made. This makes possible speedy decisions, keeps executives from spending time coordinating their decisions with many others, reduces the amount of paper work, and improves the quality of decisions by reducing their magnitude to manageable proportions.

Exactly what this size is cannot be arbitrarily stated. Some managers believe it to be 1,000 persons, others believe it to be closer to 100 or 250, and some would hold that 2,500 employees can be grouped into manageable divisions, each with considerable decentralized authority. In any case, there is evidence that, where the unit exceeds a certain size, the distance from top to bottom may impair the quality and speed of decision making.

Also important to size is the character of the unit. For decentralization to be thoroughly effective, the unit must possess a certain economic and managerial self-sufficiency. Functional departments such as sales or manufacturing or engineering cannot be the independent unit that product or territorial departments of the same size can be, encompassing as they do nearly all the functions of an enterprise. It therefore follows that, if the uneconomic aspects of size are to be reduced, it is preferable to departmentize along product, territorial, or distribution channel lines.

In the zeal to overcome the disadvantages of size by reducing the decision-making unit, certain shortcomings of decentralization should not be overlooked. When authority is decentralized, a lack of policy uniformity and of coordination may follow. The branch, product division, or other self-sufficient unit may be so preoccupied with its objectives as to lose sight of those of the enterprise as a whole. What headquarters executive has not had the feeling that a division or a branch is at times "running away with the company"? Independence may mean, too, that the talents of top line and staff officials and specialists—whose experience and training are expensive business assets—are not sufficiently used by the subordinate managers in the decentralized units.

History of the Enterprise

Whether authority will be decentralized frequently depends upon the way the business has been built. Those enterprises which, in the main, expand from within—such as Marshall Field and Company and International Harvester Company—show a marked tendency to keep authority centralized, as do those that expand under the direction of the owner-founder. The Ford Motor Company was, under its founder, an extraordinary case of centralized authority; Henry Ford, Sr., prided himself on having no organizational titles in the top management except that of president and general manager, insisting, to the extent he could, that every major decision in that vast company be made by himself.

On the other hand, enterprises that represent amalgamations and consolidations are likely to show, at least at first, a definite tendency to retain decentralized authority, especially if the unit acquired is operating profitably. To be sure, this tendency not to rock the boat may be politically inspired rather than based on pure managerial considerations. Certainly, the claim of autonomy of the once-independent units is especially strong, and a full managerial generation may have to pass before the chief executive of the amalgamation dares materially to reduce the degree of decentralization.

In some cases the first influence of an amalgamation may be toward increased centralization. If the controlling group wishes to put in its own management or take immediate advantage of the economies of combined operation, the requirements of policy uniformity and quick action may necessitate centralization.

Management Philosophy

The character of top executives and their philosophy have an important influence on the extent to which authority is decentralized. Sometimes the top manager is despotic, brooking no interference with the authority and information he jealously hoards. At other times, the top manager keeps authority, not merely to gratify a desire for status or power, but because he simply cannot give up the activities and authorities he held before he reached the top or before his business expanded from an owner-manager shop.

Some men find decentralization a means to make big business work. In those cases, top managers may see decentralization as a way of organizational life that takes advantage of the innate desire of men to create, to be free, and to have status. Many successful top managers find in it a means to harness the desire for freedom to economic efficiency, much as the free enterprise system has been responsible for this country's remarkable industrial progress.

As an example of this attitude Robert E. Wood, former chairman of the board of Sears, Roebuck and Company, said:[8]

We complain about government in business, we stress the advantages of the free enterprise system, we complain about the totalitarian state, but in our industrial organizations, in our striving for efficiency, we have created more or less of a totalitarian organization in industry—particularly in large industry.

The problem of retaining efficiency and discipline in these large organizations and yet allowing people to express themselves, to exercise initiative, and to have some voice in the affairs of the organization is the greatest problem for large organizations to solve.

Desire for Independence

It is a characteristic of individuals and of groups to desire a degree of independence. A region may resent various aspects of absentee control. Observe the hostility of the Chicago Board of Trade and the Chicago newspapers toward the absent managers of its railroads during the fifty years prior to World War I; the establishment of twelve Federal Reserve banks to meet regional banking needs; the frequent exasperation of branch managers with their head offices.

Individuals may become frustrated by delay in getting decisions, by long lines of communication, and by the great game of passing the buck. This frustration can lead to dangerous loss of good men, to jockeying by the office politician, and to resigned inertia by the less competent seeker of security.

Availability of Managers

A real shortage of managerial manpower would limit the extent of decentralization of authority, since dispersal of decision making assumes the availability of trained managers. But too often the mourned perennial scarcity of good managers is used as an excuse for centralizing authority; the executive who complains that he has no one to whom he can delegate authority is trying to magnify his own value to the firm or is confessing his own failure to develop subordinates.

There are managers, also, who believe that a firm should centralize authority because it will then need very few good managers. Indeed, if this can be well done, savings will result. One difficulty is that the firm that so centralizes authority may not be able to train managerial manpower to take over the duties of the centralized top managers, and external sources must be relied upon to furnish any necessary replacements.

The key to safe decentralization is adequate training of managers. By the same token, decentralization is perhaps the most important key to training. Many large firms whose size makes decentralization a necessity consciously push decision making down into the organization for the purpose

---

[8] Quoted in Dale, *op. cit.*, p. 116.

of developing managerial manpower because they feel that the best training is actual experience. Since this usually carries with it chances for mistakes by the novice, it is good practice to limit, at least initially, the importance of his decisions.

Control Techniques

Another factor affecting the degree of decentralization is the state of development of control techniques. One cannot expect a good manager at any level of the organization to delegate authority without some way of knowing whether it will be used properly. Not knowing how to control often explains unwillingness to delegate authority and makes valid the manager's belief that it takes him more time to unmake mistakes or oversee a job than it would to do the job himself.

Coupled with the manager's need to understand and use appropriate control techniques is the state of their development. Improvements in statistical devices, accounting controls, and other techniques have helped make possible the current trend toward extensive managerial decentralization. Even the most ardent supporters of decentralization, such as General Motors, du Pont, and Sears, could hardly take so favorable a view without adequate techniques to show management, from the top down, whether performance is conforming to plans. To decentralize is not to lose control, and to push decision making down into the organization is not to abdicate responsibility.

Decentralized Performance

This is basically a technical matter depending upon such factors as the economies of division of labor, the opportunities for using machines, the nature of the work to be performed (thus, a railroad has no choice but to disperse its performance), and the location of raw materials, labor supply, and consumers. Although this kind of decentralization may be geographical or physical in nature, it influences the centralization of authority.

Authority tends to be decentralized when performance is decentralized, if for no other reason than that the absentee manager is unable to manage, although there are exceptions. For example, some of the large chain-store enterprises are characterized by widely decentralized performance, yet the local manager of a store may have little or no authority over pricing, advertising and merchandising methods, inventory and purchasing, or product line, all of which may be controlled from a central or regional office. The head of a local manufacturing plant of a large organization may have little authority beyond the right to hire and fire, and even in these cases he may be circumscribed by company policy and procedure and by the authority of a centralized personnel department. At the same time, the decentralization of performance limits the ability to centralize authority. The most despotic top manager of a national organization cannot completely supervise his San Francisco plant as closely as he could if it were adjacent to his New York office.

It does not follow that when performance is centralized, authority is centralized as well. True, authority can be more easily centralized if performance is, and if a company wishes tight control over decision making, centralized performance will aid this. But there are too many other factors to give geographical concentration a controlling influence in centralization.

Business Dynamics

The dynamic character of a business also affects the degree to which authority may be decentralized. If a business is growing fast and facing complex problems of expansion, its managers, particularly those responsible for top policy, may be forced to make a disproportionate share of the decisions. But, strangely enough, this very dynamic condition may force these managers to delegate authority and take a calculated risk on the costs of error. Generally this dilemma is resolved in the direction of delegation, and, in order to avoid delegation to untrained subordinates, close attention is given to rapid formation of policies and accelerated training in management. An alternative often adopted is to slow the rate of change, including the rate of that causing change, expansion. Many top managers have found that the critical factor limiting their ability to meet change and expand a business is the lack of trained personnel to whom authority may be delegated. Often, also, authority is delegated to untrained and undirected hands in order to meet the requirements of change, with the recognized future task of taking in the reins and rectifying mistakes when the pace of change has slowed.

In old, well-established, or relatively static businesses, there is a natural tendency to centralize or recentralize authority. Where few major decisions must be made, the advantages of uniform policy and the economies of having a few well-qualified persons make the decisions dictate that authority be centralized. This may explain why in many banks and insurance companies and in certain railroads, decentralization is not extensive. Nevertheless, in static businesses too much centralization may carry danger. New discoveries, vigorous competition from an unexpected source, or political change are only a few of the factors that might introduce dynamic conditions, and if this occurs, the overcentralized firm may not be able to meet a situation requiring decentralized decision making.

Environmental Influences

The determinants of the extent of decentralization dealt with so far have been largely interior to the firm, although the economics of decentralization of performance and the character of business dynamics include elements well beyond the control of an enterprise's management. In addition, there are definite external forces affecting the extent of decentralization. Among the most important of these are government controls, national unionism, and tax policies.

Government regulation of many facets of business policy makes it difficult and sometimes impossible to decentralize authority. If prices are regulated, the sales manager cannot be given much real freedom in determining them. If materials are allocated and restricted, the purchasing and factory managers are not free to buy or use them. If labor may be worked only a limited number of hours at a minimum rate of pay, the local division manager cannot freely set hours and wages.

But the restriction on decentralization goes further: top management itself no longer has authority over controlled aspects of policy and cannot, therefore, delegate authority it does not have. It may only delegate authority to execute controlled policy. Much authority could still be decentralized. But the manager often does not dare trust subordinates to interpret government regulations, especially since the penalties and the public opprobrium for breaking the law are so serious and since the interpretation of laws is a matter for the specialist.

In the same way, the rise of national unions in the past four decades has had a centralizing influence on business. So long as the departmental or divisional manager may control the terms of the labor contract, either by dealing with company unions or with employees directly, authority to negotiate may be delegated by top management to these subordinates. But where, as is increasingly the case, a national union enters into a collective-bargaining contract with headquarters management, with the terms of the contract applicable to all workers of a company wherever located, the company can no more chance decentralization of certain decision making than it can in the case of government controls.

The tax system of the national, state, and local governments has had a marked regulatory effect on business. The tax collector, especially the federal income tax collector, sits at the elbow of every executive who makes a decision involving funds. As a matter of fact, with high rates applicable to corporate income, the impact of taxation is often a policy-determining factor that overshadows such traditional business considerations as plant expansion, marketing policies, and economical operations. Uniformity of tax policy becomes a consideration of primary importance to company management. This spells centralization, because the manager without appropriate tax advice cannot be expected to make wise decisions. It may even require a central tax department acting not only in an advisory capacity and as a tax service agency but also with a degree of functional authority over matters with tax implications.

RECENTRALIZATION OF AUTHORITY

At times an enterprise can be said to recentralize authority—to centralize authority once decentralized. This process is normally not merely a reversal of decentralization, for the authority delegations are not wholly withdrawn by the managers who made them. What occurs is a centralization of authority over a certain type of activity or a certain kind of function, wherever in the organization it may be found.

Thus, the growing importance of taxes, the requirements of uniform labor policy, and the realities of government regulation may dictate that authority over these areas be recentralized or managed by a department with functional authority over them. This recentralization may also occur when, through growth and extensive decentralization, top managers feel that they have lost control over the business. Or if a business falls on difficult times, managers may wish to reinforce their authority over the expenditure of funds, the level of costs, or the character of sales effort. Such recentralization, sometimes intended to be temporary, often becomes permanent. Many top managers take pride in their cost control, budget, or internal auditing departments and in the authority of these departments not only to advise but to supervise many previous prerogatives of lower managers.

DECENTRALIZATION AND ENTERPRISE FUNCTIONS

As will be recalled, the principal functions of any business enterprise are the creation of utilities (production), the exchange of utilities (sales), and the financing of this exchange and of the enterprise itself (finance). In addition, through the need for specialization, there have been split off such functions as personnel, accounting, data processing, statistics, purchasing, and traffic and distribution.

Production

Authority over production is usually the first to be delegated by the chief executive of a company, although the extent of this delegation varies with such factors as the nature of the product, the scale of production, markets, and supply of labor and materials. As the production scale increases or as the processes become more complex, authority is likely to be further decentralized. However, budgets and other controls exert a centralizing influence, as also do the functional staff departments.

Sales

Authority over sales is also likely to be decentralized early. As soon as the geographical area covered by salesmen becomes extensive, or salesmen numerous, the sales department begins to feel strongly the advantage of decentralization. As a matter of fact, delegation of decision-making authority in most aspects of sales is usually greater than in any other function.

The reason for this is easy to find. Sales effort must be brought to the customer, and the branch or district sales manager needs a wide area of discretion. Decentralizing is usually accentuated when a manufacturer has several product lines.

Although selling is usually decentralized, related staff or service activities are not so likely to be. For example, advertising and market research and pricing decisions are likely to be centralized, mainly because of the need for specialized talent, economy, and the requirements of uniform policy.

Finance

The finance department is the last stronghold of highly centralized authority. Even when a company has widely adopted a policy of decentralization, the finance function is far less decentralized than any other.

The reason for this is simple. Enterprise objectives almost always include profitability, availability of funds, and financial stability. In addition, many treasurers and controllers mistakenly assume detailed control over the *activities* of spending, purchasing, and accounting. The important considerations should revolve around reporting on the use of funds, in accordance with approved plans, and assurance that the accounting system reports an accurate and honest record.

Centralization is customarily exerted through budgetary controls over both expenses and capital expenditures, those over the latter usually being stricter than those over the former. The authors know of a sales manager who could sign sales contracts to $5,000,000 but could not approve a capital expenditure of more than $100. The reason for this distinction is usually that operating expenses can be more easily budgeted and that more effective corporate controls can be placed over them. Capital expenditures, on the other hand, are difficult to budget accurately, and they represent a commitment of scarce permanent resources.

Personnel

Certain areas of personnel activities are highly centralized. One of these is the collective-bargaining contract and its administration. Other sensitive areas are wage and salary administration, job evaluation, and managerial selection and appraisal. Except for these areas, the personnel function should be as decentralized as is managership, since all managers must be responsible for their personnel.

Statistics and Data Processing

With the eyes of top managers fixed on the necessity for over-all controls and with the economies of concentrating statistics and data processing, the predominant trend of recent decades has been to centralize authority over these functions, except, of course, in the actual gathering of data. More recently, however, alert managements have begun to decentralize a large portion of this activity.

Central control of statistics and data processing may be most economical and serve top managers well, but the managerial group on the firing line—the group that can really control costs, production, and sales—have often been denied information necessary to their jobs or have received it too late. As a consequence, industry has developed a kind of centralized decentralization, with centralization of authority over the statistical activities necessary for top management and for accumulating those data, but with decentralization of data gathering and report making for the lower levels.

Purchasing

It is difficult to generalize with respect to decentralization of authority over purchasing. The purchase of capital equipment and the acquisition of major materials that constitute a large share of costs are almost invariably handled centrally. So are almost all other purchases in single-plant enterprises and in companies having several plants in a fairly small geographical area. When a company, however, has many plants or branches geographically dispersed or where it has departmentized along product lines, purchasing decisions are likely to be decentralized. Authority over national contracts will almost always be centralized.

Traffic and Distribution

Traffic and distribution functions are likely to be subject to centralized authority in cases where a steady flow of work depends upon a unified and efficient system of routing materials. In most companies, studies of transportation rates, negotiation with carriers, and the establishment of basic shipping policies are centralized. In recent years, with the development of planning and control of physical distribution as a logistics system, there has been a definite trend toward centralizing authority and activities in this area.

OBTAINING THE DESIRED DEGREE OF DECENTRALIZATION

Underlying the discussion to this point has been the assumption that managers can obtain the degree of decentralization upon which they have decided. In other words, the emphasis has been upon how much decentralization, rather than on whether the desired degree can be realized and maintained.

Many managers who believe that authority should be pushed down in an organization as far as it will go are faced with the practical problem of how to push it down there. It is a rare top manager who does not find in his organization somewhere an authority hoarder who simply will not delegate. One of the authors had occasion once to observe a division controller whose office was piled high with major policy matters requiring his attention, while he engaged in minute examination of employees' expense accounts, excusing himself with the statement that none of this work could be entrusted to his subordinates.

In obtaining the degree of decentralization desired, an understanding of decentralization is essential. This concept is based upon the knowledge that decentralization cannot mean autonomy, that it implies establishment of policies to guide decision making along the desired courses, that it requires careful delegation of authority by managers who know how and want to delegate, and that, not being an abdication of responsibility, it must be accompanied by controls designed to ensure that delegated authority is used properly. Although the art of authority delegation lies at the base of proper decentralization, it is apparent that the mere act of delegation is not enough to ensure decentralization.

No manual can indicate how to ensure authority being properly decentralized or appropriately withheld, but several techniques may be used with some chance of success. One of these is merely a technique of organization, the provision of a statement of each manager's duties, the degree of authority delegated to him, and his responsibility. Besides being clear and, preferably, written, the statement should be issued in such a way that all employees may know what it contains. This can serve a vital purpose in settling jurisdictional squabbles and excursions beyond the authority area of a given manager.

Another important technique lies in the example and teaching of the superior, starting at the top of the organization. The character of top leadership in an enterprise permeates any organization. There are in every firm of any size those who will reach out for power, impinge upon activities assigned to others, and bully the timid. Rules and job descriptions are often subject to differences in interpretation, which can be conveniently stretched or circumscribed, depending upon the political environment. Their unreliability, despite their obvious usefulness, stands as a warning to executives that the most dependable foundation for achieving the desired degree of decentralization is the education of subordinate managers in the rights of others—teaching them restraint as well as aggressiveness.

One of the best means of forcing delegation of authority, particularly in middle and lower levels of organization, is to require managers to have a large number of subordinates and, at the same time, hold them to a high standard of performance. When a manager's span of management is stretched, he has no alternative but to delegate authority. At the same time, in order to protect his own performance, the manager learns to select good subordinate managers, train them well, establish clear-cut policies, and find efficient means of control.

Another technique used to force decentralization has been the policy of promoting managers only when they have subordinates able to take their places. To accomplish this end, managers are forced to delegate authority. Moreover, this policy removes a major cause of hoarding authority, the desire of a manager to gain indispensability by making sure that his duties cannot be handled by any of his subordinates.

Occasionally the problem concerns how to retain a predetermined degree of authority. Division and branch managers—because they are far away from the home office, wish to build empires, or want to do a complete job—may assume too much authority and resent the outside auditor, sabotage centralized controls, and oppose central management. The answer, of course, to this problem is primarily one of leadership, clear policy determination and authority delegation, and proper training of subordinate managers. But perhaps the principal problem lies in the character of the top executives. If they temporize, do not support the authority delegations they have made, ignore the organization structure, condone serious deviations from policy, and neglect in other ways to do a thorough managerial job, little can be done to retain any predetermined degree of decentralization.

CLARIFYING DECENTRALIZATION

As in so many areas of managing, conflict, friction, and inefficiencies result from lack of clarification of individual roles. This is nowhere more true in practice than in clarifying the extent and nature of decentralization. This problem can be greatly simplified and clarified by means of a chart of executive approval authorizations. The chart is a technique by which, normally on a single sheet of paper or chart, the various authority delegations of a company are outlined and clarified. Since most of these delegations have to do with the right to commit the company for money, most of the chart has to do with expenditure limits. However, there are other matters, such as policies and programs, which can be and are often shown on such a chart.

An example of a chart of approval authorizations for a small to medium-sized company is shown in Fig. 18.1. It will be noted that a list of major decision areas appears on the left-hand side of the chart. It was found useful in this company to group these decision areas under the classifications of personnel, operating expenses, capital expenditures and commitments, prices and sales commitments, and general. Across the top of the chart are listed those various managerial levels which have approval authority, along with certain staff personnel who have functional authority in a decision matter or whose consultation is required for advice or information.

In the development of a chart, it is apparent that the authority and responsibility for doing so must rest at the top of a company. Because it even distinguishes between decision matters that the board of directors reserves for itself and those delegated to operating management, the board must necessarily be called upon to approve at least this area of delegation. The effective board may wish to do more. If its organizational policy is really one of decentralization, with centralized decision making in certain matters at the top, it may wish to approve the entire chart, at least enough so as to perceive that its policy is being followed in practice.

In addition to clarity to individuals with authority, the chart has other advantages. It acts as a medium of communication of the entire structure of decision making in a company so that people down the line, or in departments whose coordination in a decision is necessary, can see what the decision-making relationships are. Also, in a multi-division company, by having separate divisional charts, as well as a corporate chart, authority may be delegated in varying degrees. Thus, in a large division, more authority may be delegated; or in a division manned by less experienced managers a smaller degree of authority could be delegated. A further advantage is that authority delegations can be changed with greater ease than where they are included in a number of individual-position descriptions.

Although the chart of approval authorizations is only a tool, it is regarded by the authors as an essential one. If it is to work, it should be made a way of life in an enterprise; it must be updated whenever there is any significant change in organization structure or authority delegation and must be communicated wherever decision-making relationships exist. It seldom, if ever, includes matters that should be held confidential. Along with position descriptions and the formulation of verifiable goals for each position in an enterprise, it helps define the roles which individuals must fill.

BALANCE: THE KEY TO DECENTRALIZATION

Any program for decentralizing authority must reflect the principles of delegation if practical pitfalls are to be avoided. There are, in addition, several other

Figure 18.1. Chart of Approval Authorization *

Nature of transaction	Department manager	Staff manager	Division director	President (corporate and domestic) Chairman of the board (international)	Board of directors
1. Personnel					
Employment of new personnel:					
Hourly	All	Personnel manager to process and review for consistency with company policy	All exceptions to company policy		
Salaried	All	Personnel manager to process	All over $800 per month	All over $1,200 per month	All over $2,000 per month
Wage and salary increases:					
Hourly	All	Personnel manager to process and review for consistency with company policy	All exceptions to company policy		
Salaried	All	Personnel manager to process	All	All resulting in salary over $1,200 per month	All resulting in salary over $2,000 per month
Moving expenses		To be processed by controller	All	All over $2,000 in cost	
Leaves of absences	All	To be processed by personnel manager	All	All over 30 days	All over 90 days
2. Operating expenses					
Procurement of materials and services (approval of manufacturing and engineering schedule by vice-president manufacturing and engineering):					
In accordance with approved schedules	Manager of purchasing on all schedules				
Not in accordance with approved schedules		Vice-president of manufacturing and engineering on all. Controller on all exceeding $5,000	All		
Consultation services			All	All corporate services	All contracts or retainers over $5,000 per year

Figure 18.1. *(continued)*

Supplies and maintenance materials and services	All	All over $5,000		All over $5,000
Travel and entertainment requests and reports	All those reporting to him	All those reporting to him	All those reporting to him and all over $1,000	President and chairman of the board approved by board of directors
Advertising and public relations: In accordance with approved program	Manager of advertising and sales promotion on all			
Not in accordance with approved program		General sales manager on all	All outside total budget	
Contributions: Budgeted	Controller		Chairman of the board	
Nonbudgeted			Chairman of the board on all except technical magazines and books	
Memberships and subscriptions	All			
Research and development projects	All	Director of research and development on all	All involving new product lines	
Miscellaneous expenses	All	All over $1,000	All over $5,000	
Tax payments and adjustments	Controller on all		President and corporate secretary where law requires	Tax adjustments over $15,000
Guarantees and replacements	General sales manager and controller on all		All over $5,000	All over $10,000
Contract cancellations	General sales manager and controller on all		All involving more than $10,000	
Leases: Temporary, not to exceed $1,000 in total commitment	All	All		
Other	Controller and secretary-treasurer on all		All	
Operating expense budgets: basic variable budget	Secretary-treasurer on all		All	
3. Capital expenditures and commitments Capital expenditures: In accordance with approved budget	Controller to check for budgetary accuracy	All	All individual items exceeding $5,000	All items exceeding $25,000
Not in accordance with approved budget	Secretary-treasurer on all	All	All items over $1,000	All items exceeding $5,000

Figure 18.1. *(continued)*

Nature of transaction	Department manager	Staff manager	Division director	President (corporate and domestic) Chairman of the board (international)	Board of directors
Capital expenditure budgets	All	Secretary-treasurer on all	All	All	All
Disposal of capital assets		Secretary-treasurer and controller on all	All	All over $5,000	All over $100,000
Patent applications, licensing and patent agreements		Secretary-treasurer on all	All	All	All basic policy
4. Prices and sales commitments					
Sales price formulas		Secretary-treasurer on all		All	
Sales commitments:					
Catalogue standard items	Manager of sales service on all	Controller on all acceptance of credit	General sales manager on all orders exceeding $100,000		
Nonstandard items	Manager of sales service on all	Controller on all acceptance of credit	General sales manager on all exceeding $10,000	All exceeding commitment of $50,000	All exceeding commitment of $200,000
Variations from standard prices	Manager of sales on all		General sales manager on all over $5,000 / Vice-president of manufacturing and engineering on all over $15,000	Inform president of variations in excess of 10% on orders exceeding $10,000	
New product lines		General sales manager on all	All	All	All
Contracts with sales representatives		Form approved by legal counsel	General sales manager on all	All nonstandard contracts	Basic items of commitment in standard form
5. General					
Bank loans for company operations:					
Line of credit		Secretary-treasurer on all		All	All
Loans within line		Secretary-treasurer on all		All	
Loans for buildings and land		Secretary-treasurer on all		All	All
Acquisition of financial interest in or loan to any company		Secretary-treasurer		All	All

*A person required to approve transactions as outlined in the above chart may authorize another person to sign for him in his absence. The person so authorized must affix the proper signature, showing his initials under such signature.

SOURCE: H. Koontz. *The Board of Directors and Effective Management* (New York: McGraw-Hill Book Company. 1967). pp. 46–49.

matters to be considered. The widespread practice of decentralization in recent years has taught important lessons.

Strong forces favor the practice of decentralization. The nature of organized effort requires coordination of people at every level, and most of the managers responsible for coordination are found at middle and lower organization levels; these cannot function without the authority to manage. The growing size of the average organized activity requires an increasing number of managers. And while enterprise does not decentralize in order to develop managers, it is nevertheless quite true that these will not be developed internally unless they have an opportunity to exercise authority. Moreover, the presence of large numbers of well-educated and ambitious young men in enterprise is a steady pressure on top managers to decentralize.

At the same time, extensive decentralization is not to be blindly applied. In many organizations the size and complexity of operations do not require it. Decentralization is not without costs, even in larger companies. In addition to the dangers from nonuniform policy and the problems of control, there are often real financial costs. As authority is decentralized, the manager becomes more and more an independent operator of a small business. He may acquire his own accounting force, his own statisticians, his own engineering staff. Indeed, he may soon be duplicating specialized services of the top company organization.

Perhaps the principal problem of decentralization is loss of control. No enterprise can decentralize to the extent that its existence is threatened and the achievement of its goals is frustrated. If organizational disintegration is to be avoided, decentralization must be tempered by selective centralization of certain areas of vital major policy. The company with well-balanced, centralized decentralization will probably centralize decisions at the top on such things as financing, over-all profit goals and budgeting, major facilities and other capital expenditures, important new-product programs, major marketing policies, basic personnel policies, and the development and compensation of managerial personnel. The key to effective decentralization is the proper balance between centralization and decentralization.

But, judging from experience, a proper balance is not easy to achieve. Many prominent enterprises have had serious problems in this area. Even the great General Electric Company lived too long with a highly centralized functional organization structure; then, when it reorganized after 1954, it decentralized too much, giving far more discretion than later proved to be wise to some 120 integrated and highly autonomous departments. The classic case of excessive decentralization without control was the General Dynamics Company in the late 1950s when its Convair Division surprised its parent with an almost bankrupting loss of 430 million dollars on its ill-fated jet airplane program. The history of many other companies shows cyclical trends in decentralization, at times dispersing too much authority and at other times overcentralizing.

The achievement of balance is perhaps one of the greatest accomplishments of Alfred Sloan in his managing of General Motors over the years. Although practicing and preaching decentralization, he and his top-management team realized that no department or division could be given complete freedom. As a result, this company, as large as it has been, has always continued to hold at the very top major policy and program decisions on those matters necessary for maintaining the soundness and success of the entire company.

FOR DISCUSSION

1. Why has there been so much written and said, in the last twenty years, in favor of decentralizing authority?
2. What is the distinction between decentralizing "some of all authority" and "all of some authority"? What is actually done?
3. In many foreign countries very little authority is decentralized. What reasons do you think would explain this phenomenon? What effect does it have?
4. If you were a manager, would you decentralize authority? State several reasons for your answer. How would you make sure that you did not decentralize too much?
5. There is considerable justification for the position of some top managers that they do not have a free choice in deciding upon the extent of decentralization of authority. Comment.
6. Should authority be pushed down into an organization as far as it will go?

19

committees

One of the most ubiquitous and controversial devices of organization is the committee. Whether referred to as a "board," "commission," "task force," or "team," its essential nature is the same, for the committee is a group of persons to whom, as a group, some matter is committed. It is this characteristic of group action that sets the committee apart from other organization devices.

THE NATURE OF COMMITTEES

Because of variation in authority assigned to committees, much confusion has resulted as to their nature.

Some committees undertake managerial functions, and others do not. Some make decisions; others merely deliberate on problems without authority to decide. Some have authority to make recommendations to a manager, who may or may not accept them, while others are formed purely to receive information, without making recommendations or decisions.

A committee may be either line or staff, depending upon its authority. If its authority involves decision making affecting subordinates responsible to it, it is a plural executive and a line committee; if its authority relationship to a superior is advisory, then it is a staff committee.

Committees may also be formal or informal. If established as part of the organization structure, with specifically delegated duties and authority, they are formal. Most committees with any permanence or standing fall into this class. Or they may be informal, that is, organized without specific delegation of authority and usually by some person desiring group thinking or group decision on a particular problem. Thus, a manager may have a problem on which he needs advice from other managers or specialists outside his department and may call a special meeting for the purpose. Indeed, this kind of motivation, plus the occasional need for gathering together in one room all the authority available to deal with an unusual problem, gives rise to many of the numerous conferences in organizational life.

Moreover, committees may be relatively permanent, or they may be temporary. One would expect the formal committees to be more permanent than the informal, although this is not necessarily so. A formal committee might be established by order of a company president, with appropriate provision in the organization structure, for the sole purpose of studying the advisability of building a new factory and be disbanded immediately upon completion of its task. And an informal committee set up by the factory manager to advise him upon the improvement of quality or to help coordinate delivery dates with sales commitments might continue indefinitely.

However, the executive who calls his assistants into his office or confers with his department heads is not creating a committee. It is sometimes difficult to draw a sharp distinction between committees and other group meetings. The essential characteristic of the committee is that it is a group charged with dealing with a specific problem.

The committee is in wide use in all types of organization. In government, one finds a large number of standing and special committees of every legislative body; indeed, state and national legislatures are committees, as are the cabinets of the chief executives of the federal and state governments. Committees manage many government agencies such as the Tennessee Valley Authority, the Atomic Energy Commission, the Federal Deposit Insurance Corporation, and the Export-Import Bank. Even the courts make liberal use of the device.

In education, faculties of great universities, jealous of academic freedom and distrustful of administrative rights, traditionally circumscribe the authority of presidents and deans with a myriad of committees. In one large university more than 300 standing committees share in administration or advise on policy, ranging from the academic senate and the budget committees, to committees on committees, coordinating committees, and committees on alumni records, university welfare, and maintenance of order during examinations.

Religious institutions likewise lean heavily on committees, partly to encourage active participation by members and partly to delimit the authority of leaders. Although their authority may vary widely, depending upon the traditions of the sect, committees—ranging from the church board to the committee in charge of a church supper—are ever-present.

Committees are also prevalent in business. The board of directors is a committee, as are its various constituent groups such as the executive committee, the finance committee, the audit committee, and the bonus committee. Occasionally, one finds a business managed by a management committee instead of a president. And almost invariably under the president there will be a variety of management or policy committees, planning committees, wage and salary review committees, grievance committees, task forces for particular projects, and numerous other standing and special committees. Moreover, at each level of the organization structure, one or more committees are likely to be found.

REASONS FOR USE

One need not look far for reasons for the widespread use of committees. Although the committee is sometimes regarded as having democratic origins and as being characteristic of democratic society, the reasons for its existence go beyond mere desire for group participation. Committees are found even in authoritarian organizations, as in Soviet Russia and Communist China.

Group Deliberation and Judgment

Perhaps the most important reason for the use of committees is the advantage of gaining group deliberation and judgment—a variation of the adage that "two heads are better than one."[1] A group of people can bring to bear on a problem a wider range of experience than can a single person, a greater variety of opinion, a more thorough probing of the facts, and a more diverse training in specialized aspects. Few indeed are important business problems that fall entirely into a single area such as production, engineering, finance, or sales. Most problems, on the contrary, require more knowledge, experience, and judgment than any individual possesses.

It should not be inferred that group judgment can be obtained only through use of committees. The staff specialist who confers individually with many persons expert in a given phase of a problem can obtain group judgment without the formation of a committee, as can the executive who asks key subordinates or other specialists for memoranda analyzing a problem and making recommendations thereon. Often group judgment can thus be obtained more efficiently, in terms of time, without the long deliberations of a committee. The keen manager can usually grasp ideas and the reasoning behind them more quickly from a concise written memorandum than from an oral presentation.

However, one of the advantages of group deliberation and judgment, not to be obtained without an actual meeting, is the stimulation resulting from oral interchange of ideas and the cross-examination techniques of the committee meeting. Leading, as it does, to clarification of problems and development of new ideas, this interchange has been found to be especially enlightening in policy matters. It is true that sometimes the results obtained by group judgment are superior to those obtained by individual judgment.

Fear of Authority

Another reason for the widespread use of the committee in organization is the fear of delegating too much authority to a single person. This fear, especially pronounced in government, dictated to the framers of the American Constitution not only the establishment of a two-house legislature and a multimember Supreme Court but also the division of the powers of government among the

---

[1] Even though, as the Scots add, "one is a sheep's head."

Congress, the Supreme Court, and the President. However, despite this fear of centralized authority, the founders of the American republic placed the *administration* of laws in the hands of a single top executive, recognizing the advantages of this system.

Fear of delegating too much authority to the individual has been experienced in educational organizations and in charitable and religious enterprises. Although the willingness of people to be bound by the authoritarianism of faith has led to concentration of authority in the head of the Roman Catholic Church, in the various Protestant denominations one finds far less willingness to trust the single executive.

This fear has had less influence in business than in other types of organization. Business enterprises have, for one thing, developed primarily from small beginnings within the institution of private property, with its implications of authority of the owner; workers, too, have been free to avoid abuse of power by moving from one company to another; and the overriding importance of efficiency, finally, has favored the single manager. At the same time, the traditional existence of a board of directors as the top managing group of the business corporation may be traced, to a great extent, to the fear of property owners of delegating too much authority to a managing director.

This motive has likewise influenced the formation of many internal business committees. A committee may be established to make recommendations on a problem largely because the president or department head does not wish to take full responsibility for making a decision or to trust the decision to a subordinate. Bonus committees often result from such motivation, and major financial and capital investment policies are developed by committees, partly because of unwillingness to trust a single individual with a complete authority to make so important a decision.

Representation of Interested Groups

The desire to have various interested groups represented in policy matters, which played an important part in the organization of the United States House of Representatives and the Senate, makes itself felt in all branches of government where either law or tradition requires that the two major political parties, various sections of the country, or various pressure groups be represented.

Representation plays a part, too, in the establishment and manning of committees in business. Boards of directors are often selected on the basis of groups interested in the company and, perhaps more often, on the basis of groups in which the company has an interest. When an executive has a particularly difficult internal problem involving managers and specialists in various departments and activities, he may choose committee members in such a way as to give these interested parties representation. He may ostensibly do this in order to get a more balanced group judgment and a more diversified point of view, but he may actually be doing it to ensure that these groups will be represented and will thereby feel a sense of loyalty and commitment to the decision reached.

Coordination of Plans and Policies

Committees are also useful for coordinating planning and the execution of programs. The dynamics of modern enterprise place a heavy burden on its managers to integrate plans and activities. With complications, change, and numerous specialized departments, it is difficult to coordinate every activity, every subordinate plan, and every expenditure with others.

A committee permits the individuals concerned not only to obtain first-hand a picture of over-all plans and of their place in them but to contribute suggestions on the spot for improvement of plans. The committee also furnishes a place where agreement may be reached on the steps in coordination.

Transmission of Information

The committee is useful for transmission of information. All parties affected by a mutual problem or project can learn of it simultaneously, and decisions and instructions can be received uniformly with opportunities for clarification. The time thus saved may be considerable; and the spoken word, with its possibilities for overtones and emphasis and the opportunities for clarification, may carry its point better than even carefully written memoranda.

Consolidation of Authority

A manager in a department, branch, or section often has only a portion of the authority necessary to accomplish a program. As noted earlier, this is known as splintered authority. Good organization practice normally provides managers with the power appropriate to their position. However, this is not possible in every instance, and some matters call for the exercise of authority that the manager at the level concerned does not possess.

One way to handle problems of this sort is to refer them upward in the organizational hierarchy until they reach a point at which the requisite authority exists. But this place is often in the office of the president, and the problem may not be of sufficient importance to be decided at that level. Suppose, for example, that a customer of a machine-tool manufacturer wished a slight but unusual change in design in a piece of equipment. He would approach the sales department, which, if there were no established procedure for handling this change, could not act without the authority of the engineering department, the production department, and the cost estimating department. In this case, the sales manager might establish a special-purpose committee to study the problem, to agree on the nature and cost of the change, and to use its combined authority to approve the request.

This informal use of the committee gives much flexibility to organization. However, consolidating splintered authority through a committee should be watched carefully to ascertain whether the organizational structure itself might not be changed to concentrate in one position the appropriate authority to make *recurring* decisions.

Motivation through Participation

Committees permit wider participation in decision making. Persons who take part in planning a program or making a decision usually feel more enthusiastic in accepting and executing it. Even slight participation can be helpful.

The use of committees to motivate subordinates to get behind a program or decision requires skillful handling. It is by no means certain that deliberations of this kind will kindle enthusiastic support, for they can also result in the deepening of existing divisions among participants. Should this occur, this use of a committee may be a mistake. On the other hand, there are people who seem to be against every move unless they have been previously consulted. One of the authors recalls a college president who had on hand a surplus of federal government funds. He had concluded an agreement with the government representatives to use these funds for the construction of a Greek theatre. At this stage the president announced the coup to his faculty. Taken by surprise and therefore hurt (being easily bruised, anyway), the faculty forced the abandonment of the project and the return of the surplus moneys to the government.

Avoidance of Action

It cannot be denied that committees are sometimes appointed by a manager when he does not want any action to ensue. One of the surest ways to delay the handling of a problem and even to postpone a decision indefinitely is to appoint a committee to study the matter, particularly if its membership is carefully selected with delay in mind. In organizations of all kinds, skillful managers resort to this delaying action when they see fit.

DISADVANTAGES OF COMMITTEES

Certain dangers of committees have been so widely publicized that many managers make little use of them. Disparaging attitudes are reflected in such definitions as "a committee is made up of the unfit selected by the unwilling to do the unnecessary," or "a place where the loneliness of thought is replaced by the togetherness of nothingness."

High Cost in Time and Money

The cost of committee action in time is likely to be considerable. A committee may require members to travel some distance to reach a meeting. During the meeting, each member has the right to be heard, to have his point of view discussed, to challenge and cross-examine the points of view of others, and to go over grounds for a considered group conclusion. The spoken word, though valuable for emphasis and clarification, is seldom concise, and the "thinking out loud" that takes place is sometimes a waste of time for those who must listen. If the committee must reach a unanimous or nearly unanimous decision, the discussion is likely to be lengthy. And if a decision can be reached quickly, the meeting may have been unnecessary in the first place.

The monetary cost of committee discussion can also be very high. One must consider not only the cost of executive time (which for even a $30,000-per-year executive runs to $15 an hour) but even more the cost to the company of the time lost by the executive from his principal job.

This cost in time and money becomes all the more disadvantageous when a committee is assigned a problem that could as well, or better, be solved by a single individual, or by an individual with the help of a smaller and lesser-paid staff. Thus, the advantages of committee action must be considerable to offset the costs.

Compromise at the Least Common Denominator

Where committees are required to come to some conclusion or to reach some decision, there is danger that their action will be watered down or even meaningless. If the matter under consideration is so simple that differences of opinion do not exist, the use of committee time is wasteful. If differences of opinion exist, the point at which all or a majority of the committeemen can agree will tend to be at the least common denominator of group agreement. Most often this is not as strong and positive a course of action as that undertaken by an individual who has only to consider the facts as he sees them and then reach a conclusion. Because of the necessity for seeking out common ground, committees often take innocuous action or defer action entirely.

The danger of compromise at the level of the least common denominator of agreement grows as the percentage of agreement felt necessary for committee action increases. Even committees whose authority delegation requires only majority agreement sometimes develop traditions of unanimity. Small groups of people frequently seek—from feelings of politeness, mutual respect, and humility—to reach conclusions on which all can agree. Since committee members are ordinarily picked from organization equals, reluctance to force a conclusion on a recalcitrant minority is understandable, increasing thereby the probability of weak decisions.

Indecision

Another disadvantage of committees is that the time required for thorough deliberation, the discussion of peripheral or tangential subjects, and the difficulty of reaching agreement often result in adjournment without actions or in redecision.

Tendency to Be Self-destructive

Indecisiveness gives the chairman or a strong member an opportunity to force the committee into a decision, for it is a rare group of men who can participate in the exercise of authority on a team basis. Almost invariably, one man emerges as the leader. But when an individual becomes dominant, the nature of the committee as a decision-making group of equals changes, and there actually emerges an executive with a group of followers or advisers. Executives often delude themselves into believing that committees operate on group-management principles with a group of equals, when, as a matter of fact, the "team" is composed of subordinate advisers or even yes-men following the superior's leadership.

A committee which does not make decisions often disintegrates into an assembly dominated by a leader or leaders of two or three opposing factions. When the committee ceases to operate as a group of equals, and especially when it becomes a battleground for warring camps, the politics of the situation may lead to decisions or recommendations even worse than those weak ones based on the least common denominator of agreement.

Splitting of Responsibility

When authority to study, make recommendations, or arrive at a decision is delegated to a group, the fact is that the authority is dispersed throughout the group. Thus, the individual member hardly feels the same degree of responsibility that he would if he personally were charged with the same task. This splitting of responsibility is one of the chief disadvantages of a committee. Since no one can practically or logically feel accountable for the actions of the group, no individual feels personally responsible for his action within it.

Minority Tyranny

As was pointed out above, committees tend to seek unanimous or near-unanimous conclusions or decisions. Minority members are, therefore, in a strong position. By their insistence upon acceptance of their position or of a compromise position, they exercise an unwarranted tyranny over the majority. The minority members of a jury have such power. The authors recall an important committee of nine members in which a tradition for unanimous agreement developed. One member actually controlled the committee, not through force of leadership but through power to withhold his vote. The matters which he blocked or on which he forced a watered-down conclusion fell in the area of committee authority and responsibility; the committee, though having failed because of his tyranny, provided cover for him. Had he borne individual authority and responsibility for his actions, he could hardly have been the obstructionist he was.

THE PLURAL EXECUTIVE

Most committees found in business are nonmanagerial in nature. However, there are many groups that are given the power to make decisions and to undertake some or all of the managerial functions of planning, organizing, staffing, directing, and controlling. It is this latter type of committee that is referred to as the plural executive.

Origin

The plural executive may be established by law, or it may result from a managerial decision.[2] Examples of the former are the board of directors of a corporation and the plural executive (commission, board) established by various legislatures to operate one of their agencies. In the case of the corporation, legislatures have traditionally required that the board be elected to act for the stockholders. State and federal legislatures have, especially in recent years, provided for direction of most government agencies by a single manager, but in many instances a plural executive is still operating.

Authority

The extent of authority to manage and to make decisions held by a plural executive is not always easy to ascertain. Some, such as the board of directors, clearly have this power, although they may not exercise it. Some companies, like the Standard Oil Company (New Jersey) and the du Pont Company, have been managed from the top, on a day-to-day or weekly basis, by a plural executive. In Standard the plural executive has been a group of inside members of the board of directors meeting weekly, with an executive committee meeting daily; and in the du Pont Company an executive committee, composed of the president and eight vice-presidents, meets weekly to make major decisions.

There are, however, many executive committees which potentially have the power to manage but which actually do not, since decisions are made by a prominent stockholder or a strong leader in the group. Usually, the president is the dominant figure, with the other members little more than advisers. In other words, the plural executive is not always what it seems, and a single executive often in reality makes the decisions. Then there are other committees established with advisory authority only. Sometimes these actually operate as plural executives if, through tradition, weakness of leadership, or insistence of the chairman on agreement before a decision is made, they actually make decisions or undertake managerial functions as a group.

Role in Policy Making

The plural executive is often found in the field of policy making. Many companies have an executive or management committee to develop major plans and adopt basic policy. They go by various names: General Motors has its executive and finance committees, United States Rubber Company its operating policy committee, the Sun Chemical Company its management committee, Lockheed Aircraft Corporation its corporate policy committee, and the Koppers Company its policy committee.

The extent of authority of these committees varies considerably, although their influence on decision making is perhaps greater in policy-making or plan-

---

[2] For a history of the corporate executive, see C. O'Donnell, "Origins of the Corporate Executive," *Bulletin of the Business Historical Society*, vol. 26, no. 2 (June, 1952).

ning than in any other. These committees also engage in control, for their concern with policies and plans must be followed up to make sure that events conform to decisions.

Furthermore, these committees often decide organizational conflicts, which are important in planning, because the adequacy of the organization structure may affect and be affected by planning. This function is especially useful in the settlement of questions of organizational jurisdiction. The plural executive is an ideal arbitrator of disputes since the determination of a group will usually be accepted by contesting parties as more impartial than that of a single arbiter. Besides, personality clashes in a given situation are more easily submerged in group action.

Where committees are successful in policy formulation, they are dependent upon accurate and adequate staff work. A committee can hardly develop a proposal, forecast probable profits and costs from alternative courses of action, or investigate the numerous tangible and intangible factors influencing a basic decision. These are matters for study, and the committee is a notoriously poor study or research device. Therefore, if group deliberation is to be productive, facts and estimates must be developed and presented so that the members need not grope for material upon which to base conclusions.

Role in Policy Execution

Many companies and management experts distinguish between policy making and policy execution. It has been said that the former is concerned with "the establishment of broad principles by which administration is guided," while the latter is concerned with "the daily conduct of the company's affairs—setting standards and procedures to guide and govern execution of policies, establishing controls to insure adherence to standards, solving interdivisional disputes, improving interdivisional coordination, and meeting various emergencies as they arise."[3]

[3] E. Dale, *Planning and Developing the Company Organization Structure*, Research Report No. 20 (New York: American Management Association, 1952), pp. 96–97.

Figure 19.1 *Committee organization in a large bank. . . . This bank has supplemented its management organization structure with a large number of committees and subcommittees. All these groups exert influence on management policy and decision, and certain committees, such as the Position Evaluation Committee, actually make decisions. Others, such as the Advisory Council of the Board of Directors and the Regional and Branch Advisory Boards, operate only in an advisory capacity. Likewise, the General Trust Committee concerns itself only with policy decisions, while the Trust Investment and Branch Trust Committees make actual trust decisions. Most of the committees have as their members senior or other key managers from all the important departments and divisions of the company. The Junior Advisory Council, however, consists of lower-level managers or those about to be placed in a managerial capacity. While it carries on important analyses and projects and advises senior management groups, its primary purpose is training junior managers for future increased responsibilities in the bank.*

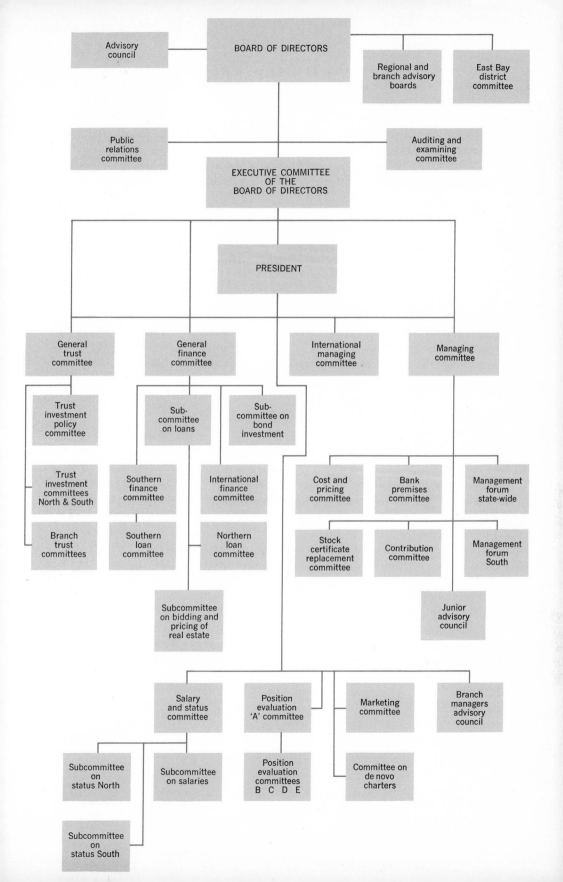

In companies where this distinction is made, special committees are established in functional areas—such as engineering, distribution, manufacturing, public relations, and labor relations—to deal with the more specialized and technical aspects of planning; such committees may make recommendations to policy committees or may bolster basic policy with detailed enabling plans and programs.

In reality, there is little difference between policy-making committees and those which are thought of as executing policy. Both committees are engaged primarily in planning. The difference between them is one of degree, with the former usually engaged in major planning and the latter in less important planning. But because the latter are often facilitative and involve technical tasks requiring specialists, use of the committee in these areas is sometimes far less effective than the single administrator.

PLURAL VERSUS INDIVIDUAL EXECUTIVE

Committees without managerial authority are far more numerous than those which are true plural executives. While much experience exists in organization with committees and with plural executives, the benefits of group management, as compared to individual management, have not been widely studied.

AMA Survey

One attempt to measure the merits of group versus individual management was made some years ago by the American Management Association.[4] Through interviews with executives and analysis of records of some twenty representative companies, the association found some interesting results. Breaking down management activity into twelve functions, the survey roughly estimated the proportion of each function that could (1) be exercised effectively by committee action; (2) be exercised effectively by committee action but more effectively by individual action; (3) be exercised by individual action, though helpfully supplemented by committee action; or (4) be effectively exercised only by individual action.

The results of this survey are summarized in Table 19.1. Although the sample is small, the breakdowns rough, and the percentages no more than approximate, the survey shows what the top executives in some well-managed companies think of group, as compared to individual, executive action. This survey indicates a strong preference for the plural executive only in the settling of jurisdictional questions. The emphasis on the superiority of individual action in practically every function of management is pronounced. Even where committee action was found effective (the first two classifications), though not in all cases as effective as individual action, the score in favor of committees, with one exception, is still not particularly high.

[4] *Ibid.*, pp. 92–93.

TABLE 19.1.   RELATIVE EFFECTIVENESS OF INDIVIDUAL AND COMMITTEE ACTION IN FUNCTIONAL ACTIVITIES, PERCENT

Management function	Can be exercised by committee effectively	Can be exercised by committee but more effectively by individual	Individual initiative essential but may be supplemented by committee	Individual action essential; committee ineffective
Planning	20	20	25	35
Control	25	20	25	30
Formulating objectives	35	35	10	20
Organization	5	25	20	50
Jurisdictional questions	90	10		
Leadership			10	90
Administration	20	25	25	30
Execution	10	15	10	65
Innovation	30	20	20	30
Communication	20	15	35	30
Advice	15	25	35	25
Decision making	10	30	10	50

Evaluation

Growing out of the foregoing discussion of the plural executive are certain clearly defined impressions. The plural executive succeeds fairly well in helping to coordinate the activities of managers. It has a high potential for aiding in defining objectives, selecting alternative ways of achieving them, and measuring the success attained. In terms of managerial functions, the plural executive is thus especially useful in planning and in certain of the broader aspects of control. However, all the disadvantages of the committee form apply with special force to the true plural executive.

BOARD OF DIRECTORS: TOP PLURAL EXECUTIVE

One of the most interesting organizational devices of the business management scene, established in the form of a plural executive, is the board of directors. Its importance to American business management is sometimes underestimated. An organization devoted to the study and rating of managerial effectiveness has made this surprising statement about boards:[5]

The Institute, after study of thousands of corporations, is convinced the greatest single weakness in American business organization lies in the composition of the average board of directors. . . . In fact, more than one-half of the correspondence of the Ameri-

[5] American Institute of Management, *The Corporate Director,* Special Issue No. 15, p. 4 (December, 1951).

can Institute of Management, in answer to inquiries from the outside, is now concerned with matters regarding directors.

State laws under which corporations are established almost invariably require that the corporation be "managed" by a board of directors composed of at least three members. The logic behind the requirement is that the corporation is an artificial entity, established by a sovereign power through contract with a group of owners (the stockholders), and therefore must have real persons responsible for managing.

Observation of boards of directors, however, shows that many of them actually do not manage, and corporate boards have often been criticized for this. Instead, managing, in its usual sense, is given completely to the president and other chief officers. The separation of ownership and management sometimes makes the inside managerial group all-powerful and the board of directors a legal sham. Prominent stockholders, often controlling with a minority interest, occasionally make boards of directors approve their wishes. Yet boards of directors have an important managerial job to do. Under the corporation laws they are charged with the duty of managing the entire corporation for the stockholders, who are often too numerous and unorganized to take part in policy determination. Moreover, directors are definitely liable for their conduct, particularly under the Securities Act of 1933 and the Securities Exchange Act of 1934. The criticism of American business in the decades after 1933, coupled with increasing legal liabilities and rising interest in the quality of managing and the need for the modern company to be responsive to its environment, has reawakened interest in the board and its proper functioning in the modern corporation.

Functions

Some of the functions of the board of directors will be discussed briefly in this section.[6]

Trusteeship   Probably the most important function of the board of directors may be summed up in the term "trusteeship," the husbanding of the corporation assets for the benefit of the stockholders. Even the most ineffectual board cannot escape this obligation.

Sometimes, especially in the large, publicly held corporation, the concept of trusteeship will extend beyond obligation to the stockholders to include obligation to the public, without whose support a corporation, as a social institution, could not endure; obligation to the employees of the corporation, whose efforts are necessary for its success; and obligation to the customers, who buy its products.[7] The position may be taken, on the other hand, that a

---

[6] For a more thorough discussion of the functions of the board of directors and its role in management, see H. Koontz, *The Board of Directors and Effective Management* (New York: McGraw-Hill Book Company, 1967).

[7] See chap. 5 for more detailed analysis of the social responsibilities of enterprise managers.

director has the duty to operate exclusively for the benefit of the stockholders because it is their funds that he manages. To manage them for the benefit of other groups might then be interpreted as misappropriation of private property. It may, however, be in the interest of the stockholder to administer for the benefit of employees and the public generally. With the lessening of privacy of the large corporation, the very proper need to take into account all influential environmental factors, the importance of labor relations forced on management by unionism, and in particular an enlightened attitude toward the human factor in business, such is often the case. Nevertheless, when directors forget that their first obligation is to the corporate owners whose funds they manage, there is a real question as to whether they are living up to their trust.

Determination of enterprise objectives   Another major function of the board of directors is the establishment of basic objectives of the business. Although making profit by furnishing economic goods and services demanded by buyers is properly the primary objective of all business, this must be translated into clearly understandable enterprise goals and into basic strategies and policies by which to achieve these goals.

Selection of executives   The board's function in selecting the chief executive of the corporation is a planning matter with long-run implications.

Basic policy making and the choice of an executive are both functions of the board of directors, and in fact they are closely related. Every action by a board regarding the choice of a chief executive involves basic policy examination. If the man chosen is expected to follow the course of his predecessor, that action is a reaffirmation of the predecessor's policies and a decision to proceed as before. When a board maps out a new course preliminary to the choice of an executive, or when it accepts policy changes as conditions of acceptance stipulated by a candidate, the board of directors is making a long-run major planning decision.

In numerous ways, therefore, the effects of the decision reached by a board of directors in choosing a new executive will be apparent for a long time in the future.

While boards of directors actually elect other corporate officers, most directors regard it as the job of the president to nominate them. This is as it should be. The president is the operating head responsible to the board, and if he cannot select his lieutenants, he can hardly be held responsible for the successful operation of the corporation as a whole. On the other hand, a responsible board must satisfy itself as to the quality of the company's entire management team and certain powers of *approval*, rather than actual *selection*, of top managers should be reserved to the board.

Assuring adequate plans and checking on results   Directors, by establishing corporate objectives and formulating major policies, are of course doing basic planning. But this is not enough. Being responsible for seeing that the company is well managed, the board should assure itself that the operating managers are making adequate plans. Thus, a board should review and approve, or be informed of, management programs in such areas as new products, marketing approaches, personnel, organization, management development, and finance. The very presentation of such programs is often assurance that adequate planning is being done.

A board should also see that results are being accomplished in accordance with plans. Such evaluation means more than a study of financial statements and the audit reports. In the financial area, it means a careful review of forecasts and expected performance. In the area of organization, reports on actual organization practice, as dictated by board policy, should be submitted to the board. Similar reports should be made in the other areas of board interest. Too often, boards of directors approve planning programs and then forget them.

Approval of budgets   Final approval of budgets is usually a key function of boards of directors. Whether applying to cash, revenues, expenses, capital expenditures, or number of employees, budgets are planning instruments whereby anticipated results are reduced to numerical terms. After adoption, they become the standard against which performance is measured for a given future period. To the extent that they are focused on over-all corporate affairs, as in the case of budget summaries, or matters of major corporate concern, such as cash and capital expenditures, they are properly subject to board approval.

Securing long-range stability   An often-overlooked function of the board of directors is securing long-range business stability in a changing environment. Even though people have a natural propensity to organize and many organizations exist at any one time, few survive for a long period, since most fail to adjust their objectives and plans to a changing environment. From the standpoint of business, these changes include new technology, markets, and tastes; varying political, ethical, and economic conditions; and the growth of new business enterprises.

Experienced directors, detached from everyday company operations, can call to the attention of management the need for changes in objectives and techniques. As Copeland and Towl[8] have pointed out, a competent board, operating as a group, has "a vitality which transcends that of the individual directors."

There are those who feel that securing long-range stability is the fundamental function of a board of directors. Board and management have a similar interest in avoiding calamity, preserving the company, and ensuring its continuity. In other words, as the corporate form is designed to furnish immortality, so the duty of the board is to accept responsibility for survival.

Distribution of earnings   Another major function that must be exercised by directors—at least to meet the requirements of corporation law and the obligation to stockholders—is the distribution of earnings. Directors must

[8] M. T. Copeland and A. R. Towl, *The Board of Directors and Business Management* (Boston: Division of Research, Harvard Business School, 1947), p. 24.

decide whether earnings should be distributed as dividends, retained in the business for expansion, or used to eliminate outstanding indebtedness.

This decision is of exceptional importance. If a director decides that earnings should be distributed, he is taking the position that the owner would rather have immediate earnings in hand than invest in future earnings of the business or in capital gains. Should he decide to keep the earnings for expansion, he is, to some extent, forcing owners to reinvest funds in the corporation. If earnings are to be used to retire debt, the director is once more exercising his trusteeship of the investor's funds. The distribution of earnings is, to the stockholder, second in importance only to the actual utilization of his original capital investment.

Checking on plans and operations through discerning questions   A director should ask discerning questions, an activity that does not depend upon a detailed familiarity with the affairs of a business. Such questions force the proponents of a proposal, usually the corporation's executives, to defend it with facts and analysis or considered judgment. Questions seek to make sure that all facets of a problem have been explored, that all facts have been considered, and that alternative courses of action have been properly analyzed and rejected.

The ability to ask discerning questions comes from experience in decision making; consequently, some of the best corporation directors are not those who know every detail of a company's operation but those who have had experience in a variety of situations. Such persons often develop an intuitive feeling about business problems and know what is likely to affect them.

Perhaps more important than the effect of discerning questions on a board's deliberations is their effect on the study and preparation of a proposal before it is submitted to the board. Although questions are not designed to represent cross-examination or to discredit management, they frequently embarrass the unprepared manager. The executive who knows he will be questioned will naturally try to anticipate it, and his assistants will take far greater care in briefing him.

Boards in Small Corporations

Boards in smaller businesses are often mere legal forms, with the owner or owners and members of their immediate families as directors. Indeed, it is not unusual for the necessary minutes of such boards to be prepared by legal counsel to cover matters required by state laws, while the actual operation of the board is practically nonexistent. At the same time, many small businesses have found the board of directors useful for improving the quality of their management, and studies have indicated that the board has an important place in the small corporate business.[9]

A dominant reason why the typical small corporation owner does not

[9] An excellent study of this subject, even though made many years ago, is that made by M. L. Mace in *The Board of Directors in Small Corporations* (Boston: Division of Research, Harvard Business School, 1948). This study should be read by every owner of a small corporate business.

attach much importance to the board of directors but makes it a family board is his distrust of outsiders. Having built his own business from a garage machine shop or a basement office in his house, he often regards it as his offspring, his life, and his prized possession. Moreover, he may feel timid about asking a banker or lawyer or a management consultant, who he feels would not have this interest, to serve on his board, and he may feel that the business could not make it worth their while to give their time. On the other hand, many public-spirited business and professional men see in the small business the heart of the private enterprise system, a challenge to professional experience and ingenuity, and a means of being of genuine service in the building of well-managed business enterprise.

A small corporation may not be able to afford specialized talent, managerial and technical, yet its problems are the same, except in degree and scope, as those of the large corporation. The owner-manager of the typical small corporation frequently has several limitations, both in education and in experience. The outside director can be extremely useful in at least partly eliminating them.

An outside director can assist materially in basic policy making in the small corporation. Such policy is often overlooked by the small business manager, who becomes overburdened by recurring operating problems and details that could easily be handled by reference to an established policy.

Managers of small businesses often fail to plan. Sales and production dips come without warning. Income taxes come due without enough cash on hand. Inventories build up and working capital becomes frozen before the manager realizes what is happening. The temptation to accept orders without thought of the capital required to meet them sometimes causes the owner to become overextended in the midst of promise of profits. An outside director, whose approach to the business is uncluttered by day-to-day problems, can often bring the necessary foresight to this kind of situation.

Again, the review and reestablishment of company objectives in the light of new technical, political, or economic developments may be overlooked by the harassed owner-manager but will be natural subjects for consideration by the more detached outside director. Problems of management succession become especially important to the small business, which normally has no ready supply of understudies trained to take over active management. Misunderstandings or jealousies between owner-managers and their key subordinates may reach exaggerated proportions if left unsolved. The interests of minority stockholders may be overlooked by the ambitious owner of a majority of the stock in a small corporation. These and other problems, although not peculiar to the small corporation, are likely to be aggravated in it. Their solution requires skill, tact, and an objective point of view—qualities that can be found in the well-selected outside board member.

Revitalization of Boards

Although subject to the various inherent drawbacks of the plural executive, boards of directors stand at the apex of the pyramid of corporate organization.

The character of the business leadership, the tone of managerial policy, and the basic direction of the enterprise are among their far-reaching concerns. There are signs that the authoritative position of boards is coming to be better recognized and their independence encouraged. Special surveys of board effectiveness made in 1955, 1962, 1964, and 1967 disclosed that more outsiders were serving on boards, more boards were made up of specialists, more was being expected of directors, more and longer meetings were being held, and directors were being paid more.[10]

This revitalization of corporate boards results from several factors. The rise in stockholder interest in corporate affairs and the instances of stockholders ousting company managements have led many top managers to seek the protection and help of an effective board. The larger holdings of institutional investors in corporate stocks and the fact that these investors have become a major source of capital funds have likewise contributed to the establishment of more effective boards with more outside members.[11] Also, the increased tempo of business competition has caused company officers and prominent stockholders to secure more outside specialists on the board and to seek their counsel in major policy matters.

In place of the former resentment of interference by outsiders on the board, there is a rising realization by top corporate managers that major decisions call for thorough analysis and deliberation on the part of the best available management brains, that some of this can come from outside the corporation, and that advantages may offset disadvantages in group decision making. With recent searching studies and the focus of attention upon corporate responsibilities, a further revitalization of boards as molders of business policy may be expected.

MISUSE OF COMMITTEES

The committee form has often fallen into disrepute through misuse. The five following abuses should be avoided when committees are set up.

In Place of a Manager

The weakness of the committee as a managing device has already been noted. Leadership is essentially a quality of individuals. If decision making is to be sharp, clear, prompt, and subject to unquestioned responsibility, it is better exercised by the individual, as is the directing of subordinates.

There are times, it must be admitted, when managerial effectiveness is

---

[10] "Directors; Doing More Directing," *Business Week*, pp. 101–104 (Mar. 12, 1955). See also John R. Kinley, *Corporate Directorship Practices*, Studies in Business Policy No. 103 (New York: National Industrial Conference Board, Inc., 1962); and J. Bacon, *Corporate Directorship Practices*, Studies in Business Policy No. 125 (New York: National Industrial Conference Board, Inc., 1967).

[11] In 1964 the New York Stock Exchange required a minimum of two outside directors for all newly listed companies and recommended the same for companies then listed, a suggestion that has actually been followed.

not an overriding consideration. In certain government agencies the danger of putting too much authority in the hands of an individual may be so great as to supersede questions of pure efficiency. As a matter of fact, before criticizing the waste, duplication, and inefficiency of governmental management, one should face the question of whether these costs are a fair price to pay for curtailing possible abuses of authority. Similarly, in business, a certain area of decision might be so important to the welfare of the company and the dangers of abuse of authority in that area so great that no individual should be entrusted with this power. But this would be an exceptional case.

One can hardly say that a committee has no place in management, but the advantages of group thinking and participation in policy questions can be gained in most cases through advisory committees. Most business committees function this way, leaving the real decision making and managing to the line executives to whom they report. As Ralph Cordiner, former president of the General Electric Company, has said, "We have no committees to make decisions that individuals should make."

For Research or Study

A group meeting together can hardly engage in research or study, even though it may well weigh and criticize the results of these. When the solution to a problem requires data not available to a committee, no amount of discussion or consideration can turn up the missing information. This is essentially an individual function, even though, of course, individuals may be coordinated into a team with individual research assignments. Most committees, therefore, need a research staff, providing at least analyses of alternative courses of action, historical summaries, or well-considered forecasts.

For Unimportant Decisions

Even where the committee is clothed with advisory authority only, the disadvantages of this device should dictate that its use be limited to important matters. Moreover, no intelligent specialist or manager can help chafing as a result of the time wasted by a group deliberating at length on trivial subjects. This impatience reaches its frustrating climax when a committee member finds himself considering a question upon which a certain decision is a foregone conclusion.

For Decisions beyond Participants' Authority

Where committees are used for decision making, if committeemen with authority attend the meetings or send duly empowered representatives, and if the agenda deals with matters within the competence of the members, no authority problem will be encountered. But, altogether too often, the executive with the requisite authority cannot or does not attend the meeting and sends in his place a subordinate who has not been delegated his superior's authority or who hesitates to bind his superior. The result is that the committee cannot function as intended. Delay results as the substitute refers questions to his superior, and much advantage of group decision making and deliberation is lost.

This misuse is probably the most usual reason for failure of the well-constituted committee. In a sense, it is inherent in the system. The committee is most useful in major policy determination, which is ordinarily the province of relatively few upper-level executives. If the same executive belongs to many committees, he cannot afford time to attend all meetings and must send subordinates. Yet he hesitates to delegate binding authority, a situation that causes many executives to be critical of committees. The way out of this dilemma is twofold: careful preparation of the agenda, so that the executive knows precisely what will come up and can give his subordinate the authority necessary for the meeting; and careful advance study of proposals, so that the executive can offer his opinions intelligently even by proxy.

There are other cases of misuse where the committee as constituted includes members whose authority does not fit the decision or discussion area. Often, to spread committee memberships, reduce the load of committee work, or increase the training and informational advantages of participation, individuals are chosen to represent points of view in areas over which they have no authority. Thus, a committee might be constituted to establish advertising policy. Although it might be entirely proper for the sales promotion manager and the market research manager to be members, unless one of them can speak for the marketing department as a whole, the committee may be unable to come to a conclusion and may result in a wasteful use of manpower.

To Consolidate Divided Authority

A disadvantage of departmentation is that authority is so delegated that, in some cases, no executive except the chief officer has adequate authority to do what must be done. Even within departments or sections, authority may be so splintered that group meetings are necessary to consolidate authority for making decisions. If divided authority can be eliminated by changing the organization structure and the delegations of authority, recourse to a committee is certainly a misuse of the device.

SUCCESSFUL OPERATION OF COMMITTEES

The costs and other drawbacks of a committee system, as well as its frequent misuse, call for more managerial attention than is usually forthcoming. Moreover, the democratic tradition in American social life, plus increasing emphasis on group management and group participation in enterprise affairs, makes this problem of great importance to management. Despite the acknowledged disadvantages, there is evidence that the use of committees in all types of organizations continues to increase. This calls for fresh attention to improving their use.

Need for Well-defined Authority and Scope

Unless a committee's authority is carefully spelled out, the members may not know whether they are responsible for a decision, a recommendation, or merely inconclusive deliberation from which the chairman may gain some insights. The members should also know the exact scope of subjects the group is expected to consider. A great inefficiency of committee action is wandering from the subject or the chairman's introducing subjects that are beyond the committee's scope.

Furthermore, with authority and scope clear, committee members are better able to gauge whether they are meeting their responsibilities to the organization. Some companies make extensive efforts to review committee work, dissolving or consolidating those whose work is no longer justified. Some companies have an evaluating committee that continually analyzes other committees in this way.

Determining Size

No precise conclusions can be drawn here. As a general rule, a committee should be large enough to promote deliberation and include the breadth of expertness required for its job but not so large as to waste time or foster indecision. This is thought by some to mean as large as five or six members but no larger than fifteen or sixteen.[12] An analysis of small-group research indicates that the ideal committee size is five, when the five members possess adequate skills and knowledge to deal with problems facing the committee.[13] It is obvious that the larger the group, the greater the difficulty in obtaining a "sense of the meeting," and the more time necessary to allow everyone to make his contribution.

If a committee is to have all interested parties participate in its deliberations, the number may be too large, and the group may be incompatible. If all interests are not represented, the committee's work may be subject to criticism. Where representation is important, the answer may be found in a structure of subcommittees, with the problems to be considered properly broken down for their action. However, in many instances, the need for representation is overstressed. The true purposes of committees are often accomplished by complete staff preparation for scrutinizing the various facets of a problem, and by limiting the membership to individuals who can look at the problem as a whole rather than regard their membership as a means of protecting a narrow interest.

Selecting Members

For a successful committee,[14] the members must be suitably representative of the interests they are intended to serve and possess the requisite authority,

---

[12] *Ibid.*, p. 90. W. H. Newman, in *Administrative Action*, p. 234, believes, however, that a committee should be held down to three or four members. C. J. Berwitz, in "The Work Committee—An Administrative Technique," *Harvard Business Review*, vol. 30, pp. 110–124 (January, 1952), suggests a maximum of seven members.

[13] See A. C. Filley, "Committee Management: Guidelines from Social Science Research," *California Management Review*, vol. 13, no. 1, pp. 13–21 (Fall, 1970).

[14] For suggestions on membership selection, see C. O'Donnell, "Ground Rules for Using Committees," *Management Review*, vol. 50, no. 10, pp. 63ff. (October, 1961).

and they must be able to perform well in a group. Not everyone has the temperament, verbal and analytical ability, and capacity for working with others to do this.

Members should also have the capacity for reaching group decisions by integrating group thinking rather than by compromise or by conclusions forced by position or political strength. Committees are more likely to reach agreement without weak compromise or power politics if the members are friendly, known to one another, and mutually respectful of one another's positions and interests. This means that the participants should generally be on approximately the same organizational level and independent enough of one another not to fear reprisal. Where committees are used as the forum of the traditional dissenter or as the rostrum of the ambitious climber anxious to use his talents, waste of time may be the sole result. Again, some individuals feel a need to engage in hypothetical discussions achieving no concrete results. It is a rare and enjoyable committee that does not have the committee bore among its members.

Selecting Subject Matter

Committee work must be limited to subject matter that can be handled in group discussion. Certain kinds of subjects, therefore, lend themselves to committee action while others do not. Other than jurisdictional questions, where the prestige and impersonal nature of group action are definitely superior, the best area for group action is policy formulation or major planning. Along with planning, subjects for committee action lie in the area of control, especially over managers responsible for implementing major plans.

The way subjects are presented is also important. Proposals made before the committee should be sharply presented. Unless the questions raised are appropriate to the deliberations desired, a well-prepared agenda is not helpful. Ideally, an agenda should be circulated to members well in advance of the meeting, so that they may know what will be discussed. Even the cleverest and best-informed committee member can hardly be expected to have a considered opinion on important matters without some notice of what to expect. Masses of carefully prepared recommendations available for cursory study at the member's place at the table seldom meet this need. Often the meeting time is consumed in laborious study of reports or in listening to various members think aloud; or else the reports are meekly accepted by the members and the results railroaded by the chairman; or the meeting may be postponed to a later date after the members have had an opportunity to study the proposals.

Importance of the Chairman

The success of a committee will never be greater than the skill of the chairman.[15] A good chairman can avoid many of the wastes and drawbacks of committees by planning the meeting, preparing the agenda, seeing that the results

---

[15] For an analysis of the role and duties of a chairman, see H. Koontz, *op. cit.*, chap. 8.

of research are available to the members ahead of time, arranging definite proposals for discussion or action, and conducting the meeting efficiently.

The chairman sets the tone of the meeting. He may wish it to be formal or informal, the argument to be casual or pointed. By anticipating objections and playing the devil's advocate, he may completely undermine many objections. When the subject matter is especially open to contention, the chairman may lead the discussion so that members are not forced into a position, at least until the subject has been fully discussed. Human nature being what it is, individuals who take a premature position are likely to defend it to the end. Since a committee is after results of group deliberation, lines should not be too sharply drawn, at least early in the discussion.

It usually falls to the chairman to integrate committee deliberation. Integration of ideas, as contrasted with compromise, builds a point of view, often quite new, from the basic positions of the group. If the chairman is weak or not fully familiar with the subject or the way individual members think, integration of ideas is unlikely to result. When leadership is assumed by a committee member, that member often becomes the de facto chairman of the meeting.

The chairman, also, must keep discussion from wandering. This often takes great skill, especially when the committee includes persons who enjoy the sound of their own voices or who lack ability to recognize essentials and to speak of them concisely. The chairman must handle the meeting firmly without imposing his own opinions or thwarting freedom of discussion, yet without yielding his powers of chairmanship.

Thus, the chairman of a committee must be chosen with great care. On his shoulders falls most of the responsibility for assuring that the committee acts effectively. Obviously, it is a great help if the members and subject matter have been well selected. Even a skilled chairman can hardly make up for the deficiencies of a poorly constituted committee.

Checking Conclusions

The use of a committee allows a group of people to participate in the discussion or solution of a problem and to be informed simultaneously concerning it. Yet individuals may walk away from meetings with varying interpretations as to what was accomplished. To avoid this, it is well to take careful minutes of the meeting, circulate them in draft for correction or modifications, and then have the final copy approved by the committee. This procedure has the advantage of forcing committee members to agree or disagree upon the results of the discussion and the further advantage of supplementing oral discussion with the written word.

Checking conclusions also provides for follow-up. If a committee makes a recommendation to a superior manager, it should be informed as to the action, if any, which is taken; if the recommendation is not followed, explanations are required in order to preserve committee morale and to educate its membership on management policy. Even if a committee makes neither decision nor recommendation but merely explores ideas, some report to the membership is of value.

The Committee Must Be Worth the Cost

Above all, in measuring the success of committee operation, one must continually question whether the committee's benefits are worth its cost. It may be difficult to count the benefits, especially in such intangible forms as morale, enhancement of status, teamwork, and training. But the committee can be justified only if the costs, often considerable, are definitely offset by tangible and intangible benefits.

FOR DISCUSSION

1. A prominent novelist-critic of the management scene has said: "I don't think we can go on very much longer with the luxurious practice of hiring 10 men to make one man's decision. With all its advantages, professional management tends to encourage bureaucratic corpulence." Comment.
2. Distinguish between a "committee," "team," and "group."
3. Where in an organization would you suggest, if any place, committees should be used? Why?
4. Boards of directors legally have the responsibility to "manage" a corporation. How should they do it?
5. If you were asked to develop a course of study to train committee chairmen, what would you put into this course?
6. Compare, in organization terms, the typical formal business organization with the usual committee with which you are familiar, the usual athletic team, and a symphony orchestra.

20
making organizing effective

Perhaps the function of organizing is the most fully developed area of management theory. Its importance was recognized before that of the other management functions, and its principles have been more completely explored, developed, and tested. Although some principles may not be as fully tested in practice as others and some important truths are probably yet undiscovered, fundamental truths, distilled from long practice, can be applied to make organization structure aid in the effective and efficient performance of individuals.

Organizing is essentially aimed at developing an intentional structure for effective performance, a network of *decision* communications centers from which to secure coordination of individual effort toward group goals. Yet to make an organization structure work, certain common mistakes—certain inflexibilities and conflicts which arise in practice—must be avoided, the organization structure must be understood, and principles put into practice.

SOME MISTAKES IN ORGANIZING

Despite their obviousness and their thwarting of personal and enterprise goals, the persistence of certain mistakes of organizing is striking evidence of either the difficulty of managing or the lack of sophistication of managers, or both.

1. Failure to Plan Properly

It is not unusual to find an enterprise continuing a traditional organization structure long after its objectives, plans, and external environment have changed. For example, a company may keep its product research department under manufacturing division control long after the business environment has changed from being production-oriented (as in a typical sellers' market) to being marketing-oriented (as in a typical buyers' market). Or a company may continue its functional organization structure when product groupings and

396

the need for integrated, decentralized profit responsibility demand decentralized product divisions.

Also, a company may need managers of a kind not currently available, or, just as likely, may find that certain managers have not grown with the company or do not fit current needs. Small, growing businesses often make the mistake of assuming that original employees can grow with the company, only to find that a good engineering designer, made a vice-president-engineering, can no longer fill the larger role of the engineering chief, or that a once-adequate production superintendent cannot head a larger manufacturing department.

Another failure in planning involves organizing around people. Organization structure must normally be modified to take people into account, and there is much to be said for trying to take full advantage of employee strengths and weaknesses. But organizing *primarily* around people overlooks several facts. In the first place, there can never be assurance by so doing that all bases will be covered, that all the necessary tasks will be undertaken. In the second place, there is danger that different people will desire to do the same things, resulting in conflict or multiple command. In the third place, people have a way of coming and going in an enterprise—through retirement, resignation, promotion, or death—which makes organizing around them risky and their position, when vacated, hard to determine accurately and to fill adequately.

Such mistakes occur when an enterprise fails to plan properly toward a future materially different from the past or present. By looking forward, the manager should determine what kind of organization structure will best serve future needs and what kind of people will best serve this organization.

2. Failure to Clarify Relationships

The failure to clarify organization relationships, probably more than any other mistake, accounts for friction, politics, and inefficiencies. Since the authority and the responsibility for action are critical in organization, lack of clarity here means lack of knowledge of the part employees are to play on an enterprise team. This implies neither a detailed and minute job description nor that people cannot operate as a team. Although some enterprise leaders have prided themselves on having a team of subordinates without specified tasks and authority lines, any sports coach could tell them that such a team is likely to be a group of jealous, insecure, buck-passing individuals jockeying for position and favor.

3. Failure to Delegate Authority

A common complaint in organizational life is that managers are reluctant to push decision making down into the organization. In some businesses, where uniformity of policy is necessary and decision making can be handled by one or a few managers, there may be neither need nor desire to decentralize authority. But bottlenecks of decision making, excessive referral of small problems to upper echelons, overburdening of top executives with detail, continual "fighting fires" and "meeting crises," and underdevelopment of managerial experience in the lower levels of organization give evidence that failing to delegate authority to the right extent is usually a decided mistake.

4. Failure to Balance Delegation

Another mistake made in organizing is failure to maintain balanced delegation. In other words, some managers—in their zeal for decentralization—may take literally the organizational bromide to "push decision making down in the organization as far as it will go." Obviously, to do this pushes it down to the very bottom of the structure and develops a system of independent organizational satellites. Even without going to this extreme, not maintaining authority suitable for the various levels of organization has caused many organizational failures.

As was pointed out in Chapter 18 on decentralization, top managers must retain some authority, particularly over decisions of company-wide impact and at least enough to review the plans and performance of subordinates. The manager must not forget that there is authority he should not delegate. Nor should he overlook the fact that he must maintain enough authority to make sure when delegated to his subordinates it is being used to discharge his own responsibility.

5. Confusion of Lines of Authority and of Information

The problems and costs of levels of organization and departmentation can be reduced by opening wide the channels of information. Unless information is confidential (and businesses and government, as well as other enterprises, overdo this classification) or is unavailable except at too great expense, there is no reason why lines of information should follow lines of authority. Information gathering should be separated from decision making, since only the latter requires managerial authority. Enterprises often force lines of information to follow authority lines, when the only reason for following a chain of command is to preserve the integrity of authority for decision making and the clarity of responsibility.

6. Authority without Responsibility

A significant cause of mismanagement is the granting of authority without exacting responsibility. Authority delegation is not responsibility delegation; the delegant remains responsible for the proper exercise of authority by his subordinate. Any other relationship would lead to organizational anarchy. Moreover, anyone to whom authority is delegated must be willing to be held responsible for all his actions.

7. Responsibility without Authority

A common complaint of subordinates is that superiors hold them responsible for results without giving them the authority to accomplish them. Some of these complaints are unjustified and based on misunderstanding the fact that subordinates can seldom have unlimited authority in any area, because their actions must be coordinated with those in other areas and must remain within defined policies. Subordinates often see their jobs as all-encompassing and forget that their authority must be limited to their own departmental boundaries and within controlling policies.

Too often, however, the complaints are justified; managers, sometimes without realizing it, do hold subordinates responsible for results they have no power to accomplish. This does not happen as frequently where organization lines and duties have been clearly set forth, but where an organized structure of roles is unclear or confused, it does occur.

8. Careless Application of the Staff Device

There are many valid reasons for using the staff assistant or the staff specialist and even building entire advisory departments. However, there is danger that the staff person will be used to undermine the authority of the very managers he is intended merely to advise.

The undermining of managerial authority may extend to subordinate line managers. There is an ever-present danger that a top manager may surround himself with staff specialists and so preoccupy himself with their work as to exclude from his schedule the time and attention needed for his line subordinates; or he may assign problems to his staff that should be more appropriately assigned, often with specially delegated authority, to his line lieutenants.

In other instances, staff personnel exercise line authority which has not been delegated to them. It is easy to understand the impatience of a staff specialist who sees clearly how a situation should be handled, while the line officer in charge of it seems to be dilatory or clumsy. The very quality that makes a staff specialist valuable—his specialized knowledge—also makes him impatient to command. Yet if he were to have this authority without clear delegation, he would be not only undermining the authority of the responsible line official but breaking down unity of command.

9. Misuse of Functional Authority

Perhaps even more perilous to good managing are the dangers in undefined and unrestricted delegation of functional authority. This is true especially because the complexities of modern enterprise often create cases where it is desirable to give a predominantly staff or service department functional authority over activities in other parts of the organization.

In the quest for the economies of specialization and for advantages of technically expert opinion, managers often unduly exalt staff and service departments at the expense of operating departments. Many line officers —from the vice-president in charge of operations to the foreman—feel, with justice, that the business is being run by the staff and service departments.

10. Multiple Subordination

The principal danger of too great proliferation of functional authority delega-tions is the breakdown of unity of command. One has only to look at the various departments of a typical medium-sized or large business to see how such a breakdown occurs. The controller prescribes accounting procedures through-out the company. The purchasing director prescribes how and where purchases are to be made. The personnel manager dictates (often according to union con-tracts or government regulations) how employees shall be classified for pay purposes, how vacations shall be scheduled, and how many hours are to be worked. The traffic manager guides the routing of all freight. The general counsel insists that all contracts bear his approval and be made in prescribed form. The public relations director requires that all public utterances of man-agers and other employees be cleared through him or meet a prescribed policy line. And the tax director reviews all program decisions for clearance on their tax aspects.

Thus, with all these staff and service specialists having some degree of line authority over other parts of the organization, plus counterparts often in divisions and regions, the key operating manager finds himself subject to the direction of a number of people with functional authority in addition to his principal superior, who usually has the final decision of his pay scale and chances for promotion. One frustrated general foreman of a factory sub-depart-ment informed the authors that he just did the best he could to satisfy everyone and that, when he did not have time and energy to satisfy all, he resorted to the "decibel" principle of management, satisfying those who made the most noise.

Multiple subordination results also from faulty organization structure and from instances of plural executives. Wherever found, it tends to cause confusion, undermines the definiteness and effectiveness of authority, and threatens organizational stability.

11. Misuse of Service Departments

These departments are often looked upon as not much concerned with the accomplishment of major enterprise objectives, when they are in fact just as immediately concerned as any operating department. Sometimes people, par-ticularly in so-called line departments, regard a service department as rela-tively unnecessary, unimportant, and therefore something to be ignored when possible.

On the other hand, many service departments mistakenly look upon their function as an end unto itself rather than a service to other departments. Thus, a purchasing department may not realize that its purpose is to purchase efficiently items ordered by authorized departments; or a statistics department may forget that it exists to furnish data desired by others rather than to produce reports of its own choosing.

Perhaps the greatest misuse of service departments is summed up in the words "efficient inefficiency." When managers establish service departments, looking more to their cost savings than to the efficiency of the entire enterprise, a highly "efficient" service may do an inefficient job of serving. For example, little is gained in putting out low-cost reports not useful to managers, nor is it sensible to set up a low-cost central recruiting section if the employees recruited do not meet enterprise needs.

12. Overorganization

Overorganization usually results from failure to put into practice the concept that the activity-authority structure of the enterprise is merely a framework for efficient performance of people. Unduly complicating the structure through too many levels ignores the fact that efficiency demands that a manager supervise as many subordinates as he well can. Narrow spans may reflect misunderstanding of the span of management principle, managerial inability to minimize the time requirements of his necessary human relationships, or lack of time to manage—a lack often caused by poor assignments and authority delegations. Likewise, the multiplication of staff and service activities or departments may be caused by inadequate delegation to line subordinates and the tendency to regard service specialization and efficiency so narrowly that larger enterprise operations are overlooked.

Managers also overorganize by having unnecessary line assistants (for example, assistant or deputy managers). Having a line assistant is justified when a manager wishes to devote his time to matters outside his department, during his long absences from the office, when he wishes to delegate line authority in a given area such as engineering, or during a limited training period for a subordinate to whom full managerial status is soon to be given. Otherwise, the separation of the manager from his other subordinates and the confusion as to who is really their superior lead the observer to conclude that this form of overorganization should be undertaken carefully.

Sometimes, excessive procedures are confused with overorganization. Overorganization—particularly if interlaced with functional authority—can lead to excessive procedures. But much of the "red tape" often blamed on overorganization really results from poor planning. The failure to regard procedures as plans—and to treat them with the respect given other areas of planning—often results in bewilderingly complex procedures.

Similarly, too many committees, sapping the time and energies of managers and their staffs, are often blamed on overorganization rather than on poor organization (particularly when committees make decisions better made by individuals). Excessive committees often result from splintered authority or vague delegation. Such excess of committees may actually point to underorganization.

AVOIDING MISTAKES BY PLANNING

As with the other functions of management, establishment of objectives and orderly planning are necessary for good organization. As Urwick has said,

"Lack of design [in organization] is illogical, cruel, wasteful, and inefficient."[1] It is illogical because good design, or planning, must come first, whether one speaks of engineering or social practice. It is cruel because "the main sufferers from a lack of design in organization are those individuals who work in an undertaking."[2] It is wasteful because "unless jobs are clearly put together along lines of functional specialization it is impossible to train new men to succeed to positions as the incumbents are promoted, resign or retire."[3] And it is inefficient because, unless based on principles, management becomes based on personalities, with the resultant rise of company politics, for "a machine will not run smoothly when fundamental engineering principles have been ignored in construction."[4]

Planning for the Ideal

Essential to organization planning is the search for an ideal form to reflect enterprise goals. This entails charting the main lines of organization, considering the organizational philosophy of the enterprise managers (for example, shall authority be as centralized as possible, or should the company break its operations down into semiautonomous product or territorial divisions?), and sketching out consequent authority relationships. The ultimate form established, like all plans, seldom remains unchanged, and continuous remolding of the ideal plan will normally be necessary. Nevertheless, an ideal organization plan constitutes a standard, and, by comparing present structure with it, enterprise leaders know what changes should be made when possible.

The organizer must ever be careful not to be blinded by popular notions in organizing, because what may work in one company may not work in another. Principles of organizing have general application, but the factual background of each company's operations and needs must be considered in applying these principles. Organization structure needs to be tailor-made.

Modification for the Human Factor

If available personnel do not fit into the ideal structure and cannot or should not be sidetracked, there is no alternative but to modify the structure to fit individual capabilities, attitudes, or limitations. Although this smacks of organizing around people, the difference is that it is organizing *first* around the goals to be met and only *then* making modifications for the human factor. In this way, planning will be available to eliminate further compromises with principle whenever changes in personnel occur.

[1] L. Urwick, *The Elements of Administration* (New York: Harper & Row, Publishers, Incorporated, 1944), p. 38.
[2] *Ibid.* In this connection Urwick quotes the following lines from Browning:
"It's an awkward thing to play with souls
And matter enough to save one's own."
[3] *Ibid.*
[4] *Ibid.*

Advantages of Planning

Good organization structure can go far to make up for deficiencies in leadership by furnishing a support for available abilities. Such a support increases managerial efficiency by cutting down on meetings to determine who has the authority to do what, or how this program or that policy is to be implemented, and relieves the manager of constantly correcting subordinates on the nature of their functions, responsibilities, or authority.

Planning the organization structure also helps determine future personnel needs and attendant training programs. Without knowing what managerial personnel will be needed and what experience to demand, an enterprise cannot intelligently recruit and train men.

Furthermore, organization planning can disclose weaknesses. Duplication of effort, unclear lines of authority, too long lines of communication, too much red tape, and obsolete practices show up best when desirable and actual organization structures are compared.

AVOIDING ORGANIZATIONAL INFLEXIBILITY

One basic advantage of organization planning is avoidance of organizational inflexibility. Many enterprises, especially those which have been in operation for many years, become too rigid to meet the first test of effective organization structure—adaptation to changing environment.

Signs of Inflexibility

Some of the older companies provide ample evidence of these inflexibilities: an organization pattern no longer suited to the times; a district or regional organization that could be either abolished or enlarged because of improved communications; or a too highly centralized structure for an enlarged enterprise requiring decentralization.

Reasons for Reorganization

Although reorganization is intended to meet changes in the enterprise environment, there may be other compelling reasons. Those related to the business environment include changes in operations caused by acquisition or sale of major properties, changes in product line or marketing methods, business cycles, competitive influences, new producing techniques, labor-union policy, government regulatory and fiscal policy, or the state of current knowledge about organizing. New techniques and principles may become applicable, such as that of developing managers by allowing them to manage decentralized semiautonomous units of a company; or new methods may come into use, such as that of gaining adequate financial control with a high degree of decentralization.

Moreover, a new chief executive officer and new vice-presidents and department heads are likely to have some definite organizational ideas of their own. Shifts may come merely from the desire of new managers to make changes from ideas formulated through their previous experience, or because their methods of managing and their personalities require a modified organization structure.

Furthermore, reorganization may also be caused by demonstrated deficiencies in an existing structure. Some of these arise from organizational weaknesses themselves: excessive spans of management, too many levels, inadequate communication, poor interdepartmental coordination, excess committees, lack of uniform policy, slow decision making, or failure to accomplish objectives, as well as through inability to meet delivery schedules, excessive costs, or breakdown of financial control. Other deficiencies may stem from inadequacies of managers. Lack of knowledge or skill by a manager, who for some reason cannot be replaced, may be avoided by organizing so as to move much of the authority for decision making to another position.

Personality clashes between managers also may be solved by reorganization. Staff-line conflicts may develop to such an extent that they can be resolved only by reorganization.

Need for Readjustment and Change

In addition to impelling reasons for reorganization, there is a certain need for moderate and continuing readjustment merely to keep the structure from developing inertia. "Empire building" is not so attractive when everyone knows that his position is subject to change. As a company president told his subordinates: "Don't bother to build any empires, because I can assure you that you won't be in the same position three years from now." Some enterprise managers, realizing that an organization structure must be a living thing, make structural changes merely to accustom subordinates to change.

Much can be said for developing a tradition of change. People used to change tend to accept it without the frustration and demoralization that result when need for reorganization is allowed to reach the stage at which change must be revolutionary. On the other hand, a company continually undertaking major reorganization may so damage morale as to harm the enterprise by losing key personnel or by causing people in all ranks to spend much of their time wondering what will happen to them.

AVOIDING CONFLICT BY CLARIFICATION

A major reason why conflict develops in organizations is that people do not understand their assignment and that of their co-workers. No matter how well conceived an organization structure, people must understand it to make it work. Understanding is aided materially by proper use of organization charts, accurate job descriptions, the spelling out of authority and informational relationships, and the introduction of specific goals to breathe life into positions.

Organization Charts

The organization chart is widely used and appropriate for making organization principles work. Every organization structure can be charted, even a poor one, for a chart merely indicates how departments are tied together along the principal lines of authority. It is, therefore, somewhat surprising occasionally to find top managers taking pride in not having an organization chart or feeling that the charts should be kept secret.

Advantages   A prominent manufacturer once informed the authors that, although he could see some use for an organization chart for his factory, he had refused to chart the organization above the level of factory superintendent. His argument was that charts tended to make people overly conscious of being superiors or inferiors, tended to destroy team feeling, and gave persons occupying a box on the chart too great a feeling of "ownership." Another top executive informed the authors that if an organization is left uncharted, it can be changed more easily, and it also encourages a competitive drive for higher executive positions on the part of the uncharted middle-management group.

These reasons for not charting organization structures are clearly untenable. Subordinate-superior relationships exist not because of charting but rather because of essential authority relationships. As for any too-comfortable feeling engendered and a lack of drive for those who have "arrived," these are matters of top leadership—of reorganizing whenever the enterprise environment demands, of developing a tradition of change, and of making subordinate managers continue to meet adequate and well-understood standards of performance. The manager who believes that team spirit can be engendered without clearly spelling out relationships is deluding himself and preparing the way for politics, intrigue, frustration, buck passing, lack of coordination, duplicated effort, vague policy, uncertain decision making, and other evidences of organizational inefficiency.

Since a chart maps lines of decision-making authority, sometimes merely charting an organization shows inconsistencies and complexities and leads to their correction. A chart also reveals to managers and new personnel how they tie into the entire structure. It has been generally found that those firms which have comprehensive organization charts appear to have sound organization structures.

Limitations   Organization charts are subject to important limitations. In the first place, a chart shows only formal authority relationships and omits the many significant informal and informational relationships. It does not even picture how much authority exists at any point in the structure. While it would be interesting to chart an organization with lines of different widths to denote varying degrees of formal authority, authority is not subject to such measurement. And if the multiple lines of informal relationships and of information were drawn, it would so complicate a chart that it would lose its value.

Many charts show structures as they are supposed or used to be, rather than as they really are. Managers hesitate or neglect to redraft charts, forgetting that organization is dynamic and that a chart should not be allowed to become obsolete.

Another difficulty with organization charts is that individuals may confuse authority relationships with status. The staff officer reporting to the corporation president may be depicted at the top of the organization chart, while a regional line officer may be shown one or two levels lower. Although good charting attempts to make levels on the chart conform to levels of enterprise importance, it cannot always do so. This problem can be handled by clearly spelling out authority relationships and by that best indicator of status—salary and bonus levels. No one is likely, for example, to hear that the general manager of Chevrolet in General Motors feels a sense of inferiority because his position on the chart is below that of the patent section director.

Position Descriptions

Every managerial position should be defined specifically. A good managerial position description informs the incumbent and others about what he is supposed to do and helps determine what authority must be delegated in order to carry out the job. Without such a description, it is difficult to know what to hold a manager responsible for.

A soundly conceived position description is not a detailed list of all the activities a manager undertakes and certainly does not specify *how* to undertake them. Rather, it states the basic function of the position, its major duties, its scope of authority, and, often, the major authority and information relationships to be observed. For example, the basic function of one vice-president in charge of marketing was described as being responsible to the president for effectively and efficiently planning, organizing, staffing, directing, and controlling company activities in market research, consumer public relations, advertising and promotion, and sales. He was given authority, among other things, to hire, dismiss, or change the rates of pay (in accordance with the established salary program and the chart of executive approval authorization) of his subordinates. One of his major relationships was to keep the general manager of the international division informed of domestic marketing plans.

Besides, position descriptions should formalize each managerial position in such a way as to reflect analysis of what must be done to attain company objectives. The descriptions should not be straitjackets but should be broad enough to permit changing plans and situations.

Such descriptions have many benefits. As jobs are analyzed, attendant duties and responsibilities are brought into focus and areas of overlapping or neglected duties come to light. The authors have found that forcing people to consider what should be done and who should do it is more than worth the effort. Further benefits of job descriptions include their guidance in training new managers, in drawing up candidate requirements, and in setting up salary levels. Finally, as a means of control over organization, the position guide furnishes a standard against which to judge whether a position is necessary and, if so, its organization level and exact location in the structure.

Need to Define Relationships

Some statement of authority and information relationships is usually included in position descriptions. People often do not cooperate because they do not know with whom their cooperation is required. People often do not communicate—not because they have nothing to say or don't know how to say it—but because they do not know to whom their message should be directed.

By showing up vague authority, inappropriate or misunderstood communication lines, and inefficiencies of organization levels or management spans, spelling out a position and its relationships is a major step toward removing conflict. As with organization charts, the very spelling out furnishes a standard against which effectiveness of organization can be measured. Perhaps the most powerful tool for defining and clarifying relationships is the chart of executive approval authorizations, discussed above in Chapter 18. By spelling out clearly what organizational positions have the responsibility of approving actions involving commitments and where final approvals lie, as well as which managers are to exercise functional authority, the whole system of authority relationships may be made clear. This clarity extends not only to the manager who is given approval authority but, if proper publicity is given to the chart, can be made available to other persons who are involved.

Goal Definition

Managerial position descriptions need to be bolstered by specific goals. Thus, a manager's major duty may be to develop plans for field sales, but this duty has no concrete meaning without goals.

In other words, a position description indicates the area of a manager's work, but goals—and accompanying plans—indicate what is expected of him in this area. The position description is not in itself enough to describe completely what is expected of a manager. While goals and some elements of plans could be incorporated in the description, and sometimes are, it is usually better practice to separate them, since immediate goals and plans may change from month to month or quarter to quarter.

ASSURING UNDERSTANDING OF ORGANIZING

To be made to work, organization structures must be well understood by its members. This requires teaching. Also, it must be remembered, formal organization, as conceived in this book, does not cover all organizational relationships but is supplemented by informal organization, which plays a part in making formal organization work. Since this is so, members of an enterprise must understand the general working of informal as well as formal organization.

Teaching the Nature of Organizing

Many soundly conceived organization plans fail because organization members do not understand them. To be sure, a well-written organization manual—

containing a statement of organization philosophy, programs, charts, and an outline of position descriptions—goes far toward making organizing understandable. Certainly, if an organization structure is put into written word and charts, it has a better chance of being clear than if it is not. However, because even the best written word and charts do not always clearly convey to every reader the same meaning, the effective manager cannot stop with written clarification. He must teach those in his operation the meaning of the organization structure, their position in it, and the relationships involved.

This may be done by individual coaching, through staff or special meetings, or by simply watching how the structure works. If subordinates pass decisions up the line when they should be making them, the manager can take this opportunity to clarify authority. Likewise, if communication between members of a group seems to be inadequate, the manager can look for causes either in a poorly conceived or a poorly understood organization structure. Too many group meetings or too much committee work is a signal for the manager to do some investigating. Thus, the manager is obligated continually to teach the fundamentals of organizing, for if he does not, his enterprise or department is likely to fail.

Recognizing the Importance of Informal Organization

Another way of making the formal organization work effectively is to recognize and take full advantage of informal organization. Since formal organization is a social tool for the conscious coordination of activities toward a goal, informal organization, as Barnard has pointed out,[5] necessarily precedes it. Before coordination and structure can be given to group behavior, there must be communication, association, and a concrete goal. People seek associations and the satisfactions that arise from them. This gregarious impulse and association to accomplish goals that an individual alone cannot gain form the basis for formal organization. When the group is coordinated, with a conscious joint purpose and a structure to gain this purpose, it becomes a formal organization.

Formal organizations, according to Barnard, create additional informal organizations. Interrelationships of authority that cannot be charted, unwritten rules of organization conduct, the necessity for "learning the ropes," and other typical phenomena lead to informal organization.

The grapevine   One of the most interesting and significant informal relationships, almost always supplementing formal organization, is referred to as the "grapevine." This relationship is generally quite structureless but comes to life when members of the formal organization who know each other well enough pass on information in some way connected with the enterprise. In the typical enterprise—the members of which spend many hours a day deriving both material security and status from it—the desire for information concerning the company and its people is strong enough so that such informa-

---

[5] *The Functions of the Executive* (Cambridge, Mass.: Harvard University Press, 1938), chap. 9. Also see discussion of informal organization above, p. 243.

tion is rapidly transmitted between persons who know and trust each other.

The grapevine, of course, thrives on information not openly available to the entire group, whether because it is regarded as confidential, because formal lines of communication are inadequate to disperse it, or because it is of the kind that would never be formally disclosed. Even a management that conscientiously informs employees through company bulletins or newspapers never so completely or expeditiously discloses all information of interest as to make the grapevine purposeless.

Since all informal organization serves essential human communication, the grapevine is inevitable and valuable. Indeed, the intelligent top manager would probably be wise to feed it with accurate information, since it is very effective for quick communication. There is much to be said for the manager gaining a place—personally or through a trusted staff member or secretary—on the company grapevine.

Benefits   As Barnard has emphasized, informal organization brings cohesiveness to formal organization. It brings to the members of a formal organization a feeling of belonging, of status, of self-respect, and of gregarious satisfaction. Barnard observes in this connection that informal organizations are rather an important "means of maintaining the personality of the individual against certain effects of formal organizations which tend to disintegrate personality."[6] Many managers, understanding this fact, consciously use informal organizations as channels of communications and molders of employee morale.

SUMMARY OF MAJOR PRINCIPLES OF SOUND ORGANIZING

Although no one would claim that the science of organizing has developed to the point where principles are infallible laws, it is surprising how much unanimity there is among management scholars and practitioners as to the existence of a number of them. These principles are truths of general application, although the generality of their application is not so precise as to give them the exactness of the laws of pure science. They are more in the nature of criteria for good organizing. They are, as Urwick has pointed out,[7] "a beginning, if only a beginning, of a comprehensive philosophy of the task of administration, whether in business or elsewhere."

In order to summarize the major principles of organizing[8] and to see them

---

[6] *Ibid.*, p. 122.

[7] L. Urwick, *The Need Is Urgent to Make Leadership a Reality* (Toronto: Manufacturing and Industrial Engineering, 1952), p. 34. This monograph is a series of six lectures given by Urwick at the University of Toronto in 1951.

[8] Included in this summary are a few principles applicable to organizing dealt with in Part I. An increasing number of companies are summarizing principles of organizing and incorporating them in their organization manuals. See, for example, *Preparing the Organization Manual*, Studies in Personnel Policy No. 157 (New York: National Industrial Conference Board, Inc., 1957); and J. J. Famularo, *Organization Planning Manual* (New York: American Management Association, 1971).

in a logical framework, the authors propose an outline in which they may be grouped under the following aspects of organizing: the purpose of organizing, its cause, the structure of organization, and the process of organizing. Or, to state these aspects as principles, it might be said that the attainment of an objective is the purpose of organizing, span of management the cause, authority the cement, departmentized activities the framework, and effectiveness the measure in supporting performance.

The Purpose of Organizing

The purpose of organizing might be summarized by the following principles:

Principle of unity of objective   An organization structure is effective if it facilitates the contribution of individuals in the attainment of enterprise objectives.

Principle of efficiency   An organization is efficient if it is structured to aid in the accomplishment of enterprise objectives with the minimum of unsought consequences or costs.

Thus, a structure must be effective, as Barnard has emphasized, in furnishing individuals *as a group* the organizational means for gaining enterprise objectives. Every division, branch, department, or section should be judged in the light of how well it contributes to the attainment of enterprise objectives. But the fact that an organization may be effective in gaining enterprise objectives, with every part contributing to this end, does not imply that it does so efficiently. Certainly the concepts of effectiveness and efficiency must be considered together. Moreover, both principles imply the existence of formulated and understood enterprise objectives.

The Cause of Organizing

One finds the basic cause of organization structure in the span of management principle. Certainly, if there were no such limitation, one could have an unorganized enterprise with only one manager.

Span of management principle   There is a limit in each managerial position to the number of persons an individual can effectively manage, but the exact number will vary in accordance with the effect of underlying variables and their impact on the time requirements of effective managing.

Much confusion has arisen in the statement and application of this principle because of the tendency to make a specific law of it through attaching some maximum number of subordinates. This is, of course, erroneous. The number of subordinates a manager can effectively manage may be few or many, depending upon his ability, his job, and basic factors that influence the time demands upon him.

The Structure of Organization: Authority

Authority is the cement of organization structure, the thread that makes it possible, the means by which groups of activities can be placed under a manager and coordination of organizational units can be promoted. It is the tool by which a manager is able to create an environment for individual performance. Authority furnishes the primary line of communication in an enterprise, since it deals with those communications which are composed of decisions. One finds, as might be expected, that some of the most useful principles of organizing are related to it.

The scalar principle   The more clear the line of authority from the top manager in an enterprise to every subordinate position, the more effective will be the responsible decision making and organization communication.

Principle of delegation   Authority delegated to an individual manager should be adequate to assure his ability to accomplish results expected of him.

Principle of absoluteness of responsibility   The responsibility of the subordinate to his superior for performance is absolute, and no superior can escape responsibility for the organization activities of his subordinate.

Principle of parity of authority and responsibility   The responsibility for actions cannot be greater than that implied by the authority delegated, nor should it be less.

Principle of unity of command   The more completely an individual has a reporting relationship to a single superior, the less the problem of conflict in instructions and the greater the feeling of personal responsibility for results.

The authority-level principle   Maintenance of intended delegation requires that decisions within the authority competence of an individual manager be made by him and not be referred upward in the organization structure.

The Structure of Organization: Departmentized Activities

This aspect of organization involves both the departmental framework itself and the problems of assigning activities to these departmental units. Although a number of fundamental truths might be summarized in this area, there are three that appear to be of major importance.

Principle of division of work   The more an organization structure reflects a classification of the tasks or activities necessary to attain goals and assists in their coordination, and the more that roles are designed to fit the capabilities and motivations of people available to fill them, the more effective and efficient an organization structure will be.

The principle of division of work has at times been incorrectly interpreted to mean that activities should be thoroughly specialized. In this instance, it has been confused with the economic principle of occupational specialization. Formal organization, rather than economic specialization, has consequently been blamed by some persons for the existence of highly specialized and limited tasks. It is true that Fayol's discussion of this principle perhaps implies this;[9] but it is likewise true that Fayol wisely recognized that "division of work has its limits which experience and a sense of proportion teach us may not be exceeded."

The principle of division of work should be distinguished from occupational specialization in its detailed and ultimate sense. Division of work does imply that an enterprise will gain from specialization of tasks. But this specialization can be in the broad area of sales or accounting, or it can even be in a project form in which a variety of fairly specialized tasks are aimed at the accomplishment of a special integrated project. The point of the principle is that the activities of an enterprise should be so divided and grouped as to contribute most effectively to objectives. In some cases, this might mean a department with the specialized task of doing nothing more than fuel accounting; or it can mean an engineering project section working to design a complicated piece of electronic gear.

Particularly with respect to the principle of division of work, further principles might be noted as means for explaining the effectiveness and efficiency of the activity groupings in meeting objectives. The various guides in using functional or product or territorial bases of departmentation are cases in point. Also, attention is directed to the guides for associating activities that are tools for the manager to use when the easier and more general criterion of similarity is found to be inapplicable or unsuitable.

Principle of functional definition   The more a position or a department has clear definition of results expected, activities to be undertaken, organization authority delegated, and authority and informational relationships with other positions understood, the more adequately individuals responsible can contribute toward accomplishing enterprise objectives.

Principle of separation   If one activity is designed to be a check on another, the individual charged with the former cannot adequately discharge his responsibility if he reports to the department whose activity he is expected to evaluate.

The Process of Organizing

In a real sense, the various principles of authority delegation and of departmentation are fundamental truths dealing with the process of organizing. But

---

[9] *General and Industrial Administration* (New York: Pitman Publishing Corporation, 1949). Fayol says (p. 20), "Division of work permits of reduction in the number of objects to which attention and effort must be directed and has been recognized as the best means of making use of individuals and of groups of people."

they deal with phases of the two primary aspects of organizing—authority and activity groupings. There are other principles that appear to deal with the process of organizing as a whole. It is through their application that one gains a sense of proportion or a measure of the total organizing process.

Principle of balance   The application of principles or techniques must be balanced in the light of the over-all effectiveness of the structure in meeting enterprise objectives. The principle of balance is common to all areas of science and to all functions of the manager. Perhaps, however, its application is more dramatic in the case of organizing than with the other functions.[10] In every structure there is need for balance. The inefficiencies of broad spans of management must be balanced against the inefficiencies of long lines of communications. The losses of multiple command must be balanced against the gains from expertness and uniformity in applying functional authority to staff and service departments. The savings of occupational specialization in departmentizing in accordance with enterprise function must be balanced against the advantages of establishing profit-responsible, semiautonomous product or territorial departments.

Principle of flexibility   The more provisions are made for building in organizational flexibility, the more adequately organization structure can fulfill its purpose.

This principle has to do with building into every structure devices, techniques, and other environmental factors in anticipating and reacting to change. Every enterprise moves toward its goals in a changing environment, both external and internal. The enterprise that develops inflexibilities, whether these are resistance to change, too complicated procedures, or too firm departmental lines, is risking inability to meet the challenges of economic, technical, biological, political, and social change. It should not be forgotten that one of the obligations of the manager, and one of the tasks role structures are designed to perform, is the perpetuation of the enterprise.

Principle of leadership facilitation   The more an organization structure and its authority delegations make it possible for a manager to design and maintain an environment for performance, the more it will facilitate his leadership abilities.

Since managership depends materially upon the quality of leadership of those in managerial positions, it is important for the organization structure to do its part in creating a situation in which the manager can most effectively lead. In this sense, organizing is a technique of promoting leadership. If the authority allocation and the structural arrangements create a situation in which

---

[10] To expect all principles to pull in exactly the same direction in every environmental situation is to overlook the facts of life. Although a principle is a fundamental truth of general applicability and of predictive value in given situations, there are often varying sets of circumstances in a single complex social (or physical or biological) system. Certainly a physicist would not argue that the principle of gravitation is void merely because it might be offset by principles of centrifugal force. Yet there are those who argue that a principle of management may be invalid because another principle, or a group of forces, tends to offset it in individual instances.

the head of a department tends to be looked upon as the leader and in which his task of leadership is facilitated, structuring has accomplished an essential task. But if the department head is buried in detail or if the actual authority for planning, organizing, directing, staffing, or controlling his department is out of his hands, the organization structure has overshadowed and thwarted its managers.

FOR DISCUSSION

1. Many psychologists have pointed to the advantages of "job enlargement," whereby tasks are not so specialized that an individual loses a sense of doing things which are meaningful. Assuming that a manager wishes to limit specialization of tasks and "enlarge" jobs, can he do so and still apply the basic principles of organizing?
2. Taking an organized enterprise with which you have some familiarity, can you find any of the deficiencies commonly found in organization structures?
3. It is sometimes stated that the typical hierarchical organization chart is an undemocratic device that emphasizes the superiority and inferiority of positions. Comment.
4. What, in your judgment, makes an organization structure "good"? How does "good" organization structure support leadership?
5. What would you need to know to plan an organization structure? How far ahead would you plan it? How would you go about making such a plan?
6. A prominent scholar has forecast that a system of well-defined organizational hierarchy will give way to one of democracy in organization. What do you think?

part four
STAFFING

Every enterprise should be vitally concerned about the quality of its people, especially its managers. The function of staffing has to do with manning the organization structure to assure that an enterprise can be competently operated. In particular, staffing involves the proper and effective selection, appraisal, and development of personnel to fill the roles designed into an organizational structure. While it is clearly a function of all managers, primary attention will be given to staffing of managerial personnel; this does not overlook the importance of staffing problems of the first-line supervisor but this subject, well treated in personnel management books, is not specially dealt with here.

In Chapter 21, the nature and purpose of the staffing function is treated with emphasis on its importance, logic, and the difficulties in dealing with it. To furnish a background for the major aspects of staffing, attention is paid to the nature of the managerial job, the shortage of managerial manpower, the source of managerial personnel, and the problem of evaluating managerial positions.

In the following chapter, the authors discuss the subject of selection of managers. In this important aspect of staffing, the problem of recruitment, qualifications, and methods of selection of managers at various levels are discussed, as well as the complex subject of promotability.

In Chapter 23, appraisal of managers is analyzed. After pointing to the deficiencies of traditional appraisal methods, the authors suggest what they regard as the most promising means of appraising. This program has two major parts. One is the evaluation of performance of managers against their ability to set and achieve verifiable objectives; this is appraising performance in managing by objectives as set forth earlier in Chapter 7. The second part of the program is one where managers are appraised as managers by utilizing as standards the basic concepts and principles of management. It is the

415

authors' view that the effective enterprise must assure itself not only that managers can achieve goals, but also that they know how to manage; goal performance is not adequate assurance, because of the element of chance or a favorable external environment, of continuing success. Also in this chapter, appraisal is related to the highly desirable technique of having an adequate inventory of present and potential managerial manpower.

Following appraisal, Chapter 24 discusses the important area of development and training of managers. Methods of accomplishing this are analyzed and programs for accomplishing effective development are suggested for first-line, middle, and upper-level managers. In every instance, care is taken to point out weaknesses as well as strengths of the programs presented.

21
nature and purpose
of staffing

The managerial function of staffing involves manning the organization structure through proper and effective selection, appraisal, and development of
personnel to fill the roles designed into the structure. Although many writers
on management theory include staffing as a phase of organizing, the authors
have separated it as a major managerial function for a number of reasons. In
the first place, the actual manning of organizational roles contemplates approaches and knowledge not usually dealt with in the practicing manager's
concept of organizing. A second reason is that managers have too often overlooked the essential nature of their responsibility in this area and have been
inclined to regard staffing as something that can be delegated to personnel
departments. A third consideration is that there has developed a considerable
and important body of knowledge and practice in this area.

THE STAFFING FUNCTION

All managers have a responsibility for staffing. The board of directors undertakes a staffing function by selecting, helping develop, and appraising a president; a manufacturing vice-president discharges this function when he selects
a plant manager or other subordinate; and the latter does likewise when he
selects, trains, and appraises his superintendents. Even the foremen or first-
line supervisors have a staffing responsibility. While the same principles apply
in nonmanagerial staffing as in staffing managerial positions, attention will
be paid here primarily to the tasks of designing and evaluating positions for
selecting, appraising, and developing managerial personnel. The staffing of
nonmanagerial positions is a complex task in its own right and has been treated
extensively in books on personnel administration.

417

The Logic of Staffing

If the staffing function were to be handled logically, it would be far more complex than is usual in practice. Since positions are filled not only for the present, but for the future, staffing must deal with future requirements. This means that the first step should be the development of an organization plan for the future since, unless an enterprise expects to replace people constantly, people selected and developed now should be able to fill future roles. But, as will be immediately apparent, an organization plan depends upon enterprise plans, since the organizational structure is always required to establish an environment for performance to accomplish objectives and plans.

In this connection, the question of how much time in the future an organization and staffing plan should encompass depends basically on the commitment principle and the degree of flexibility an enterprise has. If a business or other enterprise expects to "grow" its own future managers, as most enterprises actually intend, rather than to hire them from outside as needed, this would mean fairly long-range planning, perhaps something in the order of twenty to thirty years. However, this is modified by the possibilities of flexibility. A company may feel that it can recruit its needs from the outside as they become apparent and discharge persons unable to fill changing positions. In larger companies, there may be so many positions that flexibility results from the sheer numbers of managers available, with the probability of there being someone in the enterprise available to fill needs as they develop.

Upon the development of a suitable organization plan with its identification of positions available for the future, needs for talent are disclosed. The next logical step is to inventory and appraise existing and potential managerial manpower and to compare this with needs forecast for the future. This will usually show a serious gap between requirements and available personnel, particularly after taking into account enterprise growth and change, retirements, probable separations, and death of those now available. As a matter of fact, there are few enterprises indeed that do not find this gap greater than anyone had realized. In inventorying studies made by the authors they have yet to see enough promising people available to meet future requirements of a company. Even those who had believed that they had enough "comers" found to their chagrin that these persons with great promise were only a small number compared to the requirements that planning disclosed.

The next step is to plan for the acquisition of future needed manpower. This can be done through developing available talent which seems to have the ability to fill future positions. Or it might be done by planning to acquire personnel from outside the company. If the decision, as is usually the case, is to "raise" talent rather than "raid" for it, the final step in staffing is to formulate plans for development.

If development is to be most efficient, logic would dictate that people be carefully appraised, that their strengths and shortcomings be carefully evaluated, and assessed against needs, and that development programs be designed to help people correct deficiencies. As can be appreciated, development programs, if one can judge from the practice of the past several decades, are seldom so specifically designed. They are, rather, designed on the questionable assumption that everyone, at least in certain levels, needs the same training.

Although many enterprises, particularly those in business, have attempted to follow the logical pattern of staffing, most have not. This is understandable. The logic demands a considerable planning and analysis effort. Yet forecasting and planning for managerial manpower requirements very far in advance are fairly rare. The same companies that carefully plan for sales, expenses, and capital expenditures for five to ten years in the future seldom do so for manpower. This is particularly dangerous since development of managerial manpower may take many years. Too many top managers wake up with a critical shortage on their hands and cannot then take the time to staff logically.

In view of the importance of having qualified persons available for future positions and of having people put into positions today who can meet the requirements of tomorrow, a logical approach to staffing would appear to be of very great importance. Many are the top managers who have had to go through the pain of dismissing a loyal subordinate manager who could once meet the requirements of a position that has outgrown him. In fact, one of the foremost entrepreneurs who founded a company that eventually grew into a very large one told one of the authors that the major mistake he made in his early days was to assume that those who started with him would grow with the company.

Staffing Involves People

While a manager must plan, control, and organize effectively, these functions may be viewed as essentially objective and even somewhat mechanistic in the sense that their processes yield rather easily to logic and principle. On the other hand, the functions of staffing and directing are concerned almost completely with people, a fact which introduces enormous complexities that do not yield so well to the efficacy of logic. Uncertainties in the selection and direction of people create baffling problems in general management and as such will probably continue to be not only a source of intense frustration to managers everywhere, but also of prime importance when measured by the cost of failure.

Responsibility for Staffing

The immediate responsibility for efficient execution of the staffing function rests upon every manager at all levels. For many managers this requirement is exceptionally difficult, and they tend to be dilatory in taking action. As a consequence, it is much too common for managers to neglect important aspects of their staffing function.

Such neglect is compensated for in some enterprises by permitting the personnel department or a consultant to handle most of the staffing. This solution is attractive to those who wish to dump an ill-understood function in the lap of someone else. But neither the personnel department nor any other service group is the proper place for this function. The development of future managers, for one thing, cannot be routinized. There is a need for direction from top policy makers. And decisions about the identity of persons to be developed are so far-reaching and are tinged with so much judgment that few people would trust any one individual to make them.

The responsibility for staffing rests upon the chief executive officer and those of his immediate subordinates who compose the internal policy-making group of executives. They have the duty of developing policy, assigning its execution to subordinates, and making certain that it is being properly carried out. Policy considerations include how to develop a staffing program, whether to promote from within or to secure managers from without, where to seek candidates, which selection procedures to follow, whether development should be formalized, and what promotion and retirement procedures to follow.

Need for follow-up   The need for top-level follow-up is as essential for the staffing program as for any other. Numerous types of resistance tend to be encountered: managers resent the loss of promising subordinates, routed, for the sake of broadening experience, to other departments; staffing may not seem pressing and be neglected; and there may be certain changes in the routines. The prestige of top officials is therefore necessary in carrying out the program according to plan. A further and overriding reason for placing the ultimate responsibility on the shoulders of the chief general officer is that the staffing function is carried out with an eye to the future of the enterprise.

Number of Managers Required

The number of managers needed in an enterprise depends not only upon its size but upon the complexity of the organization structure, its plans for expansion, and the rate of turnover in managerial personnel; and the ratio between the number of managers and the number of employees does not obey any law of proportion. It is possible, by enlarging or contracting the delegation of authority, to modify organization structures so that the number of managers in a given enterprise will increase or decrease.

The rate of annual appointments to executive positions can be readily determined by a review of past experience and future expectations. Analysis will also reveal the relative importance of retirement for age and vacancies created by ill health, demotions and separations, and the steady demand of other enterprises for able young subordinates whom the firm has trained but is unable to hold.

The New Sense of Responsibility

In recent years, there has arisen among better-managed business firms and other types of enterprise an important new sense of responsibility for staffing. As the chief executive of one of America's largest manufacturing enterprises told one of the authors, he and his chairman of the board thought they were spending some 40 percent of their time on various aspects of the staffing function. Not only did they spend much time in responsibly dealing with their own subordinates but also in seeing that various programs of careful selection, appraisal, and development were formulated and effectively administered throughout the company. Part of this was accomplished through administration of the company's compensation and bonus system where staffing matters were given heavy emphasis. And part of it was done through special analyses and studies demanded by the top executives. The president, despite the fact that he headed a company with more than 400,000 employees world-wide, even knew how well M.B.A.'s recruited from various graduate schools were progressing in the company!

This involvement of top executives in staffing policies and operation is becoming increasingly widespread. Derived from their realization that effective manning of an organization structure is one of the best assurances of successful operation and growth, this new attitude of responsibility is encouraging. One can expect, as a result, that the many subordinate managers in such enterprises will follow this kind of leadership with a sense of importance that staffing, even a decade ago, did not often command.

WHAT IS A MANAGER?

Before selecting a person for a position, as much as possible must be known about its nature. Just what are managers asked to do? Some time ago Barnard described the nature of the job in these words:[1]

. . . for executives, . . . the world of the future is one of complex technologies and intricate techniques that cannot be adequately comprehended for practical working purposes except by formal and conscious intellectual processes. To understand the formal aspects of a complex organization; to analyze formal relationships between organizations; to deal appropriately with combinations of technological, economic, financial, social, and legal elements; and to explain them to others so manifestly call for ability in making accurate distinctions, in classification, in logical reasoning and analysis, that the point requires no argument.

Management is a most difficult activity, and men in these positions must be effective decision makers. They are often called upon to decide issues on short notice, and management issues tend normally to be very complex in terms of all the factors which affect them. The manager must recognize these elements, weigh them correctly, mentally formulate sets of simultaneous equations, and often solve them while the person who requests the decision awaits the answer. And the answer had better be correct, because on it may hang profit or loss, an industrial strike or peace, a facilitated or blighted career of a subordinate, a bold or timid response to challenge, a helping or a dead hand in making free enterprise work, an assist in achieving cultural values or a disregard of them which could help to destroy civilization. All these factors are

---

[1] Chester I. Barnard, *Organization and Management* (Cambridge, Mass.: Harvard University Press, 1949), p. 197.

grist in management decision making. Correct choices are of crucial importance to the enterprise and conceivably to our way of life.

The managerial job is complex, even in small firms. No way has ever been found to place an enterprise in a laboratory. The engineer, the physicist, and the chemist are aided in their quest to discover the nature of a force or an element by the facility with which they can control the test environment. The scientist is able to exclude the influence of factors not currently being studied, either by creating a situation in which they cannot intrude or by permitting them to exert an unvarying influence. The manager cannot do this. His decisions must not only take into consideration such forces as the stage and trend of the business cycle, the political, economic, and social policies of government in its national and international phases, trends in the markets, and his immediate and future competitive situation, but he must also evaluate all these forces simultaneously. For him there is no easy assumption as to "other things being equal" or "other factors remaining constant."

Varying Views of Managers

There are those who assume that managers must have certain qualities or traits if they are to be successful. No scientific basis is laid for this deduction. One merely looks around and decides that a rather long list of (frequently) overlapping characteristics is just what the successful manager must have. He achieves this state of excellence through knowing what qualities he should have and acquiring them through practice. Few would deny that most enterprises would benefit from being managed by such godlike creatures, but many would question the correlation between each of the qualities and enterprise success. Managers are exhorted to acquire and practice these qualities. This is good advice insofar as behavior can be learned. Whether it is really worthwhile in terms of enterprise success, and whether we have efficient means of changing behavior, are quite other questions.

Those who are concerned with the operation of research laboratories sometimes look upon the manager in quite a different light. Knowing that scientists want to report to technically competent men, many individuals specify that the research manager must be respected for his scientific capability as demonstrated by his engaging part-time in personal research and spending the rest of his time in crystallizing the creative ideas of his subordinates, in advising with them about approaches to their problems, and in smoothing away the administrative clutter that scientists are presumed to dislike so much. However, the manager who is solely a technical catalyst is no manager at all.

In his *The Managerial Mind*, David W. Ewing[2] draws a fundamental distinction between the front-line and middle-level managers, who are primarily concerned with the execution of the managerial functions, and the top manager, who cultivates—like a gardener—his enterprise that it may live and grow. The latter will use the productive factors with a skill that rests upon a deep

[2](New York: The Free Press of Glencoe, 1964).

knowledge of technical factors and of human nature, and he will observe the external scene with a view to taking both defensive and offensive action. This is a useful view of the manager because it draws the distinction between the man who looks upon the execution of the manager's functions as an end and the man who looks upon those functions as the means to achieve a healthy and growing enterprise. The implication that there is a necessary distinction between managerial levels with respect to this view of the top manager is, however, highly questionable.

When Abram T. Collier[3] looked at the manager, he saw a man who was concerned about the enterprise in its total complexity. He established for the manager's guidance five sets of values. The "A" values are composed of self-teaching, the virtues of hard work, self-realization, personal responsibility, and the search for justice and honor. The "B" values include organizational skills, sales techniques, administrative genius, communication power, and the integration of mental and physical health. Among the "C" values are professional training, desire for facts, legal realism, and historical objectivity. The "D" values relate to people-centered teaching, customer-oriented selling, service, participative management, and self-transcendence. Finally, the "E" values are ultimate values: the capacity to adapt to change, ability to integrate viewpoints, and the power to go beyond the above four value structures. In essence, Collier thinks that a man must be able to look at the results of his work and call them "good." The enterprise is thus looked upon as part of the existence of the manager.

The manager has also been looked upon as a technician.[4] He operates an open system, seeking his objectives through an organization which functions in an extraordinarily complex environment. He protects the enterprise through decision making that reflects the changing laws of the land, shifting markets, and many pressures exerted by unions, competitors, politicians, and educators. He also maintains his internal system by evaluating the pressures of technology, financial forces, and the social interrelationships of his employees. He develops an operating system which provides for feedback and review.

Variation in Job Descriptions

Although there is a managerial job to be done, there is no standardized managerial position. This fact is traceable to variations in assigned duties and to semantic difficulties. The common usage of such terms as "sales manager," "personnel director," and "president" implies that these positions are standardized, yet nothing could be further from the truth. A person entitled "president" may devote his time almost entirely to finance or engineering; he may grant a title to a subordinate but assign to him few, if any, of the duties implied in the title; or he may create a responsible position without a title.

---

[3] *Management, Man and Values* (New York: Harper & Row, Publishers, Incorporated, 1962), chap. 11, pp. 226–227.

[4] Leonard R. Sayles, *Managerial Behavior* (New York: McGraw-Hill Book Company, 1964), chap. 14.

Position titles may be both misleading and unrevealing. The organization structures of department stores provide several examples of these two difficulties. One store may have a position with the title of sales manager. There is no way of determining from the organization chart just what this title implies, and it is not comparable to the commonly accepted title of merchandise manager, because the product-line merchandise manager reports to the president. Four stores may employ four different titles for the manager in charge of publicity, display, and advertising—publicity manager, advertising manager, manager of sales and publicity, and publicity director.

In order to communicate more specifically about the activities associated with a position title, enterprises have long relied upon job descriptions. A great deal of frustration has always accompanied this technique because it is usually impracticable to identify all the elements of a given position or role. As noted in Chapter 18, it is much easier and clearer to identify authority delegations through a chart of approval authorizations. Also, as pointed out in Chapter 7, the development of verifiable objectives, which are an integral part of any managerial role, is naturally highly dynamic and cannot easily be put into a position description unless one is satisfied with generalities with respect to what is expected or is willing constantly to revise these descriptions. Furthermore, it is highly unlikely that sources of needed information can be adequately described in such descriptions.

It must be recognized, therefore, that any given managerial role is understandably complex. Even so, with the modern tools of clarifying goals, of specifying delegations, of grouping and identifying at least major duties, and of making available and communicating needed information, any role can be made clear to those selected to fill it and to those with whom the occupant is expected to coordinate his activities. Moreover, in the purely *managerial* aspects of a position, an adequate knowledge of what managing is and the intelligence and perseverance to apply this knowledge to reality should leave little to doubt in the responsibility for staffing.

THE SHORTAGE OF MANAGERIAL MANPOWER

Enterprise managers are becoming more and more aware that potential competent executive manpower is extremely scarce. In general, this has been the case ever since the rapid business, governmental, and educational expansion following the Second World War. But it is expected to be even more serious in the 1970s. As one expert in the field of staffing has said:[5]

Evidence is accumulating that a "no holds barred" scramble for executive talent— already in short supply—will develop in the next few years. Indeed, there are signs the demand for this increasingly rare commodity could reach such boom proportions by 1975 that even the best-managed companies, which have executive talent in considerable depth today, would be unfavorably affected.

[5] A. Patton, "The Coming Scramble for Executive Talent," *Harvard Business Review*, vol. 45, no. 3, pp. 155–171 (May–June, 1967).

The shortage forecast for the 1970s is due to a number of causes, including the low birthrate of the 1930s, the expansion of size of the average corporation in recent years, the increasing complexity of the task of managing, the large demand for executives outside of industry particularly in government and education, and the fact that executives have become increasingly mobile with continuing decline of loyalty to their employing enterprise. What is particularly interesting is that executive positions have increased faster than enterprise growth. One study reports that, between 1955 and 1965, the number of corporate officers in the 100 largest U.S. companies increased by 28 percent and during a similar time the number of federal government employees of so-called "executive grades" increased by 58 percent.[6]

This study and forecast of managerial manpower underscore some fundamental reasons that have long existed in developing managerial personnel to meet requirements.

Modern Enterprise and Managers

The growth in size of modern business, government, and other enterprises, has increased the demand for persons with managerial skill. Whereas small firms sometimes cannot fully enjoy the economic advantages of the division of labor between manager and nonmanager, large enterprises profit from this specialization. The roles of foremen, frontline supervisors, office managers, and the numerous department heads, as well as general officers, are filled with people who engage primarily in carrying out managerial functions. Consequently, a clear-cut demand for managers is felt in all enterprises as they grow larger.

Tardy Recognition of the Problem

Tardy recognition of the problems of staffing is evidenced by the somewhat slow steps that managers have taken to develop suitable candidates, and considerable uncertainty has characterized programs. Part of this uncertainty can be explained by the relatively recent growth of many large enterprises.

Another reason for delaying attention to staffing has been slowness to understand what a manager does. As long as it was believed that a manager just "managed" and that whatever this entailed was indistinguishable from the exercise of technical skills, there was very little chance that the importance of the staffing function would be realized. Before any of the functions of managers could be studied with profit, it was necessary to identify them, define them, and understand their relationship to enterprise objectives.

A third reason for the tardy recognition of the managerial staffing problem is the late discovery that the qualifications for managers are, in part, psychological in nature and that success in staffing depends, therefore, upon the development of ways of measuring such factors as intelligence, personality, leadership potential, and judgment. Psychologists have thus far been unable

[6] *Ibid.*, p. 159.

to help as much as desired, and there is, consequently, an understandable hesitancy on the part of business managers to proceed with assurance in the selection of potential candidates.

Lack of Managerial Teaching

The lack of managerial teaching in educational institutions was deplored by Henri Fayol as early as 1916,[7] but little or no attention was paid to his views at that time. Indeed, despite the development of business schools, there were few academicians interested in the subject until recent years. Such inattention may be largely responsible for the highly developed educational activities of consulting firms and the American Management Association, an organization whose membership is predominantly drawn from business executives.

The inadequacy of university teaching in the area of management theory stems from two factors. One is that skilled teachers in this area need ideally to be persons with a combination of academic training and business or other management experience. To some extent, a few enterprises are trying to remedy this fault through providing internships for university professors, lasting from a week or two to three months. Such firms as Boeing, Swift, and du Pont have been pioneers in this movement.

A second reason for the lack of managerial teaching concerns the nature of the subject; clearly, universities cannot teach management in the same sense that they teach chemical research, accounting, and mathematics. The manager must work through *people,* and the ability of the potential manager to do this cannot be discerned without on-the-job experience. However, there are some things that can be done by the universities. These are to transmit to the student an understanding of the managerial functions and the principles underlying them, to provide him with a background of knowledge and skill in the application of scientific methodology, conceptual skills, and tools for communicating.[8] From this point on, it is largely the responsibility of the employer to give managerial candidates an opportunity to learn through development on and within the job.

Uncertainties of Top Executives

Further causes for the shortage of executive manpower may be found in the uncertainties that plague top executives. Many executives hesitate to do enough about developing managers because they are not sure just what to do. Many are uncertain, too, about their future needs for managers. Those who are concerned mainly with the immediate and short-term problems of an enterprise are often inclined to delay attention to the flow of future managers. And

[7] Henri Fayol, *General and Industrial Management* (New York: Pitman Publishing Corporation, 1949), p. v.

[8] For a more complete analysis of what universities can do, see H. Koontz, *Requirements for Basic and Professional Education for Scientific Management* (London: British Institute of Management, 1964).

for those that find the expense of training able managers high, delays are understandably not uncommon.

Executives have sometimes been slow to realize their personal responsibility for the development of future managers. There are still too few operations that assign to their officers the specific duty of training subordinate managers. This duty is, of course, clearly implied. But it is easily neglected by men who consider themselves too busy to execute it, who shy away from the expense of development—especially when candidates are free to leave the enterprise after their training—and who themselves were brought up by older men who trusted to chance and experience and believed in an innate ability to hire good outside executives when needed (and when there was no shortage).

Finally, top managers contribute to the shortage through their uncertainty about the proper training methods to use. Many executives who recognize the need for managers and conscientiously accept their responsibility for developing them are stymied, because principles of training are yet unsettled.

SOURCES OF MANAGERIAL PERSONNEL

Although there is a shortage of managerial manpower, those who feel the shortage most may have failed to develop all the available sources. This is not merely a question of overlooking certain sources; it can also result from not knowing how to use them.

Promotion from Within

The phrase "promotion from within" has had such wide currency for about half a century in all kinds of enterprises that its meaning has long since lost precision. It has even acquired an emotional content that contributes to its indiscriminate use. In its original and literal meaning, promotion from within implied that advancement into managerial positions proceeded from rankers, or workers, into front-line supervisory positions and thence upward through the organizational hierarchy. Thus, the firm was pictured as receiving a flow of nonmanagerial employees from among whom future managers emerged. As it used to be said in the railroad industry: "When a president retires or dies, we hire a new office boy."

So long as the matter is considered theoretically, there is little question but that employees overwhelmingly favor a policy of promotion from within. The proscription of outsiders places severe limits on the competition for positions and gives employees of the firm an established monopoly on managerial openings. Employees come to doubt the wisdom of the policy only when they are confronted with a specific case of selection of one of their own number for promotion. This feeling is present at all levels of the organization. Indeed, the difficulty of selecting a general officer from among the sales, production, finance, or engineering managers, or a dean from among a group of professors, grows so large that managers are often inclined to choose the easier way and select an outsider.

The attitude of managers toward a policy of promotion from within is conditioned by similar conflicts of interest. To placate the employees, the firm is likely to publicize bravely its adherence to this policy. William B. Given, when president of the American Brake Shoe Company,[9] wrote, "It is our policy to give our own people the benefit of advancement as openings occur. We believe that unless we have no one who can possibly qualify it is not fair to our people to hire an outsider." Even more emphatic is the position taken by Sears, Roebuck and Company. In a booklet given to prospective employees is the statement, "At Sears the policy of 'promotion from within' is not just a phrase or a slogan. It is a fact, insured by specific administrative measures to make sure that it happens." Similarly, General Petroleum Corporation stated that its policy was to fill all jobs, whenever possible, from within; and Procter & Gamble asserts that its policy of promotion from within is strictly adhered to.

Such statements on the internal source of managerial candidates probably represent the general and official attitude of many corporate executives. There can be little question that they place heavy emphasis on the policy for the purpose of encouraging prospective nonmanagerial candidates to accept employment, with the view of long-run commitment and of bolstering employee morale. It is not always clear whether these same firms give similar assurance to their middle and top functional executives. The saving phrase "whenever possible" is quite sufficient to provide an escape.

Making promotions from the personnel within the enterprise not only has positive values relating to its morale and reputation, but it also permits taking advantage of the presence of potentially fine managers among its personnel. Even though these positive but unmeasurable values are important, their pursuit should not blind executives to the dangers of either overemphasizing this source or relying upon it exclusively.

The assumption underlying the policy of promoting from within is either that new employees are hired with a view to their managerial potential or that from among the new and old employees there will emerge a sufficient number of qualified candidates for promotion. The latter assumption is unsafe for modern enterprise. It is increasingly dangerous as a population becomes differentiated in the degree to which its members seek education, since well-educated persons are more likely than the less well-educated to be the successful candidates for managerial positions.

The assumption that all employees are hired with a view to their managerial potential is contrary to fact. Indeed, most employees are hired for their skills as machinists, electricians, PBX operators, typists, accountants, engineers, or statisticians. Those who are wanted because of such skills are not refused because they may have low managerial potential.

An exclusive policy of promoting from within leads to inbreeding, which is the selection of persons for promotion who have prepared by imitating their superiors. Inbreeding is not a fault if only the best methods, routines, and

[9] "Experience in the Development of Executive Leadership," in Marvin Bower (ed.), *Development of Executive Leadership* (Cambridge, Mass.: Harvard University Press, 1951), p. 79.

viewpoints are cultivated. But such a circumstance is likely to be an unapproachable ideal. Enterprises depend upon new blood to introduce new ideas and practices, the very elements that competition forces the firm to cultivate. Consequently, there is every reason to avoid a policy that contributes to inbreeding.

The Policy of Open Competition

Reliance upon a policy of promotion from within enhances the monopolistic position of current employees with respect to managerial openings and denies to the enterprise the benefits of open competition. Since there is neither a legal nor a moral obligation to promote employees, it is incumbent upon those who manage an enterprise to decide whether the benefits of such a policy outweigh its shortcomings. There are forthright reasons for implementing the principle of open competition in which vacant positions are open to the best qualified persons available, whether inside or outside the enterprise. It gives the firm, in the final analysis, the opportunity to secure the services of the best-qualified candidates. It counters the shortcoming of inbreeding, permits a firm to adopt the best techniques in the recruiting of managers, and eliminates the complacent heir apparent. To exchange these advantages for a part-time morale factor would appear to be questionable.

It should be noted that the dangers of inbreeding and the creation of monopolistic advantages for existing employees can be largely avoided in a large, diversified firm even though it follows a policy of promotion from within. Promotion from within in these companies can provide competition over a fairly broad area of activity if the policy of the firm permits it. Unfortunately, many diversified firms confine selections for promotions to candidates in the requesting division or department. In so doing, they encounter the same evils of promotion from within as much smaller firms.

A policy of open competition is a much better means of assuring managerial competence and is more honest in that it avoids use of that usually overlooked qualification, "so long as a qualified person is available," found in promotion-from-within policies. However, it does put the managers who use it under a special obligation. If morale is to be protected in applying an open-competition policy, the enterprise must have a fair and objective method of appraising its people and should do everything possible to help them develop so that they can qualify for promotions.

With these requirements, it would be expected that every manager, in considering an appointment to a vacancy or a new position, would have available to him a roster of qualified candidates within the enterprise. If people know that their qualifications are being considered, if they have been well appraised and have been given opportunities for development, they are far less likely to feel a sense of injustice if an opening goes to an outsider. Other things being equal, present employees can and should be able to compete with outsiders. If they have the ability for a position, they have the considerable advantage of having been identified with the enterprise and knowing its personnel, history, problems, policies, and objectives. For the superior candidate, competition with all others from whatever source should hold no hazards.

Selection of Key Executives from Outside

The key executive is the one who supplies the force that sparks a program and carries it to completion. These executives may be identified at all organizational levels. They may be the men who make the functional, service, and staff departments operate with vigor and efficiency. But more probably, the key executive will be found at or near the top of the organization structure. He provides the tone, imagination, and judgment with which the enterprise attains its objective. Since subordinate managers tend to reflect the attitudes of their superior, their contribution to a program may often be ascribed to the inspiration of the dominating personality.

The negative reason for recruiting key executives from the outside has already been suggested—the morale problem of dealing with grumpy, frustrated, uncooperative executives who have not been selected for a given promotion. Rather than create such conditions, which are extremely disagreeable, it is not uncommon for an enterprise to recruit a key man from outside, though he may be superior in no way to the internal candidates for the position.

Often there are positive reasons for selecting a key executive from the outside. The outside candidate may be considered superior to the internal contenders for one or more reasons. For instance, when firms reach a position in their development where the outstanding need is for their energies to be directed vigorously toward the solution of marketing problems, they almost certainly will turn to the outside. Promotion of inside men would be unthinkable, since they have brought the enterprise to its stagnant position. Indeed, this is the situation that faced many firms during the 1950s when key marketing executives were brought in to guide firms through a highly competitive period. For similar reasons, production men were imported during the nineteenth century; and engineers have more recently been brought into conspicuous positions with firms in the aerodynamics, electronics, and plastics industries. Here the factor being sought is vision, new ideas, and new applications.

THE REWARDS OF MANAGING

Concentration upon the qualifications of managers and the sources of suitable candidates obscures the point that managers do not work for enterprises: they work for an enterprise. Hence, the firm is faced with persuading the prospective candidate to select it from among all others competing for his services. Business enterprises in particular have scrambled for candidates with managerial potential, persuaded to do so by growing awareness that the manager's functions are different from others, and that there is a shortage of promotable candidates for executive positions.

But what incentives should be offered the candidate? Such a question could not be answered until something was known about motivation. The motive of monetary income in an era of prosperity was not enough. Firms that paid good salaries often failed to attract good candidates. Gradually they learned that statistical averages and general observations obscure the fact that every individual has desires and requirements that do not square with those of the "average" man. Consequently, a successful approach to motivating prospective managerial candidates must be broad enough to encompass dominant human desires and still be personal enough to cover individual needs. Some progress has been made in understanding human incentives: we feel we have a better understanding of the manager.

Managerial candidates differ widely in age, economic position, and maturity. Nevertheless, it may be helpful to consider the potential executive as one who begins his career with no other assets than innate drive and a good education. And he wants many things—opportunity, income, power, prestige, and respect. A lifetime may not be long enough to satisfy in some measure all these desires. Circumstances undoubtedly deprive many potential managers of opportunity; few, indeed, succeed to positions of power. Perhaps in this may be found the reason for the human tendency to imbue with gradations of status every occupation, every department in a firm, every enterprise, and every classification of enterprises.

Opportunity for a Progressive Career

The main concern of a managerial candidate who stands on the threshold of his career is to find an enterprise that will give him maximum opportunity to gain breadth, as well as depth, of business experience. He is aware that he lacks practical experience and that the only way to fill this void is through employment. A job, he knows, is not enough to qualify him for a supervisory position. He requires a variety of work broad enough to permit an understanding of the total operation of the enterprise and the departmental interrelationships as well as internal problems, handicaps, limitations, and merits.

As he scans the business horizon, the candidate will be assessing the opportunities for promotion after such experience has been acquired. Clearly, preparation for advancement is no end in itself. It is at this point that the prospective employer, because of poor communication, is likely to lose patience with a candidate "who wants to be a top manager". The only assurance the firm can give, and the only one sought by the candidate, is in terms of the average number of promotions made by the firm per year and its future plans. The candidate will favor the firm which annually fills many supervisory positions over the firm that has a record of promoting few employees.

Challenge in Meaningful Work

Closely related to the opportunity for a progressive career and perhaps one of the most dominant forces inducing managers throughout their career is the challenge found in meaningful work. Young candidates as well as older managers thrive on the desire to accomplish, on feeling a sense of mission. This is akin to Veblen's "instinct of workmanship" and is probably one of the least utilized inducements in modern enterprise, particularly at lower levels of an organization.

To be sure, what might look dull to one person might be challenging to another, a fact that those appropriately preaching the importance of job enrichment should not forget. For example, an accountant in a large railroad who had spent years keeping careful records of fuel consumption felt that his job was one of the most important and demanding in the company; needless to say, the vice-president and controller regarded it as a boring assignment and could not understand the accountant's feeling of challenge.

If the reward of accomplishment is to be realized, a man must know what his job is, what his discretion or authority is, what is expected of him, and the environment in which he operates must be conducive to performance; moreover, the results expected must be challenging to him. To a very great extent, the desire for accomplishment is central to the theme of this book in which the authors take the view that furnishing an environment for performance is the task of all managers.

Financial Reward

The young candidate thinks in terms of financial security as soon as he feels confident that he can gain experience toward an opportunity to compete for future promotions. It is at this point in his career that his family expenses usually begin to rise, he develops a keen desire to live in the manner of his colleagues, and he achieves a realistic conception of the importance of laying a solid foundation for financial independence. These considerations will be high on the list of incentives for much of his active life. Money is often more than mere dollars; it usually reflects all other motivating forces. Consequently, those who say it is unimportant tend to overlook what money represents.

Power

By the time he may enjoy seeing action follow his decisions, the manager will probably already have proved his ability to settle issues, demonstrated he can get things done, developed judgment, and gained the confidence of his superiors. At this point a freer rein can be given to exercising the authority that enables him to influence people and events in the direction in which he wishes them to go. Power is derived largely from the authority to use both material and human resources. Hence, the manager who has reached this stage has considerable leeway in changing policies, practices, products, and objectives. There is a strong element of creativeness in such changes. The manager wants to try out new ideas, improve the orientation of the enterprise, and be able to point with pride to his handiwork.

Prestige

As the desire for power becomes less important, the desire for prestige becomes greater, although status is a strong motivating force at all times. The manager comes to value more highly that ascendancy which is derived from the admiration of his fellow human beings, whether they be his superiors, subordinates, or individuals unconnected with the enterprise. Such admiration may spring from the estimation of a man's worth based upon his reputation; it may reflect acceptance by peers; it may arise from the favorable opinion of subordinates; or it may adhere to the executive who occupies or succeeds to a position surrounded by an aura of prestige. Whatever its source, the desire to acquire the satisfaction of being well thought of by other human beings can become intense. The top executive may then feel that he can afford to seek actively the approbation of mankind. Like our Presidents, he begins to think of his place in history. The enterprise in which he has made his career may not afford opportunities for an executive to be satisfied with the prestige involved. Consequently, he may turn to the broad field of public service, employing his talents in diplomacy, government, research, philanthropy, or education.

DESIGNING AND EVALUATING MANAGERIAL POSITIONS

It is not quite enough to look to the organization structure to furnish complete answers as to the number and kinds of managerial positions in an enterprise. To be sure, if a complete structure of roles is developed, the number and kinds of positions are identified, with results to be expected, major activities to be undertaken, authority to be exercised, and coordination required. With the structure as a guide and through other managerial actions in the areas of planning, directing, and controlling, information sources and understanding of relationships can be provided.

Positions and Motivating Factors

However, since positions are filled by people and people respond to various motivations, as was preliminarily discussed in the previous section, motivating factors must also be built, to the extent possible, into positions. Inducements designed into management positions will be discussed in Chapter 26.

Evaluating Managerial Positions

One of the most difficult tasks of managing is the evaluation of managerial *positions*, a task which should be distinguished from evaluating the *performance of a person* in it. Should a company controller's position be rated higher than that of assistant to the president? Is a personnel manager's position less or more valuable than that of an engineering manager or a plant manager? Should the vice-president for marketing outrank the vice-president for manufacturing? Should the position of sales manager over one product line be more or less highly placed than the position of a sales manager over another product line? Should controllers of similar size companies be rated equal?

Obviously the evaluation of positions within an enterprise has great importance for such matters as compensation, prestige, office allocations and furnishings, and the many other things that are so meaningful to incumbents of managerial (as well as all other) positions. One would think, therefore, that this would be one of the most highly developed areas of management. But, unfortunately, it is not.

Comparison Method

The most common method of evaluating managerial positions in practice is through comparing, or "slotting," them. Given a few key positions on which some standard of pay and status exists, such as president, manager of accounting, or plant superintendent, others are compared to them and a largely subjective judgment is made as to whether, in a given company, one rates higher than another in the hierarchy of organization. The exact extent of the difference is usually expressed in differences in salary levels. These, in turn, tend to be fixed, at least for selected key positions, by statistics on salaries paid by similar companies, as disclosed in surveys made by the American Management Association or other various agencies. It is thus a kind of recognition that market competition sets the salaries for like positions.

Job Factor Method

Some companies evaluate managerial positions by using variations in the common practice of evaluating lower-level jobs, such as factory or clerical employees. This is done by selecting job factors, assigning them weights and points, and then giving a numerical expression to each factor. Such factors include education required, experience, mental or physical effort, responsibility, and work conditions. On the basis of these point evaluations, a series of grades is developed, and by reference to those grades where competitive salaries or wages are known, compensation levels and ranges are set for each grade. These point-rating systems have been used for many professional positions and in some cases even for managerial positions, understandably with different job factors and weightings. But, traditional point ratings have not been widely used for middle- and upper-level managerial jobs.

However, one of the more popular adaptations of the point system to managerial job evaluation is what is called the "guide-chart" profile method, developed over the years by Edward N. Hay and Associates.[10] In this approach, positions are evaluated in three areas: (1) know-how required; (2) problem solving involved; and (3) degree and extent of accountability, or responsibility. Within each area factors are analyzed and weighted and the score profile is used as a basis of comparing positions.

Time-span of Discretion Method

One of the most original and promising, but not yet proved, approaches to evaluating any kind of position, but with particular interest for managerial positions, is the "time-span of discretion" technique developed by Elliott

---

[10] J. Doulton and D. Hay, *Managerial and Professional Staff Grading* (London: George Allen & Unwin, Ltd., 1962), esp. chap. 2.

Jaques, distinguished management scholar, psychologist, and consultant of England.[11] Jaques believes, and has considerable research to make his point persuasive, that the worth of any job can be measured by the time-span of discretion in the position. This he defines as follows:[12]

The longest period which can elapse in a role before the manager can be sure that his subordinate has not been exercising marginally sub-standard discretion continuously in balancing the pace and the quality of his work.

In other words, the time-span of discretion is that longest period of time that must elapse before it is known whether a subordinate is not measuring up in those tasks that have the longest time involved to see whether the discretion exercised was correct. For example, with a foreman in an assembly operation, mistakes due to low skill or poor judgment might show up rather quickly, but for a company president it might take years to ascertain the correctness of discretion in certain tasks.

Jaques's technique involves measuring the length of time-span of discretion by analyzing tasks in a position. His research shows that the longer the time-span, the more a position should be paid. While greater practical application of the technique is necessary to show its value, it is nonetheless true that this approach is both original and offers one of the better hopes for obtaining objectivity in managerial job evaluation.

Deficiencies in Managerial Job Evaluation

All methods of evaluating managerial positions suffer from deficiencies. Titles vary so much in terms of what is included in a job that slotting may be extremely imprecise, and even point-systems or time-span approaches may not adequately detect what a job really is. Even though the latter two systems reduce greatly the element of subjectivity so prevalent in the position comparison method, they still suffer from a significant degree of subjectivity.

Perhaps the greatest reason for concern in position evaluation is that not everyone who fills a given position does the same things in the same way. Managerial positions, like many other professional jobs, have a high degree of elasticity and much depends upon what incumbents make of their jobs. This is particularly true with higher-level positions, but it is even an implicit factor in middle- and lower-level managerial jobs. To be sure, differences in performance should normally be weighed by evaluation of the person in the position, but the fact is that many positions depend to a greater or lesser degree on the persons who have them. The spectrum of important tasks and results expected is not easy to define completely in managerial roles.

---

[11] See his *Equitable Payment* (New York: John Wiley & Sons, Inc., 1961) and *Time-Span Handbook* (London: William Heinemann, Ltd., 1962). For a description of the system, see E. F. Beal, "In Praise of Job Evaluation," *California Management Review*, vol. 5, no. 3, pp. 8–17 (Summer, 1963).

[12] Jaques, op. cit., p. 23.

FOR DISCUSSION

1. What differences do you see in the problem of staffing for managers and non-managers?
2. It is sometimes argued that good managers make or break an enterprise and that, therefore, staffing is the most important managerial function. To what extent is this accurate and what are the issues involved?
3. Most observers would agree that good managers, particularly for top positions, seem to be very scarce. What explanation of this situation seems most acceptable to you?
4. Although it is usually assumed that managers are mobile, a survey of large companies by *Fortune* indicated that top managers typically have worked for only two firms. Does the survey refute the assumption?
5. Why is the function of staffing so seldom approached logically?
6. What are the dangers and difficulties in applying a policy of promoting from within?
7. Apply the time-span of discretion technique to some highly paid positions with which you are familiar. Does it reasonably apply?

22
selection of managers

If it is not too much to say that the well-being of an enterprise depends largely on the quality of its managers, then it may also be said that no enterprise activity can be more important than that of choosing these managers.[1] Since the maturing of these men is a long process involving training, practice, and the creation of developmental opportunities, it is critical for the future of the enterprise to identify, if possible, these men at all levels in the organization structure.[2]

Three general difficulties should be kept in mind when judging the qualifications of managerial candidates. First is the variation in management positions from front-line supervision through middle to top posts. Second is the variation in what is known about a candidate's past managerial experience; whereas the candidate for front-line supervision normally will have had no management experience, the candidate for higher-level positions will probably have had such experience, but records of it, even if available, are likely not to be comparable or adequate. Third, variation occurs in the matter of who makes the selection; this can run the gamut from immediate superior to a series of committees at several levels in the management hierarchy.

THE RECRUITMENT PROBLEM

The execution of a policy of developing managerial personnel logically proceeds from an understanding of the sheer magnitude of the job. The firm must know how many candidates need be considered each year in order to provide

[1] See P. F. Drucker, *Concept of the Corporation* (New York: The John Day Company, Inc., 1946), p. 31. Or, as L. F. Urwick remarked, ". . . businesses are made or broken in the long run not by markets, or capital, patents or equipment, but by men. . . ." See *Sixteen Questions about the Selection and Training of Managers* (London: Urwick, Orr & Partners Limited, 1958).

[2] Cf. James W. Walker, "Trends in Manpower Management Research," *Business Horizons*, Vol. 11, no. 4, pp. 37–46 (August, 1968).

the requisite number of selections. There must also be an understanding of the meaning of recruitment. To some firms this term will be confined to the college graduates selected for management development each year. To others, it may be expanded to include those who are selected from among the ranks. Still others will include the selection of experienced men from both within and without the firm to fill middle- and higher-level positions.

Scope of a Recruitment Program

Definition of the jobs to be covered can be troublesome. Specifically, shall the program include front-line supervisors? There are many reasons—relating to their educational qualifications and the nature of their jobs—for excluding them. The front-line supervisor, whether a foreman, a section chief, or an office manager, requires considerable technical skill in the operation of machinery or equipment, or of the activities supervised, in order to evaluate the quality of work turned out. He also needs this foundation to be able to teach new hands and to direct all subordinates in the work group. To obtain this skill and knowledge, he may be most efficiently trained in a nonmanagerial position.

Even though these requirements for technical knowledge tend to set apart candidates for front-line supervision from candidates for higher-level management positions, there appear to be good reasons for including supervisors in the management selection program. They are managers. They execute every one of the manager's functions. In their positions they acquire invaluable experience in developing a successful leadership pattern. They deal directly with the people who do the work of enterprise. They are, by all odds, the most promising source of supply of middle- and top-level managers.

How Many Selections?

The actual magnitude of the recruitment program is affected by several factors. The first step in arriving at a reasonable figure for the average number of selections to be made each year is to count the number of managerial positions that currently exist. Such a task is easy for any firm that maintains its organization chart in a complete and up-to-date manner.

The next step is to estimate the turnover in managerial personnel. A better estimate can be obtained if the immediately preceding five-year period is considered as a sample, rather than a shorter span. The purpose is to arrive at a stable figure that represents the annual average number of appointments made to management positions. It is most useful to express this average in the form of an index or as a ratio.

At this point a careful inventory of the current position of the firm with respect to its existing managers should be made. This is developed by classifying managers as (1) prospects for promotion, (2) those who should be retained in their jobs but are not promotable, (3) those who should be replaced, and (4) those who are about to retire. This information, supplemented by a time and position schedule for each promotable manager, is useful for determining whether the demand for selectees will be greater than average for the next year. The firm following such inventorying consistently will be able to forecast its needs quite accurately.

Since it is necessary to determine the number of selections to be made for the succeeding year, it is important to allow for any foreseeable changes in the organization structure. This requires an evaluation of plans for the expansion or contraction of enterprise activity, and translation of these plans into the number of required managerial positions. Application of the turnover index to this total will yield the probable number of changes to be made in managerial personnel during the succeeding year.

The final step involves the determination of the number of trainees to be selected. Enterprises vary widely in their practices here. Some follow the conservative 1 to 1 ratio between the number of selections and the number of probable openings. Others adopt ratios of 2, 5, and even 10 to 1.[3] Every firm runs into an attrition rate of large or small proportions. Selectees leave the firm for many different reasons.

There are other factors involved in this problem. Businessmen know that the number of people who can be interested in their firm also depends upon such factors as climate, geographical distances, and personal interests. It is for reasons of this nature that New England firms are reluctant to recruit in California. They can keep down the number of separations by drawing upon potential managers from nearby localities, because the personal ties of these people condition them to local employment.

The Recruitment Process

The managers of enterprise seem ever prone to use simple techniques to solve complicated problems. However, in the recruitment of managers at all levels, those who select are faced with imponderables that will not yield to simple procedures. These have been tried. Recruiters spend heavily on the screening process, often applying not science but their own subjective measures. Managers often proceed in the same way, or simply ignore the problem until it will not go away, or have a blind faith that good candidates will emerge randomly.

An aura of science tends to be associated with psychological testing. Considerable impetus was given to this technique during World War I, when the United States Army administered an intelligence test to its personnel. These tests were originally developed for use in schools. The postwar period saw a great increase both in the types of tests and in the fields of application. Exaggerated claims about the efficacy of testing have grown into a strong chorus as the procedure has become commercialized.

Enterprise executives have responded to these claims in a variety of ways; some exhibit profound bewilderment; many rely implicitly on the tests; others

---

[3] Urwick urges four, on the basis that by the time they are sixty years old one-quarter will be dead, one-quarter will have fallen by the wayside, and there should be at least two qualified for each position. See *Sixteen Questions about the Selection and Training of Managers, op. cit.*, p. 13.

administer them for fear they might otherwise be missing a bet; and still others have nothing to do with them.

Although by now there are several hundred "standard" tests, they may be readily classified in four groups:

1. Intelligence tests, designed to measure mental capacity and test memory, speed of thought, and observation of interrelationships
2. Proficiency and aptitude tests, constructed to discover, respectively, existing skills and the potentiality for acquiring such skills
3. Vocational tests, designed to discover the most suitable occupational area
4. Personality tests, last to be developed, designed to measure potentiality for leadership

On the basis of present knowledge, certain conclusions with respect to the use of psychological tests can be reached. In the first place, the writers on the topic of testing tend to fail to distinguish between tests for nonmanagerial and managerial positions. Important claims are made for tests for certain types of nonmanagerial jobs. For instance, Schein[4] refers to the success of testing in the selection of Air Force pilots and insurance salesmen. Other applications include aptitude, intelligence, specific skills, comprehension, interests, attitudes, and personality testing.

In the second place, psychologists have yet to develop reliable tests for use in selecting managers. Despite many attempts made, the basic reason for their failure is that the managerial job or, more accurately, the qualities on which managerial success rest, are extremely difficult to isolate. Without knowing for what one is testing, there is no expectation, except perhaps by coincidence, that a successful test can ever be developed. As Schein says, ". . . selecting managers, for example, has been much more difficult because of the problem of describing the managerial job and reliably judging relative performance." He cites other technical difficulties in developing such a test, but these are scarcely important in view of the fundamental problem.

SELECTION OF FRONT-LINE SUPERVISORS

Every supervisor needs guidance in the difficult and risky task of selecting from among his nonmanagerial subordinates a candidate to fill a vacant or potentially vacant supervisory position. Neither time-honored practices nor psychological tests will help him because they are not discriminative enough in identifying potential management ability. He would be able to make the selection efficiently if he knew (1) what qualities were required; (2) in what degree each was essential; (3) what combinations of qualities were required and in what degree; and (4) how to identify the required qualities in candidates.

[4]Edgar H. Schein, *Organizational Psychology* (Englewood Cliffs, N.J.: Prentice-Hall, Inc., 1965), chap. 3.

The inductive approach to these issues has been barren, and such an approach may be impractical in view of the nature of the managerial job. But a deductive approach has much to commend it. From a thorough knowledge of the executive functions and the environment in which they are discharged, certain qualities important to success should be identifiable. Knowing what a front-line supervisor will be asked to do, his success, it is believed, will depend directly on the degree to which he wants to manage, his intelligence, his analytical and communication abilities, and his integrity. He will also require leadership ability, but this quality can best be assessed as management is practiced. Based upon available records and especially upon observation and personal knowledge of subordinates, the supervisor can evaluate those who aspire to management positions. For purposes of summary, he might consider Figure 22.1 useful.

Factors in Selecting Front-line Supervisors

Some of the most important managerial qualities are discussed briefly below.

Desire to manage   Perhaps the most pervasive requirement for successful performance of the managerial function is an intense desire to manage. There is a close correlation between good managerial performance and the possession of a driving desire to achieve purposes through the teamed efforts of subordinates. Too many people drift into management because they are attracted by its rewards in terms of salary, status, and perquisites and fail to understand that it has its frustrations and responsibilities. Those who select supervisors must probe beneath the superficial reasons of candidates for management and search for individuals who will derive a basic satisfaction from accomplishing objectives through the teamwork of their associates. These men, in all likelihood, will have the drive and determination essential in effective managers.

Intelligence   An estimate of the candidate's intelligence level can be a simple matter. If he is a graduate of a university known for its high standards, the transcript of his scholastic record will provide the requisite information. In case of doubt about the reliability of the grade index or if the candidate is in some other category, the supervisor will probably evaluate intelligence on the basis of performance of work assignments. However determined, above-average intelligence is an absolute requirement.

Analytical ability   The supervisor has many opportunities to assess the facility of a candidate in the use of analytic methods. Subordinates are often given special assignments beyond the routine of their jobs, such as reporting on a new proposal, a change in policy or procedure, or a marketing program. If the supervisor learns to assess not only the recommendation in the report but the investigative procedure used in making it, he will have a good measure

FIGURE 22.1   Supervisor Selection Form

This form to be used in weighing the managerial potential of nonmanagerial candidates for supervisory appointments.

Policy

The future of this company is largely dependent upon its ability to attract, select, and develop personnel with superior managerial potential.

This form, when completed, becomes an important instrument in the selection of our future supervisors. It becomes part of the permanent personnel record of those who are accepted.

Detailed instructions

This form is to be completed by the immediate supervisor of each candidate. Read the definition and explanations of each characteristic before selecting the degree to which it is possessed by the candidate.

Attention should be devoted to a single characteristic at a time.

Personal data:

Name:_____

Age:_____

Date:_____

Supervisor:_____

1.   **The desire to manage**

This quality can be recognized only by knowing a candidate well. Discussions about management, its problems, and the candidate's reasons for desiring a management career are probably essential in coming to a considered opinion.

Candidate:	
Wants to manage	☐
Is not sure	☐
Prefers technical work	☐

---

of the candidate's analytical ability as well as of his ability to proceed logically.

Ability to communicate   The supervisor can judge the candidate's ability to transmit ideas from his written reports, letters, oral discussions, and any committee assignments in which he may participate. These activities will reflect his facility in choice of words, organization of thought, phrasing, sentence structure, paragraphing, and over-all clarity and forcefulness of expression.

Integrity   Our social system demands that managers be morally sound and worthy of trust. They exercise considerable authority, they cannot be closely supervised, and they are responsible for numerous actions which could compromise the enterprise. Integrity in managers means many things. It goes beyond a conception of honesty in money and material matters and in the use of time, important as these are. It requires a subordinate manager to keep his superior fully informed, to adhere always to the full truth, especially in briefing superiors, and to have the strength of character to live and act in accordance

2.   Intelligence

This quality may be determined from the transcript of the college record of the candidate and/or from observation of him as he performs his tasks.

Grade point_____ Graduate of_____ Degree_____

	Low			High
Estimate of Intelligence:	1	2	3	4

3.   Ability to make a logical analysis

Consider the candidate's performance of work assignments and special projects in terms of his logical approach and indicate your judgment of his facility with scientific methodology.

	Low				High
Check one:	1	2	3	4	5

4.   Ability to communicate

Evaluate the candidate's facility with language. Note particularly grammar and spelling, choice of words, flow of words, clarity of thought and expression, and ability to maintain interest while conveying information.

	Low				High
Check one:	1	2	3	4	5

5.   Integrity

Consider the candidate's honesty and responsibility in using time, company equipment, in reporting expenses and use of funds, in reporting both positive and negative factors concerning his performance of assignments, and his moral soundness.

	Low				High
Check one:	1	2	3	4	5

with the moral standards of our society.

While it is not an easy matter to evaluate the integrity of a subordinate, close acquaintance with him in the work environment provides the best opportunity for a correct assessment. His use of time and expense reports, his dealing with co-workers and other business associates, his probity in handling assignments, his sincerity about his work, and his attitude toward life combine to give the observing superior many opportunities to evaluate integrity.

Many managers, in selecting a candidate for front-line supervision, may wish to consider additionally such other factors as cooperation, ability to lead others, imagination, and appearance. There is no particular reason to dissent from such elaboration and no doubt that such qualities are important to a manager.

Who Shall Select?

The immediate supervisor is in the best position to nominate candidates for promotion from among his subordinates. He should know them well in work situations; he has trained and coached them. If he can show that he has evaluated them objectively on the basis of the qualities set forth in the preceding section, his judgment is very important.

From among such candidates the common superior of the superiors— usually the department head—should make his selection. When he decides who will work for him, he can be held responsible for the performance of his department and will be deprived of the alibi that someone else selected his subordinates.

Limitations of the Selection Process

The approach outlined in this section is not without its limitations, which must be understood along with the positive features. Only then may its value be judged.

The recommended approach rests upon two premises. First, there is no known way positively to identify potential managers in advance. Second, certain qualities, deduced from the nature of managing, will improve the chances of becoming an efficient manager. Whether the man *really* can manage remains unknown until he can be judged on the basis of performance. Mistakes in selection at the front-line level are numerous. For this reason it is only fair that the successful candidate be forewarned of the risk of eventual failure and be told frankly that if he is not successful he will be removed. Superiors have a moral responsibility to make this clear so that candidates may choose their course of action intelligently. The timid may decline promotion while the confident will risk it, and both these reactions will be in the best interest of the enterprise.

Figure 22.2 *Relation of managerial charters to enterprise objectives.*

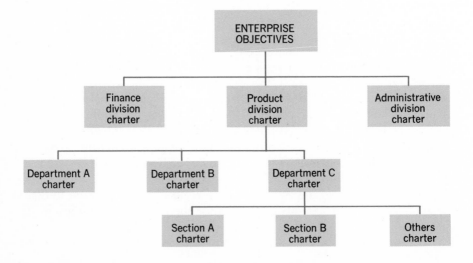

SELECTION OF MIDDLE- AND UPPER-LEVEL MANAGERS

The program suggested for selecting middle- and upper-level managers is quite different from that recommended for front-line supervision. First, the functions of managers are the same at all levels; second, all candidates for promotion at this level have management experience behind them; and third, the most reliable forecast of a manager's future is his past accomplishment *as a manager.* Since selection is made from among candidates *who have achieved,* the process can be largely results-oriented. The critical question becomes, To what degree has the candidate measured up to the requirements of his job? In order to answer this question, it is first necessary to have a clear concept of what that job is.

A Manager's Charter[5]

The purpose of any organized undertaking is to achieve specific objectives in an efficient and effective manner. As an essential requirement, each enterprise selects a manager,[6] who establishes a formal organization at the top level. By this means the manager divides the work to be accomplished in accordance with some principle. He may select a functional basis, as does the President of the United States in his organization of the Cabinet and a business manager in carving out areas of activities such as production, marketing, and finance. He may select a service basis, as does the hospital manager in dividing activities between surgery and internal medicine, or a product basis, as when activities are divided between group executives who are concerned about ground systems and aerospace systems. He may decide upon still other methods of grouping activities. The essential point is that the work of realizing the ultimate objective is divided up (specialized). As is illustrated in Figure 22.2, the manager of each division is assigned a charter or mission to produce certain goods or services, under appropriate conditions of time, cost, and quality, and with verifiable goals established from time to time, which, with proper integration with the charters of other peer managers, is designed for accomplishment of enterprise objectives. To do this properly, each manager, depending upon the amount and variety of resources placed at his disposal, will subdivide activities within his command and establish a charter for each subordinate manager. Thus, the manager's charter reflects what he is supposed to accomplish; the simultaneous accomplishment of the charters of peer managers will thereby achieve the charter of this common superior. The essential feature of this concept is that *the manager is responsible for accomplishing his charter* within

[5] This section is based on Cyril O'Donnell, "Managerial Training: A System Approach," *Training and Development Journal,* vol. 22, no. 1 (1968). For a restatement of current thinking about the qualities of top managers, see Robert N. McMurry, "Avoiding Mistakes in Selecting Executives," *Michigan Business Review,* vol. 22, no. 4, pp. 7–14 (July, 1970).

[6] There must be a "top" to secure unity of command, despite the rather fuzzy experimentation with divided authority by some corporations. See "Management Problems of Tomorrow," *Dun's Review,* vol. 89, no. 2, pp. 24–26, 78–79 (February, 1967), and Pearson Hunt, "Fallacy of the One Big Brain," *Harvard Business Review,* vol. 44, no. 4, pp. 84–90 (July–August, 1966).

the broad limitations of the law, acceptable public practice, and ethical principles.

To illustrate these relationships, we may turn to a firm in the aerospace industry. Its objective is to be a cost-conscious, efficient, advanced-technology enterprise as it strives for profitable growth. Its organization structure breaks into product and functional divisions. Each of these divisions has a charter. For example, one product division conceives, designs, sells, manufactures, installs, and supports its (specified) systems and subsystems. Each department and section within this division also has its charter. One department provides logistic support for division products. In total, the accomplishment of all subordinate organizational charters will add up to the achievement of the product division charter, and this, added to similar accomplishment on the part of peer divisions, should enable the enterprise to accomplish its objectives.[7]

In order to accomplish its charter, each organizational unit will achieve certain goals and produce certain end products. As the term implies, an end product may be hardware, paper (reports), or service produced by the unit in question and turned over to other organizational units or directly to a customer. For instance, a logistics department has an end product consisting of engineering service to be performed according to a contract which spells out skills, man-hours, location, cost, and other constraints. A controller's end products consist mainly of specific reports, such as balance sheets, profits and loss statements, financial forecasts and analyses, and reports to government agencies.

It is especially important to distinguish between charter and end products. The latter are the means by which the charter is accomplished. This may be readily understood if one considers a controller. It is commonly understood that his charter is to keep safe the assets of the enterprise.[8] One of the means by which he accomplishes his job is to produce information for the use of others outside his department.

The Selection Process

Every manager's job is to accomplish his charter. Since he lives in a dynamic world, charter, goals, and end products are likely to change with time. So also will standards for measuring the quality of his ultimate accomplishments. At a moment in time, these standards may be contained in a contract which is being fulfilled. Sometimes they are established in the plan of operation (including physical and budgetary plans). Sometimes they are somewhat vague, as in the case of the end products of administrative divisions where there are no standard services, or costs thereof, except those that may be agreed upon

[7] See George S. Sanders, "The Management of Research," Chemistry and Industry, pp. 2076–2079 (Dec. 25, 1955).

[8] Technically this is inaccurate, because the controller can only develop reporting procedures which become the basis for decisions by his superior. Thus, the responsibility for safeguarding assets is his superior's and peers' and not the controller's.

method. On the other hand, there is no question but that operations are streamlined and each manager can effectively be held accountable for his total activity.

Balancing the Age Factor

It is not too uncommon to see a company manned by people in the same age group. The vice-presidents may cluster about the age of forty or fifty-five or sixty, depending upon the history of the firm. Similarly, the middle managers approximate the same age. Inattention to this factor can be very embarrassing to any enterprise. When several managers on the same level retire within a short period of time, a serious gap in operating effectiveness is likely to occur. Furthermore, if a level of managers grows old simultaneously, it puts an effectual cap on the promotion process for their subordinates. These difficulties can readily be avoided by paying close attention to the age factor when appointments are originally made.

Who Selects?

It is an undeviating rule that the manager to whom the successful candidate will report should make the selection. This requirement is paramount because the selector will be held accountable for all events in his department or division. This rule works very well in practice, but it is frequently challenged by those who prefer a "committee" approach. There are several reasons for rejecting this technique. It obviously reduces the authority, and therefore the responsibility, of the superior manager. Even if the committee is designated as advisory, it can and does wield considerable power by talking the appointment to death, by overemphasizing the factors that certain members want stressed, and by intimidating the prospective superior.

The committee process is widely prevalent in making university appointments, as it is in some government agencies. It seems to have the widest application in those enterprises where accountability for results is somewhat diffused. Certainly no competitive enterprise could stand the strain of group deliberations on candidacies for promotion. This is not to say that opinions of others who have had a working relationship with the candidate should not be solicited. Indeed, they should. The major responsibility, however, is the primary right of the candidate's prospective superior.

At the same time there are likely to be cases where automatic approval of a superior's selection may not be desirable. In fact, many companies, particularly for upper-level appointments, follow this practice. They do it for two basic reasons. In the first place, they wish to assure themselves that the superior is selecting an adequately high-caliber subordinate. Second, it is often recognized that from a man's subordinates will likely be selected his replacement or the replacement for others at the level of the superior. While this exercise of the approval function is understandably wise as a matter of assuring that the best quality of manager will be hired, it still is unwise if the actual selection is made by any person other than the immediate superior.

FOR DISCUSSION

1. Do you see any relationship between the selection process and the scarcity of good managers?
2. Although top managers are fond of saying that a liberal arts education is preferable for potential managers, their recruiters look for particular skills. What seems to be wrong?
3. What are the factors which make it difficult to select effective front-line supervisors?
4. Delay in identifying potential successors to managers often leads to quick and inadequate selection when a position suddenly becomes vacant. Discuss the steps which might be taken to avoid this problem.
5. The "Peter principle" has been widely quoted in management circles. What do you think of it? Do you believe that it could ever apply to you?
6. Take any managerial position you wish and draw up a chart, including a set of typical verifiable goals and end products. After doing so, attempt to draw up a list of requirements against which a candidate could be measured.

23

*appraisal of managers**

Managerial appraisal has sometimes been referred to as the "Achilles' heel" of management development. But one could say more. It is probably a major key to managing itself. It is, of course, important to management development because if a manager's strengths and weaknesses are not known, it would only be accidental that development efforts would be aimed in the right direction. Appraisal is, or should be, an integral part of managing itself. Knowing how well a manager plans, organizes, staffs, directs, and controls, and taking steps to correct deficiencies, are really the only way to assure that those occupying managerial positions are actually managing effectively. If a business, a government agency, charitable organization, or even a university is to reach its goals effectively and efficiently, ways of accurately measuring management performance must be found and implemented.

THE PROBLEM OF MANAGEMENT APPRAISAL

There has long been a reluctance on the part of managers to appraise subordinates.[1] However, in an activity as important as managing, there should be no reluctance in measuring performance as accurately as we can. No one should get excited about the concern of those who fear that measuring the performance of others tends to put a manager in the untenable position of measuring the worth of his subordinates and of acting on these judgments. It is sometimes difficult to comprehend the fear of "playing God" in a culture where individual performance has been rated at least from the time a person enters kindergarten and throughout his school and university life. In almost

---

*Much of this chapter has been drawn from H. Koontz, *Appraising Managers as Managers* (New York: McGraw-Hill Book Company, 1971).

[1] See, for example, B. F. White and L. B. Barnes, "Power Networks in the Appraisal Process," *Harvard Business Review*, vol. 49, no. 3, pp. 101–109 (May-June, 1971).

all kinds of group enterprise, whether in work or play, performance has long been rated in some way. Moreover, most people, and particularly people of ability, *want to know* how well they are doing.

It is difficult to believe that the controversy, misgivings, even the disillusionment, still so widespread, with respect to managerial performance appraisal have come from the *fact* of measuring and evaluating. It rather appears that they have arisen from the things measured, the standards used, and the way measurement is done. A manager can understandably take exception, feel unhappy, or resist when he believes that he is evaluating, or is being evaluated, inaccurately or against standards that are inapplicable, inadequate, or subjective.

A bright beam of light and hope has emerged in the past decade and offers promise of making evaluation effective. The exploding interest in evaluating managers by comparing actual performance against preset verifiable objectives or goals is one of the most exciting developments in management in the past quarter century. However, examination of actual programs in operation raises questions as to how many of these are truly effective. Indeed, a fair question may be raised as to whether there is still more talk than action. In addition, one might question whether this outbreak of attention may become a fad and like other fads, even though based on sound principles, may fade from the scene. People have a way of becoming disenchanted and resistant when new ideas or programs do not work as intended.

However, appraisal against verifiable objectives is not enough. As will be noted presently, this needs to be supplemented by appraisal of managers as managers. Moreover, neither system is without difficulties and pitfalls, and neither can be operated by simply adopting the technique and doing the paper work. One needs to do more. In the first place, it is essential that managing by verifiable objectives, as explained in Chapter 7, be a way of life in an enterprise. In the second place, there is needed a clear concept of the managerial job, the fundamentals underlying it, and the ability to apply these in practice.

WHAT SHOULD BE MEASURED

It hardly seems necessary to say that managerial appraisal should measure *performance as a manager* in meeting goals for which the manager is responsible. Yet, obvious as this is, or at least should be, examination of a large number of appraisal systems used by business, government, and other enterprises shows a lack of understanding of this truism, or at least an unwillingness or inability to translate understanding into practice.

Note then that appraisal should measure both *performance* in accomplishing goals and plans and *performance as a manager*. No one would want a person in a managerial role who appeared to do everything right as a manager, but who could not turn in a good record of profit making, marketing, controllership, or whatever his area of responsibility might be. Nor should one be satisfied to have a performer in a managerial position who cannot operate effectively as a manager. Performers tend to be "flashes in the pan," and many are the performers who have succeeded through no fault of their own.

Performance in Accomplishing Goals

In assessing performance, the newer systems of appraising against verifiable preselected goals represent the best method that has yet been devised. Given consistent, integrated, and understood planning designed to reach verifiable goals, the best measuring criteria of the manager are his goals, including the intelligence with which he selects them, the planning programs he devises to accomplish them, and his success in achieving them. Those who have operated under some variation of this system have often claimed that this is adequate and that elements of luck or other factors beyond the manager's control are taken into account in arriving at any appraisal. To some extent this may be true. But there are too many cases of the sparkling performer being promoted despite these factors and the performing failure being inaccurately blamed.

Performance as Managers

Although an impressive record of setting and accomplishing goals is persuasive evidence of any group leader's ability, it is proposed in this book to supplement this standard of performance by an appraisal of a manager *as a manager*. One must grant that a manager at any level undertakes nonmanagerial duties and these cannot be overlooked. The primary purpose for which a manager is hired, and against which he should be measured, however, is his performance as a manager. This should indicate that he be appraised on the basis of how well he understands and undertakes the managerial functions of planning, organizing, staffing, directing, and controlling. For standards in this area we must turn to the fundamentals of management.

TRADITIONAL TRAIT APPRAISALS

For many years, and even commonly today, managers have been evaluated against standards of personal traits and work characteristics. These typical trait-rating evaluation systems might list ten to fifteen personal characteristics, such as ability to get along with people, leadership, analytical competence, industry, judgment, initative, and so forth. The list might also include such work-oriented characteristics as job knowledge, ability to carry through on assignments, production or cost results, or seeing that plans and instructions are carried out. However, at least until recent years, personal traits have far outnumbered work-oriented characteristics. Given these standards, the rater was then asked to evaluate his subordinates on the basis of one of five or six ratings ranging from unacceptable to outstanding.

Typical trait-oriented appraisal is that used by the United States Navy for many years in appraising officers. While the total "Report on the Fitness

TABLE 23.1. QUALITIES AND RATING FORM OF U.S. NAVY REPORT ON FITNESS OF OFFICERS

A MARK TO THE RIGHT OF THIS LINE

	Not observed	Outstanding	Excellent	Average	Unsatisfactory
(a) Intelligence (With reference to the faculty of comprehension; mental acuteness.)		Exceptionally quick-witted; keen in understanding	Grasps essentials of a situation quickly.	Understands normal situations and conditions.	
(b) Judgment (With reference to a discriminating perception by which the values and relations of things are mentally asserted.)		Unusually keen in estimating situations and reaching sound decisions.	Can generally be depended on to make proper decisions.	Fair judgment in normal and routine things.	
(c) Initiative (With reference to constructive thinking and resourcefulness; ability and intelligence to act on own responsibility.)		Exceptional in ability to think, plan, and do things without waiting to be told and instructed.	Able to plan and execute missions on his own responsibility.	Capable of performing routine duties on own responsibility.	
(d) Force (With reference to moral power possessed and exerted in producing results.)		Strong, dynamic.	Strong.	Effectual under normal and routine circumstances.	
(e) Leadership (With reference to the faculty of directing, controlling, and influencing others in definite lines of action and of maintaining discipline.)		Inspires others to a high degree by precept and example. Requires a high standard of discipline.	A very good leader.	Leads fairly well.	
(f) Moral courage (With reference to that mental quality which impels one to carry out the dictates of his conscience and convictions fearlessly.)		Exceptionally courageous.	Courageous to a high degree.	Fairly courageous.	
(g) Cooperation (With reference to the faculty of working harmoniously with others toward the accomplishment of common duties.)		Exceptionally successful in working with others to a common end.	Works in harmony with others.	Cooperates fairly well.	

CONSTITUTES AN ADVERSE REPORT

(h) Loyalty (Fidelity, faithfulness, allegiance, constancy—all with reference to a cause and to higher authority.)	Unswerving in allegiance; frank and honest in aiding and advising.	A high sense of loyalty.	Reasonably faithful in the execution of his duty.
(i) Perseverance (With reference to maintenance of purpose or undertaking in spite of obstacles or discouragement.)	Determined, resolute.	Constant in purpose.	Fairly steady.
(j) Reaction in emergencies (With reference to the faculty of acting instinctively in a logical manner in difficult and unforeseen situations.)	Exceptionally cool-headed and logical in his actions under all conditions.	Composed and logical in his actions in difficult situations	Fairly logical in his actions in general.
(k) Endurance (With reference to ability for carrying on under any and all conditions.)	Capable of standing an exceptional amount of physical hardship and strain.	Can perform well his duties under trying conditions.	Of normal endurance.
(l) Industry (With reference to performance of duties in an energetic manner.)	Extremely energetic and industrious.	Thorough and energetic.	Reasonably energetic and industrious.
(m) Military bearing and neatness of person and dress (With reference to dignity of demeanor, correctness of uniform, and smartness of appearance.)	Exceptional.	Very good.	Fair.

14. A report containing adverse matter must be referred to the officer reported on for statement pursuant to article 1701 (8) USNR. His statement should be attached to this report. Statements of minor deficiencies either in character or performance of duties must be brought to the attention of the officer reported on either orally or in writing.

Has This Been Done? _____ What Improvement, If Any, Has Been Noted? _____

_____

(Signature of reporting senior)

of Officers" required additional information on duties, study courses carried out, whether the reviewing officer would desire to have the subordinate in his command, and any open-ended comments, the major portion of the evaluation was involved in the trait analysis shown in Table 23.1.

Managers resist doing trait rating or tend to go through the paper work without knowing exactly how to rate. Even where earnest attempts have been made to "sell" such programs, to indoctrinate managers, and to train them in the meaning of traits so that they can improve their appraisal ability, few managers can or will do them well.

One practical problem of the trait approach to appraisal is that, because trait evaluation cannot be objective, serious fair-minded managers do not wish to utilize their obviously subjective judgment on a matter so important as performance. And employees who receive less than the top rating almost invariably feel that they have been unfairly dealt with. Most regard this "playing with people's souls" as possibly being the province of the professional psychiatrist, but hardly that of the manager.

Another problem is that the basic assumption of trait appraisals is open to question. The connection between performance and possession of traits is doubtful. It also tends to be outside of, separated from, a manager's actual operations. It substitutes what someone *thinks* of an individual for what he actually *does*. This is made even more constraining when we find in trait appraisal forms too few references to the actual job being done.

The results of resistance by managers are several. Many look upon it as only a paper-work exercise that must be done because someone has ordered it. When this happens, people go through the paper work and tend to make ratings as painless (on the subordinate and the manager) as possible. Consequently, they tend not to be very discriminating. It is interesting, but hardly surprising, that a study of ratings of Navy officers a few years ago came up with an arithmetic paradox: that of all officers of the U.S. Navy rated over a period of time, some 98.5 per cent were outstanding or excellent and only 1 per cent were average.

Trait criteria are at best nebulous. Raters are dealing with a blunt tool, and subordinates are likely to be vague about what it is they are being rated on. In the hands of most practitioners it is a crude device, and since raters are painfully aware of this, they are reluctant to use it in a manner which would affect the careers of their subordinates. One of the principal purposes of appraisal is to provide a basis upon which to discuss performance and plan for improvement. But trait evaluations provide little tangible to discuss, little on which participants can agree as fact, and therefore little mutual understanding of what would be required to obtain improvement.

Attempts to Strengthen Trait Rating

As the deficiencies of trait rating have come to be recognized, a number of changes and additions have been introduced. Some are aimed at making the traits more comprehensible to raters. As will be noted with reference to the U.S. Navy form, instead of saying merely "judgment," the report defines this quality as "discriminating perception by which values and relations to things are mentally asserted." In a form of a well-known-business corporation, "judgment," for example, is explained to mean "how capable is he in recognizing the significant from the less significant in arriving at sound conclusions?" Likewise, attempts are made, as was done on the Navy form, to give meanings to various grades under each category.

Often, too, trait and work quality forms are supplemented by open-ended evaluations in which, without specific guidance, the appraiser is asked to supply whatever evidence on performance he feels is pertinent. Sometimes, also, this approach is used for the entire appraisal. The appraiser may be given a broad outline to guide him, such as asking for comments under such items as "operations," "organization," "personnel," and "financial," and he may be asked specifically to consider such things as quality, quantity, time element of work, customer relations, and subordinate employee morale. While these are helpful, experience has shown that they do not greatly improve the quality of ratings.

Attempts have also been made to improve the effectiveness of the rating process. In some systems, the subordinate is required to rate himself, and his superior must compare his rating with that made by the subordinate. In other instances, the superior's superior is asked to rate the former's subordinate or at least carefully review the evaluation made by the immediate superior. Sometimes, discrimination in rating is forced by a system of requiring a rater to rank his subordinates from the best to the least able. In still other cases, rating has been done through the use of critical incidents that are assumed to give meaning to grades given.

These and other devices have been used for improving ratings. They have helped, but they cannot overcome the fact that traits and work qualities are, at best, subjective and consequently neither very accurate nor necessarily truly applicable to what a manager's job really is.

APPRAISING MANAGERS AGAINST VERIFIABLE OBJECTIVES

One of the most promising tools of managerial appraisal that has developed in recent years is the system of evaluating managerial performance against the setting and accomplishing of verifiable objectives. As noted in Chapter 7, setting a network of meaningful and actionable objectives lies at the base of all managing. This is simple logic since no one can be expected to accomplish a task with effectiveness or efficiency unless he knows what the end points of his efforts should be. Nor can any organized enterprise in business or elsewhere be expected to do so.

The Appraisal Process

Once a program of managing by verifiable objectives is operating, a major phase of appraisal is a fairly easy step. What is involved is seeing how competently managers set objectives and how well they performed against them. In those cases where appraisal by results has failed or been disillusioning, the cause can usually be traced to the fact that it was seen *only* as an *appraisal* tool. Even though search for a better appraisal method probably did give managing by objectives its strongest impetus, the system is not likely to work if only used as a means of appraisal. Management by objectives must be a way of managing, a way of planning, as well as the key to organizing, staffing, directing, and controlling. When it is this, appraisal boils down to whether or not the manager established adequate but reasonably attainable objectives and how he performed against them in a certain period.

This can be done by looking at the system of managing and appraising by objectives, as is done in Figure 23.1. As can be seen, appraising is only a last step in the entire process.

But there are problems. Were the goals adequate? Did they call for "stretched" performance? These questions can only be answered by the judgment and experience of the man's superior, although this judgment can become sharper with time and trial and can take on a high degree of objectivity in those instances where goals of other managers in a similar position can be used for comparison.

In assessing goal accomplishment, the evaluator must take into account such considerations as whether the goals were reasonably attainable in the first place, whether intervening factors beyond a man's control unduly helped or hindered him in accomplishing his goals, and what the reasons for accomplishment or nonaccomplishment were. Another matter which the reviewer should watch is whether an individual has continued to operate against obsolete goals when his situation changed and he should have established revised goals.

As in any case of control, progress toward goals should be regularly reviewed as it may be dangerous to limit appraisal to looking at performance once a year. For a top manager, such as a president or a division general manager, progress should probably be reviewed and appraised quarterly in fair detail and more broadly in the light of probable accomplishment, three or four additional quarters in the future. Alert and intelligent managers hardly wish to risk having obsolete objectives, naturally prefer to have both goal setting and evaluation be a regular activity, and certainly, in most instances, would not wish to wait an entire year to know how they and their subordinates were doing.

For individuals below the top level, quarterly reviews may be enough. And they may not. The real determinant is the time span necessary to determine whether a goal is still valid and whether satisfactory progress is being made. It is probable that for certain positions, such as those of first-level supervision, reviews should be usefully made each month. Note that this does not necessarily involve separate appraisals. This is merely carrying on the function of managing, and actual appraising becomes a relatively easy by-product of the process.

Strengths

The strengths of appraising against accomplishment of objectives are almost the same as those of managing by objectives. Both are part of the same process,

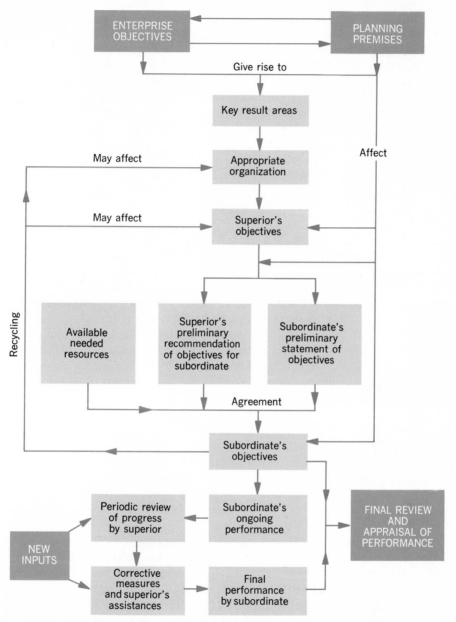

Figure 23-1   *The system of managing and appraising by objective.*
Source: H. Koontz, *Appraising Managers as Managers* (New York: McGraw-Hill Book Company, 1971), p. 78.

both are basic to effective managing, and both are means of improving the quality of managing.

In the area of appraising there are special and important strengths, especially when compared to the traditional methods of evaluating people against personal traits or work characteristics. Appraising on the basis of performance against verifiable objectives has the great advantage of being operational. Appraisals are not apart from the job a manager does, but a review of what he actually did as a manager. There are, however, always questions of how well a man did, whether goals were missed or accomplished through no fault of his own, and how much by the way of goal attainment should be expected.

But information on what a man has done, against what he agreed was a reasonable target, is available. It thus furnishes strong presumptions of objectivity and reduces the element of pure judgment in appraisal. Moreover, the appraisal can be carried on in an atmosphere of the superior working with his subordinate and not sitting in Olympian judgment on him.

Weaknesses

As noted in Chapter 7, there are certain weaknesses in the system and practice of managing by objectives. These weaknesses, of course, apply with equal force to appraisal. One of the great weaknesses from the latter point of view is that it is entirely possible for a man to meet or miss goals through no fault of his own. Luck often does play a part in performance. It is possible, for example, that a new product will take off in the market far beyond expectations because of completely external factors and make the sales or marketing manager look exceptionally good, when the quality of the marketing program and its implementation might actually be poor. Or an unpredictable cancellation of a major defense contract might make the record of a division manager look deficient.

Most evaluators will say that they always take uncontrollable or unexpected factors into account in assessing goal performance, and to a very great extent they do. But it is extremely difficult. In an outstanding sales record, for example, how can anyone be sure how much was due to luck and how much to competence? The outstanding performer is always a "fair-haired boy," at least as long as he performs. The nonperformer likewise can hardly escape having a cloud cast over him.

With its emphasis on accomplishing operating objectives, the system of appraising against these may overlook needs for individual development. Goal attainment tends to be short run in practice. Even where longer-range considerations are put into the system, seldom would they be so long as to contemplate adequate long-term development of managers. The manager concerned primarily with results might be driven by the system to take too little time to plan, implement, and follow through with programs required for his development and that of his subordinates.

On the other hand, it can be argued that, since management by objectives gives better and more accurate visibility to managerial needs, development programs can be better pinpointed. As possible as this is, if development is to be assured, goals in this area should be specifically set.

From an appraisal as well as an operating management point of view, perhaps the greatest deficiency of management by objectives is that it appraises operating performance only. Not only is there a question of luck mentioned previously, but there are also other factors to appraise, notably an individual's *managerial* abilities. This is why the authors of this book feel that an adequate appraisal system must appraise performance as a manager as well as performance in setting and meeting goals.

APPRAISING MANAGERS AS MANAGERS

A number of companies have recognized the importance of evaluating the quality of a manager, although these have been relatively few. Some have been satisfied to ask for appraisal in such broad areas as planning, organizing, co-ordinating, leading, motivating, and controlling. Others have broken down these areas into such broad categories as, in the case of organizing, job assignments, clarity of staff, responsibilities and authorities, and delegation. One company, at least, the St. Regis Paper Company, aided managers in their appraisals by preparing and distributing a booklet on *Guidelines for Managing* which was really a brief summary of basic principles of management.[2] However, the standards thus far used for appraising managers as managers have seemed to be too broad and too susceptible to general and subjective judgment.

A Suggested Program

It has been the authors' position for many years that the most appropriate standards to be used for appraising managers as managers are the fundamentals of management. It is not enough to appraise a manager on such broad areas as the basic functions of the manager. While important, these are too broad to be used as standards of appraisal. To do as the St. Regis Paper Company has done and give these terms some concrete meaning is a help. But for appraisal we should go further.

The best approach the authors have found is to utilize the basic concepts and principles of management as standards. If they are basic, as they have been found to be in a wide variety of managerial positions and cultures, they should serve as reasonably good standards. As crude as they may be and even though some judgment may be necessary in applying them to practice, they do give the evaluator some bench marks to weigh whether his subordinates understand and are following out the functions of managing. They are definitely more specific and applicable than evaluations based on such broad standards as work habits, integrity, cooperation, intelligence, judgment, or loyalty. They at least focus attention on what may be expected of a manager *as a manager*. And, when taken in conjunction with the performance of plans and goals, they can help remove much of the weakness in many management appraisal systems.

In brief, the program involves breaking down the functions of the manager as done in this book, and then each function is dealt with by a series of questions designed to reflect the most important fundamentals of managing in each area. While the total list of key questions, the form used, the system of ratings,

[2] As reported in W. S. Wikstrom, *Managing By and With Objectives* (New York: National Industrial Conference Board, Inc., 1968), pp. 38–56.

and instructions for operating the program are too extensive to be treated in this book,[3] some sample checkpoints may be given.

For example, in the area of planning, a manager would be rated by such check questions as the following:

Does he set for his departmental unit both short-term and long-term goals in verifiable terms that are related in a positive way to those of his superior and his company?

Does he understand the role of company policies in his decision making and assure that his subordinates do likewise?

Does he check his plans periodically to see if they are consistent with current expectations?

In choosing from among alternatives, does he recognize and give primary attention to those factors which are limiting or critical to the solution of a problem?

Also, in the area of organizing, such questions are asked as the following:

Does he delegate authority to his subordinates on the basis of results expected of them?

When he has delegated authority to his subordinate, does he refrain from making decisions in that area?

Does he regularly teach his subordinates, or otherwise make sure that his subordinates understand, the nature of line and staff relationships?

Does he distinguish in his operations between lines of authority and lines of information?

The other areas of managing are dealt with similarly for a total of seventy-three checkpoints over the five areas of planning, organizing, staffing, directing, and controlling. Also, in order to solve the problem of semantics so prevalent among managers, practitioners are advised to use as a guide a standard book on management with reference to where every check question is treated in the book.

In developing this system, it was hoped to make the ratings completely objective by designing the checkpoints and questions to be "go-no-go," that is, the manager being rated either did or did not. This was not found to be possible, and degrees of "how well" had to be inserted in each question, with rankings from 0 ("inadequate") to 5 ("superior"). In order to give the numerical ratings some rigor, however, each is defined; "superior," for example, is defined as "a standard of performance which could not be improved upon under any circumstances or conditions known to the rater." Other attempts to reduce subjectivity and lack of discrimination in rating include (1) the requirement in the final annual appraisal that incident examples be given to support certain ratings, (2) review of ratings by the superior's superior, and (3) raters being

---

[3] All these may be found in H. Koontz, *Appraising Managers as Managers* (New York: McGraw-Hill Book Company, 1971), chaps. 5 and 6 and appendixes 2–5.

informed that their evaluation would depend in part on discrimination shown in ratings. A degree of objectivity is also introduced by the number and specific nature of the checkpoint questions.

Advantages

Clinical experience with the program in a multinational company showed certain advantages. By focusing on the essentials of management, this method of evaluation gives operational meaning to what management really is. Also, by use of a standard reference text for interpretation of concepts and terms, many of the semantic and communication difficulties so commonly encountered are removed. Such things as "variable budgets," "verifiable objectives," and "delegation" take on consistent meaning. Likewise, many management techniques become uniformly understood.

The system, furthermore, has proved to be a tool for management development by calling to a manager's attention certain basics that he may have long disregarded or not understood. In addition, the approach has been found useful in pinpointing areas where weaknesses exist and to which development should be pointed. Finally, as intended, the program acts as a supplement and a check on appraising managers with respect to their effectiveness in setting and achieving goals. If a manager has an outstanding performance in goal accomplishment but is found to be a less than average manager, those in charge would look for the reason. Normally, one would expect a truly effective manager to be also effective in meeting goals.

Weaknesses

There are, however, a number of weaknesses or shortcomings in the approach. It only applies to managerial aspects of a given position and not to such technical qualifications as marketing or engineering abilities that might also be important. These, however, should be weighed on the basis of goals selected and achieved. There is also the problem of the apparent complexity of the total of seventy-three checkpoints; to rate on all these does take time, but it is believed that the time is well spent.

Perhaps the major shortcoming of the proposed approach to appraising managers as managers is the question of subjectivity. As was mentioned earlier, it was found that some subjectivity in rating each checkpoint was unavoidable. However, the program still has a high degree of objectivity and is far more objective than having managers appraised on the broader areas of the managerial functions, as has been common in the few cases where attempts have been made to appraise managers as managers. At least the checkpoints are specific and go to the essentials of managing.

APPRAISAL AND THE MANAGEMENT INVENTORY

Annual evaluations of the over-all efficiency of managers are important in addition to their use as a basis for appraisal or merit review. They provide the data for the development of a manager inventory which reflects specific information about every manager in terms of his promotability. Viewed from this point, both superior and subordinate are in a position to understand the implications of the evaluations. The superior can review the need of the enterprise for managers and the action he must take to safeguard its future in this regard; the subordinate can determine the status of his career in management.

Inventory Chart

Every responsible manager needs to know where he stands with respect to the capability of present subordinates and their potential for promotion. This knowledge is necessary to his staffing function. The periodic appraisal of subordinates provides information on age, efficiency, and readiness for promotion. For an over-all perspective of where he stands, an inventory chart is recommended. This is simply an organization chart of his unit with all managerial positions indicated and keyed as to the promotability of each incumbent.

Figure 23.2 is a typical inventory chart. At a glance the controller can see where he stands with respect to his staffing function. His own successor is the manager of general accounting, and this man in turn has a successor ready for promotion. Supporting him in turn is a subordinate who will be ready for promotion in one year, but below him is one man who does not have potential, and two new hires.

The cost accounting manager represents the all-too-frequent case of a man who is acceptable but not promotable. He stands in the way of one subordinate who is promotable now. The remaining men in this department represent extremes of nonpromotability and good potential. Over-all, the staffing pattern in this department is not satisfactory.

The manager of budget and analysis has considerable development to accomplish before he is ready for promotion. He does not have an available successor. And to complicate matters, no further potential exists among his remaining subordinates.

Contract pricing portends some problems. Its manager is not promotable but he has good potential in his subordinates.

Actions to Be Taken

On the basis of the inventory chart, a plan of action can be developed, geared to both the short term and the long run. For the short term, action may be taken to replace an unsatisfactory manager, to begin the training of a successor for the next higher level, to transfer a manager in order to broaden his experience specifically for his next promotion, or to transfer surplus men, now ready for promotion, to other departments where managerial vacancies exist.

For the long run, age may play as important a part as efficiency.[4] If it is true, as is sometimes asserted, that a manager's most productive age is from

[4]J. F. Garde, Jr., "The Insidious Management Cycle," *Dun's Review*, vol. 79, no. 4 (April, 1962).

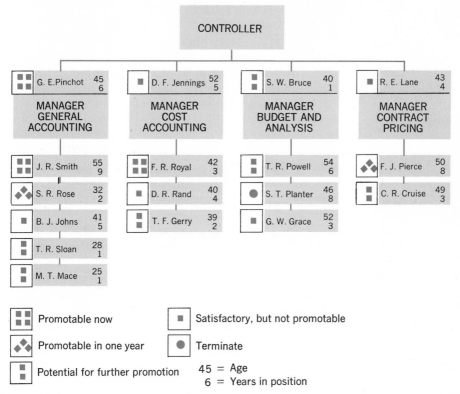

Figure 23-2 *Manager inventory chart.*

forty to sixty years, then it is important to the future welfare of a firm that its managers—especially its top managers—be at varying ages above forty. If they are not scattered along the productive age range, it might happen that in ten years' time all top managers would be over sixty. Such a situation may be avoided by judicious promotion of persons in the right age group. The long-run plan of action for qualified managers needs to be integrated with short-run action. For instance, it is clearly inadvisable in the short run to identify a backup man (successor) who is the same age as his immediate superior, for they will both grow old together. It may be clearly advantageous to name as immediate successor a man even older than the incumbent and to begin to train as ultimate successor a third man a number of years his junior. This arrangement will satisfy the short-run requirements for a trained successor in the person of the older man, and the long-run needs in the person of the trainee.

One question that the manager inventory chart does not answer is: Promotable to what? It is not enough to become aware that a man is promotable. Provision needs to be made for its actualization. One may take the position that, with respect to his area of specialization, the promotable person in the controller's division or in the manufacturing division simply remains there until an opening occurs vertically above him. Is he really promotable if he happens to be listed in this way by the production control manager and an opening occurs for a manager of industrial engineering or general superintendent? In the case of Figure 23.2, is J. R. Smith in general accounting promotable to manager of budget and analysis?

This common difficulty of the promotion process can scarcely ever be solved in the short run. It is essential for the top managers of every enterprise to insist that young men with managerial potential be identified in the very early years of their employment and be given real opportunities to broaden their experience through lateral assignments. Breadth of experience is essential during the years *prior to* succession to upper managerial positions. From a practical point of view, at lower levels of management such experience might be provided on an intradivisional, but not interdivisional, basis. This practice will maintain the integrity of the divisional staffing plan and permit the promotable manager to be an active candidate for interdepartmental openings. Interdivisional training for promotable candidates for upper-level management positions is considered in the following chapter.

Another difficulty encountered in large enterprises is the hoarding of promotable men by their immediate superiors. Quite naturally, these managers are averse to depriving themselves of able subordinates, but the interests of the enterprise are paramount. Therefore, vigorous surveillance of the manager inventory must be maintained by the division manager. Only he can make the basic staffing strategy of top managers work.

Importance in Staffing

By systematically examining his staffing needs, a manager will give adequate attention to this often-neglected function. He will be alert to the requirements for potential managers to be at specific levels of preparation at a given time, and he will funnel off to other departments excess subordinates *before* they become disenchanted with their prospects and leave the firm.

This manager will also be serving the best interests of his subordinates, who want to know their prospects so that they can determine whether *their* needs may best be served by remaining with the firm or by leaving to take advantage of other opportunities. They can now be answered with confidence by their superior. He has a moral responsibility to be honest in his answer, even though this may mean that the subordinate will resign. This situation is not seen fairly by superior managers who think only of what the resignation will mean to themselves. They should realize that the highest good for the company may arise from recognition of the career interests of the individual.

TOWARD MORE EFFECTIVE APPRAISALS

After many years of frustration from traditional approaches to managerial appraisal, primarily based on evaluating traits, there is real hope that this key aspect of managing is becoming meaningful. Appraisal of managerial ability based on performance against preselected verifiable objectives is a tremendous step in the right direction. It concentrates, as it should, on what a manager *does* rather than on what someone subjectively thinks of him. When utilized as a standard for evaluation along with appraisal of a manager as a manager, there is hope that we are, at long last, beginning to approach the area of evaluating managers with logic and effectiveness.

But devices and approaches will not solve the problem. There is ever the danger that people will adopt techniques without accompanying them with an understanding of the philosophy back of them, without the tools and assistance subordinates need, the hard work, time, commitment, and leadership to make them work. No management technique is self-actuating. It requires patient leadership, intelligent application, and willingness to take the time required.

In the area of managerial appraisal, the results should be worth the effort required. As has been said before, there is little dispute that the quality and vigor of managers make the difference, at least in long-term success of any kind of enterprise. There should likewise be no doubt that if we are to have competent managers in an enterprise, this cannot happen without effective selection, appraisal, development, and motivation. These are all links in the chain, and appraisal has historically been the weakest one.

FOR DISCUSSION

1. Do you think managers should be appraised regularly? If so, how?
2. What problems may arise from the fact that different managers, on the same level, appraise differently, some generally rating higher than others?
3. Many firms still evaluate middle and top managers on such personality factors as aggressiveness, cooperation, leadership, and attitude. Do you think this makes any sense?
4. The argument has been made in this book for appraising managers on their ability to execute their functions. Should anything more be expected of them?
5. How do you feel about an appraisal system based upon results expected and realized? Would you prefer to be appraised on this basis? If not, why?
6. Do you feel that a manager inventory should be kept confidential?
7. What is your assessment of the degree of objectivity or subjectivity involved in the appraisal approaches suggested in this chapter? Can you suggest any further means for making appraisal more objective?

24
development
and training
of managers

Good executives look to the future. Every firm has the responsibility of helping in the development of men who have the requisite potential to contribute their full measure to the management of an enterprise.

In the days before World War II when management was less clearly understood, the generally accepted viewpoint was that somehow or other men acquired whatever it took to be a manager. Given sufficient exposure to practical experience, by starting from the humble jobs made so famous by Horatio Alger and by Sir Joseph Porter of *Pinafore*, the man destined to rise to high managerial position was thought to be marked in some fashion easily distinguished by his superiors, who saw to it that he was put through the fires of nasty jobs and fierce trials to be properly chastened for the welcome burdens of later positions of great trust.

This dreamworld of the business tycoon, based on an economy of Victorian vintage, was rudely shattered in the depression years of the 1930s. Executives lost their aura of omnipotence. Probably for the first time in industrial history they began to question their views about business success and, by the time World War II was upon them, decided they needed help fast. The first answer was training at the foreman level. At middle and higher levels, men were simply assigned responsible jobs with a prayer that nothing too disastrous would happen.

The lessons learned from these experiences were so valuable that the idea that managers possessed special skills which could be explained took firm hold. By 1950 training was at a critical stage. Although it was then making inroads into enterprises heretofore firm in their skepticism, it was also being reexamined with a critical eye by its early adherents. The conclusions seemed to be that it had value but had been marred by the barnacles of fad and ignorance.

MANAGER DEVELOPMENT VERSUS MANAGERIAL TRAINING

Terminology is ambiguous in this area, but it need not be. The authors of this book use "manager development" to refer to the progress a manager makes in learning how to manage, and "managerial training" to refer to the programs devised to facilitate this learning process. Thus, the firm is seen as providing training opportunities; the manager, as developing proficiency by interfacing practical experience and training.

THE NATURE OF MANAGER DEVELOPMENT

Manager development is an elusive concept. Like education, it is associated with stages of progress, but unlike education the stages are not marked by certificates and academic degrees. There is no objective standard or level of proficiency with which one might compare attainments and be able to say that he is a developed supervisor, a developed division manager, a developed hospital administrator, or a developed general officer. Clearly, manager development is not something *to have achieved* because none would admit that development is ever complete any more than one would say that one's education is complete.

If one thinks of manager development as a never-ending process, he is at once confronted with the phenomenon of "topping-out." Some managers seem to reach a point in their development beyond which they are unable to grow. It is probable that all manager selections are made with some trepidation. Sometimes, to the great pleasure of all concerned, the individual seems to blossom out and handle the more responsible position with élan. Such a man is developing, but is he developed? On the other hand, some selections turn out to be failures. Can it be said that such men are developed? Or cannot be developed?

Attempts to view manager development in these terms seem to offer little encouragement. Perhaps the concept of objective standards is inappropriate. It may be more fruitful to think of manager development in terms of the individual. If this were the viewpoint, then the developed manager would be one whose capabilities are fully utilized.

Assuming that development is the process of individual growth toward the full utilization of managerial capabilities, the determinants of progress are probably three. The first is a high order of intelligence and the desire to manage. These matters were considered in Chapter 22. The second factor is the way men learn. The manager has a need to know the principles underlying his functions and how to apply them. Whatever the proportions of science and art in managing, and some would say 1 in 4, it is certain that principles can be taught in a short time but that skill in their application can only come from years of practice. Provisions for learning opportunities are the subject of the present chapter. The third determinant is a chance to manage. One *has* to be appointed to a position before he can practice management, but the determinants of an opportunity to manage run the gamut of all the motives of human nature. Even what "ought" to be is not clear.

CURRENT APPROACHES TO MANAGER TRAINING

Executives who have given thought to manager training have displayed considerable ingenuity in devising ways of achieving results. Some have relied exclusively on certain favored methods, while others have combined any promising approaches that appeared to fit their needs. The following analysis of the more prominent techniques describes their merits and shortcomings.

Planned Progression

The technique of planned progression is concerned with blueprinting the path of promotion that lies before the manager in any given position. Sometimes the path is traced through the successive levels of the functional organization structure. Thus, the foreman may be told that his path will lead to general foreman, superintendent, works manager, and production manager. Or the supervisor in the sales department may be informed that his path of promotion lies through branch manager, district manager, and assistant general sales manager to sales manager. This, however, gives an overoptimistic picture to the subordinate; it encourages undue specialization; and it provides insufficient training.

There is, however, a concept of planned progression with proved merit. A committee, responsible for developing candidates for promotion, can settle in conference the alternate positions into which a man occupying a given post may be promoted. Thus, three or four positions at the next higher level in a number of different departments may be specified. If this progression *into the next higher level* is worked out for *each* candidate, the advantages are obvious. The superior who is asked about promotion opportunities will have a definite answer to give; the alternatives are broad enough to provide for needed diversity of experience; and the candidate can be informed with some exactitude about the requirements of the next alternative positions and the most appropriate means of achieving them. From the psychological point of view planned progression has the merit of being geared to immediate rather than distant opportunities.

Job Rotation

Few terms are as common in management literature as "job rotation," and it is safe to say that few are as misunderstood. In general, job rotation refers to a technique for providing diversified training. The questions are: Who is to be trained? Why? At what levels? Those concerned with the answers seem to have one or more of five potential situations in mind.

Rotation in nonsupervisory work Firms that confine job rotation to nonsupervisory work visualize the process as one in which selectees for management training are assigned to predetermined jobs within several departments for a given period of time. At the end of each stage, the selectees are reshuffled among the same group of jobs until all have had diversified experience. The trainees may learn how to sell, receive and mark merchandise. recruit and interview applicants, read blueprints, and write bills of materials. There are long lists of such jobs to be selected for their experience value and in which trainees will quickly earn their way. The evident purpose is to acquaint trainees with the range of activities undertaken by the firm.

There are several serious disadvantages to this type of job rotation. The trainee can learn the details of these work assignments in a short time, and keeping him on such jobs for weeks and months will add nothing to his progress. In fact, the actual selection of work for its experience value is extremely difficult. Furthermore, after the trainee has been rotated through the series of jobs, no one can guarantee him a supervisory position. If none is available, he is likely to leave the firm in discouragement. Or if a permanent opening occurs before he has completed the cycle, should he accept and thus miss the remainder of the program, or should he refuse and take his chances on a later opening? The first alternative fails to achieve the purpose of training; the second risks losing out entirely. Finally, the departments offering the training may object to bearing the allocated salary expense; and other employees, jealous of the opportunity provided trainees, may resent what they consider taking jobs away from the permanent help.

Rotation in observation assignments A second concept of job rotation allows trainees to observe a group of department managers on a rotating basis. Its purpose is to acquaint the trainee with the work of department heads. For the trainee, the advantages of this method include acquaintance with various techniques in handling diverse situations, the possibility of "selling" one's self to a given manager, and an opportunity to get a close-up of the work one thinks one wants to do. The firm, on the other hand, considers that it has developed a pool of potential managers.

There are disadvantages, however. Many department heads feel that the trainee does not know what to observe, that it is wasteful to watch the decision-making process in so many situations, and that the training expense should not be borne by the departments. As far as the trainee is concerned, there is a great gap between watching and doing, and there is a question whether he will be able to apply anything he has observed. This concept of job rotation, therefore, lacks the basic ingredient of practical experience.

Rotation among managerial training positions A third concept involves the designation of certain managerial positions, on the same level in the organization structure, as training stations, to be successively occupied by selectees. Although the positions are a regular part of the organization structure of the enterprise and, consequently, bona fide managerial posts, they are filled solely by successive trainees and not by promotion from lower-level jobs. The purpose of this type of rotation is to give trainees actual supervisory experience in a variety of positions in several departments.

There are two evident advantages of this type of rotation. First, the trainees obtain actual experience in managing, an important matter since it is the best known means of discovering whether they have leadership ability and good judgment. Secondly, the trainees develop an appreciation of the viewpoints of various departmental personnel and acquire, as well, an understanding of interdepartmental relationships.

The disadvantages of any plan to rotate trainees among predetermined supervisory positions include the difficulty of identifying appropriate positions for this purpose; the resentment of subordinates because these jobs are reserved for management trainees; and the frequent delay in making permanent assignments to those who have completed their training.

In deciding which supervisory posts may be appropriately reserved for training purposes, the value of the experience to be obtained must be weighed and some post found in which turnover would be rather unimportant. How long it will take a new man in these positions to become productive seems to depend upon the degree to which the department activities are standardized, the presence of experienced subordinates, and the stability of the operation. Posts that fit these requirements might include the supervision of accounts payable, personnel recruitment, production follow-up, and the requisitioning of raw materials.

No matter how much publicity is given the training program and the jobs reserved for training, it seems impossible to eliminate the resentment of qualified subordinates who are passed over when such positions are filled by trainees. The young and capable subordinate is almost certain to leave the firm in protest; the older subordinate, who would find openings elsewhere scarce, harbors a smoldering resentment against the trainees. Only the routine nature of the operation keeps it from disintegrating in hostility.

Finally, this type of rotation suffers from the disadvantage of all pool arrangements: those who complete their training are eager to be placed permanently; disillusion grows greater the longer the period of waiting.

Rotation in middle-level "assistant" positions   There are firms that conceive of job rotation as the process of shuffling managerial trainees among positions as assistant managers in several departments. The advantage for the men involved is the broadening of their experience at a high level. The firm gains from the creation of a pool of trainees for later appointment to department managerships.

As with other types of rotation, this does not solve the difficulties of permanently locating a man whose training is completed. It also creates considerable resentment among subordinates in the several departments. The most serious disadvantage concerns the type of training received. There is a good deal of difference between being a high-grade messenger or observer and making analyses and decisions for department managers. Clearly, if the "assistant" position involves the latter kind of experience, it is valuable training.

Unspecified rotation in managerial positions   By resorting to an unspecified, and often unplanned, rotation of managers, some companies have effectively used job rotation without encountering the difficulties enumerated in the alternative approaches outlined above. These companies make it a practice to move promising managers from one department or activity to another. These are often lateral rather than vertical moves and are made in the spirit of giving the manager a "permanent" job. Thus, a manager in the production department may be offered a position in sales and, later, one in finance or on an important staff. In each of these changes the manager is given no indication as to how long he will be in the job, and there is usually no specified time actually in the minds of those responsible for his training. The manager may be in the position for several years, and if he does not show promise of growth he may not be rotated further.

The purpose of this kind of program is to give managers responsible continuing experience in a variety of situations. It avoids the feeling, so prevalent in most kinds of job rotation, that the incumbent is on a visit. It likewise avoids making him look to his fellows like a "crown prince." And it eliminates the dangers and costs of reserving special managerial positions for training purposes. Indeed, this type of informal program appears to be the most effective kind of managerial job rotation.

Creation of "Assistant-to" Positions

The "assistant-to" position, frequently used as a training device, permits the trainee to broaden his viewpoint by exposing him to many areas of managerial practice. This technique should be by no means routine. The position may have been specially carved out for training purposes and may be eliminated after it has served this purpose. However, many needed and permanent "assistant-to" positions exist, and they are valuable posts for training the potential manager.

The advantage of "assistant-to" positions from the viewpoint of the superior is that he can most satisfactorily exercise his function as a teacher, tailoring the training period to the assistant's needs and making assignments to test his judgment. Facets of his experience that need buttressing can be filled out by carefully chosen tasks, and his decision-making and leadership ability can be tried in selected cases.

The disadvantage of this type of training procedure becomes apparent when the superior executive fails to teach properly. If he lacks understanding of the assistant's needs, if he is authoritarian, or if he feels that he is being pushed into this relationship, the training will certainly be poor and the trainee's position is likely to degenerate into a reviewing stand. Attention soon flags in repetitious exposure to activity in which the observer is charged with no duty. Able assistants, placed in such an environment, would soon be lost to the firm.[1]

Psychological Approaches to Training

During the past decade social scientists,[2] particularly psychologists, have been active in training experiments using two basic techniques, role playing and sensitivity training.

Role playing   This technique is commonly applied by clinical psychologists since they discovered that a patient appears to gain understanding of an emotionally disturbing situation when encouraged to act out the roles involved. As applied in enterprises with (we hope) normal people the purpose of role playing is to aid trainees to understand certain business problems and enable observers to evaluate various reactions to them. Thus, for the problem of handling grievances, two individuals from a class would be selected to act out the parts of employee and supervisor. When this situation is enacted by various pairs among the class and the techniques and results are discussed, the auditors are presumed to reach conclusions about the most effective means of handling similar situations.

There are several obvious drawbacks to this technique. It is not possible to recreate the environment of the work situation. The roles played have no necessary relation to actual practice, and, consequently, the players feel no practical *responsibility* for handling their roles realistically. Also, the technique is not subject to validation. On the other hand, it is an interesting device that may have some value in broadening the viewpoints of the participants.

Sensitivity training   This technique, with its variations, is based upon the experience of group psychotherapists that people with mild emotional disturbances can be helped through the device of group discussion. It has apparently been successful in the rehabilitation of war prisoners, delinquents, and alcoholics, and its practitioners believe that it can be successful in leadership training. Sensitivity training is well known in academic circles and many enterprises. Subjected to it, individuals become involved in a cathartic group experience which presumably results in self-knowledge and insights into interpersonal relationships. Out of this strong emotional experience one is supposed to gain an awareness valuable to his future behavior.

Since psychologists deal with people, their training activities have piqued the interest of human beings, which probably accounts for the great popularity

[1] See L. F. Urwick, *Profitably Using the General Staff Position in Business*, General Management Series No. 165 (New York: American Management Association, 1953), and C. O'Donnell, "The Role of the Assistant: A Modern Business Enigma," *California Management Review*, vol. 2, no. 3, pp. 65–69 (Spring, 1960).

[2] See I. L. Heckmann, Jr., and S. G. Huneryager, *Human Relations in Management* (Cincinnati: South-Western Publishing Company, 1960), pp. 748–753; R. J. House, "T-Group Training: Good or Bad?" *Business Horizons*, vol. 12, no. 6, pp. 69–78 (December, 1969).

of their techniques. As for sensitivity training, a wide variety of opinions of its value and place in management development may be found. Many participants claim tremendous benefits, particularly in understanding their impact on others. Other participants have reported virtually no benefit. And lasting benefits, especially if the participant returns to his pretraining environment, do not appear to be great. However, for those who understand, preferably in advance, what to expect and who can enter into this experience without too great a traumatic effect, it has often proved to be an interesting device. But still too little evidence exists to weigh it adequately as a management training tool.

Temporary Promotions

Although many firms may occasionally resort to temporary promotions, the use of this technique for training purposes entails difficult problems of organization. The large enterprise that desired to train a group of candidates by this method would need to make certain that a given number of departments or sections would be without a permanent head or that this position could be vacated on schedule, an arrangement obviously impossible. Nor would it be possible to assess personal responsibility for the conduct of departmental affairs.

On the other hand, the medium-sized and the small firm may find temporary promotion an ideal way to train a candidate. Since training in such firms is necessarily discontinuous, the man tapped for future greatness may very well be moved up to acting head when the permanent head is temporarily absent. The candidate would then presumably be responsible for departmental conduct during this period of service.

Certain drawbacks are inescapable. Is it possible to hold a man responsible for the conduct of a temporary position? Can the performance of a temporary appointee be evaluated? A large degree of drift or procrastination is permitted the occupant of any managerial position surrounded by well-known and tested policies and procedures. Furthermore, the attempt of a candidate to do something different, such as to reverse a previous decision or to introduce new working relationships, is quite unlikely to be productive of good results. If expectations are moderate in view of these limitations, temporary promotion can be useful, but it is much inferior to the real test of a permanent appointment.

Committees and Junior Boards

When used as a training technique, the committee and the "junior board" have come to be known as multiple management.[3] These committees are com-

---

[3] The original idea is commonly credited to McCormick and Company, Inc., Baltimore. See Charles McCormick, *Multiple Management* (New York: Harper & Row, Publishers, Incorporated, 1938).

posed of a group of middle-level managers, selected on the basis of merit ratings, who meet regularly to consider any proposal affecting the firm's welfare. Decisions reached by these "idea men" are forwarded to the responsible general officer of the firm, who may adopt, reject, or table them, refer them back for further consideration, or send them to the board of directors. The advantages claimed for this type of training are that the perspective of the committee members is broadened and a sense of responsibility for the welfare of the firm is developed.

Where this technique has been used, there have been strong overtones of paternalism exercised by senior officers, despite loud protests of noninterference. One cannot afford not to interfere when he designates the persons receiving the training, evaluates their deliberations, and promotes from among them. Perhaps the firm can "afford" to devote an enormous number of man-hours to the proposed solution of issues, especially when the candidates are investing their own time.

There is, of course, universal recognition of the value a manager may gain from membership on a regularly established company committee. The new junior man is soon likely to be placed in one or more of these groups. Here he acquires a broader viewpoint, develops an understanding of enterprise needs and purposes, and gets experience in leadership. But this is in the ordinary course of employment; it is not in any sense extracurricular.

Conference Programs

Another widely used training device is that of conference programs. This consists of group exposure to ideas developed by a leader or speaker. It is a direct and economical method of transmitting information that applies to all members of a group. Thus, a class of junior trainees or a new foreman group may be effectively instructed in the history of the firm, its purposes and policies, and its attitudes toward customers, employees, consumers, and other groups.

It is easy to overestimate the values derived from conference training. Its employment represents the adoption of time-honored teaching techniques and its failure often follows poor teaching methods and a lack of understanding of what can be taught by this means. It is as wrong to assume that any manager can teach in such conferences as to believe that any teacher can manage.

University Management Programs

In recent years many universities have organized courses, institutes, conferences, and extensive formal programs for the training of managers. These efforts may be as simple as offering an evening course for management students and as complex as offering a full graduate curriculum.

Such programs present opportunities for the exposition of management principles, a review of these principles in the light of practical experience, and explanation of new ideas with possible application to the enterprise. There is the added advantage of valuable group contacts.

The drawbacks of university management programs are related to the quality of the instructor and of the subject matter. Managers, in their eagerness to learn, are often misled by extravagant claims. Unless those who teach in these programs *really* know what managing is, the "training" is all too likely to degenerate into social clubs or the teaching of specialized skills in engineering, accounting, statistics, human relations, or other areas.

American Management Association's Workshop Program

The educational efforts of the American Management Association include workshop or seminar instruction in an unusually wide variety of subjects. In most instances, the particular subject is narrowly defined so that it can be handled effectively in one to three days. Classes are confined to a limited number of participants, and the discussion method is employed to facilitate interchange of varied experiences. The leader of each workshop is usually an operating business executive who has had considerable experience.

The advantages of such training are knowledgeable leadership, cooperative learning through the exchange of ideas, and concentration upon a limited subject. The program has certain disadvantages, however. Most of the sessions are held in a few large cities, restricted problems are treated from the viewpoint of "how to do it," and there is a failure to generalize on the basis of principles applicable to all enterprises.

Needed: A Philosophy of Training

In summary, let us reflect upon the wide variety of approaches and subject matter offered under a heading such as "management training." Do the "trainers" really know what they are doing, or are they simply taking advantage of the willingness of enterprises to pay for anything called "training"? The authors of this book are not the only ones who raise this question. After sending forth their managers to be "trained," top executives are beginning to ask for a demonstrable payoff from the training dollar. They have paid huge sums to get their men registered in anything called "training," and it is time to consider whether they are getting their money's worth.

It would appear, from two decades' experience with various schemes, that there is a need for a philosophy of training. This philosophy should rest on principles from which there can be projected specific kinds of opportunities for men who want to be managers or want to improve their management skills.

MANAGEMENT TRAINING: SUGGESTED PROGRAM

In formulating a training program, there are certain elements of which we have some knowledge: purpose, general premises, the nature of positions at various levels, past experience in training, and the nature of man himself.

Building upon these is precarious, because no theory of learning is generally accepted. Still, there is a pressing need to examine this matter as comprehensively as possible, for managers must manage even while theorists theorize.

Purpose

One reason for the dissatisfaction managers feel for training programs is that the *over-all* purpose is rarely clarified. The major purpose of training should be the creation of opportunities for managers to develop knowledge and skills directly related to the execution of their functions.

Premises

Selection of the training methodology is served by a specific exposition of the basic facts or assumptions on which a program rests. The validity of the training programs rests on seven premises.

1. Top managers must actively support the program   The support of top managers, such as presidents and executive vice-presidents, is essential if a program is to apply throughout the enterprise at all levels. Subordinates look to their superiors for signals as to what to support enthusiastically and what to ignore. If the superiors' signal indicates understanding and support of a training program, the program will be actively embraced by subordinates.

2. Top managers should be trained first   In order for top managers to prove their interest in the program, training should start at the top. Top managers who are opposed to this are in a poor position to encourage training. And yet it may be too optimistic to expect many company presidents to submit to training;[4] those who have reached their position without a comprehensive philosophy of management are almost sure to feel that training is probably unnecessary, especially for themselves. Thus, the best that can be expected is that their more or less immediate subordinates will take kindly to the exercise. When they have had training in management principles, there is no problem, for they are certain to support a feasible program. If they have not had such training, they should certainly be exposed to it prior to implementing the program at lower levels. Only then will their support be characterized by understanding and vigor. Awareness must precede action.

3. Learning is voluntary   Since there is no generally accepted theory of learning, this premise must be qualified. Some psychologists feel that learning occurs through emotional experience, as on the level of fear. For instance, many of us can remember our refusal to learn to swim, but, on being thrown into the water, we learned—involuntarily, as it were—because of our fear of drowning. Similarly we, as all animals, learn through unstudied observation, or chance.

---

[4] There are a few programs offered "for presidents only."

However, these basic motivations have little to do with the learning processes of an enterprise manager. Even clarity and brilliance in teaching won't make a man learn; you can lead him to class, but you can't make him think.

4. Training needs vary with manager levels On an organization chart, managers are classified by levels. Top management usually includes the general managers and their immediate line and service subordinates. Thus, in a functionally organized firm, the top managers would include the president and the heads of functional divisions such as marketing, manufacturing, engineering, finance, and accounting. At the other extreme are front-line supervisors—managers on the lowest administrative level, who stand between their superiors and workers and technicians. Between these two clearly defined levels stand the inchoate middle managers who may occupy one or more levels of management.

The training needs of these three groups are somewhat different. The front-line supervisor must learn to carry out efficiently the programs allotted to his shop or section; the middle managers, having been supervisors, stand to benefit most by learning management theory; and the top managers, who are candidates for general management positions, need a broader and deeper understanding of the firm and its environment as well as the theory and techniques of management.

5. Training needs determine methods Training needs should be satisfied optimally, and the methods chosen should be most effective for the purpose. The needs of the three levels of managers should be specifically identified and the most economical and precise method of fulfilling them selected.

6. Methods must be effective at all levels It will not do for training methods to be ineffective for front-line supervisors but effective for middle managers. Poor results at any level would make promotion from within a hazardous process. Managers should prove themselves at each successive level.

7. Theory and practice must go hand in hand Learning what a manager does, does not make a manager. It is one thing, in halls of learning, to suggest that managers should make subordinates happy, that authority relationships should be turned upside down, or that subordinates must sometimes revolt against the formal organization. Academicians can do this, because they have little responsibility for results. It is also one thing to demonstrate budget making and to lecture on a philosophy of management. It is quite another to demonstrate proficiency in management when theory is applied to actual environments calling for the attainment of goals. This takes meaningful practice, for which theoretical training is no substitute. Consequently, training is a coin, one side of which is the teaching of theory and the demonstration of techniques, the other, the actual practice of management.

THE PROGRAM ITSELF

Based upon the foregoing premises, a practical program can be constructed to provide learning opportunities for aspiring managers at the front-line, middle, and top-management levels and—within each of these categories—for individual managers to satisfy specific personal requirements.

Front-line Supervisory Training

Candidates for front-line supervisory positions and incumbent supervisors need the same kind of training opportunities.

Objective   Men need to know how to develop and carry out approved programs within a budget, to obtain and use service and staff help, and to meet the requirements of their superior managers. In each category they need special information about the firm, the division, the department, and the section.

Programs are needed wherever supervisors are found, whether it be in scheduling, engineering drawing, area sales and service, record keeping and financial reporting, servicing delinquent accounts, or purchasing. Every supervisor engages in certain activities such as recruiting, training, and motivating subordinates; providing for adequate space and equipment; integrating operation rates with the requirements of other departments; selecting and training a successor; reporting progress and anticipating trouble; carrying out the provisions of the labor contract; and keeping an eye on public relations.

Technique   On-the-job training by the incumbent supervisor is best, if he has the interest and patience, because no one knows the job better.

From an organizational point of view, there is great merit in having a special training slot created and titled "assistant to the supervisor,"[5] and placing the trainee in this position. This has the advantages of cutting off his responsibility for technical assignments, permitting full attention to the learning process, and keeping him available for instruction.

The training technique recommended here is the time-honored and proved one of explanation, demonstration, practice, and critique. The supervisor explains why an activity is performed, demonstrates it, has the trainee practice it under supervision, and criticizes the performance until it is mastered. This works well with respect to the areas of procedures and policies, organizational interrelationships, budget formation and other planning activity, control processes, and to some extent the hiring of technicians (skilled nonmanagers). It is less effective in areas of interpersonal relationships, such as communication, instruction and motivation of subordinates, and cooperation and competition with peers. Here there is no science, no generally accepted guiding principle. In these areas the supervisor can but explain the techniques which work well for him; he cannot instruct the trainee to go and

[5] For more detail on this suggestion see C. O'Donnell, "The Role of the Assistant: A Modern Business Enigma," *California Management Review*, vol. 2, no. 3, pp. 65–69 (Spring, 1960).

do likewise, because the techniques are personal, depending partly on character and personality, and may not work for others. The trainee knows that he must communicate, instruct and motivate, cooperate, compete, and perhaps oppose, but his learning will come from trial and evaluation, followed by correction and more trial and evaluation, until workable techniques result. He will find that even empathy and the golden rule—the best and most generalized guides available for interpersonal relationships—need, at times, to be supplemented by discipline and by strategies of attack and retreat, in order to achieve department goals.

Specific problems Specific problems center on both instructor and trainees. In regard to the instructor, his effectiveness will depend on his ability to teach. If among professional educators teaching ability varies from poor to excellent, among supervisors there will be similar variation. The question is whether the poor teacher should be permitted to instruct. If there is no alternative, the answer must be affirmative and the instruction accomplished under the watchful eye of the supervisor's superior. But in many firms, and especially within divisions of firms where there is no technological barrier, it is a good practice to identify the able instructors among the supervisors and have them train all candidates. This is readily done, for it is almost as easy to train two or three men in "assistant-to" positions as it is to train one.

In regard to trainees, there will be some who fail to learn. These, of course, should be removed from their trainee position and permitted either to return to their former post, to transfer, or to resign. Those who satisfactorily complete training will be ready for assignment as supervisors, but if there are no openings they will be on a stand-by basis which may require them to return to their old jobs. This is far from satisfactory if it involves much waiting, because the men are likely to become restless and to terminate. As a consequence, enterprise managers try to keep the number of trainees at a minimum or to adopt an expansionist policy in order to absorb surplus managers.

When the number of trainees is minimized, those who want to manage but have little prospect of being trained are very likely to terminate. This is why college men so often leave their first employer summarily. Again, there are others who think they do not want a management career and who continue in nonmanagement positions until they reach the top of their salary brackets. After perhaps ten years of this, they suddenly decide they want to manage. Engineers typically have this experience.

The refusal of enterprise managers to train able subordinates is inexcusable. The manager has a moral responsibility to train, or to provide training opportunities, for every *qualified* subordinate,[6] irrespective of number. Why? Because it is a national concern that every man be permitted to develop his

---

[6] That is, those who are acceptable on the basis of a screening process. The problems, however, are even more complex than may appear. Screening standards are likely to be flexible. As in every activity, from sports to education, to business, standards are more strict the more candidates there are. Another aspect of this problem is that one never knows exactly how many potential candidates will be needed. In practice, the manager does his best to train good men and help the surplus to transfer if this seems best for their careers.

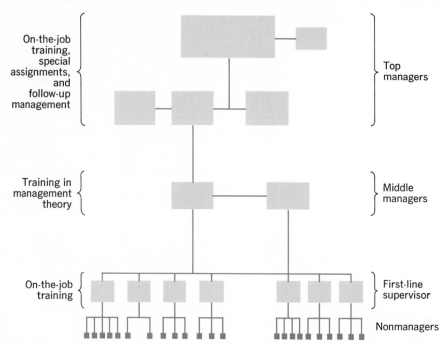

Figure 24.1 *Training methods for three levels of management. Training for first-line supervision is most often done on the job by operating supervisors who can explain, demonstrate, and criticize. If possible, the trainee should experience all the activities and functions of his future job. After some years of supervisory experience, the same man may be selected for a middle-management position. At this point he should receive thorough training in the theory of management. This can be done effectively in formal training sessions. When a man at the middle-management level is promoted to a top-management position, the most appropriate training is again on-the-job, although refresher work is often useful. Such training can often be best accomplished by appointing the individual as an assistant to executives in a wide variety of top-level positions or appointing him to a position in which he performs all varieties of top-level work, though not at the very highest level.*

socially approved capabilities whatever they may be. Only the enterprise can provide full opportunities for management development.

    Practice of supervision   At the point where a trainee is assigned to a supervisory position, the practice of management begins. Over a range of time of some several years, the new incumbent practices, with full responsibility for results, what he has learned about supervision and refines his peculiar techniques of interpersonal relationships. His further career depends upon his developed skills, for an unsuccessful supervisor must be demoted, transferred, or terminated; the average performer will be acceptable at the front-line level but will have no promotability; and the outstanding men will become candidates for promotion to middle-management positions.

Middle-management Training

The men training to enter the middle-management group are generally supervisors who have had several years of successful on-the-job practice. They will most likely have achieved specified goals in such major matters as production, expense control, budgeting, recruiting, training and directing subordinates, and dealing with peers and superiors. What further development is required of these men?

Objective   These men stand most in need of a knowledge of management theory. True, they will have spent a great deal of time developing techniques of directing, achieving teamwork among subordinates, handling grievances, fitting specific skills to program requirements, planning budget proposals, and reporting progress. Thus, on the practical side, there is much about management that they know informally.

Now, when they are about to manage managers and not technicians, they will find themselves removed from close contact with the people who actually do the work. No longer can they rely so much on their technical proficiency to get things done. To manage managers they particularly need a comprehensive understanding of the functions of managers because these are the means they must utilize to accomplish their jobs.

Technique   To teach the theory of management, it is best to borrow the technique employed for the same purpose in our universities. Basically, this consists of lectures, discussions of theory, and case studies relating to enterprise functions and general management. It is applicable to groups ranging from ten to forty, and its effectiveness depends on timing, location, and the instructors.

Timing relates to the relative net advantages of live-in courses, in which the participant devotes from a week to three months full time to his training, as opposed to part-time courses, in which instruction is given on an after-working-hours basis. Either type can fail or succeed, and there are variations of the two extremes. The amount of time required obviously depends on the scope of the curriculum, the efficiency of the instructor, and the aptitude of the students. It is probable that sharply diminishing returns will be encountered after three full weeks, even under optimum circumstances, because concentrated and continuous mental effort is fatiguing; there is a limit to what can be learned in a given period of time; and trainees long disassociated from the environment of their firms grow restless, and their learning tends to become an experience separate from the realities of their jobs.

The relative quality of results from different course formats is still uncertain.[7] Full-time training permits a participant to concentrate on the intellectual fare, get to know his colleagues, and avoid the daily problems at the plant. On the other hand, material presented too fast to be absorbed is not

[7] See R. M. Powell, *The Role and Impact of the Part-time University Program in Executive Education: A Case Study* (Los Angeles: Division of Research, Graduate School of Business Administration, University of California, 1962).

learned. Weekly exposure to instruction in the same subject matter has the great advantage of permitting trainees the opportunity to think through and perhaps apply on their jobs what is learned from week to week; it also permits training of men who could not be spared to attend a live-in course.

The management of the training program may also be either external or internal to the firm. From an economic point of view, the enterprise seeking to train one or a few middle managers will necessarily apply for admission to university-, association-, or consultant-managed courses. There the trainees will mix with those from other enterprises. On the other hand, large firms with many men to be trained sometimes establish their own programs for their exclusive use, using owned or leased facilities and inside or outside instructors. The type of program management does not seem to be critical in terms of results achieved. There are failures as well as successes in both external and internal forms, depending on subject matter and the quality of instruction.

Again, who should teach? Echoes of this question have sounded throughout this discussion of training, because, assuming that proper objectives and subject matter have been selected, success depends largely on the instructor. Lack of appreciation of this simple point has permitted use of the ill-equipped, the charlatans, the men who simply can't teach, the actors with irrelevant gimmicks. Surely, it should be obvious that the successful instructor knows his material and teaches it with confidence, skill, and insight, and thereby attracts the attention of his students and inspires them to learn, apply what they learn, and become themselves creative. Such instructors are rare, as every college student knows, but they should be deliberately sought, for they are much more effective in encouraging men to develop than are those chosen solely for books they have written, the school they represent, the managing experience they have had, or convenience.

Top-management Training

The men to be trained at this level are normally functional, plant, and division managers who are candidates for general management positions designated by such titles as general manager, executive vice-president, or president. Assuming that they have had training comparable to that suggested for front-line and middle managers, plus enough years of practical management experience to create an emerging maturity, the problem becomes one of determining their needs for additional training and the best means of providing it.

Objective What additional knowledge should a successful division manager have in order to manage a whole enterprise? Functional managers who have stepped up the promotion ladder within their division—controllers coming up through accounting, sales managers through marketing, engineering directors through engineering—require training in the management of functions which are strange to them. Although a director of engineering may have learned something about accounting, he normally has no deep understanding of the controller's management problems. The manager of a plant organized on a product-line basis is in an entirely different position. He has functional subordinates reporting to him and thus is already knowledgeable in these areas. However, all potential top managers have some need for training, whether it be in labor relations, in relations with the financial community, trade association work, governmental relations such as negotiation and perhaps lobbying, or foreign relations.

Although it is assumed here that top managers have a substantial grounding in the fundamentals and techniques of management, unfortunately this is not always the case. Moreover, the knowledge and technical aspects of managing are rapidly changing and the perceptive top manager will never assume that his education in management is complete. Consequently, one of the objectives of top-management training should be the review of management theory and principles and the updating of knowledge and technical developments in managing.

Technique The basic technique recommended is on-the-job training, supplemented by flexible variations such as special seminars and guided reading. Should one be available, a concentrated seminar of a week or two consisting of management theory and new techniques and designed especially for top managers would be highly desirable for those preparing to go into top management.

In the case of the functional manager, he should be relieved of his job and should enter a deliberate program of learning the jobs of his peers. Thus, the head of manufacturing needs to understand in depth the operations of marketing, engineering, and accounting. Two alternatives are available: he may be slipped into "assistant-to" positions and receive direct instruction from the department head of each of the functions to be studied or act for a period as assistant to the chief executive.

Or, as some enterprises do, he may be placed in direct control of the function to be learned and, for a year, be responsible for its operation. The deficiencies of the latter alternative are that no instruction beyond the superior's normal direction is available, and that it is a rare function which can survive for a year while its head is training elsewhere or which can operate while its trainee-head is learning. Consequently, the first alternative is much the better in terms of quality of results and the continuing efficiency of the functional operation.

If the "assistant-to" device is used, there is the question whether to leave open the old position of the trainee, in anticipation of his temporary return, or to fill it with another and rely on the ability of the firm to absorb the newly trained man in a general management position. The second alternative is recommended, because it would be unwise to have the old position without an active head during the internal training period. And not many enterprises could live under a program which embodied the rotation of several functional heads.

Training in its external aspects can be most effectively accomplished through special assignments. The trainee may participate in contract negotiation or renegotiation, in union bargaining, in trade association assignments, or he may be sent abroad to survey a market or run a foreign subsidiary. No training could be more effective than this exposure to actual responsibility for operations.

The number of trainees for general management positions would likely be small, possibly limited to one or two, occasionally none at all. The actual number at a given time would depend on the needs of the enterprise for available successors or to fill vacant positions. There would be few of these unless a vigorous expansion program were being followed or the firm were quite large. As a consequence, the dangers of uncertainty and change due to the training program would always be minimal.

If the training program were looked upon as a necessary exercise grudgingly undertaken and happily concluded, its value would be largely lost. Such an attitude would reflect managerial disinterest, and nothing kills an activity faster than executive indifference. Training is a continuing process which lasts a lifetime.

FOLLOW-UP TRAINING

So many executives look upon a formal program as the end of training that it seems necessary to answer the question: After formal training, what should we do? Follow-up training is achieved by coaching, refresher courses, and personal reflection upon the meaning of practical experience.

Coaching

As a training technique, coaching begins when a subordinate is promoted to a managerial position. It is a continuing process that is essential for all subordinates, whether they are titled supervisors, managers, or vice-presidents. Perhaps coaching is most effective when an individual has had other formal or informal training, and in this sense it may properly be looked upon as a follow-up training technique.

Coaching is face-to-face counseling. Its success depends upon the proper combination of personal qualities of superior and subordinate and upon the environment. The superior takes pride in grooming able managers, develops the ability and patience to teach, and delegates authority wisely. The subordinate should have confidence in his superior, be interested in his own work, analytical in his approach to problems, and should possess the strength of character to use his authority. The environment for successful coaching requires easy access to the superior.

Such counseling is a good way for a subordinate to become oriented in his job. It helps him understand the way his superior looks at interdepartmental relationships and personalities. Analysis of a specific performance gives both superior and subordinate an opportunity to learn why the results were good or bad. The superior can then demonstrate the importance of considering alternative ways and give the trainee some idea of how to weigh intangibles. Particular managerial skills may come up for discussion, covering the gamut of interpersonal relations, leadership, getting things done, and follow-up. Eventually, the trainee will develop a variety of skills and judgment.

Standardization of counseling techniques is obviously impossible. Blind imitation by one superior of an effective method employed by another gives no assurance of similar results. The superior should use a method effective for *him,* but even this is varied to fit the different personalities of his subordinates.

Confidence and coaching   The belief on the part of the subordinate that his superior has confidence in him is a strategic element in coaching. In such a climate the exchange of information can be extremely valuable. The trainee may even feel that no harm will come to him if he brings bad news. Indeed, the superior can, through expressions of encouragement and confidence, create in the subordinate a feeling that under no circumstances would he disappoint his boss. Many assignments that look too big are carried off by men who "couldn't let their superior down."

The edifice of confidence is very difficult to build up and can be easily impaired or destroyed. It requires immense patience and wisdom. The superior can, through carelessness, ambition, or pressure of other matters, undermine this carefully constructed relationship with a frown, a slight, an impoliteness. Or sometimes a weak superior permits a subordinate to exhibit boldness, poor taste, boastfulness, and the appearance of special favor. The dignity of the superior's position is clearly assailed by such behavior.

Maintenance of the correct level of confidence is the responsibility of the superior. If he is an able man, he has two advantages over his subordinates: the authority and tradition of his office and the assurance that rests solidly upon a sense of superior ability.

The superior acts as a superior is supposed to act, according to traditionally approved behavior patterns. He is supposed to have an air of success, be a decision maker and a leader, and obey with conscientiousness the mores of society. This means that the superior must be both a moral being, who does nothing to offend his subordinates, and an aggressive, effective manager, who decides issues positively and with wisdom.[8]

The personal dignity of the superior rests upon self-respect. He earns the respect of his subordinates by his moral courage, his skill as a manager, and his personal attitudes. Whether he is gruff, amiable, or shy is really of no importance, but he must be fair.

Encouraging executives to coach   The superior who is sure that training capable future managers is a major service enjoys coaching, but this attitude is difficult to retain because immediacy is given such high priority in organized operations. The question is whether the present or the future is more important to the firm. If "there is nothing about an organization more important than its future,"[9] then superiors should be encouraged to adopt this viewpoint. Men who have been wisely chosen will exhibit unexpected talents in the hands

---

[8]See E. P. Learned, D. N. Ulrich, and D. R. Booz, *Executive Action* (Boston: Division of Research, Harvard Business School, 1951), pp. 53–58.

[9]P. E. Holden, L. S. Fish, and H. L. Smith, *Top-management Organization and Control* (New York: McGraw-Hill Book Company, 1951), p. 4.

of a superior who takes pride in training executives, who evaluates mistakes in terms of the lessons they teach, and who is content unobtrusively to watch a subordinate use delegated authority to carry out an exacting assignment.

Refresher Courses

There is a general feeling that the time devoted to refresher courses should be short—from one day to a week—but there is no consensus about subject matter. The views on this phase of training vary from "more of the same" through "advanced training" to "group problem solving."

Those who favor the first approach base their case on two reasons. Because they were happy with the results of the original training and have no idea what else could be done, they would like to reactivate the spirit achieved by the original trainees. This position is questionable because diminishing returns might be accompanied by disappointment. Others argue that managers, engaged in pressing daily problems, forget much of what they learned and should have the opportunity, after two or three years, to repeat their training.

The advocates of "advanced training" are often confused. If they wish to extend their knowledge of management, they apparently need only will power to study independently; university libraries and publishers provide what should be read. However, most people need the discipline of regular classes and this is the main thing a refresher course can provide. Sometimes advocates of advanced training are thinking of opportunities to acquire certain technical knowledge omitted from the original training, such as corporation finance, bank relationships, and labor relations. But this is not advanced training; it involves additional technical knowledge to be acquired through college or extension courses, reading, using available services, or employing a consultant.

The enterprise which views refresher courses in terms of group problem solving is usually one whose managers have had some training and which yet is faced with serious problems. Top management of such firms often retreats to a quiet environment for the purpose of reaching a consensus on how to solve their problems. On their return, announcements may be made of new or redefined policies or of other decisions, and the firm presumably starts off on a new tack. This technique is excellent if the decisions are within the responsibilities of the men present. Examples include decisions on pricing, recentralization, or the adoption of a budget.

The Vertical Slice

For solving problems which adversely affect operating efficiency at all levels, the technique of the "vertical slice" may be effective. A group composed of all managers—or representatives of all managers, in large firms—from front-line supervisor to division head or company president, meet to identify and solve specific management problems facing the division or firm, such as lack of cooperation, excessive decentralization, and poor communication. Variations in technique, such as introducing competition between subgroups and insisting on representation from all enterprise activities, may be adopted. But the essential feature of the vertical slice should always be maintained, because it provides all managerial levels with insights into selected problems and into the way others see them.

The disadvantages of the vertical slice include fear of repercussions caused by the presence of superiors and, especially, fear of group criticism, both of which may lead to innocuous discussion. Furthermore, managers at different levels view situations differently and they may take untenable positions too early as a result of limited knowledge. On the other hand, the advantage of multilevel exchange of views can be marked. Communication can be facilitated. Once the whole problem is seen, effective solution is made easier. This advantage can outweigh the disadvantages if the members of the vertical slice consider problems and not personalities. Not that people can be overlooked, for the sessions will make clear who are the effective managers and who are merely part of the problem; action on the latter can be taken later by the appropriate superior. Nor is it possible to wave a wand and eliminate status. Admonitions to do so and the adoption of the artifice of first names are impractical measures. A concerted determination to stick to issues is the mature way to reap the advantage of the vertical slice.

SPECIAL PROBLEMS IN TRAINING AND DEVELOPMENT

Undoubtedly there are several practical problems that are not easily solved through the device of three-level training as described above. They certainly would include time in position, integration of managers acquired through mergers and purchases, improving the accountability of managers for the training and development of their subordinates, and the attitude of managers toward self-development.

Time in Position

Potential as well as operating managers are often concerned about this problem. It is typical that the person who wants to be a manager is first assigned to technical jobs that are quite unrelated to the managing process. They may wait a long time before they are promoted to supervisory positions because no openings occur. These same people know that if they do not get started up the promotional ladder before they are thirty, they probably will not make it at all.

Under these circumstances, it is essential for the top managers of the enterprise to assess their needs for new supervisors and to develop some tangible means of letting potential candidates know that they are important in the firm's future. The former problem was discussed in Chapter 21. A variety of approaches suggest themselves in communicating the need for managers. Certainly, it is important to carve out for these men a scope of work that is challenging and important. In these days, when future managers are most likely to be well-educated people, it is wasteful and humiliating to assign routine and menial work. The candidate with potential will not wait around to be claimed by the future. Neither will he respond positively, unless he is given a responsible job as soon as he is ready for it and is held accountable for its performance. Superior managers must not hold back because the candidate is young or make excuses about his unreadiness. On the other hand, it is notorious that the restless want prompt promotion, while there still is much they need to learn about their present job. This issue is best joined through the coaching process; readiness is a vague concept and two-way communication about it is the best means of reaching an understanding.

Some business, government, and other enterprises are experimenting with the technique of positively identifying potential candidates and providing some distinct opportunities prior to their selection for frontline training. For instance, a cadre of potentials may be developed through a careful recommendation and screening process. These men may be exposed to a two- or three-day orientation, at which time they are addressed by high-level managers who tell them the needs of the enterprise for managers, the philosophy of management adhered to, the details of the program, and the bases for their own selection. Special programs, task forces, and challenging assignments are created for training purposes, although most often these are entirely productive activities. Most of the time, the special work is simply added to the regular assignments of the candidates; sometimes they may expect to travel to carry out special assignments. From among those who profit by this training, and still want to become supervisors, selections are made. Thus, the group is a select one about which a good deal is known; the risk of making a mistake in selecting front-line supervisors is considerably reduced. Certainly, the men in the group like this approach; and, equally certainly, the superior managers who want to promote a favorite employee are considerably restrained. It is quite probable that, in large enterprises where many appointments are annually made at the supervisory level, this technique will prove very rewarding.

Time-in-position is also a concern to middle and top managers. The able and ambitious man who works for a superior who, for one of many reasons, is not promotable is in a frustrating position. So also is the man who is ready for promotion but has no opening to aspire to. The time that these men spend in a particular position can be unreasonably long. The only real solution is for the top managers to promote an expansionary program that will absorb the energies and satisfy the ambitions of these able people.

Integration of Managers Inherited from Acquisitions

This is a pressing problem for those firms that grow through mergers, purchases, and consolidations. In the case where the acquisition was a profitable one, the best practice is to leave in place the managers who brought the firm to this desirable state. However, if the firm has not been successful, or if it has been merged or consolidated, there are always difficult problems relating to the newly inherited managers. Sometimes they come as part of the package deal; sometimes jobs are created for them. Over all, the experience of firms with this kind of problem is that most of these managers will be replaced sooner or later. The few who are retained have important potential, and these are not difficult to integrate. They catch up quickly in the training programs of their new employer; they absorb the new management philosophy without trouble.

Accountability for Training

Superior managers *are* accountable for the training of their subordinates, though, in many institutions, this is not accomplished. Too often the practice is to assign training to someone else and ignore the whole event. One way to give encouragement for the training of subordinates is to hold managers strictly accountable and let their accomplishment be appraised as part of the regular program of measurement. Men readily attend to goal achievement if they know it will be appraised, and subordinates more easily identify with superiors if the latter take a personal interest in their development. Another, and more subtle, way is to involve middle and top managers in the in-plant training programs. These can be readily structured in such a way as to provide opportunities for operating managers to instruct through such devices as case histories, incidents, and illustrations of the applications they have made of management principles. This technique has a high payoff value. The manager takes great pride in doing well, he gets to know the group of subordinate managers in the conference, and they likewise get to know their superiors.

Attitude toward Managing

When all is said and done, we come around to the conclusion that most managers are forced to learn management. True, there are the self-starters who see to their own progress. But too many occupants of management positions will not learn to manage unless they are compelled to by their superiors. They perform routine tasks, make decisions as they seem necessary in isolated conditions, and enjoy the status of their jobs. One does not see them reviewing management principles, reflecting upon their experiences, and consciously developing a philosophy of management. These things they will do only if their superiors force them—and too many superiors behave in the same manner, or get tired of the continual effort to make subordinate managers keep abreast of new developments in management.

MEASUREMENT: THE TRAINING PAYOFF

As was mentioned earlier, there has risen a question among all types of enterprise about the productivity of training programs. Specifically, executives want to know whether they are repaid for the expense of classroom training. And well they might, for the quality of training has not always been high. Logically, a case can be made for the right kind of training; the question is, Does it really pay off?

At this stage in our knowledge it must be confessed that no one knows. In fact, training is in somewhat the position of basic research. Does basic research really pay, and if so, how much? Over all, we may not be sure, but we are convinced that it must be undertaken. So with training. This area requires concentrated attention to creating a means of measurement. There are many instances where managers credit improvement in their skill to their training, but it is really not possible to generalize these views, for who can assign specific credit for a skill that may be an end product of personal aptitude, logic, imitation, and pressures in the environment, as well as of exposure to formal study and discussion?

SUMMARY OF MAJOR STAFFING PRINCIPLES

Although no generally accepted principles of staffing have, as yet, been codified, careful consideration leads to the following formulations underlying the purpose and means of staffing.

The Purpose of Staffing

The purpose of staffing can be summarized in the following principles:

Principle of staffing objective   The objective of managerial staffing is to assure that organization roles are filled by personnel able and willing to occupy them.

Principle of staffing   The better the definition of organization roles, their human requirements, and the techniques of manager training and appraisal, the more assurance there will be of managerial quality.

The first principle stresses the fundamental importance of desire and ability to undertake the responsibilities of management. There is understandably a good deal of evidence that failure in managerial assignments results when these qualities are lacking. The second principle rests upon an important body of knowledge concerning management practices. Those firms which fail to establish the requirements for job definition and the appraisal and training of managers are forced to rely upon coincidence or outside sources for able managers. On the other hand, management succession is no problem for firms that implement the principle of staffing.

The Process of Staffing

A number of principles appear to explain the means by which staffing is most effectively accomplished.

Principle of job definition   The more precisely known the results a manager is expected to attain, the more the parameters of his position can be deduced.

Principle of managerial appraisal   The more specific the management results intended, the more closely managers should be appraised in their terms.

Principle of open competition   The more an enterprise is committed to the assurance of quality management, the more it will encourage open competition among all candidates for management positions.

Principle of management development   The more that development programs aim at improving the abilities of managers in their present positions, at making them promotable, and at involving top managers in the process, the more effective they will be.

Principle of continuing development   The more an enterprise is committed to managerial competence, the more it requires managers who practice continuing self-development.

As can be seen, the principle of job definition is quite similar to the principle of functional definition noted in the discussion of organizing. Since formal organization structure creates roles by establishing objectives, grouping of activities, specifying authority delegations, and clarifying information relationships, it follows that functional execution should be assigned to department managers. The first step in tailoring the process of staffing to its purposes is to make the organization roles of a department or division consistent with and supportive of objectives. Since organizational roles must be filled by people, it is obvious that built into these roles must be those many elements—such as pay, status, power, discretion, and possibility of accomplishment—that induce people to perform.

The principle of managerial appraisal highlights the fact that an enterprise can hardly wish to have managers who apparently know management but who cannot perform. And, since performers are often "flashes in the pan" or perform well or poorly sometimes because of factors beyond their control, there is danger in having a performer who cannot manage. The best assurance for the future is a person who is both a good performer and a good manager. Therefore, appraisal methods should encompass both areas of a manager's role.

Violation of the principle of open competition in promotion has led many firms to appoint managers whose ability is inferior. Although the social pressures are strongly in favor of promoting men from within the firm, these should be resisted whenever better candidates can be brought in from the outside. Otherwise, it is not possible for the superior to discharge his responsibility to stockholders, employees, and society in general, for these interests cannot be adequately served by mediocrity.

Since many diverse practices are undertaken in the name of management development, it is fair to assume that diverse objectives are sought. Management development means one thing: improving the ability of existing managers to perform their functions. As a consequence, it will always be a process of education directed toward overcoming the weaknesses of individual managers as these are identified through the appraisal program.

The principle of continuous development may seem unduly harsh, yet the competitive demands upon an enterprise and its social responsibilities are such that it cannot afford to muddle through with managers who have no interest in developing themselves. The authors have seen firms in which managers have lacked the desire for competitive effectiveness. Invariably, such enterprises are sluggish, they fall behind their competition, and they fail to measure up to their social responsibilities.

FOR DISCUSSION

1. It has been argued that firms have an obligation to train all employees with managerial potential. Would you agree?
2. What differences do you see in policies to train managers for promotion and to train them to perform better in their existing positions? Should a firm have both policies or choose one of them?
3. Who are the "middle managers" in enterprise? Would you advocate on-the-job training for them? Why?
4. Job rotation is sometimes used as a means of training managers. Does such rotation involve promotion? What gains may be expected from this practice? What difficulties do you see in actually carrying out this policy?

part five
DIRECTING

To direct subordinates effectively, a manager is concerned with motivation, communication, and leadership. Faulty directing can completely nullify all the work that has gone into organizing and staffing the enterprise, and it can make the attainment of objectives impossible. The first chapter of this part gives the reader a view of the entire subject and relates directing to the other management functions. In the other three chapters, motivation, communication, and specific techniques of leadership are dealt with in more detail.

Motivation is a difficult subject to approach because the management theorist now is using ideas and discoveries of the sociologist and the psychologist. Chapter 26 gives the reader a useful orientation to the best modern techniques from disciplines primarily outside management. The authors, being of the "management process," or "operational," school, believe that work of any kind ought to be directed at attaining enterprise objectives.

Communication in management is a constant problem. Organized enterprises grow and move at a constantly increasing pace. It becomes more and more difficult simply to keep everybody in management informed of current developments. But communicating with superiors and subordinates so that they really understand can be done effectively. Chapter 27 develops some very useful techniques. To obtain the greatest benefit from them, the most important point to remember is that selectivity is essential. Clear, crisp, precise language is useless if the content of the message is not worth communicating.

The final chapter of this part deals with leadership. A good leader evokes zeal and confidence in subordinates. Without this quality, the enterprise may be superbly organized and staffed and may have excellent plans but its performance may be mediocre. Leadership techniques are quite as difficult to grasp as are techniques of communication. They are treated in abstract language, and their adaptation requires a great deal of native insight on the part of the practitioner.

25
nature of directing

Directing is the interpersonal aspect of managing by which subordinates are led to understand and contribute effectively and efficiently to the attainment of enterprise objectives. This function is difficult because the manager is dealing with a complex of forces about which not enough is known and over many of which he has no control.

The reader who wishes to examine this function and try to understand it is at a considerable disadvantage. As he looks into the literature on the subject, he is appalled by its volume, the varied claims of truth, the diverse interpretations of the same research data, and the assurance of many writers that their specialty comprises the sum total of "management." The executive looks at the same materials and wonders just what use he can make of them. Perhaps the first step in understanding the nature of directing is to review the purpose of enterprise, the productive factors necessary for achievement and the nature of the human factor.

THE OBJECTIVE OF ENTERPRISE

All organized effort is undertaken to produce wealth, a term that includes goods and services. This effort is by no means restricted to business activity; it is also applied to universities, hospitals, associations, and governments. The economist has long looked upon the process of turning out end products as a system. The individual or group that conceived the enterprise applied capital, land, and manpower in judicious proportions to the essential activities required to produce a flow of goods or services. This conception comprised a true system of interdependent parts whose proper interactions were essential for survival.

The objective of every business, at least, and most other enterprises, is to survive. To do this, it cannot even stand still, let alone decline in vigor. It ordinarily must grow, especially if it is a competitive business. It must also produce goods or services that are in demand, that is, that others want, in a volume and quality and at a price that will keep the firm competitive. The degree to which the objective is attained is the measure of success. The productive factors are the means used to secure the objective. The manager selects them in terms of quantity and quality and maintains them to that degree which is most efficient. This means that the human factor in production must be managed in such a way as to promote its full contribution. Thus the purpose of enterprise is not to provide for the whole life of the employee but to establish an environment that caters to those needs whose fulfillment contributes to the achievement of its objective.

This viewpoint sometimes encourages critics to leap to the conclusion that the human factor is merely a purchased commodity. Nothing is further from the truth. The individual is much more than a productive factor: he is a consumer of the produced goods and services and, thus, he vitally influences demand. He is a member of such organizations as the family, school, business, church, and fraternal associations, and he is a citizen. In these several capacities, he exercises influence that establishes laws which govern managers, ethics which guide his behavior, and a vision of human dignity which is the special contribution of our society.

Nor should the reader think of organized enterprise as being an arena for one big boss. Managers are human, too. They manage other managers as well as nonmanagers. It is true that they exercise authority over others and that this sometimes leads to forms of exploitation. But this phenomenon is as typical of one enterprise as it is of another; exploiters are rather evenly dispersed in government departments, schools and universities, hospitals, churches, and businesses.

The human factor of production is much more than this phrase implies. He is a complex individual with a long series of needs that are often changing. He embodies productive power that is required in any enterprise. The manager's problem is to evoke this power. This is his function of directing. Thus, it simply is not true, as Schein states when he evaluates the implication of the classical school's view of man, that "management's responsibility for the feelings and morale of people is secondary."[1] Quite the contrary; managers are very much concerned about human feelings and morale. Management is not a one-way street; all of us have superiors. It is human to be more concerned about one's own feelings than about others', but a manager cannot achieve his objectives if he treats his subordinates as a commodity. The manager, in the interests of his job, cannot be held responsible for the total care of subordinates. He is held responsible, however, for exercising such care as will encourage subordinates to contribute fully to enterprise objectives.

THE HUMAN FACTOR

In applying the objective and inanimate land and capital factors of production, managers have developed a great deal of skill. Guided first by economists, and

[1] Edgar H. Schein, *Organizational Psychology* (Englewood Cliffs, N.J.: Prentice-Hall, Inc., 1965), p. 49.

later by such specialists as industrial engineers, financiers, and technologists, they have learned much about the nature of these resources, and they have been able to estimate accurately the cost-output relationships. The human factor has remained largely an unknown element of production. It was utilized, none-theless, because it was indispensable. Managers, as well as other men, held varying views of the nature of man, and these have changed as our knowledge has broadened. Thus, when the economic historians of the industrial revolu-tion reported on the exploitation of labor that was so characteristic of that age, they were observing the end product of implicit assumptions concerning man's nature that were held by employers. The latter acted as though labor was a com-modity. As time passed, the employers in the great Western tradition have gradually changed their views; since they are a part of a larger society, they have adopted the changing viewpoints of that society. Of course, in any society there will be different levels of aspiration, and this is true of our own. The creators and innovators are out front, always dissatisfied with "progress." This is as it should be, but one should not assume that the managers of enterprise are the typical laggards.

One of the early writers to dramatize the question of the human factor explicitly was Douglas McGregor. In his well-known *The Human Side of Enter-prise*,[2] he set forth—at opposite extremes—two pairs of assumptions about human beings which he thought were implied by the actions of autocratic and permissive managers. It is important to note that these were intuitive deductions and were not based on any research whatsoever.[3] The autocratic, or "Theory X," manager is presumed to make the following assumptions about his employees:

1. The average human being has an inherent dislike of work and will avoid it if he can.
2. Because of this human characteristic of dislike of work, most people must be coerced, controlled, directed, threatened with punishment, to get them to put forth adequate effort toward the achievement of organizational objectives.
3. The average human being prefers to be directed, wishes to avoid respon-sibility, has relatively little ambition, wants security above all.

At the opposite extreme the permissive, or "Theory Y," manager assumes:

1. The expenditure of physical effort and mental effort in work is as natural as play or rest.
2. External control and the threat of punishment are not the only means for bringing about effort toward organizational objectives. Man will exercise self-direction and self-control in the service of objectives to which he is committed.
3. Commitment to objectives is a function of the rewards associated with their achievement.

[2] (New York: McGraw-Hill Book Company, 1960).
[3] *Ibid.*, Preface, p. vi.

4. The average human being learns, under proper conditions, not only to accept but to seek responsibility.
5. The capacity to exercise a relatively high degree of imagination, ingenuity, and creativity in the solution of organizational problems is widely, not narrowly, distributed in the population.
6. Under the conditions of modern industrial life, the intellectual potentialities of the average human being are only partially utilized.[4]

The experienced teacher will see at once an effective use of the device of comparing extremes. It is an excellent technique by which to make a point. The harm that it does is to leave the clear impression that managers *are* Theory X practitioners and that they *ought* to be Theory Y adherents. Actually, these are straw men set up to be attacked or approved. In the real world of management, it would be most difficult to find a manager who was all one or the other. Managers do not hire "average" men: they employ individuals. The more definite their accountability, the more care they will exercise in utilizing the factors of production—human factors included. In fact, they employ all degrees of directing and controlling, depending upon the nature of the subordinate, for in the end they want the full effort of employees.

Following the McGregor lead, an increasing degree of attention has been given to the need for a more explicit statement of assumptions about man. Inevitably and properly, more detailed analyses have been made. For instance, Schein[5] sees four conceptions of man in the order of their historical appearance. The assumptions which are deduced from the concept of a rational economic man are:

1. Man is primarily motivated by economic incentives and will do that which gets him the greatest economic gain.
2. Since economic *incentives* are under the control of the organization, man is essentially a passive agent to be manipulated, motivated, and controlled by the organization.
3. Man's feelings are essentially irrational and must be prevented from interfering with his rational calculation of self-interest.
4. Organizations can and must be designed in such a way as to neutralize and control man's feelings and therefore his unpredictable traits.

To this list Schein adds the McGregor deductions about the assumptions of the Theory X manager.

Schein does not say who, specifically, held these ideas about man, or how he deduced the ideas, or when these ideas were prevalent. It must have been sometime before the Hawthorne studies, because these and others are cited as the basis for conceiving social man. The assumptions about human beings that are implicit in the reports of Elton Mayo and others are said to be:

[4] *Ibid.*, chaps. 3, 4.
[5] Schein, *op. cit.*, pp. 49–63.

1. Man is basically motivated by social needs and obtains his basic sense of identity through relationships with others.
2. As a result of the industrial revolution and the rationalization of work, much of the meaning has gone out of work itself and must therefore be sought in the social relationships on the job.
3. Man is more responsive to the social forces of the peer group than to the incentives and controls of management.
4. Man is responsive to management to the extent that a supervisor can meet a subordinate's social needs and needs for acceptance.

According to Schein, there are psychologists—among whom he includes Argyris, Maslow, and McGregor—who believe that the ". . . loss of meaning from work is not related so much to man's *social* needs . . . as to man's inherent need to use his capacities and skills in a mature and productive way."[6] The assumptions which these writers seem to make about self-actualizing man are:

1. Man's motives fall into classes which are arranged in a hierarchy: (a) simple needs for survival, safety, and security; (b) social and affiliative needs; (c) ego-satisfaction and self-esteem needs; (d) needs for autonomy and independence; and (e) self-actualization needs in the sense of maximum use of all his resources.
2. Man seeks to be mature on the job and is capable of being so.
3. Man is primarily self-motivated and self-controlled.
4. There is no inherent conflict between self-actualization and more effective organization performance.

Schein's own views about man seem to be embodied in a set of assumptions which he makes about complex man:

1. Man is not only complex, but also highly variable.
2. Man is capable of learning new motives through his organizational experiences.
3. Man's motives in different organizations or different subparts of the same organization may be different.
4. Man can respond to many different kinds of managerial strategies.

Even though it is precarious to lean too heavily on a stage theory of the evolution of ideas about the nature of man, it is nonetheless refreshing to note that research has contributed a great deal to our knowledge. The reader should feel that man is less a stranger, but only slightly less; the manager will feel that though he may know men better, they still must be managed.

Gibson[7] has looked at the same problem and reached an essentially similar classification of views about man. With rational-economic man, he equates

[7]J. L. Gibson, "Organizational Theory and the Nature of Man," *Academy of Management Journal*, vol. 9, no. 3, pp. 233–245 (September, 1966).

the mechanistic view; with social man he associates the humanistic view; and with self-actualizing and complex man, he identifies the realistic synthesis. With each group he deduces essentially the same assumptions regarding man as Schein. It is significant that both authors seem quite unwilling to build organization theory solely on any of the assumptions attributed to rational or humanistic approaches. The eclectic view, whether it is called rational synthesis or complex man, is preferred.

If one sets out to consider the nature of man, it is quite essential that the whole man come under review. This has not been done by the writers considered above. Man is indeed complex. That part of his nature that seems to be involved in organized effort cannot be studied apart from his own nature without producing a caricature. One cannot manage part of a man; all aspects of his nature are "hired" when he becomes an employee. Not only do all aspects interact, their priorities change quickly and, as yet, largely unpredictably.

In facing up to the problem of describing the nature of man, the authors of this book continue to look for the answer to the musical line: "How do you hold a moonbeam in your hand?" We are not at all sure that the question can be fully or adequately answered; neither are we certain that the best approach has been taken. The concept of man's nature is achieved through the research and observations of many writers. They have seen many aspects, but have they seen all of them? When the aspects that have impressed various scholars are considered, there arises the problem of classification. For our purposes, it has seemed best to describe man's nature as a complex composed of his animal inheritance, his individualistic-social tendencies, and his spiritual endowment.

The fact that man has evolved from primitive life forms is of overwhelming significance.[8] *Man retains all of the aspects of his animal nature.* His strongest instinct is for territorial preeminence. He has a recurring need for food. He considers his safety—the keeping-alive aspect—of first-rate importance. He has a recurring need for sex and group associations. Man can be calculating and cunning. In earlier times, he exercised dominance over others whenever he could, but he readily saw that, before the greater power of others, the safest strategy was retreat and/or submission. These may not be considered admirable qualities by the present generation, but they certainly enabled man to survive. The reader can readily illustrate each of these aspects with examples from the animal kingdom.

In some ways the dichotomy of individual-social aspects of man's nature may appear to be an unhappy basis for classification. We propose this basis because the difficulties in treating these aspects separately are even more formidable, and because we prefer to look at man as an individual in a social environment. The individual is the paramount factor. He helped create the social environment and, while he is certainly affected by it, he still remains influential, as he can change it to suit his collective desires.

[8] For a summary of the implications of evolution to man, see *Scientific American*, vol. 203, no. 3 (September, 1960). This view is contested by Robert Ardrey, *African Genesis* (New York: Dell Publishing Co., Inc., 1961).

While we may agree with the oft-repeated remark that man is a social animal, we think it is important to inquire into the relationship of group size to personal satisfaction and into the need for solitary retreat. While man has been able to build large societies and large institutions, he is not always well prepared to live in them or to be a part of them. The stresses and strains of a life lived in close proximity to large numbers of people are all too evident in our own times. There is a real question whether man will ever be able to cope with this type of environment.

Man has superimposed an intelligence upon his animal nature and has succeeded in modifying that nature. His mind and conceptual ability have enabled him to create an imaginative world, to realize a degree of foresight, and to acquire the conviction that the demands of his basic nature can be modified and channeled to such a degree that their satisfaction can indeed lead to his perfection. This view of the nature of man, if correct, makes it possible to deduce certain conclusions that are of utmost importance to the manager. These may be listed as follows:

1. The individual is the primary concern of man.

    Man looks after himself both in the extremities of life or death and in the modern affluent society. It is he who wants preferment, who wants to win. He may very well enjoy the success of others *after he has achieved,* although his jealous and skeptical nature shows through. True, we do have our unselfish heroes, men who willingly have laid down their lives for others, the wholly unselfish mother, the man who will step aside for the benefit of others. The rarity of these people makes them subject to comment and to award.

2. The individual will work to satisfy the demands of his basic nature if the benefits exceed the costs.

    It is often said that man enjoys work. This is certainly true if the effort is directed toward satisfying the demands of his complex nature. He is doing this even when he tinkers. As he approaches the point of marginal satisfaction, he scarcely has the will and verve to apply himself to the specific labor *for the same reason.* For instance, he may work at his bench with unusual productivity in order to save time at the end of the day to experiment with a new tool or a new method he has invented. In this view, the objective of work may change for the worker several times a day.

3. The individual can be led.

    Man responds to leadership. He can be persuaded through many devices to take the desired road, but the devices themselves must be selected, tuned, and timed to the individual's need to satisfy his basic nature. Appeals to pride, status, greed, and many other aspects of man's nature are sometimes successful. Ancient armies were led with promises of booty; modern armies would have none of this. The leader must be imaginative in identifying the persuasive device to which another, at a given time, will respond positively.

4. The individual wants to live and work in a social environment.

    This seems to be true most of the time. There is a definite need for solitude, however; sometimes people cannot bear people; many scientists still work best alone. In general, these periods of time are much shorter than those when man desires group associations. Both aspects rest squarely upon man's basic nature. Man may be largely a social animal, but he is not entirely so.

5. **The individual helps to create organizations to serve his needs.**
   There are many needs that man alone cannot satisfy. He can achieve them only through cooperative effort. If they promise a surplus of benefits over costs, he is likely to accept the implied limitations upon his individuality. For these reasons man creates government, educational, religious, health, and many other organizations. His chief problem in large-scale society is to retain his mastery of the organizations he has created and not become their slave.

6. **There is no average man.**
   Attempts to take the arithmetical average of mankind, on the assumption that people are all alike, are bound to fail. People are not all alike. Natures are different and, for the individual, his nature may differ from time to time. Man does not, even as an individual, proceed to accommodate all aspects of his basic nature in the same degree at a given time. He exhibits priorities and these are kaleidoscopic.

7. **The individual can rise to the challenge of his full capabilities.**
   Man is usually impatient to use his abilities to their fullest extent. He then resents the lack of opportunities to apply his knowledge and skills and to shoulder the responsibility for results. He becomes bored working at half speed, with routine. He is curious to learn the maximum level of his capabilities and he wants to operate at this level.

The implications of this concept of the nature of man are especially critical in managing an enterprise. Man is an important factor of production, but he cannot be treated as if he were inanimate. Neither can he be treated solely as rational-economic, or social, or self-actualizing. He is all of these in varying degrees and at varying times. The instability of this complex creature makes it quite impossible to measure his capabilities and apply them on the basis of an exact input-output calculation. The manager is probably better able to approximate such an equation than is most anyone else, as he has more experience in directing the efforts of men. Nevertheless, he would be the first to acknowledge how poorly the job is done. This is why his directing function is often ineffectively executed.

MANAGING THE HUMAN FACTOR

In turning to a more detailed examination of the implications of this view of the nature of man for the management process, it is important to stress that the manager himself possesses as variable and complex a nature as does any of his subordinates. He is part of the problem; he cannot deal as objectively with the human factor of production as he can with land or capital. His spirits rise as he views excellent results; they are depressed by troubles. He brings to work attitudes that are allowed to influence his reactions to events. He is responsible for results and often feels helpless to achieve them. Indeed, the interactions between superior and subordinates are endless, but they must be managed.

It is also important to recall that the aspects of human nature set forth above are those with which the manager is directly concerned. The human being is a total man, interested in himself, and therefore conscious of the inputs he receives from external factors, such as family, neighbors, schools, churches, unions or trade associations, political associations, and fraternal groups. He cannot divest himself of the impact of these forces as he presents himself before the firm that employs him. He brings within the gate, and within the work situation, a whole man that is only partially motivated by the need to work. What he cannot do is to leave outside the gate the influences, the ambitions, and the means of satisfaction of many of his natural demands that no firm can satisfy. He may be intent upon family formation, the education of his children, the purchase of a house, his candidacy for political office, or his religious life. None of these concerns can be sloughed off as the worker passes through the gate of the employer's premises, even though he enters this gate solely because he needs an income and has contracted to exchange services for that income. His manager must recognize this fact and be prepared to deal with it.

How to deal with this problem has been the subject of considerable discussion during recent years. Some psychologists have been so concerned about the problem that they have tended to take the position that the enterprise has an obligation to satisfy the needs of the whole man. This is, of course, untenable on its face. No enterprise could live under these requirements. None, especially those who criticize business managers, would accept the manager's decisions to provide for family life, political associations, religious ties, and other social necessities of employees. And the firm itself could not maintain its competitive position vis-à-vis those enterprises that are operated on the assumption that the business of business is business.

On the other hand, the manager who thinks and acts as if he is hiring *only* the working man is bound to be inefficient and ineffective. The employee's nature is an indivisible whole. It is also something else: it is a whole within which the establishment of priorities is a viable process. When a man reports for work, he has clearly established an income, and perhaps a social, priority. For the time established by the employer, effort will be exchanged for progress toward achieving the employer's objectives. True, it will not be undiluted effort. It will be affected by the impact of noneconomic influences, but these can be modified to a greater or lesser extent by the leadership ability of the manager.

The Manager Must Act His Part

Exactly because he *is* the manager and thus exercises a superior authority position, it is important that the manager first be in command of himself. He should see himself as objectively as possible and act his expected part.[9] In the first edition of this book, the authors expressed this view as follows:

The superior must act as a superior is supposed to act. Society has traditions of approved behavioral patterns, and the particular role expected of the boss is no exception. He is viewed as an isolated individual who has an air of success, is a decision maker, is an inspired leader, and obeys with unusual conscientiousness the mores of society.[10]

Nothing has occurred to modify this concept in the intervening time. What has occurred is that managers seem to be more conscious of the impact of their behavior on others, and their activities are now undertaken with more circumspection.

Individual Arrangements

In view of those aspects of man's nature which bear upon his role as a factor of production, the manager should attempt to create an internal environment that will induce subordinates to work at the level of their full capabilities. Since it is known that the individual is primarily concerned with what happens to him in the work situation, it is important that procedures be established that take this attitude into account. The selection, appraisal, and promotion processes should be tied in with individual competence. Training should be directed to personal needs. Work assignments should challenge the capabilities of the individual. When personal trust in subordinate managers is established, authority to make decisions should be decentralized if possible. Those who want responsibility should have it; those who do not want it should not have it. Salary and perquisites should be related to job responsibility. The environment that is constructed along these lines will resolve preferment on a competitive basis and will enable the individual to take care of himself along lines that redound to the achievement of group purpose.

Why Men Work

Work is effort directed to the accomplishment of some objective. Work is certainly accomplished outside organized enterprise, not only as a requirement for making a living but also as activity with no economic end in view. In unorganized activity, a great deal of freedom is often permissible, since the individual can choose not to tinker, not to go to his law office, or not to go to the clinic. The individual is much more restricted when he works for organized enterprise. To make them viable, it is necessary to establish rules concerning attendance, hours, place of work, behavior on the job, and what comprises the job itself. Inevitably, the employee feels a loss of freedom. Why,

[9] Many years ago, D. N. Ulrich, E. P. Learned, and D. R. Booz wrote with deep insight on this aspect of the manager's behavior. See their *Executive Action* (Boston: Division of Research, Harvard Business School, 1951), pp. 53–58.

[10] H. Koontz and C. O'Donnell, *Principles of Management*, 1st ed. (New York: McGraw-Hill Book Company, 1955), p. 379.

then, do men work in organized enterprises? One reason must be because this is their best opportunity to make a living. The need for income to purchase scarce, and therefore costly, goods and services requires men to work. Taking stock of their existing knowledge and skills, men will choose—in the United States—to secure income in ways which will achieve their best input-output ratio. This is why doctors may desert a clinic for private practice, scientists will work in industry, and engineers will shift jobs "for ten cents an hour."

However, since men must work, they will hope to find an environment in which nonmonetary income is also received. They prefer pleasant to unpleasant surroundings, pleasant to unpleasant co-workers, interesting to uninteresting work, recognition to nonrecognition, and the opportunity to accomplish rather than not to do so. The essential point is that all of these are in the nature of fringe benefits; all of these could be obtained if they did not work at all. Thus, they do not work *for* these benefits alone. If they had to, they would work without them, because they need a job that will yield income.

As a manager looks at this aspect of man's nature, he will attempt to satisfy it by paying the value of the employee's contribution (insofar as this can be measured) and by doing his best to provide other benefits in terms of work environment, group size and personality, freedom and encouragement in innovation, and personal recognition, to the extent that each of these will contribute positively to achieving enterprise objectives efficiently and effectively.

The Individual Can Be Led

There is abundant evidence that this is true. The reasons why men follow a leader may not be fully understood. They include safety, income, power, and admiration. The leader is followed if it is believed that he can best provide, within the limits of time, place, and ability of the subordinates, the satisfactions for which men strive. On the other hand, the leader has no followers if he misjudges their needs and moods and the way they see to best accomplish these ends. The zeal of followers correlates positively with the quality of leadership.

Managers should surely take advantage of this aspect of human nature in the work situation. Subordinates want to be led, and led effectively. They will work just hard enough to get by if there is little or no leadership; with effective leadership they will work with zeal and confidence toward the peak of their capabilities.

The implication of this aspect of human nature for the enterprise is that managers should develop and apply their leadership abilities. This is not something that can be taught in its entirety; one may be guided by the techniques of other leaders, but these procedures and those he himself develops need to be tried out in the work situation. Only in this way, through trial and evaluation of effects, can managers improve this elusive skill. The payoff for effective leadership can be immense. As a consequence, the need to develop leadership skill in all managers, at all levels, is pressing. It should ever be in the minds of managers everywhere.

Social Nature of Man

It is sometimes difficult to arrange for subordinates to work in association with other people to the degree to which they want, but managers should, at least, recognize the need. For those who want to be alone, it is often possible to arrange the work and the place of work to minimize personal contacts. Of course, these concessions will not be a major item for the enterprise. They can be effected by positioning the work place, providing partitions, etc. However, the factor of a preference for isolation is often given little attention. It may be because its incidence is small, or it may be because the costs of catering to it are inconvenient.

On the other hand, the propensity for people to enjoy a social environment is probably much more pertinent for managers to consider. The need for company, for conversation, for companionship, is very real for most people. Insofar as these needs can be satisfied without interfering with productiveness, they should be catered to; indeed, productivity may well be much greater if this is done. On a broader scale, the informal organization is a reflection of the individual's social needs. It should not be interfered with unless its objectives are a deterrent to the accomplishment of enterprise goals.

While recognizing the social needs of subordinates, the manager has a rather difficult time deciding just what size the social group should be. At the extreme, the large bullpen with hundreds of employees is clearly inefficient because of the noise level, the encouragement to visiting, and even the fear that some have of being in crowds. Despite the lack of behavioral guides, managers have tended to cut down on group size in order to minimize its disadvantages. But they can go too far in this regard.

The manager must cope with this phenomenon. He is torn between noninterference in the personal freedom of subordinates and the potential for this desire to interfere with productivity and with the achievement of enterprise objectives. Productivity may well be affected adversely where company time is used for group activities. A compromise may be reached wherein the group may use company time either wholly or partially. Such a decision may not adversely affect output because encouragement of voluntary group activities can have a favorable impact on zeal. In the latter case, managers are especially concerned.

No Average Man

That there is no average man managers would be the first to acknowledge. Yet certain exigencies of organized enterprise require that the assumption be made. Order and discipline are prime requisites for organizational success. To this end, rules and procedures are developed; concerted hours of work are essential, safety is imperative, division of labor is often paramount in achieving maximum productivity, wage and salary levels must be harmonious, and equality of opportunity must be preserved. In all of these fields, individuals must apparently be treated alike.

Despite these standardized techniques designed to treat the undifferentiated, managers do have considerable opportunity to make personal adjustments within the established environment. The needs of the enterprise for order and discipline do not wholly preclude their devising adjustments for the differentiated individual. Opportunities for marginal differential treatment should be vigorously sought. Work can be rearranged and various degrees of job enlargement can be achieved. Merit, promotions, and other symbols of success can be individually treated. Hours of labor can sometimes be modified, or a choice of shifts can be provided.

The tendency of managers to treat individuals in a standardized and routine way is very strong because such a practice greatly simplifies the manager's job. However, this attitude should be resisted consistently, for individuals want individualistic—but fair—treatment. Standardization is contrary to the nature of human beings, and it should be avoided within the enterprise so far as is possible. It is perfectly obvious not only that the needs of individuals vary at a given moment of time, but that they vary within the working day for the individual himself. These little-understood characteristics of human nature are important nonetheless as far as output is concerned; therefore, it behooves the manager to respond constructively to them, as far as it is economical to do so.

The Desire for Responsibility

Of course, it would be a mistake to assume that all employees will rise to a challenge of their full capabilities. One need only walk through a plant, a hospital, or the premises of any organized enterprise to see that many employees work at a level much below their potential, even after they are invited and exhorted to earn the rewards of higher effort. They simply do not rise to a challenge—for reasons that may include work restrictions by unions, work definition spelled out in the union contract, job security protected by law, ineffective discipline, tolerance by managers, lack of belief in the importance of their work, or acceptance of the propaganda that they are somehow being exploited. These attitudes and beliefs are exhibited not only in the shop, but by work gangs outside the premises, engineers, stenographers, nurses, and clerical employees, whether in business or in universities, libraries, and government agencies. Indeed, they are observable wherever men are employed.

The proportion of employees who refuse to accept the challenge of greater responsibilities is unknown. Those whose biases are with the employee seem to ignore the question or to minimize it; those whose biases are with the employer are concerned with the problem and may exaggerate it. There is a need to know. However, the employer, insofar as he is permitted by law or union contract, should recruit with a view toward selecting those employees who will respond to the challenge of responsibility, *and he should provide the challenge.*

The authors of this book are not strangers to the frustrations of able employees that arise from a lack of job challenge. For instance, banks as an institution often have widely advertised their training processes as a device to attract college graduates. They were largely successful in this purpose, but the program tended to be very costly because many of the recruits soon resigned. Here was a case where most of the jobs as established did not require the talent sought and could not challenge this class of recruit. At the technical level a similar phenomenon sometimes occurs. It is not unusual to see engineers in their late thirties searching for a career in management because they have outgrown their positions. Both technically and financially their positions cease to challenge.

The provision of challenging opportunities, especially for able managers, requires a radical change in the attitudes and practices of superior managers in all organized enterprises. It is very human to want to standardize, routinize, and specialize procedures. This course, however, minimizes the discriminatory attention that should be paid to individuals. It may contribute to over-all productivity and provide an environment of "equal" treatment for employees, but it also creates just those conditions that are so frustrating to subordinate managers who long to feel the bit of responsibility. The steady hand of the superior is needed to make certain that these men understand that they need time to assimilate their experience. Just when a subordinate is ready for a promotion is something of a no-man's-land, but surely the best way to find out is to challenge his ingenuity to expand his contribution to the enterprise and to keep the rein of accountability taut.

THE DIRECTING FUNCTION

As a manager concerns himself with the directing function, he begins to grasp something of its complexity. First of all, he is dealing with people, but not on an entirely objective basis, for he is a person himself and often becomes part of the problem. He is in direct contact with people, both as individuals and as groups. He soon discovers that, as a productive factor, people are not singly interested in enterprise objectives; they have objectives of their own. In order to direct human effort toward enterprise objectives, the manager soon realizes that he should think in terms of the issues related to orientation, communication, motivation, and leadership. A consideration of the more general aspects of directing is provided in the following sections. Separate chapters will be devoted to the major directing activities of managers.

THE MANAGER'S RELATION TO SUBORDINATES

Although the manager is part of the group, it is convenient for many reasons to look upon him as apart from his subordinates. Resources—human and otherwise—for achieving enterprise objectives are assigned to him, and he must integrate them. Easy when it comes to capital, buildings, and land, this is difficult when it comes to people, for they require skilled directing.

It is also convenient to think of the manager apart from the group because he is its leader. As leader he is not so much one of the group as he is the one to persuade the group to do his will. Leadership involves wise use of a motivational system plus a personality which engenders zeal in others.

The manager is also perceived by his employees as one apart for other reasons. He knows more than they do about company goals, policies, new programs, and expected changes; he is considered to have good judgment because of his varied experience.

On the other hand, his foibles had better be socially acceptable, else he will lose the respect of his subordinates. The image of what a superior manager should be like is quite different from what is so often observed in practice.

Finally, the superior is ever apart from the group, because he holds in his hands the careers of his subordinates. His opinion is important above all others, because he decides who will be promoted, transferred, or terminated, and who will be given merit and salary increases.

The behavior of a group largely depends on the kind of manager it has. His leadership style, the quality of his communications, the respect of his peers, his general character, the degree to which he can be trusted, his human attitudes—all these influence the morale of subordinates, which, in turn, reflects his skill in directing them.

IMPORTANT PRINCIPLES

The first two of these principles applies to the purpose of directing; the third, to the directing process.

The Principle of Directing Objective

As can be readily ascertained from the above discussion, the basic purpose of directing is contained in the principle that *the more effective the directing process, the greater will be the contribution of subordinates to organizational goals.* While effective directing cannot do this alone, since plans, organization structure, adequate staffing, and effective control necessarily make their contributions, the job of getting people to understand their goals and roles and how to accomplish them—the interpersonal aspects of managing—is clearly an integral and essential part of the process.

The Principle of Harmony of Objective

Confusion has accompanied the many efforts to describe the harmony that exists between subordinates' objectives and those of the firm. Different viewpoints reflect different ways of visualizing social cooperation. Preoccupation with labor-management issues, military organization, or the question of the individual's place in society has led to biased views.

Fayol,[11] writing a half century ago, pointed out that the manager who

[11] Henri Fayol, *General and Industrial Management* (New York: Pitman Publishing Corporation, 1949), p. 33.

retained his authority in a high degree could direct employees with few counterinfluences and, consequently, could maintain a unity of view among them with respect to enterprise objective. On the other hand, when orders were filtered down through several echelons of intermediaries, they became altered, even unintentionally, permitting the growth of divergent views of the firm's objectives among personnel. Fayol's sixth principle states that the business interest must prevail over the interest of employees.[12] He also suggests that ignorance, ambition, selfishness, laziness, and other human weakness are forever at war with the best interests of the firm.

As Barnard[13] has pointed out, "The preponderance of persons in a modern society always lies on the negative side with reference to a particular existing or potential organization." In other words, usually only a very small minority of persons in an enterprise, or in a department of it, actually identify their objectives with those of the organization. Nor should a manager expect the goals of his subordinates and the goals of the group to be identical. But in directing subordinates, he must take advantage of individual motives to gain group goals; in interpreting plans and job assignments, he must harmonize individual and group objectives. A "company" man may make the manager's job easier, but the manager must never assume that selfless devotion exists in many, if any, of his subordinates.

Although employees work to satisfy needs not necessarily the same as the firm's objectives, these needs must be in harmony with and complementary to the interests of the firm, and not contrary. A good motivation system should encourage the fulfillment of those human needs which employees will work to satisfy while at the same time contributing to the achievement of enterprise objectives. From this can be deduced perhaps the most important principle dealing with the purpose of directing: *the more effective directing is, the more individuals will perceive that their personal goals are in harmony with enterprise objectives.*

The Principle of Unity of Command

The principle of unity of command is a directing, as well as an organizing, principle. As described in the discussion of organizing, it reflects the desirability of subordinates being responsible to only one superior. This principle, it will be recalled, is: *the more completely an individual has a reporting relationship to a single superior, the less the problem of conflict in instructions and the greater the feeling of personal responsibility for results.* It is well known that employees work better this way, which avoids division of loyalties, problems of priorities, and conflicting orders. The importance of such a restriction was not realized by F. W. Taylor[14] when he experimented with an organization structure that permitted eight functional foremen to give orders to the individual workmen.

[12] *Ibid.*, p. 26.

[13] Chester I. Barnard, *The Functions of the Executive* (Cambridge, Mass.: Harvard University Press, 1938), p. 84.

[14] F. W. Taylor, *Scientific Management* (New York: Harper & Row, Publishers, Incorporated, 1947).

In military organizations, unity of command is followed "so that its [organizational element] responsible head can be held solely accountable for results to higher authority."[15] The emphasis is placed upon protection of the superior, through the personal obligation of a subordinate to see that assigned activities are properly performed. Little thought is given, apparently, to the improved efficiency of the subordinate as a result of this unity of command.

The complex of personal forces that every manager manipulates to accomplish a task through other people permits no outside interference in supervision of subordinates. Directing can be most efficiently carried on by one person. He knows, better than others, the nature of the subordinate, to which motivation he best responds, and his technical proficiency. Consequently, the immediate superior is in the best position to select whichever directing techniques maximize productivity, not of the individual employee particularly, but of the group of subordinates.

ORIENTATION

Orientation is used here in the sense of providing information necessary for intelligent action. Starting with the introduction of each new employee to his physical and human environment, it more importantly includes the briefing of all employees on both immediate and continuing enterprise activities. Obviously, the more one knows about one's work and its environment, the more intelligently one can work. It is up to the superior manager to determine what information is essential for good performance and how and by whom it will be transmitted.

Orienting New Employees

Managers too often leave the orientation of new employees to the personnel department, which is skilled in providing both general and specific information about the nature of the firm and its history and about details of employment, such as pay, hours, and fringe benefits. But much more information is required from a new employee's immediate superior.

Every manager is responsible for the specific orientation of a new subordinate. It is part of his directing function to take the time and to exercise the patience required to give the employee information essential to his assignment.

Above all, any employee, new or old, should be encouraged to understand the goals of his position in as verifiable a way as possible. The employee's job and its relationship to other activities require detailed explanation. The job itself, its scope, purpose, and authority delegation, must be clearly described. The subordinate should be informed about how to report and how his performance will be evaluated. To portray organization relationships, an

---

[15] J. R. Beishline, *Military Management for National Defense* (Englewood Cliffs, N.J.: Prentice-Hall, Inc., 1950), pp. 89–90.

organization chart is helpful, showing how activities are divided and related to each other.

The subordinate's relationships with other employees need careful explanation. He should be introduced personally to managers with whom he will have considerable contact, so that information and transactions will flow smoothly and help will be readily available. For instance, the new head of a contract administration group will have continuous contact with the heads of production control, engineering, pricing, administration, purchasing, and finance and with the armed services' representative. Subordinates who have to establish rapport with complete strangers may be slow to develop their jobs.

The new subordinate must also know how to utilize support services. He needs to know what services are available, where they are, what they can do for him, and what procedures to follow in requesting them. Failure here often results in the subordinate establishing his own service that duplicates an existing activity, with attendant high cost.

Continuing Orientation

There is a constant need for orientation to new or revised goals, new assignments, changes in company activities—as related to products, policy, organization, and customers—and changes in managerial personnel. For continuing orientation, managers use techniques including written communication—memoranda, bulletins, control reports, duty assignments—and oral information at staff meetings, conferences, committee meetings, and daily coaching sessions.

The difficulty in continuing orientation is that human beings grow indifferent to activity that must be repeated indefinitely. People don't mind doing what they can finish. The orientation of a new employee can be readily and definitely accomplished, but managers need tenacious will power to provide continuing orientation. There is, for example, the continual problem of getting subordinates to coordinate their activities. Their original orientation convinced employees of the need for this, yet they often fail. It is so much easier to act alone than to bother about checking with others who will be affected.

Orientation of Superiors

Poor as the orientation of subordinates often is, it is at least a recognized aspect of directing. But the orientation of superiors is often not done well or at all; it is often not even a recognized necessity. True, superiors try to keep themselves informed through control reports and group meetings, but this is inadequate.

Every subordinate should keep his superior informed. The subordinate is in command of operational detail, and some of this is reported periodically in control reports. But daily the nagging question arises, What should be reported to the boss? The subordinate will try to protect his superior from the burden of too much information and, therefore, he will select what to report.

What is to be the basis for this discrimination? Basically, it should be to convey only information that the superior needs to keep out of trouble. No superior wants to be surprised on a matter of importance to him. This vague rule is difficult to follow, for it opens wide the discretionary door; the subordinate must correctly apprehend his superior's needs and overcome a strong temptation to censor information adversely affecting himself. The proper discharge of this responsibility requires men of character.

ISSUING ORDERS

Orders are important in directing subordinates. An order initiates, modifies, or stops an activity; it is the impetus by which an organization is activated or disbanded. Managers must thoroughly understand its meaning, uses, and limitations.

In American enterprises, from a purely legal point of view, the right to command proceeds from a contract involving the services of subordinates. The superior alone possesses this right. He (or his enterprise) employs the subordinate to perform certain duties and undertakes to explain what is needed and to pay for the service as or after it is accomplished; the employee undertakes the specified activities and receives his remuneration.

Definition of an Order

The term "order" has many connotations, as any standard dictionary will confirm. As a directional technique, an order is understood to be an instruction by a superior requiring a subordinate to act or refrain from acting in a given circumstance. Several elements in this definition require clarification. A personal relationship in direct line of command from superior to subordinate is implied. The relationship is not reversible. Two managers of equal rank cannot qualify in this relationship. And, except for functional authority, the relationship cannot exist between a superior in one department and a person of lower rank in another.

Another implication of this definition is that the content of an order be germane to the achievement of the enterprise objective. Just what this includes is not always clear. On the one hand, there may be no question that a production manager may have his foremen work a nine-hour shift. On the other hand, there may be a real question whether foremen can be ordered not to fraternize with their employees, or whether a sales manager can require his advertising head to misrepresent a product.

Finally, the definition of an order implies that it is enforceable. The manager's position would be untenable if, as a last resort, he could not employ sanctions against a subordinate who either refuses to carry out an order or who does so in an inappropriate manner. The ultimate sanction is the loss of a job. But before this stage is reached, intermediate steps may be taken, such as holding hearings, coaching, and possible transfer to other departments.

Techniques

The techniques of issuing orders have received very little consideration in management literature, although military establishments have given the problem considerable attention.[16] The relevant questions to be considered here are whether an order should be general or specific, written or oral, and what its degree of formality should be.

General or specific   Whether an order should be specific or general seems to depend upon the preference of the manager, his ability to foresee attendant circumstances, and the response made by the subordinate. Managers who have a rigid view of delegation of authority seem predisposed to phrase orders in specific terms. Such managers prefer to direct their subordinates very closely. They feel that they have clearly in mind just what is to be done and the best way to accomplish it, and they want the subordinate to carry out the order in this particular way.

In situations where it is not possible to foresee all the circumstances attendant upon carrying out the order, it is more likely to take a general form. When it must be carried out far from the personal supervision of the superior, specific orders should be given with care. For instance, district sales managers, regional plant managers, and representatives located at a distance from the home office are, perforce, likely to operate under general orders, because local influences, unforeseen factors in a negotiation, and other questions may affect the way in which the orders are carried out.

The response of a subordinate to the type of order received is important in determining its nature because some employees prefer close supervision and, consequently, do best under specific orders. On the other hand, many subordinates chafe under this treatment. They prefer to exercise initiative and are quite willing to be judged by the results. This type of person does not work well under close direction and may resent specific orders.

Written or oral   In deciding between written or oral orders, consideration is given such questions as the permanency of the relationship between superior and subordinate; the quality of trust that exists between them; and the necessity of some device—especially in large firms—for avoiding overlapping orders and acquainting all personnel concerned with the fact that an order has been issued. If it were safe to assume that the superior-subordinate relationship would continue between the same two persons, it would often be unnecessary to write orders. If the rate of job turnover is high, it is unsafe for a firm to operate without written general orders, especially those which will require considerable time to carry out.

The quality of trust existing between superior and subordinate affects the desirability of writing orders, since in this relationship the major risk is carried by the subordinate, who may prefer written orders for several reasons. He may be averse to accepting responsibility and, when this is forced upon him, may want to be covered by a written, specific order. Or he may have been

[16]*Ibid.*, chap. 14.

accused of exceeding his authority in the past and now seeks the protection of a written order. Or he may have had bitter experience with a superior who fails to remember giving an order, who changes an order and forgets that he has done so, or who blames the subordinate for poor results attendant upon carrying out his orders.

The written order is often used for preventing overlapping instructions and preventing jurisdictional disputes. If, perchance, confusion does develop, it is considerably easier to straighten matters out if the original orders were in writing.

In addition, it is often convenient to announce a particular assignment to all interested personnel by a written order. The need to do this arises particularly when the order involves a somewhat unusual assignment. A president may instruct his personnel director to make a study of accidents, their causes and incidence, and develop a program for minimizing them. Should no public notice be given and no public request for the cooperation of all division, department, and section heads, such an assignment might meet with resistance, sabotage, and other forms of noncooperation.

Formality and informality   In most enterprises—exclusive of the military—such terms as "command" or "order" are rarely used. The manager is accustomed to command by informally suggesting, "Let's do this," "Suppose you go ahead with this thing," or "Why not confer with production on this?" The outsider might not recognize these as orders, but the subordinate seldom mistakes them. Sometimes, however, a formal written or spoken order, phrased exactly as a military officer would give it, is salutary. Some employees require this sort of formal direction at all times, while others would instantly quit their jobs if anyone gave them such orders. There is a subtle skill in selecting precisely the right degree of formality to use with each subordinate, and doing this well often spells the difference between good and bad motivation.

Timing

Contrary to military practice, the informality and spontaneity with which businessmen reach decisions and give orders often result in little apparent attention to timing. This can be deceptive. If decisions are customarily reached after permitting broad participation by subordinates, relatively little explanation is needed, and timing of implementing action is often implied. In businesses operated on the basis of opportunism and immediacy, action is probably simultaneous with the decision. On the other hand, firms engaging in considerable planning necessarily follow the planned steps quite rigidly and the timing of orders is given careful attention.

DELEGATION AS A MEANS OF DIRECTING

Delegation of authority is a more general form of directing than issuance of orders. In delegation, the superior customarily gives a subordinate authority to act in a large area of affairs by means of a general statement. As the previous section pointed out, orders are issued when a superior knows (or thinks he knows) exactly what the results of the specific order will be. In many circumstances, the result cannot be anticipated or known in detail. When this is the case, more general delegation is appropriate.

Although delegation was discussed in Chapter 18, the subject deserves further attention as a specific technique of directing.

Difficulties in Assignment

It might appear that to assign duties one has only to specify which man is in charge of purchasing, production control, maintenance, or some other task. Upon a closer look, however, what is involved in these assignments? Breakdowns are attempted in job descriptions, but it is difficult to make these clear and definite, on the one hand, or distinguishable from similar assignments on the other. For example, one firm assigns to the purchasing agent the following duties: (1) to advise his superior on the formulation of procedures relating to procurement; (2) to make the necessary contacts with vendors and to study the commodity market constantly; (3) in accordance with authorized requisitions, to purchase materials and supplies; (4) to negotiate with vendors claims arising from inspection rejections; (5) to administer personnel and financial policies as they apply to his operation; and (6) to accumulate information for the preparation of his budget.

At first glance, the assignment may appear clear and exact. But let one place himself in the position of the purchasing agent. Just what, when, and how much effort is called for? Does "advising his superior" about procedures mean constructive written suggestions, based upon an analysis by an industrial engineer? What are "necessary" contacts with vendors? What does one do to study the commodity market "constantly"? Does claims negotiation mean exclusive power to conclude an agreement? Raising these questions illustrates the common inexactitude of work assignments. The man who undertakes a job described in this fashion will have to play it by ear. In fact, perhaps most managers do!

Overlapping of work assignments made to two or more subordinate managers is another common difficulty. So long as assignments are made in general terms, this is certain to happen. For instance, in negotiating sales contracts or claims on vendors, the legal department will be involved as well as the sales and buying departments. Just where the duty of one manager leaves off and that of the other begins can scarcely ever be made completely clear. Managers learn to live with these uncertainties, to interpret them in the light of the facts in any given situation, and to voluntarily coordinate their activities in the best interests of the enterprise.

Difficulties in Delegation

Delegation of authority may be even less exact, often stating merely that the subordinate is authorized to carry out the assigned duties. Since the duties themselves are not clear, the subordinate will have difficulty in interpreting his authority to do anything. For instance, in the case of the aforementioned purchasing agent, just how free is he to negotiate claims with vendors? Can he settle for any percentage of the claim? Can he cut off the vendor if there is not full satisfaction? Can he require or recommend prosecution? Even though he asks his superior for clarification, he may not get it. But this can be largely clarified by a chart of approval authorization.

Detailed versus Broad Authority

This is often not a matter of choice. It involves the question, How detailed should a grant of authority be? The answer depends upon how detailed the work assignment is. In an assignment to discipline subordinates, the delegation of authority will be broad. On the other hand, if the assignment specifies that disciplinary action is limited to a referral to the grievance committee or a request that the employee be transferred, authority to discipline is strictly spelled out. Generally, (1) detailed authority is associated with detailed work assignments; (2) delegation of authority is broad at the top of the organization structure and becomes increasingly narrow as lower echelons are reached.

Implied Authority

Purely from the point of view of efficiency, the implication of authority adheres to all managers. The importance of acting in the best interests of the enterprise overrides any nice delegation of limited authority. Probably there is no manager of any experience who has not exceeded his delegated authority. An unforeseen bargain tempts many buyers to exceed their contractual powers; a sale that rests upon a relaxation of price or terms is often confirmed by superiors, notwithstanding strict orders forbidding such practices; violations of company rules are sometimes condoned; and the firm is often committed financially by a manager who is believed to have the authority but who does not. The pattern emerging from these examples shows that trusted managers are presumed to act in the best interests of the organization, whether they occasionally override their authority or not. In this way an enterprise can benefit from unforeseen opportunities and avoid stultification.

Rigidly Delegated Authority

Some managers view authority delegation with untoward rigidity. They dislike to delegate and, when forced to do so, endeavor to circumscribe the grant with a neat exactitude. They feel that delegations can be made accurately and that the results which they personally anticipate will be achieved. Disappointments are likely to be followed by harsh judgments on the ability of their subordinates. When everything seems neat and clear to these managers, they feel frustration when their plans fail.

The effects of this attitude are serious. In the first place, such a manager is incapable of developing a successor. Many types of subordinates refuse to work for him, and the quality of those willing to work in this environment is subject to question. Subordinates learn to manage by managing. Deprived of opportunities to make their own decisions, to exercise their own judgment, and to act on their own volition, they will neither make errors for which they are personally responsible nor learn much about managing.

In the second place, a rigid concept of delegation limits the size of the enterprise and stultifies its growth. This follows naturally from the principles of departmentation. A manager who makes little use of his subordinate managers must, of necessity, make the decisions himself. The span of management places limits on what one person can do. Even if the regular work day is supplemented by long hours of nightwork, this restriction still holds. Beyond a certain point nothing can get done. This span binds the organization in iron and prevents its growth.

Positively Delegated Authority

Executives with a positive attitude toward delegating authority view their directing function entirely differently. Personal security is not a consideration, and—with the confidence resulting from intelligent selection and an appraisal program—they willingly trust their subordinates. Such executives consider their greatest service to be one of developing future managers.

This does not imply neglect of daily tasks, but errors made in them are turned into object lessons for subordinates and not looked upon simply as catastrophes. Errors are, of course, minimized by appropriate safeguards, a point that will be developed later. Proper analysis of the issue and the way it was attempted is valuable in developing judgment. Such attention to training subordinates reflects the belief that nothing is more important to an organization than its future.

Also according to the positive attitude, subordinates are encouraged to accept responsibility. Their superiors want them to become self-starters and grow in the exercise of authority. For this, the superior must study each subordinate, give him gradually expanding authority, and hold before him the challenge of unusual accomplishment.

With the positive attitude, it is necessary to keep open the channels of communication between superior and subordinate. The superior must be *available*, although unobtrusive, and must permit the subordinate to "pick his brains," because this is a short cut to experience. At the same time, the temptation to tell the subordinate what to do and how to do it must be firmly resisted. In fact, "telling" is an actual revocation of delegated authority.

Finally, the positive attitude implies immense patience. It takes a long time to acquire good judgment and develop leadership ability. The temptations of short-run opportunism are often overwhelming. It takes patience to put up with mistakes, fumbling, and the slow acquisition of good business sense. The supervisor can only obtain his satisfaction from success in developing capable men.

Degrees of Delegation

It is clearly unwise to carve out a group of duties and the authority to undertake them and hand this bundle to an inexperienced supervisor. He needs time to grow. Consequently, his authority should be gradually expanded, as the superior oversees, instructs, and tests the subordinate through successive assignments. Thus, the group of duties is completed under relatively close supervision, and, as the capacities of the subordinate increase, his superior will relax the overt overseeing and expand authority, allowing the employee to devise ways to accomplish assignments.

Since the degree of delegation is highly correlated with proved capacity, in delegating authority to several subordinates in different stages of development the extent of delegation to individuals will vary. Several subordinates will ordinarily be at various stages of development at any given time. Those who have shown ability will be tested by having their authority expanded; those who have not handled authority well will lose it.

FOR DISCUSSION

1. It is in the directing function that managers "get things done by, with, and through people." Is this also true of the organizing and planning functions?
2. Do you believe managers must have authority to command their subordinates? If not, what would you suggest?
3. Do you, as a student, work at your top capacity? Do you believe employees in enterprise do?
4. Do you believe "continuing" orientation of subordinates is desirable? Why? How should it be accomplished?

26

motivation

THE NECESSITY

It has been taught for many decades that men cooperate in an enterprise in order to accomplish a desired goal that they cannot attain individually. This explanation seems to fit well the building "bees" of Western farmers, the creation of the United States, the establishment of a university—events, large and small, wherein *equal* participators combine effort to produce a result that is shared with approximate *equality*. The anticipated satisfaction of sharing the results seems to be individually articulated, and, therefore, contributed effort seems to be largely self-motivated. This apparent lack of a need for someone to motivate others seems to be particularly characteristic of those ventures which can be shortly achieved. The distant goal, or the result that seems far distant, does not receive the same degree of self-motivated effort from co-operators. Many of these are abandoned, many become laggards, and some are changed beyond recognition.

The equal-cooperation theory also seems a poor explanation of why a person applies for a position in a church, a university, or a business. He surely does not feel like an equal cooperator; he often sees these organizations as monolithic enterprises, vigorous (at least in their outward appearance), and little in need of the services of the applicant. His motivation is seldom to share in the group goal; he usually wants a job with a salary that will pay his bills. If his motivation were not economic, he might find some other way to fulfill his noneconomic needs. For this reason, enterprise managers are required to understand the motivational process.

How Much Responsibility?

There are almost as many views of the responsibility for motivating subordinates as there are concerned people. Historically the prevalent assumption was that employers or superiors *could* motivate subordinates and should be held responsible for so doing. In this view, the degree of responsibility would be limited by the delegated authority of the individual manager. A department head is obviously limited by company policy on wages and salaries, fringe benefits, promotion, and centralization of authority. Company presidents, though less restricted, are limited by policies of the board of directors, the legal system, and competition. Thus, managers at each organization level have limited authority to do those things that motivate subordinates, and the restrictions become more severe the lower down the manager stands.

Every manager is responsible, within his authority, for motivating his immediate subordinates *and* for motivating all subordinates down to the bottom of the relevant organization structure. A president should feel responsible for motivating, primarily, those reporting directly to him and, secondarily, *all* the enterprise employees; an army corps commander and a plant manager should view their responsibilities for motivation in the same primary and secondary light.

At the other extreme are those who feel that the individual cannot be motivated by others—there is nothing that a superior or company can do to motivate an employee. In this view the assumption is that the individual can get a job anywhere he wishes, can do anything in that job that he pleases, and that the quality of his work depends upon his own inner drive to learn or to create. This set of assumptions sometimes fits a gifted scientist, providing prospective employers, whether universities or businesses, know that he exists, that he is available, that he has been productive (and, it is hoped, will continue to be), and that they can provide the equipment and space he will require on a continuing basis. If these circumstances were really realized in an organization, then there would be no responsibility resting upon superiors to motivate.

The authors of this book believe that, on the one hand, a manager has more to do than merely get out of the way of a subordinate so that he can produce. On the other hand, they do not believe that he must drive his employees with a whip. In a varied environment, with employees who differ widely from each other, with a superior who is also part of the problem, they believe that there still exists a responsibility for a manager to motivate.[1]

Understanding Human Needs

To motivate is to induce people to act in a desired manner. Inanimate objects can be made to perform certain functions with a certain degree of reliability by the direct application of force. No one can exercise similar control over

---

[1] The vagueness of certain terms used in the motivation literature is distressing. For instance, we would inquire: motivation to do what? One assumes that the intention is to move people to contribute to organization objectives at their maximum capability. Yet, individual capabilities are probably different, and in addition, they are unknown. Neither do we know whether "all-out" effort can be sustained over various time periods.

These considerations lead one to conclude that managers and leaders are trying to persuade subordinates and followers to contribute to organization ends at some higher rate than the minimum acceptable level. The effective professor, for instance, tries to motivate his students to achieve a level of excellence that most of them would not otherwise strive to attain.

human beings. They cannot be made to perform quality activities; they either perform of their own volition or they are persuaded to perform.

To rely upon the volition of people to get the world's work done is obviously futile. There are few enough who can visualize the objective of purposeful work, who have the will to proceed purposefully, who can work cooperatively and integratively, and who have an interest in producing the wealth that those who cannot, need not, or will not work, require. Consequently, the application of human resources to the production of the world's goods and services can only be accomplished by effective persuasion. This is why the processes and techniques of motivation are of vital interest to those who would cause others to act in particular ways.

Behavioral scientists, who needed a "handle" with which they could explore the causes of the actions or activities of people, selected human needs as their starting point. They reasoned that if people act to satisfy their needs, and if one knows what these needs are, then people could be motivated by satisfying, or keeping from satisfying, needs. The underlying assumption, and in our days it is quite correct, was that people were not self-sufficient—they *had* to exchange effort in cooperative activities if they were to satisfy some of their needs.

The term "need" itself requires some explanation. The overtone of "requirement" is clearly not meant by behavioralists. Instead, they seem to imply that needs include all those feelings which may be satisfied by posterior stimuli. Thus, they embrace such concepts as the need for preserving life, for social relationships, for distinction, and for status. In their concentrated study of needs during the past two decades, they appear to assume that needs are a cause of behavior. On the other hand, there is emerging from the field work of the biological scientists, especially during the 1960s,[2] potentially significant contributions to an understanding of human needs. Their point of departure is that needs are not a cause but a result of anterior stimuli. In other words, behavior is what we do and not why we do it.

The human needs that the manager is primarily interested in are those that can be satisfied within the enterprise structure. He is not interested in, and indeed, cannot afford, the paternal luxury of satisfying all the needs of an employee. He does want the scientists' help in clarifying those needs of employees which the enterprise is in the best position to satisfy, and whose satisfaction will be a powerful persuader of effective action.

SOME VIEWS ABOUT MOTIVATION

It is probable that mankind has been concerned about the motivation of children and subordinates, members of cooperative associations, peers and supe-

---

[2] Summarized and interpreted in beautiful language by Robert Ardrey in *The Territorial Imperative* (New York: Dell Publishing Co., Inc., 1966). Ardrey appears to make no scientific contribution himself, nor does he claim to, but he is an excellent publicist for such solid scientists as the late Professor K. R. L. Hall, Dr. K. P. Oakley, and Professor R. A. Dart, to name a few.

riors, and those who serve in armed forces since the beginning of its existence. We are dealing with a very old problem. Even though we know more about the issues involved, we are still far from having a good grasp on what it takes to move men to act in a desired manner.

It is fashionable to think that for the great part of history, say until the last decade or two, fear has been the chief motivator—fear of the negative incentives. There is no question but that the potential loss of food, shelter, family, safety, society, and freedom itself has been a universal motivator. But there were other incentives of equally hoary age, and they were employed depending upon time and circumstance. The distribution of booty to successful armies, bribery, marriages, political favors, and the lowly polished apple were alternatives, in some cases, to the negative incentives. So also was the invention of money which could induce work from employees. And the system of patronage which enabled gifted artists to self-actualize. In the 1970s there is an opportunity to improve on the historic motivational techniques of our ancestors because a deeper knowledge of human nature is at hand.

The twentieth has been the century in which much has been added to the knowledge of human nature. As the outstanding contributors are noted, it is important to remember that everyone had to base his conceptions upon the then-current assumptions and conclusions of related sciences. This is a shifting foundation, and the end is not yet.

Frederick Taylor   The motivational aspect of Frederick Taylor's contribution[3] was to prove that workers will respond to an incentive wage under conditions that reflect a careful assessment of environment, tools, fatigue, and the value added by work. It is not possible to generalize on the basis of Taylor's work because personal responsibility for results is growing more difficult to assess, fewer jobs favor the piece rate system of wages, strong unions restrict output, and information is lacking about where diminishing incentive sets in as piece rates increase.

Elton Mayo   In 1927 Elton Mayo and his associates at Harvard began their pioneering work in industrial behavioral research.[4] They were originally interested in the relation of fatigue and monotony to the work situation. They were unable to prove a direct relationship between environmental factors and output but discovered something heretofore unexpected. Workers were not merely a collection of individuals: they perceived themselves as *members of a group.* Interpersonal values were superior to individual or managerial values and therefore this made members vulnerable to group pressures. In practice this means that managers who do not have the enthusiastic support of the groups they supervise will be unable to motivate individual members to a significant degree.

[3] F. W. Taylor, *Scientific Management* (New York: Harper & Row, Publishers, Incorporated, 1947).

[4] See F. Roethlisberger and W. J. Dickson, *Management and the Worker* (Cambridge, Mass.: Harvard University Press, 1939).

Kurt Lewin   Study of group dynamics was revived in the late 1930s by Kurt Lewin.[5] He provided a theoretical structure for such studies. He was able to prove that groups have a personality all their own; this personality is somewhat like a composite of members' personalities; and group forces can overpower the interests of the individual. Lewin provided the impetus for numerous studies in organizational psychology and organizational behavior, and furnished the theoretical construct for the current popular training provided by T-Groups, Managerial Grid, and D-(Development) Groups. From the motivational viewpoint, Lewin's work confirmed the importance of group control over output.

Douglas McGregor   The 1960s was a decade of great productivity by the behavioral scientists. Douglas McGregor[6] stressed the importance of a manager clarifying his assumptions about the nature of man within the work situation. If a manager understood his subordinates, he would be able to select a motivational network that would better direct effort toward desired goals. Of course, the shortfall here is that much of man's nature still remains an enigma.

A. H. Maslow   On the basis of his classification of human needs, A. H. Maslow[7] assumed an hierarchical relationship from which he was able to deduce that *satisfied needs are not motivators*. This is a most important conclusion. On the surface it appeals to one as entirely reasonable, but it may be too simplistic. There is the problem of recurring need satisfaction, which Maslow recognized. This implies that the satisfaction of a need for food, say, is a motivator *whenever* one is hungry. There is also the problem of human foresight. In an affluent society a man may feel that he has arranged quite well for his need satisfaction; but does he allow for the numerous uncertainties, such as loss of job, technological obsolescence, age, injury, and product demand? In the short run these elements may be ignored; in the long run they are certain to affect need satisfaction. The manager who wishes to take Maslow's conclusion into the motivational system is uncertain how to proceed. Should he assume that his employees have satisfied some of their needs or none?

Frederick Herzberg   On the basis of his field research, Frederick Herzberg has proposed a two-factor theory of motivation.[8] In one group he includes company policy and administration, supervision, working conditions, interpersonal relations, salary, status, job security, and personal life. These environmental factors are dissatisfiers; if they are high in quantity or quality they yield no dissatisfaction, not satisfaction. In the second group are the job con-

[5] See his *A Dynamic Theory of Personality* (New York; McGraw-Hill Book Company, 1945) and *Field Theory in Social Science: Selected Theoretical Papers* (New York: Harper & Brothers, 1951).

[6] *The Human Side of Enterprise* (New York: McGraw-Hill Book Company, 1960) and *The Professional Manager,* Caroline McGregor and Warren G. Bennis, eds. (New York: McGraw-Hill Book Company, 1967).

[7] *Motivation and Personality* (New York: Harper & Brothers, 1954).

[8] F. Herzberg, B. Mausner, and B. B. Snyderman, *The Motivation to Work* (New York: John Wiley & Sons, Inc., 1959).

tent factors composed of achievement, recognition, work, responsibility, advancement, and growth. Their quality will yield feelings of satisfaction or no satisfaction (not dissatisfaction). The first group has been called "hygiene" or "maintenance" factors. Their presence will not motivate subordinates, yet they must be present or dissatisfaction will arise. The job content factors are the real motivators because they have the potential of yielding a sense of satisfaction. If this theory of motivation is sound, the manager of the future will be upgrading the job content.

Chris Argyris   Chris Argyris has focused his research upon the coexistence of individual and organizational needs.[9] He agrees with other behavioral scientists that man has strong self-actualization needs, and he makes the point that organizational controls leave the employee feeling submissive and dependent. Argyris asserts that the operational techniques employed in large-scale enterprises ignore the social and egoistic needs of the employee. Paired with this assumption is a second that maintains the inability of one person to motivate another. Having what Argyris calls "psychological energy," the subordinate will attach top priority to the satisfaction of his own needs. The greater the disparity between individual needs and company needs, the more an employee is likely to reflect dissatisfaction, apathy, conflict, tension, or subversion. In this conception, the technique of achieving motivation would involve offering job challenge and opportunity to employees who may need training to take advantage of the changed environment.

Rensis Likert   Rensis Likert has been a student of organizational relationships for many years.[10] He is a strong proponent of participative management. He sees the effective manager strongly oriented toward his subordinates, relying upon communication to keep all parties working as a unit. All members of the group, including the manager, adopt a supportive relationship in which they feel a genuine common interest in terms of needs, values, aspirations, goals, and expectations. Likert sees this relationship as essential to personal motivation. Any manager concerned about the motivation of his subordinates would have to think this through very carefully. It is not clear whether the manager is supposed to dissolve himself within his group or whether proof of his genuine interest in the development and goals of his subordinates is sufficient. Can a successful manager ever be "one of the boys"?[11]

Arch Patton   Most of the work of the behavioral scientists on motivation has dealt with first-line supervisors and hourly workers. Little has been done on what motivates executives. One of the nation's leaders in the area of execu-

---

[9] *Personality and Organization* (New York: Harper & Brothers, 1957) and *Integrating the Individual and the Organization* (New York: John Wiley & Sons, Inc., 1964).

[10] See his *New Patterns of Management* (New York: McGraw-Hill Book Company, 1961) and *The Human Organization* (New York: McGraw-Hill Book Company, 1967).

[11] Students of motivation will find much of interest in M. G. Evans, "Leadership and Motivation: A Core Concept," *Academy of Management Journal*, vol. 13, no. 1, pp. 91–102 (March, 1970).

tive compensation has identified a series of motivators. Arch Patton has found the following:[12]

1. The challenge we find in work: if this is to be maximized a man must know the purpose and scope of his job responsibilities; what his authority is; what is expected of him; and have a belief in the value of what he is doing.
2. Status: although recognized for centuries in church, military, and government, industry has come to recognize it only in recent years; it includes titles, promotions, and such symbols as office size and appointments, "executive" secretary, company car, and club memberships.
3. The urge to achieve leadership: while difficult at times to distinguish from power, it is really a desire to be a leader among one's fellow men.
4. The lash of competition: this important motivating factor is present in many aspects of life.
5. Fear: this takes many forms, including fear of errors, of loss of a job, or of reduction of a bonus.
6. Money: while placed last, this by no means indicates that it is the least effective motivator; quite the contrary, it is most often more than mere money, being generally a reflection of other motivators.

Newer Researches

While students of motivation are well acquainted with the contributions of the scientists who have been cited in this section, they should also understand that many newer scholars are currently engaged in testing the older theories, attempting to restate them, and even suggesting new theoretical positions.[13] What seems to be emerging is the conviction that motivation of people is enormously difficult due to man's complex and dynamic nature. As a consequence, the earlier tendency to generalize on the basis of small samples and the attempts of practitioners to apply these generalizations were bound to yield disappointing results. It is not likely that the nature of man can be compassed by broad generalizations that have specific validity. And from a philosophical point of view, it may be well that man is denied this power.

MOTIVATION OF MANAGERS

Although much of what is said in the following section applies equally well to nonmanagers, it is the motivation of managers which concerns us here. These men are responsible for the results attained in organized enterprise. Special care needs to be taken in any generalization made about their motivation, because they are still people and vary a great deal from one to another. Yet their similarities are even more impressive.

---

[12] See his *Men, Money and Motivation* (New York: McGraw-Hill Book Company, 1961), chap. 2.

[13] For a competent and yet succinct summary of their work, see Alan C. Filley and Robert J. House, *Managerial Process and Organizational Behavior* (Glenview, Ill.: Scott, Foresman and Company, 1969), pp. 355–387.

Motivation-related Characteristics

Motivation is by no means a science. It is probable that very little is really known about it; but enterprise is not in a position to wait until science catches up. People have been and are being moved to action. It is desirable to seize upon what is known about man and what appeals to common sense and try to establish a motivation system that will focus action on the results desired.

Man's natural inheritance includes the need to avoid boredom, to achieve an identity, and to have security. These drives are common to all mankind; they are "set" by millions of years in the selection process. But this is not to say that all men have them in equal degree. Varying as managers may in this respect, it is probable that a motivation system that enables a man to fulfill these drives is a positive one.

Managers have in common certain environmental factors. In the United States nearly three-quarters of them have good educations, which can help to maximize rational rather than emotional decision making. They have a high degree of mobility within a firm, between industries, and geographically.

This is a composite view of the manager, the man on whom enterprise relies to achieve its ends. But this is only part of the puzzle. It is necessary to define carefully the assumptions which underlie a motivation system.

Basic Assumptions

The Maslow theory that human needs are satisfied in an order of progression is questionable when applied to managers. Common observation indicates many obvious exceptions. The actions of managers differ too widely, in view of their differences in drives, age, economic status, and environmental preferences to enable anyone to say, for instance, that they fulfill first their need for security.

Whether a manager *can* be motivated may be viewed as a matter of semantics. From one point of view, a swept path before a manager is an invitation for him to drive for the satisfaction of his goals. He is self-motivated. On the other hand, someone may place those golden apples in such a way that the intended results of organized activity will, at the same time, be achieved. In other words, someone must have established the available prizes, the rules of the game, and removed the barricades to self-fulfillment. The resulting system is viewed as motivating.

The motivation system itself has certain characteristics. It has to be productive in the sense that the results it yields are in excess of the cost. For instance, it surely would not do to develop a corporate conglomerate just to provide managers with the security of expanding positions. The system has to provide competitive rewards so that managers of desired caliber will be attracted and retained. It should be comprehensive in the sense that there will be a variety of rewards appealing to the productive drives of individual managers. This will also provide the needed flexibility for application as time changes the individual and the environment.

Finally, the motivators can be both positive and negative. They have always had this feature. Although the positive elements seem to outweigh the negative, there can be circumstances when this is not true.

The Motivators

Under some circumstances, the need for *security* or the need to be free from anxiety can be a motivator, though probably a comparatively weak one. In some work situations, anxiety for job security will influence the behavior of those managers who have not attained a measure of economic independence.

On the other hand, complete freedom from an anxiety for job security is not advocated. There are too many instances of security in social arrangements with consequent poor job performance. Neither is there solicitude for the mediocre and inefficient manager even though he has some concern about his position prospects; rather, it is for the security of the able, but economically imperiled, manager whose efforts should not deteriorate through a need for security.

Since the enterprise is normally interested in reducing, but not eliminating, the incidence of position anxiety for its able managers, it should actively pursue a policy of growth. In fact, many have found without growth the desire to maintain position may act as a strong barrier to the hopes and desires of the ambitious.

Man lives in search of his *identity* and does not cease his striving at least until he has established himself at the plateau of his ability. Managers, too, strive for uniqueness for this is the only way they can achieve recognition for their accomplishments and for their personal worth.

The promise of recognition is a powerful motivator. For those who perform unusually well to accomplish beneficial results, the enterprise can offer various forms of appreciation. It has unique titles; it has, and can create, unique positions; it can promote; it can secure prestige for accomplishment; it can adjust salary and grant bonuses; and it can encourage participation. The administration of this motivator can be difficult because there are many degrees of recognition; they must be awarded fairly. Recognition should be prompt; someone must care enough to act, and that person is the superior of the manager in question.

A second motivator is the need for stimulation or the *avoidance of boredom*. The active, educated, ambitious manager wants action, challenge, and responsibility. There should be no place in organized effort for any riskless, routine sinecures. Stimulation to action and drive can be provided in several ways. A variety of compensation alternatives are available. Managers strive for economic competence: they want the freedom of economic independence. They greet with relish those opportunities to earn bonuses that exceed base salary; to receive stock options; to merit fringe benefits; and in their later years, to enjoy deferred payment and pensions for past service. Compensation plans are dynamic in American industry; they need to be flexible in order to adjust to cyclical changes. Their administration is especially critical when they are employed as motivators.

A third way to stimulate managers is to increase their control over a job. This, of course, is normally assumed in position descriptions. As a man is promoted to higher management positions he does have greater authority and responsibility for the work to be done. It is not necessary to go outside this structure for the means of stimulating action. It can be achieved within the structure, *providing* it is used as intended and authority is not withdrawn from designated positions. No greater invitation to frustration can be given than for the superior manager to go around or through his immediate subordinate managers and work directly with *their* subordinates.

Control over the activity of his group can provide other types of motivation. The opportunity to encourage participation by his subordinates where they have special knowledge that can be useful in redefining objectives or leading to improvement in quality, quantity, and diversity of product, and perhaps to a requirement for different skills, should be seized. It could improve morale—the zeal and confidence of his subordinates.

Control over the group may also affect the élan with which the supervisor manages. As everyone is aware, the way in which positions are viewed can be quite various. There is the manager who goes about his work in a routine fashion—and in many positions this is about all that can be done. Then there are managers who innovate. This is the process of combining known elements in new ways to produce an entirely different effect. For instance, the occasional use of a task force, or program management, is a resort to innovation. Finally, there is the level of creativity—a rare plateau indeed—where the genius of the manager evolves an entirely new conception.

A fourth stimulant is the provision of opportunities for managers to prepare themselves for greater responsibilities. This incentive may take the form of lateral transfers; of making educational, especially technical, opportunities available to those who earn them; and of foreign and important domestic assignments.

The motivators recommended in this section are not new. One or the other of them has been used widely, though rarely does any enterprise bring them to bear as a comprehensive *system*. Unfortunately, they are often interspersed with such nonmotivators as working conditions, interpersonal relations, job security, and interference in personal life. If managers are to be motivated, their attention should be directed to those incentives whose pursuit will satisfy their needs for identity and stimulation.

Administration

The creation and administration of a managerial motivation system are the most hazardous of all enterprise functions. The inputs are largely experimental and the outputs are unknown. Managers just hope and do the best they can because action is required. In the process they would do well to consider their administrative problems from the point of view of the system itself, the environmental influences, and the individual decision maker.

Managers should be continually concerned about the *motivation system* of their operation. One key question concerns its ability to elicit personal, constructive response. It is not enough to be in consonance with what is known about human beings. Does it act as an incentive for the *individual?* Unless it results in a personal contribution that exceeds what would be achieved from simply paying a salary, it is too costly to operate.

The administrator is also worried about whether the system should assume that all managers will react in the same way at any given time. Or should the incentives be administered on an individual basis, and should they allow for the age factor, the economic factor, the family situation factor? Important as these considerations may be, it is unwise to allow them greatly to influence administration. The costs of differential treatment would be too great, and paternalism would be quickly charged.

The question of authority is bound to arise in the administration of any system. The fact of the matter is that authority motivation cannot be centralized in any one person. Even though policy decisions are made by a board of directors concerning what groups qualify for option, for deferred income, for bonuses, for salary adjustments, there is always the problem of how each manager will interpret policy in given situations. So long as alternatives exist and decision making is decentralized, there will be wide differences in the actual administration of any incentive program.

The administration of a motivation system is also affected in important ways by changes in the *environment*. The business cycle can play havoc with the effectiveness of stock options and bonuses. Funds to pay bonuses may simply not exist during recessions. Most managers, however, understand these circumstances very well, and their actions are guided by the promises of cyclical recovery. This is not quite the response to stock options that are issued, say, at $35 and the stock falls to $5. What should a board do? It can, within certain legal and tax limitations, perhaps effectively cancel out the old and issue new options, but does it want to do so for each manager? Furthermore, stock options are normally outstanding at different issue prices. Should anything or nothing be done? Good answers to these questions are hard to come by.

Finally, the administration of a motivation system seems to be involved in nothing but problems as managers make *decisions* concerning individual salary adjustments for their subordinates, promotions, bonuses, etc. Always there is the question of fairness. And always, there will be some dissent. People never outgrow being people.

MOTIVATION AND CREATIVITY

There appears to be much mystery about creativity. One hears over and over again that what modern enterprise needs is more creativity, more innovativeness. Motivation is sometimes perceived as the key to creativity, and there is often the mistaken notion that managing itself tends to stifle it by placing heavy demands on conformity.

There are even differences in the concept of creativity held by various people. Some would say that creativity exists only when an individual brings forth something—an idea, a principle, a set of relationships (for example, Einstein's $E = MC^2$), a product, or an approach to a problem—that had not been conceived or thought of before in any major respect. Or creativity may be essentially equated with innovation as an instance where an individual puts together two or more known elements or factors in a combination that did not exist before. The latter use of the term is what is normally thought of as creativity. The former concept would exclude such generally thought of creations as the Wright brothers' airplane or the atomic bomb.

This is consistent with Haefele's concept of creativity as "the ability to formulate new combinations from two or more concepts already in the mind."[14] This is what innovation is—the use of present knowledge in a combination to solve a problem that has never been solved before. When the Wright brothers invented the airplane, they were only pulling together in a new way such elements of knowledge as those existing in aerodynamics and high horsepower in small weight. Even the basic knowledge necessary for the invention of the atomic bomb was available some years before. Likewise, the innovation involved in creating the first chart of approval authorizations was nothing more than combining into one technique the elements of authority delegation, organization hierarchy, the need for clarity, and the recognition that authority involves the right to commit for direction, money, or reputation.

It is widely agreed that creativity arises when there is a problem to be solved *and* the problem is seen in the light of the critical variables involved and their relationships. Often realization and seeing the problem are the true innovative acts and the answer the easier part of the process.

It can readily be realized that managing itself is a creative process. The effective manager is ever coming up with a solution that did not exist before to a policy, program, procedure, organizational structure, and countless other elements of his task. It is sometimes not realized that effective managing is one of the most continually creative of all pursuits.

In encouraging creativity within an enterprise, certain things need to be recognized: (1) creativity is not, as sometimes thought, a rare human quality, although socially significant creativity is a much more rare achievement; and (2) creativity is largely a matter of placing a person in an environment where he *can* be creative, where he can and will recognize the existence of problems and where he will have the organizational authority and resources to solve them—that is, the freedom to innovate and create. This is, to a very great extent, the essence of the concept of managing used in this book—the design and maintenance of an environment where individuals, working together in groups, can perform effectively and efficiently.

FOR DISCUSSION

1. What social, psychological, and physical pressures are present to force men to work?
2. If there are external pressures which force men to work, why is it necessary to motivate them on the job?
3. Should managers and leaders try to motivate subordinates and followers? Why?
4. What do you believe to be the major motivating factors for you?
5. "You cannot motivate a manager. He is self-propelled. You just get out of his way, if you really want performance." Comment.
6. How would you like to be motivated?

[14] J. W. Haefele, *Creativity and Innovation* (New York: Reinhold Publishing Corporation, 1962), p. 5.

27
communication

Although communication has pervasive application to all phases of manager-ship, it is particularly important in the function of directing. Good communica-tion has been defined by the American Society of Training Directors as the interchange of thought or information to bring about mutual understanding and confidence or good human relations. Newman and Summer[1] define com-munication as an exchange of facts, ideas, opinions, or emotions by two or more persons. Communication is also defined as intercourse by words, letters, symbols, or messages; and as a way that one organization member shares meaning and understanding with another.[2]

In this book communication is viewed as the transfer of information from one person to another, whether or not it elicits confidence. But the information transferred *must* be understandable to the receiver.[3] It should never be for-gotten that nothing can logically be called information unless it informs some-one!

IMPORTANCE OF THE COMMUNICATION FUNCTION

It is no exaggeration to say that communication is the means by which orga-nized activity is unified. It may even be looked upon as the means by which social energic inputs are fed into social systems. Whether we are considering a church, a family, a scout troop, or a business enterprise, the transfer of infor-mation from one individual to another is absolutely essential. It is the means by

[1] W. H. Newman and C. E. Summer, Jr., *The Process of Management* (Englewood Cliffs, N.J.: Prentice-Hall, Inc., 1961), p. 59.

[2] R. Bellows, T. Q. Gilson, and G. S. Odiorne, *Executive Skills* (Englewood Cliffs, N.J.: Prentice-Hall, Inc., 1962), p. 59.

[3] See C. G. Browne, "Communications Means Understanding," *Personnel Administration,* vol. 31 (1958).

which behavior is modified, change is effected, information is made productive, and goals are achieved. Communication as a topic of inquiry is of rather recent origin, not because the ancients were ignorant of its critical function, but because "everybody knew" its essentiality and took part in it.

The topic of communication has emerged in management literature in rather recent times. It is fashionable today for writers to criticize the "classical" school for lack of attention to this matter,[4] but this attitude is just as inappropriate as asking where were today's behavioralists when Fayol wrote his book. The earlier writers largely assumed the need for communication and the importance of its understanding. When they mentioned the topic at all it was in the context of directions issued by officers or managers.

Barnard was one of the first and at least the best-known of authors who gave serious consideration to communication in large-scale enterprise.[5] He viewed it as the means by which people were linked together in an organization in order to achieve a central purpose. This is still the fundamental function of communication. Group activity is impossible without information transfer because, without it, coordination and change cannot be effected.

Several years later, when psychologists became interested in the topic, the emphasis was placed on the human problems of transmission. Much of their research related to sending and receiving messages, and the barriers they found to "good" communication. Out of this work certain principles of communication have been developed; these are reported at a later point in this chapter.

The main stream of communication at the present time embodies the contributions of both sociologists and psychologists and the use of these for the welfare of the enterprise. Purpose and goals are uppermost in the minds of those who manage enterprises. To achieve these ends, they seize upon the social principles and techniques of many contributors, including communication experts. It is the view of the authors of this book that the achievement of enterprise goals is of paramount importance and that communication is one of the important tools available to the manager in seeking to attain them.

RESPONSIBILITY FOR COMMUNICATIONS

In all the attention given to communication during the past two decades, the subject of responsibility for information transfer has largely been ignored. It is a matter of some importance to understand that every person in organized enterprise shares the responsibility for good communications. It is not only a top manager who may initiate while all others receive, nor is it only the subordinate who originates while superiors listen. It is a fact that everyone is

---

[4] See, for example, E. P. Learned and A. T. Sproat, *Organization Theory and Policy* (Homewood, Ill.: Richard D. Irwin, Inc., 1966), p. 77.

[5] C. I. Barnard, *The Functions of the Executive* (Cambridge, Mass.: Harvard University Press, 1938).

both an originator and a receiver of information, depending upon the authority relationships, functional relationships, and cooperative relationships which exist in any enterprise.

The real meaning of this set of arrangements is that everyone in the enterprise has a need to know when and what to communicate to whom, as well as to know the available means for information transfer, including the use of both formal and informal avenues. The enterprise requires skill in communication from every one of its employees, although it often has to cultivate this skill internally. The effort of educational institutions in this regard falls far short of the needs of organized institutions.

PURPOSE

In its broadest sense, the purpose of communication in enterprise is to effect change—to influence action in the direction of corporate welfare. In a simple system in which the owner also supplies the labor, communication is totally external. The farmer, for instance, requires information flow from every external source that has knowledge which he can utilize for the prosperity of his operation. He needs the inward flow of knowledge about prices, competition, technology, and finance, as well as information about the business cycle, government activity, and the conditions of peace or war itself. This knowledge supplies the basis for decisions affecting product lines, production ratios, marketing strategy, quality, and the mix of productive factors.

The communication process of large-scale enterprise is largely the same, although the most important additional input concerns internal information flow. The immediate absorption and action taken in response to inputs become impossible when the top manager has a large number of employees. The human factor requires special treatment, for it has to absorb and take action in turn; when several thousand subordinates are involved, the problem becomes monumental in scope and always something less than complete in solution. The principles of communication, cited later in this chapter, are important for their own sake but are applicable only after one considers what are the needs for information transfer.

The problem of classifying information needs for purposes of achieving clarity in understanding is important in itself. On the other hand, attempts to fractionate the subject into detail, such as memoranda, bulletin-board techniques, letter writing, or computer printing, would not contribute to the central idea of promoting a useful conception of the communication needs of a large enterprise. Neither would the written-oral dichotomy be helpful. To bridge these problems, it is hoped that the classification selected here will be helpful.

COMMUNICATION AND THE DECISION PROCESS

Of concern here is the information needed and what is done with it to enable managers to make operational decisions. The locus of most decisions is internal to the firm and much of the information required is generated by the firm itself.

However, as we all know, even operational decisions rest partially upon external data.

The Manager's Need to Know

If one were to observe the information, in all its variant forms, that flows to a manager in the typical enterprise, he would have a word for it: chaos. Subordinates want to be helpful, or to promote themselves, or to reflect discredit somewhere, and they originate or serve as a transmission belt for information *they* think the manager should have. Furthermore, it is the nature of the business process that information is generated where it is most easily reflected and is very scarce in areas or phases where data are not readily available. If one could project a tape which showed "information" density through time, he would find areas of heavy concentration and areas of little or no activity. This means two things: First, people seem to have an inner drive to report available information in many ways, many forms, and for many users. Note what an accountant or statistician can do with a few figures—or a mathematician without any figures at all! Second, the lack of information in specific areas means only that it is not available; it does not mean that it is unnecessary. Indeed, the blind areas may be of the greatest importance for decision-making purposes.

The results of this state of affairs are not inconsequential. Duplications, overlaps, a mixture of the frivolous and the important, variant timing and rates of flow, and the irritations of nonavailability spell nothing but high cost and poor decisions. When one adds the immense cost of warehousing legal documents, engineering drawings, financial data, and other types of information—all often stored in quadruplicate—it is readily seen that enterprise and government have created a monster. While newer technologies are helpful in keeping pace with storage problems, not enough has been done to ensure discrimination in selecting information required for decision making.

Nothing can be done, in reality, until the manager himself poses and responds to the question, "What do I need to know?" This is the proper place to start if one is seriously concerned about the communication of relevant information for making decisions. Furthermore, one should not assume that two successive managers of the same plant will answer the question in exactly the same way. There will certainly be some common information, but there will also be unique data requirements. As will be seen in Chapter 29 where information for control purposes is discussed, the best control system is one tailored, among other things, to individual manager needs. This fact is a serious reflection upon the success of efforts to create a uniform information system for any firm.

An Information System

The considerable discussion about the possibilities of an information *system* in recent years reflects a concern for improved communications in enterprise. Theorists see a real possibility of conceptualizing information flow as a system. They have not succeeded because there has been an absence of a definition of manager needs, because they have not understood the problem of hierarchical information needs, and because of the unique factors in managerial information requirements.

The information system which is normally conceptualized is one providing for a manager to specify, or have specified for him, certain inputs flowing from subordinates who tap internal and external sources. The received information is evaluated and decisions are set forth for the consideration and action of subordinates. This is a one-loop system; in modern enterprises, the loops are interrelated at each successive level of management. This concept provides for the flow of required information from bottom to top, and from top to bottom, in the organization structure on the assumption that the top executive has defined his needs.

Besides the lack of the pivotal assumption above, the development of an information system suffers from other unsolved problems. There is the problem of how long the existing system will suffice for the needs of the enterprise. Conceivably, the system should be changed with every change in the personnel occupying management positions. This, of course, can readily be arranged—but at what cost? There is a constant turnover of managers in large-scale enterprises and a constant change in the nature of required information. Second, the system will have to provide for the acceptance of certain types of new information (not in the programmed system) at almost every level of the organization. This is not an insurmountable problem, but it is a considerable accommodation problem. Third, the system will require centralized direction. He who heads it will be a service manager, but of a type not widely existing in enterprise.

Upward Flow of Information Summaries

One conception of the information flow for decision purposes is closely related to organization levels. Information moves upward from the supervisory level and is summarized for the consumption of department managers, who take action within the scope of their authority. They, in turn, move this information upward one level, say to the division managers' level, at which point it is summarized for their action and for transmittal to the general officer, where it is summarized and serves him for decision purposes. This conception fits the thinking of systems- and computer-oriented people, but it is not realistic. First, every manager has other sources of information that he brings to bear on his decisions; he is not solely dependent upon data flow. For instance, personal observation is notably important in this regard. Second, the conception is essentially static. New factors enter the picture continuously, such as internal and external changes in price, quality, markets, competition, technology, etc. Finally, changing managers weigh information differently, and much of the summarized information may not be needed for varying time periods.

Downward and Lateral Information Flow

Timing, scope, and means are all involved in the flow of information downward in the decision process. Selecting the correct time and communicating a decision are the prerogatives of the manager. Most decisions flow through the organization structure level by level.

Obviously, downward flow of information through organization levels is a time-consuming process. Indeed, it is so time-consuming that most alert top managers insist on information flowing directly to where it is required. One company chief executive, for example, adopted the positive rule that no superior was to receive information concerning a subordinate's area of operation *before* the subordinate received it. He thus instituted a lateral flow of information so that everyone in the company would be informed as soon as possible about his area of operation and have an opportunity to undertake needed corrections expeditiously.

The scope of the communication is a highly variant matter. It is considered good practice to explain the reason for the decision to all those affected by it—not to get their approval, but to improve the quality of their response. Staff meetings are the usual technique chosen for this purpose.

EMPLOYEE COMMUNICATIONS

The human factor is a special case so far as the purpose of communication is concerned. From an internal point of view, one does not have a communication problem with land or capital. In all aspects of dealing with the human factor, however, from recruitment to retirement, the need for effective communication is paramount.

Recruiting

The purpose of communication in this process is to persuade potential employees of the merits of working for the enterprise. It is essential to inform prospective recruits about the firm in general—its location, size, product lines, competition, and financial standing—so that a favorable image will be generated. The recruits also need information about internal policies and practices, organization structure, where they will fit in, and their alternative careers. Drawbacks are not overlooked but they are not stressed. They are dealt with in a manner that provides a favorable comparison with the conditions that are generally known to prevail in other enterprises.

Orientation

The purpose of communication in this area is to provide the employee with a sense of familiarity and security in his job. Believing that people are more productive and more inclined to remain on the payroll if they are emotionally comfortable, considerable effort is directed toward making them acquainted with peers, superiors, and subordinates, toward familiarizing them with social and business groups, explaining procedures, policies, and practices, acquainting them with staff and service facilities, and making certain that they understand the operating philosophy of the enterprise.

Operation Information

In order to execute his functions effectively, every employee stands in need of considerable information. The literate and responsible employee does not respond well to detailed directions and close supervision. He looks upon himself as accountable for a total job and, to do this well, he needs to know its relationship and importance to the over-all operation. Based on this information, he can take more intelligent action—he can better judge the importance of time and quality factors. Furthermore, some degree of zeal and confidence will creep into his work if he has more information about its nature.

Individual Appraisal

The need for the superior manager to communicate to his subordinates his evaluation of their contribution to enterprise activity is critical. This is their best means of knowing how they stand, what he considers their major attributes with respect to accomplishing their assignments, how their contributions can be improved, and what the future may hold for them. This evaluation contributes greatly to employee morale, provided it is intelligently done, a matter discussed in Chapter 23.

Personal Safety

Enterprises go to great lengths today to provide information about employee safety on the job. From the employer's viewpoint, this is an essential activity because it keeps down the human cost of accidents, lowers the compensation insurance premiums and legal costs of defense, decreases recruitment and training costs for replacements, and contributes to the productivity of employees. From the employee's point of view, the communication of safety information and the enforcement of safety standards can only be morale builders. His life and welfare are, naturally, of primary importance to him.

Discipline

Everyone, and especially employees, recognize the need for discipline in organized activities. The purpose of communication on this subject is to acquaint employees with the rules and regulations of the enterprise so that they can accommodate themselves to them. Such things as hours of work, parking, special clothing to be worn, care of equipment, and peaceful interpersonal relations come into focus here. Regulations relating to work output and work flow, maintenance and safety of work place, visiting, proper handling of complaints, and reward distribution are all subjects requiring clear and accurate communication with employees.

THE ENTERPRISE IMAGE

The image which an enterprise projects externally is a matter of great concern. The very future of the enterprise may be the measure of success in this regard.

The recognition of this fact by universities, hospitals, governments, and businesses accounts for the extent and cost of "public relations" activities. The importance of broadcasting information about what an enterprise is doing, what it hopes to do, and why it is especially designed to accomplish these things is rather obvious. It may romanticize the firm, it may stress efficiency, need, power, convenience, opportunities, or safety. These appeals are notably important in improving the capability of the enterprise to attract employees, customers, and stockholders, to excite students and scholars, to soothe the trepidations of the sick and forlorn, and to project what so often is not. To do these things, resort can be had only to communication.

MAJOR PROBLEMS IN COMMUNICATION

It is important that the practical needs for communication be fully understood, and it is equally important that the issues involved in achieving good communication be clarified. These issues include getting ready to communicate, recognition of the barriers to communication, the principles of communication, the choice of techniques, crosswise communication, and the special problem of oral versus written communication.

GETTING READY TO COMMUNICATE

A review of the purposes of communication, similar to that of the foregoing section, leaves the impression that there exists a ready-made package of information which needs to be directed toward the decision makers, the motivation of subordinates, and the establishment of the enterprise image. Of course, this package is a result of getting ready to communicate. This is an interesting process if only because we carry it out so poorly. The evidence is everywhere that people start talking and writing without thinking. Getting ready to communicate is a very serious matter; it requires the time and the logic suggested in the previous discussion of the planning process. The objective must be clear, the premises known, the alternatives weighed, and the message selected. Thereafter the choice of communication techniques, and who is to execute the message, become critical. Treating the communication issue as a matter important enough to carry the cost and time of good planning techniques is most unusual, but it is essential if the change sought by a message is to be fully achieved.

BARRIERS

How can large enterprises such as the federal government, a stock exchange, an airline, and a steel corporation operate with inadequate communications? Yet, if one inquires into the degree of understanding of necessary information at any given moment, one will be taken aback by its inadequate quality. This is possible because, even while successful in the long run, enterprises respond by fits and starts, and the flow of understanding among the cooperators tends to be discontinuous.

Notable improvement in efficiency could be made if communication barriers were torn down. Perhaps the following review will encourage the improvement of information transfer, for "improvement" is all that can be realistically expected. There is no such thing as perfect communication.

Badly Expressed Messages

Irrespective of how a communication is delivered, vagueness and murkiness are all too common. Such faults as poorly chosen and empty words and phrases, careless omission, lack of coherence, poor organization of ideas, awkward sentence structure, inadequate vocabulary, platitudes, numbing repetition, jargon, and failure to clarify implications are common. This lack of clarity and precision leads to costly errors, costly corrections, and the need for otherwise unnecessary clarifications.

Faulty Translations

Managers sit at the communication centers of enterprise and function as receivers and transmitters of messages. They receive many types of communications from superiors, peers, and subordinates and, in turn, must translate information destined for subordinates, peers, and superiors into language suitable to each. It is often not enough to pass on a communication word for word; either it must be put into words appropriate to the framework in which the receiver operates, or it must be accompanied by an interpretation which will be understood by the receiver. This process calls for skill which is often nonexistent. Since enterprise members operate generally with only approximate understanding, efficiency continuously suffers, with attendant heavy cost.

Loss by Transmission and Poor Retention

Successive transmissions of the same message are decreasingly accurate: In oral communication something in the order of 30 percent of the information is lost *in each transmission*. Therefore, in large-scale enterprise, it is quite impossible to rely on oral communication from one level to another. Even written communications accompanied by interpretations are subject to some loss of meaning in transmission.

Equally serious is poor retention of information. When studies show that employees retain but 50 percent of communicated information, and supervisors but 60 percent,[6] is it any wonder that enterprise operates under a cloud of ignorance? The necessity for repetition is obvious.

Inattention

The simple failure to read bulletins, notices, minutes, and reports is common. In regard to failure to listen to oral communications, psychologists and educa-

[6] Bellows et al., *op. cit.*, pp. 60–61.

tors have noted that the nonlistener's "earphones" are often turned off while he is preoccupied with his golf score, with his family problems, or with what he can hardly wait to say—which, incidentally, may have nothing to do with the "message being sent." Unfortunately, nonlistening seems to be a chronic human failing. This is illustrated by the common practice of arguing about an *agreed* matter. The reasons vary from impressing the speaker with one's virtuosity and self-centeredness to anxiety or plain contempt for another's viewpoint. In any case, effort to communicate with someone not listening will fail.

Unclarified Assumptions

Often overlooked but critically important are the uncommunicated assumptions which underlie practically all messages. For instance, an authority delegation may appear specific, but how should a subordinate interpret it when he knows he should make a decision not specifically covered, but which he assumes to be implied? He can assume either that his superior meant only exactly what was specified, or he can assume an implication of freedom to make unforeseeable decisions in the interest of the firm. The seeming clarity of the original delegation leads to this uncertainty—and, perhaps, to delayed action or costly lack of action—because of an unclear assumption.

Or, a customer sends a message that he will visit a vendor's plant at a particular time. Then he may assume that the vendor will meet his plane, reserve hotel accommodations, make transportation available, and set up a full-scale review of his programs at the plant. But the vendor is not clairvoyant, and he may assume that the customer is arriving mainly to attend a wedding and will make a routine call at the plant. These are unclarified assumptions in both instances, with possible loss of good will.

Insufficient Adjustment Period

Sometimes communication announces change which seriously affects employees: shifts in the time, place, type, and order of work, shifts in group arrangements or skills to be used. Some communications point to the need for further training, career adjustment, or status arrangements. Changes affect people in different ways, and it may take time to think through the full meaning of a message. Consequently, it is important to efficiency not to force change before people can adjust to its implications.

Distrust of Communicator

Some superiors are noted for the number of countermanding or modifying messages that follow an original communication. These usually result from ill-considered judgments or nonlogical decisions. Repeated experience with these messages gradually conditions subordinates to delay action or to act unenthusiastically.

Premature Evaluation

Rogers and Roethlisberger's famous article[7] on barriers to communication continues, and rightly, to make the rounds of management literature. The barrier they stressed was the tendency prematurely to evaluate communications, rather than to keep an uncompromised position during the interchange. They felt that such evaluation stops the transfer of information, leaving the message sender with a sense of futility. In their thesis, those who would communicate should be listened to in noncommittal, unprejudiced fashion and thus be encouraged to state their full position before any response is generated. In this environment the complete message may be transmitted and received. Sagacious decision and action can follow.

Fear

Experienced managers recognize that they must depend on their subordinates for information; but no foolproof classification of subject matter or of urgency has yet been developed to guide a subordinate in exactly what he should communicate upward. The timing and accuracy of control reports, problem reports, and special reports normally do not provide the superior with a sense of security.

Here the door is open to poor selection, partial truths, or entire omissions. Why do subordinates behave this way? Either because they truly believe the information is not important enough to communicate—this is a matter of judgment; or, too often, fearing the consequences of a full disclosure, they deliberately mislead a superior.

Failure to Communicate

To the uninitiated, this "barrier" seems both astonishing and unforgivable, and yet it is a fact that managers fail to transmit needed messages. The reasons are found in well-known human tendencies to be lazy, to assume that "everybody knows," to procrastinate, to "hog" information, or deliberately to embarrass. Since one cannot communicate everything, it is obviously necessary to select. This leaves the door wide open to selecting nothing, of which all managers are sometimes guilty.

PRINCIPLES FOR EFFECTIVE COMMUNICATION

The following principles are useful guides for establishing good communications because they direct attention to four critical areas: message quality, conditions for reception, maintenance of integrity of organized effort, and taking advantage of informal organization.

Principle of clarity   Although communication is often thought of as

---

[7]C. R. Rogers and F. J. Roethlisberger, "Barriers and Gateways to Communication," *Harvard Business Review*, vol. 30, no. 4, pp. 46–52 (July–August, 1952).

applying to a message from a sender, if it is to have value it should meet the test of the principle of clarity: *a communication possesses clarity when it is expressed in language and transmitted in a way that will be comprehended by the receiver.* As simple as this principle is, most managers would be surprised if they knew how poorly even their most carefully phrased and thought out communications were comprehended by the receiver. Some managers have tried the test of having their communications fed back to them and having communications of others to them clarified by asking follow-up questions, such as "As I understand it, you mean so and so?" The results of such tests, even though tedious, have invariably proved to be a shocking eye-opener.

It is the responsibility of the sender to formulate the communication and express it understandably, in writing or speech. This requires a literate approach to language and familiarity with language patterns of subordinates, peers, and superiors. Adherence to this principle will overcome several barriers to communication: badly expressed messages, faulty translations and transmissions, unclarified assumptions, and the need for follow-up clarifications.

Even though the principle of clarity is observed, no communication is completed unless the message is understood, and this requires attention. Getting full attention for even well-composed messages is no easy matter, because of both the quantity of messages competing for attention and the brevity of our human attention span. The receiver cannot listen or read with understanding unless he concentrates. Listening in a discontinuous and desultory fashion, behaving listlessly, or ignoring or skimming over written words ensures lack of understanding, to say nothing of being extremely discourteous to the communicator.

Adherence to the need for attention will gradually overcome certain barriers to communication: inattention, loss in transmission, and poor retention. It will also improve the quality of listening and reading, and the communicator will most certainly feel encouragement for his efforts.

Principle of integrity Managerial communications are means rather than ends. As the principle of integrity makes clear: *the purpose of managerial communications is to support understanding by individuals in their achieving and maintaining the cooperation needed to meet enterprise goals.*

One aspect of this principle needs particular attention. The integrity of the enterprise depends in part on supporting the position of subordinate managers. Since they occupy centers of communication, they should be encouraged to use their positions for this purpose. Superiors often forget this and send messages bypassing subordinates in an effort to contact the ultimate employees directly. This can be approved only in those circumstances where simultaneous communication is essential: orders for evacuating a burning building or for taking cover from attack, information of a crisis nature such as a general wage cut or cutback in employment or the need for special effort to complete a contract, or news of equal concern to superiors and subordinates, such as the announcement and interpretation of policies of an enterprise-wide application.

Principle of strategic use of informal organization   The nature of this key principle is: *the most effective communication results when managers utilize the informal organization to supplement the communication channels of the formal organization.* Informal organization arises from the need for transmisssion of information that is not suitable for formal transmission. Existing outside the formal structure, it should be mobilized to transmit and receive information supplementary to that provided by the formal organization in the coordination of enterprise effort.

Messages do flow, and sometimes are required to flow, formally from superior to subordinate and from subordinate to superior, but this channel is inadequate and unreliable for handling all messages expeditiously and with understanding. Therefore, managers often informally approach subordinates—personally or through others—to establish contact with situations which would evade them otherwise. So long as no orders are given or implied, the intelligent use of this practice is highly recommended.

Implementation

Putting the foregoing guides to work requires voluntary application by all members of an enterprise. This calls for a special provision in the motivational system. No one can point to dollar savings, for the cost of poor communication cannot be calculated; but that there will be cost improvements from better communication no one doubts.

Managers may send subordinates to classes in communications; they should coach them constantly; and they should overlook no opportunity to point out the need for good communication.

TECHNIQUES

The sheer mass of communication in the typical enterprise is overwhelming. Everybody initiates and receives messages in some form or other. Man is almost constantly either talking, writing, listening, or reading. He usually becomes more addicted to loquacity as the size of the organization to which he belongs increases. Indeed, the volume of communication may increase in geometric progression as the enterprise grows. In an attempt to determine the time spent in communicating, one investigator[8] reported that 232 technical employees of a research organization spent 61 percent of their eight-hour workday in this activity: speaking and listening 35 percent, writing 16 percent, and reading 10 percent. A manager's whole day may be occupied in reading, writing, speaking, and listening. Thus, from 60 to 100 percent of working time may be spent sending and receiving messages.

Under these circumstances, unnecessary messages are obviously costly. Yet differentiating between necessary and unnecessary communication is complex, because there is no pat answer to the question, What does each individual in an enterprise need to know? Everyone has requirements of which he alone is aware, although sometimes even he is not aware of needing certain

[8]Bellows et al., *op. cit.*, pp. 61–63.

information. This situation makes communication largely a matter for personal decisions, for which no standards exist.

That repetitious, overlapping, and irrelevant messages are expensive is borne out by the number of persons, both inside and outside the firm, employed to review, revise, consolidate, and simplify written messages. People like to be on distribution lists whether they use the information or not; they do not want to miss anything. They even insist on slightly different forms or arrangements of data, losing sight of the cost. All these practices burden communication channels.

Choice of Presentation

Managers must often choose between presenting information in narrative, statistical, or graphic form. Trend data are easiest to understand in a graphic presentation; some items are more easily grasped in statistical form; and the unusual or complicated may be clearer in a narrative.

Electronic Data Processing

In speeding up the transfer of information, managers have studied and gradually adopted improved techniques for processing and reproducing data. The ultimate in these is electronic data processing. Electronic equipment has made it possible to communicate immense quantities of data on a regular schedule and to secure hitherto unavailable information for enterprise use.

The economy of providing computerized data is in serious question. Protagonists of electronic data processing make many unprovable claims. Equipment and programming costs are large; individual reports are costly, even on a continuing basis; the demand for computer time often forces priority scheduling; and the equipment is so interesting that its reports acquire status even though they may not be as useful, timely, or economical as an old-fashioned pencil jotting. On the other hand, a computer is indispensable for reducing large masses of data quickly and for producing new information from these data. But it must never be forgotten that data are not necessarily information; to be this, they must inform someone.

A manager must evaluate integrated data processing carefully. He will discover that many data transmissions are more economical and faster with simpler methods and that as much as three-quarters of the gain from employing high-speed computers *could be obtained by better planning*, a prior requirement for computer programming. Moreover, much of the disillusionment arising from use of electronic data processing is traceable to poor or inadequate planning and lack of definition of the end products desired.

CROSSWISE COMMUNICATIONS

All enterprises not only permit but insist on voluntary crosswise[9] or horizontal channels of communications at all levels, to speed information and improve

---

[9]For a good discussion of this subject, see M. C. Niles, *Middle Management* (New York: Harper & Row, Publishers, Incorporated, 1949), chap. 4.

understanding. Crosswise relationships exist between personnel in one division and personnel of equal, lower, or superior status in other divisions. Direct communication between them substitutes for making a message follow the chain of command upward through one or more superiors, horizontally across a level of organization, and thence downward to the particular recipient. Enterprises simply cannot operate in such stilted fashion because the communication time would be excessively long and the quality of understanding would be inferior.

The proper safeguards of crosswise communication rest in an understanding between superiors that (1) crosswise relationships will be encouraged, (2) subordinates will refrain from making policy commitments beyond their authority, and (3) subordinates will keep their superiors informed of their interdepartmental activities.

Every manager should guide his subordinates in their conduct of crosswise relationships. In addition to their objectives of getting the work done and developing potential managers, division heads are conscious of the impact that crosswise relationships may have on themselves: Every time a subordinate communicates horizontally, his superior is evaluated by others as to his general efficiency as a manager, the quality of his directive skill, his choice of subordinates, and his planning and organizing ability. In such circumstances, the superior may feel quite as helpless as a parent who wants his child to make a good impression on friends but cannot control the situation.

Overcoming Barriers

Departmentation automatically creates barriers to free communication between personnel and provides numerous points of friction. Proliferation of subdivisions based on geographic, product-line, or customer classifications, on the one hand, and the multiplication of staff and service groups, on the other, create further barriers to direct communication. People do not have time to become acquainted with the organization structure or with one another, and, as a consequence, they develop group loyalties that breed intolerance and untoward rivalry. But since organization is necessary, managers ameliorate these adverse results by carefully directing subordinates' crosswise relationships.

In guiding and supervising subordinates in these respects, managers attempt to anticipate points of friction. These usually involve lack of knowledge about the enterprise, personality clashes, and unsuitable grouping of activities.

Orientation   Getting acquainted with the objectives, structure, and authority relationships of a large-scale enterprise is formidable, especially for new employees. The superior will try to orient the subordinate and see that he masters organizational relationships. The superior will acquaint him, first, with the purpose and major functions of other divisions and, secondly, with the staff and service departments. The former present an integrated picture of the whole enterprise; knowledge of the latter may prevent the subordinate from duplicating such specialized functions within his department.

Several techniques are employed to orient subordinates in these areas. Most common are general tours and classes of instruction for new employees. They are given organization charts and manuals to study, are taken on tours through the firm or some of its divisions, and are lectured to by major department heads and perhaps general officers. A second technique is to give subordinates rotating assignments throughout the firm. Its obvious objective is to familiarize the individual with the purposes and problems of the various departments. Such familiarity helps prevent the growth of suspicion and intolerance.

Interpersonal relations Getting along with people is important in organized activity, particularly where democratic traditions are strong. This point is always stressed by managers because most work is accomplished by getting others to do it. In directing, managers should maintain respect for the authority and personal dignity of their subordinates. Such qualities as kindness, thoughtfulness, and an eagerness to understand others may seem too obvious to mention, yet lack of these is the cause of many poor personal relationships. Managers also need to caution subordinates to clear everything with everyone involved, not only as a matter of courtesy, but also to avoid presenting others with an unwelcome fait accompli which may or may not be workable.

An effective control on the quality of interpersonal relationships in crosswise communications is the requirement that subordinates keep their superior informed about their dealings with other departments. Periodic reports are often sufficient to take care of this, but on especially touchy matters or on subjects that require new policy formation immediate communication with the superior is essential.

Reorganization Sometimes crosswise relationships are unnecessarily time-consuming and perhaps even unnecessary. If this is a recurrent problem, it may be possible for the manager to modify departmental processes or groups. For example, if the geographic factor is not carefully analyzed, it can occasion much loss of time. To counter this problem it is often possible to change the location of an activity. Sometimes reorganization of an activity along product lines will bring related functions into close physical proximity.

WRITTEN VERSUS ORAL MESSAGES

It is traditional in the literature that consideration be given to formal and informal communication. The authors of this book feel that such a classification creates more problems than it solves. It is often impossible to distinguish the one from the other. The objective of communication is change, whether or not it is achieved formally. It makes more sense, therefore, to retain the common purpose of communication, that is, achieve change, and inquire into the merits of written and oral information transfer.

Written

Written communications have certain advantages: they can be retained as legal records and reference sources; they are often more carefully formulated than oral communications; and they can sometimes save time and money. They are used for the mountainous paper work concerning transactions, proposals, and agreements; organization charts and rule sheets; corporate charters and other legal documents; bulletins, memoranda, contracts, and claims; advertising and public relations announcements and press releases; policy statements and procedures manuals; authority delegations, and job descriptions; and many other things. Often their use is a matter of the communicator's preference and prudence.

There are also disadvantages to written communications. Although the writer has the opportunity to be carefully accurate in composing his message, he often fails. Poorly written messages, followed by numerous written and oral "clarifications," make the ultimate message expensive as well as confused.

A second disadvantage of the written message also involves expense but for a different reason. Because—particularly in large enterprises—there exist opportunities for shifting blame to others and also for taking undeserved credit, people respond by keeping voluminous written documentation as a means of defense or attack. Unfortunate as this situation may be, it is a fact of cooperative life, and expensive. It may cost an enterprise from $10 to $15 to write a letter or issue a check and millions of dollars to write a proposal for a government contract.

Retention for legal purposes   Every enterprise is required to retain particular information for various periods of time. It also elects to retain certain data to protect itself against charges, claims, and lawsuits that normally burden every concern. Examples include property titles, contracts, financial records, charters, and the minutes of boards of directors' meetings. The advantage of retention is often obvious, but there are numerous occasions in which retention for legal purposes is unnecessary and is duplicative. For instance, a firm doing business with the United States Defense Department may be required to retain a particular document, but several individuals are likely to save their personal copies to meet the over-all requirement. Furthermore, the uncertainty of eventual need for legal purposes results in squirreling information. However, managers can develop sensible standard practices in regard to retention if they put their mind to it.

Oral

The chief advantage of oral communication is its potentiality for speedy and complete interchange. Questions can be asked and answered at once. The speaker is forced into direct contact with the listener and challenged to make himself understood. Unfortunately, for one reason or another, many listeners fail to ask the right questions and are left with inadequate or garbled information which can result in costly error.

Furthermore, oral communication does not always save time, as anyone who has observed the lavish expenditure of conference time knows. And when each participant may be costing from $15 to $50 per hour, face-to-face group communication is hardly economical either.

Communication by Implication

Often neglected or unnoticed, communication may include implications conveyed by how something is said or what is left unsaid, and the important devices of nonverbal communication. Subordinates watch their superior intently for signs indicating what he thinks is important and signs which affect their own self-image. For example, if it is official policy to balance civilian and military business but a division superior prefers the latter, his subordinates will certainly neglect the former; and if by frown or continued unavailability the superior communicates to a subordinate a lack of respect, the chance of contented cooperation is lost.

Expediter or Liaison Man

In the foregoing discussion of written and oral communications it was assumed that the message was aimed at a willing recipient. This may not be the case at all. The recipient may have prejudged the message and decided he has no interest; he may distrust or be hostile to the sender; he may not listen and he may not read. Then there may be conflicting messages from the same or from different sources. The receiver may either do nothing or choose the message he prefers. And finally, multiple messages may require action involving time and resources far beyond those available to the receiver and, therefore, the need arises to establish priorities in handling conflicting or excessive requirements.

To take care of these frequent situations, managers sometimes resort to the expediter and the liaison man. The former is chiefly used to help the receiver of the message assign the "proper" priority to work. If this is an internal arrangement, it can be a crutch to poor communication; if it is external and results in the expediters of customers storming the facilities of a vendor, it can be not only ridiculous but an open invitation to waste.

The function of the liaison person is quite different. He is a middleman communicator who carries messages between sender and receiver in the interests of saving time, and interprets the message in the interests of better understanding. But he, too, is a crutch to poor communication. His mere availability encourages careless communication, delay of reorganization, or procrastination in adopting more efficient communication techniques.

CONTROL OVER THE COMMUNICATION PROCESS

In every enterprise, the practical difficulty of exercising control over communications is apparent to all managers. It does little good merely to describe the variety and techniques of communication; information explosion and concealment practices must be controlled in the interests of strong, progressive management. One suggestion has considerable merit.[10] Recognizing that there is a need for communicating upward information that is not reported in established channels, it has been suggested that, starting with front-line supervisors, subordinate managers should submit monthly a brief narrative statement of any item deemed important for the consideration of his superior manager. Shortly thereafter the line subordinates meet with their superior and discuss these issues, with the result that some may disappear, some may be resolved at once, some may be postponed, and some may become the subject for submission to the next higher level of management. This process is recommended sequentially for all management levels until it reaches the office of the president.

Several advantages of this technique appear at once. It forces every manager to think about his problems or potential problems. It requires each manager to select the issues he thinks should be reported. In the follow-up discussion, the relative maturity of subordinate managers becomes very clear. The technique also assures that both subordinates and superior will be prepared for the meeting. It makes certain that issues of importance, that would ordinarily be reported not at all or only too late for action, will be given appropriate attention. It gives operational purpose to staff meetings by bringing authority to bear on significant issues and thus eliminates the need for many meetings on the occasional problem, as well as many meetings called to solve crises.

There is but one important disadvantage. Narrative reporting on a regular basis is a dangerous thing to require. This type of report easily gets out of hand in terms of irrelevancy, redundancy, scope, extent, mixing of the serious with the frivolous, and poor quality of writing. Managers on the same level compete with each other in the length, content, and appearance of their reports. And, of course, sheer volume practically guarantees that few, if any, of them will be read. It is perhaps much better to follow the practice of having the problem merely cited and defined, allowing the person who submits it to bring with him any substantiating information he needs.

There may also be a need to caution managers that the information contained in their regularly scheduled reporting system should not be allowed to intrude unduly into this monthly conference. Those reports should be examined for exceptions to planned performance, corrective action should be taken at once, and only those rare instances wherein the manager has need for his superior's help should be referred upward for person-to-person attention.

A second suggestion is that each manager should make a list of the written reports he submits to his superior, and also a list of regularly scheduled meetings held with him. The frequency of these reports and meetings should be identified at the same time. Likewise, the manager should require that each of his subordinate managers do the same thing. This technique will cause

---

[10] H. Saxenian, "Prescription for Old-Fashioned Leadership," *Business Horizons*, vol. 8, no. 3, pp. 45–53 (Fall, 1965).

everyone to evaluate the need and frequency of both reports and meetings—a first step in assessing their usefulness.

There is every reason to believe that communication will continue to be numbered among the unsolved problems of every enterprise. The only hope of keeping it within manageable proportions is to hold each executive responsible for the information he demands and transmits. Such an accounting would cause him to think seriously about the problem, to take action to see that what should be communicated is identified, and to insist that the most efficient technique is used for its transmission.

FOR DISCUSSION

1. Communication is a spotty, voluntary phenomenon. Why?
2. What should a manager do to make certain his communications are understood? Cite the principles involved.
3. Develop a plan to transmit decision-making data to the officer charged with buying the assets of another company.
4. From your own experience in the past week, list the barriers to communication you detected. Why did they occur?
5. If you were president of the Students Union, what information would you require?

28
leadership

Although it is the practice of some social scientists to treat the terms "managership" and "leadership" as synonyms, the authors of this book believe they should be distinguished. As a matter of fact, there can be leaders of completely unorganized groups, but there can be managers, as conceived here, only where organized structures create such roles. There are also important analytical advantages in separating leadership from managership. In this manner leadership can be singled out for study without the encumbrance of qualifications relating to the more general issues of managership.

The reader is by now well aware that a manager performs all five functions of management. These are essential as he combines resources to accomplish certain social objectives. He puts the process into operation by means of his authority. As one writer remarked:[1]

Having a common position with reference to the source of originations or direction, subordinates develop cooperative patterns toward one another that facilitate the work process. These would be much more difficult to develop were there not a common source of authority acting on them; witness the difficulties inherent in cooperative endeavors among individuals who have not had this experience.

The manager can approach his objectives by exercising his authority in a more or less autocratic manner to obtain and allocate resources. In other words, he establishes through a rational-intellectual process[2] the internal environment in which work will be done and objectives achieved. He will get some results, as is illustrated in Figure 28.1. But they are likely to be close to the lowest level of acceptable performance in terms of quantity, quality and timeliness.

When a new nonmanagerial employee reports for work, he may be first concerned with determining how hard he must work to achieve minimum performance, that is, the level at which he will not jeopardize his employment and which is acceptable to his superior. Even though he may prefer to work

---

[1] Leonard Sayles, *Managerial Behavior* (New York: McGraw-Hill Book Company, 1964), p. 145.

[2] Social scientists sometimes call this aspect of managership "instrumental leadership."

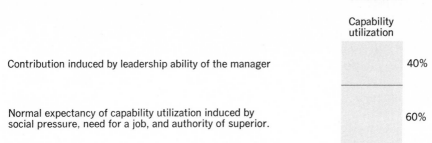

Capability
utilization

Contribution induced by leadership ability of the manager   40%

Normal expectancy of capability utilization induced by
social pressure, need for a job, and authority of superior.   60%

Figure 28.1 *Impact of leadership on employee utilization of capability. . . . Leadership is the ability of a manager to induce subordinates (followers) to work with confidence and zeal. If subordinates are guided only by rules and requirements enforced by managerial authority, they may work at about 60 or 65 percent of capacity—just enough to satisfy the requirements for holding their jobs. To raise effort toward total capability, the manager must induce zealous response on the part of efficient subordinates by exercising leadership. He does this through numerous means, all solidly based on the needs of subordinates, especially their ego and self-development needs.*

above this level, he is often restrained from doing so by output restrictions imposed by trade unions or by the mores of his group. The manager who would raise the productivity of employees toward their maximum capability should remove the artificial barriers strewn before those who are self-motivated and induce zealous response on the part of all others. To accomplish the latter calls for a high order of leadership ability.

LEADERSHIP DEFINED

Among the rare qualities of managers the ability to lead is highly prized. It may be defined as the art of inducing subordinates to accomplish their assignments with zeal and confidence. Zeal reflects ardor, earnestness, and intensity in the execution of work; confidence reflects experience and technical ability. To lead is to guide, conduct, direct, and precede. These terms identify the leader as part of a group and yet distinct from it. The leader acts to help a group attain its objectives with the maximum application of its capabilities, but he never loses his own identity. He does not stand behind a group to push and to prod; he takes his place before the group as he facilitates their progress and inspires them to accomplish organizational goals. The case of the orchestra leader is pertinent: his function is to produce coordinated sound and correct tempo through the integrated effort of the instrumentalists. Depending upon the quality of the director's leadership, the orchestra will respond in desultory fashion or with wit and élan.

FUNCTIONS OF LEADERSHIP

If enterprise managers could rely upon all subordinates to contribute toward group goal accomplishment with zeal and confidence, there would be no need to develop the art of leadership. Morale would always be high and all would produce to their maximum capability. Unfortunately, such ideal behavior cannot be found in organized activity. Whether as a result of lack of motivation or opportunity, or of adverse environmental circumstances or mediocre managers, few subordinates work with continuing zeal and confidence. Perhaps it is not within the gifts of human beings to do so, at least over considerable periods of time.

It is not known what proportion of a group of subordinates or followers are "self-starters" in the sense that they *naturally* work with zeal and confidence. Undoubtedly, many factors contribute to their number. Even among them there are those who would benefit from the manager's leadership as he directs their efforts toward organizational goals.

History is replete with instances of mediocre performance in the absence of leadership and superb performance with it. It is clearly in the interest of every enterprise, if it has other than "make-work" goals, that its employees work with zeal and confidence. Only then can their morale be said to be high; only then will they achieve greater efficiency. Indeed, in competitive situations this condition is the way to preserve organizational existence if it is true, as has been said, that morale is three-quarters of victory. The function of leadership, therefore, is to induce or persuade all subordinates or followers to contribute to organizational goals in accordance with their maximum capability.

NATURE OF LEADERSHIP

Any group of subordinates or followers that performs near its total capability has some person at its head who is skilled in the art of leadership. This skill seems to be a compound of two major ingredients—the ability to invent and use appropriate motivators and the ability to inspire.

It is one thing to know the categories of motivators. As was explained in a preceding chapter, they are concerned with man's need for identity and stimulation. It is quite another thing to discern the strength of the individual's needs, to define ways to satisfy them, and to administer the motivators in a manner that will ensure the desired response. And to make success even more problematical, there is the fact that he who would lead is also a human being and to this extent cannot objectively solve the issues. With little science to guide them, the success of those who would lead depends almost entirely upon the quality of their art and the timeliness of its application.

The second ingredient of leadership seems to be a rare ability to inspire, that is, to animate or to enliven followers to apply their full capabilities to a project. While the use of motivators seems to center about the subordinate and his needs, inspiration emanates from the group head. He has charismatic qualities that induce loyalty, devotion, and a zeal on the part of followers to promote his welfare. This is not a matter of need-satisfaction; it is, rather, a matter of giving altruistic support to a chosen champion. The best evidences of inspirational leadership come from hopeless and fearful situations such as a nation on the eve of battle, a prison camp with exceptional morale, a defeated leader undeserted by faithful followers. Some may argue that such devotion is not entirely altruistic; that it can also explain why those who face catastrophe will follow one whom they selfishly trust. But few would deny the function of charisma in either case.

The emergence of a charismatic leader in organized enterprises, especially during economically affluent years, appears to be unusual. One has only to look about him. Search as industriously as he can, he would be hard put to name many inspirational managers in such times in any university, church, business, trade union, or government organization. Perhaps there is something deadly, something that kills, or something that supersedes the need for inspirational leadership in societies enjoying economic affluence. There may be no urgent reason to be greatly inspirational, except for the gifted self-starters alone. Employees of organized enterprises are most concerned about providing for the long run satisfaction of their basic needs, about achieving identity and enjoying stimulation. Consequently, the truly inspirational ingredient in leadership is likely to lie dormant, only to become a potent art in times of crises.

On the other hand, this is not to deny the continued existence of leaders at all levels and in all kinds of enterprise. Essentially leaders exist because of the need of people for someone to follow. It is probably true that a study of leadership is really a study of followership; and people tend to follow those in whom they see a means of satisfying personal desires. Since almost every possible role in organized enterprise is made more satisfying (whether in money, status, power, or pride of accomplishment) by those who can help others meet these motivations, it can be seen that leaders must always exist in social life. As a matter of fact, perhaps the fundamental principle of leadership is: *since people tend to follow those in whom they see a means of satisfying their own personal goals, the more a manager understands what motivates his subordinates and how these motivations operate, and the more he reflects this understanding in carrying out his managerial actions, the more effective as a leader he is likely to be.* It can also be easily seen that an effective manager, carrying out his managerial functions well, will greatly aid in meeting these personal desires.

LEADERSHIP THEORY AND RESEARCH

Because of its importance to all kinds of group action, one is not surprised to find a considerable volume of research and theory concerning leadership, although most has occurred in the period beginning with World War II. Analyses have disclosed an average of twenty-one studies per year in the decade of 1930 to 1939, thirty-one studies per year between 1940 and 1944, fifty-five studies per year in the period of 1945 to 1949, and 152 studies per year from 1950 to 1953.[3] Even if this exponential expansion of interest in leadership has slowed down somewhat in the intervening years, it can be readily seen that there has been no shortage of speculation, theory, and research in this field.

---

[3] As reported in F. E. Fiedler, *A Theory of Leadership Effectiveness* (New York: McGraw-Hill Book Company, 1967), p. 6.

To give the reader an idea of the focus of this research and interest, a classification of analyses may be formulated. In general, it falls in the categories of theory and study based on personal traits, leader behavior, and leadership situations, and many of the more recent studies show an eclectic tendency to develop leadership theory from a combination of all three.

Personal Traits

Earlier studies concentrated on analysis of personal traits, such as desire for achievement, decisiveness, enthusiasm, drive, fear of failure, and good health, possessed by those who had displayed leadership capabilities. However, studies soon showed this approach to be an inadequate explanation of leadership, although one study by Ghiselli in 1963 did reveal significant correlation between leadership effectiveness and the traits of intelligence, supervisory ability, initiative, self-assurance, and individuality in the way work was done.[4] As can be noted, most of these so-called traits are really patterns of behavior or operation and correlate with various aspects of managership.

Leader behavior   More recent research on leadership has dealt with the behavior patterns of leaders rather than their personal traits. It has been found that this approach puts emphasis on what leaders do rather than on what they are perceived to be. In general, these behavior patterns may be identified as autocratic, participative or supportive, instrumental, or instrumental-supportive ("great man").

The autocratic leader is seen as one who commands and expects compliance, who is dogmatic and positive, and who leads by his ability to withhold or give rewards and punishment. Participative or supportive leadership, on the other hand, is based on the assumption that people want to participate, want to accomplish, and will work best when general supervision is employed and where the superior not only allows them to use their own initative but supports them in accomplishing their tasks.

A considerable volume of research has been undertaken on these two styles of leadership behavior. In general, the results are not as conclusive as one might expect. In their analysis of these studies, Filley and House find that although "there is a general tendency for supportive leadership to have a positive effect on member satisfaction, no consistent relationship has been found between leadership style and production."[5] In general, as these authors point out, application of one or the other managerial style depends upon the situation with respect to the tasks and the characteristics of subordinates. They thus conclude that participative leadership is most effective when (1)

---

[4] See E. E. Ghiselli, "Managerial Talent," *American Psychologist,* vol. 18, no. 10, pp. 631–641 (October, 1963). Earlier studies yielded somewhat similar results. Stogdill found that only the traits of intelligence, scholarship, dependability, responsibility, social participation, and socioeconomic status correlated between leaders and non-leaders. See R. M. Stogdill, "Personal Factors Associated With Leadership: A Survey of the Literature," *Journal of Psychology,* vol. 25, pp. 35–71 (1964).

[5] A. C. Filley and R. J. House, *Managerial Process and Organizational Behavior* (Glenview, Ill.: Scott, Foresman and Company, 1969), p. 403.

the task involves nonroutine decisions, nonstandard information and decisions need not be made quickly; and (2) where subordinates feel a strong need for independence, feel that they should be involved in decision making and can contribute to it, and are confident of their ability to work without close direction.[6]

Instrumental behavioral theory of leadership emphasizes the leader's role as a manager in the rational aspects of management—planning, organizing, and controlling. A leader may use autocratic or supportive-participative styles, but the emphasis is on the central task of allocating human and material resources. It is interesting that a considerable volume of research done at Ohio State, the University of Southern California, and University of Michigan give support to the belief that those who manage well are also effective as leaders.[7]

Largely as the result of lack of clear-cut results from any of the above styles of leader behavior, an understandable tendency is to combine participative and instrumental behavior patterns in what has sometimes been called "great man" theory. Perhaps one of the most widely known of such leadership studies approach is the "managerial grid" developed by Blake and Mouton.[8] This is based on the idea that the most effective leader or manager is one who has both concern for people and concern for production. The authors have shown this on a grid scaled to nine degrees as shown on Figure 28.2. This analytical tool is a simple way of indicating the wide variety of leadership approaches that might be taken. The authors themselves declare that there is no single "best" mix and that the extent of concern practiced should depend on the people being managed and the situation in which the manager finds himself.

Leadership situations   A large number of studies has been made on the premise that leadership is strongly affected by the situation from which the leader emerges and in which he operates. That this is a persuasive approach is indicated by the situation that gave rise to a Hitler in Germany in the 1930s, the earlier rise of Mussolini in Italy, the emergence of Roosevelt in the Great Depression of the 1930s in the United States, and the rise of Mao Tse-tung in China in the period after World War II. This approach to leadership recognizes that there exists an interaction between the group and the leader. It supports the follower theory that people tend to follow those in whom they perceive (accurately or inaccurately) a means of accomplishing their own personal desires. The leader, then, is the person who recognizes these desires and does those things, or undertakes those programs, designed to meet them.

This multidimensional approach to leadership was detected early in the studies of Stogdill and his associates when it was discovered that, in anal-

---

[6] *Ibid.*, pp. 404–405.

[7] See, for example, A. L. Comrey, J. Pfiffner, and W. S. High, *Factors Influencing Organizational Effectiveness* (Los Angeles: University of Southern California Book Store, 1954); R. M. Stogdill and A. E. Coons, *Leader Behavior: Its Description and Measurement* (Columbus, Ohio: Bureau of Business Research, The Ohio State University, 1957); D. Katz, N. M. Maccoby, and N. Morse, *Productivity, Supervision and Morale in an Office Situation* (Ann Arbor, Mich.: Survey Research Center, University of Michigan, 1950).

[8] See R. R. Blake and J. S. Mouton, *The Managerial Grid* (Houston, Tex.: Gulf Publishing Company, 1964).

Figure 28.2 *The managerial grid.*
SOURCE: *Adapted from R. R. Blake and J. S. Mouton,* The Managerial Grid, *op. cit.,*
p. 10.

yzing 470 Navy officers occupying forty-five different positions, their leadership ability was heavily affected by such situational factors as their jobs, the
organizational environment in which they operated, and the characteristics
of people they were assigned to lead.[9] Other studies made over the years have
shown that effective leadership depends upon response to such environmental
factors as the history of the enterprise, the community in which the organization operates, the psychological climate of the group being led, group member
personalities and cultural influences, and the time required for making decisions.[10]

[9]R. M. Stogdill, C. L. Shartle, and Associates, *Patterns of Administrative Performance*
(Columbus, Ohio: Bureau of Business Research, The Ohio State University, 1956), sec. IV.
[10]For a summary of these researches, see A. C. Filley and R. J. House, *op. cit.,* p. 409.

One of the interesting long-time research projects relating leadership effectiveness to situational factors is that undertaken by Fiedler and his associates at the University of Illinois.[11] Postulating that there are two basic kinds of leadership styles, one task oriented and the other people-satisfaction oriented, Fiedler has based his findings on two types of scores: scores on the least preferred co-worker, ratings made by people in a group as to those with whom they would least like to work; and scores on assumed similarity between opposites, ratings made as to the degree a leader perceives a group member to be like himself, on the assumption that people will like best and work best with those who are believed to be most like themselves.

From a considerable body of research of various groups and leaders, Fiedler comes to some interesting conclusions. Recognizing that personal perceptions may be ambiguous and even quite inaccurate, Fiedler has found that:[12]

Leadership performance depends then as much on the organization as it depends on the leader's own attributes. Except perhaps for the unusual case, it is simply not meaningful to speak of an effective leader or an ineffective leader; we can only speak of a leader who tends to be effective in one situation and ineffective in another. If we wish to increase organizational and group effectiveness we must learn not only how to train leaders more effectively but also how to build an organizational environment in which the leader can perform well.

In reviewing Fiedler's research, one finds that there is nothing automatic or "good" in either the task-oriented or the people-satisfaction-oriented style. Leadership effectiveness depends upon the various elements in the group environment. This might be expected. Casting a manager in the desired role of leader, the manager who applies his knowledge to the realities of the group reporting to him will do well to recognize that he is practicing an art. But, in doing so, he will necessarily take into account the underlying motivations of people and his ability to satisfy them in the interest of attaining enterprise goals.

DEVELOPING LEADERSHIP ABILITY

If one were to contemplate the teaching of leadership, he would consider the problems of teaching the use of its two major ingredients. If a leader is to select and apply specific motivators to each of his subordinates, he obviously must know what these people will favorably respond to. This requires an ability to *know* one's subordinates. Can this be taught? Is it possible to teach the busy manager to discern the essence of personality? Theories and knowledge about people and their motivations certainly can be taught, but plans of action based upon this knowledge are largely a matter of art.

The inspirational ingredient is even less amenable to teaching. Perhaps

[11] See F. E. Fiedler, *op. cit.*
[12] *Ibid.*, p. 261.

the major problem is that it is a dynamic personal process—dynamic in the sense that techniques vary with circumstances and with the people involved, and personal in the sense that inter-personal influence is exercised. This does not always mean face-to-face contact, for, obviously, General MacArthur, Napoleon, Caesar, Churchill, De Gaulle, and Jefferson were personally known to few of their followers. Close interpersonal relations were felt to exist, nevertheless, and this is what counts. Devices for humanizing the distant leader rely on communications (Roosevelt's fireside chats) or on some dramatic display of heroism or of pomp and circumstances to create a feeling of close personal contact in the followers: the leader projects his personality and is viewed with favor and even with adulation.

THE ENVIRONMENT AND LEADERSHIP

The environment in which interpersonal group relationships occur has a bearing on the quality of leadership. This environment is affected greatly by the leader's successes and failures, and these, in turn, result partly from managerial skill and partly from external factors. The hygienic factors—supervision, interpersonal relations, working conditions, wages, policies, and job security—come easy in times of prosperity. In times of adversity, when the hygienic factors may be gradually reduced in volume, scope, and quality—at least, when fringe benefits and even salary are reduced—human relations and supervision may even improve; certainly effort may be more productive, and more attention is given to leadership ability. It can be decisive if the self-development and inspirational aspects of the motivational system are made prominent.

It thus appears that adversity fosters zeal and that some people prefer inefficiency when they can afford it. Take the great contrast between the zeal of the British worker during the 1930s and during World War II, or between that of American railroad employees before and after the intrusion of unions and of government regulation. In both cases the quality of leadership was decisive, but in the former case it shifted from desultory to brilliant, and in the latter case, from brilliant to desultory. In the thirties, when the British were pacifist-minded and bent on curious schemes for attaining security and sharing the wealth, they chose political leadership which promised these benefits. But when, through critical challenges, preservation of their freedom became more important than anything else, a leader was chosen who could satisfy this need. In the instance of the American railroads, employee morale was high in the dynamic years of construction, under the leadership of men like James Hill; but with the coming of the rail unions and with government regulation, the employees looked to others than managers for fulfillment of their needs, and managerial leadership suffered.

However, whatever the environment, leaders emerge to make decisions and take charge. The leader in a play group selects the game and settles disputes; at the scene of an accident a doctor may lead the rescue work.

Disappointed groups readily replace leaders who fail to satisfy their interests—when they have this prerogative—in the hope of experiencing greater satisfaction through the new leader's efforts. In formal organizations such as a school, a hospital, or a business, manager-leaders are ordinarily elected or appointed without subordinate participation. While subordinates may not be able to remove their leaders, they can react negatively by slow-downs, by output restrictions, and even by quitting the job. This is why author-ity is sometimes insufficient to effect coordination, and why managers are forced to exercise their leadership ability.

CULTIVATED ATTITUDES OF LEADERS

The interpersonal relationships of leader and followers can be improved con-siderably as the leader cultivates certain attitudes. This is the area in which the more important contributions of psychologists aid us to understand the bases of influence. It becomes even more important than mere knowledge because these attitudes can be learned and used with skill.

Empathy

Webster defines empathy as "the imaginative projection of one's own con-sciousness into another being." As commonly used, it is the ability to place one's self in the position of another, simulating that person's feelings, prej-udices, and values.

The manager without empathy has objectives, ambitions, values, and biases like any other man, and he often assumes that his subordinates have the same ones. It is not likely they would have. People widely differ from each other in every respect but one: They all are guided less by reason than by emotion, and the causes of emotion are deeply personal. Therefore, the leader could not be more wrong than to assume that his followers feel as he does. This wrong assumption underlies paternalism. Many a manager provides subordinates with benefits he likes himself. The big difference is that he has freedom to choose, while his followers may value the freedom to choose more than they value any "given benefits." Then they are charged with a lack of appreciation.

As the manager contemplates his subordinates with a view to under-standing their feelings and attitudes, he is severely handicapped. Outside of their work, he knows very little about them—their personal relationships, economic and health conditions, ambitions, spiritual values, and loyalties. Each of us hardly knows himself that well, let alone our subordinates!

Placing one's self in the position of a subordinate is but half the problem, because, even so, would you know his reaction to issues? Yet, a forthright and conscientious effort to understand a subordinate is much better than none. The mere practice of asking, How would I react if I were he? is an attempt to learn, and with practice may come skill.

Objectivity

Managers should strive to observe and trace the causes of events unemotion-ally. Even though managers must depend heavily on subordinates and often become emotional about them, it is important to evaluate from a distance, determine the actual causes of results, and take intelligent steps to correct poor ones and encourage good ones.

This is a tightrope to walk, particularly if empathy is overemphasized, because empathy requires an attitude opposite to remoteness and unemotional analysis. A neat balance between empathy and objectivity is difficult to achieve, but each has its place in effective leadership.

To cultivate objectivity by schooling himself to analyze before taking action, the leader needs strong will power. With determination he can overcome a natural tendency toward snap judgment, anger, vituperation, or undue exuberance, even if he must follow the folk rule of counting to ten. Restraint and the habit of analysis are learned behavior.

Self-knowledge

The injunction to "know thyself!" is used in the context of making people aware of why they behave as they do and also what they do to draw forth certain response, lack of response, or even hostility from others. It is impossible to empathize or to be objective without self-knowledge. The plain fact is that some people irritate others unwittingly by their habitual attitude, words, or actions. Of course, in other cases, this may be their intention! In some situations this may be the correct technique to obtain a desired response. More usually friendliness, cooperation, and approval get better results. It is well to know what one is doing.

The manager—like everyone else—should, therefore, learn the effects on others of his attitudes and habits so that he can correct those which elicit negative responses; that is, he should cultivate self-knowledge and put it to work intelligently by watching for favorable and unfavorable reactions to his behavior and identifying their causes. He can make discreet inquiries, either direct or indirect, to learn the cause of an observed response. He can use the vertical slice technique (Chapter 24). For all this, he must not be touchy or let false pride show.

One major point should be remembered here: People do not all respond in the same way to anything. People are different; not all are irritated by the same thing. Furthermore, people respond differently at different times to the same stimulus depending on their immediate interior climate. Some personalities clash with few but please the many; some, conversely, seem bad-tempered but are amenable to certain personalities they find congenial. These variations in people explain, in part, why the much-publicized T training (sensitivity training) often demonstrates essentially that people respond differently to the same stimulus.

LEADERSHIP AND THE INFORMAL ORGANIZATION

"Informal organization"[13] applies to groups of two or more people who communicate more or less regularly for purposes of exchanging information, for

[13]For a discussion of informal organization in relation to formal organization, see pp. 243–244.

pleasure, or for the development of a consensus with respect to future action. The term is really incongruous, because regularity of meeting and permanency of membership lend an aspect of formality to these groups, which have no organizational relationship to the employing firm but which do have structure in terms of the leader-follower relationship of their members.

Types

There are several types of informal organizations, depending, in large part, upon their purposes.[14] Sociologists have classified them as kinship-friendship groups, cliques, and subcliques. The first, readily identified by its descriptive title, is most often confined to two persons between whom compatibility is of prime importance. Sociability is the chief objective, both at and away from work, but collateral purposes include the communication of information, whether fact or gossip, and mutual aid in achieving improved status through such means as promotion or transfer.

Cliques are composed of persons commonly in close working association: selected members of the payroll, personnel, engineering, or machineshop "crowd," or persons representing different functional activities who feel the need for cooperation. Sometimes the group has certain standards to maintain or practices to retain, and members drift together for purposes of protection. Acceptance into such a group may require the approval of all the members. There is unlikely to be any democracy here.

Subcliques include one or a few persons identified with a clique. Other members of the subclique may be employed by another firm. Often, such a subclique can control the destinies of a clique or even of a professional or trade association by its insistence that standards or customs be adhered to by prospective members. The subclique may control a clique which, in turn, may control a whole formal group. In this way, a large number of people in an organized group may be controlled by a very few who have no formal authority.

Genesis

The existence, variety, and virility of informal organizations lead to the conclusion that they satisfy human needs in a way that formal organizations do not. What are these needs? One of them is to perpetuate the culture of a group. For instance, a group may be unified in its desire to maintain a certain standard of education, discipline, or training. If a given department employs engineers exclusively, an informal group of them might oppose the use of technicians for some of the jobs. Or the insistence of an informal group upon the continuance

---

[14]C. I. Barnard, in *The Functions of the Executive* (Cambridge, Mass.: Harvard University Press, 1938), states on p. 114, in his pioneer chapter on informal organizations, that such groups have no ". . . specific conscious *joint* purpose. The contact may be accidental, or incidental to organized activities, or arise from personal desire or gregarious instinct; it may be friendly or hostile." Whatever the incident which originally throws people together, it appears that the continuing informal organization implies some kind of purpose, even though members may not be aware of it.

of hazing new members of a department or of trade apprenticeship reflects the desire to perpetuate a highly prized cultural figment.

Need for information is a second reason for the existence of informal organizations—both the need for news and the need for prompt news. If organizational information were communicated as soon as it was available, there would be no need for an informal organization to perform this function. In practice, enterprises often circulate news slowly, transmit it poorly, or even withhold it. Informal organizations provide the channels, or grapevine, for speedy communication with their members. Management, however, cannot fully rely upon this method because persons not members of informal organizations cannot tap this grapevine.

Since informal organizations can either aid or interfere with enterprise interests, their activities should be directed into constructive channels. Once leaders of informal groups are identified and their cooperation gained, organizing and directing become markedly easier. The good will, energy, and initiative of informal organizations supplement the purposes of the formal organization, and each stands to gain from the satisfaction of the other's needs. Conversely, should the manager fail to win the cooperation of the informal group leaders, his leadership ability may be low and his performance inevitably harmed.

LEADERSHIP AND THE MANAGEMENT OF CHANGE

Managers are continuously concerned with change. Two broad categories are common. Firms modify objectives and policies, location, organization structure, product lines, corporate structure, management philosophies, and methods of doing business. Sometimes these changes are voluntary; sometimes they are forced.

The other category of change involves human behavior. Managers are always faced with influencing subordinates to change. In all organization modifications there is a corresponding need to change the activity of subordinates. Many of them do not want to change; they must be induced to do so in the interest of enterprise efficiency.

In his function of directing, a manager strives to overcome resistance to change—not only that of employees, but also that of customers, suppliers, and even government people to the extent that they may be involved. Without human resistance, achieving change would be a comparatively simple matter. People fear or welcome change depending on how it may affect them, how it may increase or decrease their well-being. The change may affect income, physical environment, status, the esteem of others, group relationships, authority relationships, opportunity for self-development, or freedom of action. People need time, before committing themselves, to calculate the possible net advantage to themselves.

In the Material Environment

Enterprises differ widely in the dynamics of operation. Some—like the electronics, chemical, and metallurgical firms—operate in an environment shifting with new knowledge and with changing competitive practices, political factors, and even power politics. Others—like financial and transportation institutions, or food producers and processors—are much less dynamic but still are affected by new competition, new markets, and even new enterprises. The manager in any of these firms continually leads subordinates in meeting and conquering the new circumstances. New plans, new money, new strategy, and even new jobs may be involved. Somehow, the manager hopes to come up with a high enough order of leadership to convert the doubtful, the pessimistic, and the conservative to meet new challenges with zeal and confidence; since the environment continues to change, dramatically or imperceptibly, this job never is done—it is always in process.

In Subordinate Attitudes

In addition to the dynamics of the material environment, the manager deals with the dynamics of people's attitudes. As one looks at, or goes to work in, a firm, one gets the impression that the personnel is static in terms of number, relationships, and attitudes, and that one may depend on the stability of these factors. But before long one sees and senses changes. There are promotions and transfers, hirings and firings, labor union raids or contests or elections with attendant disputation. These changes, and many others, are disturbing to employees. They are also disturbed by changes in business volume, and their attitude toward the firm changes as their expectations change.

A manager should realize that attitudes do change, sometimes very quickly. He should feel the pulse of morale, assess the real cause of changed attitudes, and apply whatever leadership technique he judges appropriate. Since there is little science in this area, different managers will select different techniques in the same situation, some good, some poor.

Means of Implementing Change

The means available for inducing changed behavior are based upon allaying fears and satisfying needs. Man has always feared the unknown, and change represents the unknown. He does not know how change in a business operation will affect him. He should be prepared in advance for this type of change, and this requires good communications, including an explanation of the purpose of the change, its timing, and the anticipated organizational effect. Then, time must be allowed for the subordinate to get used to the idea and to assess the effect of the change on any informal organization to which he belongs, on personal relationships outside the firm, and on such situations as housing and transfer expenses. Numerous questions will demand answers by the superior, among them the question of the penalty for refusal to change.

Another kind of change may be desired in the behavior of the subordinate manager. How do you influence him to manage efficiently? To treat *his* subordinates with respect? To improve the efficiency of *his* subordinates? To induce *his* subordinates to act with dignity and respect? To take prompt action? To face reality? The available techniques here are communication and a review of the motivation system as applied in particular cases. The importance of bringing about change will, of course, be a subject for thorough discussion between superior and subordinates. It is much easier to make clear the need for change from the point of view of the institution than it is to discover the needs of a subordinate that can be satisfied by a change in his behavior. Nevertheless, this is the road to follow even though the prospect of success is minimal.

Since the success attending a change depends partly on overcoming the resistance of affected people, managers must use leadership to achieve acceptance. Suppliers of capital, customers, and employees must be convinced that they stand to gain. Achieving change in circumstances involving two equal parties may be accomplished by direct negotiation, intrusion of third parties, or open warfare. Obviously, change can be imposed, though usually at great cost, and imposition is an inferior method.

The manager may give notice to all affected by a proposed change, evaluating the change as he sees it. This one-way communication usually produces poor results except under emergency conditions. Even the conference method, in which the affected persons may ask questions, is poor, because so many questions go unasked and there are so many possible interpretations of answers in this environment.

One means of implementing change[15] has been found sometimes to be effective, given the necessary time for application. Here, the manager attempting change broaches the matter to his immediate subordinates. Small conferences—and there will be many—will achieve understanding of the reasons behind and expectations of the change. The subordinates will call conferences of their people to discuss the matter. This time-consuming method does inform people about how they will be affected, provides time for each person to evaluate his net position, and usually elicits suggestions for modifying the change to make it more effective, more acceptable, or both.

The behavioral scientists have provided some insights into the relationships of group members and the nature of informal organization. Managers have also long taken into their confidence recognized leaders of affected informal groups in order to enlist their help in effecting change. This method is frequently successful, particularly when it is combined with the group discussion technique. But it may also be attended by rebellion of the group, rejection of the group leader, and even character assassination. It may fail because the leader assesses the situation improperly or because he is induced to act against his better judgment.[16]

---

[15] See D. Cartwright, "Achieving Change in People," *Human Relations,* vol. 4, no. 4, pp. 381–392 (1951); W. G. Bennis, K. D. Benne, and R. Chin, *The Planning of Change* (New York: Holt, Rinehart and Winston, Inc., 1961); R. H. Guest, *Organizational Change* (Homewood, Ill.: Richard D. Irwin, Inc., 1962); C. Argyris et al., *Social Science Approaches to Business Behavior* (Homewood, Ill.: Richard D. Irwin, Inc., 1962); and T. Burns, "Micropolitics: Mechanisms of Institutional Change," *Administrative Science Quarterly,* vol. 6, no. 3, pp. 257–281 (1961).

[16] See, for example, A. Zaleznik, C. R. Christensen, and F. J. Roethlisberger, *The Motivation, Productivity and Satisfaction of Workers* (Boston: Division of Research, Harvard Business School, 1958).

TECHNIQUES OF LEADERSHIP

It has been fashionable to believe that a manager's leadership style may range from autocratic to laissez faire. For those holding this view, each manager can and should assume a predominantly autocratic, democratic, or laissez faire attitude, depending on its appropriateness in a given situation. When selecting the autocratic technique, the manager relies on his authority to command subordinates. When choosing the democratic technique—in what is more accurately called participative management—he solicits advice and perhaps accepts majority recommendations from subordinates. Choosing laissez faire or free rein, the manager goes so far as to practically abdicate his decision-making authority and becomes a mild consultant.

The historical position of most behavioral scientists has been anti-authoritarian and in favor of participative management.[17] Roethlisberger felt convinced enough of the righteousness of this position to comment in 1964 on how astonishing was the extent to which the findings of different investigators checked on the inadequacies of the traditional leadership style[18] and emphasized the need for more participative management, two-way communication, and permissive leadership.

Now, however, it appears that their spokesmen are beginning to accept the position maintained by the authors of this book from the beginning, namely, that the manager will choose the most effective means *for him* to achieve enterprise objectives, quite irrespective of whether they are permissive, authoritarian, or in between. As a matter of fact, the authors believe that the effective manager will vary his techniques and approaches to fit enterprise needs, people, and the environment in which they operate. Thus, the principle of direction techniques is seen to be: *as people, tasks, and organizational environment vary, techniques of directing should be appropriately varied.*

Among those who have declared themselves in this regard are P. R. Lawrence and A. Zaleznik. The former is quoted by Learned and Sproat as saying:[19]

There is now beginning to be some research evidence to support what many intuitive managers have known for a long time. And that is that the different departments, in which innovators and stabilizers work, function best when they are structured and run and led in quite different and distinct ways.

Innovators are commonly found in research and development organizations. The scientist especially insists upon participating in goal-setting, once the general area of research is fixed for him. For instance, a firm may decide to build a plutonium laboratory for the purpose of engaging in research and development work in this product. Just what will be undertaken will almost certainly depend upon the interests of the scientist, and such a person will want to have freedom

---

[17] E. P. Learned and A. T. Sproat, *Organization Theory and Policy* (Homewood, Ill.: Richard D. Irwin, Inc., 1966), p. 61.

[18] H. Koontz (ed.), *Toward a Unified Theory of Management* (New York: McGraw-Hill Book Company, 1964), pp. 41–67.

[19] *Op. cit.*, p. 62.

of communication even though he may use it very little.[20] On the other hand, the stabilizers whom Lawrence finds in the typical functionalized organizations, where procedures and policies are well established and where the educational level is not so high, are likely to perform best under more authoritarian leadership.

Even more emphatic is Abraham Zaleznik in his rejection of participation when he writes:[21]

I view with considerable pessimism the attempts . . . to develop a social movement around theories of permissive leadership, participation, and sensitivity training. . . . The research setting creates the condition for the redistribution of emotional investments that affect the levels of productivity and morale. When the researchers leave the setting, another redistribution takes effect that may result in, at best, a return to the prior situation, or, at worst, cynical and disillusioned individuals.

The manager who tries to use the results of behavioral research runs into difficulties. According to Zaleznik, he cannot act with the confidence and purpose which come from the utilization of his personal capacities because confidence is not built from without. Unless normative principles are really a part of the personality of the manager, a slavish adherence to them will develop a guilt-ridden and compulsive personality. The manager is a whole man. He must act consistently with his total personality, however it is developed, and whether this causes him to be cited as authoritarian or as permissive.

This view of human nature questions the opinion that a manager can and does readily shift his leadership style from one extreme to another, depending upon the situation with which he is confronted.[22] The authors of this book view this concept with some skepticism. Managers who are permissive by nature tend to choose a permissive style; an authoritarian manager tends to follow an authoritarian style. As a manager matures, he adopts a style that suits his personality and is effective and he is not likely to deviate much from it throughout his active employment.

The usually undefined terms "participative" and "permissive" applied to management have caused a great deal of unproductive discussion. The one thing that no manager should do is to abdicate his decision-making prerogative. If he needs information that one or more subordinates have in order to make a decision, he surely should obtain it from them. If he is uncertain how a decision will affect some of his people, he should find out *before* he makes the decision. Productive participation can be achieved through work assignments, as is the case in planning. He should not assume that his subordinates always want to or like to or can participate in decision making. Where a manager has the responsibility for making a particular decision, he should not pretend that he is not deciding. Quite on the contrary, subordinates want clear, purposeful, and effective action. They are the first to detect in their manager incompetence,

---

[20] C. O'Donnell, *The Productivity of Scientists* (unpublished manuscript, 1967).

[21] Quoted by Learned and Sproat, *op. cit.*, p. 64.

[22] See, for example, R. Tannenbaum and W. H. Schmidt, "How to Choose a Leadership Pattern," *Harvard Business Review*, vol. 36, no. 2, pp. 95–101 (March–April, 1958).

indecision, or yearning to be popular; and they complain about these qualities because they are adversely affected by them in terms of production, cost saving, ability to accomplish, growth, and pride.

On the basis of believing that the leader *must* lead, the United States Army and the United States Marines have what appears to be a sound approach. In demonstrating leadership one day the late General Patton called for a plate, a very wet noodle, and a fork. Tipping the plate, he tried to get the noodle from the bottom edge of the plate to the top edge by pushing the noodle with the fork. The futility of this became apparent. But when he pulled with the fork, the noodle readily rose to the top edge. A leader must be out in front to lead, but not so far that he loses contact with his subordinates.

Before discussing specific techniques, let us heed a warning about a pitfall dangerous to all managers: misinterpretation by subordinates of their boss's attitudes. This may be avoided by managerial alertness and insight.

A manager's every word and action are interpreted by his subordinates, who watch him closely for signs of his opinion of them and of other matters. Subordinates usually try to please their superiors by acting in approved ways and attending to whatever seems to command the boss's attention. When the superior scowls, complains, or smiles, the over-self-conscious subordinate may assume that these signals are meant for him, although, of course, they may not be. A second kind of misinterpretation is even more undesirable. Managers must concentrate on matters that need special attention, although in so doing they do not lose interest in matters that are going well. The subordinate is then apt to misread signals and—concentrating on whatever the manager is looking at—neglect other duties.

Confidence Building

A subordinate manager gains confidence in his ability to carry out his assignments effectively as his job knowledge grows and as managerial success expands. Confidence is largely acquired from experience. Some aspects of position knowledge can be explained in the continuing orientation process and perhaps special conferences. But the impact of what is taught will become apparent only when the individual attempts to apply it in his managerial position. This is the cutting edge of knowledge. Continued in-depth exposure to all the elements of the environment is the most effective way to provide the information base on which confidence partially rests. Its qualitative interpretation calls for a skill that emerges from an evaluation of experience.

The building of confidence requires further attention. There is needed a record of success in the practice of management. It is not enough to learn the principles and techniques available to managers: the manager must successfully apply them. He refines the art of their application through the process of continually evaluating this experience. It is not that continuous success is required—there will always be failures—but the experience must be generally and increasingly successful.

The confidence that results from this building process provides the manager with a deep sense of personal security. In fact, it is the only job security that has any real meaning. Internal to his enterprise he will be marked with success; to other enterprises he can bring a proven record of success. He is a free man and has no patience with the job safeguards that unions, civil service, and enterprises grant even to the incompetent.

Zeal Building

The elusive nature of zeal permits it to escape scientific analysis. For what, after all, inspires enthusiasm or ardor resulting in effort beyond the merely acceptable? Sometimes a subordinate takes this path because he stands in great need of a superior's approval; on the other hand, his zeal may win only the disapproval of his competitive or envious peers. Sometimes a subordinate takes this road to secure promotion, to become eligible to join an elite group, or to achieve power; on the other hand, the costs in effort, tension, frustration, and hostile colleagues are great. Sometimes the subordinate greatly admires his superior and determines not to let him down; on the other hand, he may only be proving his boss wrong by effectively executing an order he is certain is faulty.

Inspiration   Since inspirational techniques to build zeal are so personal, they can only be described. *This aspect of leadership probably cannot be taught.* Within the confines of enterprise policies, procedures, and rules, each manager should develop his own inspirational techniques.

The power of words and actions to inspire zeal is proverbial. The leader—standing between his group and the goals of all—beckons subordinates on with words and his own actions. It sounds old-fashioned when put into words, but old tactics and old knowledge are not necessarily obsolete. People want to be led and will work hard to satisfy the goals of an admired superior.

Then, to inspire his subordinates, a manager probably must be a success. Subordinates lose confidence in unsuccessful superiors and leave them as quickly as possible; if they cannot leave, as in the armed forces, they become dispirited. Success is an elusive concept. It may result from many factors, but its outward sign is the accomplishment of managerial objectives. In business, success may be measured in sales or profit, by expanding activities, or by rising stature within and without the enterprise. People enjoy the secondhand glory, the implied security, the prestige, of working for a successful manager whether the area is politics, religion, education, business, or war. And for superlative superiors they will work beyond the call of duty.

Strengthening personal qualities   Creating enthusiasm in subordinates seems also to be largely a matter of the superior's personal attributes and of his judgment in making use of occasions. Probably most important in terms of the durability of inspiration is the quality of character or moral vigor with which the leader lives up to the social code and, by example, induces subordinates to do likewise.

Another quality essential to leadership is that the manager act his role. Subordinates want to work for a manager who really acts like one. People develop stereotypes which they do not want altered—an image of how someone should behave—and are disappointed if this vision is not made real. In the managerial stereotype, managers bask in the aura of success and competence, possess superior knowledge, are conservative in their habits, stand somewhat aloof from subordinates, are fair and just, and strongly defend subordinates while raising their efficiency. Needless to say, such paragons may be largely imaginary, but subordinates want their managers to play this part believably. It is the way to earn respect, and zealous effort of subordinates correlates highly with the respect of subordinates for their leader.

A manager must be conscious of his effect on subordinates and, if necessary, wear a mask or adopt a demeanor which will direct subordinates as he intends, without altering the scope of positions or subtly changing the organization structure. It is hard to maintain this effect, yet this is exactly what leadership requires.

From this review of zeal-building techniques, it can be seen that the power to inspire zeal is a personal quality. There are few principles or rules for all to follow, and the masters cannot easily be imitated successfully.

What, then, is a manager to do? Lead he should, whether he occupies a high or a low step on the organization ladder. His leadership responsibility cannot be delegated. There are a few things he can do. He should remember to develop confidence in subordinates by making them technically proficient. He should develop his own zeal-building techniques by trial and error, weeding out unsuccessful techniques and cultivating successful ones. He need not be hasty, and many elements in the environment will work for him. A sound motivational system alone will go far to produce acceptable performance, and his delegated authority and organizational position place him in a strategic position. So he presumably has time to grow into being a good leader.[23]

SUMMARY OF MAJOR PRINCIPLES OF DIRECTING

Reflection upon the foregoing chapters on the managerial function of directing generates confidence that a tentative statement of some general truths can be developed. As in other areas of management, they may be grouped around the purpose of directing and the process of directing.

The Purpose of Directing

The purpose of directing can best be achieved through adherence to:

Principle of directing objective The more effective the directing process, the greater will be the contribution of subordinates to organizational goals.

Principle of harmony of objectives The more effective directing is, the more individuals will perceive that their personal goals are in harmony with enterprise objectives.

[23] Even as there are few who are eager to lead at all. See Zaleznik et al., *op. cit.*, p. 396.

Basically, directing of subordinates is undertaken as a means to facilitate their contribution to the enterprise in accordance with their highest capabilities. This purpose is achieved most effectively if the individual and organizational goals are mutually supportive and the undivided energy used to attain them is applied with confidence and zeal.

The Process of Directing

The process of directing concerns the manner by which its purpose is executed. The principles upon which the execution of directing rests are:

Principle of unity of command   The more completely an individual has a reporting relationship to a single superior, the less the problem of conflict in instructions and the greater the feeling of personal responsibility for results.

Unity of command is a principle of both organizing and directing. People respond best when they are directed by a single superior. They then have no divided loyalties and are thus in a position to give single-minded attention to the requirements of their superior. Of course, it is true that sometimes the net efficiency of an enterprise is improved by the introduction of multiple command, such as functional authority, but this should be done only when the gains clearly outweigh the costs.

Principle of direct supervision   The more direct personal contact with subordinates is, the more effective will their direction be.

While it is possible that a manager may be able to utilize objective devices to evaluate and correct activities of subordinates to assure accomplishment of plans, there can be no substitute for face-to-face contact. Not only do people like to feel that their superior is personally interested in them and their work, but objective nonpersonal data are never adequate to give the manager all the information he needs. Through face-to-face contact he is often better able to teach, to communicate, and, above all, to receive suggestions and a feeling for problems than in any other way.

Principle of leadership   Since people tend to follow those in whom they see a means of satisfying their own personal goals, the more a manager understands what motivates his subordinates and how these motivations operate, and the more he reflects these in carrying out his managerial actions, the more effective as a leader he is likely to be.

In a very real sense, this principle combines motivational considerations with managerial actions. Even though exactly how and what motivates people have not been completely proved by empirical research, the basic factors are well enough known to be used for practical guidance. Moreover, there is much a manager can do to enhance opportunities for money, status, power, sense of accomplishment, and other motivation factors in the way he structures roles and plans, in the way he staffs, in his directing abilities and techniques, and even through effective systems of control since most people want to know how well they are doing. This is not to manipulate people; this is rather a recognition that people are people, have desires and goals, and are most likely to follow superiors in whom they see a means of achieving these.

Principle of direction techniques   As people, tasks, and organizational environment vary, techniques of directing should be appropriately varied. It is important that actual selections be made in terms of effectiveness. Because subordinates differ widely in their responsiveness to various need satisfactions, superiors should select the most efficient means of evoking outstanding performance.

The Efficiency of Communication

Since communication is the means by which people in organized enterprise exchange information concerning the environment, operational requirements of superiors, program status, and ideas for improving operational efficiency, managers have a special need for excellence in communication. The following guidelines are pertinent to this subject:

Clarity   A communication possesses clarity when it is expressed in language and transmitted in a way to be comprehended by the receiver.

Integrity   All communications should be framed and transmitted in such ways as to support the integrity of the formal organization.

Strategic use of informal organization   The most effective communication results when managers utilize informal organization to supplement the communication channels of the formal organization.

Research in the efficiency of communication highlights the fact that every message must be expressed in a language understandable to the auditor and that full attention should be paid to the transmission. The superior needs to make certain that he personally is a good sender and receiver of communications, and he should train his subordinates in the same facility.

The guidelines of integrity and the strategic use of informal organization concern the transmission of communications within an organized group. Since it is important to maintain the integrity of the formal organization, all communications must support its objectives.

Informal organization is a phenomenon which managers must accept. It operates on entirely different bases than formal organizations but is always a part of them. Information, true or not, flows quickly through informal organizations. As a consequence, managers should take advantage of this device to correct misinformation and to provide for transmission of information not appropriate for formal communication.

FOR DISCUSSION

1. There is a marked tendency in management literature to confuse managing and leading. How do you feel about this semantic problem?

2. Ability to lead is an important quality for the manager. What other abilities does he need?
3. Cite various definitions of leadership. Which appeals to you, keeping in mind the importance of semantic clarification?
4. If leadership is the ability to induce zeal and confidence in subordinates or followers (as in a political party), just what effect would it have in a business firm?
5. How is leadership related to motivation?
6. How would an effective manager also tend to be an effective leader?

part six

CONTROLLING

Controlling implies measurement of accomplishment of events against the standard of plans and the correction of deviations to assure attainment of objectives according to plans. Once a plan becomes operational, control is necessary to measure progress, to uncover deviations from plans, and to indicate corrective action. Corrective action may involve simple measures such as minor changes in directing. In other cases, adequate control may result in setting new goals, formulating new plans, changing the organization structure, improving staffing, and making major changes in techniques of directing. In reading the chapters on the control function, it is important to bear in mind that it involves much more than mere measurement of deviations from plans. True control indicates that corrective action can and will be taken to get wayward operations back on course. It is thus, to a great extent, the function that closes the loop in the system of managing.

The process of control is discussed in Chapter 29. Simple definition of the control function makes it apparent that it remains essentially the same no matter what activity is under consideration. The essential of control is some sort of feedback—the operating principle of a thermostat or a steam governor. When temperature or speed becomes too great, or too low, a thermostat or a governor corrects the condition through feedback. Although the cycle in management is more complex and of longer duration, good managerial control should function in the same manner. Because of the problem of time lags, this chapter emphasizes the importance of forward-looking control. "Ready-made" control techniques, currently popular in the literature, do exist and can be of use. But Chapter 29 makes the point that really good control involves the tailoring of control devices and information to suit the individual plan, the organization, the specific needs of the enterprise, and the personal requirements of the manager. This chapter gives special attention to various traditional techniques of which the budget, or "profit plan," is the most widely used.

Chapter 30 considers some of the special control techniques in current use. Many of these are actually improved planning techniques which enable the manager to check on performance more accurately than was possible in the past. A brief review of Part 2 of this book will assist the reader in appreciating these techniques since planning and control are so closely related.

Special attention is given in this chapter to information systems which have become so important because of the increasing complexity of managing and the resultant needs for information, coupled with the great technical advances of electronic data processing. Attention is paid also to the urgent and largely unsolved practical problem of procedures design and control. Also, the use of certain quantitative and conceptual devices derived largely from the physical sciences is discussed. In addition, special treatment is given to program budgeting, recently so important in government planning and controlling, and to the utilization of formal organization structure to help in assuring program achievement. In reading this chapter, the reader should familiarize himself with such devices as PERT (Program Evaluation and Review Technique), but the primary import is still the basic method which is used in all control devices—measurement of achievement against plan and correction of negative deviation through feedback. It should not be forgotten that older forms of control devices fit this pattern, too. The more modern techniques have not yet replaced accounting, budgeting, and auditing.

Most controls are partial; they concentrate on one facet of operations—quality of product, cash flow, costs, or some other rather narrow aspect. In many enterprises, a difficult problem is the development of over-all control so that managers may have a check on the progress of the entire organization or of an integrated product or territorial division. Chapter 31 discusses the most widely used solutions. As one might expect, these over-all controls tend to be financial. The reader should recognize that financial or money measurement is a natural basis for control since inputs and outputs of an enterprise are most easily expressed in the common denominator of money. Over-all financial controls are also very useful in nonbusiness organizations. Their expenditures for personnel, material, and facilities are always an important factor against which to weigh results, and these are usually reflected in expenditures of money. The most valuable over-all control devices are budget summaries, profit and loss statements, rate of return on investment, and the enterprise self-audit. An interesting new development in over-all control is the measuring and controlling of the human organization. While applicable to individuals as well as organizations, the primary thrust has been to find ways of accounting for and controlling the human assets of an entire organization or enterprise.

In spite of traditional emphasis on financial controls, Chapter 32 demonstrates that the most direct form of control is assurance of the quality of managers. The chapter, of course, does not advocate scrapping other controls, but it does make the point that many deviations from plans will not occur *if the enterprise is well managed. A major point made in this book is that almost all the devices traditionally thought of as control tools are indirect. They are based on the fact that human beings make mistakes. Controlling performance through control of the quality of managers is direct in that it is based on the belief that qualified managers make the fewest mistakes and therefore do not require as much "indirect" control. The authors believe that this direct control is more satisfactory to all the groups interested in the fate of the enterprise—investors, employees, customers, vendors, its managers, and society as a whole.*

In addition, the concluding chapter of the book attempts to summarize some of the most general and important challenges that all managers face and what needs to be done to assure effective management. Even this brief analysis indicates that the problems and opportunities are great and will take continuing effort on the part of everyone who is responsible for the performance of others. Managing is far from realizing its potential. But in an area so important to social development in all its aspects and where the task is so complex, even small improvements can have a remarkable effect on the quality of any society.

29

the process of controlling

The managerial function of controlling is the measurement and correction of the performance of activities of subordinates in order to make sure that enterprise objectives and the plans devised to attain them are being accomplished. It is thus the function whereby every manager, from president to foreman, makes sure that what is done is what is intended. Some managers, particularly at lower levels, forget the principle of control responsibility that *the primary responsibility for the exercise of control rests in the manager charged with the execution of plans.* As Fayol so clearly recognized decades ago,[1] "In an undertaking, control consists in verifying whether everything occurs in conformity with the plan adopted, the instructions issued and principles established. It has for object to point out weaknesses and errors in order to rectify them and prevent recurrence. It operates on everything, things, people, actions." Or, as Goetz put it in his pioneering analysis,[2] "Managerial planning seeks consistent, integrated and articulated programs," while "management control seeks to compel events to conform to plans."

Since control implies the existence of goals and plans, no manager can control without them. He cannot measure whether his subordinates are operating in the desired way unless he has a plan, however vague or for however brief a period. Naturally, the more clear, complete, and coordinated plans are and the longer the period they cover, the more complete controlling can be.

A manager may study past plans to see where and how they missed fire, to ascertain what happened and why, and—on the assumption that history repeats itself—to take steps to avoid recurrence of mistakes. However, the best control prevents deviations from occurring by anticipating that they will occur unless action is taken *now*. This is what is referred to as "forward-

[1] Henri Fayol, *General and Industrial Management* (New York: Pitman Publishing Corporation, 1949), p. 107.
[2] Billy E. Goetz, *Management Planning and Control* (New York: McGraw-Hill Book Company, 1949), p. 229.

looking" control. The next best control detects them as they occur. As the navigator continually takes readings to ascertain where he is relative to a planned course, so should the manager take readings to see whether his enterprise or department is on course, and if it is not, should make corrections accordingly. In fact, it is the function of controlling to make the intended occur.

Occasionally, in view of the authority of upper managers and their resultant responsibility, top-management control is so emphasized that the impression is given that little controlling is needed at lower levels. Although control varies among managers, it is an essential managerial function at every level.

BASIC CONTROL PROCESS

Control techniques and systems are essentially the same for cash, office procedures, morale, product quality, or anything else. And they always assume that both plans and organization structure are clear, complete, and integrated to the extent that managers are sure of their course and that authority delegations and relationships are definite. If a manager is unsure of his assignment or if a subordinate does not have the power or does not know he has the power to carry out plans, it is unreasonable and difficult to hold anyone responsible.

The basic control process, wherever it is found and whatever it controls, involves three steps: (1) establishing standards, (2) measuring performance against these standards, and (3) correcting deviations from standards and plans.

Establishment of Standards

Standards are established criteria against which actual results can be measured. They represent the expression of planning goals of the enterprise or the department in such terms that the actual accomplishment of assigned duties can be measured against them. They may be physical and represent quantities of products, units of service, man-hours, speed, volume of rejections, etc.; or they may be stated in monetary terms, such as costs, revenues, or investments; or they may be expressed in any other terms which measure performance.

Standards are usually stated in specific units, but this need not be the case. A company may, for example, have for a goal a high level of foreman loyalty and morale, or it may develop a public relations program to gain acceptance as a constructive community force. Such goals can seldom be stated in numerical terms, but there are verifiable means of determining whether action is toward or away from them with techniques of measuring such intangibles as customer, employee, and public opinion. Obviously, if enough thought is given, verifiable goals can be developed for virtually any operation, and, whether they are quantitative or qualitative, they become useful and positive standards for control.

Measurement of Performance

Although it is not often practicable to do so, the measurement of performance against standard should ideally be on a future basis, so that deviations may be detected in advance of their actual occurrence and avoided by appropriate remedies. The alert, forward-looking manager can sometimes predict probable departures from standard. In the absence of such ability, deviations should be disclosed as early as possible.

If the standard is appropriately drawn and if means are available for determining exactly what subordinates are doing, appraisal of actual or expected performance is fairly easy. But there are many activities in which it is extremely difficult to develop sound standards, and there are many that are hard to measure. It may be quite simple, especially with present techniques of time and motion study, to establish man-hour standards for the production of a mass-produced item, and it may be equally simple to measure performance against these standards, but if the item is custom-made, the appraisal of performance may be a formidable task.

Furthermore, in the less technical kinds of work, not only may standards be difficult to develop but appraisal may also be exceedingly hard. For example, to control the performance of the finance vice-president or the industrial relations director is not easy, because definite standards cannot easily be developed or performance accurately measured. The superior of these managers often relies on vague standards, such as the financial health of the business, the attitude of labor unions, the absence of strikes, the enthusiasm and loyalty of subordinates, the expressed admiration of business associates, and the over-all success of the department (often measured in a negative way by lack of evidence of failure). His measurements are often equally vague. At the same time, if the department seems to be making the contribution expected of it at a reasonable cost, without too many serious errors, and if the measurable accomplishments give evidence of sound management, the unavoidable general appraisal may be adequate. The point is that, as jobs move away from the assembly line, the shop, or the accounting machine, controlling them becomes more complex and often more important.

Nevertheless, as already noted, as managers at all levels develop verifiable objectives, stated in either quantitative or qualitative terms (see Chapter 7), these become standards against which all position performance in the organization hierarchy can be measured. Also, as new techniques are developed to measure, with a reasonable degree of objectivity, the quality of managing itself in upper, as well as lower, positions, useful standards of performance will emerge.

Correction of Deviations

If standards are drawn to reflect organization structure and if performance is measured in these terms, the correction of deviations is expedited, since the manager then knows exactly where, in the assignment of individual or group duties, the corrective measures must be applied.

Correction of deviations in performance is the point at which control coalesces with the other managerial functions: The manager may correct by re-drawing his plans or by modifying his goal. (This is an exercise of the principle of navigational change referred to in Chapter 6.) Or he may correct deviation by exercising his organizing function, through reassignment or clarifica-tion of duties. He may correct, also, by additional staffing, by better selection and training of subordinates, or by that ultimate of restaffing—firing. Or, again, he may correct through better directing—fuller explanation of the job or stronger leadership.

It can be argued that correcting deviations is no step in the process of control at all but merely the point where the other managerial functions come into play. Surely, control is not confined to measuring performance against standards without doing anything when performance falls short. This overlap of the control function with the others merely demonstrates the unity of the manager's job. It shows the managing process to be an integrated system. As has been previously emphasized in this book, controlling has been sepa-rated from the other managerial functions, particularly planning, because (1) it is a useful, operational way to organize knowledge, and (2) practicing managers have long understood their functions this way.[3]

Control as a Cybernetic System

Managerial control is essentially the same basic process as is found in physical, biological, and social systems. As pointed out by Norbert Wiener,[4] communi-cation, or information transfer, and control occur in the functioning of many systems. Wiener used "information" in the general sense to include a mechan-ical transfer of energy, an electric impulse, a chemical reaction, a written or oral message, or any other means by which a "message" might be transmitted. In the science he called cybernetics, Wiener showed that all types of systems control themselves by information feedback which discloses error in accom-plishing goals and initiates corrective action. In other words, systems use some of their energy to feed back information that compares performance with a standard. Simple feedback is charted in Figure 29.1.

The steam engine governor is a simple mechanical cybernetic system. In order to control an engine's speed under different load conditions, weights (balls) are whirled. As the speed increases, centrifugal force makes these weights exercise an outward thrust which, in turn, transmits a force (a mes-sage) to cut down the input of steam and thereby reduce the speed. As speed is reduced, the reverse occurs. Likewise, in the human body, a number of cyber-netic systems control temperature, blood pressure, motor reactions, and others. In electrical systems such as a voltage regulator, the principle of feedback is used. And in social systems, even other than the managed formal organizations, one also finds feedback. For example, in the social system of baseball, there are

---

[3]But there are those who believe that most of the functions of planning and control should be combined in one—control. See, for example, R. N. Anthony, *Planning and Control Systems: A Framework for Analysis* (Boston: Division of Research, Harvard Business School, 1965), pp. 10–15.

[4]*Cybernetics: Control and Communication in the Animal and the Machine* (New York: John Wiley & Sons, Inc., 1948).

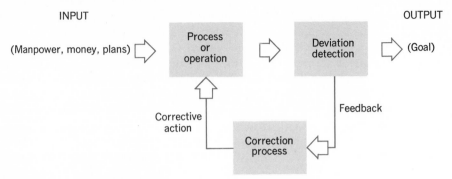

Figure 29.1   *Simple feedback.*

such standards as three strikes and out and even the seventh-inning stretch which are accomplished, essentially, by the feedback of information which corrects those who would deviate.

TEN REQUIREMENTS OF ADEQUATE CONTROLS

It is understandable that every alert manager should want to have an effective and adequate control system to assist him in making sure that events conform to plans. Much of the time and effort of accounting, statistics, and similar departments in the typical enterprise is spent on furnishing information for control. It is sometimes not realized that the control system used by managers, like any other control system, must be designed for the task it is intended to perform. While the principles of control are universal, the actual system requires special design. In this tailoring of control systems or techniques, there are certain requirements that the manager should keep in mind whether he is a top executive, checking whether new products are developed as planned, or a supervisor, checking only the operations of his work force.

1. *Controls must reflect the nature and needs of the activity.* All control systems should reflect the job they are to perform. A system useful for the vice-president in charge of manufacturing will almost certainly be different in scope and nature from that of a shop foreman. Controls of the sales department will differ from those of the finance department and these from the controls of the purchasing department. And a small business will need some different controls from a large business. This is merely a requirement of reflection of plans: *the more that controls are designed to deal with and reflect the specific nature and structure of plans, the more effectively they will serve the interests of the enterprise and its managers.*

    Certain techniques, such as budgets, break-even points, standard hours or costs, and various financial ratios have general application in many situations. However, it should never be assumed that any of these widely used techniques is applicable in a given situation. The manager must be aware of the strategic factors in his plans and operations requiring control and use techniques suited to them.

2. *Controls should report deviations promptly.* As will be noted below, the ideal control system detects projected deviations before they actually occur. In any case, the information must reach the manager in a timely manner so that he can head off failures.

Because failures are not reported expeditiously, typical business accounting is often weak in furnishing control information. Accounting, having for its original and basic purpose the recording of transactions, naturally looks backward. Moreover, in the attempt to make accounting data comprehensive and accurate, it often reaches the manager weeks or months after the event. It does a manager little good to find in October that he lost money in July for what he did in May, though, if no better data are available, this information may be worth having. Even though electronic data-processing machines are greatly speeding the flow of accounting data, most managers find that normally it must be supplemented with an accounting estimate of the present and future.

3. *Controls should be forward looking.* Although ideal control is instantaneous, as in certain electronic controls, the facts of managerial life include a time lag between the deviation and corrected action. Perhaps the first principle of control in assuring achievement of objectives is: *the task of control is to detect potential or actual deviation from plans early enough to permit effective corrective action.* Therefore, the manager, in striving to apply this principle, would surely prefer a forecast of what will probably happen next week or next month—even though this contains a margin of error—to a report—accurate to several decimal points—of the past about which he can do nothing.

That this is possible is illustrated by such forward-looking devices as cash control. A company manager cannot very well find out in April that he ran out of cash in March. Properly, he forecasts his cash requirements to handle his payroll and other cash needs as they arise. This approach to control can surely be applied on a much broader front than is now the case.

4. *Controls should point up exceptions at critical points.* The time-honored exception principle, that the manager should only watch for and deal with exceptions, is not enough for effective control. Some deviations from standards have little meaning and others have a great deal. Small exceptions in certain areas have greater significance than larger deviations in other areas. A manager, for example, might be concerned if the cost of office labor deviated from standard by 5 percent, but unworried if the cost of postage stamps deviated from budget by 20 percent.

The importance of this requirement for control may be summarized in two companion principles. The principle of critical point control stresses that *effective control requires attention to those factors critical to appraising performance against an individual plan.* The exception may be stated as: *the more a manager concentrates his control efforts on exceptions, the more efficient will be the results of his control.*

5. *Controls should be objective.* Management necessarily has many subjective elements in it, but whether a subordinate is doing a good job should ideally not be a matter for subjective determination. Where controls are subjective, a manager's or a subordinate's personality may influence judgments of performance inaccurately; but people have difficulty in explaining away objective control of their performance, particularly if the standards and measurements are kept up-to-date through periodic review. As summarized by the principle of standards, *effective control requires objective, accurate, and suitable standards.*

   Objective control should be definite and determinable in a clear and positive way. Objective standards can be quantitative, such as costs or man-hours per unit, or date of job completion; they can also be qualitative, such as a training program with specific characteristics or accomplishing a specific kind of upgrading of the quality of personnel. The point is that, in either case, the standard is determinable and verifiable.

6. *Controls should be flexible.* Controls must remain workable in the face of changed plans, unforeseen circumstances, or outright failures. As Goetz has remarked:[5] "A complex program of managerial plans may fail in some particulars. The control system should report such failures, and should contain sufficient elements of flexibility to maintain managerial control of operations despite such failures." In other words, according to the principle of flexibility, *if controls are to remain effective, despite failure or unforeseen changes of plans, flexibility is required in their design.*

   The need for flexible control can readily be illustrated. A budget system may project a certain level of expenses and grant authority to managers to hire labor and purchase materials and services at this level. If, as is usually the case, this budget is based on a forecast of a certain level of sales, it may become meaningless as a system of control if the actual sales volume is considerably above or below the forecast. Budget systems have been brought into ill repute among some companies because of inflexibility in such circumstances. What is needed, of course, is a system that will reflect sales variations as well as other deviations from plans. This has been provided, as will be noted presently, by the flexible, or variable, budget.

   In production scheduling, the production manager must be prepared for failures occasioned by the breakdown of a machine or the illness of a key worker. If his control system is too inflexible to account for such hitches, the slowdown, even though temporary, may impair his control. Much flexibility in control can be provided by having alternative plans for various probable situations. In fact, flexible control is normally best achieved through flexible plans.

7. *Controls should reflect the organization pattern.* Organization structure, being the principal vehicle for coordinating the work of people, is also

---

[5] Goetz, *op. cit.*, p. 229.

a major means for maintaining control; and the manager is the focal point of control, just as he is the focal point for the assignment of tasks and the delegation of authority. This need is summarized in the principle of organizational suitability: *the more controls are designed to reflect the place in the organization structure where responsibility for action lies, the more they will facilitate correction of deviations from plans.* For example, product cost accumulation is used to control unit cost in production. Unless costs are accumulated so as to fit the organization pattern of the production department, and unless each factory superintendent and foreman is shown cost accumulation in *his* department, actual costs may be out of line without the manager's knowing whether the cause was within his control. Fortunately, in recent years, cost accountants have recognized the importance of relating cost data to organization structure, and the cost centers now typically used in industry provide usable data for each manager concerned. In every area of control it does no good to know that things are going wrong, unless it is known where in the organization structure the deviations are occurring.

8. *Controls should be economical.* Controls must be worth their cost. Although this requirement is simple, its practice is often complex, for a manager may find it difficult to know what a particular control system is worth, or to know what it costs. Economy is relative, since the benefits vary with the importance of the activity, the size of the operation, the expense that might be incurred in the absence of control, and the contribution the system can make.

A small company cannot afford the extensive control system of a large company. The elaborate charts and detailed analyses used by the top management of the Monsanto Chemical Company or the du Pont Company doubtless represent hundreds of thousands of dollars in investment of time and many more thousands each year for their maintenance. Expensive preparation, approval, and administration of complex budgetary control programs may be well worth their cost to the large enterprise but uneconomical for the small. Likewise, a finance vice-president may feel that many thousands of dollars have been well spent for historical and forecast data on cash flow or capital investment, but in the same company a much smaller expenditure for tracing the handling of scrap inventories might be too costly.

Since a limiting factor of control systems is relative economy, this, in turn, will depend a great deal on the manager's selecting for control only critical factors in areas important to him. If tailored to the job and to the size of the enterprise, control will probably be economical. On the other hand, one of the economies of largescale enterprise results from being able to afford expensive and elaborate control systems. Often, however, the magnitude of the problems, the wider area of planning, the difficulty of coordinating plans, and poor management communication in a large business require such expensive controls that their over-all efficiency suffers in comparison to controls in a small business. As may be stated in the principle of efficiency of controls: *control techniques and approaches are efficient when they detect and illuminate the causes of actual or potential deviations from plans with the minimum of costs or other unsought consequences.*

9. *Controls should be understandable.* Some control systems, especially those based upon mathematical formulas, complex break-even charts, detailed analyses, and computer printouts, are not understandable to the managers who must use them. Sometimes the manager could understand them if he would take the time to learn to do so; but whether his lack of understanding results from complex techniques or impatience in learning them, the effect is the same: the control system will not function well. This requirement is incorporated in the basic principle of individuality of controls: *effective controls require consistency with the position, operational responsibility, ability to understand, and needs of the individual concerned.*

   Many so-called experts in graphs, charts, advanced statistical methods, or exhaustive analyses fail to communicate the meaning of their control data to the manager who should use it. "Control" staffs and departments in business often develop information that cannot or will not be used by managers because it is not simple enough or adapted to the manager's understanding. This is, of course, one of the problems of the electronic data processing systems. The output may be thousands of sheets of printouts that few people can or will understand or use. What may be valuable and comprehensible to one manager may not be so to another, and it is up to the manager (or his staff assistant) to make sure that he has an adequate control system that he understands.

10. *Controls should lead to corrective action.* A control system that detects deviations from plans will be little more than an interesting exercise if it does not show the way to corrective action. An adequate system will disclose where failures are occurring, who is responsible for them, and what should be done about them. It cannot be forgotten, as the principle of action emphasizes, that *control is justified only if indicated or experienced deviations from plans are corrected through appropriate planning, organizing, staffing, and directing.*

THE KEY IMPORTANCE OF FORWARD-LOOKING CONTROLS

Perhaps there is no more important element of an adequate and effective control system or technique than the need for forward-looking controls. As is indicated in Figure 29.2, the actual feedback loop involved in usual management controls is comprised, as a minimum, of a number of very separate and identifiable steps. Mere observation of the steps in this loop will show that many of them can be very time-consuming. With the faster flow of information now available, even if it were possible (as it is now, but it is often not economically practicable) to measure actual performance quickly and to get a fast comparison of actual against standards, and even if it were possible (as it is in some, but not all, information systems) to get quick identification of deviations, there are still unavoidable time delays in the other steps. The analysis of causes of deviation in many instances requires considerable time. In nearly

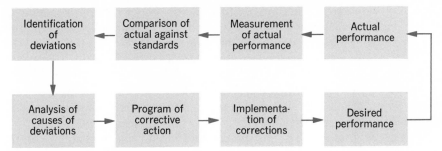

Figure 29.2 *Feedback loop of management control.*

every case, the development of a program of correction and implementation of correction take time, varying from a few days to many months.

Thus, mere inspection of the actual feedback loop involved in management control will underline the fact that fast information itself will not solve the problems of such control. Even the fastest data collection, known as "real time" information (that is, information immediately available at the time events are occurring), will not meet the requirements of quick control. To be sure, saving time in collecting information on actual performance or comparing it against standards, or even identifying deviations, will shorten the loop. But the time interval of the other steps shows clearly that this will not result in automatic correction of deviations from plans.

There is sometimes fanciful thinking about expanding real-time information to management systems of real-time control. If real-time control implies, as it is usually defined, a system of information collection, feedback, and deviation correction fast enough that outputs in a system can be effectively controlled as deviations occur, then, for most areas of managing, real-time control is impracticable. It is not that information on deviations cannot be quickly collected and processed in many areas; it is rather due to the fact that the correctional process requires time, normally varying from days to months.

This means that the intelligent manager, while encouraged by new systems of data collection and processing, will not be carried away with an exaggerated notion of their potentialities. He will, instead, recognize that what he needs is a system which will give him indication of deviations *before* they occur. This has been done, as noted above, with cash planning and control. It is being done by such devices as the networks approach (as in PERT, which is discussed in the next chapter) to planning and control. And the authors predict that, with the clear need recognized and new techniques developing, other devices will be invented in the near future to help in establishing an effective form of quick control.

CRITICAL CONTROL POINTS

The establishment of standards furnishes the basis against which actual or expected performance is measured. In a simple operation, a manager might control through over-all observation. However, as operations become more complex or a manager's authority broader, this becomes impracticable. The manager must then choose points for special attention and, by watching them, assure himself that his whole operation is proceeding as planned.

The points selected for control should be critical, in the sense either of being limiting factors in the operation or of showing better than other factors whether plans are working out. With such standards a manager can handle a larger group of subordinates and thereby increase his span of management, with resulting cost savings and improvement of communication.

There are, however, no specific catalogs of controls available to all managers because of the peculiarities of enterprise and department functions, the variety of products and services to be measured, and the innumerable policies and plans. An almost unbelievable number of standards can be used to measure certain kinds of performance. The dimensions and contents of a product can be spelled out in great detail. Production can be gauged in rate per minute, hour, day, shift, month, or year. Cost can be measured in terms of its components, per unit or per varying lots. Business income can be measured by such widely different standards as profits before and after taxes and profits as a percentage of sales or return on investment. Standards for measuring financial soundness include desired inventory levels, cash availability, working capital, depreciation reserves, and the many ratios useful in analyzing balance sheets, such as the ratio of current assets to current liabilities or net worth to debt or net quick assets to short-term liabilities. Likewise, in personnel selection and training, supervision, purchasing, traffic, public relations, and all the many activities of business varying measurements of performance exist.

The ability to select critical points of control is one of the arts of management, since sound control depends on them. In this connection the manager must ask himself such questions as: What will best reflect the goals of my department? What will best show me when these goals are not being met? What will best measure critical deviations? What will inform me as to who is responsible for any failure? What standards will cost the least? For what standards is information economically available?

Types of Critical Standards

Every broad planning objective, every goal of the many planning programs, every activity of these programs, every policy, and every procedure become standards against which actual or expected performance might be measured. In practice, however, standards tend to be of the following types: (1) physical standards, (2) cost standards, (3) capital standards, (4) revenue standards, (5) program standards, and (6) intangible standards.

Physical standards   These deal with nonmonetary measurements and are common at the operating level where materials are used, labor employed, services rendered, and goods produced. They may reflect quantitative performance, such as man-hours per unit of output, pounds of fuel per horsepower produced, ton-miles of freight traffic carried, units of production per machine-hour, or feet of wire per ton of copper. Physical standards may also reflect quality, such as hardness of bearings, closeness of tolerances, rate of climb of an airplane, durability of a fabric, or fastness of a color. As Goetz has said,[6] these standards are the "building blocks of planning," since "whether management must choose between alternate policies, organizational configuration, procedures, or resources, it must always analyze the rival programs in terms of their physical elements, determine the financial implications of these elements, integrate or synthesize the elements into programs, and select the best program it can devise." As physical standards are the building blocks of planning, they are also the fundamental standards for control.

Cost standards   These deal with monetary measurement and, like physical standards, are common at the operating level. They attach monetary values to the costs of operations. Illustrative of cost standards are such widely used measures as direct and indirect cost per unit produced, labor cost per unit or per hour, material cost per unit, machine-hour costs, costs per plane reservation, selling costs per dollar or unit of sales, and costs per foot of well drilled.

Capital standards   These are a variety of cost standards, arising from the application of monetary measurements to physical items. But they have to do with the capital invested in the firm rather than with operating costs and are therefore related to the balance sheet rather than the income statement. Perhaps the most widely used standard for new investment, as well as for over-all control, is return on investment. The typical balance sheet will disclose other capital standards, such as ratios of current assets to current liabilities, debt to net worth, fixed investment to total investment, cash and receivables to payables, notes or bonds to stock, and the size and turnover of inventories.

Revenue standards   These arise from attaching monetary values to sales. They may vary from such standards as revenue per bus passenger-mile and dollars per ton of steel shapes sold, to average sale per customer and sales per capita in a given market area.

Program standards   A manager may be assigned to install a variable budget program, a program for formally following the development of new products, or a program for improving the quality of a sales force. While some subjective judgment may have to be applied in appraising program performance, timing and other factors can be used as objective standards.

Intangible standards   More difficult to set are standards not expressed in either physical or monetary measurements. What standard can a manager use for determining the competence of the divisional purchasing agent or personnel director? What can he use for determining whether the advertising program meets both short- and long-term objectives? Or whether the public relations program is successful? Are foremen loyal to the company's objectives? Is the office boy alert? Such questions show how difficult it is to establish

---

[6]*Ibid.*, p. 93.

standards for goals that cannot be given clear quantitative or qualitative measurement.

Many intangible standards exist in business because thorough research into what constitutes desired performance has not been done above the level of the shop, the district sales office, the shipping room, or the accounting department. Perhaps a more important reason is that where human relationships count in performance, as they do above the basic operating levels, it is very hard to measure what is "good," "effective," or "efficient." Tests, surveys, and sampling techniques developed by psychologists and sociometrists have made it possible to probe human attitudes and drives, but many managerial controls over interpersonal relationships must continue to be based upon intangible standards, considered judgment, trial and error, and even, on occasion, sheer hunch.

Goals or standards   However, with the present tendency for better-managed enterprises to establish an entire network of verifiable qualitative or quantitative goals at every level of management, the use of intangible standards, while still important, is diminishing. In complex program operations as well as in the performance of managers themselves, modern managers are finding that through research and thinking it is possible to define goals that can be used as performance standards. While the quantitative goals are likely to take the form of the standards outlined above, definition of qualitative goals represents a new development in the area of standards. For example, if the program of a district sales office is spelled out to include such elements as training salesmen in accordance with a plan with specific characteristics, the very fact of the plan and its characteristics furnish standards which tend to become objective and, therefore, "tangible."

TRADITIONAL CONTROL DEVICES: THE BUDGET

A widely used device for managerial control is the budget. Indeed, it has sometimes been assumed that budgeting is *the* device for accomplishing control. As will be noted, however, many nonbudgetary devices are also essential. In fact, many companies attain a high degree of control without formal budgets, although budgeting principles are usually necessary. In a number of companies, primarily because of the negative implications of budgeting in the past, the more positive phrase "profit planning" is used and the budget is known as the "profit plan."[7]

Concept of Budgeting

Budgeting is the formulation of plans for a given future period in numerical terms. As such, budgets are statements of anticipated results, in financial

---

[7] For a discussion of the newer program planning and budget systems (PPBS), usually applied to government, see Chapter 30.

terms—as in revenue and expense and capital budgets—or in nonfinancial terms—as in budgets of direct-labor-hours, materials, physical sales volume, or units of production. It has sometimes been said, for example, that financial budgets represent the "dollarizing" of plans.

Purpose of Budgeting

Through numerical statement of plans and breaking of these plans into components consistent with the organization structure, budgets correlate planning and allow authority to be delegated without loss of control. In other words, reduction of plans to definite numbers forces a kind of orderliness that permits the manager to see clearly what capital will be spent by whom and where, and what expense, revenue, or units of physical input or output his plans will involve. Having ascertained this, he can more freely delegate authority to effectuate the plan within the limits of the budget.

Budgets sometimes serve purposes beyond that of control. A budget not only requires planning but is an instrument of planning. Moreover, a budget, to be useful to a manager at any level, must reflect the organizational pattern. Only when plans are complete, coordinated, and developed enough to be fitted into departmental operations can a useful departmental budget be prepared as an instrument of control.

Types of Budgets

Since budgets express plans and since the typical enterprise has a large variety of plans, there are many types of budgets. These may be classified into five basic types, with a budget summary portraying the total planning picture of all the budgets: (1) revenue and expense budgets, (2) time, space, material, and product budgets, (3) capital expenditure budgets, (4) cash budgets, and (5) balance sheet budgets.

Revenue and expense budgets   By far the most common business budgets spell out plans for revenues and operating expenses in dollar terms. The most basic of these is the sales budget, the formal and detailed expression of the sales forecast. As the sales forecast is the cornerstone of planning, the sales budget is the foundation of budgetary control. Although a company may budget other revenues, such as expected income from rentals, royalties, or miscellaneous sources, the revenue from sales of products or services furnishes the principal income to support operating expenses and yield profits.

Operating expense budgets of the typical business can be as numerous as the expense classifications in its chart of accounts and the units of organization in its structure. These budgets may deal with individual items of expense, such as direct labor, materials, supervision, clerical, rent, heat, power, travel, entertainment, office supplies, shop supplies, and many others. Sometimes the department head will budget only major items and lump together other items in one control summary. For example, if the manager of a small department is expected to take one business trip a year at a cost of $240 budgeting this cost each month at $20 would mean little for monthly planning or control.

Time, space, material, and product budgets   Many budgets are better expressed in physical than in monetary terms. Although such budgets are usually translated into monetary quantities, they are much more significant at a certain stage in planning and control if dealt with in physical quantities. Among the more common of these are the budgets for direct-labor-hours, machine-hours, units of materials, square feet allocated, and units produced. Most firms budget product output, and most production departments budget their share of the output of components of the final product. In addition, it is common to budget manpower, either in labor-hours or man-days, by types of manpower required. Obviously, such budgets cannot be well expressed in monetary terms, since the dollar cost would not accurately measure the resources used or the results intended.

Capital expenditure budgets   The capital expenditure budget outlines specifically capital expenditure for plant, machinery, equipment, inventories, and other items. Whether for a short or a long term, these budgets require care in giving definite form to plans for spending the funds of the enterprise. Since capital resources are generally one of the most limiting factors of the business, and since investment in plant and equipment usually requires a long period for recovery of its cost from operations, thereby leading to a high degree of inflexibility, capital expenditure budgets must be diligently tied in with long-range planning.

Cash budgets   The cash budget is simply a forecast of cash receipts and disbursements against which actual cash experience is measured. Whether called a budget or not, this is perhaps the most important single control of a business. The availability of cash to meet obligations as they fall due is the first requirement of business existence, and handsome profits do little good when tied up in inventory, machinery, or other noncash assets. Cash budgeting also shows availability of excess cash, thereby making possible planning for profit-making investment of surpluses.

Balance sheet budgets   The balance sheet budget forecasts the status of assets, liabilities, and capital account as of particular times in the future. Since the sources of change in balance sheet items are the various other budgets, it proves the accuracy of all other budgets.

In addition to the balance sheet budget, many of its items may be budgeted in various degrees of detail. The more common, in addition to cash and capital investments, are special budgets of accounts receivable, inventories, and accounts payable.

Budget summaries   Complete balance sheet budgets are a form of budget summary. In addition, a master budget gathers together all the budgets for the several departments of a business and summarizes them, first in a forecast income statement, and then in a forecast balance sheet. The former may be in detail, or it may be in a summary form showing only the principal items of revenue, expense, loss, and profit (for example, net sales, cost of sales, gross profit, administrative and selling expenses, net operating profit, other income and charges, income taxes, and net profit). The latter reflects the principal items of the balance sheet.

Dangers in Budgeting

Budgets should be used only as a tool of planning and control. Some budgetary control programs are so complete and detailed that they become cumbersome, meaningless, and unduly expensive. There is danger in overbudgeting, through spelling out minor expenses in detail and depriving the manager of needed freedom in operating his department. For example, a department head was thwarted in important sales promotion because expenditures for office supplies exceeded budgeted estimates; new expenditures had to be limited even though his total departmental expenses were well within the budget and he had funds to pay personnel for writing sales promotion letters. In another department, expenses were budgeted in such useless detail that the cost of budgeting of many items exceeded the expenses controlled.

Another danger lies in allowing budgetary goals to supersede enterprise goals. In his zest to keep within budget limits, a manager may forget that he owes primary allegiance to the enterprise objectives. The authors recall a company with a thorough budgetary control program in which the sales department could not obtain information needed from the engineering department on the grounds that the latter's budget would not stand such expense! This conflict between partial and over-all control objectives, the excessive departmental independence sometimes engendered, and the consequent lack of coordination are symptoms of inadequate management, since no budget system can be so perfect or omniscient as to replace common sense and every budget should support enterprise objectives.

A latent danger sometimes found in budgeting is that of hiding inefficiencies. Budgets have a way of growing from precedent, and the fact that a certain expenditure was made in the past becomes evidence of its reasonableness in the present; if a department once spent a given amount for supplies, this becomes a floor for future budgets. Also, managers sometimes learn that budget requests are likely to be pared down in the course of final approval and therefore ask for much more than they need. Unless budget making is accomplished by constant reexamination of standards and conversion factors by which planning is translated into numerical terms, the budget may become an umbrella under which slovenly and inefficient management can hide.

Perhaps inflexibility is the greatest danger in controlling through budgets. Even if budgeting is limited to major items and is not used to supplant management, the reduction of plans to numerical terms gives them a kind of illusive definiteness. It is entirely possible that events will prove that a larger amount should be spent for this kind of labor or that kind of material and a smaller amount for another, or that sales will exceed or fall materially below the amount forecast. Such differences may make a budget obsolete almost as soon as it is made; and if the manager must stay within the straitjacket of his budget in the face of such events, the usefulness of the budget is reduced or negated. This is especially true where budgets are made for long periods in advance.

One of the primary problems of budgeting in government, for example, is that plans for expenditures must be made, and budgets thereby created, sometimes two or three years ahead of actual expenditures, to give ample time for appropriations to be presented to and approved by the legislature. It is not easy for the dean of a state college to foresee exactly for sometime ahead his needs (for stationery, supplies, and travel expense, as well as instruction) or for the head of the research department of a state of federal regulatory agency to foresee his needs for manpower and other expense provisions so far in advance.

In business the danger of inflexibility can be extremely important. With the dynamics created by change and competition, the manager must be ready to change his plans materially at short notice. Since budgetary rigidities may make it difficult or impossible for him to do so, some top managers shy away from such programs.

Variable Budgets

Because of the dangers arising from inflexibility in budgets and because maximum flexibility consistent with efficiency underlies good planning, attention has been increasingly given to variable or flexible budgets. These are designed to vary usually as the volume of sales or production varies and so are largely limited in application to expense budgets. The variable budget is based upon an analysis of expense items to determine how individual costs *should* vary with volume of output. Some costs do not vary with volume, particularly in so short a period as a month, six months, or a year. Among these are depreciation, property taxes and insurance, maintenance of plant and equipment, and the costs of maintaining a minimum staff of supervisory and other key personnel on a readiness-to-serve basis. Some of these standby, or period, costs—such as for maintaining a minimum number of key or trained personnel for advertising or sales promotion, and for research—depend upon managerial policy.

Costs that vary with volume of output range from those that are perfectly variable to those that are only slightly variable. The task of variable budgeting is to select some unit of measure that reflects volume, to inspect the various categories of costs (usually by reference to the company's chart of accounts), and, by statistical studies, methods-engineering analyses, and other means, to determine how these costs should vary with volume. At this stage, each category of cost is related to volume, sometimes with recognition of "steps" as volume increases and sometimes with a factor allowing increases in expenses with rising volume. Each department is given these variable items of cost, along with definite dollar amounts for its fixed, or standby, costs. Periodically—usually each month—department heads are then given the volume forecast for the immediate future, from which is calculated the dollar amounts of variable costs that make up the budget. In this way, a basic budget can be established for six months or a year in advance but be made variable with shorter-term changes in sales and output.

This type of budget may be illustrated by Figure 29.3 which depicts the fixed and variable portions of business cost. A chart of a departmental budget would have essentially the same appearance, with suitable cost components. Although this chart uses units of monthly output as the base for volume, and direct labor and materials are included, many variable budgets assume that volume will automatically control direct labor and materials and are consequently used only to control indirect and general expense.

A difficulty in all kinds of variable budgets is that the department manager must still make future plans. It may be easy to tell a foreman that during the month of May he can have twelve trained electronic assemblers, then, several weeks later, that he may have fifteen in June, and a month later that his budget for July will permit hiring only ten. But the problems of hiring and training competent personnel make accomplishing these variations more costly than their advantages are worth. In other words, efficiency may demand that the department manager not vary certain of his expenses with short-term variations in volume. In the quest for flexibility in budgets, as with other tools of management, the intelligent manager will not lose sight of basic objectives and efficiencies by blindly following any system.

Observation of many variable budgets in practice leads to the conclusion that these work best when sales or other measures of volume can be reasonably well forecast and reasonably long-range plans made, so that the level of expenses will not have to be changed so often and on such short notice as to make

Figure 29.3   *Variable budget chart. . . . As volume increases, certain costs remain fixed; others vary accordingly.*

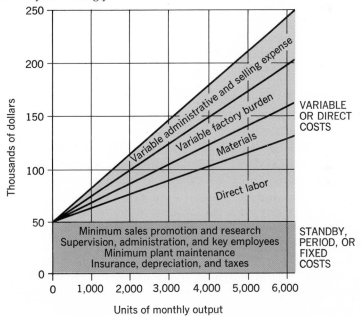

the job of supervisors intolerable. Under these circumstances, one might well ask what are the advantages of variable budgeting. Although a fixed budget will work as well with good plans and sales forecasts, a variable budget *forces* study of and preoccupation with factors which translate work load into manpower or expense needs. Carefully worked out conversion factors—worked out and applied in advance—are necessary for any good budgeting. This, rather than flexibility itself, appears to be the principal advantage of variable budgeting.

Alternative and Supplementary Budgets

Another method of obtaining variable budgeting is to establish alternative budgets for alternative eventualities. Sometimes a company will establish budgets for a high level of operation, a medium level, and a low level, and the three budgets will be approved for the company as a whole and for each organizational segment for six months or a year in advance. Then, at stated times, managers will be informed as to which budget to use in their planning and control. Alternative budgets are a modification of variable budgets, the latter being virtually infinitely variable instead of limited to a few alternatives.

Budget flexibility is also obtained via a plan referred to as the "supplemental monthly budget." Under this plan, a six-month or one-year budget is prepared for the primary purpose of outlining the framework of the company's plans, coordinating them among departments, and establishing department objectives. This is a basic or minimum budget. Then a supplementary budget is prepared each month on the basis of the volume of business forecast for that month. This budget gives each manager authority for scheduling output and spending funds above the basic budget, if and to the extent that the shorter-term plans so justify. It also gives top managers the advantages of close control, at the same time giving department managers a minimum level of operations for long-term planning. Besides, it avoids some of the detailed calculations necessary under the typical variable budget. But these budget approaches do not usually have the advantage of forcing complete analysis of all costs and relating them to volume.

Making Budgetary Control Work

If budgetary controls are to work well, managers must remember that they are designed only as tools and not to replace management, that they have limitations, and that they must be tailored to each job. Moreover, they are the tools of all managers and not alone of the budget administrator or the controller. The only persons who can administer budgets, since they are plans, are the managers responsible for budgeted programs. No successful budget program can be truly "directed" or "administered" by a budget director. This staff officer can assist in the preparation and use of budgets by the responsible managers, but, unless the entire company management is to be turned over to the budget officer, he should not be given the job of making budget-commitment or expenditure decisions.

To be most effective, budget making and administration must receive the wholehearted support of top management. To establish an office of budget administrator by decree and then forget about him leads to haphazard budget making and to saddling subordinate managers with another procedure or set of papers to prepare. On the other hand, if top management actively supports budget making and grounds the company budget firmly on company plans, encourages divisions and departments to make and defend their budgets, and participates in this review, budgets encourage alert management throughout the organization.

Related to the participation of top management, another means of making budgets work is to make sure that all managers expected to administer and live under budgets have a part in their preparation. Just as wide participation is advisable for developing understanding and loyal acceptance of plans, so is it advisable for department managers to have a part in preparing their own budgets. Although these managers must often be overruled and some of their budget requests cannot be honored, managers should be told why and how the approved budget better serves the objectives of the enterprise. Real participation in budget making, rather than pseudoparticipation, is necessary. As one student of the subject found, most budget administrators and controllers recognize that participation is crucial to budget success, but too often in practice this amounts to pressured "acceptance."[8]

Important, too, for successful budgeting is taking care that budgets are not overdone to the extent of seriously compromising the authority of managers. Although budgets do furnish a means of delegating authority without loss of control, there is danger that they will be so detailed and inflexible that little real authority is, in fact, delegated. Some executives even believe that the best budget to give a manager is one that lumps all his allowable expenditures for a period of time into a single amount and then provide for him complete freedom as to how these funds are to be spent in pursuance of the company's goals. This kind of decentralization has much to commend it, although better planning and control might be forthcoming, without centralizing authority unduly, by allowing the department manager real participation in budget making. It may also be well to allow the department manager a reasonable degree of latitude in changing his budget and in shifting funds, so long as he meets his *total* budget.

One of the keys to making budgeting work is to develop and make available standards by which the manager's work can be translated into needs for manpower, operating expenses, capital expenditures, space, and other resources. Many budgets fail for lack of such standards, and many upper-level managers hesitate to allow subordinates to submit budget plans for fear that there may be no logical basis for reviewing budget requests. With conversion factors available, the superior manager can review such requests and justify his approval or disapproval of them. Moreover, by concentrating on the resources required to do a planned job, a manager can base his request on what

---

[8] Chris Argyris, "Human Problems with Budgets," *Harvard Business Review*, vol. 31, no. 1, p. 108 (January, 1953).

he needs to have for meeting output goals and improving performance. He no longer must cope with arbitrary across-the-board budget cuts—a technique more frustrating to the superior than to the subordinate who, on the occasion of the next request, has the foresight to pad for the inevitable slice. In fact, it can be said that across-the-board cuts are the surest evidence of poor planning and loss of control.

Lastly, if budgetary control is to work, the manager needs ready information as to actual and forecast performance under budgets by *his* department. This must be designed to show him how well *he* is doing, preferably before the fact, but unfortunately, such information is usually not available until too late for him to avoid budget deviations.

TRADITIONAL NONBUDGETARY CONTROL DEVICES

There are, of course, many traditional control devices not connected with budgets, although some may be related to and used with budgetary controls. Among the more important of these are statistical data, special reports and analyses, analysis of break-even points, internal audit, and personal observation.

Statistical Data

Statistical analyses of the innumerable aspects of a business operation and the clear presentation of statistical data, whether of a historical or forecast nature, are, of course, important to control. Some managers can readily interpret tabular statistical data, but most managers prefer presentation of the data on charts. Comprehensible presentation of statistical data, whether in tabular or chart form, is an art that requires imagination.

It is probably safe to say that most managers understand statistical data best when it is presented in chart form since trends and relationships are not easily seen, except by those accountants and statisticians accustomed to them, in the tabular sheets of computer print-outs. Moreover, if data are to be meaningful, even when presented on charts, they should be presented in such a way that comparisons to some standards can be made. What is the significance of a three or ten percent rise or fall in sales or costs? What was expected? What was the standard? How significant is the deviation? Who is responsible?

Moreover, since no manager can do anything about history, it is essential that statistical reports show trends so that the viewer can extrapolate where things are going. This means that most data, when presented on charts, should be made available in time averages to rule out variations due to accounting periods, seasonal factors, accounting adjustments, and other variations associated with given times. One of the simplest and best devices for giving perspective is the moving average. In the twelve-month moving average, for example, twelve consecutive months, divided by twelve, are used. The difference in clarity may be shown by the comparative data presented graphically in Figure 29.4.

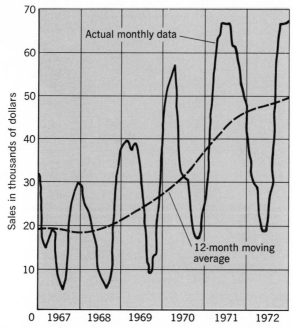

Figure 29.4 *Actual monthly data versus twelve-month moving average. . . . Sales of company X, 1967–1972.*

Special Reports and Analyses

For control purposes, special reports and analyses help in particular problem areas. While routine accounting and statistical reports furnish a good share of necessary information, there are often areas in which they are inadequate. One successful manager of a complicated operation hired a small staff of trained analysts and gave them no assignment other than investigating and analyzing operations under his control. This group developed a surprising sense for detecting situations where things did not seem just right. Almost invariably, their investigation disclosed opportunities for cost improvement or better utilization of capital that no statistical chart would have disclosed.

It may be that some of the funds being spent for elaborate budgetary control and information programs could be more profitably spent for special analyses. Their very nonroutine nature can highlight the unusual and, in so doing, reveal places for significant improvement in efficiency. In routine search for pennies and accounting for them, opportunities for saving dollars may be overlooked.

Break-even Point Analysis

An interesting control device is the break-even chart. This chart depicts the relationship of sales and expenses in such a way as to show at what volume revenues exactly cover expenses. At any lesser volume, the company would suffer a loss, and at a greater volume it would enjoy a profit.

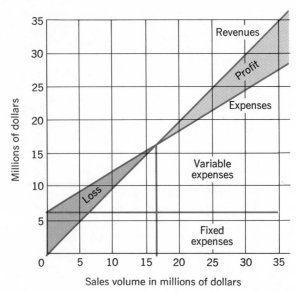

Figure 29.5 *Break-even chart. . . . The break-even point is reached when revenues equal expenditures.*

Figure 29.5, a simple form of such a chart, shows the level of revenues and expenses for each volume of sales and indicates that at $17 million of sales the company would break even. (The break-even point can be expressed as well in units of goods sold, percent of plant utilized, or similar terms.) It will be noted that the chart is similar to the variable budget chart (Figure 29.3), and break-even analysis is often confused with variable budgets. Although both use much the same kind of basic input data, the variable budget has as its purpose the control of cost, while the break-even chart has as its purpose the prediction of profit and, consequently, must incorporate revenue data. Moreover, utilized for budgetary control, the variable budget must reflect organizational units, while the break-even chart is ordinarily used to determine profitability of a given course of action as compared with alternatives.

Break-even analysis is especially useful in planning and control because it emphasizes the marginal concept. Ratios, such as percentage of profits to sales, tend to overlook the impact of fixed costs, while the use of break-even points emphasizes the effects of additional sales or costs on profits. Likewise, in dramatizing the effect of additional expenses or incremental changes in volume, it brings to the manager's attention the marginal results of his decisions.

Internal Audit

Another effective tool of managerial control is the internal audit or, as it is now coming to be called, the operational audit. Internal auditing, in its broadest sense, is the regular and independent appraisal, by a staff of internal auditors, of the accounting, financial, and other operations of a business. Although more often limited to the auditing of accounts, in its most useful aspect internal auditing involves appraisal of operations generally, weighing actual results in the light of planned results. Thus, internal auditors, in addition to assuring themselves that accounts properly reflect the facts, might also appraise policies, procedures, use of authority, quality of management, effectiveness of methods, and other phases of operations.

There is no persuasive reason why the concept of internal auditing should not be broadened in practice. Perhaps the only limiting factors are the ability of a company to afford so broad an audit, the difficulty of obtaining men who can do a broad type of audit, and the very practical consideration that no one likes to be reported upon. While persons responsible for accounts and for the safeguarding of company assets have learned to accept audit, those who are responsible for far more valuable things—the execution of the plans, policies, and procedures of a company—have not so readily learned to accept the idea.

Where the broad form of internal audit has been employed constructively and where auditors operate as a group of internal management consultants with a view to helping operating managers, their acceptance has understandably been very high. In one large company, in which the emphasis of internal auditing is less on "snooping" and more on the "outside" look of the consultant, and where the auditors are conversant with management principles and company policies and plans, line managers welcome the auditors and use them to improve operations. As one of the manufacturing managers informed the authors, the audit staff had immeasurably assisted him and his superintendents by advising on company policies and plans; raising questions about operations which had never been raised because of preoccupation with the work; and suggesting solutions for vexing managerial problems. Thus, the success of this program depended largely upon the concept of the task, the leadership given by the head auditor, and the quality of his subordinates.

Personal Observation

In any preoccupation with the devices of managerial control, one should never overlook the importance of control through personal observation. Budgets, charts, reports, ratios, auditors' recommendations, and other devices of control can be helpful, if not essential to control. But the manager who relies on these devices and sits, so to speak, in a soundproof control room reading dials and manipulating levers can hardly expect to do a thorough job of control. Management, after all, has the task of seeing that the enterprise objectives are accomplished by *people*, and, although many scientific devices aid in making sure that people are doing that which the manager has hoped and planned for them, the problem of control is still one of measuring activities of human beings. It is amazing how much information an experienced manager can get from personal observation even from an occasional walk through a plant or an office.

FOR DISCUSSION

1. Planning and control are often thought of as a system; control is also often referred to as a system. What is meant by this? Can both statements be true?
2. If you were asked to institute a system of "tailored" controls in a company, exactly what steps would you take?
3. "Variable budgets are flexible budgets." Discuss.
4. It is often claimed that an operating expense budget must be set at levels lower than expected in order to assure the attainment of goals. Do you agree?
5. To what extent, and how, can budgeting be approached on a "grass roots" basis, that is, from the bottom of the organization upward?
6. If you were going to institute a program of special control reports and analyses for a top manager, how would you go about it?

30
special control techniques

Although the basic nature and purpose of management control do not change, special tools have brought it into sharper focus and promise increasingly to improve the quality of control. These tools, closely related to recent advances in planning techniques, have brought the scientific approach to problems of control—a recognition that better planning is of no avail without better control.

Even though these techniques cannot relieve the manager of responsibility for developing his own controls or making his own decisions, they can show the way to their improvement. They take advantage of the basic techniques of the physical sciences emphasized so strongly in this book: treating operations as systems with information feedback control; the application of mathematical methods to express these system relationships in terms of goal optimization; the use of electronic machines to store and process data; and the use of time-event network analyses. In addition, there are control techniques based upon the sociopsychological needs of human beings.

Only a superficial analysis of the most significant of these techniques can be given here; but some appreciation of them is needed by every manager at every level in modern enterprise.

IMPROVED INFORMATION TECHNOLOGY[1]

Electronic equipment permits fast and economical processing of huge amounts of data. While the machine cannot design relationships of data or originate basic information, it can, with proper programming, process data toward logical conclusions, classify them, and make them readily available for the manager's use. In fact, data do not become information until they are processed into a usable form.

[1] Although many writers use this term to apply to the entire field of information handling, including operations research and simulation techniques, it is used here in the sense of providing information most suitable to the manager for planning and control.

As an astute business manager has observed, "The reach of an executive is determined by the information system at his command."[2] Note that the information must be at a manager's command; he must be able to use it. A good information system must furnish knowledge that is material to the manager's job, that can be weighed against goals; it must be designed to determine how and where goals are being missed. It must furnish intelligible data. Above all, its success depends on managers who will listen and act intelligently.

Expanding Basic Data

The focus of attention on management information, coupled with its improved processing, has led to the reduction of long-known limitations. Managers for years have recognized that traditional accounting information, aimed at the calculation of profits, has been of limited value. Yet in many companies this has been virtually the only regularly collected and analyzed type of data. Managers have known that they need all kinds of nonaccounting information, including information on the social, economic, political, and technical climate in which plans must operate, as well as information on internal operations.[3] And such information should include both qualitative and quantitative data.

While not nearly enough progress has been made in meeting these requirements, the computer, plus operations research, has led to enormous expansion of available managerial information. Problems in developing information inputs to fill existing gaps still exist, but now the gaps are apparent, and company after company is beginning to undertake research to make basic data available. One sees this especially in relation to data on marketing, competition, production and distribution, product costs, technological change and development, labor productivity, and qualitative goal accomplishment. The expansion of such information—primarily required for planning but also for control—is indicated for the marketing department of an oil company in Figure 30.1.

Sharpening Accounting Data by Direct Costing

The expansion of basic data is occurring not only in nonaccounting areas. Accountants themselves have made great strides in developing more useful data. The increasingly used technique of direct costing gives promise of revolutionizing managerial accounting.

Direct costing is simply recognition by accountants of certain basic economic principles. It is grounded on the fact that many costs, whether formerly classified as direct or indirect, vary in whole or in part with volume of output, while other costs (such as depreciation, advertising, general management salaries and expenses, and building rentals) are related to time. Thus, some costs are "direct" in the sense that they are based on producing as compared

---

[2] Stahrl Edmunds, "The Reach of an Executive," *Harvard Business Review*, vol. 37, no. 1, pp. 87–96 (January–February, 1959).

[3] For an analysis of the problem, see D. R. Daniel, "Management Information Crisis," *Harvard Business Review*, vol. 39, no. 5, pp. 111–121 (September–October, 1961).

	Defects	Environment	Competition	Internal
Division and district expenses	No information on the total market for gasoline and other automotive products—its size, its location, its rate of growth, etc.	10-year industry sales by product, by marketing division, and other where possible by trading area	10-year share-of-market reports by product, by division, and where possible, by trading area	5-year sales and realizations by product, by division, by class of trade
	No information on competitors—what they are doing, where, and how well	10-year car registration records by state and trading area (where possible)	Special price reports intended to show (a) competitor's price strategy and (b) areas of the country classified by the nature of price conditions—stable, volatile, strong, weak, etc.	Division and district expenses per gallon (without allocations of headquarters expenses)
Sales volume by product for divisions and districts	Marketing "profit and loss" concept encouraged faulty planning because of arbitrary transfer prices	10-year population records by trading area		Marketing "net back" statements by product, by division, by district, and by bulk plant (realizations less expenses)
	No information that discloses the company's marketing strengths and weaknesses by class of trade, for example, company-owned stations, independent dealers, distributors, etc.	10-year record of new road-mile construction by state and trading area (where possible)	5-year record of new station construction by competition, by division and trading area	"Laid-down" costs by product, by terminal and bulk plant
		5-year projection of 100 fastest growing trading areas in country—by percentage and absolute numbers	5-year summary of new refinery, terminal, and bulk plant construction by competition	Frequency distribution studies of gasoline sales by size or retail station, by division and district
Marketing department profit and loss	Marketing expense information misleading because of allocations of headquarters' overhead	5-year projection of car registration by state and trading area (where possible)	Analysis of 100 largest and 100 fastest growing markets (trading areas) showing leading competitors in terms of volume, market share, laid-down costs, facilities, construction or acquisitions activity, etc.	Share of company's total sales by product for each state
	Inadequate data on size "mix" of stations, for example, number and percentage of stations selling different volumes of gasoline	Report on Federal road-building program		5-year report of number of stations by type (owned, leased, etc.) by division and district
Capital budgets by division for five years	Inadequate data on the sales performance of newly built or acquired stations	5-year report (and 5-year projection) on composition of country's automobile population by size, weight, horsepower, etc. for each division	Special reports on key market developments, for example, rebrander activity, additional qualities of gasoline, multiple octane pumps, etc.	5-year report of capital budgets by division and district (amounts authorized and spent)

Purpose (Environment): to provide an over-all picture of the market, its composition, its size, its location, significant trends affecting any of these factors, etc.

Purpose (Competition): to identify who competitors are, how well they've been doing, and the likely direction of their future efforts

Purpose (Internal): to assess the company strengths and weaknesses, thus permitting a correlation between the company's capabilities and the opportunities of the market place

Figure 30.1 Comparative analysis of marketing planning information needed by an oil company. SOURCE: D. R. Daniel, "Management Information Crisis," Harvard Business Review, vol. 39, no. 5, p. 118 (September–October, 1961). Reproduced by permission.

to not producing, or on selling as compared to not selling. Other costs are "period" costs in that they are committed to provide capacity which expires with time.

In traditional, or absorption, accounting, direct costs include only the direct material used in a product and the factory or engineering labor directly working on the manufacture or engineering of a product. All indirect costs are then allocated to the product in accordance with some formula, utilizing as a base direct-labor-hours or costs, or sales dollars, or some other measure. Also, in accounting for inventory, it has been customary to accumulate in inventory a pro-rata allocation of factory burden, thus inventorying many costs really related to time rather than to volume of production. This practice can distort product costs and profits when inventories are rising or falling. When inventories of goods in process or finished goods are rising, for example, burden costs are absorbed—that is, carried into inventory—and cost performance and profits tend to be better than when those burden costs not related to volume are charged off in the period incurred.

Direct costing gives the manager better information visibility in two major respects. From the standpoint of inventory and profit calculation, he knows that period costs have been written-off as incurred, that an inventory does not include the "air" of costs not related to product volume, and that profits are more real when they reflect the write-off of costs related to time. From the standpoint of cost analysis of individual products or projects, a manager can now look at cost in more nearly marginal terms. If direct costing is thoroughly done, the manager can see whether the product is covering the costs ascribable to volume and how much remains as a contribution to period costs and profits. Thus, a product might show a loss by the customary formula of taking direct labor and material and allocating burden plus selling and administrative costs; but the same product may very well show a handsome contribution to period costs and profits by the direct-costing method.

Even though direct costing is difficult to put into effect and faces some resistance, particularly from traditional accountants and tax authorities, it offers managers a number of advantages.[4] Direct costing was first suggested in 1936.[5] It was not until 1947 that a major company, the Pittsburgh Plate Glass Company, started using it. Even as late as 1953 only seventeen companies using it could be found by the National Association of Accountants, but by 1962, *Business Week* estimated, some 250 companies had adopted direct costing and more were converting to it. Experience with companies using direct costing has convinced the authors that this trend has continued rapidly and will accelerate in the future. In fact, there is a real possibility that direct costing will become the standard accounting in the future.

---

[4]For an excellent analysis of the advantages and disadvantages of direct costing, see Willmar Wright and Felix T. Kollaritsch, "Direct Costing, Pro and Con," *The Controller,* vol. 30, no. 7, pp. 322ff. (July 1962).

[5]These and the following data are from "Direct Costing to the Rescue," *Business Week,* pp. 45–48 (Mar. 24, 1962).

Information Indigestion versus Information Design

Managers who have experienced the impact of better and faster data processing are justly concerned with the danger of information indigestion. Their appetite for figures whetted, the data originators and processors are turning out material at an almost frightening rate. Managers are complaining of being buried under reports, projections, and forecasts which they either do not have time to read or cannot understand, or which do not fill their particular needs.

Control techniques or information not properly aimed at the man and his job, or of a kind a manager cannot or will not understand, will not work. As one experienced executive declared:[6]

If a little learning is a dangerous thing, too much—that is, knowledge not put to good use—can be a costly waste. Too many undigested facts can turn a man of action into a Hamlet, paralyzed by indecision. Like the raw materials of industry, information must be converted into something. What is required is a discriminating selection which can deliver relevant data in a form usable at the echelon of decision. The research study that collects dust on shelves may well have merit; the fault is failure to relate its data to the problem it was designed to solve.

Information may involve anything from the most minute and finite to the universal. Processing information today calls not only for distinguishing the forest from the trees, but distinguishing leaves and chlorophyll—while still not losing sight of the forest.

To combat information indigestion, there arises the need to design information suited for special use at all levels and in all functions of management. Special design of information may seem to be in opposition to the mass-production techniques and economies of the electronic computer, but computer experts claim this is not so. They insist that it is up to managers to ask for what they need to carry on their tasks of planning and control. Within limits of basic data input availability, desired information can almost invariably be designed for individual managers by proper programming. All the more modern machines permit tailoring this information by merely inserting appropriate cards or tape. So far as the machine is concerned, even changes in desired information outputs may be easily made. However, it should not be forgotten that small changes in information desired can mean considerable changes in a program and programmers understandably complain that "small changes" can mount to a considerable cost in time and money. The important point to bear in mind is that it is not the computer that causes a deluge of data and a dearth of information, nor is it the computer specialists; the basic problem is that information users—operating managers—often do not know what they want.

[6]Marion Harper, Jr., "A New Profession to Aid Management," Charles Coolidge Parlin Memorial Lecture, p. 13 (Philadelphia: Philadelphia Chapter, American Marketing Association, 1960).

Intelligence Services

Attempts are being made to solve the dilemma posed by managers needing special digested and digestible information and by information processors who do not know what managers require. One such attempt consists of establishing in a company an intelligence service and developing a new profession of intelligence experts. The service would be manned by experts who would know (or find out) what information managers need and who would know how to digest and interpret such information for management use.

This approach to making the new mass of information more usable has much to commend it, and a number of companies have already adopted it. However, few have gone so far as to design information for individual managers down the line of organization as well as at the top. Under such names as "administrative services" or "management analyses and services," many companies are recognizing that some sort of information design service is necessary if expansion of basic data is to result in useful information. Some companies feel that this service should be centralized, and, in many cases, it can be. However, despite the efficiencies of a central department, doubt exists as to whether in medium-large and large companies centralization can satisfactorily cater to *all* managers or whether a number of such departments might understandably serve best those to whom they immediately report. It appears that the future will see multiple intelligence services located throughout an organization so that they can be more responsive to various information needs.

Information Systems

With the increasing use of the computer a great deal of attention has been given to the development of information systems. This is a recognition of the fact that many items of input data may be useful for a number of different outputs. Thus, input data on inventory are useful for different kinds of reports, including those to accounting for asset recording, to purchasing for reorder action, to production for planning assembly operations, and to sales for availability of product. Payroll data, likewise, are useful for accounting, labor cost control and production, labor turnover, and other concerns of managers.

It is consequently obvious that data should not be independently gathered for special purposes, but rather the same basic input data should be made available for multiple end uses. Moreover, some data are developed in large part as a kind of by-product from the operation of procedures designed to get something done, such as material flow in production or computation of labor payroll. Likewise, many procedures are designed primarily to furnish data to guide managers in their decisions, such as inventory procedures so useful to accurate accounting and financial planning and for procurement decisions.

As a consequence of these multiple uses of data and the demands of economy in data development and processing, it is understandable that specialists in this area, as well as managers, should hope to view and utilize data processing and information flow as a complete system. This becomes particularly urgent if the almost incredible conclusion of one information specialist is even somewhat true: that "at least 50 percent of the cost of running our economy is information cost."[7]

When one looks on the one hand at the tremendous information requirements of managerial and nonmanagerial personnel in a typical enterprise for their innumerable decisions and evaluations of operations, and, on the other hand, at the tremendous mass of input data necessary to produce this information, he is appalled at the possibility of tying all this into a single system. Perhaps the best approach is that recommended by Dearden: to recognize that we are dealing, in the typical company, with three major information systems and many minor systems.[8]

Dearden points out that the three major information systems typically found are financial, personnel, and logistics. The basis of the financial system is the flow of money through a company. The personnel information system has to do with the flow of data concerning people. The logistics system applies to those data reflecting the physical flow of goods through an enterprise. Other information systems identified by Dearden are those dealing with marketing, research and development, strategic planning, and executive compensation. While there are definitely interrelationships between all three, the interfaces are particularly noteworthy between financial, personnel, and logistics information systems.

Since most companies have traditionally kept information on financial and personnel matters, and a number have considerable logistics information, Dearden's suggestion has the merit of building on a practicable base. Also, by so classifying information into several systems, the approach recommended has the advantage of breaking the almost incomprehensibly complex total enterprise information system into more manageable parts. With the amount of hopeful talk aimed at using the computer as a catalytic agent to set up an entire system, and the relatively small real advances toward this goal thus far observed in practice, this appears to be an excellent way of approaching information systematization.

In the understandable anxiety of alert managers to perfect information and utilize the computer for the improvement of managing, no one should overlook the fundamental problem of information as the authors of this book see it. Unless managers actively embrace the approach of tailored controls by deciding what end product they need for effective management, no information system can be successful. In the computer, systems analysis, and programming of data conversion, we have what has been referred to as an automated factory. And what has been often done is to pick up such raw materials as may be left lying around in the form of available data, put them in this automated factory, and then wonder why the end product is unsatisfactory. No manager would follow this process in manufacturing a product for sale. In-

[7] A. M. McDonough, *Information Economics and Management Systems* (New York: McGraw-Hill Book Company, 1963), p. 5. While the authors believe the cost is great their own estimate would more nearly be 20 percent.

[8] J. Dearden, "How to Organize Information Systems," *Harvard Business Review*, vol. 43, no. 2, pp. 65–73 (March–April, 1965).

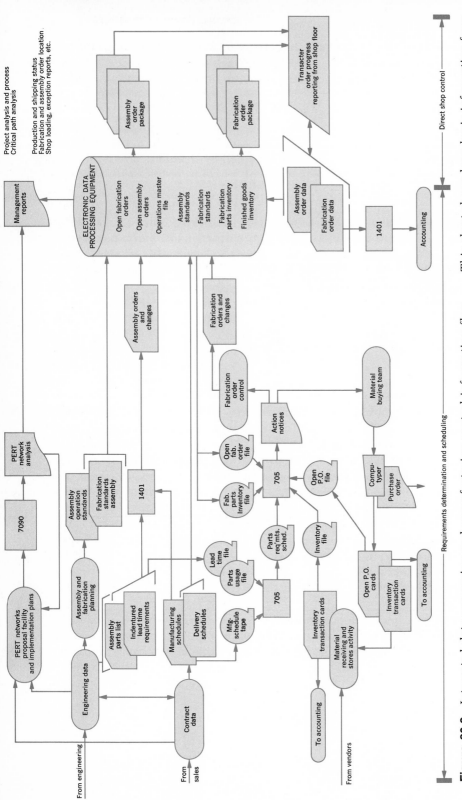

Figure 30.2 *Integrated data-processing and manufacturing control information flow. . . . This chart shows how basic information from engineering, customers (sales), and vendors is combined with internal manufacturing standards and operational requirements to develop a complete and integrated system of manufacturing control information. This not only furnishes information required for buying, fabricating, assembling, inventorying, and accounting, but also provides needed management reports from the same source.*
SOURCE: *J. B. Friauf, Advanced Techniques for Manufacturing Control, Instrument Society of America, Conference Reprint 187-LA61 (1961).*

stead, he would design the end product and work back through the production system to determine what raw materials were required. Unless this approach to management information is more thoroughly and rigorously followed all the systems and hardware that experts can design will never solve the problem.

PROCEDURES PLANNING AND CONTROL

Procedures are also closely related to information, because they apply not only to operating tasks—such as purchasing or selling—but also, outstandingly, to accumulating information for planning and control.

Procedures present a rewarding area of planning and control to which a systems approach can be applied. The extraordinary complexity of procedures and their inflexible channeling of action were discussed under types of plans in Chapter 6. While desirable tools for efficiently getting things done in a given way or for control when it is necessary not to deviate from this way, procedures can make for departmental rigidity that thwarts innovation and response to change. Although they *should* be designed to implement plans and to respond to change, they too often do not.

In addition, procedures can be expensive. Modern enterprise has created a sensational increase in the number of people doing paper work. As was pointed out by Neuschel,[9] since 1870 clerical personnel in the nation has increased a hundred times, while the total number of gainfully employed increased five times; and it was estimated that, when the nation's employed work force numbered 65 million, more than 9 million were clerical workers.

Effective planning and control of procedures depend on recognizing that they are inherently systems. Procedures normally extend into various departments, and it is a rare procedure which does not concern itself with more than two. This increases the importance of their control. Accounting departments, for example, tend to regard procedures as purely concerned with their function, yet a simple payroll or expense account procedure reaches into every nook and cranny of the company and affects many nonaccounting activities. Personnel, purchasing, and other functional departmental procedures do likewise.

How Procedures Get out of Control

Procedures often get out of control because of the specialized approach of each organization function in setting them up for its particular operation. Accounting procedures may conflict with or overlap purchasing procedures, differ but slightly from personnel procedures, and somewhat duplicate sales department procedures. Duplication, overlapping, and conflict are usually elusive and partial; there is rarely either complete duplication or clear disagreement. Commonly, different forms and records are called for though they use the same subject matter.

[9] R. F. Neuschel, *Management by System* (New York: McGraw-Hill Book Company, 1960), p. 3. It should be pointed out, of course, that not all this increase in clerical work force can be ascribed to procedures, but unquestionably most has.

Procedures also get out of control when managers try to use them to solve problems instead of solving the problems through better policies, clearer delegations, or improved direction. Then again, many procedures are instituted to correct a mistake which might never be made again. In one case, a division head ordered development of a complete system of procedures to prevent overlooking one serious customer complaint. This had only happened once. A clear policy statement, simple routing of complaints, and assigning the handling of complaints to the service manager would have taken care of the situation.

Procedures also evade control by becoming obsolete, either because they are not kept up-to-date or because failure to police them permits deviations in practice. Moreover, procedures have a way of becoming customs, ingrained in departments and individuals who have a stubborn resistance to change. And managers find it expedient to impose new procedures on the old, a haphazard practice.

Finally, a major cause of procedures that get out of control is the manager not being clear as to what procedures should do, how much they cost, when they are duplicated, how to overhaul them, and how to control them. And to top all this, managers often fail to obtain the interest and support of top management in the tedious and unromantic planning and control of procedures.

Guidelines

In planning and control of procedures, managers may find it advantageous to follow these guidelines.

Minimize procedures   The first and perhaps most important guideline for the manager is to limit procedures to those which are clearly called for. The costs of procedures in paper handling, stifled thinking, delay, and lack of responsiveness to change are such as to make a concerned manager think twice before initiating them. In other words, he must weigh the potential gain in money or necessary control against the disadvantages and costs.

Make sure they are plans   Since procedures are plans, they must be designed to reflect and help accomplish company (not just departmental) objectives and policies. Have they been planned? If they are necessary, are they designed effectively and efficiently to accomplish plans? For example, a procedure to handle orders for spare parts or repair defective parts, should expedite a job so as to meet customer service standards without undue delay.

Analyze them   Procedures should be carefully analyzed to assure a minimum of duplication, overlapping, and conflict. To do this, the procedures must be visualized. This, in turn, necessitates mapping them with their various steps identified and interrelated. That this is not always easy is exemplified by a defense company material procurement procedure which, when charted, took a piece of paper 27 feet long and involved over 250 definite related required actions!

Recognize procedures as systems   One of the failures of procedure design is to neglect to regard them as systems. Any given procedure, whether one specifying the handling of payroll, procurement, inventory planning and control, or other of many uses, is in itself a system of interrelated activities normally in a network rather than a pure linear form. Likewise, various procedures with special purposes are usually interrelated. Accounting procedures, for example tend to be intertwined with personnel, purchasing, and other procedures. Therefore, groups of procedures are usually interrelated systems.

The problem of procedures planning and control is not likely to be solved unless their complex systemic structure is recognized. And, when this occurs, it would be natural to expect that their design and improvement would call for the same kind of analytical talent so readily applied to the design of a complex instrument or machine. But seldom do companies give procedures planning and control this kind of treatment or bring to bear on them the same high level of engineering and design talent they give to products. It is obvious that this should be done, particularly when one considers the cost in money, time, and organization friction that they cause.

Estimate their cost   The analysis of a procedure should be accompanied by an estimate of what its operation will cost. While some costs cannot be ascertained, such as the cost of possible frustration to those involved, an estimate may bring into sharper focus the answer to the question: Is this procedure worthwhile?

Police their operation   Procedures are merely plans until they are executed. Execution involves three steps: First, knowledge of procedures must be made available in manual or other form to those who must follow them. Second, employees must be taught how to operate under them and, ideally, why the procedures are necessary and what purpose they are designed to serve. Third, there must be machinery to assure that people do understand and are employing up-to-date procedures, and that the procedures are doing the job intended. This step involves constructive auditing.

Procedures Analysis and Electronic Data Processing

An encouraging consequence of present systems and procedures planning and the analysis of procedures as systems is that they are often programmed on electronic data-processing (EDP) equipment. There remains the danger that the systems and procedures expert will become so enamored of programming as to forget, however, that electronic automation of procedures can only reflect the system of procedures as it exists.

Despite this danger, EDP has stimulated broad analysis and improvement of procedures. It is so frightening and expensive for top management to see a personnel, accounting, or purchasing procedure put on a machine that a strong effort is normally made to assure that it is workable and clear before it is automated. Moreover, the systems approach of the programmer forces an orderly approach to procedure analysis. Since, at the very least, a procedure cannot be put on a machine without having been mapped, the very process of mapping often shows up the existence of overlapping and the need for simplification, as well as the means of achieving it.

So far, analyzing and rationalizing procedures for EDP have mainly brought the subject to the surface and have unearthed the need for experts in this kind of planning and control. The universities are not doing much about training such experts. One wonders whether, if some of the intelligence and effort now applied to designing sophisticated instruments were applied to the more mundane problems of procedures analysis, the improvement of enterprise efficiency would not be vastly accelerated. The need is great for experts who understand the nature of procedures as a management tool and their importance in accomplishing enterprise objectives. Systems and procedures analysis—like improved information technology—is high-level, difficult, and challenging work. It should be treated as such.

LOGISTICS SYSTEMS

As was made clear from the discussion of operations research in Chapter 9, research methodology is a study of logical relationships. It is thus a study of systems so conceptualized as to show the way to manipulating variables in order to optimize some desired goal. It was also pointed out that the best use of operations research occurs when inputs are quantifiable, but that the method can be useful even when variables are little more than broad approximations. Operations research, therefore, has shown its greatest promise in logistics systems, because in areas involving labor input and the flow of materials, the variables can be credibly quantified. Consequently, operations research has proceeded from subsystem areas, such as production and inventory, and by linking these subsystems has gone on to planning and control of the broader field of production and distribution combined.

Operations Research for Inventory Control

Although space does not permit a discussion of the application of operations research to all types of production or distribution subsystems, its early application to inventory control is selected as an example. For one thing, perhaps in the history of operations research more attention has been directed to inventory control than to any other area in business and industry.[10] For another thing, the path from inventory control has led to utilization of broader forms of systems control.

If one wished to see the essential systems relationships as a little "black box" without going into detailed mathematics, he could depict it as is done in Figure 30.3.

---

[10] C. W. Churchman, R. L. Ackoff, and E. L. Arnoff, *Introduction to Operations Research*, p. 195 (New York: John Wiley & Sons, Inc., 1957).

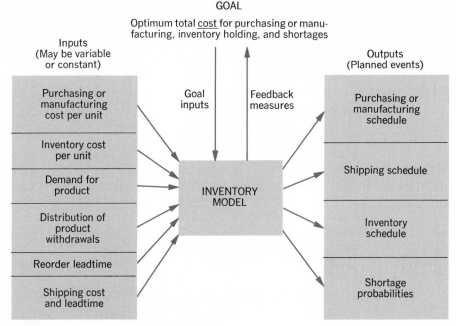

Figure 30.3 *Inventory control model.*

Or, if these conceptual relationships were placed into one of the simpler mathematical forms covering approximately the system in Figure 30.3, it might look something like this:[11]

$$Q = \sqrt{\frac{2R[S + E(s)]}{I}}$$

where Q = Reorder quantity

R = Sales requirement per year
S = Setup cost (per order)
I = Interest and carrying cost, including storage, all expressed per piece, per year
$E(s)$ = Expected cost of stockouts per order cycle

and where $E(s)$ is defined by this equation:

$$E(s) = \pi \sum_{u = r + 1}^{u\text{max}} (u - r)p(u)$$

where u = Usage during any lead time
$p(u)$ = Probability of usage greater than u

---

[11] E. H. Bowman and R. B. Fetter, *Analysis for Production Management* (Homewood, Ill.: Richard D. Irwin, Inc., 1961), pp. 330–331.

r = Reorder point in units
u = Expected usage during lead time
π = Stockout cost per unit demanded but not available

As can be seen, even the simple "black box" representation of a subsystem of control can be very complex. Each of the inputs can be variable or constant. Each can be discrete or continuous, and the rate of distribution over time can be variable or constant. Moreover, as this is a planning model, feedback of information—to make sure the model attains the goals desired—should be added to make it a planning and control system.

With all its complexities, the model illustrates several things. It forces consideration of the goals desired and of the need for placing definite values on outputs and inputs. It also furnishes a manager with the basis for plans and with standards by which to measure performance. However, with all its advantages, this is a subsystem and does not incorporate other subsystems, such as production planning, distribution planning, and sales planning.

Distribution Logistics

One of the more exciting and profit-promising ways of using systems logistics in planning and control is in the expansion of inventory control to include other factors, referred to here as distribution logistics.[12] In its most advanced form, currently in operation in a few companies, this treats the entire logistics of a business—from sales forecast through purchase and processing of material and inventorying to shipping finished goods—as a single system. The goals are usually to optimize the *total* costs of the system in operation, while furnishing a desired level of customer service and meeting certain constraints, such as financially limited inventory levels. This gathers into one system a large mass of relationships and information, so as to optimize the whole. In doing so, it is entirely possible that transportation, manufacturing, or any other single area of cost will not be optimized, but the total cost of materials management will be.

Schematically, a distribution logistics system might appear as shown in Figure 30.4. This model, represented by a "black box," would be expressed mathematically in an operating system.

This figure shows the relationships between the goal desired, the input variables and limits, and the expected outputs. The company represented by this model is a consumer goods company with a fairly broad line of products, a number of plants (some producing the whole line, others producing only part of the line), a number of finished-goods warehouses, and national distribution to grocery chains and wholesalers. It will be noted that customer service standards (that is, maximum time permitted between receipt and shipment of an order) are here inserted as a constraining input.

---

[12] Often referred to as "distribution management," or "physical distribution management," and called by some specialists "rhochrematics," the science of materials flow. See S. H. Brewer and J. Rosensweig, "Rhochrematics and Organization Adjustments," *California Management Review*, vol. 3, no. 3, pp. 52–71 (Spring, 1961).

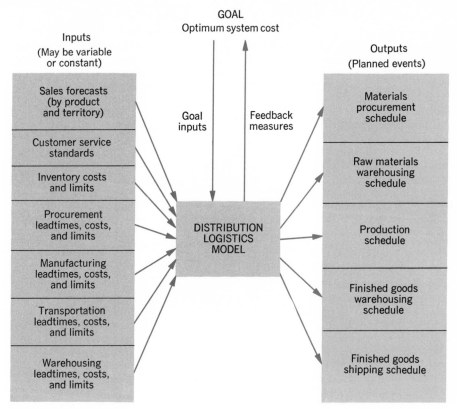

Figure 30.4   *Distribution logistics model.*

That the mathematics of this model would be exceedingly complex can be appreciated when it is known that the company had a line of 200 products (including sizes), 16 plants, 60 warehouses, and 70 sales districts. Also, this system would require fast feedback for control, adequate inventories to meet unforeseen contingencies, good sales forecasting, and territorial distribution managers able to override the system by quick change of local plans if schedules go out of control.

A fully developed distribution logistics system is a fine instrument of planning and control. By optimizing *total* costs in a broad area of operation, the system might show it would be cheaper to use more expensive transportation on occasion rather than to carry high inventories. Or it might show that production at less than economic order quantities would be justified in order to get better transportation or warehousing utilization or to meet customer service standards with limited inventories.

Moreover, such a system gives a manager a means of control which a disparate system of isolated, unconnected plans could not. By seeing how activities interlock and by setting up a system of interrelated plans, control of the entire production and distribution system can be obtained. That this could not be done on such a scale without mathematics and electronics computation is beyond question. But what is interesting, in the experience of one of the authors, is that where distribution logistics has been undertaken intelligently and patiently, its costs of operation have not been really high, while the benefits, although difficult accurately to assess, have been extraordinary.

To be sure, even such a broad distribution logistics system is not a total system of a business enterprise, but it does apply to a considerable part of the total business operation. And it applies to those parts where the inputs can be quantified with a reasonable degree of accuracy.

Industrial Dynamics

Another systems approach to planning and control is called "industrial dynamics" by Prof. J. W. Forrester, of the Massachusetts Institute of Technology.[13] This approach is based on the idea that a company is "not a collection of separate functions" but a system in which the *flows* of information, materials, manpower, capital equipment, and money set up forces that determine the basic tendencies toward growth, fluctuation, and decline. In other words, industrial dynamics anticipates adding to a distribution logistics system many factors of change, with their influence on each other, and many inputs currently not quantifiable enough to satisfy managers, such as consumer response to advertising, policies regarding work-force reduction, and the likelihood of results from research expenditures.

Industrial dynamics also takes into account fluctuations caused primarily by delays in the system. For example, if a sudden increase of sales should occur in January, delays in decision making and information flow (such as those in mailing, accounting, purchasing, and production schedule changes) may cause a cyclical effect. Thus, because of delays, sales may increase 10 percent at the retail level but might peak at 16 percent at the distributors' level, at 28 percent at the factory warehouse level, and at 40 percent at the factory production level. This fluctuation, brought on by accumulated lags, can be further amplified by random fluctuations in the consumers', retailers', or distributors' behavior.

Forrester's concept of industrial dynamics thus brings into the planning and control model the very important input of cyclical business behavior under conditions of change. He also includes more variables in his model than have been included in models so far suggested. However, being grounded on delay factors and lack of adequate sales forecasts, one might ask whether many dynamic lags would better be solved by control of delays and of poor information inputs that lead to exaggerated fluctuations. In fact, Forrester recognizes that better sales data, faster order handling, and better inventory planning are needed to improve control. However, introduction of the concept of flow of manpower, money, technology, and equipment to flow of materials does promise improvement in planning and control. And what is perhaps

---

[13]"Industrial Dynamics," *Harvard Business Review*, vol. 36, no. 4, pp. 37–66 (July–August, 1958). See also by the same author *Industrial Dynamics* (New York: John Wiley & Sons, Inc., 1961).

most exciting about Forrester's work is that he is undertaking to include in the system of a business the larger system of its environment.

Operations Control Systems

Another interesting type of planning and control system is designed to integrate information on virtually an instantaneous basis, thereby cutting down considerably the delays that Forrester finds cause inefficient fluctuations. With development of the necessary hardware and software, it is now possible for virtually any measurable data to be reported as events occur. Systems are available to provide for fast and systematic collection of data bearing on a total operation, for keeping these data readily available, and for reporting without delay the status of any of thousands of projects at any instant. They are thus primarily information systems designed to improve planning and control.

In establishing a system, its developers aim to meet three requirements: (1) to produce reports ideally suited to give each level of management the tools needed for purposeful decision making; (2) to utilize as inputs only basic data necessary to accomplish the reporting (developers have found that much data believed necessary were, on critical evaluation, not required); and (3) to design a dynamic system that would feed information into a computer simultaneously as events occur and make it immediately available for control purposes. Interesting, too, is the attempt to feed data immediately into a central part of the system to avoid manual preparation of the same data for use in many different reports.

Such systems, now fairly frequently used and specially useful for a business making many items, can nonetheless be useful in any complicated operation. Applied widely only to the complex of purchasing, storing, manufacturing, and shipping, they operate through dispatch stations, widely dispersed in the plant, and input centers, also located throughout the plant. At the dispatch centers, events are recorded as they occur and the information dispatched immediately to a computer. For example, when a foreman finishes his assigned task on the assembly of a product, the work-order timecard is put into a transactor which electrically transmits to a computer the information that item x has passed through a certain process, has accumulated y hours of labor, and other pertinent data. The input centers are equipped automatically to originate, from programmed instructions, purchase orders, shop orders, and other authorizations. These data are likewise fed into the computer to be used as standards against which the actual operations, transmitted from the dispatch stations, may be compared.

In addition to fast entry, comparison, and retrieval of information, such an integrated operations control system furnishes needed information for planning programs in such areas as purchasing, production, and inventory control. Moreover, it permits almost instananeous comparison of results with plans, pinpointing where they differ, and provides a regular (daily or more often, if needed) system of reports on items behind schedule or costs running above budget.

Other planning, control, and information systems have been developed to reflect quickly the interaction between production and distribution operations and such key financial measures as costs, profit, and cash flow. For example, Boulden and Buffa have described the development in a few companies of real-time corporate models that give operating managers virtually instant analysis of such "what-if" questions as the effects of reducing or increasing output, reduction in demand, the sensitivity of the system to labor cost increases, price changes, and new equipment additions.[14] To be sure, these system models, simulating actual operations and their impact on financial factors, are primarily planning tools. But so are most control techniques. However, by making possible exceptionally quick responses to the many "what-if" questions of operating managers, the time elapsed in correcting for deviations from plans can be greatly reduced and control materially improved.

These and the other systems sketched here—as well as many more which use the technology of science and fast computation—clearly promise to hasten the day when planning can be more precise and control more effective. The main drawback is not the cost but, rather, the failure of managers to appreciate the potential. They are often unwilling to put in the mental effort to conceptualize the system and its relationships or to see that someone in the company does so.

TIME-EVENT NETWORK ANALYSES

One of the interesting planning and control techniques is a time-event network analysis called Program Evaluation and Review Technique (PERT). There have also been other techniques designed to watch how the parts of a program fit together during the passage of time and events.

The first of these were the chart systems developed by Henry L. Gantt early in the twentieth century and culminating in the bar chart bearing his name. Although simple in concept, this chart, showing time relationships between "events" of a production program, has been regarded as revolutionary in management. What Gantt recognized was that total program goals should be regarded as a series of interrelated derivative plans (or events) that people can comprehend and follow. The most important developments of such control reflect this simple principle and also such basic principles of control as picking out the more critical or strategic elements of a plan to watch carefully.

As the result of developing further techniques from the principles of the Gantt chart, and with better appreciation of the network nature of programs, "milepost" or "milestone" budgeting and PERT have been devised in recent years, contributing much to better control of research and development.

Milestone Budgeting

Used by an increasing number of companies in recent years in controlling engineering and development, milepost or milestone budgeting breaks a

---

[14] See J. B. Boulden and E. S. Buffa, "Corporate Models: On-line Real-time Systems," *Harvard Business Review,* vol. 48, no. 4, pp. 65–83 (July–August, 1970). The detailed applications of such a system to a plywood and a steel operation are shown in this article.

project down into controllable pieces and then carefully follows them. As was pointed out in the discussion of planning, even relatively simple projects contain a network of subsidiary plans or projects. In this approach to control, milestones are defined as identifiable segments. When accomplishment of a given segment occurs, cost or other results can be determined.

Engineering control was long hampered because few people have known how much progress was being made on a project. The common device of estimating completion time, with planned inputs of manpower and materials, runs into the difficulty that, although accurate records of personnel and material costs can be kept, estimates of percentage of completion tend to reach 85 or 90 percent and stay there, while time and costs continue.

The best way to plan and control an engineering project is to break it down into a number of determinable events, for example, completion of preliminary drawings, a "breadboard" model, a package design, a packaged prototype, and production design. Or a project might be broken down vertically into subprojects—for example, the design of a circuit, a motor, a driving mechanism, a sensing device, a signal feedback device, and similar components—that can be designed, individually, in a time sequence, to be ready when needed. Milestone budgeting allows a manager to see a complex program in its simpler parts, thereby giving him some control through knowing whether it is succeeding or failing.

Program Evaluation and Review Technique

Developed by the Special Projects Office of the United States Navy,[15] PERT was first formally applied to the planning and control of the Polaris Weapon System in 1958 and worked well in expediting the successful completion of that program. For a number of years it was so enthusiastically received by the armed services that it became virtually a required tool for major contractors and subcontractors in the armament and space industry. Although PERT is no longer much heard of in defense and space contracts, for reasons that will be noted presently, its network fundamentals are still essential tools of planning and control. Moreover, in a host of nongovernmental applications, including construction, engineering and tooling projects, and even the scheduling of activities to get out monthly financial reports, PERT or its companion network technique, CPM (critical path method), is widely and profitably used.

Major features   In a sense, PERT is a variation of milestone budgeting. It uses a time-event network analysis, as shown in Figure 30.6. This very simple example illustrates the basic nature of PERT. Each circle represents an event—a subsidiary plan whose completion can be measured at a given time. Each arrow represents an activity—the time-consuming element of a program, the effort that must be made between events, "activity time" is the elapsed time required to accomplish an event.

---

[15] But also separately developed as the Critical Path Method by engineers at the du Pont Company at virtually the same time. Only PERT is discussed here because the Critical Path Method, although different in some respects, utilizes the same basic principles.

I. GANTT CHART

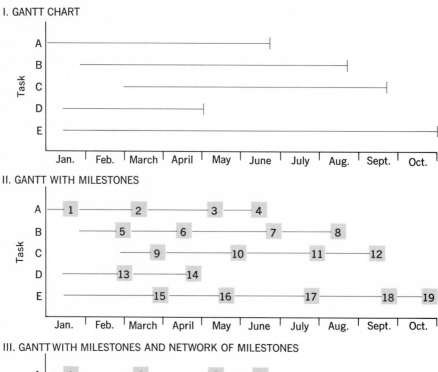

II. GANTT WITH MILESTONES

III. GANTT WITH MILESTONES AND NETWORK OF MILESTONES

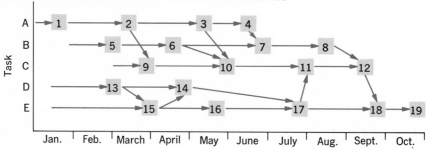

Figure 30.5 *Transition from a Gantt chart to PERT. . . . The Gantt chart in I above shows the scheduled time of accomplishing a task, such as procurement (Task A), and the related schedules of doing other tasks, such as manufacture of parts (Task B). When each of these tasks is broken down into milestones, such as the preparation of purchase specifications (Task A-1), and then network relationships between the milestones of each task to those of other tasks are worked out, the result is the basic elements of a PERT chart.*

In this example only a single time is shown, but in the original PERT program there were three time estimates: "optimistic" time, an estimate of time required if everything goes exceptionally well; "most likely" time, an estimate of what the project engineer really believes necessary to do the job; and "pessimistic" time, an estimate based on the assumption that any logically conceivable bad luck—other than a major disaster—will be encountered. These estimates are often included in PERT because it is very difficult, in many engineering and development projects, to estimate time accurately and partly, it is believed, because engineers will be willing to make a variety of estimates and will do their level best to beat the pessimistic estimate. When several estimates are made, they are usually averaged, with special weight given to the most likely estimate, and a single estimate then used.

The next step is to compute the "critical path," that sequence of events which takes the longest time and which involves, therefore, the least slack time. In Figure 30.6, the critical path is indicated as from events 1-3-4-8-9-13. Over this path, the activity time for the entire sequence of events is 131.6 weeks; if promised delivery is in 135 weeks, even this critical path would have a slack of 3.4 weeks. Some of the other paths are almost as long as the critical path. For example, the path 1-2-9-13 is 129.4 weeks. This is not un-

Figure 30.6 *PERT flow chart: major assembly of an airplane. . . . Events (each major milestone of progress) are: 1—program go-ahead; 2—initiate engine procurement; 3—complete plans and specifications; 4—complete fuselage drawings; 5—submit GFAE requirements; 6—award tail assembly subcontract; 7—award wings subcontract; 8—complete manufacture of fuselage; 9—complete assembly of fuselage-engine; 10—receive wings from subcontractors; 11—receive tail assembly from subcontractor; 12—receive GFAE; 13—complete aircraft. (*NOTE: *GFAE is government furnished airplane equipment.)*

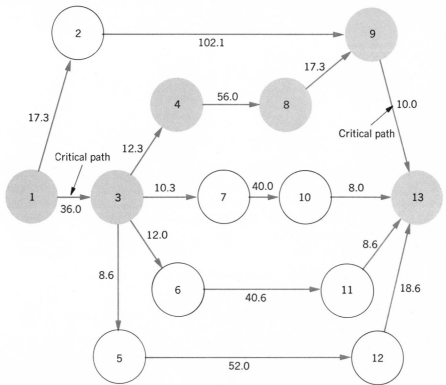

usual in PERT charts, and it is customary to identify several critical paths in order of importance. Although the critical path has a way of changing, as key events are delayed in other parts of the program, identifying it at the start makes possible close watching of this particular sequence of events to assure the total program being on schedule.

Typical PERT analyses run into hundreds or thousands of events. Even though smaller PERT analyses—including the input of event accomplishment and the frequent calculation of critical path—can be done manually, it is estimated that when upward of approximately 700 events are involved, it is virtually impossible to handle the calculations without an electronic computer.[16]

It is customary to summarize very large and complex time-event networks by subnetworks and to prepare the summarized network for top-management consideration. Thus, the top-management network might include some forty or fifty major events, each a summary of a number of subsidiary events. In fact, it is possible to group, or to break down, events so as to have a PERT network appropriate to every level of management.

Strengths and weaknesses   There are five strong advantages of PERT. First, it forces managers to plan, because it is impossible to make a time-event analysis without planning and seeing how the pieces fit together. Second, it forces planning all down the line, because each subordinate manager must plan the event for which he is responsible. Third, it concentrates attention on critical elements that may need correction. Fourth, it makes possible a kind of forward-looking control; a delay will affect succeeding events, and possibly the whole project, unless the manager can somehow make up the time by shortening that of some action in the future. Fifth, the network system with its subsystems makes possible aiming of reports and pressure for action at the right spot and level in the organization structure at the right time.

PERT also has certain limitations. Because of the importance of activity time to its operation, it cannot be useful when a program is nebulous and no reasonable "guesstimates" of schedule can be made; even here, however, insurance can be "bought" by such devices as putting two or more teams to work on an event when costs permit. PERT is also not practicable for routine planning of recurring events, such as mass production; while it could be used here, once a repetitive sequence of events is clearly worked out so elaborate a continuing control is not required. A major disadvantage of PERT has been its emphasis on time only, not costs. While this is suitable for programs where time is of the essence or where, as so often is the case, time and costs have a close direct relationship, the tool is more useful when considerations other than time are introduced.

---

[16] As estimated by Ivars Avots, "The Management Side of PERT," *California Management Review*, vol. 4, no. 2, pp. 16–27 (Winter, 1962). Most experts would estimate far fewer than 700 events.

PERT/COST   The above description of PERT is called PERT/TIME and has led logically to the development of PERT/COST with the application of costs to activities in the PERT network. While this would appear to be an easy transition, a number of complications exist. In the first place, the PERT network must be complete enough to reflect any activity which incurs cost. In the second place, in any complex project, the number of events is so great that it becomes difficult and expensive to establish job center cost accounts for each activity. As a result, in practice, the events are grouped in what are known as work packages for purposes of accumulating costs. A third complication is one of working into the cost structure a number of overhead costs not directly related to an activity or even a work package. For example, the cost of over-all project management would be one extending over the entire network while the cost of project direction for a portion of the network would be spread over that series of events. Likewise, the progress of a program against the time budget is not likely to be the same as against a cost budget.

There is no question that PERT/COST has added considerably to the managerial effectiveness of the PERT approach to planning and control. But it is also true, particularly in many large programs such as those contracted for by the Department of Defense, that the complexity of the PERT system has been greatly increased.

It is interesting that in recent years, one hears little or nothing in military and aerospace contracts or companies about PERT. In a survey made a few years ago by one of the authors, he was surprised to find out that many companies were keeping network plans and information but that they were not being used for actual control of operations. What had apparently happened to PERT and CPM in these industries at least is what happens to so many good management techniques. The specialists in the field promise too much and users become disillusioned. But, even worse, specialists, particularly those in the Pentagon, made the programs so complex that people responsible for operations, not being able to understand them, simply could not or would not use them. However, the fundamentals of network planning and control still exist in many defense and aerospace programs, even though the acronym of PERT has been replaced by a succession of others.

PERT is not a cure-all. It will not *do* the planning, although it *forces* planning. It will not make control automatic, although it establishes an environment where sound control principles may be appreciated and used. And it apparently involves rather less expense than might be thought. Setting up the network, its analysis, its interpretation, and reporting from it probably requires little, if any, more expense than most other planning and control techniques, unless, of course, these are made unduly complicated.

PROGRAM BUDGETING

One of the widely publicized tools of planning and control, used primarily in government operation but applicable to any kind of enterprise, is program planning and budgeting (PPB), or, more simply, program budgeting. While really not more, at least in its fundamentals, than what budgeting should always be, its emphasis and approach, as well as current popularity, deserve analysis as a special tool of managing.

What Program Budgeting Is

Program budgeting is basically a means for providing a systematic method for allocating the resources of an enterprise in ways most effective to meet its goals. By emphasizing goals and programs to meet them, it transcends the ordinary weakness of all kinds of budgets, even in business, of being too tied to the time-frames of accounting periods of months, quarters, or years. By concentrating on goals and programs in the light of available resources, it puts stress on the desirability of assessing costs against benefits in selecting the best course toward accomplishing a program goal.

Special Application in Government

Program budgeting has offered particularly great actual and potential benefit in government where budgeting has too often been regarded as a mere control technique—with the objective of controlling the allocation and expenditure of funds, rather than as a planning *and* control tool. For too many years, government budgeting—at federal, state, and local levels—has been handled largely on a "line" basis with allocation of funds to such functions as personnel, training, office supplies, transportation, and printing, rather than budgeting for programs designed to accomplish an identifiable goal. Also, with the fragmentation of program responsibility often among various agencies, bureaus, or divisions, and with most objectives set in such generalities as "providing adequate police protection," budgeting has tended to be an exercise by various government departments of competing and negotiating for funds rather than getting necessary support to accomplish specific desired program goals.

Following the pioneering work of Novick and Hitch at the Rand Corporation,[17] former Defense Secretary Robert McNamara introduced program budgeting in the Defense Department in 1961. It was subsequently regarded with such favor as an effective management tool that former President Lyndon Johnson later decreed its application to all federal departments. In recent years, state and local executive officers have also ordered its use in these government agencies.

---

[17] See, for example, D. Novick, *Efficiency and Economy in Government Through New Budgeting and Accounting Procedures* (Santa Monica, Calif.: The Rand Corporation, 1954); D. Novick (ed.), *Program Budgeting: Program Analysis and the Federal Budget*, 2d ed. (Cambridge, Mass.: Harvard University Press, 1967); D. Novick, "Long-Range Planning Through Program Budgeting," *Business Horizons*, vol. 12, no. 1, pp. 59–66 (February, 1969); and C. J. Hitch, "The New Approach to Management in the U.S. Department of Defense," *Management Science*, vol. 9, no. 2, pp. 1–8 (October, 1962).

Problems in Applying Program Budgeting

In the Defense Department, at least, program budgeting has worked fairly well, primarily because it has been easier to make defense objectives and strategies fairly clear and definite. It has likewise appeared to work well in such essentially program-oriented agencies as those dealing with water resources and housing programs. However, for most government agencies, one cannot say that program budgeting has been the great tool in practice that its logic would imply. There are a number of reasons for this.

In the first place, many federal, state, and local executives, particularly at the middle and lower levels of management, do not understand the philosophy and theory of the technique; they have tended to be given directives and forms without really knowing what the system entails. A second major hurdle has been the lack of clearly defined goals; obviously no one can program plan and budget for an unknown or fuzzy goal. Another difficulty is the lack of attention to planning premises; even with clear program goals, the program budgeter is in the dark without knowledge of critical planning premises. Another problem arises from the long tradition in government of doing line budgeting, and most legislators, accustomed to this kind, often will not tolerate program budgets unless they are recast in a line-item form; also many government budgetary divisions or staffs have been reluctant to make the change from their practice and procedures of annual budgets to longer-range program budgets. Other roadblocks include the fact that accounting data are seldom consistent with program budgeting, the lack of information in many areas to make meaningful cost-effectiveness analyses, and the political problems of reorganizing government departments to improve concentration for program responsibility.

The problems in government have been such that there is some question whether program budgeting will ever be made to work as it should. But a tool that makes so much sense in an area where effective management is so important and so difficult should not be allowed to fall into disuse. Unfortunately those who introduced it in most government agencies, or ordered its introduction, apparently failed to realize that much is required to make this technique successful. Attention must be given to teaching the system to managers and staffs at all levels who are expected to operate under it; even the nature of the system should be taught to those legislators who ultimately control taxpayers' pursestrings. Also, emphasis should be placed first on developing verifiable program objectives and consistent planning premises; accounting systems need modification to fit programs, rather than line activities; means should be developed for making possible better cost-benefit analyses and enthusiastic experts must realize that mathematical analyses often leave out critical intangibles; and administrators and legislators must have the perception and will to modify organization structures to fit programs.

All this might seem like a large order. And it is. But as a strategic start to develop sound government budgeting, it is worth it. Moreover, such features as the time-span of program budgeting and the use of cost-benefit analysis are features that even business would do well to adopt.

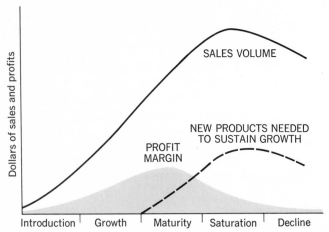

Figure 30.7   *The basic life cycle of products. . . . Profit margin tends to rise until maturity while sales volume increases until saturation is reached. But profit margin tends to fall as the market is saturated because of increased expenses and competing products. The curves demonstrate that most companies must introduce new products if they are to survive. A new product (dotted line), introduced during the maturity of the first, can sustain the company's income. It, in turn, must be followed by another new product. Product life cycles differ. Fashion goods and novelties have cycles, from introduction to saturation, of only a few months; most products have much longer lives.*

FORMALIZED PRODUCT DEVELOPMENT

Organizational devices may also furnish an important kind of control technique. The best of these involve setting up an organization structure, ordinarily with some formal processes, so that a desired end result will be given the attention it needs and where control becomes an inescapable part of a program. A good example of this is the practice of formalizing new product development.

The Need

Because new products mean future sales, because their development uses up scarce resources and time, and because new products may make existing products obsolete, well-managed companies emphasize product planning. It has been estimated that some 75 percent of the nation's growth in sales volume comes from new products, that most new-product ventures fail, and that unsuccessful products take about four out of five hours of scientific and engineering time.[18] Companies traditionally have had difficulty in developing products efficiently, fitting them to the company's strengths, and making them profitable.

[18]Booz, Allen & Hamilton, Inc., *Management of New Products* (Chicago: Booz, Allen & Hamilton, Inc., 1966), p. 2.

The Steps

Formalization of product development may be undertaken in several ways: Some companies establish a special department reporting high in the organization structure; some create a special committee; and many set up special implementing procedures. In any case, the program normally establishes the following steps with built-in control machinery:

1. Encouraging of ideas   It is usual to open up all possible channels for ideas both inside and outside the company. A company executive may ordinarily be assigned to search out product ideas by studying markets and technology, soliciting ideas from sales and research departments, or developing idea-generating groups to be guided by company strengths and weaknesses.

2. Screening   Because the objective of most formalized programs is to get maximum exposure to new-product ideas and spend money and time only on the most promising, preliminary screening is important. First, an idea's potential is given quick, inexpensive analysis, being weighed against company product policy and its marketing or technical strength in the light of immediately available cost, market, and technical information. Screening by a committee of varied specialists readily eliminates product ideas of little promise.

3. Evaluating   Product ideas surviving the screening may be subjected to a preliminary evaluation involving expenditure of some money and manpower in market, technical, or other investigations and in an estimate of the cost of a complete study of the feasibility of going ahead with the new product. At this step—because important money may be spent—the question of whether to make the expenditure for a feasibility study may be submitted to the new-product committee and even to higher authority.

4. The feasibility study   If the feasibility study is undertaken and if it indicates favorable prospects for the product, the findings are usually submitted for approval to the president or the firm's top-management committee. The study ordinarily includes analyses of design, development, and manufacturing costs; selling costs; and marketing and profit potentials. It also includes the nature of development assignments to the technical, marketing, and other company organizational areas.

5. Development of the product   If the recommendations of the feasibility study are positive and if they are approved, technical development of the product—usually a prototype or "first article"—is accomplished. Also, at the same time, preliminary marketing (including packaging) and manufacturing plans are made. This is, of course, the step in product planning where fairly large sums of money are likely to be spent.

6. Testing   After the product has been technically developed and manufacturing and marketing (including packaging) plans made, the product may be subjected to technical and market tests to see if it meets specifications and is acceptable or whether it needs any change in design or marketing approach. If the product passes the tests, the company is ready to move into the final phases of the program.

7. Final design and operational plans   When product design and marketing approach are found satisfactory, the next step is to make a final product design, detailed production plans, and complete plans for putting the product on the market.

8. Commercializing   The final step is to "commercialize" the product, making it an actuality by releasing it to manufacturing and marketing.

The Advantages

The above eight steps in formalized product development point to a number of advantages. This procedure—when reflected in the organization structure, with specific delegations of authority, and subject to upper-level management review—develops new products in accordance with company product policy and in the light of company strengths and weaknesses. Its milestone approach allows managers to see a complex program in its parts and to control and evaluate it at each step.

It is interesting that a study made in depth of some 200 companies disclosed that management problems, rather than the difficulty of getting new ideas or of creativity or personnel qualifications, were the major ones that counted in effective new-product development.[19] Of all the problems reported by these companies as interfering with their opportunities for new-product development, 55 percent were organizational (definition of responsibilities, working and reporting relationships, communications, organization structure, etc.), 12 percent were in management control, and 9 percent were in definition of objectives. Thus, in what is normally regarded as a technical or marketing area, 76 percent of the problems reported were purely managerial. There is probably no more convincing proof of the need for managers to establish and maintain an environment for performance.

While product development is the example used here, a formalized program, with adequate review, can be used in any significant area of control. The important thing is to chart the area, establish an organizational environment for doing the job, and see that the process has the attention of responsible management as it proceeds and money is spent. Proper organization can always be used as a means for focusing and channeling special effort.

FOR DISCUSSION

1. The special techniques of control appear to be as much techniques of planning as they are of control. In what ways is this true? Why would you expect it to be so?

[19] *Ibid.*, pp. 16–17.

2. PERT is a management invention that takes basic principles and knowledge and, through design to get a desired result, comes up with a useful technique of planning and control. Analyze PERT with this in mind.

3. Why would one call distribution logistics a complex system of operations research? Can this system be conceptualized without mathematics and the computer? Can it be operated in the typical multiproduct, multiplant, multicustomer firm without mathematics and the computer?

4. How would you set out to solve the problem of "information indigestion" that faces many managers today?

5. Why has program budgeting been regarded as so important in government? If you were to introduce it in a government department, how would you proceed?

6. Product planning, performance and planning review, and other techniques of assuring planning and control are increasingly being formalized. Why is this? Do you agree that this should be done?

31
control of over-all performance

Control techniques and systems must be tailored to the areas they are designed to measure and correct. Most controls are designed for specific things: policies, wages and salaries, employee selection and training, research and development, product quality, costs, pricing, capital expenditures, cash, and other areas where performance should conform to plans. Such controls are partial in the sense that they apply to a part of an enterprise and do not measure total accomplishments against total goals.

There is not space in this book to discuss in detail all types of control. However, to the extent that any control technique is sound, it will reflect the basic nature of control and its prerequisites as outlined in Chapter 29. Moreover, it is not possible to be precise about practical details of partial control without, at the very least, reference to a given plan, to the position and personality of the manager involved, and to specific enterprise goals.

As was shown in the previous chapter, planning and control are being increasingly treated as an interrelated system. Along with these special techniques, and preceding many of them, control devices have been developed to measure the over-all performance of an enterprise—or an integrated[1] division or project within it—against total goals.

There are many reasons for control of over-all performance. In the first place, as over-all planning must apply to enterprise or major division goals, so must over-all controls be applied. In the second place, decentralization of authority—especially in product or territorial divisions—creates semiautonomous units, and these must be subjected at least to over-all controls to avoid

---

[1] "Integrated" here is used as meaning that an operation includes the functions necessary to gain an over-all objective. Thus, a product division of a company would normally include engineering, manufacturing, and marketing, and this represents enough of a total operation for the division manager—even though subject to some direction and control from headquarters—to be held basically responsible for a profit. To a lesser degree, but nonetheless important, an engineering design operation might be regarded as integrated: if its head has under him all the engineering functions and specialties necessary for complete product design, he can then be held responsible for the efficient accomplishment of the project.

the chaos of complete autonomy. In the third place, over-all controls permit measuring an integrated area manager's *total* effort, rather than parts of it.

To a great extent, over-all controls in business are, as one might expect, financial. Business owes its continued existence to profit making; its capital resources are a scarce, life-giving element; and, in the environment in which it operates, the best gauge of effectiveness is the dollar. Since finance is the binding force of business, financial controls are the most important single objective gauge of the success of plans.

Financial measurements also summarize, through a common denominator, the operation of a number of plans. Further, they accurately indicate total expenditures of resources in reaching goals. This is true in all forms of enterprise. Although the purpose of an educational or government enterprise is not to make monetary profits, any responsible manager must have some way of knowing what his goal achievement has cost in terms of resources. Therefore, in all forms of enterprise, control of over-all performance is likely to be financial. Moreover, financial analyses furnish an excellent "window" through which accomplishment in nonfinancial areas can be seen. A deviation from planned costs, for example, may lead a manager to find the causes in nonfinancial factors.

In recent years, however, we have come increasingly to realize that one of the key areas of control, both for individual segments and for an entire enterprise, is the measurement of the quality of the human organization. While this area of overall control is only in its embryonic stage, there is hope that measurement and correction for unwanted deviations can be developed so as to give warning to those responsible for an enterprise when human resources lag.

BUDGET SUMMARIES AND REPORTS

A widely used control of over-all performance takes the form of a summary of budgets. A budget summary, being a résumé of all the individual budgets, reflects company plans so that sales volume, costs, profits, utilization of capital, and return on investment may be seen in their proper relationship. In these terms, it shows top management how the company as a whole is succeeding in its objectives.

The comprehensive nature of this final budget may be readily grasped if consideration is given to the preliminary steps required. These involve the sales forecast and its translation into expenditure budgets with statements of costs, output, and attendant requirements. As these are summarized, the budget maker is in a position to develop a pro forma balance sheet and statement of profit and loss to accompany the final budget. These three documents permit top management to weigh the effect of departmental activities on the enterprise as a whole or on an integrated division.

Explanation of variances is often overlooked in budget reports, but if they—whether in summary for the whole enterprise or for a department or function—are not supplemented with reasons for any significant differences between budget and actual costs, the manager may be frustrated in using them for control. Although the manager of a minor department may know, from intimate acquaintance with his operations, why his performance has diverged from plans, the higher in the organization structure the budget summary is prepared and presented, the less likely a manager will know the reasons for deviations.

Especially important in making budgets operate for control purposes is the promptness of issuance. Historical data, such as normally found in budget reports, are useful only when (as is often the case) what has happened will continue to happen. Obviously, the more promptly a report is issued, the more useful it is for purposes of control.

Uses

For the best control through a budget summary, a manager must first be satisfied that total budgets are an accurate and reasonably complete portrayal of the company's plans. The budget reports and any material accompanying them should be scrutinized to determine whether the comparison of budget and actual costs shows the real nature of any deviations. As an example of where this was not done, a company head criticized his factory manager for being considerably over his labor budget in a month when the labor force had been materially reduced and the temporary increase in expenses was due to severance pay.

Minor discrepancies should receive appropriately little attention. The purpose of a control system is to draw attention to important variations, and both the budget reports and the attention paid to them should reflect this. Above all, the manager should never forget that a budget summary is no substitute for profitable operation. There is danger in manipulating budget figures and forcing revenues and expenses to conform. Moreover, budgeting is never more perfect than the planning behind it, and plans—especially long-range plans—are subject to the imperfections wrought by change and uncertainty. There may even be times when the manager must forget his budget and take special action to meet unexpected events. Budgets are meant to be tools, and not masters, of managers.

On the other hand, the value of budget summaries, in providing an effective means for over-all control in the face of decentralization of authority, should not be underestimated. They furnish a means whereby enterprise objectives can be clearly and specifically defined, and departmental plans can be made to contribute toward such objectives. Should the budget summary and the reports of actual events indicate that the enterprise as a whole is not tending toward its objectives, the top managers have a convenient and positive means of finding out where the deviations are occurring. The summaries thus furnish a useful guide for corrective action.

PROFIT AND LOSS CONTROL

The profit and loss statement for an enterprise as a whole serves important control purposes, largely because it shows the constituent parts of a profit or a loss for a given period and, therefore, is useful for determining the immediate revenue or cost factors that have accounted for success or failure. Obviously, in the form of a pro forma forecast, it is even a better control device, in that it gives a manager a chance, before the event, to influence revenues, expenses, and consequently, profits.

Since enterprise survival usually depends on profits and they are a definite standard against which to measure business success, many companies use the profit and loss statement for divisional or departmental control. Because this is a statement of all revenues and expenses for a given time, it is a true summary of the results of business operations. Profit and loss control is usually applied to divisions or departments, based on the premise that if it is the purpose of the entire business to make a profit, each part of the enterprise should contribute to this purpose. Thus, the ability of a part to make an expected profit becomes a standard for measuring its performance.

In profit and loss control, each major department or division details its revenues and expenses—normally with a pro-rata share of the company overhead—and calculates periodically a statement of its profit or loss. Some units have their own accounting group, while in others the statement is prepared by the central accounting department. In either case, the organizational unit, in being expected to turn in a separate record of profitable operation, is considered by the enterprise in much the same way that a holding company considers its subsidiary companies.

Profit and loss control usually is practicable only in major segments of the company, since the paper work in building up profit and loss statements for smaller departments tends to be too heavy. Also, profit and loss control usually implies that the manager of the division or department has a fairly wide authority to run his part of the business as he sees fit, with profit the primary standard of success. However, many companies that do not so decentralize authority have nonetheless found profit and loss control valuable. The focus on profit and the sensitiveness of the organizational unit to it are worthwhile even when the manager has limited independence to seek profit as he wishes.

The more integrated and complete the organization unit, the more accurate a measuring stick profit and loss control can be. For this reason, it works best in product or territorial divisions, where both sales and production functions for a product or service are under one jurisdiction. For example, it is much easier to use the standard of profit for measuring the operations of the general manager of the Buick division of General Motors than it would be to use it in the motor-block boring section of the manufacturing department of this division.

At the same time, companies organized on a functional basis do occasionally employ profit and loss control. The heat-treating department may produce and "sell" its service to the machining department, which in turn "sells" its product to the assembly department, which in turn "sells" a complete product to the sales department. This can be done, although the paper work required is often not worth the effort, and the problem of determining the right transfer price may occasion much negotiation or difficult executive decisions. If the transfer is made at cost, clearly only the sales department would show a profit. If it is made at a figure above cost, the question becomes one of what price to charge.

In most instances, profit and loss control is not applied to central staff and service departments. Although these departments could "sell" their services, the most satisfactory practice is to place them under some other form of control such as a straight expense budget.

Limitations

Profit and loss control suffers its greatest limitations from the accounting expense and paper transactions involving intracompany transfers. The duplication of accounting records, the efforts involved in allocating the many burden and overhead costs, and the time and effort required to calculate intracompany sales can make this control too costly when its application is carried too far.

Profit and loss control also may be inadequate for complete over-all performance. Top managers may not wish to yield so much authority to division managers and may at least desire the additional assurances of good budgetary control. In addition, profit and loss control in and of itself does not provide a standard of desirable profits or policy controls in the areas of product line, development, or other matters of long-term over-all company concern.

Another limitation of profit and loss control, especially if carried very far in the organization, is that departments may come to compete, with an aggressive detachment not conducive to enterprise coordination. On the other hand, in many companies there is not enough feeling of departmental responsibility for company profit, and departments may develop the smugness of a monopolist with an assured market. The fabrication department that knows its products must be "bought" by the assembly department, the manufacturing or service department that can force its output on the sales department, and the engineering group that has a monopolistic hold on both production and sales are dangerous monopolists indeed. Profit and loss control can break down these islands of monopoly. So, in spite of limitations—and especially if accompanied by an intracompany pricing policy requiring departments to meet outside competitive prices rather than being based on cost—profit and loss control can give top managers an extraordinary measure of over-all control.

CONTROL THROUGH RETURN ON INVESTMENT

One of the most successfully used control techniques is that of measuring both the absolute and relative success of a company or a company unit by the ratio of earnings to investment of capital. This approach has been the core of the control system of the du Pont Company since 1919 and has received much attention in recent years. A large number of companies have adopted it as their key measure of over-all performance.

This yardstick is the rate of return that a company or a division can earn on the capital allocated to it. This tool, therefore, does not look at profit as an absolute, but as a return on capital employed in the business. The goal of a business is, accordingly, not to optimize profits but to optimize returns from capital devoted to business purposes. This standard recognizes the fundamental fact that capital is a critical factor in almost any enterprise and through its scarcity limits progress.

Some Examples

As the system has been used by the du Pont Company, return on investment involves consideration of several factors. Return is computed on the basis of capital turnover multiplied by earnings as a percentage of sales. This calculation recognizes that one division, with a high capital turnover and a low percentage of earnings to sales, may be more profitable in terms of return on investment than another with a high percentage of profits to sales but with low capital turnover. Turnover is computed on the basis of total sales divided by total investment, and investment includes not only the permanent plant facilities but also the working capital of the unit. In the du Pont system, investment and working capital represent amounts invested without reduction for liabilities or reserves, on the grounds that such a reduction would result in a fluctuation in operating investments, as reserves or liabilities change, which would distort the rate of return and render it meaningless. Earnings are, however, calculated after normal depreciation charges, on the basis that true profits are not earned until allowance is made for the write-off of a depreciable asset.

Return-on-investment control is perhaps best summarized in chart form, as in Figure 31.1. Here, an analysis of variations in rate of return leads into every financial facet of the business. Rate of return is the common denominator used in comparing divisions, and differences can easily be traced to their causes.

However, other companies have taken the position that the return on investment should be calculated on fixed assets less depreciation. Such companies hold that the depreciation reserve represents a write-off of the initial investment and that funds made available through such charges are reinvested in other fixed assets or used as working capital. Such a treatment appears more realistic to operating people, partly because it places a heavier rate-of-return burden on new fixed assets than on worn or obsolete ones.

In any control through return on investment, the number of ratios and comparisons behind the final yardstick figure cannot be overlooked. Although improvement in rate of return can come from a higher percentage of profit to sales, improvement could likewise come from increasing the rate of turnover by reducing return on sales. Moreover, the ratio of return on investment might be improved by getting more product (and sales) out of a given plant investment or by reducing the cost of sales for a given product.

Application to Product Lines

A typical functional-line organization without integrated product divisions has applied return-on-investment control to its various product lines. By grouping its many products into a number of major classifications, this com-

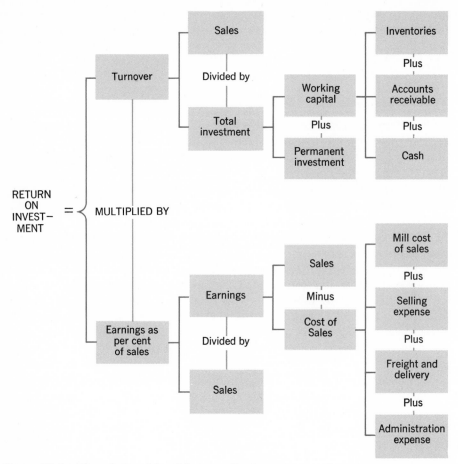

Figure 31.1   *The relationship of factors affecting return on investment.*

pany follows through with the allocation of sales, costs, and investment in fixed assets and working capital to arrive at the same kind of rate-of-return analysis used by multi-division companies. A simplified example of these results is shown in Table 31.1.

To operate the rate-of-return yardstick for product lines, the company has allocated certain expenses and assets, but these allocations apparently have not caused much difficulty. Most production costs are maintained by product, and common costs, such as sales branch expenses, are allocated by volume of sales. More difficulty is incurred in determining asset usage by product lines, but cash, accounts receivable, and administrative and sales facilities are allocated in accordance with sales: inventories and factory and plant equipment are prorated to the various products on the basis of special analyses.

In addition to comparative rates of return as between products, as indicated in Table 31.1, the company compares actual experience with trends for the various products (identified for purposes of simplicity as the "base year" in the table). An advantage of these comparisons is that the company is able to maintain a sharp look at its product lines, with a view to determining where capital is being most efficiently employed and as a guide toward obtaining a balanced use of capital for maximum over-all profit. Thus, the company has been able to identify products that are either strong and established, new and improved, or past their peak in growth and profitability.

Advantages and Limitations

One of the principal advantages of using return on investment to control over-all performance is that it, like profit and loss control, focuses managerial attention on the central objective of the business—to make the best profit possible on the capital available. It measures the efficiency of the company as a whole, its major divisions or departments, its products, and its planning. It takes attention away from mere increase in sales volume or asset size, or even from the level of costs, and draws attention to the combination of factors making for successful operation.

Another advantage of control by return on investment is that it is effective where authority is decentralized. It not only is an absolute guide to capital efficiency but offers the possibility of comparing efficiency in capital employment, both within the company and with other enterprises. By holding departmental managers responsible for performance in terms of the dollars invested in their segments of the business, it forces them to look at their operations from the point of view of top management. Managers often insist on heavy capital for new equipment or drive for lower prices to increase sales without

TABLE 31.1 COMPARATIVE RATES OF RETURN: MULTIPRODUCT COMPANY (in thousands of dollars)

	Total sales		Assets employed		Operating income*		
	Amount	*Percent of total*	*Amount*	*Per dollar of sales*	*Amount*	*Percent return on sales*	*Percent return on assets*
Base year:							
Product A	$ 39,300	40	$ 20,700	52.9%	$ 4,800	12.2	23.1
Product B	29,500	30	16,900	57.3	2,800	9.4	16.4
Product C	19,600	20	8,900	45.1	2,100	10.8	23.9
Product D	9,800	10	2,700	27.5	500	5.1	18.5
Total	$ 98,200	100	$ 49,200	50.1%	$10,200	10.4	20.8
Current year:							
Product A	$ 48,100	25	$ 28,400	59.0	$5,600	11.6	19.7
Product B	96,200	50	75,300	78.3	8,500	8.8	11.2
Product C	38,500	20	19,500	50.7	3,900	10.2	20.1
Product D	9,600	5	2,900	29.9	500	5.2	17.2
Total	$192,400	100	$126,100	65.5%	$18,500	9.6	14.6

*Before interest on borrowed money and federal income taxes.

taking into account the possible effect of their requests on the company as a whole. They also often feel isolated, particularly in large businesses, with respect to their performance. If they are furnished a guide to efficiency that reaches into many facets of the business, managers develop a keener sense of responsibility for their department or division, and top managers can more easily hold subordinate managers responsible.

A further advantage of return-on-investment control, if it is complete and shows all the factors bearing upon the return, is that it enables managers to locate weaknesses. If inventories are rising, the effect will be shown on the rate of return, or if other factors camouflage inventory variations and leave the rate looking good, tracing back influences will disclose any weakness of the inventory situation and open the way for consideration of a remedy.

With all its advantages and with its increasing use by well-managed and successful companies, this method of control is not foolproof. Difficulties involve availability of information on sales, costs, and assets and proper allocation of investment and return for commonly sold or produced items. Does the present accounting system give the needed information? If not, how much will it cost to get it, through either changes in the system or special analyses? Where assets are jointly used or costs are common, what method of allocation between divisions or departments shall be used? Should the manager be charged with assets at their original costs, their replacement costs, or their depreciated values? Setting up a return-on-investment control system is no simple task.

Another question is, What constitutes a reasonable return? Comparisons of rates of return are hardly enough, because they do not tell the top manager what the optimum rate of return *should* be. Perhaps as good a standard as any is one that meets or surpasses the level of competition of other firms, since, in a practical sense, the optimum tends to be measured not by an absolute level but rather by the level of the competition for capital.

One of the dangers of overemphasis on the rate of return is that it may lead to undesirable inflexibility in investing capital for new ventures. Many companies using this important measuring tool have set minimum rates which a division, new product program, or investment must meet before the allocation of capital would be approved. It is said that even du Pont, for many years, would not approve a new product program which would not promise a yield of a minimum of 20 percent return on investment. According to one executive of the company, this rigid minimum caused it to pass up such great product opportunities as xerography and the Land (Polaroid) camera.[2] More recently, the company has used a more flexible minimum rate of return, requiring a higher rate when risks are greater and a lower rate when results are very promising, more certain, or when an investment supplements an established business.

Perhaps the greatest danger in return-on-investment control, as with any

---

[2] See "Lighting a Fire Under the Sleeping Giants," *Business Week*, pp. 40–41 (Sept. 12, 1970).

system of control based on financial data, is that it can lead to excessive pre-occupation with financial factors, either within a firm or within an industry. Undue attention to ratios and financial data can cause a firm to overlook environmental factors such as social and technical developments. It might also lead the company to overlook the fact that capital is not the only scarce resource from which a business can grow, prosper, and endure. Every bit as scarce are competent managers, good employee morale, and good customer and public relations. A well-managed company would never regard any financially based control as the sole gauge of over-all performance.

CONTROL THROUGH KEY RESULT AREAS

While not widely used, another interesting approach to control of over-all performance was instituted by the General Electric Company (GE) some years ago.[3] Realizing the central importance of profit as a measure of over-all control but aware of the limitations involved, that company undertook a program of measurements aimed at eight key areas. This program contemplated establishment of indexes of performance that could be applied against goals in comparing one organization unit with another in a uniform and meaningful way.

The Areas

The key areas in which it attempted to measure results are profitability, market position, productivity, product leadership, personnel development, employee attitudes, public responsibility, and the balance between short- and long-range goals. Indexes developed for these were to be used to measure performance against established goals, modified from time to time and used as standards against which both objective and subjective measurements were to be applied. The content of each key area is briefly outlined below.

Profitability This area heads the list. GE felt that rate-of-return-on-investment or other profit indexes had certain shortcomings and that pure profit indexes encouraged concentration on percentages—rather than on total dollar profits—and might dampen the incentive to growth. In other words, the company believed that capital should be looked upon as a cost and that the manager should optimize profits after all costs, including the costs of capital, rather than concentrate on any percentage return on investment.

Market position The second key area for which GE attempted to develop measurements was the acceptance of the company's products and services by the market. This position reflected the company's intelligence in choosing the "right" markets as well as its ability to meet competition in quality and price, in distribution and promotion, and in technical advancements.

---

[3] See *Planning, Managing and Measuring the Business*, especially part 5, contributed by R. W. Lewis (New York: Controllership Foundation, 1955). See also W. T. Jerome, III. Executive Control: *The Catalyst* (New York: John Wiley & Sons, Inc., 1961), chap. 14.

Share of the market was, of course, an important index. In addition, attempts were made to measure customer satisfaction with GE and with its competitors, and to find out what the customer wanted but was not getting.

Productivity   In measuring the area of productivity—the "ability of a business to utilize its human, capital, and material resources to the best advantage and to the best balance"[4]—GE concentrated on the physical aspects—goods and services produced and sold compared to the physical inputs required to provide or manufacture and sell them. In this index, the company sought to measure the productivity of the *company's* operations, as contrasted to those of a supplier, and to distinguish between productivity of labor and that attributable to capital and management.

Product leadership   The area went beyond immediate considerations of market position and took in the ability of the company to meet customer needs at minimum costs for developing, manufacturing, and marketing new products. In it was measured the ability of the company—or an integrated segment of it—to exploit new scientific and technical knowledge (in manufacturing and marketing as well as engineering) and to lead competition in aggressively applying such knowledge in the creation and marketing of new products.

In approaching its measurement of product leadership, GE took into account not only innovation, but also the ability to capitalize on new ideas at the right time and at a cost—depending on quality desired—that would appeal to the customer and make a new product a success. Granting that much of this evaluation was subjective, the company periodically tested existing and new products for leadership.

Personnel development   In the fifth area, the company recognized that, because competent people at all levels are necessary for business growth, this objective must be planned systematically. GE objectives in personnel development required (1) all employees to perform on their current assignments to the limit of their capabilities; and (2) an adequate supply of promotable manpower for new and more complex job assignments as well as for filling vacancies as they occur.

Perhaps the best index to good performance here was whether or not qualified people were available when needed. The basic index was supplemented by personnel inventories (particularly those emphasizing promotability), record of promotions from within, the extent of advancement traceable to development programs, and the adequacy of available manpower as compared to requirements.

Employee attitudes   GE claimed to use employee attitudes as a key area of control, because (1) they reflect the extent to which managers have acted responsibly in satisfying personnel needs and goals of employees; (2) they play a major part in the appraisal of the company in a plant community; and (3) an employee attitude of active and willing cooperation is of great impor-

[4]Lewis, *op. cit.*, p. 34.

tance to business success. Thus, this area included not only the employee in his job, but also the company in the community.

Employee attitudes toward the company could be measured by such generally accepted indicators as labor turnover, absenteeism, safety records, and the extent that employees make suggestions for improvement. Another means of measuring was to approach employees directly through surveys.

Public responsibility The seventh area that the company aimed to measure was its conduct as a good citizen. The large industrial corporation is an institution that must be responsive to the social, economic, and political environment in which it operates. A component of the larger complex, each integrated division, operating essentially as a smaller and separate business, must make its contribution. In this area GE did not imply that an economic enterprise should be transformed into a welfare institution, but rather that one measurement with long-run implication is how seriously the company regards its public responsibilities in conducting its business.

To get this index, a variety of approaches were aimed at employees, at vendors, and at the plant and business communities. With respect to employees, measurements included such factors as job and family security, wages and working conditions, and standard of living. With respect to vendors, there might be an attitude survey comparing vendor appraisals of the company with vendor appraisals of competitors. Plant community standing can be ascertained by surveys supplemented by quantitative data on comparison of community wage rates, number of applications for work, local purchases, charitable contributions, and participation of leading employees in noncompany organizations in the community. Position in the business community was ascertained by studying how the company was regarded by retailers and competitors.

Integration of short- and long-range goals The eighth key area aimed at ascertaining how well managers integrate their short-range planning with long-range plans and goals. Control through this area emphasized the extent and nature of each manager's long-range plans and goals, how well outlined and specific they were, and what accomplishments were expected at what costs. The company expected that, by merely making sure that long-range plans were made and reviewed, short-range plans would reflect longer-range goals. At least, in reviewing short-range plans, managers would be able to gauge whether this balance was being achieved.

A Comprehensive System

General Electric was not able to develop desired measurements for all these areas, whose breadth and importance, nevertheless, are significant and impressive. Even though a company might wish to use other areas in measuring over-all performance, measurements over so broad a territory as incorporated in these eight areas should give an excellent appraisal of the management of an entire company, a subsidiary, or a division.

There might be some concern that this wide-ranging control technique, in which seven of the eight key areas did not immediately deal with profits, could dull the sharpness of the profit motive. If, however, it is realized that each of these areas is closely related to a company's success in its unavoidable political, economic, and social environment, detraction from profit goals should not occur. In other words, only if employee attitudes and public responsibility become ends in themselves might they impair other desired results. This need not happen. Those who measure over-all performance via key areas need enough insight and judgment to view the results as interrelated in their effect on the company's basic goals.

Although there is no evidence that GE or any other company has been able to develop and maintain a complete ongoing program of over-all control of this kind, the use of key result areas as a means of controlling individual manager and department performance has, of course, been often used. The key result areas selected by GE many years ago do represent an interesting framework for gauging overall performance. With the strides in recent years in setting up verifiable goals and in measuring the quality of human organization, discussed in the following section, something like the GE result areas may well become a means of control. Certainly, it would be superior to exclusive emphasis on such key financial factors as profit and rate of return.

To a very considerable extent, this is often done when a company evaluates a firm it wishes to acquire. Without, in any way, detracting from the major importance of financial performance, it is realized that a firm's value depends upon its future rather than its past. To make this evaluation, financial factors need to be supplemented by such considerations as product lines and basic competition, marketing strengths, research and development record, personnel and public relations, and the quality of management.[5] If this is of importance to a buyer of a company, one cannot help but wonder why it should not be significant on a regular and continuing basis to a firm.

MEASURING AND CONTROLLING THE HUMAN ORGANIZATION

One of the interesting special areas of control is measuring critical human variables on the valid and widely recognized fact that the human organization of any enterprise makes the most difference in end results. To a very great extent, this is what managing is about and throughout this book, by emphasizing the manager's task of creating and maintaining an environment for performance, the authors have recognized this fact. However, it is true that, except in the area of appraising managers as managers, control subjects and techniques have been largely devoted to measuring *activities* and *results* in such areas as profits, costs, sales, production output, and program performance.

[5]For such a summary, see, for example, R. B. Buchele, "How to Evaluate a Firm," *California Management Review*, vol. 5, no. 1, pp. 5–16 (Fall, 1962); and, by the same author, *Business Policy In Growing Firms* (San Francisco: Chandler Publishing Company, 1967).

Likert's System 4 Management

One of the pioneers in developing means of measuring human variables is Rensis Likert who has directed the nation's largest academic social science center, the Institute for Social Research at the University of Michigan. His research over the years has indicated to him that the best managerial producers: (1) are supportive in that they lend support to those reporting to them; (2) facilitate people's work with the necessary tools, training, inside or outside help, and other things necessary to assure that assigned tasks will be accomplished; (3) encourage interaction, talk, and mutual help among all members of the work group; and (4) expect high performance standards.[6] Likert has referred to this type of management as "System 4," or participative-group, management, as contrasted to three other types: exploitive-authoritative, benevolent-authoritative, and consultative. Since his research indicates that shifts toward system 4 management brings, at least over time, an improvement in goal performance, as well as in satisfaction of subordinates, he has sought out the underlying variables that indicate the type of managing an individual is undertaking and has developed means of measuring them. While the ability of subordinates or even specialists to measure these objectively is open to some question, there are a fairly large number of check-points and, within limits, the measurement does appear to be worthwhile.

Measuring Causal and Intervening Variables

Likert's main thesis is that the causal variable of managerial behavior and organization structure affect and are affected by certain intervening variables (such as motivating factors, goal performance, extent and nature of communication, and the character of the interaction-influence factors) to cause end-result variables in the areas of profits, sales, costs, and other enterprise goals, plus the end-result of human satisfaction. A view of the interaction of these variables is given in Figure 31.2 where a comparison is made between exploitive-authoritative (system 1) or benevolent-authoritative (system 2) and participative-group (system 4) managing.

The control aspect of Likert's approach is two-fold. One is the measurement of individual managers and their groups. Another is primarily a matter of human-asset accounting and over-all control of the human organization of an enterprise. In other words, through measuring the causal and intervening variables periodically, it is Likert's conviction that any enterprise can see what is happening to the ability of a group to perform. In this connection, however, he makes it clear that there may be a time lag before end results may be appar-

---

[6] See, for example, his *New Patterns of Management* (New York: McGraw-Hill Book Company, 1961) and *The Human Organization* (New York: McGraw-Hill Book Company, 1967). See also M. R. Weisbord, "Management in Crisis," *The Conference Board Record*, vol. 7, no. 2, pp. 10–16 (February, 1970). Ideas similar to Likert's have been long advocated by other behavioral scientists. See, for example, C. Argyris, "The Organization: What Makes It Healthy?" *Harvard Business Review*, vol. 36, no. 6, pp. 107–116 (November–December, 1958).

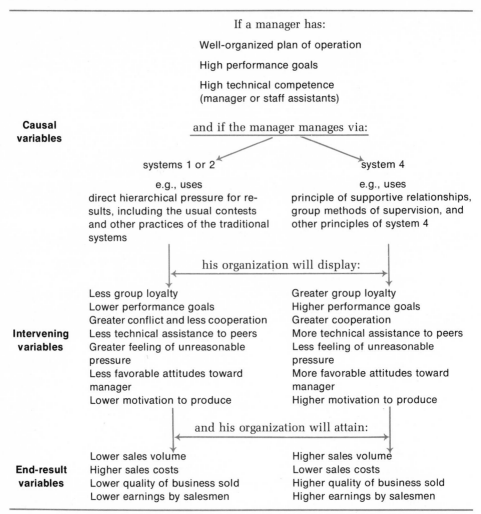

Figure 31.2 *Sequence of developments in a well-organized enterprise, as affected by use of system 2 or system 4.*
SOURCE: *R. Likert, Human Organization, p. 76. (After Rensis Likert, New patterns in sales management. In Martin R. Warshaw (ed.), Changing Perspectives in Marketing Management, Ann Arbor, Mich.: University of Michigan Bureau of Business Research, 1962. By permission of the publishers.)*

ent. His research has indicated a number of cases where costs were reduced and profits increased by highly authoritative managing, as in the instance of a rapid and arbitrary budget-cutting program; however, in some cases, while performance immediately improved, later performance suffered through the negative influence of the underlying human variables he has identified.

While this system of measurement is still rather crude and much more empirical research is needed to verify its utility, the measurement and control of human variables are important and techniques for doing so can surely improve the quality of management. While Likert has, perhaps, made too much of his system 4 type of managing and appears to be overly biased toward a highly permissive managing style, the underlying facts of his approach belie this. For example, few managers could disagree with the following characteristics he identifies with system 4 managing: (1) communication initiated at all levels; (2) full use of economic, ego, and other motives; (3) high performance goals; (4) personnel feeling responsibility for the organization's goals; (5) decision makers being well aware of problems; and (6) widespread responsibility for review and control. Nor would most managers disagree with Likert's conclusion that "a manager who has high performance goals and excellent job organization but who relies solely on economic needs and direct pressure to motivate his men is very likely to be disappointed by their achievements."[7] These and many other behavioral variables are those regularly associated with good managing.

Individual and Over-all Control

As indicated earlier, control of the human organization may be looked upon both as control of individual managers as well as the overall control of the human side of enterprise. In other words, by measuring the causal and the intervening variables identified by Likert, one can look at and predict probable results in end-result variables. Likewise, the same thing can be done for an entire enterprise. This becomes especially significant in view of the well-known fact that all enterprises tend to reflect the managerial styles of the top managers. Therefore, measuring the quality of the causal variables of managerial behavior and organization structure, as well as of the intervening variables, is likely to be an essential and helpful approach to the over-all control of performance.

Human Asset Accounting

This approach has led Likert and his associates to attempt methods for measuring the value of the human assets of an enterprise. It is, indeed, common to read in shareholders' reports the statement that "our human resources are the company's greatest asset." Also, many top managers, when asked to estimate how much it would cost to replace the human organization, come up with very high estimates exceeding three times annual payroll, or about 24 to 25 times annual earnings.[8] Yet, in commonly accepted accounting, the value of this asset is not shown in balance sheets or accounted for in earnings statements, and no rate of return is calculated on it.

To offset this deficiency, Likert and his associates have undertaken ex-

---

[7] *The Human Organization*, p. 64.

[8] According to Likert who claims to have asked "thousands" of managers this question. See M. R. Weisbord, *op. cit.*, p. 13.

periments in "human asset accounting."[9] To cover the entire spectrum of human resources, the originators of this kind of accounting would have it include not only the asset represented by people within the enterprise, but also values represented by customer good will. They point out two deficiencies of ordinary accounting. When an enterprise is investing in human capabilities and values, conventional accounting practice involves writing off these costs through operating expenses, thus actually understating profits; likewise balance sheet values are understated. In the second place, a company might be using up its human assets and showing high current earnings at the expense of almost certain lower future earnings.

In moving towards this kind of accounting, two approaches have been suggested. One is the cost approach through measuring dollar investments (recruiting, transfer, training, and investments in customer good will) offset by reductions (through obsolescence, retirement, transfers, separations, and loss of customer franchise). In one company, where human resource accounting supplementary to traditional financial accounting has been undertaken, the balance sheet and income statements were reported as shown in Figure 31.3.

The second approach is to obtain a regular evaluation of the current worth of human resources through assessing the present value of individual members of the organization. It is believed by the originators that this can be done by applying the Likert measurements of causal and intervening variables—obtaining the individual's performance and potential value as modified by expected remaining tenure, and by assessing the value of the productive capabilities of various organizational groupings.

To date, only a few experiments have been undertaken to measure the investment costs and losses in human resources. While it is believed that present "value" of human resources, at least for those internal to the enterprise, can be reasonably well approached through the use of the Likert measurements, there is little evidence that this has been done with an acceptable degree of creditability. At the same time, there is much to be said for continuing efforts in this direction. No one interested in effective control of enterprise can afford to disregard the importance of maintaining the value of human assets. These, after all, are the best assurance of the future. But, again, perhaps the best way of assuring this is through applying the fundamentals of effective managing. Even Likert and his associates seem to recognize this.

THE ENTERPRISE SELF-AUDIT

J. O. McKinsey, who achieved an outstanding position in the realm of management four decades ago, came to the conclusion that a business enterprise should periodically make a "management audit," an appraisal of the enter-

---

[9]See, for example, Likert, *The Human Organization*, Chapter 9; R. L. Brummet, W. C. Pyle, and E. G. Flamholtz, "Accounting for Human Resources," *Michigan Business Review*, vol. 20, no. 2, pp. 20–25 (March, 1968).

"THE TOTAL CONCEPT"—R. G. BARRY CORPORATION AND SUBSIDIARIES PRO-FORMA (FINANCIAL AND HUMAN RESOURCE ACCOUNTING)

Balance sheet	1969 Financial and human resource	1969 Financial only
Assets		
Total current assets	$10,003,628	$10,003,628
Net property, plant and equipment	1,770,717	1,770,717
Excess of purchase price of subsidiaries over net assets acquired	1,188,704	1,188,704
Net investments in human resources	986,094	
Other assets	106,783	106,783
	$14,055,926	$13,069,832
Liabilities and stockholders' equity		
Total current liabilities	$ 5,715,708	$ 5,715,708
Long-term debt, excluding current installments	1,935,500	1,935,500
Deferred compensation	62,380	62,380
Deferred federal income taxes as a result of appropriation for human resources	493,047	
Stockholders' equity:		
Capital stock	879,116	879,116
Additional capital in excess of par value	1,736,253	1,736,253
Retained earnings:		
Financial	2,740,875	2,740,875
Appropriation for human resources	493,047	
Total stockholders' equity	5,849,291	5,356,244
	$14,055,926	$13,069,832

Statement of income	1969 Financial and human resource	1969 Financial only
Net sales	$25,310,588	$25,310,588
Cost of sales	16,275,876	16,275,876
Gross profit	9,034,712	9,034,712
Selling, general and administrative expenses	6,737,313	6,737,313
Operating income	2,297,399	2,297,399
Other deductions, net	953,177	953,177
Income before federal income taxes	1,344,222	1,344,222
Human resource expenses applicable to future periods	173,569	
Adjusted income before federal income taxes	1,517,791	1,344,222
Federal income taxes	730,785	644,000
Net income	$ 787,006	$ 700,222

Fig. 31.3 *Financial statements reflecting human resources at the R. G. Barry Corporation*

SOURCE: *1969 R. G. Barry Corporation Annual Report, p. 14. From W. C. Pyle, "Monitoring Human Resources—'On Line'," Michigan Business Review, vol. 22, no. 4, pp. 19–32, at p. 28 (July, 1970).*

prise in all its aspects, in the light of its present and probable future environment. This type of audit has been referred to by Goetz[10] as "much the most comprehensive and powerful of these problem-seeking techniques" because it seeks in an over-all way "to discover and correct errors of management." Although McKinsey called this a management audit, it is actually an audit of the entire enterprise.

The enterprise self-audit appraises the company's position to determine where it is, where it is heading under present programs, what its objectives should be, and whether revised plans are needed to meet those objectives. In most enterprises of all kinds, objectives and policies become obsolete. If the enterprise does not change course to suit the changing social, technical, and political environment, it loses markets, personnel, and other requirements for continued existence. The enterprise self-audit is designed to force managers to meet this situation.

Procedure

The self-audit may be made annually or, more likely, once every three or five years. The first step is to study the outlook of the firm's industry. What are recent trends and prospects? What is the outlook for the product? Where are the markets? What technical developments are affecting the industry? How may demand be changed? What political or social factors may affect the industry?

A second step in the self-audit is to appraise the position of the firm in the industry, both currently and in prospect. Has the company maintained its position? Has it expanded its influence and markets? Or has competition reduced its position? What is the competitive outlook? To answer such questions, the company may undertake studies on competitor standing, development of competition, customer reactions, and other factors bearing on its position within the industry.

On the basis of such studies, the next logical step for the company would be to reexamine its basic objectives and major policies to decide where the company wishes to be in, say, five or ten years. After this reexamination, the company may audit its organization, policies, procedures, programs, facilities, financial position, personnel, and management. This examination should identify any deviations from objectives and facilitate the revision of many major and minor plans.

Contribution

Most top business managers do not think in terms of the company's future or evaluate over-all performance in relation to long-range objectives. The enterprise self-audit has the distinct advantage of forcing them to appraise over-all performance in terms not only of current goals but also of future ones. Top

[10]Billy E. Goetz, *Management Planning and Control* (New York: McGraw-Hill Book Company, 1949), p. 167. For a discussion of the management audit, see below, pp. 662–666.

managers who expend mental effort for this kind of audit will almost certainly be well repaid and will be surprised at how many day-to-day decisions will be simplified by a clear picture of where the business is attempting to go.

FOR DISCUSSION

1. Why do most controls of over-all performance tend to be financial in nature? Should they be? What else do you suggest?
2. "Profit and loss control is defective in that it does not emphasize return on investment; the latter is defective in that it places too great an emphasis on present results with possible endangering of future results." Discuss.
3. In applying rate of return on investment as a control tool, would you favor using an undepreciated or a depreciated asset base?
4. Selecting any federal, state, or local government agency you wish, could you develop an appropriate set of key result areas for it? How?
5. If steps are taken to assure effective managing throughout an enterprise, do you believe that it would be necessary or helpful to undertake an evaluation of the human organization?
6. A start has been made in human asset accounting including mainly costs incurred and values used for the internal human organization. But there are important human values external to the firm, such as customer good will. How do you believe we could account for this and measure its current value?
7. J. O. McKinsey's enterprise self-audit has seldom been used in industry. Why do you feel this has happened? Do you believe this device would be worth its cost?

32
assuring effective managing

The preceding analysis of control stresses the variety of approaches that managers follow to make results conform to plans. If managers believed plans would be automatically accomplished, control would be unnecessary.

At the base of control is the fact that the outcome of plans is influenced by people. For instance, a poor educational system cannot be controlled by criticizing its product, the unfortunate graduate; a factory turning out inferior products cannot be controlled by their consignment to the scrap heap, or a firm plagued with customer complaints cannot be controlled by ignoring the complainers. Responsibility for controllable deviations lies with whoever has made unfortunate decisions. Any hope of abolishing unsatisfactory results lies in changing the *future* actions of the responsible person, through additional training, modification of procedures, or new policy. This is the crux of controlling the quality of management.

There are two ways of seeing that the responsible person modifies future action. The normal procedure is to trace the cause of an unsatisfactory result back to the person responsible for it and get him to correct his practices. This may be called "indirect control." The alternative in the area of management is to develop better managers who will skillfully apply concepts, techniques, and principles and thus eliminate undesirable results caused by poor management. This is called "direct control."

INDIRECT CONTROL

In every enterprise hundreds, and even thousands, of standards are developed to compare the actual output of goods or services—in terms of quantity, quality, time, and cost—with plans. Excessive deviation from standards may necessitate indirect control, as defined above. A negative deviation indicates—in terms of goal achievement, cost, price, personnel, man-hours, or machine-hours—that performance is less than good or normal or standard, and that results are not conforming to plans.

Causes of Negative Deviations from Standards

The causes of negative deviations will often determine whether control measures are possible. Although an incorrect standard may cause deviation, if the standard is correct, plans may fail because of (1) uncertainty, and (2) lack of knowledge, experience, or judgment.

    Uncertainty   Elements affecting a given plan may be grouped into facts, risks, and uncertainty. Facts are known, such as number of employees, costs, or machine capacity. Considerably less is known about the element of risk. Insurable risks are readily converted to factual status through the payment of a known premium. Noninsurable risks may be included in a business decision on the basis of probability. The total of facts and risks is small, compared to the element of uncertainty, which includes everything about which nothing is certain. For instance. the success of a plan to manufacture aluminum pistons will depend not only on known facts and risks but on such uncertainties as future world conditions, competition of known and yet unknown metals, and power technology that may eliminate all piston prime movers. Not even probability can be estimated for all the uncertain factors, yet they can wreck a plan.

    Managerial errors caused by unforeseeable events cannot be corrected. The fixing of personal responsibility by indirect control techniques is of no avail in such situations.

    Lack of knowledge, experience, or judgment   Plans may misfire and negative deviations occur when men appointed to managerial posts lack the necessary background. The higher in the organizational structure a manager is placed, the broader the knowledge and experience he needs. Long years as an engineer, a sales manager, a production executive, or a controller may be inadequate in qualifying a man to be a general officer.

    Good judgment marks the mature man who intelligently applies his educational and enterprise experience and is known for his common sense. Unfortunately, some top managers who have gone through the motions of formal education, training of various kinds, and practical experience seem incapable of sound decisions and display poor judgment about such matters as product lines, expansion policy, innovation, and decentralization. At the top level, the chance of correction through separation from the firm is very small. On the other hand, continuing errors of judgment at middle and lower levels are often followed by demotion, transfer, or separation.

    If the cause of error is poor judgment, whether due to inadequate training or experience or to failure to use appropriate information in decision making, correction can be made. The manager may improve his education, be transferred to acquire broader experience, or be cautioned to take better stock of the situation before making decisions.

    From this discussion, an interesting question arises. How often can negative deviations from standard be corrected? At present, little is known about this. But it is vital. If, for instance, only 40 percent of errors in decision making are subject to correction, then the effort made to place responsibility is of no avail 60 per cent of the time. Such a ratio is likely to place on indirect controls an insuperable burden.

Questionable Assumptions

In addition to its cost, the shortcomings of indirect control rest on certain questionable assumptions: (1) that performance can be measured; (2) that personal responsibility for performance exists; (3) that the time expenditure is warranted; (4) that mistakes can be discovered in time; and (5) that the person responsible will take corrective steps.

That performance can be measured At first glance, almost any enterprise appears to be a jungle of controls. Input, output, cost, price, time, complaints, and quality are subject to numerous standards; and the standards may be expressed in terms of goal achievement, time, weight, tolerances, averages, ratios, dollars, and indexes. In terms of usefulness, the standards may be correct, acceptable, or merely better than nothing. Close analysis will often reveal shortcomings of two types. In the first place, the ability of a manager to develop potential managers, the effectiveness of research, the amount of creativity, foresight, and judgment in decision making can seldom be measured accurately.

The second shortcoming concerns the location of the control. Managers know that critical stages exist in acquiring input factors, manipulating them to produce a finished product, and selling and delivering the product. In a factory operation, for example, critical stages would include receiving inspection, inspection for each assembly process, shipping, and billing. These are critical because effective control here will minimize costs. No amount of control at other points can make up for lack of control at these stages.

That personal responsibility exists Sometimes no manager is responsible for poor results. Government action to increase interest rates caused the costs of many activities to rise precipitously. Scarcity of a particular fuel may necessitate use of less economical sources of power. And markets may shrink for reasons unconnected with the firm.

That the time expenditure is warranted Whether a manager undertakes the inquiry himself or assigns it to others, executive time must be spent in ferreting out causes of poor results. Large scrap losses, for example, may call for meetings attended by men representing quality control, production planning, engineering, purchasing, and manufacturing. Besides, passage of time may make the recall of facts quite difficult. These drawbacks may convince the manager that the cost of investigation exceeds any benefit he may derive. This often precludes investigation of clear violations of standards.

That mistakes can be discovered in time Discovery of deviations from plans often comes too late for effective action. Although true control can be applied only to future action, most controls depend on historical data—all that a manager has available. The manager should, of course, interpret such data in terms of their implications for the future.

The costs of errors in major areas—such as cash or inventories—have led to the use of forecasts as the basis for control. Since forecasts are difficult to make and subject to error, the natural tendency to rely on historical reports seriously blocks adequate controls. No manager really has control unless he can correct mistakes. And the best way to correct mistakes is to avoid them.

That the person responsible will take corrective steps Fixing the responsibility may not lead to correction. High production costs, for example, might be traced back to a marketing manager who insists that "slight" product modifications will make selling easier and that this involves "really" no change in a production run. If the marketing manager is a member of top management, a subordinate investigator may be intimidated; the president may attempt to mediate between marketing and production executives; and the marketing manager will remain unreconstructed. Although great effort may be made to correct subordinate managers, it is sometimes very difficult to correct superior executives.

THE PRINCIPLE OF DIRECT CONTROL

The principle of direct control embraces the idea that personal responsibility for negative deviations from standards can be fixed by applying fundamentals of management. It draws a sharp distinction between performance reports, essential in any case, and determining whether managers act in accordance with established principles in carrying out their functions. The principle of direct control, then, may be stated as follows: *the higher the quality of managers and their subordinates, the less will be the need for indirect controls.*

It is possible that the principle of direct control was vaguely perceived by Fayol, who possessed a mature and practical understanding of management. In a 1925 interview with the editors of *Chronique Sociale de France,* Fayol said that the best method of looking at an organization and determining the necessary improvements was "to study the administrative apparatus. . . . One can ascertain immediately that forecasting and planning, organization, command, co-ordination, and control are properly provided for, that is to say, that the undertaking is well administered."[1]

The extensive adoption of direct control must await a wider understanding of managerial principles, functions, and techniques as well as management philosophy. While such an understanding is not achieved easily, it can be gained in universities, through on-the-job experience, through coaching by the superior, and by means of constant self-education. Moreover, as progress is made in appraising managers as managers, as indicated in Chapter 23, we can expect direct control to have more practical meaning and effectiveness.

[1]Quoted by L. Urwick in his foreword to *General and Industrial Management* (New York: Pitman Publishing Corporation, 1949), p. x.

Assumptions of the Principle of Direct Control

The desirability of direct control rests upon four valid assumptions: (1) that qualified managers make a minimum of errors, (2) that managerial performance can be measured, (3) that management concepts, principles, and techniques are useful diagnostic standards in measuring management performance, and (4) that the application of management fundamentals can be evaluated.

That qualified managers make a minimum of errors   J. P. Morgan has been often quoted as saying that the decisions of good managers are right two-thirds of the time. However, an accurate analysis of the quality of decision making should not rely upon quantity of errors but be concerned with the nature of the error. As J. Paul Getty once told one of the authors, his concern in his world-wide empire was not percentage of time an executive was right or wrong; he could be wrong only 2 per cent of the time and seriously endanger a company by these errors if they were critical. Managers can logically be held strictly accountable for the performance of their functions, because these functions should be undertaken in conformance with the fundamentals of management. However, accountability cannot be exacted for errors attributable to factors beyond the manager's authority or his ability reasonably to forecast the future. An approach to the proper evaluation of managers as managers was set forth in Chapter 23. Some of this is indicated by the ability to set and achieve verifiable objectives. But much depends on being able to evaluate the performance of a manager as a manager. As crude as these standards of measurement may be at the present state of the art of managing, they are still able to highlight the extent of knowledge and ability of an individual to fill the requirements of his role as a manager.

That management fundamentals may be used to measure performance
The chief purpose of this book has been to draw together concepts, principles, and basic techniques or approaches of management and relate them to managerial functions. As was stated in previous chapters, the completeness and certitude of these vary considerably, depending largely upon the state of knowledge concerning the managerial functions. There is, for instance, greater general acceptance of some of the principles of organizing than there is of the principles relating to other functions. Nevertheless, the authors are convinced that the fundamentals set forth here are useful in measuring managerial performance even though their statement will undoubtedly be refined and better verified by future experts.

That the application of management fundamentals can be evaluated
Evaluation can provide for periodic measurement of the skill with which the manager applies management fundamentals to his five functions. This can be done not only by judgment of performance against these but by casting them into a series of fairly objective questions as suggested in Chapter 23.

Advantages

Directly controlling the quality of managers and thus minimizing errors has several advantages. In the first place, greater accuracy is achieved in assigning personal responsibility. The on-going evaluation of managers is practically certain to uncover deficiencies and should provide for specific training to eliminate them.

In the second place, direct control hastens corrective action and makes it more effective. It encourages control by self-control. Knowing that errors will be uncovered in an evaluation, managers will try to determine their responsibility and make voluntary corrections. For example, a report of excessive scrap will cause the department foreman to determine quickly whether the excess was due to poor direction of subordinates or to other factors. The same report will cause the chief inspector to look into whether his men acted properly, the purchasing agent to check the material purchased with engineering specifications, and the engineers to determine whether appropriate material was specified. All this action is immediate and voluntary. Any manager who concludes privately that he was in error will do his best to prevent a recurrence, for his future is in jeopardy.

The third advantage of direct control is its potentiality for lightening the burden now caused by indirect control, largely of determining personal responsibility. This is a net gain, since the evaluation of managers is already part of staffing. The amount of potential savings is as yet unknown, although it must be considerable.

Last, the psychological advantage of direct control is impressive. The feeling of subordinates that superiors do not rate fairly, rely on hunch and personality, and use improper measuring standards is almost universal, but direct control removes this feeling. Subordinate managers know what is expected of them, understand the nature of managerial functions, and feel a close relationship between performance and measurement. The intelligent superior manager will reciprocate this feeling, because he will know what he is expected to evaluate in subordinates and will have a technique for doing so.

MANAGEMENT AUDITING

Application of the principle of direct control has led to action in several directions. One of the most promising and active has been the improved programs in recent years to appraise individual managers. Primarily, this has taken the form of appraising performance against the standard of setting and achieving verifiable goals; even in this widely accepted approach much must still be done to make it effective. A second essential aspect of this appraisal, yet to be done except on a limited and experimental basis, is the appraisal of managers in their role *as managers*. Both of these approaches have been discussed in Chapter 23.

Another direction in which the principle of direct control has led is in the developing interest in management audits. Compared to the practice of other forms of management evaluation, these do not aim at evaluating managers as individuals but rather at looking at the entire system of managing an enterprise. While little progress has been made in such management audits, some pioneering programs have been undertaken. Certain specialists are working in this direction, and some major buyers—the Department of Defense in particular—have used elements of the concept in appraising companies for the award of major contracts.

Management Audits and Operational Audits

A distinction should be made between auditing the quality of managing as a system and auditing the quality of operations. To some extent, this is similar to appraising managers in their ability to manage and in their ability to set and accomplish objectives. Both are important, but even where so-called management audits have been undertaken, this distinction has not always been made. It clearly should be since any enterprise may succeed as a marketing or engineering organization, while being ineptly managed; it may even succeed because of a favorable environment, such as a sellers' market as often happens in wartime, despite inadequate management. If, as believed to be the case, the quality of managing will ultimately make the difference in success or failure, certainly this quality should be given an assessment separate from the ability to do well in marketing, engineering, producing, or financing.

At the same time, so long as operational auditing is clearly separated from management auditing, there may be distinct advantages in auditing both. In the case of the auditing approach suggested by Greenwood,[2] for example, the audit is divided into two parts. One is a management function audit covering evaluation in the fields of planning, organizing, staffing, directing, and controlling. The other is a management decision audit, dealing with the quality of decisions in the areas of long-range and company-wide planning, marketing, operations (production and material), personnel, accounting and finance.

American Institute of Management Program

One of the earliest programs of management audit was developed by the American Institute of Management. This institute, founded and operated by Jackson Martindell, developed some years ago a procedure for direct control.[3] Using an extensive list of 301 questions, Martindell undertook to rate companies in the areas of economic function, corporate structure, health of earnings, fairness to stockholders, research and development, directors, fiscal policies,

---

[2] See W. T. Greenwood, *A Management Audit System,* revised edition (Carbondale, Ill.: School of Business, Southern Illinois University, 1967). See also his *Management and Organizational Behavior Theories: An Interdisciplinary Approach* (Cincinnati, Ohio: South-Western Publishing Company, 1965). pp. 813–816, 868–880.

[3] See *The Scientific Appraisal of Management* (New York: Harper & Row, Publishers, Incorporated, 1962), and *Manual of Excellent Managements* (New York: American Institute of Management, 1957).

production efficiency, sales vigor, and executive ability. Each of these ten areas were, in turn, assigned point weightings, ranging out of a total of 10,000 points, from 400 points assigned to economic function and 600 to health of earnings to 1,400 for sales vigor and 2,400 for executive quality. Out of the total of 10,000 possible points, only some 3,500 points were assigned to managerial elements, the rest applying to other areas. In order for a company to obtain an "excellent" rating, the institute arbitrarily picked the requirement of 7,500 points.

In view of Martindell's long experience and interest as an investment counselor, his appraisal system was understandably heavily oriented to the considerations of an investor. Moreover, examination of the many questions used for rating indicates that there was a high degree of subjectivity. While Martindell's American Institute of Management program leaves much to be desired, its pioneering nature deserves praise. It did focus attention on control of over-all management and on the results that can be expected from "excellent management."

Other Approaches

A number of other approaches to this interesting and important area of direct control have been made. That of William Greenwood has been mentioned. It has 203 checkpoints for use in auditing decisions and 170 for use in auditing management functions. While not all of the 373 questions asked give or imply any standard of what is good or poor and many of the operational and managerial questions tend to overlap, there can be no doubt that any enterprise following Greenwood's approach would get for itself a comprehensive and searching analysis of itself and its system of managing.

A comprehensive study of the management audit was also made by William P. Leonard in 1962.[4] Although this study deals more with methods of organizing, initiating, interpreting, and presenting a management audit than with the content of the audit itself, and it is valuable from this point of view, it does indicate what a management audit should cover.[5] Leonard's check list deals with a number of searching questions on the subjects of (1) plans and objectives (for example, "Have definite plans and objectives been established?"); (2) organization structure (for example, "Is there any overlapping or duplication of functions?"); (3) policies, systems, and procedures (for example, "Are the policies positive, clear, and understandable?"); (4) department personnel (for example, "What is the rate of turnover?"); (5) layout and physical equipment (for example, "Is the office laid out in a manner to get maximum utilization of space and efficient work areas?"); and (6) operations and methods of control (for example, "What consideration has been given to the adequacy, clarity, and promptness of management reports?"). While the suggested check list and audit approach made by Leonard does not distinguish carefully between operating-performance factors and management factors, and

[4] *The Management Audit* (Englewood Cliffs, N.J.: Prentice-Hall, Inc., 1962).
[5] *Ibid.*, pp. 120–126.

while many significant management factors are overlooked or are not gone into in any depth, it is an interesting starting point for anyone wishing to study the possibilities of a management audit.

Another approach to a management audit is the activity of the Department of Defense, which has undertaken from time to time, particularly under Robert McNamara in the 1960s, to evaluate companies bidding on major defense contracts. Not only has the Department been interested in engineering concepts and capabilities, probable price and delivery promises, but it has delved deeply into the kind of organization and management the company has and, particularly, the company's plans to manage the defense contract should it be the successful bidder. The authors have seen cases where this investigation was very penetrating and information was required from the bidder, and audited by the buyer, in virtually every function of managing. Among other things, the bidder was required to submit his proposed organization structure, his precise staffing in key positions, and his approach to and methods of planning and control.

That this makes sense from the standpoint of the Department of Defense is clear. After all, in a major program there is almost certainly no single factor more important to economical and dependable performance than the quality of the company's management. Also, an interesting and beneficial result of this evaluation, particularly after word is circulated that a certain company lost a contract because of management deficiencies, is that a number of defense contractors have overhauled their management system to remove identified weaknesses.

Management Audits and Accounting Firms

Although many management consulting firms have undertaken various kinds of appraisal of enterprise management systems, usually as a part of an organization study, the greatest interest in pursuing management audits has been demonstrated by accounting audit firms.[6] One of the significant developments of recent years has been their entry into the field of management services of a broad consultancy nature. While this has been an attractive field of expansion for these auditing companies since they are already inside the enterprise and financial information furnishes a ready window to problems of managing, it does open some question of conflict of interest. In other words, the question is often raised whether the same firm can be in the position of a management consultant furnishing both advice and services and still be completely objective as an accounting auditor. To be sure, accounting firms have attempted to avoid this problem by organizationally separating these two activities.

Regardless of whether an auditing firm should be in management services, the fact is that they are. Since many are experienced both in auditing and

[6] See, for example, J. C. Burton, "Management Auditing," *The Journal of Accountancy*, vol. 125, no. 5, pp. 41–46 (May, 1968): A. E. Witte, "Management Auditing: The Present State of the Art," *The Journal of Accountancy*, vol. 124, no. 2, pp. 54–58 (August, 1967): and J. W. Buckley, "Management Services and Management Audits by Professional Accountants," *California Management Review*, vol. 9, no. 1, pp. 43–50 (Fall, 1966).

management services, it is only a short step to management auditing. If it is possible for these firms to set up a completely detached and objective management auditing operation and if this can be manned by individuals with truly professional knowledge and ability in management, it is very possible that this may result in acceleration in the practice of management auditing. At least, so long as the various professional and academic associations with a specific interest in management seem to be doing little in this field, perhaps accounting firms will show the way.

The Certified Management Audit

Another possibility for the future is the development of a certified management audit, an independent appraisal of a company's management by an outside firm. For years investors and others have relied on an independent certified accounting audit designed to make certain that the company's records and reports reflect sound accounting principles. From the standpoint of investors and even from that of managers and those desiring to work for the company, an independent audit of management quality would be extremely important. It is probably not too much to say that an investor would get more value from a certified management audit than from a certified accounting audit, since the future of a company is likely to depend more on the quality of its management than on any other single factor.

To assure objectivity, the certified management audit should be the responsibility of a recognized outside firm, staffed with individuals qualified to appraise a company's managerial philosophy and the quality of its managers. Although this would require considerable study from the inside and a set of reasonably objective standards, it probably would take little more time than that necessary for a thorough accounting audit. Moreover, except for final responsibility, the audit of top-level managers, and the seeing of a company's entire management as a total system, much work on the management audit could be done, as in the case of accounting audits, with the help of suitable inside managerial and staff personnel. Furthermore, as with the accounting audit, when a group of special auditors once becomes familiar with a company, subsequent audits take less time than the first. In order to assure real objectivity, a management audit should be made by a recognized and qualified group of management appraisers with a reporting responsibility, like that of most accounting auditors, to the board of directors.

It is quite obvious that any management audit report must go far beyond the typical accounting auditor's statements. It must do more than say that an enterprise management group has followed "generally accepted standards of management." To be meaningful it would require that the quality of managers and the system within which they manage be assessed objectively in fairly specific terms. This, as one can see, gives rise to problems. How many accounting or management consulting firms can really be expected to be objective where, as so often occurs, managerial deficiencies exist at the top and when they are retained by and report to these same top managers? This is not an easy hurdle to overcome, at least until almost completely objective standards can be agreed upon, learned by true professionals, and applied impartially. One cannot help but wonder if this might not necessitate a specially licensed group independent of present accounting auditing and management consulting firms.

As standards for appraising, fundamentals of management as outlined in this book would be appropriate.

THE CHALLENGING TASK OF THE MANAGER

Despite recognized deficiencies and crudities in the state of organized knowledge underlying the task of managing, the fact is that a science of management is developing. As the behavioral sciences give us better understanding of people, groups, cultural factors, and motivations, we are becoming better able to design environments for performance. Likewise, managerial techniques and tools are evolving rapidly, borrowing, as so many other fields have, from the systems approach long applied with benefit in the physical sciences. Moreover, as practicing managers have more thoroughly understood the importance and nature of their task, they have been able to contribute considerably to the growing body of knowledge. As the science has improved, so has the art of managing, for organized knowledge furnishes the working basis of any art.

Management and Reality

Yet, there is ever the danger that management knowledge will not be used to obtain results in practice. It has been one of the major purposes of this book to present fundamental knowledge regarding managing in a way that it can be useful. Such knowledge should be operational. It must be for reality since managing, as an art, requires the use of knowledge to solve real problems, to develop operating systems and environments in which people can perform.

This means several things. In the first place, knowledge of management is not enough. There is always the danger in any field of developing a science aimed at elegance or polish rather than results. Every science has its "educated derelicts" who know a field but cannot apply it to reality to gain useful results. Moreover, it must ever be remembered that the reality with which a manager must deal is always tomorrow. Reality is always a moving target.

Major Unsolved Problems

While it is not possible to summarize all the problems modern managers face, a few major continuing ones might be noted. One is the problem of maintaining flexibility to meet change in the face of the number of inflexibilities built into the operation and environment of any enterprise. Effective management is flexible management. Not only must an effective manager be able to recognize the need for change, but, in order to have time to meet it, he should forecast and anticipate it. He needs to design methods of obtaining organizational change in such areas as stultifying procedures and policies, obsolete organization patterns, and the normal human tendency to resist change. His task must also be to design around inflexibilities, such as government regulations or labor rules that he may be unable to modify.

Another major problem area challenging the modern manager is how to design and maintain a balanced environment for creativity and conformity. Perhaps there are in many enterprises too much conformity, too much togetherness, and too little individual responsibility and opportunity. However, it can never be forgotten that all group activity of any kind requires some conformity—speaking the same language, working certain hours, fitting into an organization structure, or contributing in a definite way toward the accomplishment of group goals. But this does not mean that the perceptive and intelligent manager cannot design roles for innovation and imagination where they are desired while still maintaining needed conformity to make group cooperation effective. This is not usually easy, but it is possible, particularly for the manager who keeps mindful of his basic task of designing an environment for performance.

There is also the major problem of building into any system of effective group cooperation the necessary inducements to take advantage of individual motivations. In societies where the passion for equality has sometimes tended to reduce the motivating force of the carrot by giving almost everyone the same carrots despite his performance, and where the force of the stick is often dulled by various security devices, the manager has a difficult problem of building necessary inducements into organizational systems. While difficult, to be sure, there are still many ways of doing so. With improved knowledge of motivation and better management science and techniques, the manager with understanding and imagination can do much.

Still another major problem facing most managers is that of coping with and using effectively the increased sophistication in all aspects of managing. Of particular importance has been the introduction of newer systems techniques in the areas of planning and controlling. But evidence indicates that practice has been slow to adopt these and other new findings. In most cases, it is believed that practicing managers have not adopted them because they do not understand them; not understanding, they are likely even to mistrust them. Much of the cause is attributable to experts who thrive on mysticism and jargon and are satisfied with elegance rather than practical application. What is needed are experts who can and will communicate and managers who can appreciate applications of such things as operations research, without necessarily understanding the mathematical models and programs, and recognize that these can contribute to better practice.

At the same time, there are still many relatively unsophisticated techniques that are too little used or too ineptly applied. When one looks at such "cloud one" techniques as managing by objectives, authority delegation, variable budgeting, formalized product planning, market-oriented organization, and appraisal of managers, one can see that these are not based on highly sophisticated techniques. Admittedly, however, even though these and many other tools and approaches are simple in concept, they may be difficult to apply in practice. But those managers who have earnestly and intelligently tried to apply them have reaped tremendous results.

Another urgent problem is one of taking advantage of the great potential of electronic data processing, direct costing, environmental forecasting, and similar advances to improve the quality and efficiency of information. Data are rather useless raw material until designed and produced to make information. No one can expect a useful end-product unless he knows what he wishes and puts into motion the steps to get it. The long-promised information revolution has been slow in coming. But come it should and will with resourceful and intelligent managing.

Perhaps one of the most urgent of all problems is to continue assuring the quality of managers. Despite widespread attention to training and appraisal in the past quarter-century, the needs appear to be greater than ever before. The growth of management knowledge, the pace of change of all kinds, and the competitive urgencies for utilizing resources well in all kinds of enterprises have tended to outdistance action. One of the most promising developments has been improvements in evaluation of managers. If these can continue and be made better in practice, if they can be tied to programs of development and reward, and if they can become an integral part of the total managing process, great progress in this area can be expected. But we still have far to go.

Managerial Obsolescence

There can be no question that the manager's role—in every kind of enterprise and at every level—is expanding and changing materially. As new knowledge and techniques become better known and applied, and as these lead to the creation of environments in which it is possible for people to perform more effectively and efficiently, the varied demands of society will force managers to take increasing advantage of this science and its resulting tools. Virtually every manager will increasingly be faced with requirements and opportunities for his improvement and for a far more intellectual approach to managing.

This means for those who manage that the danger of becoming obsolete for the task will continually be greater. So long as managing was a task only learned from experience, obsolescence was fairly unimportant. But now experience and new knowledge have been distilled into meaningful and useful principles, theory, concepts, and basic techniques which can be made useful to the manager who does not wish to risk the danger of becoming relatively more ignorant. There is no longer time for individuals to reach the state of required managerial excellence through trial and error. Absorption of new knowledge on a continuing basis *plus* the ability to use it for practical purposes is surely the only insurance against obsolescence.

DEVELOPING MORE EFFECTIVE MANAGERS

Although the introductory analyses of the task of the manager are presented in this book as a start toward understanding the science underlying managerial practice, more is required. Among the more important considerations in assuring effective managers, the authors would like to offer the following. Surely effective future managerial practice will depend at least on these.

A Willingness to Learn

If a manager is to avoid the stultifying effect of basing too much of his learning on experience, he must be aware of the dangers of experience. As was indicated earlier in this book, undistilled experience can lead an individual toward assuming that events or programs of the past will or will not work in a different future. But the manager needs more than this. He needs to be *willing* to learn and to take advantage of new knowledge and new techniques. This necessitates a humble approach to his successes and limitations. It demands a recognition that there is no finishing school or terminal degree for management education.

Acceleration of Management Development

The above discussion underlines the urgent importance of an accelerated program of management development. This implies not only more pertinent management seminars and conferences, but other means of transmitting to practicing managers in as simple and useful a way as possible the new knowledge and tools in the field of management.

One of the major challenges in this connection is one of compressing and transmitting that knowledge which is available. Every field of art based on a burgeoning science has the same problem. No field has completely solved it, although certain areas, such as specialized aspects of medicine and dentistry, have made considerable progress.

The authors have no adequate answer for this problem. It does appear that those on the management faculties of our universities have an obligation to practicing managers to do much of the task of compressing and transmitting this knowledge as easily and quickly as possible. There is still inadequate evidence that many university professors see the social importance of this role. Also, one might expect a greater contribution from various management associations, as well as from the management consultants, who can certainly greatly improve their value to clients by doing this. Perhaps more can be done through intelligent digesting of articles and books. An admirable start has been made by the publishing in recent years of *Management Research* (P. O. Box 4, Dolton, Illinois 60419). Also, it is entirely possible that there might be regularly established a series of special management clinics in which managers at all levels in alert companies would spend a day every few weeks being brought up-to-date on a specific area of new knowledge and technique. But more and better techniques must be found if the widening gap between knowledge and practice is to be narrowed.

Importance of Planning for Innovation

As competition becomes sharper, problem solving more advanced, and knowledge expands, one would expect that the manager of the future would have to place greater importance on planning for innovation. Even now it is widely recognized that a business enterprise, at least, must "innovate or die," that new products just do not happen, and that new marketing ideas do not often occur by luck. The manager of the future must place more emphasis than ever before on developing an environment for effective planning. This means, even more than at present, planning goals which call for stretch, creating policy guidelines to channel thinking toward them without stifling imagination, designing roles where people can be creative, keeping abreast of the entire external environment which affects a business, and recognizing the urgency of channeling research toward desired ends.

To develop these and other environmental elements for effective planning requires the highest order of intelligence and skill. Reference to those principles, techniques, and requirements for effective planning outlined in this book underlines the difficulties the manager of the future might expect. Moreover, as the future unfolds, the manager concerned may be certain that new and improved techniques and approaches will be discovered.

Measuring and Rewarding Management

One of the significant areas of proper concern to the manager of the future is the importance of both objectively measuring managerial performance and rewarding good performance or of imposing sanctions on poor operation or providing corrective action where it is indicated. Managers must be willing to work toward establishing objective measures of performance through both a verifiable results approach and the measurement of abilities of individuals as managers.

Tailoring Information

Another important area for the manager of the future is to obtain the right information in the right form and at the right time. Tailoring information, as outlined in this book, requires a high order of intelligence and design. Until managers realize that very little of their operation can be planned and controlled through "handbook" approaches, and until they recognize that they themselves must become involved in tailoring the information they require, little progress may be expected in this area. So long as information design is confused with the clerical work of information gathering and summarizing, managers will understandably continue to fret about the inadequacy of the data on which they are forced to act.

Need for Management Research and Development

As can be seen from the above areas where the future should command managerial attention, perhaps one of the most challenging is that of obtaining more real research and development in management tools and techniques themselves. The level of research effort and support in the field of management is woefully low. It is also not particularly great in the disciplines underlying management and, for that matter, in the entire area of social science. Nevertheless, it is probable that research in underlying disciplines far outpaces that in the central area of management.

There are many reasons for this. General management research is a difficult field, exceedingly complex and dynamic. It is one where facts and proved relationships are hard to come by and where the controlled experiment of the laboratory is difficult to use without dangerous oversimplification. Likewise, management research is expensive and the funds that have gone into it are abysmally inadequate. It has been estimated that not more than 2 per cent of the total being spent annually for all research in this country, or approximately one-twentieth of one per cent of Gross National Product, goes into research in *all* social sciences. In turn, if funds spent on management and management-related research are more than one-tenth of this, or one-two-hundredth of one per cent of Gross National Product, the authors would be surprised.

Still another reason for the low state of management research is that there is a lack of clinical analyses, despite a considerable volume of clinical experience. Consulting efforts of both professional consultants and individual academics, extensive management case collections, and studies and analyses made internally in business, government, and other enterprise almost certainly encompass a huge mass of undigested, largely unsummarized, and relatively useless information. If this clinical experience could be given the analytical and summarizing work so common in the health sciences, there might be now considerable evidence of what is workable in practice and where deficiencies exist.

In undertaking this research, patience and understanding are needed. Perfection of analysis to include all kinds of variables is a laudable goal for a researcher. But, particularly in the field of management, a little light can be a massive beam in a hitherto dark area of knowledge. We must often settle for small advances so that cumulatively, and over time, we may gain larger ones.

But research without development is insufficient. One of the major challenges for the manager of the future is the need for developing more managerial inventions. It is an interesting thing how so much creative talent has been channeled into the invention of physical designs and chemical compositions and how little into social inventions. The GANTT chart has sometimes been regarded as the most important social invention of the first half of the twentieth century. Other management inventions include the variable budget, rate-of-return-on-investment analysis, linear organizational charts, and PERT (Program Evaluation and Review Technique). Mere reference to these inventions underscores the fact that they are inventive tools developed from a base of principles on one hand and needs on the other. Reference to them indicates also that they are useful devices in improving the art of management.

Inventions tend to reflect the cultural level of an art. There are few of them in management. Surely even the present inadequate cultural level can be coupled with urgent needs to give rise to many more management innovations, particularly if those concerned are willing to spend some time and money to direct their energies toward these inventions. It is very easy to see that one significant management invention, such as those mentioned in the previous paragraph, can make important contributions to management effectiveness and economy of operation. Applied research and development in this field surely justifies a considerable expenditure of time and money.

NEED FOR INTELLECTUAL LEADERSHIP

That intellectual leadership in management is urgently needed can hardly be denied. Managing can no longer be only a practical art requiring merely native intelligence and experience. The rapid growth of underlying knowledge and the obvious need for even more, particularly that knowledge which is organized and useful for improvement of practice, are requirements which have tremendous social significance. It is not difficult to anticipate a 10 per cent rise in productivity in the American economy due to improved management, or an effort, in sheer economic terms, worth to the United States alone over $100 billion per year. Even these dramatic data give no direct recognition to the potential rise in human satisfactions involved in such improvement.

This means that key elements in any society would do well to give the area of managerial scientific research and development a high priority. Our college and university administrators and scholars—leaders in what former President Clark Kerr of the University of California has called the "knowledge industry"—should take the lead by giving management research and teaching the support their social importance deserves. Private foundations have an obligation as instruments of social betterment to support meaningful research in this field. Likewise, there can hardly be a more important area of research for a government to support. Every part of society would do well to seize the opportunity to support management research and development with the same vigor they have pursued such goals as new products, improved physical health, defense, and public welfare. In short, what is needed is an awareness that the intellectual and practical requirements of management are urgent, manifold, and socially important.

The challenges for a better society through improved management practice in every type of enterprise and those involved in intellectual leadership in the field are impressive. History teaches us that when needs exist and are recognized and when the cultural level reaches the point of ability to meet these needs, leadership usually arises to inspire solutions. The challenging needs are here. The cultural level appears to be rising to the point where many answers are feasible. The question is simply where and how this leadership can be developed.

SUMMARY OF MAJOR CONTROL PRINCIPLES

The basic principles of control can be grouped into three categories, reflecting their purpose and nature, structure, and process. In view of the unity of management and the tendency for functions to coalesce in practice, certain of these principles are understandably similar to those of other managerial functions.

The Purpose and Nature of Control

The purpose and nature of control are reflected in the following principles:

Principle of assurance of objective   The task of control is to detect potential or actual deviation from plans early enough to permit effective corrective action.

As with the other functions of management, the purpose of control is the attainment of objectives. This it can accomplish by detection of failures in plans that are, in turn, designed to attain objectives.

Control, like planning, must be forward-looking. This principle is often disregarded, largely because control has been dependent upon accounting and statistical data instead of upon forecasts and projections, and managers have been preoccupied with decimal accuracy, only to be attained—if at all—from past events. To regard planning as looking ahead and control as looking back is fallacious. Lacking means of looking forward, reference to history, on the assumption that "what is past is prologue," is better than not looking at all. But no manager attempting control should be satisfied with using historical records, adequate as they are for tax collection and for the determination of stockholders' earnings.

Ideally, a system of control should operate with instantaneous feedback, like the servo system of an automated machine tool, so that tendencies to stray from desired performance are corrected before the straying goes too far. In the absence of servomechanisms for most managerial tasks, control can be based on forecasts carried far enough into the future to foresee deviation tendencies in time to act. Even though forecasts are subject to inaccuracy, they are likely to be more satisfactory for control than reliance on history. Many firms rely on cash forecasts, and many owe their solvency to foreseeing cash shortages and preventing them. Such new techniques as PERT also make possible control that is forward-looking.

Principle of efficiency of controls   Control techniques and approaches are efficient when they detect and illuminate the causes of actual or potential deviations from plans with a minimum of costs or other unsought consequences.

The principle of efficiency is particularly important in control, because techniques have a way of becoming costly, complex, and burdensome. A manager may become so engrossed in control that he spends more than it is worth to detect a deviation. Also, should a control technique be employed by a manager with such vigor and thoroughness as to negate the authority delegation to his subordinate, or should it seriously interfere with the morale of those who must execute plans, it can easily result in costs beyond any possible value. Detailed budget controls that hamstring a subordinate, complex engineering controls that thwart innovation, and purchasing controls that delay deliveries and cost more than the item purchased are instances of inefficient controls.

Principle of control responsibility   The primary responsibility for the exercise of control rests in the manager charged with the execution of plans.

Since delegation of authority and assignment of tasks make a manager responsible for certain work, it follows that control over this work should be exercised by him. His responsibility cannot be waived or rescinded without changing the organization structure. This simple principle clarifies the often-misinterpreted role of controllers. These may act in a staff or service capacity to furnish control information to managers, but they cannot exercise control without assuming the managerial responsibility and managerial authority for the things controlled.

Principle of direct control   The higher the quality of managers and their subordinates, the less will be the need for indirect controls.

Most controls used today are grounded on the fact that human beings make mistakes. They are usually used as simple indirect controls aimed at catching errors, often after the fact. Wherever possible, direct controls—aimed at preventing errors—should be used. Unquestionably, the best means of assuring that plans work out is to secure the best possible quality of managers at all levels. Such managers make the fewest mistakes and carry out all their functions to the best advantage.

The Structure of Control

These principles that follow, dealing primarily with making control devices and practices fit in with plans and with organization structure, cast light on the structure of the controls themselves.

Principle of reflection of plans   The more controls are designed to deal with and reflect the specific nature and structure of plans, the more effectively they will serve the interests of the enterprise and its managers.

This principle recognizes the fundamental truth that, plans being a prerequisite of control and control the task of making sure that plans are accomplished, control devices or techniques must reflect plans. In cost control, for example, the control must be based on planned costs of a definite and specific type; in control of application of policy, the nature of the policies and where they are to apply should be clear; and so on in all enterprise areas.

Principle of organizational suitability   The more controls are designed to reflect the place in the organization structure where responsibility for action lies, the more they will facilitate correction of deviations from plans.

Since plans are carried out by managers and their subordinates, controls must fit a manager's authority area and therefore be designed to reflect organization structure. Consequently, any device of control must be tailored to the organization structure, and information to appraise performance against plans must be suitable to the position of the manager who is to use it. Urwick expresses this idea as the principle of uniformity and emphasizes that "all figures and reports used for purposes of control must be in terms of the organization structure."[7]

Principle of individuality of controls   Effective controls require con-

---

[7] L. Urwick, *The Elements of Administration* (New York: Harper & Row, Publishers, Incorporated, 1943), p. 107.

sistency with the position, operational responsibility, ability to understand, and needs of the individual concerned.

Although some control information and techniques can be utilized in the same form by various companies and managers, as a general rule control should meet the individual needs of each manager. The scope and detail of information requirements vary with managerial level and function. Furthermore, managers differ widely in their preferences for various methods of presenting information and in the type of units selected for reporting. Certainly, the corporate president, the controller, the vice-president in charge of manufacturing, the plant superintendent, and the foreman would not use the same type of control. The authors have seen both company presidents and factory foremen throw up their hands in dismay (for quite different reasons) at the unintelligibility and inappropriate form of control information that was a delight to the figure- and table-minded controller. Control information which a manager cannot or will not use has little value.

The Process of Control

Control, being largely a matter of technique, rests heavily on the art of management, on "know-how" in a given instance. However, these principles, arising from experience with control, have wide applicability.

Principle of standards   Effective control requires objective, accurate, and suitable standards.

There should be a simple, specific, and verifiable way to measure whether a planning program is being accomplished. Control is accomplished through people. Even the best manager cannot help being influenced by personal factors, and actual performance is sometimes camouflaged by a dull or a sparkling personality or by a subordinate's ability to "sell" a deficient performance. By the same token, good standards of performance, objectively applied, will more likely be accepted by a subordinate as fair and reasonable.

Principle of critical-point control   Effective control requires attention to those factors critical to appraising performance against an individual plan.

It would ordinarily be wasteful and unnecessary for a manager to follow every detail of planning execution. What he must know is that plans are being executed. Therefore, he concentrates his attention on salient factors of performance that will indicate, without watching everything, any important deviations from plans. There are no easy guidelines to determine the critical points he should watch, since their selection is predominantly a matter of managerial art. Perhaps the manager can ask himself what things in *his* operations will best show *him* whether the plans for which he is responsible are being accomplished.

The exception principle   The more a manager concentrates his control efforts on exceptions, the more efficient will be the results of his control.

This principle holds that the manager should concern himself only with significant deviations, the especially good or the especially bad situations. It is often confused with the principle of critical-point control, and they do have some kinship. However, critical-point control has to do with recognizing the points to be watched, while the exception principle has to do with watching the size of deviations, logically at these points.

Principle of flexibility of controls If controls are to remain effective despite failure or unforeseen changes of plans, flexibility is required in their design.

According to this principle, controls must not be so inflexibly tied in with a plan as to be useless if the entire plan fails or is suddenly changed. Note that this principle applies to failure of plans, not failure of people operating under plans, although the latter is the primary subject of control.

Principle of action Control is justified only if indicated or experienced deviations from plans are corrected through appropriate planning, organizing, staffing, and directing.

There are instances in practice where this simple truth is forgotten. Control is a wasteful use of managerial and staff time unless it is followed by action. If deviations are found in experienced or projected performance, action is indicated, either in the form of redrawing plans or in making additional plans to get back on course. It may call for reorganization. It may require replacement of a subordinate or training him to do the task desired. Or there may be no other fault than a lack of direction in getting the subordinate to understand the plans or be motivated to accomplish them. But, in any case, action is implied.

Because this action must necessarily be that of the manager in whose department the deviation occurs, this principle underscores the importance of responsible managers' being given the means not only of controlling their operations, but of undertaking the other managerial functions. It affirms the essential unity of management, the fact that no one can effectively manage who cannot appropriately undertake the functions of planning, organizing, staffing, directing and controlling.

FOR DISCUSSION

1. If direct control were completely effective, would a company need any indirect controls?
2. What distinction would you draw between management appraisal, as dealt with in Chapter 23, and the management audit discussed in this chapter?
3. How would you proceed to make a management audit? Are there any similarities between it and an accounting audit?
4. Taking any major area of management theory and principles, how can they be applied to reality?
5. By reference to specific management problem areas, such as new-product development, organization structure, or budgets, what are the ways managers can introduce flexibility and what are the inflexibilities usually encountered in each?

6. How may a manager design an environment for imaginativeness and creativity?
7. How would you anticipate that the computer will affect the manager's role at the top-management level? The middle-management level? First-line supervision?
8. If you were asked to organize and operate an effective management research and development staff, how would you proceed?

case incidents for part one. the basis of management

1. HART ELECTRONICS

Hart Electronics, Incorporated was built up in the early 1960s to design and manufacture special instruments for the Apollo Moon Landing Program. Its founders were two eminent physicists, Dr. Smith Lane and Dr. Raymond Morey. Adequately financed by Robert Hart, well-known multimillionaire, the two founders soon attracted a large group of scientists who developed acceleration instruments and test equipment useful in space programs and in airborne missile systems. Within a few years, they found themselves as the designers and producers of entire space control systems. Within ten years the company prospered and reached $100 million in annual sales with some 4,000 employees.

The company was not well organized and managed during its rapid growth, but, because of its new and imaginative products, it did succeed in making reasonable profits. However, as it grew, competition came into the field and Mr. Hart became worried about the company's ability to market and produce efficiently. On discussing this problem with his consultant, Mr. Hart was told that the top scientists in managerial positions running the company must learn to become more effective managers. At this point, he asked the consultant to start a management development program. With the approval of the company's top officers, who felt compelled to follow the suggestions of their major owner, a management development committee was established with the consultant as chairman. The committee's task was to design and implement a development program for the company. The consultant was given a committee comprised of the company's financial vice-president, director of personnel, and two top scientific leaders who headed major divisions of the company.

At the first meeting of the committee, the two top scientists were obviously unsympathetic with the program, feeling with some justification that a company with such a rapid and successful growth could hardly need any management training. One of them, obviously trying to stop the whole program, said at the start of the meeting:

"How can we even be talking about instituting a management development program? No one has even been able to tell me what management is. I have heard it said that it is getting things done through people. If that is all it is, I have been doing this in my work for years. How can we be taking our time to develop a program of any meaning for something as simple as this?"

2. THE PARAGON RADAR CORPORATION

The Paragon Radar Corporation was organized in 1955. It was managed by three engineers who formerly worked for the McDonnell Aircraft Company. They were instrumental in developing a radar capable of handling transmissions over distances far beyond those formerly permitted by the curvature of the earth. The Paragon people were adequately financed and decided upon a market policy of dealing only with government agencies, especially the Air Force, Navy, Army, and NASA. The budgets of these agencies grew steadily as the years passed and business was very good.

The Paragon people did not have a marketing department in the usual sense of this term. The heads of each department were expected to develop their own business. Consequently, the engineers would keep in close touch with their counterparts in the several agencies, help them identify their needs, help them sell these needs to their relevant policy-making executives and contracting officers, and write the proposal as soon as the request came through.

As the decade of the 1970s began the federal government drastically cut back the budget for the Department of Defense and NASA. Business was scarce and hard to get. The Paragon people bid more and more contracts with less and less success. This state of affairs became the subject of a staff meeting at the corporate level.

"Gentlemen," said the president, "you all know the causes for the decline in our business. The corporation is gradually approaching a precarious posture. We do have excellent technical abilities, and there are still some $75 billion being spent on national defense so our potential is still there. I have pointed out to the department heads that you must get new business if you are to remain part of the organization. It seems that my words have fallen on unhearing ears. But I assure you that I am really serious. The time has come when we either get well or be acquired by another firm."

James Simpson, one of the department heads, spoke up, saying, "You fellows may think that there is something lacking in my loyalty but I really believe that we are not organized in an effective way to do what we must do. In the good years we did very well. Business was good, our bids were highly successful, indeed, so much so that department managers would turn down business if the technical content did not interest them. Now that we need business we don't have the contacts. The way we have approached the problem no one is responsible for getting business: we all are, but none can say how much. Authority is widely diffused. We all share the blame and yet none accepts it."

The members of the staff were shocked. The president had the good sense to let time run on while each examined his position. One member eventually reached for his alibis, "I don't view the matter in that light. Here we have been successful for going on two decades, we get business like other aerospace companies do, and you can't expect a department head to accept and work on a contract that he is not interested in. You know, the defense business is not like selling soap."

"I know," said Simpson. "I used to believe that too. Recently I have been looking at the management literature to see if there is some principle we have overlooked. These chaps seem to be saying that the best results occur when a man has a definite objective to achieve, when he is personally held responsible for achieving it, when he has the authority to make decisions that must be made in order to bring in the business. We operate this way in everything except marketing. Why is this an exception?"

The meeting adjourned at this point. The president said he would reexamine the matter and hopefully bring in a proposal at the next meeting. Two weeks later, and after many hours of study and consultation, he opened the regular staff meeting with an announcement.

"Gentlemen," he said, "I think it is time we stop fighting management principles; let's use them for our own benefit. I think we should have a 'business-getting' activity centralized in the hands of one man and reporting to me. We might call the function 'Advanced Program Development,' for semantic purposes. I visualize this activity being comprised of three functions. One would be staffed by engineers with marketing ability, another with engineers who will write the proposals, and another with market research capability. The head of this whole group would be responsible for bringing in new business and he would have the necessary decision-making authority. He would be expected to run a tight shop. I do not want an expanding bureaucracy. He should be able to borrow technical men as needed from the operating departments. In order that the technical men in the new department will not grow stale and useless, I feel that whoever is the head of a proposal committee should be made program manager when and if he secures the contract. Thus, I can see a great deal of lateral movement among the engineers in all our activities."

The proposal was too revolutionary to expect anyone to take a position on its feasibility. The staff was dismissed with the injunction to study it and bring back suggestions that would make it more viable.

3. THE ENTERPRISE AND ITS ENVIRONMENT

The day was Thursday. The dozen members of the Seminar on Social Control were assembling. There was anticipation on their faces because they were going to deal with a really live subject. There had been so much irresponsible talk on the campus about social responsibility that at last they would be able to acquire a rational view of the matter.

"Our topic for today," began the professor, "concerns the enterprise and its environment. The term 'enterprise' includes all organized effort and thus we are equally concerned about the management of government agencies, trade unions, churches, universities, and business. The term 'environment' includes the physical, biological and social forces that affect and are affected by organized activity. I would suggest that we first identify some of these forces. Then we can consider what, if anything, should be done about them, and what principles should underlie our recommendations."

"The most commonly mentioned forces," one student spoke up, "are pollution, crime, poverty, competition, government regulations, and concentrated population."

"That is a considerable list," the professor remarked. "Are you talking about the United States or the aborigines of Australia?"

"That idea never occurred to me. When you come to think of it, I doubt if any of these forces are at work among those aborigines."

"Assuming you are close to the truth," spoke another student, "then we would have to conclude that the external environment becomes more critical and even desperate the more advanced the society in question."

"Take pollution, for instance," a third student warmed to the subject, "all through his history man has polluted his environment. But this has only become a critical problem when the ratio of pollutants to resources increases geometrically with rising population."

"You mean to say that everybody pollutes our resources? I thought only business firms did that."

"Well, you are wrong. And did you ever think of the cost of fighting pollution? I don't think consumers are about to pay the cost of keeping our resources clean, fresh, and healthy."

"I would just have the government spend its tax money to pay the cost," responded a fourth student.

"Taxes are levied on people. How would you like to pay a tax of $5 per day into government funds for the disposal of your personal contribution to pollution?" asked the third student.

"Some people are discouraged," offered the professor, "when they see how government is now taking an amount equal to 40 percent of our disposable income to pay for the inept and costly activities that politicians support because they think this is the way to stay in office. Our whole democratic process seems to feed on affluence, just as crime is so largely a product of permissiveness, ineffective education, and crowded living conditions. It is a wonder that managers can cope with such a chaotic external environment."

The students were more and more thoughtful as the time for the seminar ran out. Things were not simple after all, and they looked for some place to start in organizing their thinking.

"It is clear that we have much more work to do on this topic," said the professor. "At our next meeting let us look into man's natural and learned behavior to see if there is a possibility that he can live a fruitful life in crowded communities, if he can be disciplined to respect the rights of others, and indeed, if he can ever learn to manage an affluent society."

4. CONSOLIDATED COMPUTERS, INC.

James Pruitt was ushered into the president's office. Three months ago he was appointed manager of the first foreign plant of Consolidated Computers, Inc. He appeared to be the ideal man for this assignment. He was forty-three years old, and a proven division manager of many talents. He was an innovator and very much interested in a foreign appointment. Now he was calling on his superior just before catching the plane for Bangkok.

"I wanted to talk to you," the president began, "about some issues you will be facing when you reach Thailand. I guess you might call what I want to say a matter of my search for a business philosophy. We have not had to experience here the new issues that you will face, and we simply do not have a set of policies and procedures to cover such matters. Perhaps out of your experience we can move in that direction in case we later establish our operations in other countries.

"I am not concerned about your encountering new principles of management. They are universal, you have developed great skill in applying them to domestic operations, and I have no doubt about your skill in applying them in a foreign environment. You will soon discover, however, that managing is different abroad precisely because it is the cultural environment that is so different.

"I think our best position is to realize that we are going into Thailand as a guest. We each need the other at this time, but there may come a time when their political forces will require us to give up ownership control of our plant. It is up to you to develop the rapport with all interested parties which will most benefit our long run interests.

"Since all of your employees will be, or soon will be, native Thais it is vital to learn as quickly as possible something about their culture. Perhaps your best move is to perfect your skill in the use of their language and really learn to think and act as a native. I am not sure. You and I were raised in the folds of Western civilization which has very different institutions and behavioral patterns than you will encounter in the

Far East. For instance, does one adhere to the ethical principles of the Thais or to our own? Do they have the same trust and reliance on people that we do? Will they always react as we here are accustomed? Is social responsibility thought of in the same terms? What intentions and actions on your part will be well received by your suppliers, customers, competitors, and public figures?

"You know, I suppose that what is really on my mind is that we don't really know at what point there may be a conflict in our two cultures, and when that is discovered, what choice you will make."

case incidents for part two, planning

5. PLANNING FOR PLANNING

In a way, the line managers of the company were relieved when they realized that they themselves were responsible for planning. They certainly did not want any outsider or staff man to tell them what they were going to do.

On the other hand, planning was entirely new to them and they had a difficult time deciding just what to do, when, and where to start. All of them seemed to go off in different directions, as the president remarked to them in his staff meeting. It appeared that independence too has its costs and that they needed help.

"Do we need to organize to plan, and if so, how do we relate organization structure to corporate growth?" asked the president.

"I think we ought to relate any organization for planning to the present. Let the future take care of itself," said the controller.

"You can't really do that either, if our plans are going to run for over a year," observed the director of marketing.

"It is important not to overlook the need for procedures and standard forms if we are going to plan," said the director of administration.

"Before we get through I'll bet our company plan will cost us thousands of dollars," the controller thought out loud.

"The more I think of it the more I'm sure we need some kind of an organization structure. I'm willing to plan but somebody has to show me when and how and about what," said the director of manufacturing.

"Perhaps the best thing for us to do," the president replied, "is to develop a plan to plan for this corporation's next fiscal year."

6. MANAGING BY OBJECTIVES

"Managing by objectives is nothing new here," said Commissioner Henry A. Bishop of the Metropolis Police Department. "We have always had important objectives toward which every one in my department strives. Our job is to maintain law and order, firmly but fairly; to protect human lives and property; and to be the conscience and spirit of the general welfare of the millions of people who call our city home. Every man in this department knows these objectives. Every man knows that he must work toward them and that, if he does not, he will be replaced. I recognize that in a manufacturing concern you can measure objectives by profits, sales, costs, and product output. We can't, of course, do that for we are a service operation. But this does not mean that we are not managing by objectives. Ask anyone in my department!''

7.   DEVELOPING VERIFIABLE GOALS

The division manager had recently heard a lecture on management by objectives. His enthusiasm, kindled at that time, tended to grow the more he thought about it. He finally decided to introduce the concept and see what headway he could make at his next staff meeting.

He recounted the theoretical developments in this technique, cited the advantages to the division in its application, and asked his subordinates to think about adopting it.

It was not as easy as everyone had thought. At the next meeting, several questions were raised.

"Do you have division goals assigned to you for next year?" the finance manager wanted to know.

"No, I do not," the division manager replied. "I have been waiting for Corporate to tell me what is expected but they act as if they will do nothing about the matter."

"What is the division to do then?" the manager of production asked, rather hoping that no action would be indicated.

"I intend to list my expectations for the division," the manager said. "There is not much mystery about them. I expect $30,000,000 in sales, a profit on sales before taxes of 8 per cent, a return on investment of 15 per cent, an on-going program in effect by June 30, with specific characteristics I will list later, to develop our own future managers, completed development work on our XZ model by the end of the year, and employee turnover stabilized at 5 per cent."

The staff was somewhat stunned that their superior had thought through to these verifiable objectives with such clarity and assurance. They were also surprised about his sincerity in wanting to achieve them.

"During the next month I want each of you to translate these objectives into verifiable goals for your own functions. Naturally they will be different for finance, marketing, production, engineering, and administration. However you state them, I will expect them to add up to the realization of the division goals."

8.   GOAL SETTING

The professor was speaking to his graduate class in the philosophy of enterprise control. He was concerned about the source of managerial goals.

"The ease with which we academicians speak of goal identification and selection may be misleading. It is easy enough to say that a business manager selects a goal of 10 percent over last year's sales and profits. But if you were that man, how would you decide that the goal should be 10 percent or 8 percent or 15 percent? The only guidance we can give is to say that whatever figure is selected should reflect the judgment that it can be achieved with effort.

"Then there is another matter. We talk about stretch in goal identification. Why? Is there some reason why people should do better than in a previous time? Is this what is meant by 'progress'? And if so, why should we insist on progress? Is the University a machine that must graduate more students each year?"

The students were somewhat overwhelmed by these considerations. Who is to say that there is a 'correct' answer? Is there any guide to the selection of proper goals?

9. OLYMPIC TOY COMPANY

"I expect every manager in my department to act completely rational in every decision he makes," declared Lee Johnson, vice-president—marketing for the Olympic Toy Company. "Every one of us, no matter what his position, is hired to be a *professional* rationalist and I expect him not only to know what he is doing and why he is doing it, but to be right in his decisions. I know that someone has said that a good manager needs only to be right in more than half of his decisions. But that is not good enough for me. I would agree that you may be excused for occasionally making a mistake, especially if it is a matter beyond your control, but I can never excuse you for not acting rationally."

"I agree with your idea, Lee," said Joe Goldberg, his advertising manager, "and I always try to be rational and logical in my decisions; but would you mind helping me be sure of this by explaining just what acting rationally is?"

10. KING'S SUPERMARKETS

King's Supermarkets was a chain of twenty-five highly successful supermarkets located in medium-sized cities in New England, New York, and New Jersey. It had always been the company's policy to have only one leading store in each of a number of cities of approximately 25,000 to 50,000 population. In each city, the best possible location was sought out and very large stores were developed with attractive buildings, large parking lots and complete product lines of food and food-related products sold at advertised competitive prices. Although the company had had to close a few poorly located markets over the years, it relied almost entirely for cities and locations on the instincts of the founder-president, Walter King. The company's record of profits indicated that his judgment had been generally correct over the twenty-five years since he had opened his first market.

After Walter King's son, Donald, graduated from the university with a degree in business administration and joined the company as assistant to the president, the researching of new city locations was made one of his major assignments. Donald King felt that the techniques of operations research might be applied to this problem. He pointed out that there must be a "best" city and a "best" location for expansion, at any given time and for the future, if only this could be discovered. He insisted that all a company needed to do is to clarify its goals, identify the constraints such as cash available, existing competition, and distance from company warehouses, and look at such variables as cost of real estate, money costs, market size and characteristics, local labor markets, and local taxes and regulations; and then put these into a model to come up with the best location.

His father and the other officers of the company maintained that operations research might be all right for an oil company, a large aerospace company, or even a large bank, but it was too complicated an approach and there were too many intangibles in a matter of a supermarket location. Moreover, for twenty-five years the company had been successful in relying on the president's judgment, and, anyway, neither he nor any of the other top officers or managers understood advanced mathematics. In addition, they felt that they wanted no part of a company where such major decisions were made by a computer. They pointed out strongly that they were merchandisers and not computer experts.

Young Donald was not convinced. He was sure that operations research would greatly help in such decisions. But he did not know what to do under the circumstances.

11.   BARTLETT DRUG COMPANY

Richard Spencer was marketing manager of the cosmetics division of the Bartlett Drug Company. The company was well known as a leader in new proprietary drug and toiletry products and had a good record of profitability. The cosmetics division had been especially successful in men's toiletries and cosmetics and in the introduction of new products. It always based its new product development on market research with respect to what would appeal to men and, after almost invariably test marketing a new product in a few selected cities, launched it with a heavy advertising and sales promotion program. It had hoped in this way not only to get a large initial share of the market, but also to become so well entrenched that competitors who soon copy a successful product would not dislodge them from their market share.

After being cautioned by the president on the necessity of watching costs more carefully, the division manager became increasingly concerned with two opposing factors in his marketing strategy: (1) test marketing of new products (offering them for sale first in a few test cities with area advertising and sales programs) tended increasingly to give competitors advance information on new products and certain competitors had been able to copy a product almost as soon as Bartlett could offer it nationally and profit thereby from Bartlett's advertising; and (2) national advertising and sales promotion expenses were increasing so fast that a single major product failure would have an important impact on division profits, on which his annual bonus was being primarily determined. On the one hand, he recognized the wisdom of test marketing, but he disliked the costs and dangers involved. On the other hand, he hardly wished to take an unknown risk on embarking on a national program until a test showed that the product did in fact have a good market demand. Yet, he wondered whether all products should be test marketed.

Richard Spencer was asked to put this problem to his marketing department subordinates and ask them what should be done. To give the strategy some meaning, he used as a case at point the company's new men's hair spray and conditioner which had been developed on the basis of promising, although preliminary, market research. He asked his sales manager whether he thought the product would succeed and what he thought his "best estimate" of sales would be. He also asked his advertising manager to give some cost estimates on launching the product.

Larry Hodgson, division sales manager, thought a while and said he was convinced the product was a winner and that his best estimate would be sales of $5 million per year for at least five years. Harold Jackson, the advertising manager, said that the company could launch the product for a cost of $2 million the first year and some $500 thousand per year thereafter. He also pointed out that the test marketing program would cost $200 thousand, of which half would be saved if these test cities were merely a part of a national program, and would delay the national program for six months. But he warned Spencer that test marketing would save the gamble of so much money on the national promotion program.

At this point, Lowell Armstrong, the new marketing research manager, suggested that the group might come to a better decision if they used a decision tree.

Richard Spencer looked at his subordinate curiously and said: "What is that? How would we do that? How would that help us in a problem like this?"

12. THE ROBERTS COMPANY

The Roberts Company was founded in 1938 with four partners, one of whom was the inventor of a special product and technique for laying wall-to-wall carpeting without using tacks. Although the carpet layers of the world were reluctant to change their long practice of tacking carpets down, through hard work and demonstration of the method to carpet layers the four partners were able to obtain acceptance of their product as the standard way of laying carpet in the following twenty years. Not only was their original product a great success but the company became the world's leader in furnishing tools for laying and stretching carpeting. They also developed and marketed a special adhesive for carpet laying and seaming and later expanded this line to a product for adhering plastic laminates in kitchens, bathrooms, furniture, and elsewhere. In addition, the company expanded its operations in the construction industry through such special products as steel folding doors for closets and wardrobes, steel door frames, and other items. Moreover, they took their products to many foreign countries where they were able to establish highly profitable wholly-owned subsidiaries to manufacture and sell products developed in the United States.

In deciding on future product diversification, and not wishing to become a conglomerate, it was determined that much effort and motion would be saved if energies in designing new products and considering acquisitions could be channeled within a clear product policy. In formulating this policy, the company considered, among other things, the following features:

1. The company had very strong marketing ability on a national and international basis in the carpet accessories field.
2. It had only regional (western U.S.) marketing in its building material products.
3. Its marketing ability and coverage in adhesives in the floor covering field were good, but were both specialized and limited in other adhesive applications.
4. Its overseas subsidiaries were well managed and operated in Canada, England, Holland, Sweden, Australia, and New Zealand.
5. While its size and resources could not be compared to the very large adhesive, chemical, and building material companies, in its special fields it was large, with $40 million of annual sales and ample resources from earnings and a receptive common stock public market; the company therefore felt that it could spend far more than its smaller competitors for marketing and specialized capital equipment.
6. Much of the specialized capital equipment used by the company was designed and built by its own engineers.
7. While a leader in some of its fields, particularly in floor-covering accessories, the company was subject in these areas to many small and vigorous local competitors.

So that both new product and acquisition programs could be effectively pursued, the board of directors asked the president to recommend a product policy for the company at its next meeting.

case incidents for part three. organizing

13. CONVALESCENTS' HOME, INC.

"The growth of enterprise in size and world-wide operations has brought an increasing weight to the presidential office. Traditionally the organization structure has provided for one person to occupy this position, and most organizations still adhere to this practice. There have been some, however, that experimented with an 'Office of the President' concept wherein several managers would share the Presidential burdens. This practice was begun by the Caterpillar Tractor Company in the mid-1950s, and was followed in some form in the 1960's by General Electric, Borden, Scott Paper, Singer, Amex, and Continental Can. Although heralded at the time by innocent academicians as a replacement for the single manager, the practice has ground to a slow halt."

Charles Renfrew, the president of Convalescents' Home, Inc., opened his weekly staff meeting by reading the above excerpt from a national newspaper. "Should we," he asked, "develop an Office of the President, consisting of four equal members specialized in promotion, construction, operation, and finance?"

John de Puy, Vice-president-Construction, was first to recover from the shock of the suggestion. "Chief," he said, "why do you propose a discussion on this topic?"

"Well, John," replied Renfrew, "I feel harassed by the number of decisions I have to make, and I would like to share this burden."

"Looking at the general inefficiency of business, government, universities, hospitals and other organizations," said Mark Thompson, Vice-president-Operations, "there is something fundamentally wrong in organized enterprise. I don't think it is the harassed top executive. I think it is his total incapacity to select able subordinates and to control their activities."

Jack Douglas, Vice-president-Finance, felt uneasy. "I am impressed by the apparent inability of Presidents to control effectively what their subordinates do. For example, look at the President of the United States. He is practically helpless to achieve control of his major departments and agencies: The heads of hospitals and universities are in the same position. I believe we do better in business than in other organizations."

"Should we go in this direction," said Renfrew, "there are certain principles we would follow. For instance, the theorists say that the members of the office of the President should be co-presidents, each able to make any decision and all support

688

every decision. Each should carefully keep all others informed about operational activities and the decisions each makes. The capabilities of each should supplement rather than duplicate the qualities of the other members."

"Those *principles*," said Jack, "are not principles and as guides they are conflicting."

"Charles," said John de Puy, "this Office of the President idea is just a crutch for poor management. Let's concentrate on improving our vice-presidential selection procedure, the exaction of responsibility from them for good performance, and the sharpening of our control procedures. Good men must share responsibility for results, all right, but I for one still want you and your successor to sit at the head of the table."

14. MEASUREMENT INSTRUMENTS CORPORATION

William B. Richman, president of the Measurement Instruments Corporation, was explaining his organizational arrangements to the board of directors. The chart was as follows:

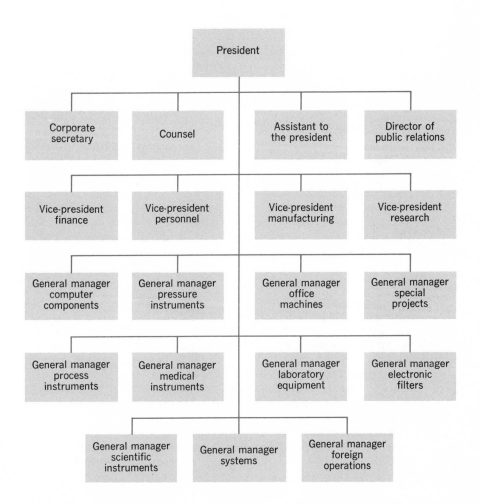

When asked by a board member whether he thought he had too many people reporting to him, Mr. Richman replied: "I do not believe in the traditional principle of span of control, or management, that a manager should only have four or five persons reporting to him. This is what makes waste and bureaucracy. All my subordinates are good men and know what they are doing. All can reach me readily with their problems when they have them. All feel close to the top because they are close to the top. Moreover, I want to know first hand how every man is doing and detect any weaknesses or errors as soon as possible. Furthermore, if a store manager at Sears Roebuck can have twenty-five to thirty men reporting to him, I ought to be able to handle nineteen. In addition, gentlemen, too few reporting to a manager doesn't give him enough to do and I assume that you hired me to give the company my full time."

15. PORTER DEFENSE MISSILES CORPORATION

A division manager of Porter Defense Missiles Corporation was discussing his top organization structure. He ticked off functions that were reporting to him:

Controller
Administrative operations, comprising personnel, employee relations, security, warehousing and facilities functions
Program management
Engineering operations, comprising field engineers, technical liaison with customer users, maintainability engineering systems, support engineering, technical training, technical manuals, training simulator engineering, and a branch plant engineering support function
Service contracts operation
Production operation, comprising a factory superintendent, engineering support for the factory, and quality control

"The problem I have is that I cannot get enough depth of insight into these operations. This is especially true of engineering, which employs about half of the division personnel. We aim to have an integrated support activity here, and if the truth were told, I have trouble seeing that engineering cooperates instead of being a stumbling block. Maybe imbalance is my problem. I think I will split the engineering operation in two, but I don't know how to do it."

16. MARKETING IN AN AEROSPACE COMPANY

The aerospace industry seems to have some peculiar ideas about the organizing structure best suited to marketing its products and services. The industry has always been dominated by engineers and scientists and these people have seldom really understood the marketing process. Instead, they strike a superior attitude in observing, "Marketing in our industry is a lot different from the soap or shoe business." This remark is intended to be intimidating to those who question the efficacy of their marketing processes. And the engineer often keeps strictly away from the statistical evidence of the very high cost of bids, successful or not.

The function that is called "marketing" in this industry is primarily comprised of learning where the dollars are and who is in a position to spend them. This activity gathers information about potential and actual procurements and its personnel are specialists in knowing who to contact in, hopefully, every situation. This information is then passed on to engineering personnel in various departments who are most likely to be interested in exploring the situation. If there is considerable business on hand the response of the engineers is quite different as compared with times when their division or department is hungry. In either case, the relevant engineering group or individual contacts the prospective procurement agency and its technical staffs, learns as much about the potential business as it can, and responds to the request for proposals with comprehensive bids that include technical, administrative, managerial and cost data.

One division manager who was in need of more business became worried about the lack of productivity of his proposal teams. They tried but failed on all too numerous occasions. A succession of managers of the narrowly defined marketing function were hired and fired; all were equally unproductive of contracts. A note of panic crossed the division manager's face when he was asked, "Can we afford to decentralize authority over marketing so far down the line?"

17.   UNIVERSAL FOOD PRODUCTS COMPANY

Alexander Owen, president of the Universal Food Products Company, was tired of being the only one in his company actually responsible for profits. While he had good vice-presidents in charge of finance, sales, advertising, manufacturing, purchasing, and product research, he realized he could not hold any of them responsible for company profits, as much as he would like to. He often found it difficult even to hold them responsible for the contribution of their various areas to company profits. The sales vice-president, for example, had rather reasonably complained that he could not be fully responsible for sales when the advertising was ineffective, or the products customer stores wanted were not readily available from manufacturing, or when he did not have the new products he needed to meet competition. Likewise, the manufacturing vice-president had some justification when he made the point that he could not both hold costs down and still be able to produce short runs so as to fill orders on short notice; moreover, financial controls would not allow the carrying of a large inventory of everything.

Mr. Owen had considered breaking his company down into six or seven small segments by setting up integrated product divisions with a manager over each with profit responsibility. But he found that this would not be feasible or economical since many of the company's branded food products were produced on the same factory equipment, used the same raw materials, and a salesman calling on a store or supermarket could far more economically handle a number of related products rather than one or a few.

Consequently, Mr. Owen came to the conclusion that the best thing for him to do was to set up six product managers reporting to a product marketing manager. Each product manager would be given responsibility for one or a few products and would oversee for his products all aspects of product research, manufacturing, advertising, and sales; he would thereby become the person responsible for the performance and profits of the products assigned to him.

Mr. Owen realized that he could not give these product managers actual line authority over the various operating departments of the company since that would cause each vice-president and his department to report to the six product managers, the product marketing manager, as well as the president. He was concerned with this problem, but he knew that some of the most successful larger companies in the world had used the product manager system. Moreover, one of his friends on a university faculty had told him that he must expect some ambiguity in any organization and that this might not be bad since it forced people to work together as teams.

Mr. Owen resolved to put in the product manager system as outlined and hoped for the best.

18. DEVELOPMENT AND ORGANIZATION FORM

The professor was concluding his lecture on the stages of corporate development. Why he thought this topic was worth such serious attention remained a moot point. However, his students were keenly interested when the principle that *the form of organization of manufacturing firms tends to vary directly with the complexity of their product-market relationships* was suggested.

In the discussion that followed it was generally conceded that the actual evidence that would demonstrate the propriety of the principle is difficult to accumulate. However, assuming that the principle was correct, what explains why firms might behave this way?

19. ABC AIRLINES

The president of ABC Airlines, seeing that costs were getting out of control, brought in as his assistant a brilliant young certified public accountant who had been in charge of the internal auditing department of a large public utility company. He told his assistant the nature of the company's problem of rising costs and asked for his help in solving the problem.

The new assistant gathered a staff of high quality industrial engineers, financial analysts, and recent top graduates from one of the nation's best known graduate schools of business administration. After laying out the company's problem, he assigned them to investigate cost problems and management methods in the airline's operations, maintenance, engineering, and sales departments. After a number of studies, the president's assistant found many sources of inefficiency in the various departments and initiated a number of changes in operating practices. In addition, he made many reports to the president outlining in detail the inefficiencies his staff had found and the measures being taken to correct them. These reports also showed, with ample supporting detail, the millions of dollars his actions were saving the company.

In the midst of these cost-saving programs, the vice-presidents in charge of operations, maintenance, engineering, and sales descended on the president and insisted that the assistant be discharged.

20. STAFF AND SERVICE DOMINATION OF LINE OPERATIONS

Several members of an American Management Association conference were discussing informally the tendency of staff and service departments to dominate line operations.

"I remember one case," said Henry Lorenz, a chief of audit in one of the Internal Revenue districts, "where many complaints from line managers were registered concerning the autocratic way the facilities and financial management men handled requests. In our business we had to make the annual fiscal budget some two years before it became operable. I'm afraid we did not anticipate our needs for equipment very well, perhaps because we thought no one could foresee that far ahead. Anyway, some of us would become distraught when the facilities department turned down our requests with the remark, 'Why did you not put that in your budget request?' At first it seemed to be rather high handed that a service group could deny a request by a line manager. Then we finally figured out that we could get most of the things we really needed if we got them approved in the budget."

"We have a different problem in our company," said George Marshall, engineering director for an aerospace company. "We really try to make plans in a democratic fashion for the following year's operation. We start early, have several reviews at group level, and eventually acquire a quite firm grasp on next year's expense, capital and manpower budgets. I notice that in allocating indirect manpower and G&A (general and administration) money to the divisions our group executive uses ratios provided by the controller or the vice-president—administration. This never sits well with us line managers, and we have often chided the group chief about using rules of thumb rather than business sense. I never get very far in my protests, however, because the group executive always says, 'Give me a better guide and I'll use it,' I have never been able to devise a substitute."

"In our business we are concerned about the arbitrary decisions of service departments," said Franz Lester, marketing director, Argon Manufacturing Corp. "For instance, their charges to our department are outrageous. I can get outside service for half the price. When these fellows submit a budget they seem to look at last year's figures, the profit projection for next year, and add 10 percent. Then they palm off a lot of services we don't want. Personnel is particularly effective in this game. Maintenance has a monopoly on service, so we get it when it suits them, not us."

Other participants added their experiences to the general topic. Finally someone remarked, "These examples do make the picture quite bleak. But I would suggest that we still have need of service and staff departments. The salient issue would appear to be how can we use them efficiently. Lorenz appears to have solved his problem. The rest of us have not. Can we generalize an effective approach?"

21. THE MIRACLE PRODUCTS COMPANY

Adam Stonebridge inherited from his father a small regional household cleansing products company. Through seeing that the three large companies in the field could not compete for quality products on a price basis because of their high advertising and promotional costs and by his extraordinary talent in setting up an imaginative sales program, Mr. Stonebridge succeeded in profitably developing the company's sales from $2 million to $20 million per year from 1957 to 1965. Because of the attractiveness of his shares to investors and their high market price, he was then able to acquire a number of smaller companies throughout the country so that by 1971, his company grew to $80 million of sales with six plants, a national sales organization, and approximately 2,500 employees.

Throughout the company's growth, Mr. Stonebridge found it difficult to delegate authority. Following the pattern when the company was much smaller, Mr. Stonebridge continued to make all final decisions on new products, advertising, pricing, sales plans and organization, hiring of people, operating budgets, production plans, capital expenditures, purchase orders above $1,000, credits given to stores, union agreements, production plans, and many other matters. As the controller who had been with the company for many years said to a new executive who asked what the company's policy was in a given area: "We don't need any policies here; whenever we want to know what to decide, we ask Adam."

Long before the company grew to its present size, the key executives—vice-presidents, plant managers, sales managers—became frustrated by bottlenecks in the presidents office. They finally approached one of the outside directors whom they trusted and knew to be a close friend of the president and asked his aid in solving the problem.

When the director investigated their complaint, he found it to be justified. He also found the president to be receptive to the idea of delegation, knowledgeable in the principles of delegation, and aware of the importance of delegating. He finally came to the conclusion that the president's unwillingness to delegate was due to a justifiable fear of losing control over the company's operations.

case incidents for part four, staffing

22. IDENTIFYING FIRST-LINE SUPERVISORS

A few years ago the executives of one of the best-managed agencies of the federal government decided that they should establish an early identification program for first-line supervisors. This agency had long been in the forefront of management education and was quite ready to heed the advice of management specialists concerning this subject. They surveyed their own experience only to find that many young men, professionally trained, were leaving the agency for private employment where the rewards were thought to be greater. This left the agency with something less than the best qualified candidates for supervision; it also left it with a notably aged group of supervisors.

A career development program was carefully worked out. Its chief features included thorough indoctrination concerning its nature and method of operation, an annual invitation to every nonmanager to apply for the career program, and an undertaking that all future supervisors would be selected from within the membership of the program. The development of the candidates comprised (1) a week of formal supervisory training; (2) assignment to an established supervisor who would act as a mentor, advising the candidate on a course of reading and enrollment in college courses wherever available, discussing the theory and practice of management with the candidate, and evaluating his progress; and (3) work on task force assignments as available and appropriate. Frequently, candidates were appointed to supervisory positions before they finished their programs; on the other hand, they would either stay within the program until assigned or resign from it to resume a technical career.

Several advantages emerged from this program. The candidates were pleased that their careers were a matter of interest and concern to the agency executives; candidates could more easily bring themselves to the attention of their superiors; the agency was provided with a cadre of youthful candidates for supervision; the brain-drain from the agency almost stopped; gradually more vigor in management levels became evident; and young men and women could establish a broader base of experience from which to decide whether they really wanted to be managers.

Certain disadvantages also became apparent. Many good candidates failed to apply for the program because they were not sure of their own career objectives; they did not want to move away from the localities in which they were domiciled; they felt too busy to undergo the training prescribed (this was in addition to their full-time position); some complained of inadequate counsel from mentors; and many who failed to apply were later disgruntled when they found themselves no longer among the candidates for supervisory appointments.

The agency is presently in a mood to reassess its experience with the program.

23. AIRBORNE INSTRUMENT DIVISION

John Simpson was an assistant department manager. He was originally appointed on the basis of his technical skill. He had been promoted through the ranks in a technical department and knew very well all aspects of the operation.

Stephen Clayton, manager of the Airborne Instrument Division, was looking over candidates to head a department. John was considered well qualified from the point of view of his knowledge of management principles and practices and of the operations.

"Why don't you select John?" Clayton was asked.

"He just wouldn't fit," the division manager responded. "The man is just impossible. Look at the way he dresses. Think of that silly grin on his face. Have you noticed those crooked spectacles he wears?

"In my division, a man has to look like a manager as well as be one."

"I don't think you have any right to dictate how a person looks," said Don Stillwell, the division controller. "It is an invasion of personal rights."

"It is not," commented Stephen Clayton. "I have a division here and it is my responsibility to run it effectively. I can select anyone I desire to fill vacant positions and I'm going to select those who facilitate rather then irritate our interpersonal relations."

"I think you are really exaggerating the impact of this person on others," replied Don Stillwell, "I feel that one is easily accustomed to seeing others in any garb they choose. I remember the hesitation of a division manager to appoint a subordinate to operations manager because he wore cowboy boots and rather low grade suits. It was his position that he would feel embarrassed to introduce such a person to higher company officials and to the admirals and generals in the Defense Department. It seemed obvious that the feelings of the division manager were at stake rather than those of the Defense Department officials or the subordinate himself."

"But," the division manager responded, "I at least know where I stand on matters of dress, appearance, deportment, and over-all image cast by my managers. If they do not want to work for me within my restrictions they can get another job. I just like it this way and I think it is important that I be pleased."

24. SELECTING SUPERVISORS

The department manager was holding a regular staff meeting with his four section heads. His practice was to confine each meeting to one chief problem, and on this day the subject was the indifferent quality of the twenty supervisors reporting to the section heads.

"We have a rather poor record in selecting good supervisors in this department," he began. "We do have five or six who are outstanding, but there are too many who are unsuccessful. What do you men look for when you recommend candidates to me?"

"I think my best technical man makes the best supervisor," said one. "He has the respect of his peers and of his subordinates. They all rate technical competence highly. I find that such a man can train new staff members very effectively, and he can also pitch in and do the most demanding jobs himself."

"Maybe that is just the trouble," said the department manager. "A fellow like that may never learn to manage because he spends his time on technical work. He is more like a lead-man."

"When I think about it," said another section head, "I have made my recommendations on the basis of seniority. It is the popular thing to do because everyone seems to expect succession on this basis."

"You think then," said the manager, "that age is the only, or at least most important, qualification for supervision? Such a practice conveniently ignores everything that has been learned about managing, or else it assumes that the candidate has the capability and the will to become proficient in management knowledge after he gets the job. Is this realistic?"

In the general conversation that followed, other elements such as getting along with people, making a good impression, having the capability for further promotion, and being able to exact responsibility were championed.

The department manager became clearly frustrated, and as he closed the meeting he remarked, "No wonder we have a 40 percent failure rate in selecting supervisors!"

25. THE PETER PRINCIPLE

The retired president of one of the leading corporations in the United States remarked in a seminar on top management that he thought there should be some system to move out managers after a five-to-ten-year term in office. It was his feeling that a newly appointed manager at any level in the organization just has one or two really new or good ideas to put into operation. After these have time to become a real part of the management practice, there is nothing new that a manager can think of to do. He has made his contribution.

This was a novel idea to the seminar members, and it created a considerable stir. They thought at once of a bishop in place for thirty years, a university president proud of his forty years as head of a large institution, a division manager who occupied his position for twenty-five years, and a foreman of thirty years on the job. If there was anything to the idea, then these organizations had been standing still for a long time.

It appeared after some discussion that the idea about limited contributions probably should be confined to the able managers. All enterprises had many mediocre caretakers for managers, and perhaps this was necessary. Someone must be a hewer of wood and drawer of water, even in management! Another reason was proposed for the existence of caretaker-type managers: they got appointed and were not about to be moved out. Able people cannot manage unless they are appointed any more than can a politician effect change unless he is actually elected to office.

Some members of the group thought that there might be a widespread fear to appoint the able; others thought that nobody was really thinking of ability when appointments were made; and still others thought that it was a mere matter of luck—no one was standing in the way of a manager who rose in the organization.

One member concluded that really what the group was talking about was the Peter Principle: that managers always rise to the level of their incompetence.

26. HARDSTONE CORPORATION

William Hardstone, president of the Hardstone Corporation, was interested in putting in a bonus plan for his top managers and their immediate subordinates. The management consultant whom he engaged to help him with the plan strongly recommended that the bonus plan be based on (1) establishing a bonus pool of 8 percent of profits after retaining 12 percent on stockholders equity plus long-term borrowing; and (2) allocating bonus shares to each man on the basis of his position, salary level, and performance in his job.

Mr. Hardstone readily agreed to having the plan based on these principles. The consultant then pointed out that, if such a plan were to be instituted, an objective appraisal of individual performance would be a necessary part.

Mr. Hardstone agreed, but told the consultant: "I don't want any formal plan of appraisal. I had one once and all that paperwork was meaningless since everyone was marked 'outstanding' or 'excellent.' I will do my own evaluation and allocate the bonuses to each man. I know how the men are doing and how well they are performing."

27. CARL WENDOVER

Carl Wendover, an assistant manager of a well-run division, was selected as head of another division. He encountered trouble from the beginning—trouble in becoming familiar with the information required by the executive vice-president, trouble with the subordinates he inherited, and trouble in really understanding that he was in trouble. Within a year he was terminated.

The man who selected him was concerned about how he came to make such a mistake. He analyzed the situation carefully, and concluded that when Carl Wendover was an assistant manager he was not trained to operate the division. His then superior simply used him as a staff man and kept him completely excluded from division operations. The assistant certainly "looked" good to all, but he was merely reflecting the reputation of the well-run division.

28. APEX MACHINE PRODUCTS COMPANY

John Willis, a prominent department manager of the Apex Machine Products Company, was being considered for promotion to division manager. His was a strong personality; he ran a tight shop; he clearly discharged his responsibility; he was known as a "good" manager. Upon closer inquiry, it became clear that this candidate was "carrying" all his section heads; they were weak yes-men and none was remotely able to succeed the department manager. The candidate was not appointed, and Dale Thompson, the group executive, was explaining to him why he was passed.

"John," he said, "You should know that we all wanted nothing but success for you. You are well thought of among all the people I talked to, and everyone wanted to see you get the chance at division management.

"This did not make the decision any easier for me, but I had other considerations to ponder. Basically, I was worried about the big risk of failure that you would run. In your present position you have carried the total load. I think this means that if you headed a division you would try to do the same thing, and you would surely fail and perhaps have a breakdown in health. Since you did not develop subordinate managers to carry the departmental load, I don't think you would or could use divisional department managers properly.

"Then there is the problem of manager succession. We don't have anybody to take your old job, and you have not prepared any of your subordinates to do so. I'm just afraid that the same thing would happen at the division level, and we just cannot afford to take that kind of a risk.

"I really don't know what the future holds for you. You are now forty years of age. I don't think it is really possible for you to change your managing style. Maybe you can, but I feel that at the first sign of pressure you would revert to doing all the managing yourself."

"Well, Mr. Thompson," replied John, "I can certainly see the problem from your point of view. What I don't see is why I have not been counseled on this point in the years past. I would have changed."

"Would you really?" mused Mr. Thompson.

29. DEVELOPING MANAGERS

The executive vice-presidents of two corporations were exchanging ideas concerning the efficiency of management education and development within their companies. Both had had considerable experience with various types of formal training. They had experimented over a ten-year period with sending selected men to universities for both individual courses and for degree work. They had extensive and costly internal programs under their personal guidance, directed by their chief training officer. At one time or another representatives of the various approaches to management theory were employed to present a series of conferences and seminars in a program and make individual speeches on the subject.

"I must say," said John, "that our experience may be summed up as very expensive in time and fees and no improvement in management skills beyond those that one would see in any able manager who is ambitious. It is not that the 'trainers' were incompetent, or uninteresting. It is not that they didn't have something to say. In fact, our people had a good time and the reports they turned in were highly complimentary. But I really don't think we made a nickel."

"A year ago I would have said the same thing," observed Jim. "We had the same results though we tried everything. And the funny thing about it was that our men thought every program was great. They were unable to discern quality and productivity. I guess this was because they could see little relevance of anything to their job. But we changed that."

"What did you do?" inquired John.

"One thing we did was to stop those programs that wander all over human experience, on the one hand, and on the other we dropped those interminable lectures. We decided to identify a particular aspect of managing that was rather poorly practiced. For instance, we thought our coaching of subordinates was being neglected, or at least poorly done. We called together a group of department heads, explained why we wanted a better coaching job done, explained how to go about it, and asked each man to confer with his boss concerning the need for coaching individual supervisors, the techniques to be used, and a later review of results. This way, we thought we had a direct line on a management need, and we insisted that the line managers do the training. On the whole, we feel we have got something that will work."

"I see," said John, who was now in a thoughful mood. "It is not enough for top managers to show an interest in the development program. They actually have to train their own subordinates."

"That is right," concluded Jim, "If there is to be training, we have to do it. The boss is the great teacher in organized enterprise."

case incidents for part five, directing

30. COUNSELING AND GUIDANCE

The manager of the university placement center was lecturing on career selection and development before the members of the executive program. To point up some of the practical problems at issue he cited several examples of career frustration.

Jim, a college graduate just returned from a tour of duty as a naval officer, set out to find a firm that would provide him with a challenging career. He was attracted by the advertisement of a bank which offered an exciting experience, broad job challenges, management training, and promotional opportunities. These factors were also stressed by the bank's recruiting officer. Jim took the job, only to resign after nine months because the bank failed to live up to its promises. It insisted on college graduates spending the same time on routine duties as was required for the training of clerks assigned permanently to the job, and it defined jobs in ways which did not require college-trained men.

A middle manager in a prosperous business phoned the professor for an appointment. "I would like to confer with you about my career," he said. A time was arranged, and the manager was prompt for the meeting.

"I am a middle manager. Although only thirty-two years old, I feel that there may be nothing further for me in the way of job challenge or promotion. As far as I know, I am appraised as a man with good potential. I am paid a good salary. However, I find time hanging on my hands. I willingly perform certain staff assignments, and I am pursuing doctoral studies at a neighboring university. I am really at the point where I am uncertain whether to change my career objectives."

Recently, a consultant was heard to remark upon the large number of engineers who attended management development conferences. "These men seem to have reached the top of their salary scales and have no place to go. All of them cluster around the age range of thirty-five to forty."

"These illustrations," he concluded, "and many others that might be cited, lead me to the general conclusion that the young need mature men with broad practical and theoretical knowledge to counsel them at most every significant stage in their education. Counseling is really applying tutoring techniques to education. If our young are to avoid costly mistakes, they need the benefit of our wise men."

"Do you know anyone who qualifies for this function?" he was asked.

"No, I do not, though there are many counselors. Our society just has not understood the vital role these people should play in guiding the young. Consequently, the profession has little status, very little influence, and most of that bad."

31.   INTERNATIONAL MEDICAL EQUIPMENT COMPANY

The International Medical Equipment Co. still maintains its headquarters in Chicago, Illinois. It was merely an idea in 1930. Its owner, operator and financier also supplied the skilled labor required to build and sell, one by one, the only product in its line—traction equipment. As may be imagined, growth was very slow and painful, but the firm did prosper. By 1960, it had sales of $17,000,000, plants in the United States and in five foreign countries, and some vigorous competition. That was also the year in which the sole owner passed away, leaving the entire enterprise in equal parts to his four sons. The eldest, John Bireley, was made president, a position he still held in 1972. His three brothers did not take an active part in the business: they were quite satisfied with the financial results of the operation. During this decade, the firm went public with a small offering that still left the brothers with a 75 percent ownership. The board of directors numbered nine, the four brothers and five outside men.

The management problems of the past decade gradually became a worrisome burden to the outside directors. It was not that they were insurmountable; they were ignored. The managers who grew up with the company, especially during the previous twenty years, were protected by the owners who sometimes maintained that they were as good as their peers anywhere, and who also sometimes admitted their weaknesses. Executive appointments and development in the foreign plants were delayed, and are still unsolved. Interplant communications concerning marketing, engineering and production are very ineffective. No long range planning of any kind is encouraged. There are additional problems of comparable magnitude. Still, the enterprise would have to be considered a success in terms of its sales trend, net earnings, and position in its industry. Technically the brothers are millionaires several times over, but their holdings are in investment letter stock, and consequently cannot be readily sold under government regulations in the open market.

The board of directors holds monthly meetings. These are always cordial. Important problems are discussed thoroughly. These range from land purchase to corporate acquisitions; from financial analyses to plant location. The president has been aggressive, insightful, and creative, on occasion, and has sometimes carried the burdens of office manfully. He was and will be supported in office by his brothers so long as their investment position in the company is sound. Indeed, their welfare as well as that of all employees was and is much in the mind of John Bireley.

At a recent meeting of the board a question arose about how much time and attention, on the part of corporate officers, was owed to the company. The conversation leisurely explored business practices in general, the way that some officers in other firms worked, and the correlation between company growth and executive energy applied.

"I used to work long hours," said John. "But during the last year or two I have eased off. I enjoy much more my duties as a member of other boards, and the operating problems of hospitals and charities. In fact, I feel that if I give this company forty hours a week that is all I owe it."

This frank assertion astonished the outside board members though it did not seem to disturb the brothers. There were visions of unsolved problems of a critical nature, of the president turning his back on things he disliked to do, of his dipping into problems and out of them without taking any action. The question going through the minds of the outside board members was, "How can we motivate the president to really be a president?"

32. SOCIAL NEEDS

A few members of the university executive development class were sitting around the dinner table. They were thinking about what the professor had just said concerning the social needs of people.

"You know, fellows," one said, "I know an executive, who following the customary practice of isolating his secretary in an enclosed office, was complaining about her work habits. He observed that she was encouraging visitors in rather large numbers, thus disrupting their work as well as her own. He recognized her need for human contact but was not sure how to handle the situation."

"Quite the contrary," another said, "I know a production vice-president who had just finished tearing down the offices of his foremen. These men," he said, "liked their offices so well, they never got out on the floor. They enjoyed the status symbol. Production has dropped off because they were not on the line keeping things moving, answering questions, and showing a new employee how to do things."

"You may be interested in the case of our president," another member said, "who was concerned about the isolation of the members of his management team. Many did not know each other, and the quality of their cooperation dwindled. At noon everyone took off for restaurants far and near. To remedy at least part of the problem, the president had an excellent executive dining room installed. His view was that managers should be encouraged to use it through an attractive price schedule and, incidentally, thereby get to know each other better. Use, of course, was voluntary.

'You won't see me in there,' said one executive. 'The company does not own my lunch hour, and I will eat with whom and wherever I choose."

The members of the group agreed that these were practical illustrations of many real problems that operating managers run into. They tried to generalize their experience but found that this was not only impossible but that any conclusions they reached would certainly not fit in with the import of the lecture they had just heard. They generally agreed that in the practical world they were almost forced to use their own common sense and consoled themselves with the thought that, "Well, old homo sapiens has done quite nicely for the last several thousand years. Why should we change him?"

33. CONSOLIDATED MANUFACTURING COMPANY

The compensation committee of the board of directors of Consolidated Manufacturing Company was holding a regular meeting on November 1, 1970. At the top of the agenda was a review of executive compensation. As in almost all corporations at that time, there was an urgent need to reconsider past practices and to devise some system that would be relevant to the times.

"As you know," A. C. Riley, the chairman, opened the meeting, "there has been pressure from our operating executives to modify our compensation program. We have deferred compensation for some, stock options outstanding at various prices (all of them much higher than the present market price of our stock), an executive bonus, and, of course, salary. Changes in tax laws, economic conditions, and competition for talent are forces that affect the quality of our compensation system. I suggest that we first clarify what we are trying to do."

"Basically," Raymond Johnston spoke up, "we are trying to keep good executives and to attract other able men."

"This seems like too much to ask of any compensation system," said James Fenway. "I don't think any system has a motivating effect; all it does is to be competitive so that managers will not stray to more promising pastures."

"That seems to be a sound observation," commented Riley. "As we look about us, we see other firms placing emphasis on one or more aspects of compensation, but they seem to retain the different elements. For instance, deferred compensation lightens the tax load during the years of high earnings and pays out after a man is retired. The bonus is a reward for outstanding accomplishment by individuals and is typically earned only occasionally. The stock option encourages managers to do things which should improve the price of the company's stock; it is their best means of building an estate."

"The trouble with the stock option is that an executive has very little influence on the future market price," said Johnston. "It is hard to see it as an incentive."

"Even so," said Fenway, "This is a competitive matter. We must have options but I am in favor of emphasizing them when the market is in a recession. Most of ours were issued at prices that will not be reached for several years. I think we should cancel them and issue new ones."

"Don't you think that our deferred compensation plan is too paternalistic?" interposed Riley. "I am in favor of letting the executive manage his own affairs, including tax affairs."

"Going back to a form of option," Ray Johnston thought out loud, "should we include phantom stock in our plans? It works the same as the real thing except that no stock is issued, no purchase money has to be raised, and the company pays the difference between the issue price and the real price at the time the executive wants to close the deal."

"I'm generally in favor of simple but effective compensation systems," said Riley. "Let us draft our policies and the system we want to recommend to the full board."

34. COMMUNICATING WITH THE BOSS

The defense electronics industry is largely managed by engineers and scientists. Insiders will stress the highly technical content of the industry's operations, and the need for technical people to talk to their technical counterparts within customer organizations if study and production contracts are to be obtained. As a result of this mixture of logic and politics the organization of the marketing function sometimes takes on strange, restrictive duties. Instead of being held responsible for the total "business getting" function, it is, instead, responsible only for market research and knowing who, in a customer's organization, should be contacted. This information is relayed to appropriate engineering and contract administration personnel who are supposed to follow these leads in order to consummate a contract.

This diffusion of accountability for getting business is not looked upon as a drawback during years of expansion. It is the recession years that bring in their train excess space, equipment and personnel, reorganization, recrimination for lack of success in securing contracts, alibis from everyone concerned with business getting, and widespread termination of personnel. This was the situation, late in 1970, in the semi-conductor division of a well-known company.

This division had a reputation for firing the marketing manager every time there was a recession. It had gone through four managers and now there was a real possibility that the present incumbent, Frank Gibson, was to be sacrificed. He was naturally worried about this possibility and asked his close friend and peer, George Handel, Manager of Administration, to come over for a talk.

"George, I think I am about to be fired," he hurriedly announced. "I just can't seem to communicate with the division manager. I barely get started explaining a marketing situation and he will break in to inquire whether I have done anything about any of a dozen possible customers. I guess I am too timid to tell him that in some cases I have not had the time, and in other cases I don't think the potential is there."

"I know," said George.

"There is another thing," continued Frank. "He seems to hold me responsible for actually bringing in the business. And in almost the same breath he will turn to the manager of engineering and tell him that his future depends on his business-getting success. I just don't understand what is going on."

"Well, Frank," responded his friend, "I can understand the division manager too. He is responsible for keeping this a viable organization. He is really concerned."

"I don't like to be held responsible if I don't have the authority and resources to do a job," Frank observed.

"This is a bad situation from an organization point of view," offered George.

"However, we have all worked together before. I think your activities and contributions are unknown to the division manager. You just don't communicate."

The next afternoon Frank was in the office of the division manager. "What bothers me, Frank, is that you just don't react to my expressed concern. No matter what I say to you, nothing happens."

35. AMERICAN AIRCRAFT COMPANY

The management consultant was lunching with Allen Murray, the president of American Aircraft Corporation. He did this quite often, largely in order to facilitate communications between them.

"This just isn't my day," he told the president. "For instance, I was out in the factory an hour ago. I happened to run into the plant manager, so I asked him, 'Why do you have that conference room filled with people every morning?' 'Well,' the plant manager replied, 'the men in there, some twenty-two of them, represent assembly, production control, purchasing, liaison personnel, quality control, shipping, and accounting. They meet each day for three hours. They iron out the problems we have in coordinating effort around here. It is effective as a means of maintaining our billings schedule.'

"Then," he continued, "just as I reached the administration building I met the contracts manager. He really looked wrung out like a rag. He told me that the weekly Tuesday meeting of department managers had just concluded. It appears that it was my friend's turn to be at stage center explaining the performance reports of his department. Every week his division manager spends a staff meeting given over to reviewing the performance of one of the departments. My friend did say with a spark of revenge that next week it will be the turn of engineering."

"I don't see why you are depressed by these events," Mr. Murray remarked.

"Well, it is just this way. I think that these techniques of communication are all wrong. They are expensive, they tend to expose individual managers to public criticism, and they create the wrong circumstance for corrective action. There are other and better means of control. It seems managers agree with theory but never let it influence their practices."

36.   HOME RADIO AND TELEVISION COMPANY

Robert Gates founded a small radio manufacturing plant in Detroit in the 1930s. From this small start came one of the nation's largest radio, television, and allied products companies. By 1965 its sales approached $300 million annually, with 15,000 employees and 10 manufacturing locations. Throughout its growth the founder remained the active, imaginative, and driving force of the company. In earlier days every manager and worker knew him and he was able to call most of them by their first name. Even after the company grew fairly large, people felt that they knew the founder and chief executive and this strong feeling of personal loyalty had much to do with the fact that the company was never unionized.

However, as the company prospered and grew, Robert Gates worried that it was losing its "small company" spirit. He also worried that communications were suffering, that his objectives and philosophy were not being understood in the company, that much wasteful duplication was occurring through poor knowledge of what others in the company were doing, and that new product development and marketing were suffering as a result. Likewise, he was concerned that he had lost touch with the people.

To solve the communications problem, he hired and had report to him a director of communications. Between the two, they put into effect every communications device they found other companies using: bulletin boards in every office and plant throughout the country; a revitalized company newspaper carrying much company and personal news affecting all locations; "Company Facts Books" for every employee giving significant information about the company; regular profit-sharing letters; company-sponsored courses to teach communications; monthly one-day meetings at headquarters for the top 100 executives; annual three-day meetings of 1,200 managers of all levels at a resort area; a large number of special committees to discuss company matters.

After much time, effort, and expense, Mr. Gates was disappointed to find that his problems of communications and of the small company feeling still existed and the results of his programs did not seem to be significant.

case incidents
for part six,
controlling

37. MAKING CONTROLS WORK

"What is your impression," inquired the professor of management of his class, "of this section on *control*?"

"My first impression," one student replied, "is one of exhaustion. The scope and detail of these various controls overwhelm me."

"Of course," put in a second student, "not all of these controls are applied to the same enterprise. But on second thought, I guess they could be."

"Do you notice that planning seems to be ignored in some of the proposals?" a third student observed. "I thought we learned that you cannot control until you have developed a clearcut plan of action including verifiable objectives."

"I think," said the quiet one in the class, "that some specialists are hired to sit in expensive offices and dream up overall control systems that no operator would touch. As soon as there is a recession these fellows are cleaned out."

"This is the affluent society?" asked the professor. And he added, less facetiously; "We could sit around here making general observations practically without end and certainly without results. The test of a control system is actually putting it into operation and really seeing if it works and at what cost. Have any of you any idea of what is involved in such an assignment?"

38. McALLISTER-STRONG PUBLISHING COMPANY

The president of McAllister-Strong Publishing Company and his friend slowly concluded their lunch. "The trouble with manager development training," one of them remarked, "is that the only one who gets smart is the trainer."

"It seems a bit harsh to say so, but I'm afraid that is true," the president took up the thought. "Let me tell you about our experience."

"I have attended a great many conferences, seminars and other executive type meetings in my time. I guess I was just an easy mark for anything that sounded like education. Anyway, times were good, we could afford the expense, and I was truly convinced that the way to develop a good manager was to expose him to the best available information sources. Of course, this worked out very well in technical areas where we had a specific need. But in manager development things were different. I had a staff survey made of what my peers were doing in this area, and what universities others recommended. I chose to get behind a vigorous and comprehensive program. I installed an internal sensitivity program and required all my managers to attend. We constantly attended the American Management Association offerings. We had our top executives attend a highly recommended university program. And we even rented a small country club for three weeks where we reviewed our experiences. I would say we had about the best exposure in our industry.

"Should we order aspirin?" his friend asked solicitously.

"That effort in manager development cost us over $200,000 in two years time. And as far as I can see I don't have a single thing to show for it."

"For an expenditure of that size I would think you should have established a control system," his friend said.

"If this were in marketing, or production or engineering, you bet I would. But how do you control a training program? I'm convinced that you have to *make* managers manage, but all I can think of doing is to pray for luck."

"By the way," his friend inquired, "do you think that any one in these management associations, training firms, or university executive programs has ever established controls for their operations?"

39. UNIVERSAL MEDICAL ELECTRONICS CORPORATION

Universal Medical Electronics Corporation was an interesting company. Its American operation was notably successful. Its managers had grown up with the business and understood it thoroughly. It maintained a strong position in the market due to its leadership position in terms of volume and quality. It had expanded into five foreign nations, investing little capital and growing from internal earnings and short term banking arrangements. These plants were earning about 8 percent on sales after taxes, and sales varied from one to six millions of dollars for each plant. Foreign managers were developing very well in most cases. They received a great deal of technical help and financial guidance from the home plant. This might be called a hand-holding operation. And, they were getting older.

Taking everything into consideration, the tempo of this enterprise was leisurely. By engineering developments and by acquisitions, especially where a key product or patent was involved, the firm expanded healthily but not vigorously. Its managers, both foreign and domestic, were comfortably overpaid if one were to judge by the quality and pay levels of comparable managers in other industries.

Control of operations was a management function that was largely accomplished by occasional decision-making. No one in the parent company was responsible for foreign operations anywhere, several functional and technical heads were dispatched unilaterally for fire-fighting purposes whenever the occasion demanded a decision. In the intervals, the local managers went their own way.

"If we ever take this thing public," the president was heard to say, "we will have to establish some controls."

40. ANCHOR CONSOLIDATED INDUSTRIES, INC.

"I heard it said in a management conference I attended last week," remarked Sidney Sims, president of Anchor Consolidated Industries, Inc., a small company whose clever new pleasure boat products had given rise to growth since its founding five years ago to a level of $5 million in annual sales, "that the sound way to run a company is to let every department and section head develop his own budgets. But I can't imagine doing that in this company. If I did, these people would spend so much money we would soon be bankrupt. No! So long as I am in charge of this company, I will tell people what they can spend. There will be no blank checks here. And I will hold my controller responsible for making sure this company makes the profits I want. I have heard of too many companies with the fast growth we have had go broke because optimism and uncontrolled spending went through the ceiling. And this idea of variable budgets is even worse. Imagine what would happen if I let everyone vary his budgets each month, quarter, or year!"

41. THE KAPPA CORPORATION

As George House, vice-president, and Henry Robbins, controller, walked into the office of Adrian Barnes, chairman and chief executive officer of Kappa Corporation, they were met with the following outburst from the company's top officer:

"Why doesn't some one tell me things? Why can't I know what is going on around here? Why am I kept in the dark? No one informs me on how the company is going, and I never seem to hear of our problems until they become crises. Now, gentlemen, I want you to work out a system where I can be kept informed and I want to know by next Monday how you will do it. I am tired of being isolated from the things I must know if I am to take responsibility for this company."

After George House had left Mr. Barnes' office, he turned to his controller and muttered: "That silly jerk! Everything he wants to know or could possibly want to know is in that shelf of reports on the table back of his desk."

42. HILLSIDE ENTERPRISES, INC.

"Our problems of control are over," said Robert Banks, director of information systems, to Charles Lamson, president of Hillside Enterprises, Inc. "With our new computer installation, transaction recorders, department and plant terminals, high-speed printers, and cathode-ray-tube display stations, every responsible manager can find out what is happening in his area as it happens. Delayed reports can now be a thing of the past. I am sure you will find that the investment we have made and contemplate in these systems is the best expenditure this company ever made. We will soon have real time control, and we can manage to a desired standard exactly like a thermostat keeps our offices at a desired temperature."

"I hope you are right," responded Mr. Lamson. "But I wonder."

43. HOSPITAL SERVICES, INCORPORATED

In the decade of the 1960s considerable interest was generated in hospital care. The aged and the poor were heavily subsidized by government programs aimed, among other things, at helping those in need to get adequate hospital care. During the same time, the cost of hospital services doubled, and still there were not enough beds for patients. Federal and state governments saw the need to distinguish between the types of care that were most suitable. It was clear that everyone did not need the full service care of general hospitals. Once discharged from such a facility the law contemplated that the patient would be sent to a convalescent hospital for a limited time, where the service level was much lower. And, theoretically, having completed the allowed time, or as much of it as was needed, in this institution, the patient could be returned to his home wherein he could receive home care services.

Jules McDonald was among several entrepreneurs who conceived the idea of building or buying a chain of convalescent hospitals to serve the growing need for beds. He thought that a chain could probably achieve some economies of operation that a single hospital would not find possible. Indeed, the idea of making a single hospital pay was very unsound. McDonald was a brilliant man. He was very imaginative and far outstripped his contemporaries in conceptual ability. He intended to broaden his business by purchasing land, securing a construction mortgage to take care of the hospital, and sell the whole package to investors; he would place his own optical and drug stores within each hospital; he would have his own stable of wholesalers in drugs and hospital equipment, and create his own construction companies. His conception was one of full and total vertical and horizontal integration.

McDonald needed money to do these things. He knew that the stocks of convalescent hospital chains were being traded in multiples from sixty to two hundred times earnings. So, he determined to tap this source for capital. He got together a few scattered assets, packaged them attractively, and took the business public. It could not be said that he could show any earnings, but he stressed his prospective earnings per share. Amazingly, the idea sold (he was not alone in this practice), and he raised about $5 million net.

With cash in the bank, an attractive vision in his head, McDonald was ready to go. Plush offices came first. Then a stable of lawyers and tax accountants was added. A salesman sold him a computer. Hospitals were purchased at fancy prices; land was bought across the country and construction begun; and ancillary acquisitions were eagerly sought. McDonald did not do this all by himself. He was specially gifted in his public relations, government relations, and negotiations skill and tended to specialize in them. Managers were hired to take care of construction, hospital management, and finance.

As the months passed, the cash raised from the public issue was fast depleted. On paper the cash flow from operations should have been adequate, but it did not actually materialize. No one, it seemed, was able to get a reading on hospital finances. In some cases there were no profits; in other cases the individual institution kept its own cash balance; and in others there was a heavy drain of funds to cover expenses. The government did not help either. Its agencies were new at this activity; interpretations were being made in the law so frequently that no one knew what practice to follow.

Throughout this period of operation there was no slowdown in activity. McDonald was in his element, but his controller failed to warn him of imminent bankruptcy. There did come a day when he ran out of money. This occurred simultaneously when his business was losing money, bankers were tightening up credit, and the stock market was falling fast.

As he contemplated the wreck he inquired, "What control system should I have had?"

44. FLETCHER CORPORATION

The president of Fletcher Corporation prided himself on being an up-to-date sophisticated manager. He had attended about all the courses, programs, and conferences
on management that he could discover. When he got back, he attempted to use the
ideas he obtained in his base of operations. Success seemed as often to elude him as
it really paid off. On this morning he was telling his staff about a disappointment.

"Gentlemen," he said, "We have long since adopted a policy of promotion of
managers from within. I think we have been very sensible to try to develop our men
and select managers from this source rather than filling positions from the outside.
However, it does not appear that our policy is accomplishing its purpose. I was looking
at the figures and was surprised to see that outsiders were appointed to our management positions during the last five years in the ratio of 60:40. Obviously, this is not
what I intend should happen."

The vice-president for administration added, "Judging by the fact that management positions in all departments have been filled in this way, it is apparent that none
of us is really executing the policy properly."

"Do we have a formal plan for manager identification and appointment?" the
president asked.

"No, we do not."

"I look to you to see that plans are drawn, executed, and controlled," the president said, looking at his administrative vice-president. "And remember that we should
have able people in management positions. We want every one to have demonstrated
under fire a capacity for using *common sense*. Each must have *integrity*. Each must
reflect *drive* and *aggressiveness* in developing their careers. And especially, they
must not deviate from any of these in their *behavior under pressure*."

selected references

PART ONE—THE BASIS OF MANAGEMENT

Books

Babbage, C.: *On the Economy of Machinery and Manufactures*, London: Charles Knight, 1832.

Barnard, C. I.: *The Function of the Executive*, Cambridge, Mass.: Harvard University Press, 1938.

Bartels, R. (ed): *Ethics in Business*, Columbus, Ohio: Bureau of Business Research, The Ohio State University, 1963.

Beer, S.: *Cybernetics and Management*, London: The English Universities Press, Ltd., 1959.

Benne, K. D.: *A Conception of Authority*, Contributions to Education No. 895, New York: Columbia University, 1943.

Berelson, B., and G. A. Steiner: *Human Behavior*, New York: Harcourt, Brace & World, Inc., 1964.

Berle, A. J., Jr.: *Power without Property*, New York: Harcourt, Brace & World, Inc., 1959.

Brown, A.: *Organization of Industry*, Englewood Cliffs, N. J.: Prentice-Hall, Inc., 1947.

Bursk, E. C. (ed.): *Business and Religion*, New York: Harper & Row, Publishers, 1959.

Clark, J. W.: *Religion and the Moral Standards of American Businessmen*, Cincinnati, Ohio: South-Western Publishing Co., 1966.

Cleveland, H., and H. D. Lasswell (eds.): *Ethics and Bigness*, New York: Harper & Row Publishers, 1962.

Cole, A. H.: *Business Enterprise in Its Social Setting*, Cambridge, Mass.: Harvard University Press, 1959.

Dennison, H. S.: *Organization Engineering*, New York: McGraw-Hill Book Company, 1931.

Farmer, R. N., and B. M. Richman: *Comparative Management and Economic Progress*, Homewood, Ill.: Richard D. Irwin, Inc., 1966.

Fayol, H.: *General and Industrial Administration*, London: Sir Isaac Pitman & Sons, Ltd., 1949.

Gulick, L., and L. Urwick (eds.): *Papers on the Science of Administration*, New York: Institute of Public Administration, 1937.

Haire, M., E. F. Ghiselli, and L. W. Porter: *Managerial Thinking: An International Study*, New York: John Wiley & Sons, Inc., 1966.

Harbison, F., and C. A. Myers: *Management in the Industrial World*, New York: McGraw-Hill Book Company, 1959.

Homans, G. C.: *The Human Group*, New York: Harcourt, Brace & World, Inc., 1950.

Katz, D., and R. L. Kahn: *The Social Psychology of Organizations*, New York: John Wiley & Sons, Inc., 1966.

Kepner, C. H., and B. B. Tregoe: *The Rational Manager*, New York: McGraw-Hill Book Company, 1965.

Koontz, H.: *Toward a Unified Theory of Management*, New York: McGraw-Hill Book Company, 1964.

Likert, R.: *New Patterns of Management*, New York: McGraw-Hill Book Company, 1961.

March, J. G., and H. A. Simon: *Organizations*, New York: John Wiley & Sons, Inc., 1958.

McGuire, J. W.: *Business and Society*, New York: McGraw-Hill Book Company, 1963.

Metcalf, H. C., and L. Urwick (eds.): *Dynamic Administration: The Collected Papers of Mary Parker Follett*, New York: Harper & Row, Publishers, 1941.

Miller, D. W., and M. K. Starr: *Executive Decisions and Operations Research*, Englewood Cliffs, N.J.: Prentice-Hall, Inc., 1960.

Mooney, J. D., and A. C. Reilley: *Onward Industry*, New York: Harper & Brothers, 1931.

Negandhi, A. R., and S. B. Prasad: *Comparative Management*, New York: Appleton Century Crofts, 1970.

Parsons, T.: *The Social System*, Glencoe, Ill.: The Free Press, 1951.

Seckler-Hudson, C. (ed.): *Processes of Organization and Management*, Washington, D.C.: Public Affairs Press, 1948.

Sheldon, O.: *The Philosophy of Management*, London: Sir Isaac Pitman & Sons, Ltd., 1923.

Taylor, F. W.: *The Principles of Scientific Management*, New York: Harper & Brothers, 1911.

Thompson, J. D.: *Organizations in Action*, New York: McGraw-Hill Book Company, 1967.

Urwick, L.: *The Elements of Administration*, New York: Harper & Row, Publishers, 1944.

Articles

Ajiferuke, M., and J. Boddewyn, "Culture and Other Explanation Variables in Comparative Management Studies," *Academy of Management Journal*, vol. 13, no. 2, pp. 153–164 (June, 1970).

Boulding, K. E., "General Systems Theory—Skeleton of Science," *Management Science*, vol. 2, no. 3, pp. 197–208 (April, 1956).

Brown, W., "What is Work?" *Harvard Business Review*, vol. 40, no. 5, pp. 121–129 (September–October, 1952).

Capon, F. S., "The Place of Business in Society," *Financial Executive*, vol. 37, no. 8, pp. 34–46 (October, 1970).

Cravens, D. W., and G. E. Hills, "Consumerism: A Perspective for Business," *Business Horizons*, vol. 13, no. 4, pp. 21–28 (August, 1970).

Dale, E., "Management Must Be Made Accountable," *Harvard Business Review*, vol. 38, no. 2, pp. 49–59 (March–April, 1960).

Ebling, A. O., Jr., "The Value of Business: The Responsibility of Businessmen," *Academy of Management Journal*, vol. 13, no. 1, pp. 79–88 (March, 1970).

Estafen, B. D., "System Transfer Characteristics: An Experimental Model for Comparative Management Research," *International Review*, vol. 10, no. 2–3, pp. 21–34 (1970).

Farmer, R. N., and B. M. Richman, "A Model for Research in Comparative Management," *California Management Review*, vol. 7, no. 2, pp. 55–68 (Winter, 1964).

Gonzalez, R. F., and C. McMillan, Jr., "The Universality of American Management Philosophy," *Journal of the Academy of Management,* vol. 4, no. 1, pp. 33–45 (April, 1961).

Hackett, J. T., "Comparative Citizenship," *Business Horizons,* vol. 12, no. 5, pp. 69–74 (October, 1969).

Koontz, H., "The Management Theory Jungle," *Journal of the Academy of Management,* vol. 4, no. 3, pp. 174–188, (December, 1961).

_____, "A Model for Analyzing the Universality and Transferability of Management," *Academy of Management Journal,* vol. 12, no. 4, pp. 415–430 (December, 1969).

Negandhi, A. R., "A Model for Analyzing Organizations in Cross-cultural Settings: A Conceptual Scheme and Some Research Findings," *Comparative Administration and Research Conference* (Kent, Ohio: Kent State University, 1969), pp. 55–87.

_____, and B. D. Estafen, "A Research Model to Determine the Applicability of American Management Know-how in Differing Cultures and/or Environments," *Academy of Management Journal,* vol. 8, no. 4, pp. 309–318 (December, 1963).

Oberg, W., "Cross-cultural Perspectives on Management Principles," *Academy of Management Journal,* vol. 6, no. 2, pp. 129–143 (June, 1963).

O'Donnell, C., "The Source of Managerial Authority." *Political Science Quarterly,* vol. 67, no. 4, pp. 583–588 (December, 1952).

Schöllhammer, H., "The Comparative Management Theory Jungle," *Academy of Management Journal,* vol. 12, no. 1, pp. 81–97 (March, 1969).

PART TWO—PLANNING

Books

Ackoff, R. L.: *A Concept of Corporate Planning,* New York: John Wiley & Sons, Inc., 1970.

_____, and P. Rivett: *A Manager's Guide to Operations Research,* New York: John Wiley & Sons, Inc., 1963.

Anthony, R. N.: *Planning and Control Systems: A Framework for Analysis,* Boston: Division of Research, Harvard Business School, 1965.

Ayres, R. U.: *Technological Forecasting and Long-range Planning,* New York: McGraw-Hill Book Company, 1969.

Beer, S.: *Decision and Control,* New York: John Wiley & Sons, Inc., 1966.

Brinkloe, W. D.: *Managerial Operations Research,* New York: McGraw-Hill Book Company, 1969.

Cannon, J. T.: *Business Strategy and Policy,* New York: Harcourt, Brace & World, Inc., 1968.

Chandler, A. D., Jr.: *Strategy and Structure,* Cambridge, Mass.: The M.I.T. Press, 1962.

Churchman, C. W., R. L. Ackoff, and E. L. Arnoff: *Introduction to Operations Research,* New York: John Wiley & Sons, Inc., 1957.

Drucker, P. F.: *The Practice of Management,* New York: Harper & Brothers, 1954.

_____: *Managing for Results,* New York: Harper & Row, Publishers, Inc., 1964.

Enrick, N. L.: *Management Planning: A Systems Approach,* New York: McGraw-Hill Book Company, 1967.

Goetz, B. E.: *Management Planning and Control*, New York: McGraw-Hill Book Company, 1949.

Hertz, D. B.: *New Power for Management*, New York: McGraw-Hill Book Company, 1969.

Humble, J. W.: *Improving Business Results*, London: McGraw-Hill Publishing Company, Ltd., 1968.

_____ (ed.): *Management By Objectives in Action*, London: McGraw-Hill Publishing Company, Ltd., 1970.

Jantsch, E. (ed.): *Perspectives of Planning*, Paris: Organization for Economic Co-operation and Development, 1969.

Kepner, C. H., and B. B. Tregoe: *The Rational Manager*, New York: McGraw-Hill Book Company, 1965.

Koontz, H.: *Appraising Managers as Managers*, New York: McGraw-Hill Book Company, 1971, chaps. 3–4.

Le Breton, P. P., and D. A. Henning: *Planning Theory*, Englewood Cliffs, N.J.: Prentice-Hall, Inc., 1961.

Miller, D. W., and M. K. Starr: *Executive Decisions and Operations Research*, Englewood Cliffs, N.J.: Prentice-Hall, Inc., 1960.

Miller, E. C.: *Objectives and Standards: An Approach to Planning and Control*, New York: American Management Association, 1966.

Odiorne, G. S.: *Management By Objectives*, New York: Pitman Publishing Corporation, 1965.

O'Donnell, C. (ed.): *The Strategy of Corporate Research*, San Francisco: The Chandler Publishing Company, 1967.

Reichard, R. S.: *Practical Techniques of Sales Forecasting*, New York: McGraw-Hill Book Company, 1966.

Schleh, E. C.: *Management By Results*, New York: McGraw-Hill Book Company, 1961.

Scott, B. W.: *Long-range Planning in American Industry*, New York: American Management Association, 1965.

Steiner, G. A.: *Top Management Planning*, New York: The Macmillan Company, 1969.

_____ (ed.): *Managerial Long-range Planning*, New York: McGraw-Hill Book Company, 1963.

Thompson, S.: *How Companies Plan*, New York: American Management Association, 1962.

Weisselberg, R. C., and J. G. Cowley: *The Executive Strategist*, New York: McGraw-Hill Book Company, 1969.

Wikstrom, W. S.: *Managing by and with Objectives*, New York: National Industrial Conference Board, Inc., 1968.

Articles

Brown, R. V., "Do Managers Find Decision Theory Useful?" *Harvard Business Review*, vol. 48, no. 2, pp. 78–89 (May–June, 1970).

Churchman, C. W., "Managerial Acceptance of Scientific Recommendations," *California Management Review*, vol. 7, no. 1, pp. 31–38 (Fall, 1964).

Edelman, F., and J. S. Greenberg, "Venture Analysis: The Assessment of Uncertainty and Risk," *Financial Executive*, vol. 37, no. 8, pp. 56–62 (August, 1969).

Hammond, J. S., III, "Better Decisions with Preference Theory," *Harvard Business Review*, vol. 45, no. 6, pp. 123–141 (November–December, 1967).

Henderson, A., and R. Schlaifer, "Mathematical Programming: Better Information for

Better Decision-making," *Harvard Business Review*, vol. 35, no. 5, pp. 49–58 (September–October, 1955).

Herrman, C. C., and J. F. Magee, "Operations Research for Management," *Harvard Business Review*, vol. 31, no. 4, pp. 100–113 (July, 1953).

Hertz, D. W., "Risk Analysis in Capital Investment," *Harvard Business Review*, vol. 42, no. 1, pp. 95–106 (January–February, 1964).

Isenson, R. S., "Technological Forecasting—Management Tool," *Business Horizons*, vol. 10, no. 2, pp. 37–46 (Summer, 1967).

Levinson, H., "Management by Whose Objectives?" *Harvard Business Review*, vol. 48, no. 4, pp. 125–134 (July–August, 1970).

Magee, J. F., "Decision Trees for Decision Making," *Harvard Business Review*, vol. 42, no. 4, pp. 126–138 (July–August, 1964).

Mason, R. H., J. Harris, and J. McLoughlin, "Corporate Strategy: A Point of View," *California Management Review*, vol. 13, no. 3, pp. 5–12 (Spring, 1971).

North, H. Q., and D. L. Pyke, "'Probes' of the Technological Future," *Harvard Business Review*, vol. 47, no. 3, pp. 69–82 (May–June, 1969).

O'Donnell, C., "Planning Objectives," *California Management Review*, vol. 6, no. 2, pp. 3–10 (Winter, 1963).

Raia, A. P., "Goal Setting and Self-control," *Journal of Management Studies*, vol. 2, no. 1, pp. 34–53 (February, 1965).

Roman, D. O., "Technological Forecasting in the Decision Process," *Academy of Management Journal*, vol. 13, no. 2, pp. 127–138 (June, 1970).

Steiner, G. A., "Making Long-range Planning Pay Off," *California Management Review*, vol. 4, no. 2, pp. 28–41 (Winter, 1962).

Swalm, R. O., "Utility Theory—Insights Into Risk Taking," *Harvard Business Review*, vol. 44, no. 6, pp. 123–136 (November–December, 1966).

Tosi, H. L., J. R. Rizzo, and J. S. Carroll, "Setting Goals in Management by Objectives," *California Management Review*, vol. 12, no. 4, pp. 70–78 (Summer, 1970).

————, and S. Carroll, "Some Factors Affecting the Success of Management by Objectives," *The Journal of Management Studies*, vol. 7, no. 2, pp. 209–223 (May, 1970).

PART THREE—ORGANIZING

Books

Blau, P. M., and W. R. Scott: *Formal Organizations*, San Francisco: Chandler Publishing Company, 1962.

Bower, M.: *The Will to Manage*, New York: McGraw-Hill Book Company, 1960, Chap. 5.

Chandler, A. D., Jr.: *Strategy and Structure*, Cambridge, Mass.: The M.I.T. Press, 1962.

Cleland, D. I., and W. R. King: *Systems Analysis and Project Management*, New York: McGraw-Hill Book Company, 1968.

Dale, E.: *The Great Organizers*, New York: McGraw-Hill Book Company, 1960.

Evans, G. H.: *The Product Manager's Job*, New York: American Management Association, 1964.

Golembiewski, R.: *Organizing Men and Power*, Chicago: Rand McNally & Company, 1967.

Katz, D., and R. L. Kahn: *The Social Psychology of Organizations*, New York: John Wiley & Sons, Inc., 1966.

Koontz, H.: *The Board of Directors and Effective Management*, New York: McGraw-Hill Book Company, 1967.

Lawrence, P. R., and J. W. Lorsch: *Organization and Environment*, Boston: Harvard Graduate School of Business Administration, 1967.

Lipperman, L. L.: *Advanced Business Systems*, AMA Research Study 86, New York: American Management Association, 1968.

Litterer, J. A.: *The Analysis of Organizations*, New York: John Wiley & Sons, Inc., 1965.

Lohmann, M. R.: *Top Management Committees*, AMA Research Study 48, New York. American Management Association, 1961.

March, J. G., and H. A. Simon: *Organizations*, New York: John Wiley & Sons, Inc., 1958.

McFarland, D. E.: *Cooperation and Conflict in Personnel Administration*, New York: American Foundation for Management Research, 1963.

Scott, W. G.: *Organization Theory: A Behavioral Analysis for Management*, Homewood, Ill.: Richard D. Irwin, Inc., 1967.

Sherman, H.: *It All Depends: A Pragmatic Approach to Organization*, University, Alabama: University of Alabama Press, 1966.

Steiner, G. A., and W. G. Ryan: *Industrial Project Management*, New York: The Macmillan Company, 1968.

Stieglitz, Harold: *Corporate Organization Structures*, Studies in Personnel Policy No. 183, New York: National Industrial Conference Board, Inc., 1961.

Thompson, J. D.: *Organizations in Action*, New York: McGraw-Hill Book Company, 1967.

Woodward, J.: *Industrial Organization: Theory and Practice*, London: Oxford University Press, 1965.

Articles

Ames, B. C., "Payoff from Product Management," *Harvard Business Review*, vol. 41, no. 6, pp. 141–152 (November–December, 1963).

———, "Dilemma of Product/Market Management," *Harvard Business Review*, vol. 49, no. 2, pp. 66–74 (March-April, 1971).

Avots, I., "Why Does Project Management Fail?" *California Management Review*, vol. 12, no. 1, pp. 77–82 (Fall, 1969).

Belasco, J. A., and J. A. Alutto, "Line and Staff Conflicts: Some Empirical Insights," *Academy of Management Journal*, vol. 12, no. 1, pp. 469–477 (December, 1969).

Carzo, R., and J. N. Yanouzas, "Effects of Flat and Tall Organization Structures," *Administrative Science Quarterly*, vol. 14, no. 2, pp. 178–191 (June, 1969).

Daniel, D. R., "Reorganizing for Results," *Harvard Business Review* vol. 44, no. 6, pp. 96–104 (November–December, 1964).

Delbecq, A. L., F. A. Shull, A. C. Filley, and A. J. Grimes, *Matrix Organization: A Conceptual Guide to Organizational Variation*, Wisconsin Business Papers No. 2, Madison, Wis.: Bureau of Business Research and Service, 1969.

Filley, A. C., "Committee Management: Guidelines from Social Science Research," *California Management Review*, vol. 13, no. 1, pp. 13–21 (Fall, 1970).

French, W., and D. Henning, "The Authority-Influence Role of the Functional Specialist in Management," *Academy of Management Journal*, vol. 9, no. 3, pp. 187–203 (September, 1966).

Fulmer, R. M., "Product Management: Panacea or Pandora's Box?" *California Management Review*, vol. 7, no. 4, pp. 63–74 (Summer, 1965).

Glueck, W. F., "Applied Organizational Analysis," *Academy of Management Journal*, vol. 10, no. 3, pp. 223–234 (September, 1967).

Henning, D. A., and R. L. Mosely, "The Authority Role of a Functional Manager: The Controller," *Administrative Science Quarterly*, vol. 15, no. 4, pp. 482–489 (December, 1970).

Hershey R. L., "Organizational Planning," *Business Topics*, vol. 10, no. 1, pp. 29–40 (Winter, 1962).

House, R. J., "Role Conflict and Multiple Authority in Company Organizations," *California Management Review*, vol. 12, no. 4, pp. 53–60 (Summer, 1970).

———, and J. B. Miner, "Merging Management and Behavioral Theory: The Interaction between Span of Control and Group Size," *Administrative Science Quarterly*, vol. 14, no. 3, pp. 451–464 (September, 1969).

Hunt, R. G., "Technology and Organization," *Academy of Management Journal*, vol. 13, no. 3, pp. 235–252 (September, 1970).

Jones, H. R., Jr., "A Study of Organization Performance for Experimental Structures of Two, Three, and Four Levels," *Academy of Management Journal*, vol. 12, no. 3, pp. 351–365 (September, 1969).

Koontz, H., "Making Theory Operational: The Span of Management," *The Journal of Management Studies*, vol. 3, no. 3, pp. 229–243 (October, 1966).

Logan, H. H., "Line and Staff: An Obsolete Concept?" *Personnel*, vol. 43, no. 1, pp. 26–33 (January–February, 1966).

Luck, D. J., and T. Nowack, "Product Management—Vision Unfulfilled," *Harvard Business Review*, vol. 43, no. 3, pp. 143–157 (May–June, 1965).

Murray, J. A., "A Sociometric Approach to Organizational Analysis," *California Management Review*, vol. 13, no. 1, pp. 59–67 (Fall, 1970).

———, "Ground Rules for Using Committees," *Management Record*, vol. 50, no. 10, pp. 63ff. (October, 1961).

O'Donnell, C., "The Role of the Assistant: A Modern Business Enigma," *California Management Review*, vol. 2, no. 3, pp. 65–69 (Spring, 1960).

Reeser, C., "Some Human Problems of the Project Form of Organization," *Academy of Management Journal*, vol. 12, no. 4, pp. 459–468 (December, 1969).

Sorrell, L. C., "Organization of Transportation and Traffic Activities," *Traffic World*, vol. 46, no. 25, vol. 47, nos. 6–8 (1930–1931).

Stewart, J. M., "Making Project Management Work," *Business Horizons*, vol. 8, no. 3, pp. 54–68 (Fall, 1965).

Thompson, V. A., "Hierarchy, Specialization and Organizational Conflict," *Administrative Science Quarterly*, vol. 5, no. 4, pp. 485–521 (March, 1961).

Ulwick, L. F., "The Manager's Span of Control," *Harvard Business Review*, vol. 34, no. 3, pp. 5–15 (May–June, 1965).

Wolf, H. A., "The Great GM Mystery," *Harvard Business Review*, vol. 42, no. 5, pp. 164 ff. (September–October, 1964).

PART FOUR—STAFFING

Books

Andrews, K. R.: *The Effectiveness of University Management Development Programs*, Boston: Division of Research, Harvard Business School, 1966.

Bower, M.: *The Will to Manage*, New York: McGraw-Hill Book Company, 1966, Chap. 6.

Drucker, P. F.: *Managing for Results*, New York: Harper & Row, Publishers, Incorporated, 1964.

Ewing, D. W.: *The Managerial Mind*, New York: The Free Press, 1964.

House, R. J.: *Management Development: Design, Evaluation, and Implementation*, Ann Arbor: Bureau of Industrial Relations, University of Michigan, 1967.

Houston, G. C.: *Manager Development*, Homewood, Ill.: Richard D. Irwin, Inc., 1961.

Jaques, E.: *Equitable Payment*, New York: John Wiley & Sons, Inc., 1961.

Jennings, E. E.: *The Anatomy of Leadership*, New York: Harper & Brothers, 1960.

Kellogg, M. S.: *What to Do About Performance Appraisal*, New York: American Management Association, 1965.

Koontz, H.: *Appraising Managers as Managers*, New York: McGraw-Hill Book Company, 1971.

Mace, M. L.: *The Growth and Development of Executives*, Boston: Division of Research, Harvard Business School, 1950.

Marrow, A. J.: *Beyond the Executive Mask*, New York: American Management Association, 1964.

McGregor, D. (W. G. Bennis and C. McGregor, eds.): *The Professional Manager*, New York: McGraw-Hill Book Company, 1967.

Odiorne, G. S.: *Management by Objectives*, New York: Pitman Publishing Corporation, 1965, 1968.

Powell, R. M.: *The Role and Impact of the Part-time University Program in Executive Education—A Case Study*, Los Angeles: Graduate School of Business Administration, University of California, 1962.

Rowland, V. K.: *Evaluating and Improving Managerial Performance*, New York: McGraw-Hill Book Company, 1970.

Sayles, L.: *Managerial Behavior*, New York: McGraw-Hill Book Company, 1964.

Schleh, E. C.: *Management by Results*, New York: McGraw-Hill Book Company, 1961.

Urwick, L. F.: *Management Education in American Business*, New York: American Management Association, 1954.

Weschler, I. R., and J. Reisel: *Inside a Sensitivity Training Group*, Los Angeles: Institute of Industrial Relations, University of California, 1959.

Whisler, T. L., and S. F. Harper (eds.): *Performance Appraisal: Research and Practice*, New York: Holt, Rinehart and Winston, Inc., 1962.

Wikstrom, W. S.: *Developing Managerial Competence: Changing Concepts Emerging Practices*, New York: The National Industrial Conference Board, Inc., 1964.

————: *Managing By and With Objectives*, New York: The National Industrial Conference Board, Inc., 1968.

Articles

Alfred, T. M., "Checkers or Choice in Manpower Management," *Harvard Business Review*, vol. 45, no. 1, pp. 157–169 (January–February, 1967).

Barrett, J. E., "The Case for Evaluation of Training Expenses," *Business Horizons*, vol. 12, no. 2, pp. 67–72 (April, 1969).

Bassett, G. A., "The Qualifications of a Manager," *California Management Review*, vol. 12, no. 2, pp. 35–44 (Winter, 1969).

Brown, R. S., "A Systems Approach to Management Development," *Financial Executive*, vol. 38, no. 4, pp. 21–25 (April, 1970).

Byham, W. C., and R. Pentecost, "The Assessment Center: Identifying Tomorrow's Managers," *Personnel*, vol. 47, no. 5, pp. 17–28 (September–October, 1970).

Coleman, B. P., "An Integrated System for Manpower Planning," *Business Horizons*, vol. 13, no. 5, pp. 89–95 (October, 1970).

House, R. J., "Leadership Training: Some Dysfunctional Consequences," *Administrative Science Quarterly*, vol. 12, no. 4, pp. 556–571 (March, 1968).

Labovitz, G. H., "In Defense of Subjective Executive Appraisals," *Academy of Management Journal*, vol. 12, no. 3, pp. 293–301 (September, 1969).

Learned, E. P., "Problems of the New Executive," *Harvard Business Review*, vol. 44, no. 4, pp. 22–28, 166–176 (July–August, 1966).

Levinson, H., "Management By Whose Objectives?" *Harvard Business Review*, vol. 48, no. 4, pp. 125–134 (July–August, 1970).

Luthans, F., J. W. Walker, and R. M. Hodgetts, "Evidence on the Validity of Management Education," *Journal of the Academy of Management*, vol. 12, no. 4, pp. 451–457 (December, 1969).

McGregor, D., "An Uneasy Look at Performance Appraisals," *Harvard Business Review*, vol. 35, no. 3, pp. 89–94 (May–June, 1957).

McMurry, R. N., "Avoiding Mistakes in Selecting Executives," *Michigan Business Review*, vol. 22, no. 4, pp. 7–14 (July, 1970).

O'Donnell, C., "Management Training: A System Approach," *Training and Development Journal*, vol. 22, no. 1 (1968).

Patton, A., "How to Appraise Executive Performance," *Harvard Business Review*, vol. 38, no. 1, pp. 63–70 (January–February, 1960).

————. "The Coming Scramble for Executive Talent." *Harvard Business Review*, vol. 45, no. 3, pp. 155–171 (May–June, 1967).

Schein, E. H., "Identifying and Developing Managers: Worldwide Shortages and Remedies," *The Conference Board Record*, vol. 2, no. 6, pp. 21–48 (June, 1965).

Teague, F. A., "International Management Selection and Development," *California Management Review*, vol. 12, no. 3, pp. 1–6 (Spring, 1970).

Thompson, P. H., and G. W. Dalton, "Performance Appraisal: Managers Beware," *Harvard Business Review*, vol. 48, no. 1, pp. 149–157 (January–February, 1970).

Urwick, L. F., "Organization and Theories about the Nature of Man," *Academy of Management Journal*, vol. 10, no. 1, pp. 9–15 (March, 1967).

Walker, J. W., "Trends in Manpower Management Research," *Business Horizons*, vol. 12, no. 4, pp. 37–46 (August, 1968).

White, B. F., and L. B. Barnes, "Power Networks in the Appraisal Process," *Harvard Business Review*, vol. 49, no. 3, pp. 101–109 (May–June, 1971).

Williams, A. P. O., "Increasing the Value of Management Appraisal Schemes: An Organizational Learning Approach," *Journal of Management Studies*, vol. 7, no. 1, pp. 23–36 (February, 1970).

Ziller, R. C., B. J. Stark, and H. O. Pruden, "Marginality and Integrative Management Positions," *Journal of the Academy of Management*, vol. 12, no. 4, pp. 487–495 (December, 1969).

PART FIVE—DIRECTING

Books

Argyris, C.: *Personality and Organization*, New York: Harper & Brothers, 1957.

————: *Integrating the Individual and the Organization*, New York: John Wiley & Sons, Inc., 1964.

Bennis, W. G.: *Changing Organizations*, New York: McGraw-Hill Book Company, 1966.

Berelson, B., and G. A. Steiner: *Human Behavior: An Inventory of Scientific Findings*, New York: Harcourt, Brace & World, Inc., 1964.

Blake, R. R., and J. S. Mouton: *The Managerial Grid*, Houston, Texas: Gulf Publishing Company, 1964.

Brown, W.: *Exploration in Management*, New York: John Wiley & Sons, Inc., 1962.

Cartwright, D., and A. Zander (eds.): *Group Dynamics Research and Theory*, New York: Harper & Row, Publishers Incorporated, 3d. ed., 1968.

Fiedler, F. E.: *A Theory of Leadership Effectiveness*, New York: McGraw-Hill Book Company, 1967.

Filley, A. C., and R. J. House: *Managerial Process and Organizational Behavior*, Glenview, Ill.: Scott, Foresman and Company, 1969, Chaps. 15–16.

Ford, R. N.: *Motivation Through the Work Itself*, New York: American Management Association, 1969.

Gellerman, S. W.: *Motivation and Productivity*, New York: American Management Association, 1968.

Haefele, J. W.: *Creativity and Innovation*, New York: Reinhold Publishing Corporation, 1962.

Herzberg, F.: *Work and the Nature of Man*, Cleveland, Ohio: World Publishing Company, 1966.

———, B. Mausner, and B. B. Snyderman: *The Motivation to Work*, New York: John Wiley & Sons, Inc., 1959.

Jennings, E. E.: *An Anatomy of Leadership*, New York: Harper & Brothers, 1960.

Katz, D., M. Maccoby, and N. Morse: *Productivity, Supervision and Morale in an Office Situation*, Ann Arbor, Michigan: Survey Research Center, University of Michigan, 1950.

Lewin, K.: *A Dynamic Theory of Personality*, New York: McGraw-Hill Book Company, 1945.

———: *Field Theory in Social Science: Selected Theoretical Papers*, New York: Harper & Brothers, 1951.

Likert, R.: *New Patterns of Management*, New York: McGraw-Hill Book Company, 1961.

———: *The Human Organization*, New York: McGraw-Hill Book Company, 1967.

Litwin, G. H., and R. A. Stringer, Jr.: *Motivation and Organizational Climate*, Boston: Division of Research, Harvard Business School, 1968.

Madsen, K. B.: *Theories of Motivation*, Kent, Ohio: The Kent State University Press, 4th ed., 1968.

Maslow, A. H.: *Motivation and Personality*, New York: Harper & Brothers, 1954.

Mayo E.: *Human Problems of an Industrial Civilization*, Cambridge, Mass.: Harvard University Press, 1933.

McClelland, D. C., and D. J. Winter: *Motivating Economic Achievement*, New York: The Free Press, 1969.

McGregor, D.: *The Human Side of Enterprise*, New York: McGraw-Hill Book Company, 1960.

Nirenberg, J. S.: *Getting Through to People*, Englewood Cliffs, N.J.: Prentice-Hall, Inc., 1965.

Patton, A.: *Men, Money and Motivation*, New York: McGraw-Hill Book Company, 1961.

Roethlisberger, F. J., and W. J. Dickerson: *Management and the Worker*, Cambridge, Mass.: Harvard University Press, 1939.

———: *Counseling in an Organization: A Sequel to the Hawthorne Research*, Boston: Graduate School of Business, Harvard University, 1966.

Rush, H. M. F. (ed.): *Managing Change*, New York: National Industrial Conference Board, 1967.

Sayles, L. R.: *Managerial Behavior*, New York: McGraw-Hill Book Company, 1964.

———, and G. Strauss: *Human Behavior in Organizations*, Englewood Cliffs, N.J.: Prentice-Hall, Inc., 1966.

Stogdill, R. M.: *Individual Behavior and Group Achievement*, London: Oxford University Press, 1959.

————, and A. E. Coons (eds.): *Leader Behavior: Its Description and Measurement*, Columbus, Ohio: Bureau of Business Research, The Ohio State University, 1957.

Tannenbaum, R., I. R. Weschler, and F. Massarik: *Leadership and Organization: A Behavioral Approach*, New York: McGraw-Hill Book Company, 1961.

Vroom, V. H.: *Motivation and Morale*, New York: John Wiley & Sons, Inc., 1964.

Whyte, W. F.: *Man and Organization: Three Problems in Human Relations in Industry*, Homewood, Ill.: Richard D. Irwin, Inc., 1959.

Zalesnik, A., C. R. Christensen, and F. J. Roethlisberger: *The Motivation, Productivity and Satisfaction of Workers*, Boston: Division of Research, Harvard Business School, 1958.

Articles

Bennis, W. G., "Leadership Theory and Administrative Behavior: The Problem of Authority," *Administrative Science Quarterly*, vol. 4, no. 3, pp. 259–301 (December, 1959).

Chung, K. H., "A Markov Chain Model of Human Needs: An Extension of Maslow's Need Theory," *Journal of the Academy of Management*, vol. 12, no. 2, pp. 223–234 (June, 1969).

Evans, M. G., "Leadership and Motivation: A Core Concept," *Journal of the Academy of Management*, vol. 13, no. 1, pp. 91–102 (March, 1970).

Ghisselli, E. F., "Managerial Talent," *American Psychologist*, vol. 18, no. 10, pp. 631–641 (October, 1963).

Glueck, W. F., "Organization Change in Business and Government," *Academy of Management Journal*, vol. 12, no. 4, pp. 429–449 (December, 1969).

Hill, W., "The Validation and Extension of Fiedler's Theory of Leadership Effectiveness," *Journal of the Academy of Management*, vol. 12, no. 1, pp. 33–47 (March, 1969).

House, R. J., and L. A. Wigdor, "Herzberg's Dual-factor Theory of Job Satisfaction and Motivation: A Review of the Evidence and a Criticism," *Personnel Psychology*, vol. 19, no. 2, pp. 153–164 (1966).

Jennings, E. E., "The Democratic and Authoritarian Approaches: A Comparative Survey of Research Findings," in *Problems and Practices in Industrial Relations*. Report No. 16, New York: American Management Association, 1958.

Kaczka, E. E., and R. V. Kirk, "Managerial Climate and Organizational Performance," *Academy of Management Proceedings*, 1967, pp. 101–112.

Lundberg, C. C., and R. W. Millman, "Comparative Views on Behavioral Science Findings," *Academy of Management Proceedings*, 1967, pp. 185–194.

McNair, W. P., "What Price Human Relations?" *Harvard Business Review*, vol. 35, no. 2, pp. 15 ff. (March–April, 1957).

McMurry, R. N., "The Case for Benevolent Autocracy," *Harvard Business Review*, vol. 36, no. 1, pp. 82–90 (January–February, 1958).

Morse, J. J., and J. W. Lorsch, "Beyond Theory Y," *Harvard Business Review*, vol. 48, no. 3, pp. 61–68 (May–June, 1970).

Murray, T. J., "How Do You Get Executives Off Dead Center?", *Dun's Review*, vol. 89, no. 4, pp. 29–30; 103 (April, 1967).

Peters, L. H., "The Acquisitive Motivation of the Businessman: Classical Views—Apologetic and Critical," The University of Wisconsin Bureau of Business Research & Service: *Wisconsin Project Reports*, vol. 111, no. 2 (March, 1966).

Roche, W. J., and N. L. MacKinnon, "Motivating People with Meaningful Work," *Harvard Business Review*, vol. 48, no. 3, pp. 97–110 (May–June, 1970).

Sales, S. M., "Supervisory Style and Productivity: Review and Theory," *Personnel Psychology*, vol. 19, no. 3, pp. 275–285.

Tannenbaum, R., and W. H. Schmidt, "How to Choose a Leadership Pattern," *Harvard Business Review*, vol. 36, no. 2, pp. 95–101 (March–April, 1958).

Wickesberg, A. K., "Communications Network in the Business Organization Structure," *Journal of the Academy of Management*, vol. 11, no. 3, pp. 253–262 (September, 1968).

Williams, E. G., "Changing Systems and Behavior," *Harvard Business Review*, vol. XII, no. 4, pp. 53–60 (August, 1960).

PART SIX—CONTROLLING

Books

Anshen, M., and G. L. Bach (eds.): *Management and Corporations 1985*, New York: McGraw-Hill Book Company, 1960.

Appley, L. A., and A. W. Angrist: *Management 2000*, New York: The American Foundation for Management Research, Inc., 1968.

Bennis, W. G.: *Changing Organizations*, New York: McGraw-Hill Book Company, 1966.

Bonini, C. P., et al.: *Management Controls*, New York: McGraw-Hill Book Company, 1964.

Buechele, R. B.: *Business Policy in Growing Firms*, San Francisco: Chandler Publishing Company, 1967.

Churchman, C. W., R. L. Ackoff, and E. L. Arnoff: *Introduction to Operations Research*, New York: John Wiley & Sons, Inc., 1957.

Forrester, J. W.: *Industrial Dynamics*, New York: John Wiley & Sons, Inc., 1961.

Goetz, B. E.: *Management Planning and Control*, New York: McGraw-Hill Book Company, 1949.

Greenwood, W. T.: *A Management Audit System*, rev. ed., Carbondale, Ill.: School of Business, Southern Illinois University, 1967.

Leonard, W. P.: *The Management Audit*, Englewood Cliffs, N.J.: Prentice-Hall, Inc., 1962.

Martindell, J. W.: *The Appraisal of Management*, New York: Harper & Brothers, 1962.

McDonough, A. M.: *Information Economics and Management Systems*, New York: McGraw-Hill Book Company, 1963.

Miller, R. W.: *Schedule, Cost, and Profit Control with PERT*, New York: McGraw-Hill Book Company, 1963.

Neuschel, R. F.: *Management by Systems*, New York: McGraw-Hill Book Company, 1960.

Novick, D. (ed.): *Program Budgeting: Program Analysis and the Federal Budget*, 2d ed., Cambridge, Mass.: Harvard University Press, 1967.

Rose, T. G.: *The Management Audit*, 3d ed., London: Gee & Company, Ltd., 1961.

Simon, H. A.: *The New Science of Management Decision*, New York: Harper & Brothers, 1960.

Suojanen, W. W.: *The Dynamics of Management*, New York: Holt, Rinehart and Winston, Inc., 1966.

Articles

Argyris, C., "Human Problems with Budgets," *Harvard Business Review*, vol. 31, no. 1, pp. 97–110 (January, 1953).

———, "The Organization: What Makes It Healthy?" *Harvard Business Review*, vol. 36, no. 6, pp. 107–116 (November–December, 1958).

Avots, I., "The Management Side of PERT," *California Management Review*, vol. 4, no. 2, pp. 16–27 (Winter, 1962).

Boulden, J. B., and E. S. Buffa, "Corporate Models: On-line Real-time Systems," *Harvard Business Review*, vol. 48, no. 4, pp. 65–83 (July–August, 1970).

Brewer, S. H., and J. Rosensweig, "Rhochrematics and Organization Adjustments," *California Management Review*, vol. 3, no. 3, pp. 52–71 (Spring, 1961).

Brummet, R. L., W. C. Pyle, and E. G. Flamholtz, "Accounting for Human Resources," *Michigan Business Review*, vol. 20, no. 2, pp. 20–25 (March, 1968).

Buechele, R. B., "How to Evaluate a Firm," *California Management Review*, vol. 5, no. 1, pp. 5–16 (Fall, 1962).

Burdeau, H. B., "Variable Budgets and Direct Costing," *Managerial Planning*, vol. 19, no. 4, pp. 4–11 (January–February, 1971).

Burton, J. C., "Management Auditing," *The Journal of Accountancy*, vol. 125, no. 5, pp. 41–46 (May, 1968).

Clayden, R., "A New Way to Measure and Control Divisional Performance," *Management Services*, vol. 7, no. 5, pp. 22–29 (September–October, 1970).

Daniel, D. R., "Management Information Crisis," *Harvard Business Review*, vol. 39, no. 5, pp. 111–121 (September–October, 1961).

Dearden, J., "How to Organize Information Systems," *Harvard Business Review*, vol. 43, no. 2, pp. 65–73 (March–April, 1965).

Edmunds, S., "The Reach of an Executive," *Harvard Business Review*, vol. 37, no. 1, pp. 87–96 (January–February, 1959).

Forrester, J. W., "Industrial Dynamics," *Harvard Business Review*, vol. 36, no. 4, pp. 37–66 (July–August, 1958).

Likert, R., D. G. Bowers, and R. M. Norman, "How to Increase a Firm's Lead Time in Recognizing and Dealing with Problems of Managing Its Human Organization," *Michigan Business Review*, vol. 21, no. 1, pp. 12–17 (January, 1969).

Magee, J. F., "The Logistics of Distribution," *Harvard Business Review*, vol. 38, no. 4, pp. 89–101 (July–August, 1960).

Newman, M. S., "Return on Investment: An Analysis of the Concept," *Management Services*, vol. 3, no. 4, pp. 15–27 (July–August, 1966).

Novick, D., "Long-range Planning through Program Budgeting," *Business Horizons*, vol. 12, no. 1, pp. 59–66 (February, 1968).

———, and C. J. Hitch, "The New Approach to Management in the U.S. Department of Defense," *Management Science*, vol. 9, no. 2, pp. 1–8 (October, 1962).

Pyle, W. C., "Monitoring Human Resources—'On Line'," *Michigan Business Review*, vol. 22, no. 4, pp. 19–32 (July, 1970).

Weisbord, M. R., "Management in Crisis," *The Conference Board Record*, vol. 7, no. 2, pp. 10–16 (February, 1970).

Wright, W., and F. P. Killaritsch, "Direct Costing: Pro and Con," *The Controller*, vol. 30, no. 7, pp. 322 ff. (July, 1962).

name and place index

subject index